Lincoln Gordon

ADST-DACOR Diplomats and Diplomacy Series
Series Editor: Margery Boichel Thompson

Since 1776, extraordinary men and women have represented the United States abroad under widely varying circumstances. What they did and how and why they did it remain little known to their compatriots. In 1995, the Association for Diplomatic Studies and Training (ADST) and DACOR, an organization of foreign affairs professionals, created the Diplomats and Diplomacy book series to increase public knowledge and appreciation of the professionalism of American diplomats and their involvement in world history. This 58th volume in the series, Bruce L. R. Smith's biography of Lincoln Gordon, presents an insightful account of the many contributions of an influential player in key events during and after World War II in Europe and Latin America and the people who helped shape these events.

Selected Titles in the Series
Peter Bridges, *Donn Piatt: Gadfly of the Gilded Age*

Gordon S. Brown, *Toussaint's Clause: The Founding Fathers and the Haitian Revolution*

J. F. Brown, *Radio Free Europe: An Insider's View*

Herman J. Cohen, *Intervening in Africa: Superpower Peacemaking in a Troubled Continent*

Charles T. Cross, *Born a Foreigner: A Memoir of the American Presence in Asia*

Hermann F. Eilts, *Early American Diplomacy in the Near and Far East: The Diplomatic and Personal History of Edmund Q. Roberts 1783–1836*

Brandon Grove, *Behind Embassy Walls: The Life and Times of an American Diplomat*

Kempton Jenkins, *Cold War Saga*

Dennis Jett, *American Ambassadors: The Past, Present, and Future of America's Diplomats*

Bo Lidegaard, *Defiant Diplomacy: Henrik Kauffmann, Denmark, and the United States in World War II and the Cold War 1939–1958*

Jane C. Loeffler, *The Architecture of Diplomacy: Building America's Embassies*

Robert H. Miller, *Vietnam and Beyond: A Diplomat's Cold War Education*

David D. Newsom, *Witness to a Changing World*

Richard B. Parker, *Memoirs of a Foreign Service Arabist*

Nicholas Platt, *China Boys: How U.S. Relations with the PRC Began and Grew*

Laurence Pope, *François de Callières: A Political Life*

Howard B. Schaffer, *Ellsworth Bunker: Global Troubleshooter, Vietnam Hawk*

Nancy Bernkopf Tucker, ed., *China Confidential: American Diplomats and Sino-American Relations 1945–1996*

For a complete list of series titles, visit adst.org/publications.

LINCOLN GORDON

ARCHITECT OF COLD WAR FOREIGN POLICY

BRUCE L. R. SMITH

An ADST-DACOR
Diplomats and Diplomacy Book

UNIVERSITY PRESS OF KENTUCKY

The University Press of Kentucky

Scholarly publisher for the Commonwealth,
serving Bellarmine University, Berea College, Centre College of Kentucky, Eastern
Kentucky University, The Filson Historical Society, Georgetown College, Kentucky
Historical Society, Kentucky State University, Morehead State University, Murray
State University, Northern Kentucky University, Transylvania University, University
of Kentucky, University of Louisville, and Western Kentucky University.
All rights reserved.

Editorial and Sales Offices: The University Press of Kentucky
663 South Limestone Street, Lexington, Kentucky 40508-4008
www.kentuckypress.com

Library of Congress Cataloging-in-Publication Data

Smith, Bruce L. R.
  Lincoln Gordon : architect of Cold War foreign policy / Bruce L. R. Smith.
      pages cm. — (ADST-DACOR diplomats and diplomacy series) (Studies in
conflict, diplomacy and peace)
  Includes bibliographical references and index.
  ISBN 978-0-8131-5655-2 (hardcover : alk. paper) — ISBN 978-0-8131-6120-4 (pdf)
  — ISBN 978-0-8131-6121-1 (epub)
  1. Gordon, Lincoln. 2. Diplomats—United States—Biography. 3. United States—
Officials and employees—Biography. 4. United States—Foreign relations—20th
century. 5. Johns Hopkins University—Presidents—Biography. 6. College teachers—
United States—Biography. 7. Ambassadors—Brazil—Biography. 8. Ambassadors—
United States—Biography. 9. Cold War. I. Title.
  E748.G687S65 2015
  327.2092—dc23
  [B]   2015003605

Member of the Association of
American University Presses

Contents

Preface vii

Introduction 1

1. Dorothy and Dad 7

2. Secular Humanism at Fieldston 19

3. Harvard in Three Years 27

4. An American at Oxford 39

5. Allison 49

6. Mobilizing for War 63

7. Controlling the Atom 84

8. Birth of the Marshall Plan, 1947–1948 118

9. The Marshall Plan in Action, 1949–1950 138

10. NATO: From Treaty to Alliance 162

11. London: A Respite 188

12. Business School Professor, 1955–1960 206

13. The Alliance for Progress and JFK Advisor 218

14. Ambassador to Brazil 238

15. Assistant Secretary 274

16. Johns Hopkins President 300

17. What Now? 343

18. Elder Statesman 381

19. Going Gently 396

Epilogue 401

Acknowledgments 413

Appendixes

    A. Lincoln Gordon's Family Tree   419

    B. Exchange of Letters with President Johnson on Departure as
       Assistant Secretary of State   423

    C. Confidential Report to the President on Vietnam Policy   427

    D. Exchange of Letters with Eugene Rostow on Panama Canal
       Treaty   431

    E. Correspondence with Richard Bissell on ERP's Early Troubles   435

Notes   441

Selected Bibliography of Lincoln Gordon's Scholarly Writings   473

Index   477

Photographs follow page 248.

Preface

Every biography, like every life, has its unique features and challenges. Writing this biography was for me a trip down memory lane. I came to Harvard about a quarter of a century after Lincoln did, and we overlapped for several years. I studied with and knew many of the same people who taught him and were later his friends and colleagues. I lived on New York's West Side, not far from his boyhood home on Riverside Drive. I, too, left teaching and settled in Washington, DC, after a stint in public service and found a congenial home at the Brookings Institution, where I first met Lincoln Gordon. He was a most congenial colleague whom I liked and admired, but it never occurred to me during his lifetime that one day I might write his biography. The idea of doing so first occurred to me in March 2010, when I attended a memorial service for him at the Cosmos Club in Washington. At this service his four children, as well as several grandchildren, gave moving tributes, a family friend offered a fond remembrance, and a great-grandson played the violin. Something in his life spoke to me, and I conceived the idea of undertaking this biography.

Since I only thought of this project after his death, I did not attempt or aspire to be a Boswell to his Johnson. I might have learned more about certain aspects of his life and his career had I been self-consciously interviewing him or recording my impressions during the time I knew him. I think I understood him, though, and what made him tick. The triumvirate of values that moved him—family, learning, and public service—was close to my heart. I thought that the story needed telling of this man who had served his country so long and so well in so many ways with so little reward or public recognition. But of course whether I have succeeded as a biographer in telling this story is for my readers and not for me to say.

Introduction

The eastern establishment that shaped the post–World War II order was made up of a circle of Wise Men (such as Averell Harriman, Dean Acheson, John McCloy, Robert Lovett, George Kennan, Charles Bohlen, and others) who have deservedly attracted the attention of biographers and historians. Some of these well-known Americans told their own stories in eloquent memoirs. But these individuals had a supporting cast of less well-known wise men and some women behind them. This supporting cast's work made possible and sometimes even outshone the achievements of the better-known figures who have gotten most of the credit. The Wise *and* the wise together built the postwar world that the United States dominated for a generation and beyond.

The major players and their close aides operated most notably in the arena of foreign policy, and most conspicuously with an Atlanticist orientation. Most of them came from outside the formal government prior to entering public service (for the most part with the onset of war, but some had previous government service and were career military officers or civilian State Department or Treasury officials). These outsiders were drawn into wartime public service from universities, foundations, industry, and finance and moved with surprising ease in and out of government to meet critical national needs. They favored free trade, free markets, and free political institutions, and for much of the wartime and early Cold War period they operated within a bipartisan framework that was not the natural or default position of American politics. This bipartisan framework, fragile though it was, insulated them from their sharp differences on domestic policy and to some degree from the vicissitudes of domestic politics. These Atlanticists achieved notable successes in wartime industrial mobilization, in rebuilding Western Europe after the war, in restoring the economic relations of the world's industrialized nations, and in building a security framework to address communist expansion. But they enjoyed less success when they applied their Europe-oriented policy premises to the Latin American context and the broader Third World framework. Military repression and torture in Brazil in the 1960s and 1970s helped to produce the human rights movement in US foreign policy, and this, along with the deep differences over American engagement in Vietnam, fractured the postwar consensus on foreign policy and ushered in a more discordant era in American foreign policy and domestic politics.

This biography tells the story of one of the most important figures in the unsung supporting cast of public servants who contributed to the World War II mobilization miracle, Europe's postwar economic recovery, and the Atlantic security framework. America's emergence as a world leader had a second, less successful chapter illustrating the limits of American power and influence, notably in the case of US policy toward Latin America, and this aspect of the story needs to be told as well. The man who figured both in the success of the Marshall Plan and NATO and in the failure of the Alliance for Progress was Lincoln Gordon. His story tells us much about both the accomplishments and the overreach of American leadership. He was not unique in his commitment to public service and his tireless efforts to build a stable international order. There are many others who worked with him in one or another phase of his career who, like him, represented the "honor, duty, country" tradition.

Gordon was representative of the professionals from law, business, and universities who did not serve in the armed forces for one reason or another but who served their country as civilians (often feeling some guilt for not serving in the military). While he was not unique, few individuals had as long or as varied a public service career as did Gordon. Because he was so young at the outbreak of World War II, he served throughout the entire war and got to know a large number of civilian and military leaders who called on him in later periods. This could almost be a collective biography of the supporting players who helped to develop and implement critical US Cold War policies. But because Gordon's career lasted so long and was so varied, he had an unusual vantage on the entire postwar era. His career thus dramatizes both the triumphs and the disappointments of the nation's Cold War policies. Gordon reflected the optimistic sense that America could tackle and solve almost any problem, but he later had to confront the reality of overreach and reckon with failure in his, and the nation's, endeavors.

Gordon participated in the early postwar effort by the United Nations to control nuclear weapons. He was one of the small team that designed the Marshall Plan and then administered the program as a key aide to Averell Harriman in Paris. He returned to Washington with Harriman when the latter became President Truman's national security adviser in the summer of 1950 and participated with Harriman in transforming NATO from a treaty to an alliance. After a shift in his intellectual interests to Latin America and to the problems of economic underdevelopment, he became a drafter of the Alliance for Progress and then President Kennedy's major adviser on Latin America. The Alliance was doomed from the beginning because it was modeled on a misleading analogy with the Marshall Plan. Gordon served as US ambassador to Brazil, the largest country in Latin America, under both Presidents Kennedy and Johnson, but his tenure came in a turbulent time, and his hopes for a Marshall Plan–style economic revival there did not materialize. He subsequently served as LBJ's assistant secretary of state during a period when Vietnam posed vexing issues for his own policy domain. He escaped from his problems at the State Department to become president of one of the nation's major research universities, but this came at just the wrong time—as antiwar campus protests erupted against US involvement in Vietnam and profound changes swept through higher education. He could not understand or cope with the generational changes that were placing extraordinary demands on university leaders. While he had excelled in previous staff roles and as part of government hierarchies, his inexperience in university administration and his shortcomings as a chief executive were exposed, and his career as university president was marked by frustration and failure.

Thereafter Gordon largely disappeared from public view but remained active for a quarter century as a policy adviser and analyst, member of advisory boards, and elder statesman. He produced a flood of books and articles that explained and defended the postwar accomplishments of US foreign policy and struggled to understand what had gone wrong with his last policy initiatives. In the early stages of his public service career, he had men like Harriman, Marshall, Lovett, Baruch, and others to buffer him from and help him navigate the winds of politics. Since he had no political standing himself or direct experience in politics, his analytical skills alone were a less certain guide to the challenges of top leadership. When the foreign policy establishment splintered in the 1960s, he was no longer an "insider," and there was no circle of elites he could advise. Like many others he was forced to invent a new role for himself. He was not a contrarian by nature but became a critic of the newer conventional thinking even as he remained wedded to the traditions of American leadership. His voluminous writings tackled large issues and dealt with the moral dimensions of policy and were marked by a strong sense of pragmatism. LBJ called him a "pragmatic idealist," a term that pleased Gordon.

While Gordon had setbacks in his public career, this is not a story of decline or a celebration of past glories. Gordon firmly believed that there was an American story, and not just a jumble of group, gender, or class perspectives. His own life exemplified for him the American experience. Born to Jewish immigrant parents from Russia, he was raised in the secular American religion of patriotism, opportunity, and hard work. The New York City of his boyhood, as he wrote many years later, was like the Sao Paulo he encountered in the late 1950s. There was an aristocratic class—the old four hundred New York families of the Edith Wharton novels—but also a rising professional class of lawyers, doctors, accountants, engineers, and philanthropists coming into prominence. Immigrants surged into New York from Europe and elsewhere, becoming a part of the booming economy. Encouraged by his talented and remarkable mother, who was the key figure in his life, Lincoln received an excellent education at the Ethical Culture Fieldston School, Harvard, and Balliol College Oxford as a Rhodes scholar, after which he joined Harvard's faculty. Becoming one of the small number of Americans with deep knowledge of events in Europe in the 1930s, he formed an internationalist outlook on the nation's problems.

I hope readers will gain from this book an appreciation of the profound changes in both thought and governmental practice that emerged in the course of Lincoln Gordon's life and career. American society at the time of Gordon's birth in 1913 may be scarcely recognizable to Americans today. The US population when Gordon was born stood at 92 million, rising to 132 million at the start of World War II and reaching 309 million in the 2010 census. In 1913 there was no radio, television, air travel, or air conditioning; little electricity outside of urban centers; and no common household appliances such as washing machines, dryers, dishwashers, or refrigerators. There were few automobiles, poor roads, and many horse-drawn carts still on city streets. Indeed, the common mode of transport in rural areas was still the horse-drawn carriage, which brought goods and people to the cities and railroad stations. Lincoln was born into a late-Victorian world in morals and social structures. He experienced unprecedented changes during his lifetime. His life story tells us something about how modern America came into being and how our governing institutions have evolved to cope with vast changes.

Gordon's perspective was neither that of the foot soldier of history nor that of someone at the very pinnacle of power. Gordon did not believe that history followed a trajectory of iron laws and predestined ends or was driven by historical "forces" divorced from human agency and human purposes. He did not place much credence in a bottom-up view of history as the spontaneous actions of "the people" apart from the visible hand of leadership and the interplay of organized interests. On the other hand, he did not adopt Thomas Carlyle's notion of a few leaders as the only significant actors in the fate of nations. He subscribed to the idea of social hierarchies and to the concept of a political class, but one that interacted with the wider public in shaping political aspirations. He felt comfortable serving in a staff role to natural aristocrats and top politicians. (The categories of political leader and aristocratic servant of the people, embodied in figures like FDR and Harriman, overlapped in his mind.) What Gordon saw as the mainspring of history was the interplay of political leaders, scientists, and other experts with broad trends in public opinion that were driven by both ideals and organized economic interests. He believed that governing institutions reflected and embodied human aspirations, along with crasser impulses. Whether higher purposes were realized or thwarted would depend in some important part on thinkers and analysts like himself whose duty it was to place themselves at the service of the nation's political leaders.

America's experience in and after World War II is familiar in broad outline, a story told and retold until it has achieved familiarity through repetition. The sacrifices of the "greatest generation" of Americans on the battlefields of Europe and Asia are firmly fixed in the nation's collective memory. The dramas in the policy corridors at home and the administrative agencies are less familiar but no less important. The events in this book can seem in retrospect almost inevitable and preordained: the United States casts off isolationism, wins the war, revives the fortunes of a prostrate Europe, and builds a strong alliance against the expansionist communist empire of the Soviet Union. The institutions that carry out the national purpose arise, so it seems, almost automatically from the logic of events. A nostalgic mist hovers over the story. Even the historians who blame the United States for precipitating the Cold War tend to portray Americans as dominating events. Reality, the choices and the twists of fortune that Americans and their allies actually faced, sometimes gets lost in this simplified narrative. History is more contingent and compelling than either the triumphalist or the revisionist narrative suggests. The past is more interesting when viewed through the eyes of those who lived it and when the sharp peaks of experience are not worn down by repetition and familiarity.

1

Dorothy and Dad

I loved turning the pages for Mummy.
—Lincoln Gordon, 2009

Lincoln Gordon was born in a post-Victorian America brimming with Progressive ideas of reform and social justice. The bustling New York City of his youth provided many opportunities for the new professional classes, which blended easily with the established aristocratic families still dominating the country's social, economic, and political life. His family, led by his gifted and assertive mother, had grown away from its immigrant and ethnic origins and embraced Americanism. Lincoln's religion, to the extent he had anything resembling religious belief, consisted of devotion to the creed of American exceptionalism and the embrace of secular humanism. His intellect and purposefulness attracted the attention of his teachers, first at the Ethical Culture Fieldston School and then at Harvard and Oxford. His education gave him several deep convictions that would continue to guide his thinking: that a strong government was necessary in domestic affairs to make capitalism work and that in foreign affairs fascism and Nazism (and later communism) imperiled world peace and had to be confronted. A unifying principle tied together these strands of thought: America was the world's indispensable nation, which provided economic well-being and opportunity at home and protected democracy and Western values in the world.

On January 10, 1891, a man named Leo Lerner arrived at Ellis Island with his family from a small town in Moldavia. The immigrant family included Leo, age forty-one, who was identified as a law student on the ship's manifest; his wife, Rose, age thirty-five; and daughters Tillie, thirteen, Katherine, eleven, Adele, six, Elizabeth, seven, and Dorothy, four.[1]

Leo settled his family on Manhattan's Lower East Side, populated by Jewish and other immigrants, and soon worked his way to a law degree from New York University Law School. He began practicing law, specializing in real estate transactions, but quickly spread his wings into real estate speculation and by 1897 had amassed considerable wealth. Leo became a philanthropist specializing in Jewish causes and brought numerous members of his extended family to the United States, where they prospered and participated in the American Dream.

Of his entire extended family, Leo's youngest daughter, Dorothy, was the most notable figure. She became a well-known singer and broadcaster in the new medium of radio and later the anchor of a popular national television show. She was gifted at languages as well as music. Her first language was probably either Yiddish or Rumanian, and she spoke all of the Romance languages and German very fluently (which came in handy in her performing career when she sang folk songs in their native languages). She was a natural storyteller from an early age and often invented stories about her own background. She created the fiction that she was the daughter of an American diplomat and that she had acquired her fluency in languages in his many postings to Europe.[2] She did travel widely in Europe in her youth, but her father was an immigrant, not an American diplomat. Despite her cosmopolitan background, she had a strong desire to be Americanized and took no interest in her Jewish heritage or her family history.

On June 29, 1910, Dorothy married Bernard Gordon, a lawyer who lived near her family's home in Brooklyn. Dorothy and Bernard had two sons: Frank H. Gordon, born on April 11, 1911, and Abraham Lincoln Gordon, born on September 10, 1913. The name "Abraham" did not last, however, and from an early age Abraham Lincoln Gordon was known only as "Lincoln" or "Linc" to his family and friends.[3] Occasionally the "Abraham" showed up on official documents and transcripts for a number of years, but by his graduate school years it had vanished.

Bernard Gordon

Allison Gordon, Lincoln's wife, described her father-in-law as "a very nice man." Family records show Bernard's birth as having taken place on July 23, 1879, in New York City. His parents were Moses (born in Russia, emigrated to the United States in 1870) and Fannie Belson Gordon (born in Russia, emigrated to the United States in 1874). Bernard was the second of ten children. He had little contact with his parents and his siblings after he married Dorothy and moved to New York's Upper West Side. In fact, Lincoln and Frank Gordon never met their paternal grandfather, who moved to Jerusalem sometime in the 1910s and died there in 1922. Dorothy and Bernard moved around in Manhattan's West Side a number of times until they settled in their permanent home in the city at 37 Riverside Drive, overlooking Riverside Park and the Hudson River, with a view of New Jersey in the distance.

In 1924 Bernard made a shrewd investment when he bought 250 acres of waterfront property at Lake Sunapee, New Hampshire, which became the family's summer home. He bought the land and a compound including a main house and several adjacent buildings very cheaply, but over the years the property appreciated enormously in value and proved to be critical to the family's fortunes. It was a majestic spot, and the Bernard Gordons and their children spent every summer there for the rest of their lives. (Winter vacations there were common as well for the Lincoln Gordon family.) Frank Gordon's widow, ninety-seven years old at the time of this writing, still lives there except during the coldest months of the winter. The combination of a place in the city and a retreat outside it during the hot, pre-air-conditioning summer days was the norm for affluent New Yorkers and added greatly to the family's quality of life.

Bernard was something of a moralist. He did not believe in gambling, and he considered the stock market to be gambling. He never invested in the booming market of the 1920s because stocks were mere speculation, whereas land had solid value. BG, as he was known to family and friends, was an ardent amateur horticulturalist and loved to identify every plant, bush, and tree on his property. The family's Lake Sunapee summer home had something of a romantic past. Over the grand fireplace in the living room hangs the antlered head of an African elk, nicknamed Hiram by the Gordons, supposedly shot by President Teddy Roosevelt, who was a friend of the previous owner. The house had been built around 1885 and originally located on the opposite side of the lake. When it was sold, around 1900, the new owner decided to sled the house using oxen teams across the frozen lake in winter to a new location on the opposite side of the lake. As the house neared its destination, it was near dusk, and the owner decided to suspend operations for the night to spare his workers from a possible accident in the dark. The workers advised him not to stop because the house could sink through the ice during the night. The owner should have listened to the workers, for the house did indeed break through the ice overnight, and about a third was underwater when they returned the next morning. With oxen and mechanical winches, the house was dragged back onto the solid ice, and from there it was hauled up the slope to its present location on top of a rocky hillside. The main house was known as Chetwood by the owner, and Bernard and Dorothy retained the name. It has been refurbished and expanded several times over the years, including a substantial renovation by the Gordons after the house suffered severe damage in the 1938 New England hurricane. The compound Bernard purchased included the main house, a boathouse, a barn, and several other adjacent buildings. In 1937 Bernard gave Lincoln a parcel of land and the means to build a house of his own—called Dark-water by the Lincoln Gordons—on a site only a short walk through the woods from Chetwood.

By the time of Bernard's death in 1944, his law practice had declined to the point that his small firm had to be closed down, and his sole partner, unable to pay the office rent, had to reach a settlement with the landlord. Bernard in fact left his wife nothing except the New Hampshire real estate, so Dorothy subsequently had to fend for herself and rely on her broadcast earnings. Bernard's health may have been a factor in the firm's decline, as Bernard had begun to suffer from poor health in his later years. He had a heart condition as early as 1928, when his son Lincoln, then fifteen, drove him from the summer home in New Hampshire to New York City to see Dr. Albert Freudenberg, the family physician and his father's close friend. Bernard did not fully trust the medical attention he received in New Hampshire, and Lincoln was proud his father had entrusted him with this important mission, which seemed to the boy a life-and-death matter.

Bernard's death came rather suddenly in 1944. He was working alone at his boat slip when he fell and struck his head on a concrete footing. He was found unconscious and half submerged by his wife's sister, Lizzie, and was dragged out of the water and revived. But he had suffered severe injuries as a result of either the fall or the stroke or heart episode that might have caused the fall. He declined rapidly and died two months later. Dorothy, distraught, suffered a heart attack herself within a month of Bernard's death. She installed an elevator, still operating in a rickety fashion when I visited the compound in the summer of 2012, so that she would not have to climb the stairs to her second-floor bedroom at the Lake Sunapee home. Dorothy placed her husband's ashes in a gravesite on a hillside in the woods overlooking Lake Sunapee (and Lincoln and Frank placed her ashes there as well when she died twenty-six years later).

Dorothy Gordon's Influence on Lincoln

The young Lincoln's first dim memories were of being carried on his father's shoulders, perhaps at the New Jersey shore. A more distinct memory was that of a newsboy calling, "Armistice! Armistice!" at the end of World War I. At five years of age he evidently had some sense of the external world and of his own identity. Dorothy Gordon took a special interest in her younger son. She regarded him as "sickly" and feared that he might not develop normally. He was small for his age at five and did not have the physical vigor and strong temperament of his older brother. Dorothy herself was diminutive, at five feet, two inches. (Lincoln grew to five feet, eight inches.) His older brother, Frank, in contrast, was boisterous, outgoing, and willful. Frank delighted in arguing with and challenging his mother at every opportunity (and this continued throughout their lives). Dorothy felt closer to Lincoln, and throughout his life he was drawn to intelligent, strong women.

Dorothy decided in any case that she would make a project of nursing Lincoln to robust health and of attending to his education. She homeschooled him and doted on him. An important part of the education she provided was cultivating in him her love of music. His quick mind and talent for learning were well suited for this project, and by the age of five or six he could read music. Dorothy, the decisive figure in her son's development and the most important person in his life, lit up any room she entered, a dramatic and alive presence who was an entertainer even when she was not on stage. To her grandchildren, who lived with her during New Hampshire summers, she remains a vivid and unforgettable personality. Because of his special bond with his mother, Lincoln felt he was something special, part of her circle, and he cherished the time he spent with her and her many friends, who were frequent guests at their Manhattan home and in New Hampshire. In 2004 he recalled a typical evening with his mother when he was a boy. He was part of the lively circle sitting at his mother's end of the table, while Frank and his father sat at the other end, removed from the action: "She [his mother] had many friends at the Metropolitan Opera, mostly Italians, making for my recollections of Saturday evenings at our apartment. That was one of two maid's nights off every week. I can still almost taste portions from an enormous bowl of pasta cooked by my mother. Then there was animated conversation in a language I could not follow and gathering around the piano for an evening of musical joking—all without any alcohol."[4]

The reference to the lack of alcohol reflects Bernard's insistence that no alcohol could be served in his house during Prohibition. Because he was a lawyer, Bernard considered that he was an officer of the court and could not violate the law even in his own home. Lincoln never saw his father take an alcoholic drink until 1923, on a family trip to Canada, when the train crossed over the border and left US jurisdiction. This abstinence policy apparently did not diminish the liveliness of Dorothy's parties.

Around 1921, at the time Dorothy was home-schooling Lincoln and teaching him to read music, she decided to embark on a career as a singer. According to family legend, it was Lincoln who gave his mother the idea. Since she liked children and had a whole repertoire of songs that she sang to her son, he suggested that she go out and sing for an audience of children and their parents. Her first love was opera, but her voice was not strong enough in those preamplification days. Dorothy included a role for Lincoln in her early plans: because he was so adept at reading music, she had him turn the pages for her as she played the piano and sang. As she refined her act later, she had a professional accompanist. A family photo from earlier days shows the smiling boy, dressed in a suit, sitting alongside his mother on the piano bench while she sings to a group of children. He is glancing down at his mother's fingers on the keys, beaming, evidently pleased with himself, and very comfortable in his role as her assistant. In the last year of his life, Lincoln told his daughter-in-law Bridget Gordon, "I loved turning the pages for Mummy when she performed."

During World War II and its aftermath, his knowledge of economics and his unique ability to navigate between his superiors and specialists made him useful to Bernard Baruch, General George Marshall, Averell Harriman, and later Presidents Kennedy and Johnson. In 1997 the national television networks, as part of their coverage of the fiftieth anniversary of the Marshall Plan, showed a film clip of Secretary of State

George C. Marshall testifying regarding the Marshall Plan before the Senate Committee on Foreign Relations. Behind him sat Lincoln Gordon, ready to provide the secretary with any technical details he might need. Lincoln, in the Senate chambers, had the same expression on his face that he had when turning the pages of his mother's music.

Dorothy made her radio debut in 1923, which increased her popularity and the size of her audience. By the late 1920s her act was highly professional. An enthusiastic *New York Times* review described how Miss Gordon (as she was known professionally) captivated an audience of children, young teens, and parents at one of her "Songs from around the World" concerts.[5] She began a regular show on radio in the early 1930s, and in 1943 she developed *Youth Forum,* which was broadcast for years on WQXR, the *New York Times* radio station. Later NBC television took the program on and broadcast it nationally. The show featured the discussion of public issues for and by children, high school students, and young adults, with prominent figures making guest appearances. Dorothy's career flourished as her son's career also took off, and she remained Lincoln's close friend and confidante. Prominent guests on Dorothy's show included such figures as Dwight Eisenhower, Averell Harriman, and Golda Meir. She may have met Harriman before Lincoln did. He became one of her favorite guests, and the two were on very cordial terms. Shortly after Dorothy's death from stomach cancer in May 1970, Harriman sent the following telegram to Lincoln:

DISTRESSED BEYOND MEASURE TO LEARN OF YOUR MOTHER'S DEATH. SHE WAS A TERRIFICALLY VITAL FORCE FOR EVERYTHING THAT IS GOOD. MARIE JOINS IN SENDING OUR DEEPEST SYMPATHY AND LOVE.
AVERELL

Lincoln, caught up in his duties at commencement, responded ten days later:

Dear Averell:
Only the fact that day-to-day campus pressures occupied almost every waking moment until our Commencement last week has

kept me from acknowledging long since your very kind telegram of May 13 concerning my mother's death last month. I am sure that you know that you were her most favorite youth forum guest, and your willingness to join her year after year was a source of great delight to her. I was in New York on Sunday morning, May 17, when NBC broadcast the tribute to Dorothy which included two splendid contributions of yours. I observed to Allison that your special rapport with my mother reflected your shared unquenchable youthfulness of spirit, which apparently has nothing to do with the calendar.

Dorothy knew that her health was failing rapidly during the six or eight months before she died, and she had set her heart on finishing this year's programs. The last one was taped on Tuesday six days before she died. Even with ample advance warning, it is hard for me to realize that she is really gone, but there is much comfort in the quality of her life and the way in which she took her leave. That she won the friendship and respect of people like yourself is itself a great tribute.

Allison joins me in regard and thanks to Marie and you.

Sincerely,

Linc[6]

Past and Future

For Lincoln Gordon there was no past, no family history, and no ethnic or group identity other than his Americanism. He was the quintessential American, starting from a fresh slate. He had never met his paternal grandfather and had no contact with his father's siblings or relatives. He had met his maternal grandfather only once and then only to shake his hand on the 1923 family trip to the Rockies, Canada, the Yukon, and back down to Los Angeles, where they stayed with one of his mother's sisters. Lincoln had no interest in his family tree, his ancestors, his origins, or his Jewish heritage. He never showed any interest in his roots because his mother had no such interest; she invented herself as an American, a pioneer in the entertainment world, an early feminist. He was, like his mother and the New York City and America he knew, forward looking, optimistic, secular, and malleable—ready to take advantage of the opportunities presented by the booming and bustling America of the Progressive Era. His mother by virtue of her talents had become a successful figure in the entertainment and media world, a kind of Oprah Winfrey of her day. His father by virtue of his hard work was a successful lawyer. Lincoln was dimly aware that there was an Edith Wharton world of the aristocracy in his native New York, a world made up of old money, landed gentry, railroad magnates, and fashionably dressed ladies. His family was not like the Roosevelts, the Harrimans, the Rockefellers, and other grand families, but there was a connection between those families and his own. Harriman's railroads, Carnegie's foundations, Rockefeller's universities, and the Roosevelt interests had to be managed by people of talent, energy, and training. The institutions and the society produced by the wealth of the old families could not be run without the talented layer of people who served them. The Gordon family belonged to a kind of minor gentry because of their large land holdings in New Hampshire and the deference this brought from the townsfolk. The Gordons did not want to battle or overthrow the aristocracy, but to join it.

From early on Lincoln and Frank Gordon knew they were part of an elite, or a meritocracy, though they would not have used such terms. They understood that they did not belong to the old New York families, but they were part of the educated circle represented by their parents and their parents' friends. All of them valued education and had risen in the world by virtue of hard work and education. The boys had a tutor during the summer so they would not forget their lessons. The family traveled often, enjoyed a trip to Europe in the summer of 1922, and had servants. Three families—the Woodruffs, the Tilsons, and the Gordons—in the 1920s and 1930s owned all of the land surrounding Lake Sunapee near the town of Gorgas Mills. As they grew up, the boys felt that they owed something to their community and country for the privileged lives they enjoyed.

The social circle in which Bernard and Dorothy Gordon moved reinforced their sons' outlook. Bernard Gordon's closest friend was George Z. Medalie, a prominent New York lawyer and Jewish philanthropic figure who became US attorney for the Southern District of New York under President Herbert Hoover and ran for the US Senate in New York in 1932 against the Democratic incumbent Robert F. Wagner. Medalie, a Republican, worked closely with Democratic politicians both upstate and in the city. New York politics, though intensely competitive and labyrinthine in their complexity, were an elite affair in those days, and the politicians knew each other well and struck bargains readily within and between parties. Medalie visited the Gordons regularly and often spent part of the summer with them in New Hampshire. Medalie knew both of the Gordon boys from birth and held long conversations with them. The boys acquired an interest in public affairs from Medalie and from their neighbors at Lake Sunapee, the John Tilsons. Tilson, who lived on the other side of Lake Sunapee and owned a large acreage, was a prominent Connecticut Republican congressman and later a member of the Republican National Committee. The Tilson boys and the Gordon boys were the same ages and shared summer activities. The two families socialized regularly during their summers at the lake.

Lincoln and Frank's interest in politics and public life was reinforced by their mother's advocacy on behalf of children in New York City. Lincoln also developed a lifelong interest in birth control issues by observing Margaret Sanger's efforts at Planned Parenthood. The Gordon boys, however, never took an interest in electoral politics for themselves. Running for office meant to Lincoln and Frank an ethnic identification that they disdained. They sought an American rather than a group identity and deemed the rough-and-tumble of electoral politics a concern of the lower class. Like other progressives of their time, they would rather deal with the small circle of aristocrats who had reached the pinnacle of power than try to climb up the greasy pole of power via seeking office in their own right. Like many other progressives who were technocratic in outlook, they shunned electoral politics as the province of party hacks, big-city bosses, and populist demagogues.

It was clear to the Gordon boys that their future lay not in commerce, but in one of the learned professions. Law was a strong possibility, and Lincoln for a time flirted with medicine. There was never any discussion in the Gordon household of the commercial world, no paper routes, no lemonade stands, no hint of the necessity of making a living through business activities. Of course their mother was skilled at marketing herself, but her involvement in music and broadcasting was an act of creative self-expression more than a commercial venture. A livelihood would come as a byproduct of one's professional life. The only businessman to appear in their home as a family friend was Margaret Sanger's husband, Noah Slee, who had made a fortune with his invention of Three-in-One Oil. He was now a philanthropist, giving away his fortune to support his wife's causes. In Lincoln's eyes, Slee was a man of science and technology, a modern man who was inventing the new devices and products that were transforming the lives of Americans and forging the new consumer economy and prosperity. So the Gordon boys, who lacked a past, looked forward in the American fashion to the future, and the future they saw was not in business or politics, but somewhere in the growing professional worlds of law, education, research, philanthropy, and public service.

World War II changed Lincoln's and Frank's lives in different ways. It propelled Lincoln into a life of public service, a role in momentous events, and a place in history as America moved into the position of leader of the Allied wartime coalition and shaper of the postwar international order. At the end of his life Lincoln started but never finished a memoir. In this draft memoir he recalls clearly his childhood and includes vignettes detailing his involvement with the wartime mobilization and the Marshall Plan. He dodges, though, the controversies of his public life and does not address the reasons behind the success or failure of the policies he pursued. He does not attempt to assess or defend his "legacy" or that of the outside professionals who moved from their jobs in the private sector into government service. Although he was a student of government, he does not attempt to analyze his own role or to evaluate the contributions and decisions of the high-level officials and political leaders for whom he worked. It seemed self-evident to him that the country needed a shared national purpose and that this meant putting aside all domestic political quarrels. The wartime and postwar emergencies required the infusion of outside talent because the government was too small and ill equipped for the enormous new challenges it faced. Gordon was proud of his public service, but he did not think in terms of his own legacy or probing deeply into his motives or those of his various associates or of assessing what he and others had actually accomplished in the light of history. He considered the wartime mobilization and the Marshall Plan to be great successes, but he was not sure about his other public service. The highs and lows of his career were linked to the successes and failures of American policy, but he does not address such questions in his memoir.

How is it that one could excel in one role and fail in another? Were Gordon's particular talents well suited for a period of consensus and shared purpose but less suited for a contentious period? Gordon, it seemed, was more successful when he was insulated somewhat from politics and served in a staff role for figures such as Marshall or Harriman and less successful when he himself was in charge. Was such a difference attributable to the personal qualities required for a political or line-manager role as opposed to a staff role, or were different historical and political circumstances the decisive factors? The United States, during the Korean War, adopted a state of semipermanent mobilization built around strengthened governmental machinery, along with a network of private contractors serving the military. Did this military-industrial complex do away with the need for the temporary services of talented outsiders? Was the World War II generation of Wise Men and their supporting cast nothing more or less than an accident of history that has nothing to say to us today about government and policy-making? Gordon's public life speaks to these questions, to the respective roles of the great and the near-great in history, to an understanding of the mysterious qualities of leadership and what leaders owe to their advisers, and to an understanding of critical chapters in the history of America and the Cold War.

2

Secular Humanism
at Fieldston

Look on my works, ye Mighty, and despair.
—Percy Bysshe Shelley, "Ozymandias"

Bernard and Dorothy Gordon chose the Ethical Culture Fieldston School for Lincoln in part because the school was hospitable to Jewish children. Indeed, the ethical culture movement had played an important role in Jewish assimilation and in the rise of secular humanism among Jews. The school was also coeducational. Girls competed at a varsity level at least in basketball and baseball.[1] That the students studied the classics of English literature probably impressed Dorothy and Bernard. The Fieldston curriculum had some of the same rigorous learning as the prestigious boarding schools of New England, but without the hazing and the social hierarchies.

The principal of Fieldston was Herbert W. Smith, who sported the bow tie favored by the redoubtable Endicott Peabody of the Groton School. But Smith was a much less intimidating figure than Peabody. He was a serious man, modest and low-key, very much the headmaster, and proud of Fieldston's reputation for academic excellence. He had high intellectual standards but did not have a powerhouse personality. He was treated with a degree of easy familiarity by the boys and girls, as apparently were the middle school principal, Ralph P. Boas, and the dean of girls, Emma Mueden. The school stressed the students' individuality and self-development rather than discipline and conformity. Athletics were important, but not quite on a par with the playing fields of Eton, which supposedly gave British schoolboys their stiff upper lips. The friendlier atmosphere must have appealed to Dorothy, who believed that Lincoln had intellectual gifts but needed room to develop in his own way. The school clearly had a college preparatory focus, a feature that the Gordons of course wanted. At this time it was not taken for granted that high school graduates would go on to college: only some 5 percent of high school graduates did so.[2]

The Gordons decided to send Frank to Andover Academy in Massachusetts. As noted earlier, he was difficult to manage at home and clashed repeatedly with his mother. His parents felt that a stay away from home in a disciplined environment might "tame" him somewhat. Boarding school tuition for their younger son thus might have been financially burdensome, and down the line there would be a need to pay college tuition for both of them. Lincoln was, in any event, a different personality from Frank, and it is likely that Dorothy wanted her younger son to be closer to her.

The yearbook picture shows the young Lincoln Gordon to have a mop of wavy hair, strong angular features, and a look that is bold, with perhaps a touch of defiance. The caption under the photo reads, "Look on my works, ye Mighty, and despair."[3] The reference is to Shelley's Ozymandias of Egypt, king of kings, whose inscriptions on two giant legs of stone, half-buried in the desert sands, are noted and commented on by the poem's traveler/narrator. The poem intrigued the young Lincoln. He puzzled over the poem for much of his adult life and was very pleased at his late success in finding an explanation for one line that had long baffled him: "The hand that mocked them and the heart that fed." Gordon's mastery of the sonnet form would show up years hence when he amused his colleagues at the War Production Board (WPB) with a verse rendering of the board's troubles that used the same rhyme scheme as did Shelley's "Ozymandias." Gordon made such a hit with his sonnet that he took to composing verse for future family ceremonial occasions and assorted tributes to friends.

Lincoln was evidently popular with his classmates, who were bemused by his sense of self, even if at times they found him too serious. In a spoof labeled "Last Will and Testament" in the school yearbook, the "Field-glass," class members bequeath certain of their traits to others. Lincoln Gordon leaves "his beautiful humility, among other things, to Aline Bernstein."[4] His classmates evidently did not consider him or Aline humble. He was, though, human enough to have a crush on Aline, and his classmates were engaging in a bit of gossip here, for Aline, indeed, was his first love. A junior, Aline has no picture in the yearbook, but articles describing her brilliant later career as an art and architecture critic call her "blond" and "attractive."[5] In a diary entry of March 1, 1937, Gordon rhapsodizes about meeting Allison Wright, the woman he would marry, and writes, "I can honestly say without exaggeration that this comes closer to an emotional revolution for me than anything since that extraordinary 22nd of February, 1930, with Aline—still the happiest single day of my life."[6]

Aline went on to Vassar in 1931, the year after Lincoln went off to Harvard. The two saw each other at Vassar, but the encounter or encounters did not go well, and they broke off contact. When Gordon looked her up upon his return from England in 1936, Aline was already Mrs. Joseph Louchhein and expecting a baby. He found her "tremendously improved since our meeting at Vassar."[7] The two had a pleasant and warm meeting, but there is no record of any future contact in their busy lives. Nor is there any indication that he was aware of her remarkable career as critic, journalist, author, TV personality, news executive, and the wife (her second husband) of the famous Finnish architect Eero Saarinen.[8]

Gordon wrote years later that the quality of the Fieldston faculty "was very high, including women who today could be university professors or leaders in business, the professions, or public affairs."[9] His teachers made a deep impression on him. Gordon did not keep in touch with his principal, Mr. Smith, as FDR and other Grotonians kept in contact with Endicott Peabody over the years.[10] But he was on good terms with his principal and seems to have absorbed some of Smith's understated leadership style. When the school moved into its new quarters in Riverdale, Smith asked for volunteers to help in transferring the school's lab equipment to the new facilities. He was especially pleased that young Lincoln devoted weekends to helping his chemistry teachers prepare the new laboratory.

During Gordon's senior year at Fieldston his class made a weeklong trip to Washington, DC, to observe both the House of Representatives and the Senate in action. This trip whetted Gordon's interest in American history and civics, which had been sparked by "an excellent course in American history with a special emphasis on the 'critical period' (1781 to 1789), the constitutional convention of 1787, and sample readings from the Federalist Papers."[11] Other Fieldston work included music, drama, drawing, and woodworking. Gordon had the lead role in his class play his senior year. He was, by his own estimate, "a dud in painting and sculpture but good in woodworking and music and not bad in athletics."[12] He took pride in installing bookshelves in his various houses and even designed a house he had built on Lake Sunapee in the late 1930s.

Lincoln was the captain of the basketball team his senior year. At five feet, eight inches, he was what we now call a point guard. He was not the team's main scorer, but his value is suggested by his teammates choosing him as captain. The team had a good year, winning nine and losing only one. Fieldston defeated such schools as Riverdale, Cathedral, Lincoln, Pratt, Franklin, and Irving and lost only to Horace Mann by the lopsided score of 48 to 32. But then in the final game of the year, the squad defeated Horace Mann in a rematch, 35–24.[13] Gordon was also on the varsity track team and the tennis team. In track he ran cross-country races and also four-hundred-yard and eight-hundred-yard races. Tennis remained a passion for him into his nineties, despite problems with his feet as he grew older. In the 1970s, after he gave up the cello, he started playing tennis four to five times a week and was constantly in search of partners. His style, as described by his son Hugh, "was unorthodox and his service weak, but, as with many aspects of his life, his terrier-like tenacity in chasing the ball made up for his lack of refined technique."[14]

The hard work in the classroom was punctuated with summers of hard physical activity at Lake Sunapee. The alteration of intense intellectual activity with periods of strenuous exercise and physical activity, the interplay of the city and the country, was beginning to form the pattern of his life. Lincoln never quite became an enthusiast for one of the more rarified sports, such as polo, a passion that drove Averell Harriman, but Lincoln and Frank both became moderately proficient at horseback riding. Lincoln was also an experienced sailor, but he did not develop the love for sailing and yachting that led to a lifelong avocation for Frank. Perhaps because sailing was Frank's passion, Lincoln preferred his own simpler enjoyments: hiking in the mountains, chopping wood, skating and cross-country skiing in the winter, carpentry, and talking with adults. He enjoyed discussing social reform with Margaret Sanger, business with Noah Slee, and law with George Medalie.

As graduation drew near, college beckoned and with it the issue of the direction he would take in life. There was still the unfinished business of winding up classes and exams and taking college boards. Something of his mindset at this time is suggested by the letter he wrote as a sixteen-year-old to his mother on Mother's Day in 1930. It is not certain where Dorothy was at this time. She was either on tour or abroad gathering material for one of her books of songs. The letter is handwritten in Lincoln's distinctive script. His parents may have complained about his handwriting, for in subsequent letters he resorted increasingly to the typewriter. He could wryly admit that his writing was not easy to read, but he took pride in the laboriously crafted characters and sweeping regular lines that were characteristic of the days when penmanship was a high art.

As usual, his mother is addressed as "Dorothy." The tone is both that of the dutiful son reporting on his activities and that of a wise friend giving her a pep talk to lift her spirits:

> Mothers' Day, 1930
> 5 1 30

Dear Dorothy,

This is an excellent traditional day on which to write to mothers—besides being a day when it's possible—so here goes.

Was overwhelmed yesterday to find a letter in the mail from none other than Peg [Margaret Sanger]. I suppose you've heard the news already, but it came as quite a shock to me. Think of Peg with bobbed hair! It seems almost impossible. But I suppose I'll get used to it. We got used to yours.

I'm slightly surprised to hear that you've been homesick. Is it really as bad as you say it is? Or were you just feeling a bit depressed when you wrote that letter? Of course it would be nice for you to be nearer home, but one cannot have everything, and success as an international singer is nothing to be sneezed at, so to speak. But you'll be back in just about a month from today, anyway, and we'll all be together for the summer—so why worry?

I've been roped in to speak to the parents of the junior and senior class next Friday night. Supposed to tell them what's wrong with the school where their children go to. I ought to be quite the public speaker by the time the year is over—as far as the valedictory is concerned, I wrote one that seems to me worse the more I think it over. But everyone is writing them—we ought to find one good one, or we may piece one together, and I seem to be the logical person to give it. I hope so, anyway.

It's been beastly hot in New York this week, and we've been putting on extreme pressure in work to get ready for the finals a week from Thursday. The end is really here now—and college boards are only a little over a month off. So we make the last grand effort that week in June, and that's the end of high school for us.

So lots of good wishes, Dorothy,—and hopes of seeing you soon.

Love,

Linc[15]

It was "us," his class as a whole, that was moving on. But it was he who was about to take a big step in life. Life had already changed. Frank had gone off, first to boarding school and then to Princeton. His mother's career was taking off, and she was gone for long stretches. His father was worrying more and working harder after the stock market crashed, even though the crash had not affected his family directly. Lincoln worried about his father's health. There would be decisions, a lot of them, for the young man to make. First things first, though: finals were coming up; summer at the lake—a last chance for some relaxing before college. And what college? Not Princeton. That was Frank's. It would be Harvard for Lincoln. In those days, students from good prep schools did not worry about getting into college. Harvard accepted over 90 percent of applicants. Lincoln's main worry might have been whether he would be excluded as a Jew. If he was accepted, what should he study, and what should he do for a living afterward?

He had a strong sense of self for a sixteen-year-old. He knew what he was good at—he was good at music, learned languages well, excelled in science, and was good in history and civics. A strong student in general, he was the valedictorian of his class. He knew that his path in life would center on his intellectual abilities. He also understood what he was not good at—he was a "dud" in drawing and art; he did not have charisma like his mother or Margaret Sanger. But he did not depreciate his considerable abilities, which included the ability to get on well and work with people who did have charisma. He could "piece together" the various valedictory statements of his classmates; it was only natural for him to be "roped in" to speak to parents. He was not a great athlete, but he thought that he was not bad either—after all, he had led his team to an eight-and-one basketball season. He was tenacious and extremely competitive.

He also had a sense of his place in the world. His mother had a wide circle of influential friends. Mr. Medalie, his father's friend, seemed to enjoy talking with him. And his Lake Sunapee neighbor Mr. Tilson, a congressman, also talked to him. He would accomplish something in life; of this he had no doubt. Of course, this would take hard work. Hard work was always necessary—after all, this was America, this was New York. The young Lincoln was hardworking, direct, competitive, and tenacious—traits one expected from New Yorkers. For those with a psychological bent, the young Gordon displayed the classic traits of the second child: he was determined to prove himself and to outshine his older brother. He was a driven young man determined to achieve his goals.

And what were those goals? He had a love of science and saw America as being transformed by science and technology. As Henry Adams viewed the steam age as a great historical divide, so Gordon saw modern science as altering the patterns of American life.[16] His science teachers had taught him, and he could plainly see, how new inventions were transforming daily life. The transformative power of technology was apparent in the host of new home appliances in the 1920s. Business would be increasingly shaped by science and research. Inventions like the telephone and electricity, and a whole range of new consumer products, affirmed the importance of science in Americans' lives and reinforced the role of reason in the conduct of human affairs. Lincoln could easily get to school via the IRT Broadway subway line, which had been opened in 1904 and completed in 1908. He could get across town via electric trolleys. Now a few gasoline-powered buses had begun to run on the cross-town routes, and it was rumored that the mayor might mandate buses for all the trolley routes. His mother could remember the old horse-drawn carriages replaced by the trolleys, the El replaced by the subways and the suburban trains.

Civics was an exciting topic, too, and was perhaps the arena where Lincoln's knowledge could be focused. Law would regulate matters and ensure that benefits were broadly shared. There was something great to be done, and it would involve science, law, and government. It was hard for Lincoln not to have a sense of history. Right outside his door, just a few blocks north of the home at 37 Riverside Drive, was the majestic Soldiers' and Sailors' Monument. It stood ninety-six feet tall, with twelve Corinthian columns, commemorating the New Yorkers who had died in the Civil War.[17] Standing before this monument, it must have occurred to him that his name, Abraham Lincoln Gordon, as it appeared on his birth certificate, was intended to place him in the sweep of American history. While the name "Abraham" was too Jewish and had been dropped, there was something in that name that spoke to him of American history. Farther north on Riverside Drive was Grant's Tomb, another reminder of the Civil War and American history.

While Lincoln felt himself to be an American, his gaze also naturally fell toward Europe. New York City was populated with people who came from Europe, its commerce was directed toward Europe, and the limited Asian and Hispanic immigrations had been halted by the restrictive immigration laws enacted by Congress in 1923. (The surge of Asians and Hispanics did not take place until the 1960s, when Congress loosened the immigration laws again, and the city's ethnic composition dramatically shifted as a result.) New Yorkers traveled regularly to Europe, as Lincoln had first done at the age of twelve, with his parents and brother. He had family roots and relatives in Europe, and educated persons like his mother spoke French, German, and other European languages. The Atlantic orientation was natural to New York's upper classes and to the emerging American establishment.

He was about to embark on a new chapter in life. He was sixteen, the class valedictorian, and one of the leading Fieldston students of recent classes, according to his principal, Mr. Smith. The future looked bright, but leaving home at sixteen must have been somewhat scary. There had been the stock market crash. He still referred to New York City as home in his college letters to his parents, but as he took up residence elsewhere, at Harvard and then in England and then again at Harvard, his home would no longer be the bustling city of his youth. He became a New Englander, saw his parents and brother mostly in New Hampshire over summers, and later alternated between Cambridge and Washington or wherever he might be posted in diplomatic service.

3

Harvard in Three Years

Is a people as politically self-conscious as us to suffer its machinery
to collapse—for the sake of tradition?
—Lincoln Gordon, "The Federal Trade Commission
and the Courts," 1933

Lincoln's first decision at Harvard was based on "an irrational desire to
catch up with my brother Frank."[1] Frank, two and a half years older, had
entered Princeton the previous year as a member of the class of '33. By
completing his requirements in three years, Lincoln could short-circuit
the process and graduate the same year as Frank. To finish in the same
year as his brother would be a coup of sorts in Lincoln's mind. The relationship between the two brothers as adults had already begun to take
shape, a relationship that was "correct but not warm."[2] His determination to finish early meant that Lincoln would not have quite the connection to Harvard College that Frank had to Princeton. Lincoln did make
close friendships as an undergraduate, but he was never an enthusiastic
or active alumnus. Frank, on the other hand, was an avid Princetonian.
After World War II, when Frank returned to the Office of the US Attorney for the Southern District of New York, he headed a team of prosecu-
tors in the highly publicized trial of leaders of the American Communist
Party. The trial was presided over by Judge Harold J. Medina, a fellow
Princeton alumnus. In securing the convictions of the communist leaders,
Frank remarked in a letter to his Princeton classmates posted in 2000 on
the Web site of the class of '33, he was helped by the cordial relationship
he had developed with the judge. The defense attorneys in the case never
realized "that Judge Medina and I were united by our love of Princeton."[3]
Over the 1930 summer in New Hampshire his father had persuaded

Lincoln to sign up as a prelaw student. The idea of finishing in three years worried Bernard, however, and he asked his good friend George Medalie, the US attorney for the Southern District of New York, to talk to the youth and try to convince him that finishing in three years was not a good idea. Medalie had an extended conversation with Lincoln but came away convinced—as he told Bernard—that Lincoln knew his mind, and there was no point in trying to hold him back. At Harvard Lincoln was assigned a senior member of the Harvard Law School, George K. Gardner, as his freshman adviser. Professor Gardner took his role seriously and tried to convince Gordon to follow the regular four-year pattern. "He went beyond the call of duty in seeking to dissuade me, including two lunches at the faculty club," wrote Gordon in his draft memoir. The professor marshaled various arguments but failed to budge the young man. Gardner must have been struck by the tenacity of the youth, who politely conceded the force of the professor's arguments but doggedly stuck to his guns.

The young man's resolve to finish in three years meant an extremely busy schedule. He rose early but not too early; he was a fanatic about getting plenty of sleep. There were typically classes all morning and most afternoons, including, in his freshman year, an afternoon chemistry lab. A C+ in his chemistry lab convinced him that he was not cut out for medical research. Somewhere each day he fitted in a squash game for a half hour or more (squash replacing tennis as his favorite sport because it could be played through the winter on convenient indoor courts). There was a one-hour rehearsal for the Harvard Chapel Choir, one of three choral singing groups he joined. Weekday evenings in his freshman year were given over to intensive study, usually in the library. By prearrangement a phone call from home might be on the evening schedule. There were no phones in the dorm rooms, and a call from New York was a long-distance call, not commonplace in those days. There was also no radio in his room until his parents finally sent him one so that he could be sure to catch his mother's broadcasts. His letters usually contained apologies for failing to write earlier, but the apologies were accompanied by accounts of how busy he was as his excuse. His weekends were more relaxed but still busy. His weekend activities included tennis, squash, cross-country runs, and hiking. He seriously considered trying out for the varsity track team as a cross-country runner but decided against it because it would take too much time. He enjoyed regular Sunday visits to the Belmont home of his favorite professor and mentor after he became part of the inner circle of William Yandell ("Wild Bill") Elliott.

Elliott was a charismatic and swashbuckling Tennessean who taught political theory and had a broad following among the students. In 1928 Elliott had published a much-admired and widely discussed book, *The Pragmatic Revolt in Politics,* but his scholarship had begun to fall off by the time of Gordon's arrival on campus.[4] Elliott was a large man with an outsized personality and equally large talents, ambitions, and pretentions. He had the air of an old-fashioned southern politician, was given to oracular pronouncements, and spent too much time cultivating a following and seeking an appointment to high office. At the same time he loved his students and was a warm friend to those who were part of his circle. He liked to entertain a select few students at his Belmont home with his gracious second wife and was invariably surrounded by his numerous cats and other pets. Elliott took a special liking to the young Gordon, recognizing in him rare intellectual gifts and strength of character under a quiet and unpretentious manner. Elliott subsequently played an important role in launching Gordon's career as a Harvard faculty member and public servant. Elliott talked often and with great enthusiasm about two of his favorite undergraduates at Harvard. One was Gordon. The other was also a New Yorker, a secular Jew with a cosmopolitan background who came along seventeen years after Gordon: Henry Kissinger.[5] In both cases, Elliott was a generous patron who unselfishly furthered the careers of these two gifted students and preached to them a gospel of public service that was genuine even if he in his own career had allowed his ambition for high office to become obsessive and to sap his intellectual energies.

In his freshman year, Gordon at times suffered from homesickness. In March 1931 he wrote his father: "Try to get up for the 21st if you can, won't you, Dad? I'd like very much to see you; my next visit to the city isn't till April 12th."[6] By the next year such references had disappeared from his letters, and his tone is brisker and more independent. He was not sure if he could make it back to the city for Thanksgiving—a decision would have to await developments in his schedule. His mother tried to entice him back home on a weekend to meet some of her literary friends, probably J. M. Barrie, the author of the Peter Pan stories, and A. A. Milne of *Winnie-the-Pooh* fame, who were both visiting from London. His mother's efforts were of no avail. Despite the important personages being in New York he was too busy for a trip down to the city.

Social Life

Not everything was hard work. After surviving his freshman year, Gordon found the pace more leisurely. It was almost too relaxed for him. He remarked unfavorably on the lack of seriousness of many of his fellow students. But Gordon was able to enjoy a lively social life, especially after he moved from Gore Hall, the freshman dorm, into Dunster House at the start of his sophomore year. Northrop "Nors" Beach became his roommate and close friend. The Harvard houses then had distinctive characters: Adams House had an artistic/performing arts tradition; Eliot House was Anglophilic, with the tutors and some students wearing three-piece suits; and Lowell House was clubby and suitable for young men from socially prominent New England families. Dunster House was the newest of the houses at that time and enjoyed a reputation as a home for earnest, hardworking, upper-middle- and middle-class students. Gordon was popular with his peers, was active in house affairs, and had a following among his fellow Dunster residents.

The closest thing to hijinks that Lincoln engaged in as an undergraduate resulted from a scheme that he and his roommate conceived to buy an old car to enhance their social lives. The car would help them get dates and do something within the strict time limits governing Radcliffe students on their evenings out of their dorms. So they pooled their resources and bought a used car. This was, in Gordon's somewhat Victorian formulation, "an enormous asset in the cultivation of girl friends, both for transportation to shows (or out-of-the-way suburban roads) and for gentle embracing before the timely return of the girl to her dormitory."[7] They found the ideal vehicle in a much-used Reo sedan, a long-since-defunct trademark, and they bought it for sixty dollars, giving it the nickname "the Dorabel." They devised a plan whereby roommate Nors would have first dibs on the car for Friday evenings and Lincoln for Saturday evenings, but Nors ended up often having first crack at the car on Saturdays as well if Lincoln had no date for the evening. One warm spring Saturday evening Lincoln found himself without a date, and Nors took the car. Nors assured Lincoln that he would only deliver a message to one of his

Radcliffe girlfriends and would be back shortly in case Linc needed the car. Feeling somewhat morose, Gordon ran into another friend, George Acheson, who announced that he had recently met a fun-loving young woman from nearby Dorchester. She had many friends, and Acheson proposed that the two of them take the car to Dorchester. Telephoning her was impossible. There was no car, Gordon explained. Nors had taken it to deliver a message. The two waited and waited.

Finally they decided to walk to Radcliffe, find the car, and leave Nors to hike back to Dunster House. After finding the car and driving to Dorchester, the two young men noticed a police car with flashing lights coming up behind them. The police car pulled up alongside them. George said, "I think the cop next to the driver is trying to signal you."[8]

"What's going on? We're certainly not speeding," said Lincoln.

"I think you'd better pull over. He's pointing his gun at you."

Lincoln pulled the Dorabel to the curb. The two officers approached the Dorabel with their guns drawn and ordered the young men out of the car.

"What's the problem, officer? I'm certain we weren't speeding," said Lincoln.

"You're driving a stolen vehicle, that's what's wrong," said the policeman.

Gordon burst out laughing.

"You think a stolen car is funny?" the officer said, having no patience with a smart-ass college type.

Lincoln explained that he was in fact the owner, or rather co-owner, of the car, and he had the papers to prove it. The cops holstered their weapons but remained wary. Lincoln produced the registration from the glove compartment and his own driver's license. The officer studied the papers and announced that the name on the registration was not the one on the driver's license. In fact the registration bore the name of the owner, who had alerted the police to the theft. Lincoln explained that his co-owner was actually his roommate, as could be seen by the fact that the addresses matched: G-41 Dunster House.

"Well, you had better come down to the station anyway," explained the officer, "because if I let you go another cop will pick you up since the bulletin has gone out."

That the police were still not wholly reassured was evident from the fact that Gordon was ordered to ride with the driver of the police car, and his partner drove the Dorabel, with George accompanying him. At the police station Nors Beach eventually was roused from Dunster House and went to the station around midnight, and finally the two young men were released. Nothing went on their records. The future diplomat was spared the prospect of explaining to security officers why he had an entry, though not a conviction, for car theft on his record.

Intellectual Development

Although Lincoln had listed prelaw as his likely major (as he had promised his father), he had made no final decision. He was torn among career choices in the hard sciences, in law, or as a college teacher in the social sciences. He consulted on his courses with Professor Gardner, his freshman adviser, and came up with a compromise that would allow him a sampling of courses while providing the opportunity to focus later without losing time. His freshman courses were "government, Greek, German, calculus, and chemistry."[9] This was a formidable schedule for the freshman just turned seventeen. The chemistry class included time-consuming lab sessions. But he persisted and in general flourished. His government course was particularly exciting, bringing him in contact with political philosophers and with the work of Professor Elliott. While becoming increasingly close to Elliott, Gordon also formed friendships with two of his younger tutors, Pendleton Herring in government and Edward Mason in economics, and found intellectual stimulation with Professor Charles McIlwain, a renowned constitutional scholar. Herring and Mason were attached to Dunster House and became Gordon's close friends after he moved there at the start of his sophomore year. Some forty years later, as president of Johns Hopkins University, Gordon would confer honorary degrees on Herring and Mason.

Gordon had a voracious appetite for learning in numerous fields when he arrived at Harvard, but he realized that he could not continue to be interested in everything. By the middle of his freshman year he decided that he had had enough of formal language training. He could not go further with Greek and German if he wanted to finish his degree in three years. He passed the French reading proficiency test so that he did not have to worry about the language requirement. The aforementioned C+ in his chemistry lab was enough to convince him that he "was not cut out for a career as a scientist."[10] The stock market crash and ensuing bank failures made economics a distinct possibility as a major. Gordon did not approach this subject out of a passion for social justice or ideological zeal. Rather, he approached the problems of the industrial economy as an intellectual exercise—as a matter of how to fashion workable solutions to practical problems. But there was something prior to economic relations—the legal and constitutional order—that provided the basic framework for economic decisions. He therefore chose government as his major, but with a heavy concentration of economics supplementing courses in government and history.

His conviction then was that the legal order and political factors came first, providing the basis for the direction of economic activity. He never wavered fundamentally from this conviction, but at various points in his career he was mainly preoccupied with economics, industrial development, and investment issues—a range of subjects more narrowly economic in nature. He studied Marxism but formed a conviction early that the evolution of the workers' movements in Western societies did not follow the path predicted by Marx. Marxism or Trotskyism, embraced by many of his contemporaries, did not appeal to Gordon even as a flirtation. He formed his basic convictions from Elliott's *The Pragmatic Revolt* and from Charles McIlwain's *Constitutionalism—Ancient and Modern*.[11] McIlwain became another mentor, and he took two courses with him. Gordon later credited McIlwain with shaping his aversion to revolutionary change. Evolutionary change offered much more promise for human progress than did revolutionary change.

Gordon's chief attraction to Elliott's ideas, however, lay in their ability to explain international trends. His imagination was clearly fired by Elliott's critique of fascism and syndicalism in Italy, which called attention to the threats to peace posed by these extremist movements. A favorite passage was this: "And now Italy's destiny has become momentous for many countries where democratic and representative government had won a slender foothold at least. In its imperialistic program and its avowed disbelief in the settlement of international disputes through any possible machinery of international justice, Fascism has international implications. It represents a complete denial of the existence as well as of the availability of any principles of morality applicable to the conduct of states—except the law of the survival of the fittest. It is the most serious existing threat to peace in Europe."[12]

As Gordon approached the end of his second year at Harvard, with only one year to go, he had immediate practical concerns on his mind. Professor Elliott had encouraged him to apply and had nominated him for a Rhodes scholarship to Oxford for the academic year beginning in the fall of 1933. Papers had to be turned in by October 1932, which meant that Gordon would have to propose a course of study for Oxford over the summer. And there was also an urgent need to formulate a topic for, and to begin work on, his honors thesis—the final version of which had to be turned in by April if he hoped to graduate in June 1933. In thinking about both of these matters, he began to formulate the themes that would occupy him for many years.

Thesis: "The Federal Trade Commission and the Courts"

For his honors thesis Gordon chose to study the Federal Trade Commission (FTC), a new regulatory agency created during the administration of President Woodrow Wilson. Although dense and at times almost unreadable, the thesis highlights vital issues of the 1930s and in particular the powerful Progressive currents in the New Deal that led to the Roosevelt administration's bitter battles with the Supreme Court over the reach of federal power. Gordon enunciated the argument that the federal courts were totally incompetent to deal with complex antitrust issues and should be replaced by a new tribunal made up of technical experts.

Gordon's letters home cautiously mention his "hopes" for the project, as if he does not want to jinx himself. Then he seems to gain confidence, and the hopes turn into "high hopes." The tone of the letters becomes that of a man who is happy in and good at his work. The thesis was a considerable labor: it was 125 pages long, with appendixes. It was copiously documented with references to books, law reviews, and other legal periodicals and references to cases, including some two hundred Supreme Court and other court cases that he had read in his father's law office. Since, as he notes, "few constitutional issues are raised in the interpretation of the Federal Trade Commission and the Clayton Acts," his task was therefore to examine the judicial review of the FTC "in order that some general principles might be evolved and that we might better appreciate the function which administrative adjudication can play in our political system."[13] The FTC provided Gordon a good case study because it involves the functions of experts trying to interpret and adapt the broad will of Congress in a complex and rapidly changing arena.

The villains Gordon attacks are rarely persons, but are rather the "legal mind," outmoded doctrines, and shortcomings in the common-law tradition. Gordon draws heavily in his analysis on Dean Roscoe Pound's much-admired treatise *The Spirit of the Common Law* (1921) in framing his critique of the courts. Gordon is willing to credit the common law with developing standards of protection for individual rights and applauds the Supreme Court for its role in extending and protecting human freedom. But while courts appropriately should devote extra attention to the protection of individual rights—the doctrine of "strict scrutiny," for example, in First Amendment freedom of speech—this judicial mindset is not appropriate, he declares, for judicial review of administrative actions and economic regulations. Law is not "found" through a long process of trial and error in a large number of cases. The normal common-law presumption that judges should always follow precedent is totally out of place in the context of economic regulation in our increasingly technological age. What is required in this area is technical and economic expertise.

Law is for practical purposes "made" by judges, Gordon argues, and hence the crux of the problem is that judges "lack expert knowledge" and do not have "the legislative facilities of committee specialization and expert testimony from all available open to them."[14]

Therefore, he declares: "We are drawn to the conclusion that the courts are not adequate entities for the performance of this function, either in applying standards of or in crystallizing them into rules of law, in the field of economic regulation. The practical desiderata behind the idea of the reign of law are certainty and justice, and the judiciary, from ignorance of the issues it is called upon to decide, can give neither."[15]

It remained for Gordon to give his ideas regarding the solutions to these problems. If not quite as compelling as his attack, his proposed solutions show originality and for that time a daring quality. His idea was that a new kind of appellate court and novel institutional arrangements were in order. This new institutional layer would be sandwiched between the Supreme Court and federal appellate courts, modeled somewhat on the Federal Reserve Board. Gordon's proposed new court would operate like a regular court, on the basis of written opinions, and would employ some of the features of normal judicial proceedings, such as following the practice of *stare decisis.* But it would be less bound by adherence to precedent than a regular court and would have some of the features of a Royal Commission in Britain. He concludes, slightly portentously, by posing a question: "Is a people as politically self-conscious as ourselves to suffer its machinery to collapse—for the sake of tradition?"[16]

Gordon's cast of mind—it is too much to claim that he has a vision of government's ideal role—is shown in his honors thesis. He is clearly in the camp of those who believe in the role of reason rather than tradition as a guiding principle in human affairs. Tradition, like the piecemeal solutions of the common law, gives us inadequate responses to the needs of a rapidly changing society. Reason—that is, applied intelligence—will produce the bolder solutions that will lift society over the obstacles and social problems that inevitably and increasingly arise in an industrial, urban society. Population growth and urbanization are facts of life, and a more complex economy calls into play a more complex governmental machinery to both regulate and stimulate the private economy. Gordon's vision is that of process—it is the vision of the progressives, the technocrats, the trained and dedicated elites with the intellectual capacity to analyze problems and devise solutions embodying broad national purposes. Of course broad moral purposes are involved, and the government must act in accord with the underlying values of society. The executive-branch agencies have the major role in policy, rather than the courts, which are too heavily invested with tradition, or the legislatures, which are too responsive to parochial and partial interests. Gordon's thesis might be almost an anticipation of FDR's "court packing" plan of a few years hence, designed to overcome judicial obstacles to the New Deal.

At the commencement ceremony there was a pleasant surprise. Lincoln discovered that Walter Salant, who had been the intellectual leader of the Fieldston class ahead of him, had been awarded a summa by Harvard's Economics Department. The two remarked on the fact that a small school in Manhattan had won two Harvard summas. Gordon had regarded Salant with something like awe at Fieldston and had not been close to him then or even in his three undergraduate years at Harvard. Salant, after the Harvard graduation, went to Cambridge University, while Gordon went to Oxford, and the two would go on to see each other frequently in England. There they would begin a friendship that lasted until Salant's death in 1997, when both men were visiting scholars at the Brookings Institution.

Looking Ahead to England

He was nineteen years old. He had graduated from Harvard College summa cum laude, and he had done so in three years. He had won a Rhodes scholarship. Now he was facing another major change in his life. It seemed like only yesterday that he was writing to his mother about tying up the loose ends as high school graduation approached. The three years at Harvard had been too rushed; he had shortchanged himself and would not do so again. He would henceforth take the full opportunity to study all the things he had missed at Harvard, staying three full years at Oxford. Then there was the matter of his career choice. He had decided to seek the DPhil, the British equivalent of the American PhD, so that he could embark on a career as a college teacher. There were some favorable signs that Harvard might beckon if he could get a dissertation published. For reasons of practicality he decided to abandon the idea of studying the evolution of Roman law. He needed a project that he could be reasonably certain to finish in three years. He decided that he would study the public corporation in Great Britain and would undertake this task through case studies of four such corporations. By the time he left for England, he had already decided on three of the four and had laid out in his mind the exact timetable he would follow to complete the project.

He traveled to England with his mother. He would have much preferred going with his Rhodes colleagues and getting the chance to become acquainted with everybody, but Dorothy insisted he come with her. They would travel first class on the *Ile de France* for the price of tourist class, because of the Depression. They would spend some weeks traveling in Europe, and then Lincoln would stay in England to make his way to Oxford. He had negotiated some of the itinerary, and to boot he would get his first plane ride. In fact there were two plane rides on the trip. They celebrated his twentieth birthday in Paris. Dorothy introduced her son to her literary friends in London, but he was unfamiliar with their writings and was not comfortable with them. Finally Dorothy and Lincoln ended up in Southampton, Dorothy to take the liner back to New York and he to travel on via bicycle to Oxford. He allowed three days for that leg. This left plenty of time for him to arrive by the start of term in October 1933. He felt confident that it was going to be a great adventure. He would travel in Europe over the summers and on holidays and get a first-hand look at developments abroad. He promised his father reports. That was the least he could do, since Bernard was helping out with his travel costs during the Oxford stay. Whatever happened in Europe, he would be there to see it.

4

An American at Oxford

Do you know that this is the most precious piece of paper in the world?
—Unidentified German woman, 1936

Seeing his mother off for America, Lincoln set off for Oxford on his new bike, which was to be his principal mode of transport for the next three years. His trunks had been sent ahead to the college, and he had carefully charted his way to Oxford with an estimated time of arrival on October 2. He encountered difficulty, with heavy rain that slowed him down for the first two days. The weather cleared up the third day, and he was able to pedal his way pleasantly along the Stratford-on-Avon Road. He arrived a day ahead of schedule and found his rooms ready for him. His quarters were quite comfortable and included a piano. His books had arrived already. He wrote to his mother that he had gotten a favorable exchange rate on the bank draft she had supplied him ($4.80 to the pound) and told her that he had already met the master of the college and that one must refer to him as "master" rather than as "sir."[1]

Gordon took to his new life with relish. At one of his first dinners he met a fellow Rhodes scholar and one of many Scots at Balliol College. The man was a lord and a substantial landholder in his native Scotland. They took a walk after dinner and engaged in a conversation about the class system in Britain and how the Depression had given rise to new class conflicts. The Scot explained that he was puzzled and saw no reason for class resentment.

"My family and my ancestors have always treated our tenants well," the Scot said. "We have kept their cottages in good repair, we give them a Christmas party every year, and if anyone gets sick we make sure that a doctor comes."[2]

Gordon inquired about the number of people working his lands.

"Well, I don't know exactly, but I think between 300 and 400," the Scot said.

This surprised the American, and Gordon began to understand more fully the British class system. What his companion described was a classic landed aristocracy. Along with class privileges, Gordon's Scottish companion shared an outlook privileging duty and obligation to society. A few years later the Scot was killed in the Battle of Britain as an RAF pilot. Although certainly American society was more fluid and open than British society at the time, the differences between the worldview of his Scottish friend and his own were not as great as Gordon imagined. Gordon referred to the community of Rhodes scholars as "our little brotherhood," which was more than a casual endearment. Lincoln shared with the Scot a sense of noblesse oblige, and he clearly was an elitist in the sense of believing that public affairs were the province of the well-educated classes. His Oxford years strengthened his Jeffersonian belief in the members of an "aristocracy of merit" as the natural leaders of society. The wider public could be persuaded to follow an enlightened course if appealed to on the basis of reason, but only if responsible leaders stepped forward and made themselves heard in the boisterous clamor of democratic politics. Gordon was suspicious of "the people," seeing in them the raw material for demagogues to exploit, especially in times of economic distress. It was the unemployed working classes, he believed, that formed the basis of support for Hitler and Mussolini. Still, Gordon was no nineteenth-century British Tory. Like most of his friends at Oxford, he had leftist political sympathies, but his leftist sympathies were those of FDR and the New Deal. Had he been a little older, Gordon would have fit perfectly as a member of the Roosevelt Brain Trust. He wanted to rescue capitalism from its own excesses, not to transform it. At Oxford, indeed, one of his regular activities was to explain the workings of the New Deal and US politics to his British colleagues. While he was sympathetic to the British Labor Party, he formed an extreme dislike for the party's far left wing (just as he later disliked the leftist anti-US intellectuals he encountered in Latin America and the American student radicals of the 1960s).

Gordon had listed Balliol at his first choice among the Oxford colleges on his Rhodes application and had been delighted to get it. Balliol had been Professor Elliott's college a decade earlier, and Elliott's enthusiastic letter of recommendation for Gordon had caught the attention of A. D. Lindsay, the master of Balliol College. Lindsay, highly popular in the college, was an unusual man to be the master of an Oxford college. Though highly learned and erudite, he was unassuming, a political activist and leader in the British Labor Party, a man who had risen from a working-class background and made his mark in education by teaching adults and union workers. Lindsay decided that he would himself provide a tutorial for the newly arrived American Rhodes scholar. Tall and good-looking, the master did not at all fit Gordon's preconception of a tweedy Oxford don, but the two men got on extremely well.

Gordon's tutorials with Lindsay consisted of Gordon reading and discussing a book a week on a topic he had not previously studied. The topics included Scottish political history, international law, and changing conceptions of good and evil. Lindsay combined a deep classical education with religion-based ethics and social democratic politics. Their most spirited intellectual disputes arose over religion. Gordon had no religious instincts whatsoever (other than a passionate belief in secularism) and often found Lindsay's explanations and defense of British religious practices baffling. How could it be, as Lindsay had once remarked, that the king of England was simultaneously an Anglican and a Presbyterian? Gordon could not quite fathom that the king was head of the Church of Scotland when he was at Balmoral Castle and that the royal religious identity then shifted back to Anglicanism when the king returned to London. The literal-minded American suggested that in this one instance ambiguity rather than strict logic might be preferable on the question of the king's religion, lest there be a return to earlier English religious wars. Lincoln enjoyed himself with Lindsay, and their exchanges developed into playful thrusts. On the question of religion, however, Gordon was always in earnest, not merely an agnostic but a militant atheist.

Gordon felt very much in his element in his two years at Oxford (before he moved to London for the harder work of writing his thesis). There were relatively few Americans studying at Oxford in those days. Few students sought the DPhil, because a first-class honors degree as an undergraduate was usually all that was needed for an appointment as don. Gordon stood out and at the same time blended in, mixing easily with the dons, who were closer to his age, but also with the Oxford under-graduates. He took up the ways of a don, wearing tweeds and flannels; he acquired a British accent. He took up pipe smoking, a habit that continued for decades. In his intellectual interests he veered between law and macroeconomics, the latter a subject then developing rapidly at Oxford. Gordon took a seminar cotaught by Redvers Opie and Jacob Marshak, the latter moving to Harvard in a few years and becoming Gordon's colleague there. This was a fertile time for the burgeoning discipline of macroeconomics, and perhaps the most significant development in the field was the work of John Maynard Keynes. Keynes had published his *Treatise on Money* in 1930 and was now hard at work on *The General Theory of Employment, Interest and Money* (1936). Gordon had read Keynes's *Essays in Persuasion* (1931) and his famous *Economic Consequences of the Peace* (1919), so it was a great pleasure for him to join a group of Oxford, Cambridge, and London graduate students who met in turn in the three cities to discuss the latest work in economics. A regular feature of the meetings in Cambridge was a teatime session at the home of Keynes, at which the great economist discussed his latest work and took questions from students. Gordon found Keynes "truly charismatic" (one of his favorite words at the time) and relished the exchanges with the famous man. Gordon regretted later that he had not sought to follow up his acquaintance with Keynes when the economist was visiting the United States during the Bretton Woods negotiations, but he presumed that Keynes was more than fully occupied at the time.

Gordon was becoming an increasingly enthusiastic New Dealer. He had had no direct contact with any actual New Dealers, but his intellectual embrace of Keynesian fiscal policies strengthened his already strong New Deal convictions. FDR's proclamation of a "New Deal" for America just months before Gordon's graduation from Harvard had fired his imagination, even if by his own assessment at the time he had only "inchoate ideas" about how the government should cope with the Depression. He took a special interest in George Norris's proposal for a Tennessee Valley Authority, which seemed to him to combine the virtues of forceful governmental action with the efficiency of corporate business practices. Gordon was often called upon to explain recent developments in America to his fellow students and dons, and of course he tried to follow events at home as closely as he could from England. Lincoln's father kept up a steady supply of clippings and articles to help fill him in on the latest news. Gordon not only gave occasional seminars on the New Deal but also gained a certain experience in the diplomatic arts by defending American policies to skeptical audiences.

An important chapter of Gordon's Oxford days was his romance with Margaret Peel, a recent Oxford graduate and a schoolteacher in London. She was an attractive and intelligent woman from a good family. Her father was a county judge and a collateral descendant of the nineteenth-century prime minister Sir Robert Peel. Margaret drove down from London frequently to visit him, and the pair traveled to Europe on holidays, usually with other companions for appearance's sake. The two were very much in love, but at the time they met, Lincoln was only twenty years old. This was too young for him to consider marriage, and he seems to have harbored some doubts about her. She apparently lacked forcefulness, and he liked strong, intelligent women like his mother.

Travels in Europe

A notable part of Gordon's stay was his extensive travel in Europe during the summers and holidays. This contributed to the understanding of Europe that he brought to his postwar work on the Marshall Plan and the North Atlantic Treaty Organization (NATO). He traveled to familiar tourist sites and to more out-of-the-way locations. His exposure gave him an immediacy of experience that was not obtainable from his formal studies. The Nazi seizure of power in the Weimar Republic had taken place in January 1933, before Gordon arrived in Europe, but the Nazi consolidation of power and other important events occurred during his years at Oxford. The Night of the Long Knives (Nacht der langen Messer), executed by Ernst Roehm, leader of the Brown Shirts, took place on June 30, 1934, while Gordon was in Heidelberg. The German reoccupation of the Rhineland, the failure of disarmament negotiations, Italian aggression in Africa, political instability in France, important shifts in the British party system, Gandhism in India and its effects on British politics, and the onset of the Spanish Civil War were some of the significant events taking place during this period.

Gordon became convinced from his first trip to the continent that the Nazis could not be dislodged from power short of war or some other major economic catastrophe. In letters to his parents he stressed the economic causes that had permitted the Nazis to rise to power. Nazism was a perverted form of a "New Deal" for Germany. Subsequent trips enlarged his grasp of the German political scene. In July 1934 he joined his friend Dick Crossman and a group of Oxford students for a conference at the University of Marburg in the German Rhineland. Crossman and Gordon were invited to dinner at the home of the German host of the conference, Professor Max Deutschbein, a leading Shakespeare scholar. After dinner the professor asked that he and his guests be excused to take coffee on the terrace. When they were alone, the professor shifted the conversation to English and launched into an agonized description of what was happening to his university under the Nazis. Jewish professors were being dismissed, Jewish students expelled; censors checked professorial writings; free inquiry and *Lehrfreiheit* were being destroyed; and anyone who protested risked his career. What should he do? Could he start over at his age in another country? Several days later another German faculty member who was married to a Swedish woman took Gordon aside and queried him on whether the American thought he might be able to emigrate to Sweden on the basis of his wife's nationality.

In a July 12, 1934, letter to his parents Lincoln described the German students as "a larger population of overgrown boys even worse than in Princeton!" He declared that "much of the teaching is in the way of propaganda" and that there was "no end of excitement over the events of the 30th of June," despite the fact that "the German press is doing its best not to say much—and thereby neatly leading itself into self-contradiction."[3] He went on to note that "these, however, are rather technical matters, which cannot interest you very much."[4]

Two years later, again in Germany with Crossman, he became convinced that Hitler had strengthened the Nazi position by restoring a measure of national pride to Germans. Gordon and Crossman were dining with a group of friends when a German at a neighboring table, noticing that English was being spoken, asked where they were from. The German went on to inquire whether they had been in Germany before. When told yes, he asked whether they noticed any difference. What kind of difference? they asked. We were *ohne Macht* (without power) then, he replied, and now we have our *Macht* back. And what did Germans plan to do with their power? "Well," said the German, as Gordon would later recount in his unpublished memoir, "we don't plan to attack anyone, but it's nice being a real country again."

In between the German trips in 1934 and 1936 with Dick Crossman, Gordon also went back to Germany during his summer holidays in 1935, on a hiking vacation in the Bavarian Alps with Margaret Peel and several other British friends. They traveled by rail to Berchtesgaden and on the first day climbed to the Zugspitze summit. The next day they hiked ten miles south to the Hintersee, a small lake with a country inn where they planned to spend the evening. They reached the inn around noon and found it crowded, with the manager distracted by a wedding party scheduled to arrive shortly. They were told to check in with the manager later. They soon picked up rumors that the "wedding party" was actually a visit by Hitler, who was stopping for lunch on his way to his summer residence at Berchtesgaden. Gordon positioned himself where he could observe the Fuehrer with the aid of binoculars. There was surprisingly little security. He could not see Hitler when he was seated, but every few minutes a cheer of "Fuehrer, Fuehrer!" came from a small crowd, and Hitler would rise and bow to the crowd. Nearly seventy years later, in his unpublished memoir, Gordon remembered Hitler's "face that was neither handsome nor ugly but with a pair of intense, almost compelling eyes."

But one trip stuck in his mind and brought home for him the realities of the European crisis. The recollection of an incident from that trip sixty-eight years later, he said, "still brings tears to my own eyes." In Danzig, on the final leg of the 1936 trip with Crossman, Lincoln found himself sitting alone at a table with one of the Danzig wives from their party. The two were watching their companions on the dance floor and engaged in an aimless conversation. Both Russian and German diplomatic activity was putting pressure on the city's inhabitants. The woman became earnest and shifted the conversation suddenly. She inquired if Gordon was an American. When told that he was, she asked if he had his passport with him. He did. She paused for some moments. Then she asked quietly if she might see it. He took out the green-bound document from his pack and handed it to her. She held it for some time and then placed in on the table. She continued to look at it and touched it again. Looking up slowly, her eyes flooded with tears.

"Do you know," she said, "that this is the most precious piece of paper in the world?"

The Public Corporation in Great Britain

Gordon had settled on his dissertation project and was well along by the fall of 1934. In the spring of 1935 he accelerated his pace because he had just one year left to complete the formidable intellectual effort of *The Public Corporation in Great Britain.*[5] He moved to London to be closer to the individuals he would have to interview, as well as his thesis adviser, G. D. H. Cole, then a fellow at University College, London. Cole was a prolific writer and popularizer of socialist doctrines and well connected in social democratic and government circles. Cole was well suited for the supervisory task, providing the American with sources and introductions to relevant officials. Gordon not only had to do a prodigious amount of reading on British administrative history but also had to interview numerous officials of the Port of London Authority, the Central Electricity Board, the British Broadcasting System, and the London Passenger Transport Board.[6] His target to complete the thesis was the spring of 1936.

His interest in the topic had been whetted by what he knew of the Tennessee Valley Authority in the United States. He first had to establish what, if anything, the four cases had in common. He showed how, in recent constitutional history, governments were replacing monopolistic competition with more accountable mechanisms. Highways, ports, rail transport, electricity, and telecommunications required huge capital outlays. Private monopolists often sought to extract rents from the public while neglecting investment and the maintenance of their facilities and did not serve certain parts of the population or always respect the wider public interest. As economies became interdependent, government intervention increased across the whole of industrial Europe. But since direct government bureaucracy was not always desirable—especially in areas requiring rapid adaptation to changing technologies—the new hybrid form of the public enterprise was gaining favor.

Gordon then analyzed how these new ideas in public administration appealed to various groups. The left (but not the far left) welcomed the effort to make sure all sectors would enjoy public services at reasonable prices. The new meritocratic classes would run the enterprises. The political right also welcomed the trend because politicians would be kept out of direct control. Only the far left, which wanted to nationalize everything, and the far right, which sought power over economic decisions, were strongly opposed to the public enterprises. Britain in 1926 created both the British Broadcasting Corporation (BBC) and the Central Electricity Board, with substantial support across the political spectrum. The BBC illustrated how the nation would cope with a totally new technology that required significant start-up costs and how control of the airwaves would be kept out of private hands. At the same time broadcasting would not be run by government bureaucrats.

The Central Electricity Board was an example of something quite different at first glance but alike in its fundamentals. This was a case of a very old system—the provision of electricity by a fragmented, decentralized, and inefficient system that had emerged in an earlier stage of industrialization—that was now badly in need of modernization. By making a large initial capital investment and amortizing the costs over a five-year period, the country had created an integrated electrical grid. The London Port Authority had been created in 1908 but had been hampered by an almost baroque system of assigning workers to the task of unloading. The system placed power in the hands of foremen, who chose workers on a basis that invited corruption. With the help of interviews with key personnel, Gordon was able to show how efficiencies could be achieved and thus helped pave the way for needed reforms in the procedures for unloading large ships and strengthening the role of unions and worker safety in the process.

Occasionally he ran into distinctively British problems. With the BBC, he was at first stymied by the excessive deference shown to the imperious Sir Arthur Reith, who ran things in the old mold and intimidated the staff. This seemed to Gordon a case of the collision between the old class system and the newer professionalism that was needed to run the BBC. Finally he found an official who would talk turkey, a man who was resigning to leave for America with his American wife, and this individual gave Gordon a frank account of the BBC's problems. The Central Electricity Board was less ideologically charged but still faced formidable challenges in converting the nation's entire electrical generating system into an integrated grid. The London Passenger Transport Board was the newest entity, and its task of linking Underground (subway), bus, and suburban rail service had just gotten under way. It was still in its honeymoon period, and its leaders and staff "felt themselves on trial to prove its practability."[7] In conclusion, the British public corporations, Gordon found, had "indeed combined most of the advantages of State ownership with those of commercial administration."[8]

Going Home to America

As his dissertation neared completion, Gordon toyed with the idea of a kind of exposé of the BBC and briefly entered into negotiations with Faber & Co. publishers, showing them a draft of the BBC section of his manuscript. The effort proved to be a nonstarter. Faber editors deemed the submission, as he wrote his parents, "insufficiently scandalous" for a popular audience.[9] Gordon decided that he should stick to his scholarly métier and put the final touches on his dissertation in spring 1936. He sent it to the Oxford authorities. By this time the good news from Harvard had arrived: he was to be appointed an instructor in government.

He had learned from his father that developments with the Supreme Court were reaching a critical point and that the dispute involved some of the very issues he had dealt with in his honors thesis. The court was challenging key elements of the New Deal, and the court's competence in economic matters and the ability of a decentralized, federal system to cope with a complex modern economy were emerging as central issues. And of course the presidential election was coming up. He must be back for that. In the meantime he needed to return to Oxford to tie up loose ends and then find time for a final trip to Europe with his friend Dick Crossman. After that trip it would be home to America.

5

Allison

The stone itself in truth is rather small.
But what it represents is large indeed.
A count in years of forty-five in all
Of troth maintained—affection, trust, and need—
Of shared experience in varied climes;
Of homes in London, Rio, and Versailles;
Of ennui and frustration too at times;
Your skill to sort the solid from the hollow;
Whether in art or men who rule the land.
Then four strong personalities to follow,
Shaped by a mother's firm but loving hand.
In part this life may've seemed like random motion,
But at its base lies unimpaired devotion.
—Lincoln Gordon, "To Allison—With a Sapphire," 1982

A human being on another plane.
—Lincoln Gordon, diary entry,
February 28, 1937

Gordon arrived at Boston harbor on August 16, 1936. A few weeks of recuperation at Chetwood was all he could muster before the start of Harvard's fall term. His appointment as instructor in the Government Department carried a salary of $2,425, supplemented by $975 for teaching the same courses at Radcliffe and $525 for teaching in the Summer School, plus free room and board as resident tutor at Dunster House. He continued to follow developments in Europe; he had been alarmed when Britain and France did nothing to oppose Germany's reoccupation of the Rhineland. But developments in Europe faded gradually into the background as the pressures of the term increased. Colleagues kidded him about his British accent, which took a little more than three months to disappear completely.

Gordon dutifully wrote to his parents that he had settled in and was busy with tutorials, grading student papers, and preparing lectures. He was not sure whether he could make a weekend that Bernard had tentatively planned for Chetwood but asked to be kept posted. He thanked his parents for the gift of a radio. He wrote his father excitedly that he was "hard at work on the Sherman Antitrust Act" in preparation for a course he was teaching with a colleague on government regulation of the economy.[1] He was teaching the course with Merle Fainsod, assistant professor of government, a soft-spoken, diffident, and brilliant scholar six years older than Gordon. Fainsod, like many other Harvard scholars of his generation, had had considerable practical experience in government, already having served as a staff member on the Louis Brownlow Commission. He had a manner and temperament that made Gordon comfortable, and Fainsod for his part found the intense New Yorker a congenial colleague. The two subsequently decided to write a book based on their course lectures. The governmental process, they posited, was made up in good measure of the lobbying activities of business, labor, and consumer groups, with the government acting both to help the various interests express themselves politically and at the same time to regulate and balance the various group interests in the interest of promoting the common good. The less well-organized interests, such as those of consumer groups, needed the government's help in setting forth their agenda. The difficulty of articulating and representing broad consumer interests, discussed at length, was one of the book's important contributions. How the legal order had retarded or promoted economic performance at various junctures in American history was another important theme. Their 836-page book, *Government and the American Economy,* became an authoritative text that was widely used in both graduate and undergraduate courses for many years. The paradigm they presented of how government operated in the economic arena stimulated a whole body of research in political science after the war.[2] Meanwhile Oxford University Press had published Gordon's *The Public Corporation in Great Britain* in 1938, giving him a good start on his academic career.

Marriage to Allison Wright

On February 23, 1937, at a Dunster House function, Gordon met Allison Wright, a young history teacher at an elite Boston prep school for girls and a graduate student in sociology at Radcliffe. It was love at first sight for him. He wrote in his diary on February 28 that he had met "a new person . . . a person whose acquaintance for four hours makes that of every other girl I have ever met seem pale—all surpassed by a human being on another plane. . . . I am literally dumbfounded."[3] The encounter with Allison "comes closer to an emotional revolution for me than anything since that extraordinary 22nd of February, 1930, with Aline—still the happiest day of my life."[4] On March 6 his diary entry was: "The relationship with Allison is proceeding rapidly, and has absorbed an extraordinarily large proportion of time all week."[5] On March 15 he wrote: "I am solidly, completely, unequivocally in love with her."[6] By March 19 he saw evidence of reciprocation and had formally proposed to her. It was evidently a more complicated matter for Allison, but she fell in love with him, too, and within a few weeks of their first meeting they became engaged. At age twenty-seven, four years older than Lincoln, Allison may have felt that this was her best chance for happiness—and at least she would escape from unhappy home circumstances and forge an independent life.

She was to him everything he lacked; she was artistic, extremely well read, and broadly cultivated in art, sculpture, and aesthetics. She was slender and attractive, and she was outspoken, something he liked in women. Her knowledge of architecture was unusual, as was her knowledge of the museum world. She was a New Englander, having on her mother's side an aristocratic Yankee lineage. This was perfectly suited for his persona as an adopted New Englander and Harvard professor. Not least, he was sexually attracted to her.

Although Allison was a proper Bostonian, she was also something of a rebel against the class-consciousness of Boston's upper crust. She had very decisive likes and dislikes. Her childhood had been at times a torment. She was close to her mother but had a more difficult relationship with her father and her brother. She had happy memories of summers at Cape Cod, her parents' farm in Brookline, and childhood friends. But her childhood had also left her with deep emotional scars. In marrying Lincoln Gordon she chose what she thought would be a quiet life as a professor's wife in her beloved New England. She hoped that she would be able to cultivate her own intellectual and artistic talents. Unlike Dorothy Gordon or Margaret Sanger, however, she was never to have an independent career. She was, as her husband described his Fieldston women teachers, a talented person who a generation later would have been a lawyer, doctor, college professor, or artist with her own professional career.

Allison's father, George, had been an orphan from Britain who stowed away on a voyage to America as a small boy. The boy met a kindly American on the voyage who adopted him and provided him with an education—at Harvard College and then at dental school. George Wright became a prosperous and prominent dental surgeon in Boston but had shortcomings as a father. He hectored his daughter unmercifully. She grew up feeling that she was never quite intelligent or pretty enough to gain his favor. Allison's one sibling, her brother, Goddard, bullied her, and she disliked him intensely. She was estranged from him as an adult. Allison's mother was from an aristocratic New England family, a lineage that contrasted with her father's orphan background. Her loving relationship with her mother and her more tense relationship with her father contributed to Allison's fractured identity. She could be the New England grande dame, but she had contempt for the idle rich and an instinctive sympathy for the underdog.

As Allison and Lincoln embarked on their married life, the future looked bright. There was a complication, though, that the couple had to deal with. Lincoln had acquired a consulting job in Washington for the summer and spent large parts of the summer away from Chetwood, leaving his bride with his parents. Dorothy ruled the roost at Chetwood, and there were tensions between Allison and her mother-in-law. According to Dot Gordon, Frank Gordon's spry ninety-six-year-old widow, Allison and Dorothy that summer "fought like cats and dogs."[7] But since Dot did not know Frank at that time and did not marry him until 1939, she must have gotten this version of events secondhand from her husband at a later point. Family legend (from the Frank Gordon family) has it that Allison at the end of that first summer told Lincoln that she could not stand another summer alone with his mother. As a result Bernard Gordon decided to split up his 250 acres of land around Lake Sunapee between his two sons, and in addition he gave Lincoln the funds to construct his own house at the water's edge, not far from the main Chetwood house. Lincoln's unpublished memoir tells a different story, with no mention of tensions between the two women in his life. His father, Lincoln writes, gave the newlyweds the funds to build a home of their own near the main residence as a wedding present. Planning for the home, which Lincoln himself designed (and later called Darkwater), began right after the wedding, but construction was delayed. Allison's residence in the main house with Dorothy was understood to be a temporary arrangement for the first summer. Whichever version is the truth, the construction of the new house began early in 1938 and was completed in the summer. The Depression made skilled labor available at relatively low wages.

Local artisans built a huge stone fireplace and a wood-burning stove, but unlike the main Chetwood house, Darkwater also had a furnace installed that could heat it in the winter. Lincoln himself built much of the furniture and contributed the main features of its design. During the Christmas holidays, Lincoln and Allison usually went to Darkwater for an adventurous winter vacation. During one of these winter vacations they had a new Scottish terrier puppy with them. The dog got himself stuck under the dock, thrashing around in the icy water and unable to climb back up on the solid ice. Without a moment's hesitation, Allison dived into the icy lake, fully clothed, to rescue the unfortunate creature. They were a happy couple, enjoying each other, in robust health, and to all intents and purposes their life together looked secure and settled. He was absorbed in his work; she had given up her teaching job but continued to pursue her studies. They were financially moderately well off. The couple had a circle of academic friends. Lincoln's best friend was Pendleton Herring, his former tutor and later Dunster House fellow tutor, who had been his best man for the wedding. Apparently Lincoln's brother, Frank, held no grudge against him for the snub, for he asked Lincoln to be his best man when he married Dorothy "Dot" Birmingham, a Smith College graduate and a friend of Kay Tilson, their Lake Sunapee neighbor.

World War II changed everything. Allison was often alone and had to act as a virtual single mother without much help from an absent husband. When the children were grown, she often faced hostess or representational duties, which she loathed. She moved sixteen times in the course of her husband's career and in each instance bore the burden of setting up the new household. Her husband, in addition to often being absent from home, was not easy to live with when he was home. He was not a good father in the conventional sense. He disliked children generally, including his own. He found them irritating, moody, and needy, and he was often impatient with them. He only began to warm to them when they were old enough to hold conversations.

Allison carried on with a New England sense of duty and stoicism. She had a fine sense of the ridiculous that showed itself in flashes of wit in the numerous letters she wrote to her children when she and Lincoln were abroad. She started writing lengthy letters, called the "Mes enfants" letters by her children, from the embassy in Brazil during her husband's tenure there. In one such letter, read by her son Hugh at the family's January 24, 1987, memorial service for her, Allison describes a ceremonial visit she and her embassy social secretary made to Mrs. Marie Goulart, wife of the president of Brazil:

> Papa is now very legal indeed. He went up to Brasilia bright and early on Wednesday taking quite a staff with him and the process was not over too simply for him. The Pres. [Goulart] kept him a long time discussing many things and the press reactions has been incredible since he made a great hit speaking Portuguese. . . .
>
> I was ordered up to Brasilia too. I got there in time to rest for twenty minutes. . . . The stone pavement in front was so waxed and polished that we both wondered if we could get to the door without falling down. Fortunately it was not slippery at all. We were met by Protocol, a most pompous gentleman, who led us across the building to the garden. . . . Mme. Goulart was not quite ready to see us. . . . We cooled our heels—or throats—for quite a time.
>
> Protocol turned up in the distance with a lady and young girl between them. The young girl turned out to be the Pres.' wife. She sat down and would not speak at all. The two aides, hers and mine, took up the conversation. I tried again. Nothing happened. After a period I looked at my watch and realized that only seven of the twenty minutes had passed. . . . I looked at her again and I wondered what would happen if I slapped her. I had traveled 600 miles since she said I was to come to see her. And we had expected a refusal and had laid on some other things for me to do here. The whole idea amused me so much that I cheered up and became

much more normal and told about the nights we spent at Yosemite with the bears and even referred to them with the new word I learned the night before for mongrel, *viralata,* garbage overturners, and she unbent a wee bit. Then I moved to go and we were taken out to be photographed, something which as you know is painful to me, and more pictures out the other door. I will say she did go to the car to say goodbye though I gave her the chance several times to duck.

I do hope that the numerous future calls will not be so difficult.[8]

Allison's mood could shift, and the letters to the children become darker. In a letter of January 21, 1962, she wrote:

I seem to find it terribly hard to write to you this week without a long series of complaints. . . . Not that I have much to complain about except the excruciating boredom of what I have to do. . . . I add nothing to the welfare of the nation, nor to the household. . . . It is a long experience . . . of sitting around and giving encouragement and praise in some things in which I feel no part, must not take a part, and feel one ought not take a part at all.

Daddy has been working like a madman so he has not been around. I hope he has enjoyed his week. I have got to get something to put my teeth into but I can't see anything which I can do and I am so done in by having meals at crazy hours that I have no energy left to do some of the obvious things. Papa is carried on by the interest he has in his job but I suspect soon his temper will give way as it did before Xmas from fatigue.

What a remarkably dull week it has been for me with the hours so cut that I could not get wholesomely dirty working in clay and God knows interrupted enough, in poor light so that I think I have ruined the one good head which I have made. No one's temper has been improved [and] the 48 hours of rain we had . . . made going out as impossible as in a blizzard and no one could show up when they were expected. The streets were like Venice.

I guess I feel mouldy.[9]

Allison seemed to enjoy some of the official duties. She also could be playful and amuse her husband and friends. At the embassy in Brazil she hatched the idea of staging a hoax exhibit, dubbed the Morrissey Collection, of paintings by unrecognized American modern artists from Kansas to be viewed by the embassy wives. With the aid of her Brazilian social secretary Ina and her young daughter Amy, Allison painted a series of large canvases featuring splashes of vivid colors and framed with the artists' names and short bios giving the background of the works. In one inspired satirical touch they glued an old tennis shoe they had found on the sand at the beach to one of the canvases as an illustration of modern art. She gave away the hoax in some of her descriptions of the works in overblown postmodern literary terminology. At the exhibit's unveiling, intended only for the embassy wives, there were skeptics, but they either went along with the ruse out of calculation or else did not want to offend her. Some wives reproached themselves for their failure to know the work of these accomplished Kansas moderns. The question arose of a public showing, and the hoax was exposed when the deputy chief of mission inquired about how pictures could have gotten through Brazilian customs without his authorization.

Robert W. Gordon in his remembrance of his mother observed that she did not like to talk about herself but would, if she were in the right mood, talk about the novel she was writing in the last ten years of her life.[10] Apparently begun not long after she returned to the United States from Brazil, the novel tells of a narrator-heroine not unlike Allison herself. The novel, which filled thousands of pages of manuscript, describes the return of the heroine, Louisa, to her native New England after a prolonged stay abroad. The death of Louisa's aunt prompts the return, and Louisa's confidante, her husband, is still detained on business abroad. So Louisa narrates her tale via letters to the absent husband. Everything in the old town has changed for the worse. Shopping malls have replaced picturesque farmhouses, the small shops are gone, rustic charm has been replaced by crass modernity, and an unscrupulous developer exercises all the political power. The America of the 1970s is cast in terms much like those of John Updike's *Rabbit Is Rich*—Updike was one of Allison's favorites—and the poor heroine finds herself bewildered by all the changes. Louisa, though scarcely comprehending the new surroundings, fights back against the despoilers of nature and the crass materialism. Here, Allison's son Bob explains, his mother's narrator-heroine runs into some difficulties in knowing how to bring the tale to an end. Allison experimented with three different endings—a happy ending, an unhappy ending, and a more realistic mixed outcome to Louisa's travails. The happy ending has Louisa outsmarting the nefarious developer, restoring the old order, and being hailed by the townspeople for bringing back the traditional New England virtues. But this is too Pollyannaish and unlikely an outcome, so Allison developed an opposite one: Louisa dies, everything goes from bad to worse, and all the wrong values and bad characters prevail. This ending, too, was not satisfactory, and Allison developed a more nuanced conclusion, with Louisa able to hold her head high and feel she has accomplished something, but with the negative trends still in the ascendancy.

Allison led a life she could scarcely have imagined when she married Lincoln Gordon. Like her heroine Louisa she endured much loneliness, and like Louisa she neither triumphed totally nor had reason to despair.

Doubts about His Career Path

In the fall of 1938 came both good news and bad news for Gordon's aspirations to become a tenured Harvard professor. After serving two one-year annual appointments as instructor, he was promoted to a tenure-track position as faculty instructor (the equivalent of assistant professor in current terms). This was a five-year appointment, to culminate in either a promotion to associate professor, carrying tenure, or departure from Harvard to another institution. A one-semester leave from teaching duties was included in the promotion. Gordon would have to complete another major piece of research for the tenure hurdle. But he experienced a temporary block and for the first time in his life could not think of what to do. Worse, to this self-confident New Yorker who had always expressed himself with crisp authority on any subject, a disturbing new element had crept into his psyche. For the first time he experienced self-doubt. He not only had difficulty formulating a new research direction, but he also was uncertain whether he was cut out for a career in basic research. He could not confide his doubts to his wife—what would she think of him? He could not speak to his colleagues and risk losing their confidence. He could scarcely admit to himself that he was unsure if he had chosen the right path. As he confessed in a draft chapter of his memoir in July 2004:

"Without quite acknowledging it, even to myself or Allison, I began to realize that I did not have a passion for basic social science research, either to formulate a new theoretical methodology of or cast explanatory light on some hitherto baffling aspect of social behavior."

In late fall 1938 he went to a cocktail party with Allison. In the big annual game with Yale, Harvard had won an unexpected victory, and the couple was celebrating with friends. The idea suddenly occurred to Gordon that a visit to New Zealand, combining the summer with his one-semester sabbatical leave, would be ideal for him to examine the novel approach that the new labor government there was taking to bolster jobs and economic development. He had read an article on the subject, and it had triggered pleasant memories of conversations with several of his fellow Rhodes scholars. New Zealand was a small country of 1.5 million inhabitants, and Lincoln was confident that he could interview everyone of note in the government. He could do something like what he had done in the United Kingdom—a study of the country's new approach to governmental intervention in the economy. And Allison would love the sightseeing they could do in the process. Somewhat to his surprise, the project still looked good the next morning.

Allison and Lincoln made plans for low-cost travel to New Zealand that would start right after Christmas in 1939, as soon as he could wind up his end-of-term duties. The doubts that still lingered were pushed to the back of his mind. They planned to drive across the United States and then leave from Los Angeles for the long sea voyage to New Zealand, returning in time for the Harvard fall term of the 1940–1941 academic year. They had in the meantime rented out their Darkwater house to British friends of Lincoln's Harvard colleague Daniel Boorstin. However, the war in Europe got in the way.

The Shadow of War

What had loomed in the background for Americans burst into the foreground on September 1, 1939, when the Germans invaded Poland. Britain two days later declared war on Germany. New Zealand as a loyal Commonwealth nation followed suit and declared war on Germany the day after Britain did. The New Zealand project was dead. Under America's neutrality legislation, Gordon could not legally travel to a belligerent nation except on official business. It seemed obvious that the United States was heading into deeper participation in the crisis of Europe, but it was not clear what form this might take. The country was far from united.[11] Isolationist sentiment remained strong in various parts of the country. Republicans in Congress and even stalwart New Dealers were hesitant about US involvement in the troubles in Europe. After the rapid surrender of Poland, the "phony war" set in and lasted until April 1940, with the Germans engaging in psychological warfare and alternating between threats and peace overtures. With the German invasion of the Low Countries and France and the air attacks on Britain, the phony war turned into hot war in Europe. FDR was maneuvering the country toward providing assistance to Britain, but he was proceeding with great caution, aware that public opinion was still not united behind deeper US engagement in the crisis.[12] Only one in six Americans in the summer of 1940 believed that the United States should get involved in the war anytime, and only one in forty favored an immediate declaration of war on Germany.[13]

Gordon still needed a research topic, with the collapse of the New Zealand project. At the suggestion of Arthur Holcombe, chairman of Harvard's Government Department, he decided to spend his leave in the spring term of 1940 in Washington, DC, working at the National Resources Planning Board (NRPB). The NRPB would give him experience in the new planning techniques of cost-benefit analysis and potentially yield a research project. It would also give him exposure to what was happening in the nation's capital in policy terms, especially in foreign policy. Gordon arranged employment for the semester and was assigned to a research group focusing on policies for energy development and water resources. A whimsical remark summing up the agency's mission by a staffer from Texas named Samuel Houston Johnson caught Gordon's attention: "Until this agency [NRPB] was created, there used to be a Rivers and Harbors Act in every session of Congress. It had to have at least 435 clauses, one for every congressional district in the country. If there were any districts totally lacking in rivers or harbors, the Army Corps of Engineers would be ordered to make some! Now, for the first time, real effort is being made to evaluate costs and benefits."[14]

Gordon contributed papers on the allocation of costs among classes of users and on the effects of energy costs on the location of industry, which gave him excellent background for his later work with the War

Production Board (WPB). Although he found the NRPB work stimulating, Gordon still had not come up with a project that he could develop into a book. But the work was enjoyable and suited his technocratic bent, even if it was not quite the basic research suitable for an academic book. He was enjoying Washington with Allison, who was now pregnant with their first child.

In May 1940, FDR announced that he would reestablish the National Defense Advisory Committee (NDAC) from World War I. Gordon learned from his friend Edward Mason that the president had decided to form a central Bureau of Research and Statistics within the NDAC. This bureau would be headed by Stacy May of the Rockefeller Foundation. May had asked Mason to come to Washington for the summer and bring some Harvard colleagues to help establish the bureau's operations. Would Gordon be interested in joining Mason over the summer for this assignment? After talking the matter over, the Gordons decided to alter their plans. With Allison's blessing Lincoln accepted the invitation and stayed on in Washington, while she went back to stay with her parents to await the baby's birth.

Working in crowded, non-air-conditioned, "temporary" buildings constructed in World War I, Gordon and his colleagues faced the problem of how to speed up the rearmament process. Gordon studied industrial mobilization and wartime finance in the United Kingdom and Canada to discern potential lessons for the United States. The papers he wrote prepared him for his later work with the War Production Board.[15] It began to be apparent that Washington was preparing for a wider governmental role in the economy in the event that the country was drawn more deeply into the European conflict. The summer sped by with the feverish pace of his work. After his return to Massachusetts in September, he was quickly immersed again in his regular academic duties. The Gordons' new home in Belmont was ready, and Lincoln was moving furniture in as Allison gave birth to their daughter Anne on September 17, 1940. Fourteen months later their son Robert was born. Meanwhile, in preparing the Government 29 course for the fall term of 1940, Gordon and Merle Fainsod added to their teaching workload by agreeing to write, in response to an invitation from William Norton of W. W. Norton & Sons of New York, the book *Government and the American Economy*, which drew heavily on their course notes. This book became the leading textbook in the field and was the research undertaking that Lincoln needed for his academic resume.

The Selective Service Act was passed in September 1940 (approved in the House by only one vote) and signed into law by FDR. The law required Gordon and all men under thirty-five to register with their local draft boards. In March 1941 Lend-Lease narrowly passed Congress, giving the president wide authority to provide aid to Britain on a "cash and carry" basis.[16] FDR had in late 1940 on his own authority transferred some fifty old destroyers to Britain in exchange for leases for bases in the Western hemisphere. The prospect of US involvement in the war was clearly rising. Gordon and Fainsod knew that they would join the war effort in some capacity if the United States in fact joined the war. But direct engagement was still not certain. Lend-Lease was sold to the country and a reluctant Congress on the theory that the best way to keep the nation out of the war in Europe was to aid the British. As Fainsod and Gordon noted in their book, the pattern of military activity to date was unusual, interspersing hostilities with periods of seeming calm. In June 1941 the war took a new turn when the Nazis turned on their erstwhile ally and launched Operation Barbarossa, the invasion of Russia. Major action shifted to the eastern front as Hitler apparently abandoned the idea of a cross-channel invasion of Britain (though he continued savage air attacks on British ports). German U-boats continued to harass US shipping both to Britain and later on the sea routes to Russia. As the United States gradually became more deeply involved in a war on the sea, FDR authorized US naval vessels to escort convoys on the open seas.

Fainsod and Gordon wrote furiously to complete their book in the shadow of war. They knew that US involvement would transform the problems they studied in the book. Indeed, the book describes the machinery of government and the policy changes set in motion by the recent military events. The book's concluding chapter discusses the problems of industrial mobilization and reviews the implications of direct US involvement in the crisis. The authors acknowledge that both the extent and the nature of the involvement could not be predicted as they went to press in early 1941. They express their conviction that any actions the government might take would be sustained by a sense of sacrifice from all groups, by our deep faith in free economic processes, and by long tradition. They were expressing more of a hope than a demonstrable truth. They were part of the eastern establishment, led by FDR and now increasingly with the support of a small circle of liberal internationalist Republicans who saw the prospect of US involvement in the war against Hitler as both inevitable and necessary. Henry Stimson and Frank Knox, both liberal Republicans, had joined FDR's cabinet in 1940 as, respectively, secretary of war and secretary of the navy, just four days before the Republican national convention (both were heavily criticized at the convention for doing so). Fainsod and Gordon took no stand on whether the nation should enter the war and wrote from the standpoint of technicians stating how the administrative problems of wartime mobilization might be handled. But they were clearly part of the liberal consensus that saw engagement as coming and sought to reassure their readers that "however complex the economic problems of the future, solutions would be sought in keeping with the traditional values of a democratic political order."[17]

6

Mobilizing for War

Seen in retrospect after a half century, industrial mobilization in World War II stands out as one of the great success stories of American history, perhaps comparable only to the postwar Marshall Plan. Both were efforts sustained over four years. Both were bipartisan in support and staffed by outstanding leadership from varied backgrounds in public and private life. Both accomplished more than had been hoped for at the outset, in shorter time and at less cost. Both were virtually free of allegations of corruption or malfeasance.
—Lincoln Gordon, 1995

It took Lincoln three years to discover Grant and you may not have hit on your production Grant first crack out of the box.
—Felix Frankfurter to FDR, 1942

As Lincoln and Allison Gordon were driving home from a midday dinner with her parents, the news flash from Pearl Harbor came on the car radio. It was immediately clear to both of them that the nation was now at war and that Lincoln would quickly join the war effort. His Harvard colleagues, his neighbors, his brother, and every able-bodied man he knew soon either joined the military or signed up for civilian duty in Washington. Lincoln was exempted from military service because he had two small children at the time of the Pearl Harbor attack. Two Harvard colleagues, Merle Fainsod and John Kenneth Galbraith, tried to recruit him for what became the Office of Price Administration (OPA), a key wartime agency. But he had other ideas. He had become an expert on mobilization issues in his prewar consulting work and hence preferred the War Production Board (WPB) over the OPA. Gordon may have also been influenced by the fact that Bill Elliott had chosen to serve at the WPB during the war. In any event, Gordon soon plunged into sixty- and seventy-hour work weeks planning the industrial mobilization effort that made the United States the "arsenal of democracy." He impressed Donald Nelson, the WPB director, John Lord O'Brian, its general counsel, and other senior officials and rose to become the WPB's number-three official by the end of the war. The effort took a toll on him. Gordon was away from his family for long periods, suffered from depression, and aged prematurely. His hair had turned completely white by his thirtieth birthday in 1943, and as his wife told their children years later, because of the unremitting and consuming effort, he had "lost his sense of fun."

Lincoln participated in hundreds of decisions and actions, ranging from broad policy issues to small administrative actions, and worked collegially with industrialists, career military officers, academics, and other outsiders like himself, which makes it difficult to single out his specific contributions or high points in his four and a half years of WPB service. The WPB's fortunes waxed and waned in the complex wartime bureaucratic struggles. There is little doubt, however, that his contributions and those of his numerous unsung colleagues contributed to the production miracle that helped to win the war.

Background

The twenty-first-century reader may find it baffling to grasp the World War II mobilization challenge. The United States in recent years has been engaged in two wars fought by a highly trained professional army that is backed by a network of civilian contractors and support agencies. Yet the recent wars and numerous other special operations have had no disruptive impact on the broad economy. Except for TV news reports, many Americans would hardly be aware that the nation was at war: the war effort may seem a distant reality for those not a part of the armed forces or the supporting agencies. Most Americans can scarcely imagine a halt to all civilian automobile manufacture; rent and other price controls (World War II controls at their peak extended to an estimated 90 percent of US retail prices); the closing down of whole sectors of the civilian economy; and the rationing of gasoline, fuel oil, sugar, coffee, shoes, tires, and meats and processed foods. This, and more, was precisely what happened in World War II.

Gordon himself in 1995 lucidly analyzed what was involved in the mobilization effort in a paper he prepared for a volume that was unfortunately never published (but that he attached as an appendix to chapter 2 of his draft memoir). World War I, as he explained, was "like combat between two super-dinosaurs—momentous assemblages of almost brainless men and materiel, decided by sheer numbers of troops and weight of munitions."[1] It was conducted along an entrenched line, and the rival armies tried to wear the other side down through attrition. No one could apply the term *intelligent weaponry* to World War I. World War II avoided the trench warfare of its predecessor and began to break the old technological mold with such examples as radar, penicillin, rocketry, the use of operations research, and the atomic bomb. But the sheer weight of men and munitions still remained decisive, he observed, for the ultimate Allied success. One hundred million men and women were mobilized in the armies of all of the combatant nations of World War II. The US total of slightly over twelve million men and women in uniform at the war's peak in 1944 was critical to the Allied war effort.[2] The US share of total wartime industrial production was even more impressive, amounting to some 22 percent of all industrial production.[3] The United States not only supplied ships, aircraft, tanks, radios, and munitions in prodigious quantities to its own forces but also sent vast supplies to the United Kingdom and Russia through Lend-Lease.

These figures are all the more impressive when one recognizes the very low base from which the nation began to mobilize. Furthermore, the process of instituting wartime controls occurred within a short time span and lasted for only a relatively limited period, thus whipsawing the economy between rapid mobilization and then an almost equally rapid demobilization.[4] The US armed forces in the 1930s had fallen to very low numbers. On the eve of the war the American army was dwarfed by the Axis forces. Germany, Italy, and Japan each had 700,000 men in their armies (both active duty and reserves), for a total of 2.1 million, while the United States' active duty army included only 187,000 troops (with some 300,000 reserves).[5] The US Army was in addition poorly equipped, with low stocks of munitions, poor artillery, and inadequate numbers and poor quality of tanks.

World War I offered few lessons in preparation for World War II industrial mobilization, for scandals and incompetence had marked procurement efforts (as was the case for the Spanish American War and the Civil War). The performance of the railways in World War I was so poor that the army had to take them over. Financier Bernard Baruch emerged from World War I with an enhanced national reputation, but the conditions he faced as wartime administrator differed from what confronted the planners on the eve of World War II. By early 1941 FDR, Secretary of the Treasury Henry Morgenthau, and Secretary of War Henry Stimson recognized the need for more urgent mobilization planning and began to put together the rudiments of the wartime administrative machinery, but the steps were halting until Pearl Harbor galvanized efforts. Part of the problem had been uncertainty over what kind of war and what theater of operations the nation might have to face. As *Time* magazine put it in a February 24, 1941, cover story, the United States was preparing "Heaven-knows-whom at Heaven-knows-where for Heaven-knows-what."[6] FDR still had to move cautiously in the face of strong neutralist sentiment in Congress and across the nation.

While Pearl Harbor by no means resolved the controversies, after Pearl Harbor the bitter partisanship that had marked the battle over conscription in 1939 and the 1940 presidential campaign was in some measure set aside in foreign and defense policy. Or, put differently, FDR's own party supporters and a nucleus of internationalist Republicans from the Northeast built a bipartisan coalition sufficiently strong to maintain a precarious national unity for the duration of the war. FDR and his supporters drew on lessons from history. In 1928 Secretary of State Henry Stimson (who had previously served as secretary of war under President William Howard Taft) helped to secure the tradition of bipartisanship in national security by refusing a request from President Herbert Hoover to campaign for Hoover's reelection, saying that as secretary of state he should stay out of politics. FDR, as president, now appointed Stimson, a Republican, as his secretary of war in May 1940 as hostilities loomed in Europe. FDR also appointed Frank Knox, an outspoken, prointervention Republican newspaper publisher from Chicago, as secretary of the navy.[7]

After the election FDR blessed a trip by Wendell Willkie, his Republican opponent in the 1940 presidential election, to Britain and gave him the status of special envoy, maneuvering him in the process into the position of presidential messenger rather than independent statesman.[8] FDR also appointed other Republicans, such as Robert Lovett, Robert Patterson, James Forrestal, and John J. McCloy, to key defense posts. The lack of consensus on New Deal domestic and economic policies was increasingly evident later in the war and in the debates over reconversion, production priorities and allocation of strategic materials, and price controls. In the war's final stages the bipartisan truce largely broke down when planning for demobilization began, and after the war the disputes over America's responsibility to aid Europe brought sharp partisan differences in defense and foreign policy.

The WPB, from its creation in 1942 as the fusion of two existing but ineffectual agencies, was caught up in bitter controversies. Some parts of the agency were staffed largely by Republicans from the business community and others by academics and New Deal supporters who were Democrats. The requirements office in which Gordon served was staffed mostly by academics and New Dealers, but its disputes with other units were rarely narrowly partisan. Clashing conceptions frequently arose, however, over how much and what kinds of government intervention were necessary. Disputes between the OPA and the WPB were constant and often turned on ideological differences between the agencies. When it came to demobilization, controversy sharpened over whether to "plan" (e.g., allocate market shares to companies and sectors) or simply to allow the "free market" to operate. The role of small business was a particular bone of contention within the WPB itself and between the WPB and the Pentagon. Americans were patriots during World War II, but patriotism did not entirely smother politics, and at the war's end politics returned with a vengeance.

Economic conditions in the 1930s had some favorable aspects for the wartime mobilization planners that should be noted and that deserve some of the credit attributed to the wartime planners. The 1930s recorded some striking productivity gains and infrastructure improvements that helped to make possible the wartime production miracles. The successes in the production of planes and ships "for the most part represented, in conjunction with massive government . . . infusions of plant and equipment, the application to the production of military hardware of organizational techniques that had been pioneered in the civilian manufacture of radios, vacuum cleaners, and automobiles."[9] Transportation improvements facilitated the movement of goods and subassembly components to manufacturing locations. Road improvements and the construction of interstate highways in particular made possible railway productivity gains, as trains could haul freight from locations supplied by greatly increased truck haulage. Railroads, though they had fewer stations, trunk lines, and employees, carried more freight and had more passenger miles in 1940 than in 1929.[10]

Unemployment, which fell sharply from 14 percent in 1940 to 9.9 percent in 1941, meant an important source of labor for the defense industry. Labor shortages developed soon enough and were partly filled by the addition of more than three million women to the workforce. Labor shortages nonetheless became one of the most critical issues facing Gordon and his colleagues in the wartime administration. Behind the many problems, though, lay the greatest asset of all in Lincoln Gordon's estimation: the zeal and patriotic engagement of Americans of all classes and regions made acceptance of controls possible. To Gordon, as he notes in his 1995 article on mobilization, "the broadest lessons of our wartime experience . . . concern the national spirit. An all-out war is unique in its capacity to engender the readiness to sacrifice personal and particularistic interests and to join wholeheartedly in a common effort. . . . This mood should be fortified by recalling the spirit and the accomplishments on the home front in World War II."[11]

The War Production Board

Gordon's first post–Pearl Harbor trip to Washington brought confirmation that the new wartime agency he was interested in would soon be established. He was advised to return to Belmont, rent out his house, and come back to Washington with his family in January 1942. By good fortune he found an unfurnished home to rent in Chevy Chase, Maryland, just one mile north of the District of Columbia line. The Gordon family set off for Washington in his 1940 Ford with what could be stuffed into the car. Lincoln reported as directed to Edwin B. George, an economist and business journalist who had been brought into government by Donald Nelson to recruit for the new agency. George presumed, though Gordon had no business experience, that traditional business experience was not quite suitable for the administration of wartime controls. Academic economists and business school professors might be good recruits for his purposes. George knew from Stacy May and other colleagues from the WPB's predecessor agencies of Lincoln Gordon's reputation for intellect and diligent work habits.

"Do you know anything about copper?" Eddie George asked Gordon.

Gordon replied that copper was a red metal, a major component of brass and bronze metals, and an excellent conductor of electricity.

"Good," George said. "Now go over to the next building and introduce yourself to Harry King, Chief of the Copper Branch. You're our copper specialist."[12]

Gordon focused on copper as his initial assignment, looking for ways to curtail ornamental and other nonessential uses. He negotiated with representatives of the Kennecott, Anaconda, and Phelps Dodge copper companies to expand their production for the defense effort. These companies had been reluctant to expand capacity because they were fearful of repeating the boom-and-bust experience of the 1920s and 1930s. Government commitments after Pearl Harbor removed the fear, and companies proved eager to expand their output. Gordon escorted Anaconda executives to the wartime Reconstruction Finance Corporation (RFC) and arranged loans for them to open their huge new mine in Chuquincanata, Chile. He achieved a minor victory when he oversaw the development of the wartime substitute penny, which replaced most of the penny's copper content while still working in the nation's thousands of candy slot machines. Gordon conceded in his memoir that the penny's "contribution to copper conservation was in truth quite small, but FDR was pleased by its symbolism to wartime conservation efforts."

Gordon made his own private contribution to energy conservation by riding the bicycle he had used at Oxford from Chevy Chase to the WPB headquarters at Fourth Street and Independence Avenue, SW, a distance of seven or so miles. This became a strain in the hot Washington summers, and he went over to carpooling with fellow WPB staff members. Although the house in Chevy Chase was somewhat shaded by trees and well insulated, the non-air-conditioned Washington summers were too much for Allison, and she and their two children summered in New Hampshire, where Lincoln managed to join them for two weeks of vacation each summer. Allison otherwise had no adult company except for her occasional visits to her mother-in-law's house and the guests that Dorothy might bring to Chetwood.

Although at first well down in the WPB hierarchy, Gordon soon rec-ognized that the WPB was facing serious administrative problems. The agency needed, and experienced, constant course corrections, and he sus-pected that its leadership was causing some of the problems by the lack of clarity regarding lines of authority. As a sign of the WPB's instability, Gordon's first boss, Bill Batt, the program vice chairman of the require-ments committee, left suddenly and was replaced in July 1942 by James Knowlson, another engineer from industry. Before the war Batt had been president of the Swedish SKF ball-bearing company's American subsid-iary and had earned kudos for his work with the Office of Production Management (OPM), a WPB predecessor unit. He typically worked from 8:00 a.m. to midnight every day, eating dinner at his desk. Batt had also traveled to Russia with Averell Harriman to determine Russia's military requirements for the Lend-Lease program. At the WPB Batt became a strong proponent of conservation. He went on the radio and in a stern voice lectured Americans on the need to recycle tin cans and other scrap metals, cooking fats, rubber gloves, and other items.[13] Gordon remained on friendly terms with Batt even after Batt left his post as program vice chairman (he later assisted Gordon by nominating him to be his successor in a senior diplomatic post in London in 1952).

William L. Batt's career in government during the war illustrates some of the cross-pressures and political currents that plagued adminis-trative tasks. While generally conceded to be an able administrator, Batt had his detractors, as did other "one dollar a year" men (i.e., those who served without government salary and remained on private payrolls while working for the government). Batt was suspected by Secretary of the Trea-sury Henry Morgenthau of being a traitor. At Morgenthau's direction a secret investigation was undertaken by a Morgenthau ally in the White House Office of Emergency Management in an unsuccessful effort to gain incriminating evidence against Batt.[14] Batt was suspected of divert-ing ball-bearing production to the Germans by shipping a part of his company's output to Latin American subsidiaries for transshipment to SKF's huge ball-bearing plant in Germany. (This accusation came from a disgruntled ex-employee who had been fired and who voiced his suspi-cions to federal authorities.) Batt's Philadelphia plant had fallen behind on deliveries to the Curtiss Wright aircraft company, a failure that Batt's detractors saw as confirmation of the sabotage allegation. SKF's Swedish chairman was an aristocrat with a reputation as a playboy who was a second cousin by marriage to Hermann Göring, the Luftwaffe chief, and was also a friend of the Duke and Duchess of Windsor (well known for having Nazi sympathies). Batt's enemies believed that Swedish spymasters were sending secret instructions to him through diplomatic courier, thus avoiding any US surveillance of his mail. Swedish neutrality was suspect for many Americans during the war. Batt nonetheless maintained throughout the war his post as director of the SKF American subsidiary. With the assistance of his adroit New York attorney, John Foster Dulles, he arranged to have himself designated the majority shareholder (voting 90 percent of the firm's shares) for the duration of the war to avoid potential confiscation of the firm by administrators of US neutrality laws.

The Batt problem was unusual, but he and most of the other industry people who served without government pay survived the criticisms they aroused. A more basic problem that the WPB and the Requirements Committee faced was the conflict between the armed services' statements of requirements and the assessments of agency analysts. The military's requests could not be accepted at face value. The Pentagon's system of establishing its needs had a built-in overestimate. This resulted from the fact that at each stage in the chain, from the combat lines to the points of supply, a safety factor would be added for "undefined contingencies." At one point in 1942 the Pentagon's requirements for small-arms ammunition alone (not counting bullets above twenty millimeters, or, in other words, what tank, ship, or aircraft guns require) exceeded the free world's total production of copper. Bert Fox, a professor of economics at Amherst College who became the WPB's point man for dealing with Pentagon requirements, devised a system that accounted for the Pentagon's routine overestimates and managed to do so without arousing the ire of the military's strong-willed representative on the WPB board, General Lucius Clay. For a time at least this system worked—but the bitterest clash with the military came after November 1943, when defense production peaked, and the WPB began to plan for reconversion to a civilian economy.

Other difficulties, too, confronted Gordon and his colleagues. A critical technical issue was whether to assign priorities "horizontally," to firms across the chain of production, or "vertically," to the end-user. In the latter case the end-user could make the necessary priority assignments on materials or subassembly parts for integration into the final assembly.

Then there was the ever-present problem of deciding which civilian sectors should be protected to help maintain the overall defense production base. The electric utility industry was an obvious case in point for priority assignment because defense plants needed power for their production lines. But the going got conceptually tougher when one moved beyond the electric utility industry and a few other obvious cases. Early in the war, for example, the civilian automobile fleet had not yet worn down, but as it did, the need for new civilian vehicles became urgent. If workers could not get to work on functioning buses, improving the civilian bus fleet would be essential to the defense effort.

Confusing Administrative Machinery

The WPB chairman, Donald M. Nelson, had gotten his job through unusual circumstances. In May 1940, Secretary of the Treasury Henry Morgenthau called General Robert E. Wood, the president of Sears, who had made a successful business career after retiring from the army. Morgenthau asked Wood for the loan of E. Penn Brooks, Sears's vice president in charge of factories, for a two-month period. It was, Morgenthau said, a matter of national urgency, and the emergency required a production genius to map out a plan for saving France. Wood demurred, saying Brooks was on a critical assignment for the company and was not available. Wood searched his mind for someone he could volunteer and whom he could spare for a couple of months. The name he came up with was Don Nelson, the Sears purchasing chief. Nelson had worked his way up through the complex prewar administrative machinery and gotten favorable press in the process. A *Time* magazine cover story of February 24, 1941, portrayed him as a miracle worker in defense production. His main virtue was that he was neither an ideological New Dealer who attacked big business and put butter ahead of guns nor a brash Republican businessman trying to undo New Deal social programs. He had cultivated a reputation for caution, deliberateness, and a judicious temperament. But his critics saw these qualities as procrastination and indecision. FDR biographer Jean Edward Smith, reviewing the wartime production controls, describes Nelson as a man who was "congenitally incapable of making tough decisions."[15] FDR evidently had some qualms when he named Nelson to the WPB post and expressed them to his friend Justice Felix Frankfurter. Frankfurter told FDR, "It took Lincoln three years to discover Grant, and you may not have hit on your production Grant first crack out of the box."[16]

Gordon had initially focused on problems in the copper industry. Copper shortages were among the most critical issues facing the WPB, and he helped the agency devise conservation policies, rationing strategies, and trade policy, as well as laying plans to expand production for the industry. While he labored in the ranks during this period, he could not help noticing a considerable churning in the agency's leadership. Gordon saw the departure of Batt and soon thereafter of Batt's successor, Jim Knowlson, followed by the arrival of Ferdinand Eberstadt, from the Army-Navy Munitions Board, as the new program vice chairman and Gordon's divisional boss. The arrival of Eberstadt represented a new and a more favorable phase in Gordon's wartime service. More politically aware after some nine months on the job, Gordon recognized an immediate improvement in the agency's decision-making process under Eberstadt. A general shift of power toward Eberstadt seemed to be in process. Gordon took advantage of the opportunity and developed a close working relationship with Eberstadt. He saw Eberstadt as a brilliant administrator, skilled negotiator, and tough in-fighter in the skirmishes that swirled around the office. Eberstadt, a New York lawyer and investment banker in civilian life, had worked in World War I in refugee policy and had held a variety of posts under Presidents Hoover and FDR.[17] At the WPB, Eberstadt developed the "Controlled Materials Plan," under which the armed services would prioritize their needs, and private industry in turn would more easily plan production schedules to meet military needs. Gordon was Bierstadt's staff person in charge of the effort, providing important analytical assistance in the plan's development and then taking on a major role in its implementation. With Eberstadt's arrival, Gordon's work shifted from being desk officer for copper to tackling wider issues, in addition to implementing the broad Controlled Materials Plan. His close relationship with Eberstadt made him a rising star in the agency. From Gordon's perspective Eberstadt was becoming the de facto head of the agency. Power seemed to flow to Eberstadt because of his ability to analyze a problem quickly and come up with a practicable solution.

However, Eberstadt then overplayed his hand and engaged in a maneuver to oust Nelson as WPB chairman. Eberstadt discovered that

Don Nelson was not quite as guileless as he sometimes portrayed himself to be. While Eberstadt's relationship with Gordon did not extend to soliciting his aide's political advice on the bold but rash move to oust Nelson and shake up the WPB leadership ranks, he might have done well to take the youthful Gordon (who had turned twenty-nine in September 1942) into his confidence. Eberstadt, considering Nelson hopelessly inept, devised a plan whereby Nelson would be ousted as WPB chairman and replaced by Bernard Baruch, a close friend and associate of Bierstadt's. Baruch in effect would be the public face of the agency, and Eberstadt would take over day-to-day management. Gordon was not in on this attempted coup. Eberstadt had the backing of James Byrnes for the plan, and Byrnes had persuaded FDR to go along. Baruch delayed the process by having second thoughts but finally decided to accept the new role if the president offered it and scheduled a trip to Washington to meet with FDR. Nelson got wind of the attempted coup on the morning of the very day in February 1943 that his replacement by Baruch was to be made public and quickly fired Eberstadt and announced a reorganization of his staff that featured the promotion of businessman Charles Wilson as his principal deputy. FDR decided that he had no choice but to back Nelson. FDR met with Baruch later in the day, but instead of offering him the WPB job, as Baruch expected, he rambled on for an hour about other matters and left it to subordinates to explain to the baffled Baruch what had happened. Eberstadt returned to the Navy Department, where he worked with James V. Forrestal for the rest of the war.

Gordon did not understand why Eberstadt had undertaken such a rash move but surmised that Eberstadt had probably been forced on Nelson to begin with because of dissatisfactions with Nelson's own performance as WPB chairman. Accepting Eberstadt as program vice chairman was a condition for Nelson to keep his own job. Nelson for his part was stung by Eberstadt's disloyalty because he had brought Eberstadt into government service as chairman of the Army-Navy Munitions Board, at the suggestion of Baruch. Nelson, though he may have been passive as WPB chairman, was not passive when it came to sniffing out conspiracies and defending himself. He had cultivated a strong following in the press and was adept at portraying himself as a moderate among contending factions.

FDR had earlier concluded that he could no longer be both chief strategist for the war and manager-in-chief of the home front. The president had a plan to shed some administrative responsibilities but did not want to surrender authority entirely. He accordingly persuaded Justice James F. Byrnes of the US Supreme Court to step down from the bench to become director of a new Office of War Mobilization in the White House. Byrnes, a former congressman and senator from South Carolina who was one of the South's New Deal supporters, was supposed to function as an "assistant president" and to have the last word on all domestic matters, including those of war production.[18] (Byrnes was for a time FDR's first choice to replace Henry Wallace as vice presidential candidate on the ticket in 1944, but political logic eventually dictated the selection of Senator Harry S. Truman instead.) Adding Byrnes and the new White House Office of War Mobilization created a new layer of bureaucracy but never quite worked as intended. The new "czar" did not in particular resolve the production issues between the WPB and the Pentagon. A simmering dispute between (and within) the WPB and the military over reconversion to a civilian economy intensified in late 1943, which Nelson called "the war within a war."[19]

Although Gordon's fortunes were on the rise within the WPB, he began to experience symptoms of depression. Doubts and uncertainties about his job, his future, and the path he had chosen plunged him into gloom. He had recently been promoted to the position of chief of staff for the requirements committee but had long felt guilt about not serving in the military. This feeling had grown more acute after Eberstadt's departure, despite his promotion. He talked the matter over with Allison and got her support for leaving the WPB and going on active duty. She could not have been happy with his decision to join the military, but she apparently did not want to add to his psychological burdens by protesting the move. Lincoln received an offer to join the navy from a naval captain he had worked with, but it would have relegated him to a routine job of contract administration, which did not appeal to him. He decided instead to join the army and to do so around the time of his birthday in September, when his current deferment would expire. He then learned that he was among a small number of WPB staff members for whom the agency's leadership was seeking a presidential deferment from the draft for the remainder of the war. With the overwhelming majority of men his age in the military, he felt his own position was indefensible. He decided to ask the WPB to withdraw his name from the deferral request list, drafting a letter to Donald Nelson to this effect. A few days later he got a call to meet with John Lord O'Brian, the WPB's general counsel.

O'Brian indicated that Don Nelson had passed Gordon's letter on to him.

"Let me ask a preliminary question," said O'Brian. "Have you any intention of running for any kind of elective office after the war is over?"[20]

Gordon replied that he had briefly thought of someday running for Congress or the Senate but upon reflection had decided that he did not have the right temperament to run for elective office.

"That's good," said O'Brian, "because for the next generation any young man who was in good health in the war years and did not serve in uniform will fail if he runs for any office, from dog-catcher up. Don Nelson and I wouldn't want to stand in your way. Now, let's get to the merits. Remind me of your age."

"Thirty in September."

"That settles it. You're too old to be thinking of combat. Do you know how to operate a typewriter?"

Gordon said that he typed quite well. O'Brian went on to describe what this meant. After basic training, he would be sent be sent to an office as a clerk and would keep track of security materials. After giving a detailed account of the triviality of these clerical duties, O'Brian wound up rhetorically: "Now do you think you would really be making more of a contribution to the war than you are doing now as a high-ranking official of the WPB?"

Gordon admitted that he probably wouldn't be making the same contribution, but O'Brian was not finished. According to Gordon's recollection sixty years later, O'Brian then added the clincher: "The rumor about our seeking a White House deferral for you is quite true. But get it out of your mind that we're doing it in *your* interest. We're doing it in *our* interest. Especially now, when you have spent several years in designing and operating the system of war production management, you would be hard to replace. Your conscience should be entirely clear."[21]

After the interview with O'Brian, Gordon returned to work but still was not quite easy in his mind. He was depressed but continued to work long hours. He was suffering from anxiety and chronic depression but admitted only to a temporary episode of depression in his draft memoir. On his thirtieth birthday, September 10, 1943, he had an episode of depression that he described as "haunting," noting that it "stuck in my memory for sixty years." His car-pool colleagues noticed that he had fallen into an unusually dark mood; when queried about what was troubling him, he replied that "as long as you're in your twenties all roads remain open. At thirty, they begin to close in." He did not reflect deeply in his draft memoir on his mental state during this period, attributing the depression to "a delayed reaction against my too hurried schooling, especially at Harvard." The dark mood, he claimed, passed quickly and never returned "with such intensity." Modern diagnosticians would probably doubt that an episode of depression would come on so rapidly or dissipate so quickly. A depressive individual can continue to function at a high level and will often battle the depression by working even harder. For Gordon the answer to his problem was not self-pity, but more determined effort.

The Final Period of Gordon's World War II Service

Gordon had developed good working relations with Julius A. "Cap" Krug, Eberstadt's successor as program vice chairman. In August 1944 Krug became WPB chairman when FDR finally fired Don Nelson. Lincoln turned his efforts to planning the country's output of landing crafts intended for Operation Overlord, the Normandy invasion. Industry's performance in this initiative exceeded even the military's estimate of what it needed. Even before D-Day, in June 1944, planning had begun for redeployment to the Pacific front once the Germans had been knocked out of the war. Gordon worked long hours, and his spirits improved as he saw his contributions leading to what now seemed like inevitable victory. The year 1943 had marked a turning of the tide in the battle of the Atlantic. Now, for the first time, the increase in production of new ships exceeded the losses to enemy submarines, as advances in convoy tactics and statistical techniques such as operations research helped to defeat the U-boat threat. During this time Gordon also got to know Richard Bissell, a brilliant economist who was a pioneer in statistical planning for convoys and who later became a close friend and colleague during work on the Marshall Plan. Milton Katz, on leave from Harvard Law School to serve as O'Brian's deputy general counsel at the WPB, was another wartime associate with whom Gordon would later work closely in the Marshall Plan administration.

There were lighter moments for Gordon and his colleagues despite the pace of work. It was customary, for example, for WPB staff to host a dinner for any departing colleague at which jocular toasts would be offered. Nobody yet used the term *roast* for these occasions. When invited to his first such dinner—a privilege reserved for those of executive rank—Gordon decided he would deliver his toast in verse. The experiment was a success. His colleagues were amused, and Gordon, pleased with himself, resolved that he would henceforth compose a sonnet for all important family and ceremonial occasions. The sonnet he composed for his toast included the following lines:

Sonnets for the Requirement Committee Chairmen

[1]
When first upon the martial scene emerged
    The War Production Board replacing SPAB,
The wiser heads among our leaders urged
    A group to settle things by gift of gab.
Requirements-Supply were its domain,
    Allotments, ratings, programs were its jargon.
It carried on its work with little strain;
    Maintaining peace 'twixt Weiner and the others,
That gallant warrior, Bill Batt,
    Who made the members act like friendly brothers.
The happy scene was marred but by one doubt:
    Decisions flowed, but were they carried out?

[2]
Implementation was the byword when
    Luther brought forth the summer's realignment,
One James S. Knowlson swam into our ken
    To take upon his head the Chair's assignment. . . .
The Chairman travelled on his way serene,
    Only one fly disturbed the honeyed ointment:
The cares for others often were unseen
    By him; he used, to others' disappointment,

That noble means for passing of the buck:
    "Gentlemen, that problem I must duck!"

[3]
With autumn's coming rose again the cry:
    "Find a Captain for the Requirement's helm!"
And Eberstadt abandoned [his old] pleasant realm. . . .
    Controlled Materials now took premier place . . .
And guided systems vertical toward first base.
    A single flaw bemused the plan's proponents
They quite forgot about those damned components. . . .

[4]
When we review the year's final roll-call
    We've had five chairmen for our lot: Our Bill,
Our Jim, our Ferd, our Cap; we love them all.
    Yet—seek to conceal it as we will—
The insidious brain sets up a whispered patter:
    "Who's Chairman—or does it really matter?"

Meanwhile the Allied armies consolidated their foothold on the continent and began to move in force toward Germany. The battle on the home front over reconversion to the civilian economy heated up. The fortunes of war seemed to be inversely related to the WPB's fortunes on the home front. The more the war turned in favor of the Allies, the more acrimonious became the divisions among the wartime agencies in Washington. Don Nelson may have been a passive WPB administrator, but there was one issue where he was anything but mild and laid back: he was a passionate believer in the free enterprise system. He became increasingly convinced that what the military services were proposing for the postwar period was nothing short of a subversion of America's free market system. The military's plans for semipermanent postwar mobilization roused Nelson to furious indignation. He considered that military leaders in their reconversion plans were entering into an unholy alliance with big business to restrict entry into various lines of business—in effect cartelizing the economy in the name of maintaining a permanent state of preparedness. There was no need, in Nelson's view, for the permanent high mobilization the military wanted. The United States had just proven that the nation could mobilize rapidly and become the "arsenal of democracy," and now administrators, with victory in sight, should plan for return to a peacetime economy that would provide opportunities for small businesses to thrive, not just large defense contractors. A deep split developed within the WPB over the reconversion plan that Nelson forced, against strong opposition from the military services. A crisis point was reached in June 1944. Lincoln Gordon was on Nelson's side in favoring opportunities for small business. He had become fond of the Willys Jeep Company and did not want the big auto manufacturers to be given market shares based on their shares of the prewar auto market. At the same time Gordon feared a too-rapid return to the civilian economy and thought that government planners should continue to exercise authority over the pace and timing of major demobilization steps. In this respect he was on the military's side, but he had shifted more to the "butter" side and less to the "guns" side now that the war was on the way to being won. Government's role should include the provision of major assistance to returning veterans in housing, education, and job placement.

The major reconversion issues could not be resolved within the WPB or the Byrnes-led office in the White House. Worst of all, from FDR's standpoint, the controversy spilled out into the press. In the face of this public dispute, FDR finally decided to replace Nelson as WPB chairman. He did this by an indirect Rooseveltian maneuver: he sent Nelson off on what he billed as an important diplomatic mission to China. While FDR liked special envoys, in this case he was more interested in getting Nelson out of the picture than in focusing on Asian policy. The president summoned Nelson to the Oval Office and asked him if he would act as a special presidential emissary to Chang Kai-chek. The two men agreed on Charles E. Wilson of General Electric Co. as Nelson's successor.[22] Wilson had been serving as Nelson's WPB deputy but had sided with the armed services rather than with Nelson on small business. Supporters of Nelson spread stories that their boss had been humiliated, and some even stoked the controversy by insinuating that Wilson was in on the scheme to oust Nelson. Wilson, infuriated, held a stormy news conference at which he lashed out against the Washington scene, his bureaucratic foes, and by implication Nelson himself.[23] The president concluded that Wilson had gone too far and burned his Washington bridges and settled on Julius

Krug as Nelson's successor, which produced some temporary calm. Nonetheless, the battle over demobilization continued and dominated the final stages of Gordon's WPB career.

The End of the War

With the coming of spring 1945 it was clear that German forces had failed in their last offensive blow. They were now fighting a rear-guard action against Allied advances on all fronts. Allied warplanes, now in complete control of the skies, pounded German cities. Soviet forces under Marshall Zhukov fought their way to the outskirts of Berlin. The Pentagon still advised caution in the relaxation of wartime controls, but Congress and a wide array of civilian interests wanted to be liberated from wartime controls and pushed to demobilize the economy. The price-control system, already rickety, began to teeter on the brink of collapse amid unmistakable inflationary signs.

The WPB, fearing a surge of inflation and high unemployment from too rapid a demobilization, tried to slow down the headlong push toward restoring the civilian economy. The military continued to favor caution and the slowing of demobilization until the war was over. The military's position was that the United States could decontrol the economy completely in one massive step once the war was over and do so without the need for central planning. If controls had to be relaxed to permit some production of civilian goods, military strategists favored a formula to allocate civilian production based on prewar production levels. Gordon opposed this approach because he thought it would work to the advantage of big business—those firms that already had a foothold in a given line of business would benefit, at the expense of small businesses, new entrants, and general innovation. The advocates for partial civilian demobilization were divided between those who favored permitting all firms in a given industrial sector to be allowed to produce civilian products and those who favored choosing which firms should be permitted the resumption of production. This was a conundrum that was only resolved by the collapse of the enemy forces, which produced complete demobilization almost overnight.

Housing was of particular interest to Gordon. Construction during the war had been limited to the building of facilities for military bases and troop barracks. Gordon and his WPB colleagues believed that civilian housing should be authorized, but priority should be given to housing for returning veterans. The housing industry wanted an unrestricted marketplace. The auto industry presented another difficult issue. The civilian fleet needed replacement, and by the end of 1944 and early 1945 pressures were building toward allowing Detroit to resume production of at least some civilian vehicles. The big three auto makers wanted to allocate quotas on the basis of prewar market shares, but this struck Gordon as wholly unfair to Studebaker and Willys Jeep. These companies were quite capable of producing civilian vehicles, but on the basis of prewar market shares they would be virtually shut out of the market. The chief executives of the auto industry were gathered at WPB headquarters on April 12, 1945, to discuss how and when civilian production would be resumed when the meeting was suddenly interrupted by the announcement of President Roosevelt's death. The meeting was adjourned in disarray.

Events moved swiftly. Hitler committed suicide on April 30 in his Berlin bunker, just weeks after FDR's death. On May 7 Admiral Karl Donitz, acting as president, signed the documents of surrender for Germany, and Victory in Europe (VE) Day was proclaimed the next day. With the war in Europe over, Gordon and his colleagues were given instructions from the Office of War Mobilization to plan for a one-front war with Japan lasting approximately one year. An invading force of one million troops with supporting materiel was projected. Only a very restricted circle of officials, which did not include Gordon, was aware of the nature of the secret project that had been receiving the WPB's highest priority for anything it needed. Lincoln Gordon knew of the project's high priority but was not cleared for direct knowledge of what was happening in the New Mexico desert. On August 6, the world learned the details at the same time as the WPB planners when the United States dropped the first atomic bomb on Hiroshima. Three days later an atomic weapon of slightly different design was detonated over Nagasaki to even more devastating effect. On August 15 Japan Standard Time (August 14 in the United States), Emperor Hirohito announced on the radio the Japanese military surrender and acceptance of the terms of the Potsdam Declaration. The greatest war in history, greater even than the Great War in terms of its costs in human life, consumption of output, and destruction, was suddenly over, and the effort that had consumed the energies of the nation was at an end.

President Truman, when he announced the dropping of the Hiroshima bomb sixteen hours after it occurred, had warned that if the Japanese "do not accept our terms, they may expect a war of ruin from the air, the like of which has never been seen on this earth." James Agee in *Time* magazine on August 20, 1945, said: "To the U.S. and the world, the harnessing of atomic power carried the explosive implications of an industrial revolution, perhaps more significant for the future than the harnessing of steam or electricity, or the invention of the internal-combustion engine had been in the past."[24] The scientists who had developed the bomb, the nation's military strategists, and civilian policy-makers now faced the task of how to control the awesome power of the atom.

7

Controlling the Atom

> While science should be free, it should not be free to destroy mankind.
> —Bernard Baruch, 1949

With VE Day, the War Production Board's mission had shifted to planning for a one-front war in the Pacific and for the transition to the postwar civilian economy. In June Gordon was promoted to program vice chairman of the requirements committee, like the varsity athlete, he said in his draft memoir, earning "his letter by appearing in the final minutes of the big game." He was being too modest, since he had in fact exercised the powers of program vice chairman for most of the previous six months. Despite his self-deprecating remark, Gordon was now officially (as he had been unofficially) one of the key officials in the agency, effectively next in power to Chairman Krug.

Even those who did not know of the secret weapon about to be tested in New Mexico understood that the enemy in the Pacific was fighting a rearguard action. Consequently many civilians who had signed on for service in the wartime agencies were fleeing for the exit. The nation's cooperative spirit, which had helped sustain the wartime regulatory machinery, weakened. Parochial interests and regional tensions reemerged with a vengeance. Certain industries had never been easy to organize. In textiles, for example, many small producers had made it difficult to formulate broad regulatory guidelines that would be observed even during the height of wartime patriotism. Large oligopolistic sectors now became less amenable to wage and price controls and to industry-wide production guidelines. Office of Price Administration (OPA) staff became concerned that inflationary pressures would explode across the economy unless production limits were linked to price controls—in effect, OPA advocated a more centralized system to shore up the controls that now appeared on the verge of collapse. Gordon had studied the Canadian system of unified production and price controls in his initial work for the National Resources and Planning Board before the war and had concluded that this system could not work in the larger and more complicated US economy. He thus resisted the suggestions of his friends in the OPA to strengthen and centralize controls.

With the end of the war in the Pacific, the WPB's sole mission became reconversion. This was, as we have seen, anything but a simple task, for it raised squarely the issues that had been present during the war between New Dealers and free marketers throughout the wartime apparatus. How much of a state of permanent military preparedness should be maintained so that the nation would not be caught flat-footed again?[1] In October 1945 the WPB was officially dissolved and replaced by the Civilian Production Administration (CPA), with Gordon becoming its director of reconversion priorities. As a New Dealer, Gordon was disposed toward maintaining a prominent government role to deal with the predictable problems of shifting back to a civilian economy. But he was also realistic enough to recognize the overwhelming pressures within Congress, industry, and the public at large for the rapid and comprehensive lifting of wartime controls. Gordon had acquired an education in practical politics and recognized the appeal of the Republican slogan in the 1946 midterm congressional elections: "Had enough [of wartime controls]? Vote Republican!" It was no surprise to him when the Republicans swept to victory in 1946 and gained control of both the House of Representatives and the Senate.

What Next in His Career?

In the war's late stages Gordon's thoughts turned to what he would do after the war. Many wartime associates had returned or planned to return to their prewar occupations. Others had been changed by their wartime service and decided to stay in government. Gordon had reentry rights to Harvard's Government Department, since he had been at the midpoint of a five-year term as assistant professor when he departed for government service. He could resume his teaching duties, reoccupy his home in Belmont that he had rented out, and resettle his family (now grown to three children with the arrival of his second son, Hugh B. Gordon, in 1945) in Boston. This course would require him to begin work immediately on a new research project since a decision on tenure would come within two years.

A return to Harvard was certainly an attractive option, but it held potential drawbacks as well. There was first the matter of Gordon's doubts about his aptitude for basic research. Something of this concern may have been involved in the episode of depression he had suffered during the war. He also did not really enjoy teaching. He particularly loathed grading exam papers, and in general he preferred research to teaching. Nor was it certain that he would be promoted to a tenured associate professorship. His coauthor Merle Fainsod had a claim on a tenure position that was much superior to his own. In later years Gordon maintained that there was no direct competition with Fainsod because of the latter's shift to specializing in Soviet studies, but in 1945 Gordon believed there was such a competition.

Another problem was the feud between Gordon's mentor William Y. Elliott and Carl J. Friedrich, two of the Government Department's professorial barons. Elliott had been influential in bringing Friedrich to Harvard originally, but their relationship had deteriorated until it turned into bitter personal animosity, as well as professional rivalry. Senior professors in that day could exercise a veto over appointments and especially over promotions to tenure. As a protégé of Elliott, Gordon had reason to fear a Friedrich veto. There is no direct evidence that Gordon and Friedrich had openly clashed previously, but a March 1958 incident suggests a lingering antipathy between them. Gordon made disparaging marginal notes on a paper given by Friedrich at the Conference on Franco-American Relations, characterizing Friedrich's argument as "utter nonsense" in marginalia on his copy of the paper. It is not known whether he made comments to this effect at the conference or afterward, but Gordon's views apparently came to Friedrich's attention and provoked the irate professor to write an angry note to Professor Al Heros of the Harvard Business School, a conference sponsor, in which he complained bitterly about Gordon's comments.[2] The only individual in the Government Department able to remain on good terms with both Friedrich and Elliott was Henry Kissinger, a sign, according to Kissinger's biographer Walter Isaacson, of

Kissinger's wiliness, ability to flatter powerful older men, and precocity as a diplomat.[3] Diplomatic guile was clearly not an attribute of Gordon's; his manner was direct, straightforward, and generally trusting. Gordon certainly had a temper and was thin-skinned; he could be blunt and was not always tactful. Further, having left the Government Department for the business school (see below), in part over the uncertainty of getting tenure, for which he blamed Friedrich, Gordon likely harbored some resentment toward Friedrich. His choice of the business school as a bird in the hand in any case pushed him in the direction of a more practical, professional school orientation to economics and business-government relations and made him less sympathetic to Friedrich's theoretical formulations. A position in the business school clearly shifted Gordon's main intellectual interests toward economics rather than politics at this stage of his career.

For Gordon, at the end of the war, there had also been the opportunity to remain in government service. In June 1945 he received an attractive invitation to leave the WPB and join the Strategic Bombing Survey team as its economist. He very badly wanted to accept this assignment but decided to reject the offer out of loyalty to the WPB. (The assignment went instead to his Harvard colleague Ken Galbraith, who was then serving at the OPA.) At the end of the war Lincoln was also sounded out by WPB chairman Julius Krug (who had succeeded Don Nelson and would soon become secretary of the interior) about coming to the Interior Department as assistant secretary to straighten out the department's tangled jurisdictional lines. Krug admired Gordon's high energy and good judgment and badly wanted to take him to Interior. After reflection Gordon declined the invitation to sort out the Interior Department's internal organization, feeling this would be a mission impossible.

While he was considering the Krug offer, Gordon also received some good news that greatly improved the appeal of returning to Cambridge. It came in a visit by Dean Donald David of the Harvard Business School.[4] Pendleton Herring, Lincoln's closest friend, had earlier discreetly asked him if he might be interested in a potential offer from the Harvard Business School if this could be arranged. Gordon had given the green light. Dean David had worked closely with Don Nelson in devising courses for WPB managers during the war and knew Gordon reasonably well. David's proposition was attractive: Would Gordon consider joining the faculty of the Harvard Business School (HBS) instead of returning to the Government Department, with an immediate promotion to associate professor with tenure and promotion the following year to full professor? The salary would be higher than what Gordon would make as a returning assistant professor in the Government Department. The dean explained that the status and reputation of businessmen had been damaged by the Depression, and he was intent on repairing relations between the business school and Harvard's arts and sciences faculty. He believed that Gordon could do this for him.

It did not take Gordon long to accept the offer. Though he shared the biases of the arts and sciences faculty toward the business school, the advantages of switching to the HBS were compelling. He discussed the matter with Herring, Harvard economist Seymour E. Harris, and probably Elliott.[5] Harris was involved in the negotiations and apparently arranged for Gordon to have an affiliation with the Graduate School of Public Administration (the Littauer School) as part of the package. Gordon was to teach a course on public administration at the Littauer School at some point after settling in at the HBS. Later Gordon thought better of this aspect of his new appointment and tried to get out of teaching a seminar in public administration. In the spring of 1947, however, he received an offer to become associate dean of the Littauer School but declined the offer and apparently severed his ties with the school.[6] The HBS exempted him from teaching during his first term back so that he would have time to prepare his courses for the fall term of 1946 and to do some consulting work in Washington on the transition to the civilian economy. He had thus arranged to spend three days, usually Wednesday through Friday on alternate weeks, consulting for the WPB's successor agency and supplementing his Harvard salary.

The UN Atomic Energy Commission

The story of the making of the atomic bomb has been well told and need not be repeated here.[7] But a few highlights will refresh the reader's recollection and set the stage for our discussion of the UN Atomic Energy Commission's work from July to December 1946. On October 9, 1941, Vannevar Bush, head of the Office of Scientific Research and Development (OSRD), proposed to FDR that the president authorize a significant expansion of US nuclear research in light of recent information on the feasibility of a bomb.[8] Bush warned that the accelerated project could cost "many times as much as a major oil refinery." FDR pigeonholed the request. On January 9, 1942, after Pearl Harbor, President Roosevelt returned the memo to Bush with a covering note:

VB,
OK—returned—I think you had best keep this in your own safe.
FDR[9]

Vannevar Bush and James B. Conant urged policy-makers to give thought to postwar organization for atomic energy even before the test of the weapon in the New Mexico desert in the summer of 1945. Bush, Conant, and other scientists had worried about the postwar control of atomic energy and wondered if the United States should take the lead in advocating an international control entity. The interim committee under Secretary of War Henry Stimson that had recommended the use of the bomb to hasten the end of the war had also endorsed the need for postwar international controls. Secretary Stimson was convinced that the United States should recognize that a new era in human affairs had been ushered in with the bomb and believed that the nation should pursue international control of all aspects of atomic energy.[10] Stimson and his deputy, John J. McCloy, found an ally in Dean Acheson, newly installed as under secretary of state but often exercising the powers of the secretary of state while Secretary Byrnes was abroad in negotiations. Secretary of Commerce Henry Wallace was an early and enthusiastic advocate of partnership with the Soviet Union and was convinced that a nuclear agreement would ease postwar relations. Wallace took advantage of his position as the sole remaining original New Dealer in Truman's cabinet and pushed hard for conciliatory polices toward the Soviet Union. But the ideas of those early arms controllers stirred intense opposition from within the bureaucracy, the Congress, and especially the military. Admiral Leahy, President Truman's military adviser, adamantly opposed any deal with the Soviet Union. Senator Arthur Vandenberg (R, Michigan), along with many of his Republican colleagues, was suspicious of the Soviet Union. Secretary of State James F. Byrnes, engaged in arduous negotiations with his Soviet and Allied counterparts, was alternately wary of Soviet intentions and eager for an accord that would burnish his credentials as a peacemaker. President Truman wanted an accord if Byrnes could get one but was more skeptical of Soviet intentions than was Byrnes and somewhat wary of Byrnes's ambitions.

The situation was thus unusually fluid. The Cold War was not yet clearly in existence. (Even the phrase—an invention of Herbert Bayard Swope's, Bernard Baruch's publicist and speechwriter, that was then picked up by Walter Lippmann—was not yet in wide usage.)[11] The nation was both engaged in the process of industrial reconversion and releasing millions of men and women from the armed services. Americans looked with relish at the prospects of disengaging from the sacrifices of the war and at the same time understood that a war-ravaged world would have to be rebuilt. The Republican Party was badly split between the internationalist eastern wing and midwestern elements anxious for a return to normalcy. Democrats were split between the Wallace "idealist" wing and the Truman-Byrnes-Acheson "realist" wing. Personal ambitions clouded the picture, as Byrnes maneuvered to score personal diplomatic triumphs in his negotiations with the Russians and Wallace pondered his political fortunes. Atomic energy was squarely in the center of the debate over the challenges facing the nation in both foreign and domestic policy. The civilian scientists who had created the bomb stressed the promise of plentiful and cheap energy supplies, health improvements, and other nonmilitary uses of atomic power. Should nuclear energy become a commercial activity, or should it require direct government ownership? Clearly a new agency would be required to deal with both the military and the civilian aspects of nuclear power. But should this entity—given its obvious closeness to security concerns—be placed within one of the military services? President Truman decided in October 1945 that he would embrace civilian control of atomic energy, but he did not resolve the question of how much secrecy would accompany the civilian control. The kind of international control that should and could be sought would obviously be influenced by the state of international relations.

Congress began drafting legislation on a domestic atomic energy agency while keeping a watchful eye on what the State Department was doing in the United Nations General Assembly in New York. With the departure of Stimson from government, Secretary of State Byrnes took the initiative in atomic diplomacy. In early January 1946, Byrnes named Under Secretary Acheson to head a committee to formulate an American plan for controlling the atom.[12] In taking over the leadership of postwar atomic diplomacy, Acheson was aided by his special assistant Herbert S. Marks, a young lawyer who had served with the Tennessee Valley Authority, the Bonneville Dam Authority, and the War Production Board.[13] Carroll S. Wilson, an engineer with the Office of Scientific Research and Development, provided day-to-day technical advice and support for the committee. The committee worked diligently and soon had the outlines of a plan to present to the United Nations for the creation of a UN Atomic Energy Commission (UNAEC).

The UNAEC was formally founded on January 24, 1946, under the authority of Resolution 1 of the UN General Assembly. Resolution 1 specified that the commission was "to deal with the problems raised by the discovery of atomic energy" and directed further to "make specific proposals: (a) for extending between all nations the exchange of basic scientific information for peaceful ends; (b) for control of atomic energy to the extent necessary to ensure its use only for peaceful purposes; (c) for the elimination from national armaments of atomic weapons and of all other major weapons adaptable to mass destruction; and (d) for effective arrangements by way of inspection and other means to protect complying states against the hazards of violations and evasions."[14]

While the general scope and mission of the international control entity were thus laid out, the specific proposals that the United States would advance when the UNAEC actually convened to achieve the broad ends still had to be developed by the Acheson-Lilienthal team. Significant effort went into the process of educating the nontechnical participants about the intricacies of the atom, an assignment that fell largely to J. Robert Oppenheimer, the technical director of the Manhattan Project. His eloquent and lucid explanations riveted his colleagues. Acheson relied on a five-member board of consultants—including Oppenheimer; Charles A. Thomas of the Monsanto Chemical Company; Chester I. Barnard, president of the Bell Telephone Company; Harry A. Winne, vice president of engineering of General Electric; and David E. Lilienthal, chairman of the Tennessee Valley Authority (TVA)—to prepare a draft report for the wider committee.[15] Policy recommendations flowed from the technical explanations, but broader political and moral factors influenced Acheson's team of consultants and shaped their plan and their recommendations to the full committee. David Lilienthal, chairman of the TVA, was experienced in dealing with complex technical issues and showed his skills as chairman of the board of consultants. He played a major role in shaping the plan that finally emerged from the deliberations of the full committee, after a final weekend of editing, on Monday, March 18, 1946. The report notably and ably picked up the challenge posed at the end of the Henry Smyth Report published in 1945: to spell out the implications for and the meaning of US policy on the scientific developments.

The Acheson-Lilienthal Report argued that it *was* technically feasible to control atomic energy and that the best way to do so was to have an international agency that owned and controlled all aspects of atomic energy production. The new agency, in short, would regulate the entire civilian nuclear industry from the ground up. The mission would include any extraction efforts by entities of national governments. The international agency would have scientific expertise of its own and would also conduct peaceful nuclear research. The United States, once the new entity was fully established, would turn over its nuclear fuels, give a full accounting of all nuclear materials it possessed, dismantle its nuclear weapons infrastructure, and pledge to manufacture no new weapons. Any existing stockpile of atomic bombs would be destroyed or turned over to the new agency, provided that other nations would forego nuclear development or pledge to turn over their weapons. (Only Britain apart from the United States at this time seemed capable of developing atomic bombs.) The Acheson-Lilienthal Report was silent on the question of whether the UN Security Council's normal operating procedures—in particular, the veto right guaranteed to each of the five permanent members—would apply to inspection actions of the new UN atomic agency. Acheson's committee had largely completed its work by the time President Truman named Bernard Baruch as the US representative to the UN Atomic Energy Commission. But the committee did not send the report officially to President Truman and Secretary Byrnes until after the president had decided on Baruch as his UN atomic representative. Although President Truman accepted the report's recommendations in general terms, numerous questions remained. The committee members were conscious of the loose ends in their report. They had finessed a number of critical issues, including the question of whether nonnuclear weapons of mass destruction would be included within the purview of the UN commission.

One key unanswered question was whether the report was to be construed as official US policy or was merely a working paper for the official who would present America's atomic proposals to the UN. The issue, in short, was the extent of Baruch's authority as the US special representative. Acheson and most of his State Department colleagues felt strongly that the report should be made public as soon as possible to provide a foundation of public support for it as official US policy. John McCloy, the Defense representative on the Acheson committee, cautioned against premature public disclosure. He urged that the American delegate must have room to negotiate at the UN.

External events meanwhile had complicated matters as Cold War tensions had begun to rise. A more fluid environment was being replaced by the emerging division of the world into opposing camps. Kennan's "long telegram" warned of Soviet intransigence and hostility to the West.[16] Rumors of suspected wartime Soviet nuclear espionage began to surface in some news media. Winston Churchill's speech at Westminster College in Fulton, Missouri, declaring that an "iron curtain" had fallen across Europe, created a firestorm and caused President Truman to distance himself from his old ally after sponsoring the speech in the first place and accompanying Churchill to Missouri. The outspoken secretary of commerce Henry Wallace, dropped from the ticket as vice presidential candidate in 1944, was among the loudest of the voices on the left that deplored the Churchill iron curtain speech as strident and warmongering. The Truman administration's attitude toward the Soviet Union, especially on the issue of concessions to the Soviets in order to gain an agreement for the international control of atomic energy, was not fully formed in the spring of 1946. But the upcoming UN session would force the United States to clarify its position, and legislation moved forward to create a domestic atomic agency that would affect, and limit, what stand the country would take on international issues. The situation did not rule out completely an accommodation with the Soviet Union on specific issues such as the international control and inspection of atomic materials to prevent the spread of military capabilities. The negotiating terrain, however, was bound to be exceedingly difficult.

The Choice of Bernard M. Baruch

Secretary of State Byrnes spent much of his time in negotiations in Europe during his early time in office, leaving the task of running the department to Acheson. Byrnes reentered the nuclear debate by recommending that President Truman appoint Byrnes's old friend and fellow South Carolinian Bernard M. Baruch as US atomic representative to the UN. Byrnes and Baruch had been close friends and political allies for years. Byrnes had first raised the matter with Baruch when he visited him at his South Carolina estate in late February 1946. In sounding him, out the secretary cited the gravity of the issues, the need for someone of high prestige to have credibility with Congress and the public, and the wide policy latitude that Baruch would enjoy. Byrnes gave his friend a copy of the UN resolution creating the UNAEC and told Baruch he would raise the matter with the president only if Baruch would accept the assignment. Baruch on March 13 informed Byrnes that he would need a deputy and scientific advisers, and that it must be understood that he was free to speak publicly on any issue. Moreover, at age seventy-six, he would work only from 10:00 a.m. to noon and from 2:30 to 4:00 p.m., but he was willing to serve under these conditions. Truman did not know Baruch but was familiar with his outsized reputation and was convinced that it would take someone of Baruch's stature to win over the Senate and the public to the administration's ideas. Baruch could not only help ensure diplomatic success but strengthen the prospects for civilian control of the domestic atomic agency Truman had in mind. Baruch's stature would also keep the Senate from holding hearings on the international aspects of atomic energy that might expose the present lack of unity within the executive branch. Truman first saw and endorsed in general the Acheson-Lilienthal Plan on March 21, three days after he sent up Baruch's nomination to the Senate.

Acheson was alarmed when he learned of the Baruch nomination. The appointment of an outsider new to the nuclear issue was bound, in Acheson's mind, to create problems of policy unity and coordination no matter how distinguished the individual. The outsider's team would duplicate the work of insiders and in this case might well undercut the policy framework set forth in the Acheson-Lilienthal Plan. Furthermore Baruch had a reputation for vanity and for tireless self-promotion by his publicist, Herbert Bayard Swope. Lilienthal pronounced himself "quite sick" over the appointment.[17] Oppenheimer considered that Acheson, Bush, or any fellow member of the Acheson board of consultants would have been a better choice. He did not consider Baruch's advisers competent in scientific matters. The president, though nominating Baruch at Byrnes's suggestion, had no illusions about Baruch's penchant for grandiosity. In notes he kept he described Baruch as a man "wanting to run the world, the moon, and maybe Jupiter."[18] Notwithstanding the reservations, the press reaction and comments from Capitol Hill, as the president had surmised, were in general favorable and matched Byrnes's and Truman's hopes. Senator Tom Connolly (D, Texas), chairman of the Senate Foreign Relations Committee, called Baruch with an offer to short-circuit the confirmation process, provided the elder statesman could give assurance that US security interests would be respected in any control plan. Baruch happily gave Connelly assurance that no atomic secrets would be divulged to anybody without express congressional approval.

The contents of the Acheson-Lilienthal Plan began to appear in press reports, and the State Department in short order released the whole report. Fearing that his role might be merely that of a "messenger boy" for the State Department, Baruch got cold feet and asked for an appointment with President Truman. At this meeting he asked for a postponement of his confirmation hearing to give himself more time to reflect on whether he could serve a useful role. Baruch wondered whether, if the Acheson plan represented official US policy, the public might think that Baruch had no role. Acheson or Lilienthal might just as easily present the plan to the UN. If on the other hand Baruch had full authority, he would formulate a clear policy that the public and the Senate would accept but that might depart from the Acheson-Lilienthal Report in certain particulars. Truman's recollection of the meeting ten years later was that Baruch was mainly interested in public recognition for himself and that he told the elder statesman he would have to operate within the framework of administration policy, which would be set by the president. Baruch's version was that the president, when asked who would be in charge of atomic policy, said, "Hell, you are."[19] Baruch told the president that he wanted to consult further with Byrnes. A master at conciliation, Byrnes gave the right assurances so that the confirmation process was unblocked, and Baruch was quickly confirmed by the Senate in April 1946.

Baruch immersed himself in the nuclear issue and in the details of the Acheson-Lilienthal Plan with the aid of four members of his inner circle. These were his business associate and former military officer John Hancock, his publicist Herbert Swope, New York attorney Ferdinand Eberstadt, and engineer John Searle. These men had other responsibilities, however, and none would be able to work full time on the project. Baruch clearly needed and invited numerous government officials to his New York City apartment to brief him. He sought unsuccessfully to have the Acheson board of scientific consultants continue to exist as a staff resource for him. He also tried but failed to persuade Bush, Conant, and Oppenheimer to work for him full time as scientific advisers. With the help of Arthur Compton and General Leslie Groves, he did persuade Richard Tolman, distinguished senior physicist from the California Institute of Technology (who had an important role in the atomic bomb's development), to come east and serve as his full-time science adviser. Oppenheimer thereupon agreed to help out on a part-time basis.

The relations of Baruch and his team with Acheson and his staff had started out on a strained basis and remained delicate. The underlying problem was that Baruch had major reservations on key points of the State Department plan. Baruch was persuaded, for example, by Searle that international control and ownership of all mining operations was impractical and unnecessary. Private companies should be allowed to mine the necessary ores and could operate facilities under licensing arrangements from and close supervision by the international control agency. Baruch believed that inspection arrangements should be more clearly spelled out from the start as a precondition for negotiations with the Soviet Union. Baruch insisted further that penalties should be automatically imposed by the international agency in the event of any violation. Moreover he sought the inclusion of nonnuclear weapons of mass destruction in the inspections. Acheson initially assessed the prospects for an agreement with the Soviets as moderately favorable so long as the United States did not demand too many inspections or make other demands at the outset. A major policy review in mid-May by the Baruch and Acheson teams did not, however, resolve their differences. Part of the problem was that the Baruch side lacked full-time staff resources and indeed had neither the size nor the depth to negotiate with the State Department on the details of the US plan.

Gordon Joins the Baruch Team

The DC-3 that carried Gordon, now thirty-two, on his commute to Washington stopped as usual at LaGuardia Airport for refueling and maintenance. Passengers had to disembark even when the same aircraft went on to Washington's National Airport. In late May 1946, shortly after the unsatisfactory review between the Baruch and Acheson staffs, Gordon was traveling to Washington and decided to stretch his legs during the stopover in New York. He strolled around the airport and was surprised to see his old WPB boss Ferdinand Eberstadt approaching. He had not seen Eberstadt since the latter's abrupt departure from the WPB in 1943. Recognizing Gordon, Eberstadt slapped his head with his hand and called out: "Linc! Why didn't I think of you before? We need your help. Have you met the Old Man? Can you come to New York for the summer?"[20]

Lincoln asked Ferd what all this was about—and what old man did he mean?

"It's Barney Baruch, of course," said Eberstadt. "And the work is the UN Atomic Energy Commission—the most important negotiation in the world right now."

Eberstadt knew his man. He explained to Gordon why they needed him. A lot of the team was only part time; they needed full-time staff, and they needed a generalist like Gordon who knew technical issues and had a quick pen. There was no more important issue in the world. Eberstadt led Gordon around the corner and introduced him to Baruch. Gordon had recently been studying Baruch's role as "czar" in World War I mobilization, and Baruch struck him as an imposing figure: six foot four, slender, silver haired, impeccably dressed as always, and exuding an air of authority. There was no time for conversation. Eberstadt took Gordon's telephone number and promised to be in touch shortly. On his return to Boston on the weekend Gordon found a message from Eberstadt formalizing an offer to join the Baruch staff.

This gave Gordon "a couple of sleepless nights." The Harvard Business School had made him a generous offer, and how would it appear if he were to depart so soon after returning? He would be leaving his wife to bear the burdens of child raising again. The Gordons, as noted earlier, now had three children, with the arrival of their second son, Hugh B. Gordon, in 1945. It helped that the obligation would be self-limiting in that the Baruch assignment was to formulate a US proposal and present it to the UN, after which the regular diplomatic machinery of the State Department would take over for the next stage. Gordon could stay with his mother in New York or at her apartment after she left for Lake

Sunapee so that he would not have to spend money on room and board. Gordon had bought a copy of the Smyth Report nine months earlier and "read it carefully enough to understand every sentence and diagram, no skipping permitted."[21] He "was fascinated by the physics involved and by possible peaceful uses of nuclear energy. On the international side," he wrote, "it seemed to me at that stage (and still does today), that coordinated action to prevent any military use of atomic energy was the only reliable means of preserving world civilization."[22]

He met with Dean Donald David and his deputy (and designated successor) Stanley Teele to review his situation, and to his relief they enthusiastically supported his request for a temporary leave. "This is a one-time opportunity," the dean told him. "Your book on industrial mobilization can wait." David and Teele were only concerned that Gordon be ready for teaching his class on business-government relations in the spring term beginning in January 1947.

The reactions to Baruch's June UN speech were highly favorable in the United States. Only the Hearst newspapers were critical, attacking Baruch for his willingness to give away US military secrets to hostile foreign powers.[23] *Pravda* predictably accused the United States of trying to perpetuate its atomic monopoly. Soviet UN representative Andrei Gromyko called for a halt to the manufacture of all atomic weapons as the basis for negotiation. There were continuing worries in the State Department over Baruch's stand on the veto question and his insistence on automatic penalties for violators. However, most nations, after Baruch's speech, were willing to credit the United States with being serious about the control and elimination of nuclear weapons. Then came the announcement that the United States planned a series of atomic bomb tests in the Pacific. The idea for conducting the tests was the US Navy's. The tests, first announced in March 1946, had been postponed in the light of Senate criticism that seaworthy ships were going to be destroyed unnecessarily. Secretary Byrnes continued to oppose the tests while the UN negotiations were under way. Secretary of Commerce Henry Wallace, in an augury of policy disputes to come, wrote to Truman, urging the president to halt the manufacture of atomic bombs altogether as a gesture of good intentions. Truman agreed to the initial postponement but told the cabinet that the tests would be rescheduled for July 1 unless somebody had a good reason for further postponement.

Gordon arrived for duty in New York just after the Baruch speech in June and as the dispute erupted over the US resumption of atomic bomb tests in the Pacific. He felt in his element as soon as he reported for duty with the Baruch team. His skills as a quick draftsman were in demand as the US delegation in July tabled new explanations and refinements of the US proposals at the UNAEC sessions. He got on well with his old WPB boss Eberstadt, speechwriter Swope, and John Hancock, Baruch's deputy and longtime associate. Gordon also formed a close working friendship with science adviser Richard Tolman, with whom he spent a daily one-hour commute from Manhattan to the UN temporary headquarters in Lake Success, Long Island, while the permanent UN headquarters on Manhattan's east side were under construction. To Gordon's delight his old friend and best man Pen Herring had become the secretary of the UNAEC and the liaison official with the US delegation to the UN.

Another pleasant aspect of the job was that he became friends with Robert Oppenheimer, who commuted from Princeton and assisted Tolman part time on scientific issues.[24] On the diplomatic front Gordon acted as the main liaison between the Baruch team and the State Department, dealing with Herbert S. Marks, Acheson's principal aide on nuclear matters, and Frank Lindsay, of the US delegation to the UN. Rounding out the group of close associates was the Canadian George Ignatieff, a fellow Rhodes scholar and a member of what Gordon dubbed "our little brotherhood." Ignatieff, the only non-native-born Canadian Rhodes scholar, was then a senior official on the Canadian delegation to the UN specializing in atomic matters. There was camaraderie on the Baruch team, and Gordon found his days energizing and highly stimulating. Gordon met alone with Baruch only twice but saw him frequently in the company of other staff members and was favorably impressed by his energy and his grasp of the issues, though the elder statesman was undoubtedly vain.

The Baruch team and the United States needed, first of all, to arrive at a unified position. Gordon was helpful on this score as he explained Baruch's views to his State Department staff counterparts and explained State positions to his Baruch colleagues. Baruch and the State Department were united in trying to combat the influence of Henry Wallace on the US posture toward the Soviet Union. Wallace had injected himself into the public debate on atomic diplomacy and other foreign policy issues. Once approximate harmony, Wallace aside, had been reached on official US nuclear policy, the Baruch team and the US delegation to the UN faced the need to educate the other UN delegates on the basic facts of nuclear energy and to spell out how the proposed atomic develop-ment authority in the United States would work in practice. This meant explaining the intricate licensing and regulatory arrangements of the pro-posal, the administrative arrangements between the new atomic agency and the regular UN decision-making machinery, and a host of other highly complex policy and technical issues that were new to most of the UN delegations. Gordon had learned enough about the technical issues that he could explain them lucidly to nonspecialists and relate them to political and administrative issues.

In retrospect, Gordon and his colleagues clearly had little chance of negotiating an agreement with the Soviet Union. The US military was not willing to give up its nuclear monopoly, and the Soviet Union was secretly committed to its own nuclear program. The UK was also determined to have its own nuclear deterrent and civilian nuclear industry. The con-tainment doctrine—which became the cornerstone of US policy toward the Soviet Union as the Cold War developed—was based initially on the assumption that the United States would enjoy a monopoly on nuclear weapons for an indeterminate future. That Stalin had knowledge of US nuclear secrets and was determined to have his own bomb was not known at the onset of the negotiations, however, and Gordon and his colleagues thought that there was a decent chance that an agreement could be nego-tiated. Many US officials at the time thought that the groundwork might be laid for future UN action even if an agreement could not be reached now. Baruch presented the US proposals in June, calling for an atomic development authority (ADA) to license nuclear technology to national and subnational entities, inspections to ensure that the atom was used for peaceful purposes, and sanctions in the event of violations and diversion of nuclear fuels to military uses. The US proposal called for the suspen-sion of the normal veto rights of the five permanent members of the UN Security Council when the new UN nuclear authority determined that a violation of its regulations had occurred and it was forced to impose auto-matic penalties and sanctions against the violator. The proposals would be embodied in a treaty that would be signed and ratified by the govern-ments of UN member nations.

The initial Soviet objections to the US proposals rested on the argument that the United States simply wanted to protect its own nuclear monopoly for both military and commercial reasons and deny the benefits of atomic energy to other nations. The United States, in the Soviet view, had to renounce atomic weapons completely and surrender or destroy its existing stockpile before it could seriously negotiate with other nations. The US side pointed out that all US nuclear weapons would be surrendered to the new UN agency once it was up and running and its machinery of inspections and sanctions was fully operational. The Soviet Union continued to downplay the need for sanctions, penalties, and inspections, insisting that the United States had to halt outright and categorically renounce the manufacture of all atomic arms before any serious negotiations could take place. The Canadian representative to the UNAEC, thoroughly briefed by Ignatieff and Gordon, effectively rebutted the Soviet position by pointing to the failure of past international efforts to outlaw dum-dum bullets, poison gas, and special categories of explosives without adequate inspection mechanisms. Further, the failure of the Kellogg-Briand Peace Treaty's attempt to outlaw war absent any collective enforcement machinery was further evidence that unilateral and unverifiable pronouncements were not effective tools of diplomacy.

A crisis point came on July 24, when Soviet representative Andrei Gromyko made a major speech announcing the official Soviet reaction to the US proposal. Despite strenuous efforts by the US delegation to resolve the differences over the previous month, Gromyko rejected categorically the US proposals "either as a whole or their separate parts."[25] "Either as a whole or their separate parts" seemed definitive and appeared to preclude further negotiations. The US proposals to which Gromyko particularly objected dealt with the relationship between the proposed new UN atomic authority and the rest of the UN structure and operating rules. Gromyko argued that the special authority was redundant, that the Security Council had adequate authority to deal with atomic issues without the special agency, and that abridging the Security Council's veto power would wreck the whole UN decision-making machinery. The hour-long Gromyko speech was first delivered in Russian, which none of the US team understood, then in French, which a few, including Gordon, understood, and then in English, there being no simultaneous translation yet at the UN. The US delegation, after listening to the English translation of the Gromyko speech, returned to its headquarters in the Empire State Building to discuss what to do next.

Swope was the first to speak. The Soviet rejection was so definitive and the tone so belligerent that it was time to fold up operations. The regular State Department diplomats could take over, Swope declared, since the talks were now only a matter of trading barbs with the Soviets. Gordon had previously tried to soften Baruch's position on the veto and bring it closer to the Acheson/State Department view that the United States might be forced to soften its position on the automatic application of sanctions with no veto or negotiations. Despite being the most junior member of the delegation, Gordon decided to speak up and argued that it would be a mistake to give up so easily. He suggested that Gromyko's modifying words "in their present form" gave some hope that a compromise could still be reached. Even if the Soviet Union proved intransigent, there was something to be gained by winning over the rest of the world to US proposals, isolating Gromyko and demonstrating Soviet unreasonableness. Baruch and Eberstadt were impressed by this line of reasoning and quickly agreed. Baruch made a show of optimism and attempted to boost the morale of his colleagues. Perhaps stung by the imputations that he was a showboat with little taste for the nitty-gritty of diplomacy, the elder statesman declared that the United States should not be deterred by Gromyko's rebuff and should find a new path forward. This path would be to make progress by stepping back and retracing the earlier steps taken by Acheson's scientific experts in order to come up with fresh ideas and something they might have overlooked.

Someone came up with the idea of reexamining the technical fundamentals of the isotope separation process with a new set of experts. Hancock demurred on the grounds that this would merely postpone facing the hard political choices that were at the heart of the problem. He insisted that the technical and political aspects of the large issues could not be separated and that everyone already understood how the isotope separation process worked. Hancock's argument did not prevail. While it was conceded that the Acheson-Lilienthal Report had thoroughly plowed the technical ground, the Baruch team decided that atomic developments were still so novel—and the need to educate other nations so urgent— that it would be useful to review the technical aspects again. And this time, for negotiating purposes, it would be useful to draw on non-American scientists as well. Baruch's response to the Gromyko speech was thus to thrust scientists—and in particular non-American scientists—into the diplomatic limelight for the next phase of the UNAEC's work. The plan had a dual aim: to soften Gromyko's opposition to a control regime and, if that failed, at least to build up a broad base of understanding and support behind US views for the future. Hancock's view in the end proved to be correct. The Soviet objections were not based on a failure to understand the technical aspects of nuclear energy, but on the political determination to develop nuclear weapons.

Under the adroit chairmanship of the internationally respected Dutch nuclear physicist Hendrik Kramers, a new UNAEC scientific subcommittee undertook an intensive review of the technical issues during the month of August. Kramers urged his colleagues to put a premium on informal discussions and keep diplomatic protocol to a minimum. The scientists came to a conceptual agreement, cautiously phrased in the negative, that there was no scientific evidence indicating that it was impossible or impracticable to regulate atomic energy production and use. Further, an international agency would be useful to set broad technical and safety standards for individual nations to follow. Kramers appeared to obtain unanimity among the scientists, but the Soviet and Polish delegates were instructed by their governments to object to the report being forwarded unanimously. The United States prevailed by a ten-to-two vote and was in position to achieve a convincing approval at the meeting of the full UN Atomic Energy Commission. But the Soviet opposition had not softened, and any US proposal that was taken up by the Security Council was certain to face a Soviet veto. Baruch decided that under the circumstances it was time for a full report to President Truman on the state of the negotiations, a report that would clarify the policy choices that the president now faced. Gordon was given the assignment of drafting the report and the accompanying letter to the president. The report went through about five drafts. Gordon records in a Truman Library oral history interview of September 1975 that Baruch was "an enormously vain man" but was very actively engaged in the substance of the debate and "was very much in command of his brief."[26] Baruch made numerous suggestions for changes in Gordon's drafts and showed mastery of the issues. Swope did some minor editing on the final version. An appointment was scheduled for

September 18 for Baruch and Hancock to present the report and discuss the next steps with President Truman.

This meeting suddenly became all the more important when Secretary of Commerce Henry Wallace gave a speech over the weekend (on Saturday, September 14) to twenty thousand roaring union delegates in Madison Square Garden excoriating US foreign policy and singling out Baruch's stance in the UN atomic talks for special criticism. Wallace misrepresented the US position and demanded a more conciliatory posture toward the Soviet Union. The errant secretary of commerce was a force to be reckoned with, though Baruch and his team may have overestimated Wallace's strength at this time. The Iowan had migrated from his family's farm-publishing business to successful entrepreneurship in the food industry to New Deal politics, becoming FDR's secretary of agriculture, a post his father had held under Presidents Harding and Coolidge. Wallace was one of the most ardent New Dealers and enjoyed brilliant success as secretary of agriculture, despite having to work around adverse court rulings on the scope of his executive powers. FDR's esteem for Wallace rose until he seemingly anointed him as his chosen successor by picking Wallace as his vice presidential running mate on the 1940 ticket. James Reston of the *New York Times* wrote in October 1941, "Meet the new Assistant President. His decisions in the next few months or years will undoubtedly affect your job, your rent, and the price of your groceries. And, what's more important, his decisions may determine the outcome of the war and the basis of the peace."[27] The high-water mark of Wallace's influence probably came at the time of his memorable speech "The Price of Free World Victory," in 1942. In this rousing leftist speech Wallace sounded the theme of the common man: "Some have spoken of the 'American Century.' I say that the century on which we are entering—the century which will come out of this war—can be and must be the century of the common man. . . . There must be neither military nor economic imperialism. . . . International cartels that serve American greed and the German will to power must go. . . . The people's revolution is on the march, and the devil and all his angels cannot prevail against it."[28]

Wallace's rousing speech so impressed Aaron Copeland that it inspired him to compose "Fanfare for the Common Man." It was less impressive to FDR. After this freewheeling display and an accumulation of spats with colleagues and other grievances, FDR began decidedly to cool on Wallace. Wallace's public quarrels with other senior officials in 1943, which made unpleasant headlines, convinced FDR that his doubts about the vice president were well founded and justified removing him from the ticket in 1944. Although he made a tepid public show of support for keeping the vice president on the ticket, FDR privately passed the word that Wallace was to be dropped in favor of Senator Harry Truman of Missouri. But Wallace missed by a hairsbreadth foiling the plan to dump him when a number of delegates from the party's left wing—led by Senator Claude Pepper of Florida—hatched a plan to keep him on the ticket. Pepper believed, and was probably correct in this surmise, that if he managed to get Wallace's name placed in nomination, there would be a stampede of delegates to Wallace. The party bosses would then have to back down, and FDR, having ostensibly expressed support for Wallace, would have to acquiesce. Unluckily for Pepper, the convention organizers got wind of his plan and were ready for him. When Pepper strode down the aisle and was about to mount the platform to nominate Wallace, the chairman gaveled the session to a close for the evening and refused to recognize him before the vote nominating Truman. With FDR's death in April 1945 Wallace became an outspoken critic of US foreign policy and of Truman from his new post as secretary of commerce. Wallace moved left and embraced policies closer to Soviet positions than to US ones in the emerging Cold War. He became a thorn in Truman's side, but the president was unwilling to discipline or fire him. Wallace represented the administration's closest link to the New Deal heritage. Unknown to the Baruch team or to Truman, Wallace's technical knowledge on atomic energy and his misinformation about US policy came from his contact in late 1945 with Soviet diplomat Anatoly Gorsky, who happened to be the NKGB station chief in Washington. Wallace was an amateur in foreign affairs and diplomacy and was easily misled by his far left advisers.

Before Baruch and Hancock left New York for their meeting with Truman, Gordon briefed them in great detail about the diplomatic context at the UN and the current state of the negotiations. In briefing Baruch, Gordon casually asked him how he could be sure the president would actually read the memo they would send him and present at the meeting.

"Oh, I have a simple device for that," Baruch said. "When I have anything important I want to talk over with the President I go in and say, 'Well, Mr. President, here it is. I know your time is more valuable than mine so I'd just as soon wait while you read it and then we can talk about it.'"[29]

Baruch did not get the chance to use his simple device. On the morning of his White House appointment, which was scheduled for 11:30, another Wallace bombshell burst into the headlines and upset Baruch's plans. Gordon and Frank Lindsay, from the US delegation to the UN, got the story when Baruch and Hancock picked them up at Mitchell Air Force Base on Long Island the day after the meeting with the president. Baruch departed immediately and left Hancock to explain what had happened. Hancock told them that on the day of the scheduled meeting with Truman, he had been awakened by an early morning phone call from Baruch, who asked him: "John, have you seen the morning papers?"

"No, Chief, I haven't."

"Well, get dressed and get up here right away for breakfast. Take a look at the morning papers before you come."[30]

The morning papers were full of news about the leak of a July 24 letter from Henry Wallace to the president. In a major bungle, Truman's press secretary Charles Ross had accidently given a mimeographed copy of the private letter to a reporter. The letter's contents were shocking. The immediate consequence was that the agenda for the presidential meeting was in a shambles, and any softening in Baruch's UN was now out of the question. It had been assumed within the US delegation that Baruch was ready to recommend new steps in America's atomic policies, but any shift now would appear to be capitulating to Wallace and enhancing his influence.

The Wallace Affair

Baruch and Hancock were shocked by the contents of Wallace's letter to the president. The press reported that the letter was filled with misrepresentations about the US delegation's role at the UN and US policy positions. The letter alluded to sources that supposedly revealed the bellicose intentions of US military planners and seemed to repeat Soviet talking points. Astonishingly, the letter implied that elements within the US military were planning for a preemptive attack on the Soviet Union. Wallace's intent was apparently to move President Truman toward a more conciliatory posture vis-à-vis Russia.[31] Baruch and Hancock surmised that the morning headlines meant that their meeting with the president would now have to focus on how to deal with the Wallace charges. They went to the State Department to confer with Under Secretary of State Will Clayton, the acting secretary, as Byrnes and Acheson were abroad on mission. Clayton, Baruch, and Hancock then went to the White House in the early afternoon. At the meeting Baruch outlined Wallace's errors and indicated he would supply the president with a point-by-point refutation of Wallace's misrepresentations of US policies. Baruch suggested three broad options for dealing with Wallace, two of them involving variations on a plan to rein in the errant commerce secretary and get him to state publicly that he had been misled. He would have to withdraw his allegations. The third option was for Baruch to resign. The president cautioned Baruch not to be in a hurry to resign.

Baruch and Hancock were pointed in their attack on Wallace: if Wallace had sources within the US government warning of ill-conceived plans for military action, he should identify these sources. Truman assured them that he would deal with Wallace, ordering him to desist from further foreign policy pronouncements. In fact Wallace had already been summoned and told to report to the White House for a 3:30 p.m. meeting that day. The meeting between Truman and Wallace followed the Baruch-Hancock-Clayton session and lasted for two and a half hours, and Wallace finally emerged to face a flock of reporters at 6:00 p.m. He appeared unbowed and unrepentant; he acknowledged only that at the president's direction he would refrain from any foreign policy statements while Secretary of State Byrnes was engaged in negotiations in Paris.

Baruch and Hancock were unsatisfied with Wallace's remarks. They considered that either the president had been too cautious or Wallace had brazenly ignored the restraints the president had placed on him. They decided to send off to the president the detailed rebuttal of Wallace's statements prepared by Gordon and to take matters into their own hands and arrange a meeting with Wallace. In the meantime Truman and Secretary Byrnes exchanged lengthy teletype messages about the Wallace speech, the leaked letter, and Wallace's comments to reporters after his meeting with the president. Byrnes was shocked when Wallace apparently told reporters he would resume his foreign policy pronouncements as soon as the secretary returned from Paris. Senator Vandenberg weighed in from Capitol Hill with the observation that the president could not have two secretaries of state at the same time. Truman finally concluded that in the wake of the Byrnes and Vandenberg reactions, he would have to fire Wallace. He did so on Friday, September 20, in a telephone call. Wallace took the news with an unusual good grace. Truman told his wife later that Wallace "was so nice about it that I almost backed out."[32] This action by the president did not, however, quite put an end to the Wallace affair from Baruch's point of view.

Baruch decided that Wallace, even if fired, was still at least a nuisance and might even be a danger. Before the firing he had telephoned Wallace to explain the US actions at the UN and now denied that he should attempt once more to conciliate Wallace. He would appeal to Wallace's statesmanship, his love of peace, and their mutual desire to protect humankind from the perils of the atom. Accordingly, Baruch proposed a meeting in New York where the two men could work out their differences amicably. Wallace at first equivocated. One of Wallace's reasons for not wanting to correct his earlier "errors" was that he was planning to publish an expanded version of them in pamphlet form.

Nevertheless, through a combination of coaxing and threats, Baruch was finally able to arrange a meeting for September 27 at the US delegation's offices in the Empire State Building. Wallace brought along Philip M. Hauser, director of the Census Bureau and a former top career aide. Present on the Baruch side were Baruch, Hancock, Eberstadt, Swope, Gordon, and several others. Gordon had prepared the memorandum that had been sent to the president with the detailed five-point refutation of the misstatements in Wallace's July 24 letter to Truman, an elaboration of the US and Soviet positions, and an explanation of the differences between the two sides. The memo now was the focus of the discussion with Wallace. The meeting lasted some three hours as the participants went over the analysis of Gordon's memo point by point. When the discussion was finished, Wallace appeared embarrassed and said, "It is obvious I was not fully posted as to the facts."[33] Wallace expressed himself as being fully in accord with the US position now that he understood it. The former farm reporter, researcher, entrepreneur, agriculture and commerce secretary, and vice president was actually a man who disliked the horse-trading aspects of politics and relished intellectual and substantive discussion.

Wallace had to leave for a luncheon appointment and asked Hauser to work out an appropriate statement with the Baruch team. Gordon was designated to work with Hauser to prepare the statement. (Baruch later mistakenly told reporters, much to Gordon's irritation, that it was Swope who handled the negotiations with Wallace.) In Gordon's version of events it was relatively easy to come up with a draft that Hauser thought would satisfy Wallace. The official history of the Atomic Energy Commission, by Richard G. Hewlett and Oscar E. Anderson Jr., suggests that the process was more protracted and contentious.[34] In any case Gordon worked out a satisfactory statement with Hauser by the end of the afternoon. It was agreed that the draft would be read to Wallace over the telephone for his final approval as soon as he could be reached.

Hauser, however, was unable to reach Wallace at the numbers Wallace had given him. He left for Washington promising to get back to the Baruch team sometime over the weekend, as soon as he had reached Wallace. Wallace, now freed from his official responsibilities and commitments, promptly gave another foreign policy speech, this time at a conference of the political action committee of the Congress of Industrial Organizations (CIO), in which he sought, and received, the CIO's endorsement of his call for the United States to halt the production of atomic bombs as a step to reassure the Soviet Union of the country's peaceful intent.

Hauser telephoned Gordon on Sunday to say that he was still unable to reach Wallace. On Monday, September 30, Eberstadt at last reached Wallace but immediately encountered bad news. Wallace had changed his mind and backed away from his endorsement of US policy and repudiated the draft statement worked out between Gordon and Hauser. Instead he proposed a new statement that he read to Eberstadt that contained nothing in the nature of a retraction or a confession of error on his part. Wallace merely restated his view that the United States must show "by deed as well as by word" its commitment to nuclear disarmament. Trust could not be established, Wallace insisted, until the United States halted its production of atomic weapons. He credited Baruch with sincerity and good intentions but went no further toward an accommodation. There followed more negotiations with Wallace for two days.

Finally Baruch decided that he had had enough of Henry Wallace and arranged for the publication of four key documents in the newspapers on October 3.[35] These were Gordon's memorandum for the president rebutting Wallace, the Gordon-Hauser statement in which Wallace admitted mistakes, Wallace's revised statement, and a telegram from Baruch to Wallace castigating him for misleading the public. Baruch arranged for General Leslie Groves and other dignitaries from Washington to stand with him in a show of unity at the press conference he called for the next day. Baruch carried on at the UN and won a split ten-to-two vote—with only Russia and Poland voting "no"—in the UNAEC in favor of the Baruch Plan, which was then forwarded for consideration to the UN Security Council (where it was certain to be vetoed by the Soviet Union). After some debate within his team and with the State Department, Baruch resigned on December 31, 1946, considering his part of the job done and handing over the atomic portfolio to the State Department and the regular US delegation to the UN. Within weeks of his meeting with Baruch, Wallace took over the editorship of the *New Republic,* from which post he launched attacks at Truman at every opportunity. He eventually took his case to the country and ran for president in 1948 on a peace platform, with American Communist Party leaders playing key roles in his campaign.[36] He conducted a vigorous campaign, but the voters did not like what he had to say, giving him a humiliatingly low total of only slightly over one million votes, or 2.4 percent of the popular vote and no electoral votes. Wallace finished fourth, behind Truman, the Republican candidate Thomas Dewey, and States Rights candidate Strom Thurmond. After the Korean War, Wallace publicly recanted his views about the peaceful intentions of the Soviet Union and began to migrate back across the political spectrum to his Republican roots, voting for Eisenhower in 1956 and meeting secretly with Nixon in 1960 but mainly staying away from politics and devoting himself to agricultural research until his death in 1965 of Lou Gehrig's disease. Baruch and Wallace never reconciled and never again met or spoke.

For Gordon, though he had no further direct dealings with Wallace, the fight with the Iowa visionary was not quite over. He had to contend with Wallace and attempt to rebut him again in the next phase of his career, when Wallace assailed the Marshall Plan as likely to turn Europe into a "vast military camp, with freedom extinguished."[37] After the Marshall Plan had been approved by Congress, Gordon did not have the time or occasion to think much about Wallace. Gordon, a few years after leaving Washington, befriended Paul Appleby, then the dean of the School of Citizenship and Public Affairs at Syracuse University (and formerly

an aide to Wallace at the Department of Agriculture), who told him stories about Wallace holding séances in his office, where staff members sat
around the table, holding hands, with the shades drawn, while the secretary attempted to commune with spirits. Gordon was out of the country
and took no notice when Wallace published an article in 1952, "Where I
Was Wrong," saying he had been fooled by Soviet propaganda and declaring the Soviet Union "evil."[38] For Baruch this apology came six years too
late. Wallace was a man whom Gordon could not understand. Though an
intellectual and a scientist, Wallace was also a mystic, while Gordon was a
down-to-earth rationalist. Gordon attributed Wallace's erratic behavior to
the fact that he was a politician, but in fact Wallace loathed the compromises and logrolling of politics as much as Gordon did. Both men, ironically, were critical of Henry Luce's concept of "the American century,"
Wallace because he thought it bespoke American imperialism and Gordon because he considered the concept vainglorious. Wallace was unfath-
omable to Gordon. All Gordon knew for sure was that Wallace was the
strangest man he had encountered in the whole of his public service. He
had occasion to think about Wallace seriously only in the last years of his
own life, when he was writing his memoirs. The intervening years had
given him no new perspective. Henry Wallace was still the strangest man
he had encountered.

Back to Harvard Again

Gordon experienced something of a disengagement from atomic issues
after the Wallace affair, but nonetheless he continued to consult and write
policy papers for the US delegation at the UN through the spring of 1947.
In a busy spring term, besides commuting to New York, he taught an
advanced management course at the business school, resumed work on his
book on industrial mobilization, and collaborated with business school
colleagues Bert Fox and Stanley Teele on a future industrial mobilization
plan for the War Department (implemented in the Korean War mobilization in 1950). He was working with his former WPB colleague Vince
Barnett on the big book, but his attention was distracted by other projects
and matters. A growing interest in Europe's problems particularly began
to occupy his attention.

Meanwhile, after Christmas with his family in 1946, he had returned to New York to prepare a memorandum on the long-term US nuclear stance, which he drafted for John Hancock to use in congressional testimony and for speeches. He saw this as something of a swan song for his work with the Baruch team. Neither he nor Hancock held any illusion that a shift in US nuclear policy would dramatically affect the situation in the near term or produce results in the negotiations with the Soviet Union. Wallace, in Gordon's view, had raised some valid concerns about the US position that needed to be explained. While Acheson, his aide Herbert Marks, Byrnes, and President Truman, along with the Baruch team, had all ended up opposing Wallace, there had been some initial sympathy with Wallace's position. Gordon shared the feeling that Baruch's stand on the Security Council veto could and should be modified if negotiations showed any signs of moving forward. If the Soviet Union had shown even the slightest willingness to negotiate seriously, Gordon believed that the United States might have been forced to alter its position on the veto. Canada and a number of other countries privately urged compromise on this point, but the implacable Soviet opposition to any concessions plus the growing evidence of Soviet nuclear espionage had rendered moot the question of softening the US negotiating posture. The negotiations were now for the hearts and minds of neutral countries and US allies. Wallace had blundered badly by seeming simply to echo Soviet propaganda points and seriously misstating the US stance. By attacking Baruch in the midst of delicate negotiations and failing to do his homework, Gordon believed, Wallace had injured his own cause. Gordon had asked Hauser why Wallace changed his mind so dramatically over the weekend, after he instructed Hauser to work out the statement with the Baruch team. Hauser told him that it was because Wallace had consulted with his political advisers, and they told him he would look weak and hurt his planned presidential campaign if he so publicly confessed error. If the political advisers he consulted were his friends from the American Communist Party who ran his 1948 presidential campaign, they probably also told him that confessing error to Baruch would validate US foreign policy and implicitly indict Soviet policies.

It was now clear in any case to Gordon (in December 1946) that the Senate was unlikely to ratify any treaty that divulged US nuclear secrets. At the least a convincing case had to be made to the senators that an international control regime would be in the US interest. The passage of the

McMahon Act in in 1946 had strengthened the military's hand in nuclear secrecy, and General Leslie Grove's decision to order British scientists to leave the Los Alamos laboratory "was a bitter blow to most of the British scientists who had worked on the bomb."[39] Britain was a puzzle for the Baruch team because Lord Cadogan, the British special representative to the UNAEC, was disinterested in the negotiations, considering them doomed and a mere repetition of futile negotiations during the 1920s. But there was more than this to the British position. Britain seemed determined to pursue its own development of nuclear weapons and a nuclear industry. International cooperation in nuclear matters was unlikely for the immediate future, but Gordon felt that the case should be made for international controls for the future. He decided therefore to try to answer all of the objections that had been raised in the course of the negotiations and to undertake this daunting task in one short, dense, and closely reasoned speech for his boss Hancock.

Even if the prospects for any international entity to own, control, and regulate the nuclear fuel cycle or military uses of the atom were dim, Gordon decided that he should outline a long-term strategy for controlling the atom and address the critical objections. So, pointing to eight principal objections to the US negotiating stance, Gordon argued in sometimes dense prose that each objection lacked merit and could not stand when assessed in the light of modern realities introduced by the atomic age and the enlightened national interests of the UN's member states, whether great powers or smaller nations. Borrowing a portable typewriter, he typed out a nine-page memo entitled "International Control of Atomic Energy . . . And the Veto" for John Hancock and also sent a copy to colleagues in the State Department's UN liaison. He began with a reminder that the very first action of the newly established UN was to create the UN Atomic Energy Commission. This action was based on recognition that atomic energy represented a new era in human affairs and called for unprecedented steps to safeguard humankind from the dangers posed by the atom, while realizing nuclear power's potential peaceful uses. Collective security was the answer to the new challenges, the collective security provided by a functioning UN and by such auxiliary bodies as were essential under overall supervision for important specific missions. Clearly, controlling the atom was one such urgent task, and the US proposals to the UN Atomic Energy Commission were intended to provide practicable steps toward that end. The Soviet Union also presented proposals, and an important point of difference was the problem of the veto. Gordon then proceeded to a defense of the US proposal and a detailed rebuttal of the objections raised against the US veto stand (of which he counted eight principal points of contention). Why should there be any departure from normal UN rules and procedures, including the veto rights granted to the five permanent members of the Security Council? Here Gordon returned to his point of departure. Military uses of the atom could threaten whole civilizations, and a single and limited restriction on the veto was thus necessary to ensure that atomic weapons would not be used or their use threatened for purposes of coercive diplomacy.

The Soviet delegation had also queried why it was necessary to create a separate bureaucracy, what the Americans called the Atomic Development Authority (ADA), to administer policy instead of relying on the regular UN machinery. Here Gordon harked back to his call for a Progressive Era technocratic appeals court in his undergraduate honors thesis and his defense of British public corporations—the separate ADA was necessary because specialists were critical to certain very specialized tasks created by new technologies—and foreshadowed his arguments regarding why the Marshall Plan needed to recruit outside experts and be administered by an independent agency. Inspections, Gordon insisted, would be necessary to determine whether technical violations were occurring, and only nuclear experts could perform such tasks. The arguments for inspections, as Gordon developed the memo for his boss, have a contemporary ring and rehearse themes that are now familiar in arms control debates. Inspectors could not do their jobs if they were subject to a veto by a few UN policy-makers at the top. The national representatives on the Security Council and the top UN generalist bureaucrats could not be expected to have enough detailed knowledge of the technical complexities of nuclear inspections to play a useful role. It was evident by this date in December that the original idea in the Acheson-Lilienthal Report, to have one central agency licensing all fissile materials, was not going to be acceptable, and hence the mission of the UN atomic agency would shift more toward the inspection of national entities or private companies operating under national jurisdictions to detect and prevent diversion of fissile materials to military uses. Gordon finessed some of the issues but brought them up for discussion and analysis. He was also fond of pointing out the shortcomings of the Kellogg-Briand Pact and other disarmament efforts of the 1920s and defended the US proposals for their practicality in accomplishing the ends sought. Abstract pronouncements about disarmament accomplished nothing, Gordon asserted, and a practical UN agency staffed with competent experts would offer strong assurances against the diversion of nuclear materials for military uses.

Gordon took up the small tactical issue of why the United States had not started with the less controversial matters to build up a working relationship with the Soviet delegates before proceeding to the more controversial veto issue. The answer to this was simply the tactical concern that the United States did not want to be charged with introducing roadblocks at the last minute to disrupt negotiations. The United States had accordingly presented the veto issue in its June proposals, but clearly in a conciliatory spirit, with a willingness to compromise. Here Gordon was exaggerating slightly because many in the State Department (and Gordon himself at times) considered Baruch's stand on the veto too rigid. He then came to a central concern: the Soviet contention that the United States was merely putting up a smokescreen with its proposals because it aimed at locking in its own nuclear superiority by blocking the access of other nations to nuclear weapons. Not so. The United States had pledged to destroy or surrender all of its existing atomic bombs to the UN agency once it was fully established and to do so within three months after the UN agency had become operational. While this was part of the US proposal, it was highly doubtful even then that the country could have delivered on this pledge. Anticipating such concerns, Gordon discussed several critical political issues. Would the US Senate ratify any agreement reached in the UN negotiations? Gordon could not swear that this would occur, of course, and could not guarantee that other nations would ratify the proposed treaty that would implement the new UN system for inspections and nuclear controls. The provisions of the treaty would apply only to signatory nations. But what would be accomplished if nations did not ratify the treaty? Furthermore, the US proposals were deficient in making no provision for chemical and bacteriological weapons of mass destruction, nonnuclear weapons that could threaten whole cities or regions.

The answer to these objections was that a partial system of collective action was superior to no system at all. The collective weight of humankind and the power to persuade would play an important part in any system. Nonnuclear weapons of mass destruction were important, but not as important in the first instance as the new atomic weapons. In the future systems could be devised, and treaties ratified, to restrict chemical and bacteriological weapons, he argued, and nations might decide to ratify the proposed nuclear and other treaties as they gained confidence that the system of collective security was working. Political remedies would have to be part of the solution. There would be near certainty that violations would be detected and brought to the attention of the world once the UN nuclear system was in operation. Many measures could then be taken to punish violators when they were exposed. Collective security would be easier, of course, when the great powers were in agreement and when the violators were small nations. Gordon anticipated that small nations might seek the "equalizer" of nuclear weapons and that nonproliferation would become an important US policy goal. If great powers disagreed or if one of them indirectly sponsored a given violation, diplomacy would have to take place and would naturally center on mobilizing the world's moral indignation against the offense and the offender. The resulting opprobrium would help deter violations. The present limited UN framework for collective security was, insisted Gordon, better than none at all. Collaboration could yet provide "the basis out of which there may evolve . . . a future closer-knit world system."[40] By creating machinery for discussing atomic control issues, and by educating world leaders about regulatory regimes to combat nuclear proliferation, Gordon believed that the efforts of the UN Atomic Energy Commission had played a useful role, even if Cold War tensions prevented a successful outcome to the nuclear negotiations in the short term. President Eisenhower's initiative in the 1950s on the peaceful uses of the atom, Gordon later believed, as well as the subsequent UN inspections systems and nonproliferation activities, benefited from the preliminary work done by the UNAEC.

Gordon was adamant, however, in dismissing the arguments advanced from time to time by critics that US policy-makers had lacked vision and blundered by failing to take advantage of historic opportunities to avert the Cold War. A 1996 *Foreign Affairs* article by James Chace particularly irked Gordon, who wrote a three-page rebuttal in a letter to the journal's editor.[41] He pointed out that the author failed to mention Soviet nuclear espionage at the Manhattan Project, which came to light in the summer of 1946; neglected to acknowledge that the Soviet delegation grew increasingly intransigent over the course of the summer of 1946; and ignored the fact that the Soviet Union had no intention of giving up its own nuclear weapons development program. The United States would have been willing to modify its position if the Soviet Union had shown any intention of serious willingness to negotiate. Moreover, the author erred in suggesting that Baruch had no scientists on his team and no scientific input in the formation of the Baruch plan. Gordon named the numerous scientists involved with the Baruch team over the summer of 1946 and observed that while the scientists agreed on the scientific "facts," they differed among themselves, and with other US delegates and officials, on the meaning of the facts for US policy. Gordon had been one of the most dovish of the Baruch team members when he arrived and talked frequently with the scientists, including Oppenheimer, which strengthened his interest in international controls. He had been influential in urging his colleagues to continue negotiations with the Soviet delegation, even after Gromyko's July rejection of the Baruch Plan, but his attitudes had hardened in the face of Soviet obsructionism. Gordon's own experience convinced him that it was Russia, not the United States, that had blocked diplomatic progress. His interaction with Wallace reinforced his suspicions of the far left and hardened his views on Soviet intentions and tactics.

8

Birth of the Marshall Plan, 1947–1948

It is logical that the United States should do whatever it is able to do to assist in the return of normal economic health in the world, without which there can be no political stability and no assured peace. Our policy is directed not against any country or doctrine, but against hunger, poverty, desperation and chaos.
—George C. Marshall, June 5, 1947

The essential function of the Marshall Plan was to make it politically and administratively possible for the Europeans to do in four years what otherwise couldn't possibly be done in so short a period.
—Milton Katz, 1975

A fourth lesson [of the Marshall Plan] involves the interweaving of market forces and institutional factors, and the need to be wary of purist dogmatisms. . . . There were many novel experiments during those years. . . . Some succeeded, and others failed, but all involved mixtures of private enterprise and governmental framework-building; none were at the extremes of pure planning or pure market forces.
—Lincoln Gordon, 1984

Gordon did not attend the June 5, 1947, Harvard commencement exercises. He was busy with end-of-term activities. After resuming his teaching duties in January 1947, and with additional research and consulting responsibilities, he found it an effort to catch up with the scholarly literature, prepare his lectures, meet with students, and attend to myriad other academic tasks. The events in Europe were on his mind, however, and he also continued to follow closely what was happening at the UN with atomic energy. The Baruch Plan on atomic energy was clearly dead, due to a combination of Soviet intransigence and Pentagon opposition. President Truman and his congressional allies had won an important victory with the McMahon bill, establishing civilian control of atomic energy, but the military services were big winners, too, by keeping nearly everything connected with nuclear energy highly classified.

Meanwhile, the domestic political climate was confusing to Gordon. The country had clearly turned to the right with the Republican victories in 1946, but did the election represent fatigue with the New Deal or only with the wartime controls? Was there a backlash against foreign involvement generally now that the war was over? He supposed the shift was probably due to some combination of factors. The election was by no means simply an expression of isolationism. Republican congressmen like Walter Judd of Minnesota, for example, as well as the Luce publishing empire, wanted strong anticommunist engagement in Asia. Democrats were split into left, right, and center factions. Wallace represented the far left, but he had such unlikely allies as Gordon's old boss Don Nelson, now serving as the Washington representative of independent filmmakers and hobnobbing with Hollywood celebrities when he was not warning anyone who would listen to his diatribes against the military-industrial complex. Wallace had increasingly become a kiss of death rather than a useful ally for others on the left who favored spheres of influence or some other formula of accommodation with the Soviet Union. The doctrine of containment could be seen as either a military or a diplomatic strategy. Senators Claude Pepper (D, Florida) and Glen Taylor (D, Idaho) and investment banker James P. Warburg took positions at odds with the Truman administration and the political establishment.[1] These and other critics on the left differed among themselves but were not, except for Wallace, idealists or one-worlders; they saw themselves as more realistic than "realists."

Gordon did not consider himself a bitter anticommunist at this time, though his experience at the UN the previous summer had stripped him of any illusions he might have had regarding Wallace and the idealist far left one-world view. Certainly the nation's approach to the Soviet empire was a central foreign policy issue and required hard thought, but the problem was to determine if the Soviet Union would be content with a sphere of influence in Eastern Europe or wanted to extend its influence westward through internal subversion of West European governments. On the economic front the United States was supporting the United Nations Rehabilitation and Relief Administration (UNRRA), headed by Fiorello LaGuardia, former mayor of New York City. Export-Import Bank funds had been increased, and other forms of US humanitarian and emergency assistance were flowing to Europe. Relief and emergency aid amounted to some $9 billion by 1946.[2] But conditions in Western Europe were far worse than previously thought in light of the severe 1946–1947 winter. This much was evident from radio and newspaper reports. Gordon remained in touch with British friends and received reports from colleagues on conditions in Europe, but he had other things on his mind. The book on industrial mobilization was pressing on him. Harvard Business School had kindly given him a year to work on it before having to assume a full teaching load. He was not holding up his end of the project, having managed to finish drafts of only a few chapters. During this summer of 1947 he hoped to get caught up with his writing and also have some relaxation at Lake Sunapee.

So when he read the Marshall speech and the story in the *New York Times,* Gordon's reaction was muted. The *New York Times* had not given the text the prominent treatment it typically did for major addresses. The Truman administration was evidently trying to come up with a plan to convert relief into a more permanent recovery assistance package. This was probably a good idea, but what was being envisaged was not clear to him. There were very few details, especially on economic issues and the criteria for aid.[3] The speech, in Gordon's mind, had properly rejected any idea that the United States would impose a solution on the Europeans; it would instead expect the nations receiving aid to come up with their own ideas about what they needed. Marshall, following the formula sketched out for him by George Kennan in the first paper of the newly created Policy Planning Staff, had also seemed to suggest that the Europeans would devise their own system for relating to US authorities.[4] There was no reference to how the United States would provide aid, how much would be provided, or what kinds of economic programs would be supported. Any plan would face a hard sell in Congress, and the international obstacles were also formidable. Lincoln supposed it was probably wise not to have too many details at the start, so that there would be no obvious flaws for critics to attack. Since he liked puzzles, he let his mind linger on the problem for a while. He was not quite sure where things stood with reparations, but it seemed the Russians felt they were entitled to reparations from the Western Zones under the agreement at Potsdam. Even if what Marshall was calling for seemed right, could the administration get past the twin embarrassment of giving money to the Soviets and having to ask Congress for more aid after it had assured Congress the year before that emergency aid to Britain would be the last such request? Without giving the matter deep thought, it appeared to Gordon that the speech's key points were on target: the problem was correctly diagnosed; the US interest in European recovery was clearly stated; the Europeans were to be primarily responsible for spelling out their needs; and no one was to be obviously excluded from the potential assistance—in practice, this meant Eastern Europe could be included. But the questions of how the whole effort was to be organized, how the new approach would differ from past recovery efforts, and what would happen to the recovery aid went unanswered.

Marshall had wound up his speech by saying that "we are remote from the scene of these troubles," making it difficult, "merely by reading, or listening, or even seeing photographs or motion pictures, to grasp at all the real significance of the situation." Much, he said, "hinges . . . to a large extent on the realization of the American people of just what are the dominant factors." Finally, Marshall posed questions rather than prescribing answers: "What are the sufferings? What is needed? What can be done? What must be done? Thank you very much."[5]

A Request for Assistance

Soon after Marshall's speech, Gordon was surprised by a phone call from an old wartime colleague, C. Tyler Wood. Wood was an investment banker from New York who had served as an aide to General Lucius Clay during the war and been Clay's principal liaison with the WPB. Gordon and Wood had met in 1943 and become friends after working together closely in the late stages of the war. In late 1944 Gordon and Wood began to lunch together every several weeks as their workloads eased in the war's final stages. Wood had decided to remain in government, staying on as deputy assistant secretary of state under William Clayton, the under secretary of state for economic affairs. Clayton was spearheading the department's efforts to promote Europe's economic recovery.

"Did you happen to attend commencement and hear the Secretary's speech?" Wood asked.[6]

Gordon replied that he had not, but he had read the speech.

"What did you think?"

Gordon thought the speech was good but that significant effort would be necessary to translate the concept into a program. How would you organize the effort within the US government, how would you deal with the Europeans, how would you bring Congress into the act, and how would you make sure of public support?

"Exactly, that's going to be your job. That's where we need your help," said Wood. "This is going to be the most important issue in American foreign policy, at least for the next four years."

Gordon demurred. He was flattered that his friend should think of him. There was no question this was a great challenge, but it was impossible for Gordon right now.

Well, if he could not come full time, could he come part time? At least help out by consulting over the summer and outlining some of the practical steps in launching the effort? The men talked more. Gordon stuck to his guns. Was he in any case planning to visit Washington soon? Gordon did have such a commitment in the next several weeks, and Wood asked if he could stop by for a talk.

In early July, Gordon stopped by his friend's office. Wood had a spacious office in the elegant War-Navy-State Building (now the Eisenhower Executive Office Building) on Pennsylvania Avenue next to the White House. At one end of the room Gordon noticed a conference table with a pile of papers. Wood said, "Before we talk, I want you to glance through these cables sent by Will Clayton from Europe."

Gordon read through the cables, with Clayton's dire description of what was happening on the ground in Europe. His reading included Clayton's memo of May 24, containing his most recent thinking and recommendations.[7] Clayton made a practice, in gaining information, of not merely talking to local dignitaries; he also often stayed at out-of-the-way hotels under an assumed name. His dispatches were unusual for their startling details and glimpses of conditions on the ground. It was Clayton's four-page report in March 1947 that had focused attention on the need for a broad European recovery program, not merely short-term emergency relief.

Emergency aid of $3.75 billion had gone to the United Kingdom in 1946—in part to support the pound sterling against the huge reserves of sterling built up in India, Pakistan, and other Commonwealth countries as a result of their wartime service. Gordon read that part of the UNRRA aid was being diverted to the Soviet Union, thus becoming in effect a down payment on the reparations that Stalin was demanding from his former Allies. The 1946–1947 winter had been the most severe Europe had experienced since Napoleonic times. Britain had been particularly hard hit, snowstorms battering it beyond anything seen since 1881. The emergency relief had provided badly needed humanitarian aid but could not keep up with the magnitude of the problem. The European economies needed US assistance that went beyond piecemeal relief to individual countries. A group of young staffers in the State Department's economic bureau began to propose ideas regarding how the United States could aid European recovery.[8]

When Gordon finished reading the Clayton cables and memos, Wood saw that they had had the desired effect. He filled Gordon in on the latest developments. The Europeans, under the leadership of Foreign Ministers Ernest Bevan and George Bidault, had convened a conference in Paris of European nations to respond to the American offer of assistance. Czechoslovakia and Poland had expressed strong interest, and it appeared initially that the Soviet Union had encouraged Eastern Europeans to participate. But just a few days before, on July 7, Stalin had apparently changed his mind and instructed Eastern European countries not to attend. According to Stalin's current thinking, the Marshall Plan was an American trick to get the East to divulge its economic secrets and to extend American influence eastward for purposes of subversion. Soviet actions had thus removed a very contentious issue for American planners. Dean Acheson had left the State Department on July 1 to return to private law practice. And Will Clayton was likely to leave shortly to return to his cotton business for health reasons and because of promises to his wife. He did in fact leave in October 1947. Gordon could expect to work closely with Willard Thorp, assistant secretary of state for economic affairs—a well-known economist and someone Gordon knew—and with Paul Nitze, of the Policy Planning Staff. And of course Secretary Marshall was also deeply involved in the planning of the European Recovery Program (ERP), as was Under Secretary Robert Lovett. Gordon could expect some contact with them as well.

Gordon's expertise was particularly needed on the organizational structure of the Marshall Plan. A related area would be to help prepare the rationale for the size of the funding needed from Congress for the projected aid program, with critics already objecting to its scope. Republican congressional leaders wanted an orderly, businesslike administrative structure for the program both to keep costs down and to keep politics out. Having acquired their first taste of power since FDR was elected, the Republicans were in no mood to defer passively to the administration. President Truman had won plaudits for nominating the great wartime leader General Marshall as secretary of state, but Congress would likely demand the most careful expert analysis of the funding requests. There would have to be a significant measure of public support before Congress voted for any large-scale recovery program. It went without saying that the program would have to be bipartisan, since Republicans controlled both houses of Congress.

His reservations having melted away, Gordon knew when he left Wood's office that he would be—and very much wanted to be—part of this historic effort. Controlling the atom was certainly a grave issue, but rescuing Europe from imminent collapse was momentous. He could not refuse a role in this endeavor. He could not have guessed that this effort would occupy him for the next eight years.

The Marshall Plan's Organizational Structure

Gordon's visit with the Harvard Business School administration went more smoothly than he had imagined. Assistant Dean Stanley Teele was enthusiastic and foresaw no problems from the university's side. Gordon could have leave for the rest of the summer and for the fall term, too, if necessary. Years later, Allison Gordon told her adult children that the Marshall Plan service, coming so close upon the end of the war, had taken a toll on and prematurely aged her husband. His once jet-black hair had already turned white, and she believed his work also brought personality changes: compulsiveness, irritability, an inability to relax. Even during his prep school days Gordon's classmates had been bemused by his frenetic activity and constant absorption with multiple tasks. His energy level and intensity, always under control but just barely, were his most striking traits. In a diary entry of October 19, 1936, at age twenty-three, Lincoln described a performance of *Hamlet* he had just seen: "Leslie Howard's *Hamlet* was disappointing. It is restrained, like Gielgud's, but without the Gielgud intensity, and therefore flaccid. It is not easy to make Hamlet a consistent character; I feel that restraint is essential . . . but restraint as understood as insight into the weaknesses *and* strengths of introversion."[9] Intensity combined with restraint was highly valued by the young Lincoln Gordon. Yet he could also be almost merry at times, chirpy like a squirrel, and have an almost childlike quality. He never lost the capacity to take delight and wonder in the simple things. But something changed, Allison felt, and she attributed this to his spending so much time with serious people in government bureaucracies and having to struggle constantly with difficult problems that he could not leave behind at the office. The consequence was that he was seldom rested, he tired easily, and his temper grew shorter. Vigorous physical activity would have its recuperative effects, but he never seemed to get enough exercise or enough sleep. Allison reluctantly understood that her husband would have to accept the Marshall Plan assignment. He apparently tried to reassure her that he would not accept any permanent position and that he would return to his teaching duties by the end of the year.

Gordon reported to Ty Wood's office on July 19 to start work. He was immediately told to prepare for and attend that evening's European Recovery Program working-group session. This was a government-wide group of officials who were preparing the executive branch's presentation to Congress on the ERP. Since the officials from various agencies were occupied with their normal departmental duties during the day, the group as a whole met Tuesday and Thursday evenings to coordinate their activities. The group's plenary sessions consisted of some fifty officials from State, War, Commerce, Labor, Treasury, Agriculture, the Federal Reserve, the Budget Bureau, and a few smaller agencies. The membership varied somewhat depending on the evening's primary topics, but State was the lead agency, with Commerce, Treasury, and Agriculture as key supporting players.

An inner circle or steering committee of the larger working group became the day-to-day working unit for coordinating all government efforts on short-term relief, technical assistance, the Marshall Plan, and the Greek-Turkish assistance provided in the Truman Doctrine. This steering committee was responsible for drafting the ERP legislation, preparing all congressional testimony, and meeting daily with those who would present testimony to Congress, principally Ambassador Lewis Douglas, Under Secretary Lovett, and Secretary Marshall. The steering committee responded to constant requests for data and information from congressional staff. One of its first assignments was to scrape up funds from the Export-Import Bank, the Treasury stabilization fund, and other legitimate sources for emergency relief to Italy and France. For the remainder of the summer of 1947 and into the fall, the steering committee largely planned the broad recovery strategy. It also backstopped an emergency request to Congress in December for interim funding until the full recovery program would be finally authorized and receive appropriations in the spring of 1948.

Members of the steering committee typically worked an eighty-hour week during the summer and fall of 1947. They met daily, usually in Paul Nitze's office in the morning. Afternoons and into the evenings they worked individually. Gordon did not get back to Boston until the Christmas break. In January 1948 Senator Arthur Vandenberg (R, Michigan), chairman of the Senate Foreign Relations Committee, observed that the ERP "was more carefully studied and more scrupulously prepared than any other bill to come before the Congress."[10] James Reston, writing in the *New York Times* on January 10, 1948, named three men as forming the steering committee's inner circle: Lieutenant Colonel Charles H. Bonesteel, forty-one, special assistant to Under Secretary Robert Lovett, identified as graduating from West Point in 1921; Paul Nitze, forty-one, of the State Department Policy Planning Staff; and Lincoln Gordon, thirty-four, identified as a professor on leave from the Harvard Graduate School of Public Administration.[11] Four others named as playing important supporting roles were Thomas E. Birdsell, assistant to Secretary Harriman at the Commerce Department (on leave from Columbia University); Frank A. Southard Jr., from the Treasury Department; J. Burke Knapp, of the Federal Reserve; and F. B. Northrop, from the Agriculture Department. Three of these seven men—Bonesteel, Gordon, and Knapp—were former Rhodes scholars. In his 1975 Truman Library oral history interview, Gordon added Colonel George "Abe" Lincoln, a professor from West Point, as a member of the steering committee, along with himself, Charles "Tich" Bonesteel, and Paul Nitze. On the fortieth anniversary of the Marshall Plan, in 1986, Gordon identified only Bonesteel, Nitze, and himself as the core of the steering committee.[12] All sources agree that the chairman of the steering committee was Nitze, who at the time was deputy director of the State Department Policy Planning Staff under George Kennan. Kennan occasionally participated in the group's work and showed up whenever the team met with Secretary Marshall or Under Secretary Lovett.

Others in the State Department also played important roles in the mammoth effort of working out the details of the plan and presenting it to Congress. Ernest Gross of the legal affairs staff at the State Department was the key drafter of the Marshall Plan legislation. Charles Kindleberger of State's Economic Affairs bureau—later a distinguished economist at MIT—provided much of the voluminous data on national income, imports and exports, and country forecasts for congressional staffers.[13]

Meanwhile, President Truman had created a prestigious outside committee, the President's Committee on Foreign Aid, under the chairmanship of his commerce secretary, Averell Harriman, to report on the situation in Europe and make recommendations reflecting the views of the distinguished private-sector members of the panel. Gordon was in touch constantly with Richard Bissell, executive secretary of the President's Committee (or the Harriman Committee) and another study committee convened by President Truman to study aspects of European economic recovery.[14] It was Gordon's job to make sure that the Harriman recommendations jibed with the State Department's recommendations. Harriman skillfully maneuvered his nineteen-person committee into a unanimous report favoring American assistance for European recovery. The report, "European Recovery and American Aid," called for a four-year program of American grants and loans to Europe, in the range of $12.5 to $17.2 billion. Gordon, who had known Bissell slightly during his wartime service, became close friends with him during his liaison work with the Harriman Committee.

The most significant assignment for Gordon, however, was his role in devising the organizational structure of the ERP (which was not yet called the Marshall Plan). He got this assignment on July 19 from Assistant Secretary Willard Thorp.

"Your first task," Thorp said, "is to handle a problem raised today by

Secretary Marshall. It concerns the organizational structure to administer ERP."[15]

Thorp suggested to Gordon that he get in touch with Miriam Camp, a young State Department diplomat who had returned from London after serving for most of the war with the Harriman Lend-Lease mission. Camp became Gordon's close ally in framing the organizational structure for the recovery program. Gordon's chief antagonists were James E. Webb, director of the Bureau of the Budget (BOB), and his assistant director Donald Stone. The BOB had come out strongly in favor of the State Department taking the dominant role in administering all foreign aid programs. The BOB was locked in a dispute with Congressman Christian Herter over what it saw as a threat to presidential authority in the Herter (and Republican) proposals on foreign aid. The congressman, aided by business and agricultural interests, wanted an independent corporation, not the State Department, to handle economic assistance. The Herter view was that the independent entity would diminish the risk of politics interfering with aid-program administration. This dispute presented a complex assignment to Gordon since he had to argue, in effect, that his own department should not have jurisdiction over an important new program. Webb and Stone, moreover, had the backing of some senior officials in State, including, at the time Gordon started working, Under Secretary Robert Lovett himself.[16]

However, many officials in favor of aid for Europe were increasingly worried that Congress would restrict the department's administration of the recovery program if the administration seemed to oppose congressional wishes. In short, the department was rethinking its position on the proper structure for the aid program, wanting to both satisfy Congress and yet maintain its central role in foreign policy. This was the context in which Gordon and Miriam Camp set out to design the structure for the Marshall Plan. Within days, Gordon and Camp had worked out what would become, after a considerable struggle, the main administrative structure of the Marshall Plan. Their plan favored the route of placing an independent agency in charge of the plan's administration, but not a private corporation, as Herter and some other congressional Republicans had proposed. Gordon and Camp's ideas called for a separate cabinet department whose headquarters would be in Washington. The head of the department would report directly to the president, and the department would have a fixed, five-year life span. It would be responsible for overall policy direction and major operations, but it would not interfere with the State Department's lead role in broad foreign policy. This new department, the Economic Cooperation Administration (ECA), would have a series of field offices, or country missions, in each participating European country. The field offices would be set up and housed within the US embassy in each country receiving aid but would report administratively to the Washington ECA headquarters. Here the going got tougher. Under standard diplomatic practice, the chief of mission in a given country (the ambassador) would be responsible for all aspects of foreign policy and all US government operations in that country. How was this to be reconciled with the independent policy direction of the ECA? Would the ECA country mission director be accountable to the US ambassador in the recipient country? The ECA official within the embassy would have to have diplomatic rank, and in Gordon's scheme that rank would be second only to that of the US ambassador. This could become a problem in practice since the deputy chief of mission (DCM) was the normal number two in any embassy. To round out the scheme there would be an Office of Special Representative (OSR) in Paris that would function like a military theater commander—that is, the OSR would transmit orders to the separate offices located in the individual countries. The chain of command would run from the president to the ECA administrator in Washington to the theater commander in Paris.

There were numerous problems that could be anticipated in developing common standards for contracting, purchasing materials, and coordinating policies among the various countries receiving aid. Here the Committee for European Economic Cooperation (CEEC), then being established by the Europeans, would deal with the Americans in program implementation. Gordon saw the role of the US special representative as coordinating all the individual US country missions in Europe.

Gordon operated in the tradition of bipartisanship, but this was clearly dictated by the fact of a divided government. In devising his plan, he was engaged in an exercise not of public administration theory but of political realism. An executive branch controlled by the Democrats could not present a plan to the Republican Congress without significant Republican input. President Truman was also going to have to choose officials for the leadership of the new structure with party affiliation in mind. He chose Paul Hoffman, a Republican businessman backed by Senator Vandenberg, to head the Economic Cooperation Administration in Washington and Averell Harriman as the US special representative in Paris.

From Ideas to Policies

Although Gordon's broad organizational plan was sketched out relatively quickly, the process of working out the details and getting agreement within the government and with the Congress proved to be laborious and time consuming. This process included resolving certain critical aspects of the plan that were ambiguous and that required protracted negotiations among executive agencies and with congressional leaders. A key issue left unresolved in Gordon's early formulations was this question: Would the Paris-based OSR report to ECA headquarters in Washington or to the secretary of state? The chain of command was finally set to run from Paris, with Harriman as field commander, to the ECA Washington headquarters, headed by Hoffman, and from Hoffman directly to the president. No ECA staffers in Washington could give orders to any individual staff member in Paris or any individual country mission. Policy direction and orders came via Hoffman to Harriman, who functioned like a theater commander. This arrangement presented practical difficulties that were worked out, as we will see in the next chapter, between the number-three official in Paris, Gordon, and the number-three official in Washington, Bissell. Harriman and Hoffman initially had a frosty relationship but eventually worked together in reasonable harmony. Harriman, who had been FDR's Lend-Lease coordinator in London, the ambassador to the Soviet Union, and a Truman cabinet secretary, initially viewed Hoffman's role as merely testifying before Congress and giving speeches around the United States, leaving major decisions to Harriman in Europe. The working relationship between the two men improved over time, but Hoffman never sought to overrule Harriman, and Harriman was wily enough never to challenge Hoffman's authority directly. Harriman's relationship to the secretary of state presented somewhat similar issues, but Harriman and his senior aides understood that the State Department would be centrally involved in all foreign policy issues. Gordon's role at the planning stage was to see that a bill got drafted with enough support to get passed by Congress and without inviting controversy by specifying every contingency that program administrators might have to deal with later.

Gordon and his colleagues in the State Department were aware of the executive branch disunity and of congressional interest in the administrative details of the proposed program and of agency operations. Before the issue could be fully joined on Capitol Hill, the Truman administration had to arrive at a unified position. Gordon met late in the summer with Secretary Marshall to discuss the State Department position on the ECA's administrative structure. Gordon was not sure where Marshall stood or whether he had followed all of the details of the debate. He was immediately struck, like nearly everyone who came into contact with the architect of victory in World War II, by Marshall's integrity and his complete devotion to the public interest. Gordon's vivid initial impressions stayed with him throughout his life: "Although my first one-on-one talk with Marshall lasted less than an hour, it made a deep impression on me—an impression reinforced by our later discussions in preparing for Congressional hearings and by his performance before the Senate Foreign Relations Committee [in January 1948]. Marshall combined high intelligence with understanding of the earth-shaking importance of European reconstruction and absolute indifference to personal advancement or flattery. In many decades since, including acquaintance with hundreds of prominent personalities, I have never met his equal for sheer character."[17]

Marshall was something special—he was like someone "out of a different century." It was rumored that his wife referred to him as "Mr. Marshall." Marshall addressed his subordinates by their last names, like a Victorian country squire or a general talking to his men. It was said that Marshall was the only man to have bristled at FDR's habitual practice of using first names. Marshall had never accepted any honor or award during the war because he felt it would be unseemly so long as American troops were risking their lives and would expect him to be at his desk. Marshall was by no means a prude. He was not above having a shot of whiskey with his men. Yet he had an aura about him that could be intimidating. Gordon was both awestruck and strangely at ease in his meeting with Marshall. The subject was one Gordon knew something about. Independent agencies, from the Federal Trade Commission to British public corporations, and how these entities related to regular departmental operations were familiar topics to him. His education, his research, and his whole background seemingly had prepared him for the meeting. He felt comfortable hearing his own ideas coming back at him, expressed forcefully and framed in greater complexity by the secretary. Marshall alluded to Gordon's wartime experience with the War Production Board. Was it not the case that some very talented managers were recruited and drawn into the war effort by relaxing civil service rules?

Gordon agreed that this was so. Would it therefore be a good idea to have an independent agency to handle operational details, with the program run by talented managers from outside the government? Gordon agreed. The training of State Department officers did not necessarily reflect significant economic or management expertise, the secretary observed. The secretary sketched out his vision of how the new agency would operate and then moved to the obstacles that had to be overcome. The BOB was a problem, Marshall acknowledged, but the budget officials had an argument that had to be answered. The BOB was concerned that an independent entity, if too independent, would make it difficult for the president to exercise his authority over policy. How could we preserve the unity of command and make sure that private interests did not unduly influence or shape US foreign policy? Could the State Department maintain a broad policy role if it did not have a say in the operational details? There were many specific questions to answer, and the State Department itself had to be sure of its own position in order to deal effectively with the BOB. And if the executive branch could finally agree, Congress still had to be persuaded of the correctness of the approach.

Gordon set out to reach an understanding with the BOB at the staff level. He went head-to-head with Donald C. Stone, the "by-the-books" assistant director of the BOB and the bureau's point man on the issue. The lanky, austere Stone was not a man easily moved from his position. Indeed, he was the perfect foil for Gordon. Stone had stormed out of his PhD oral examination at Columbia University in a rage over the pedantry of his examiners and carried on a crusade for the rest of his life against the PhD as an obstacle to the more practical "nuts-and-bolts" training that should be given public administrators. Stone disliked academics even though—or perhaps because—he spent an important part of his career as an academic dean. In his later career he was an energetic figure in the public administration field for years, invariably siding with practitioners against academic theorists. Gordon in contrast believed that a public administrator should be a philosopher king, broadly educated and learned in history, moral philosophy, and political theory, as well as having technical expertise in a given field. It would be hard to imagine two men less likely to hit it off, and indeed they did not. They carried on bruising trench warfare at the staff level. Stone later worked for Paul Hoffman in a senior ECA post and brought his formidable administrative skills to the Marshall Plan, where he and Gordon were allies but never became friends. Gordon was unable to soften Stone's and the BOB's position on the independence of the proposed agency. Gordon in the meantime was still caught up in an intense effort to forge a unified State Department position and to gain Commerce and Agriculture support for his plan.

In September Lovett appointed a special committee under Gordon's chairmanship to resolve the differences and draft the plan for the administration to submit to Congress.[18] The committee's report, finished in late October, called for the new independent agency and spelled out in detail the ECA's role and mission.[19] The report attempted to reassure those who were worried about preserving State's central role in foreign policy by limiting the ECA's role to "operational matters" only. All "policy" decisions were to be left to the State Department. The country missions would be housed within the US embassies—and hence be subject to the ambassador's supervision; this would ensure that State had a role in day-to-day operations as well. The secretary of state would remain the chief adviser to the president on foreign policy, with Commerce and Agriculture playing important roles in export promotion but subject to overall State Department supervision.

The Department of State became unified behind the Gordon committee report: an independent operating agency would recruit talent and direct overall operations but would be subject to supervision and policy direction from the State Department. Commerce and Agriculture backed the proposal as well. But the BOB continued to balk. Stone and his BOB colleagues doubted that the distinction between policy and operations was a workable one and argued that State would be better off having direct control over all aspects of foreign assistance. Lovett, now having reached a consensus within the State Department and other departments behind the Gordon plan, fought back against the BOB staffers, who claimed to be better judges of the State Department's interests than the departmental leadership itself. He cabled Marshall, who was now in London, and got his backing to stand firm with the budget officials. Budget director Webb escalated the battle by sidestepping Lovett and arranging a private meeting with President Truman, at which he secured an endorsement of the BOB position. Lovett countered by arranging a meeting of his own with the president and, armed with a telegram from Marshall strongly affirming his support for the State position, convinced the president to overrule his budget officials and embrace the State Department plan. The BOB finally gave up the fight. Donald Stone advised Webb that the president "could hardly assign operational responsibilities to a department unwilling to accept them."[20]

The executive branch had consolidated its position, but this was only half of the battle. The State Department had managed to persuade budget officials and its own internal skeptics that an independent agency posed no threat to departmental primacy in foreign policy. Now the challenge was to persuade Senate Republicans, and Vandenberg in particular, that the State Department's control over "policy" would pose no threat to the independence and the businesslike practices of the new agency.

Selling the Marshall Plan to Congress and the Country

Gordon, after helping to prepare for an emergency December request for interim funding for European assistance, returned to Boston in time for the Christmas holiday with his family. For now he considered his work done, except for his scheduled return to Washington to accompany Secretary Marshall for his appearance before the Senate Foreign Relations Committee in January 1948. Marshall brought only Gordon and Willard Thorp as his aides for his Senate testimony. Marshall endured a grilling from the senators, who treated him with great courtesy but bore down repeatedly on several key issues. Granted that the State Department had to be responsible for foreign policy, how could the nation be sure that overall policy control did not interfere with the business side of things? Would the ECA administrator be able to run his own show? Senator Vandenberg worried that the ECA head could not even appoint any of his subordinate officers overseas.[21] He wanted to make sure that the ECA administrator could do his job in a businesslike, nonpolitical, and efficient manner and be guaranteed direct access to the president.

Marshall reassured the senators that the structure spelled out in the bill would work in practice. He acknowledged that policy and operational matters were not easily separated in practice and that one would have to guard against overstepping proper bounds. In an exchange with Senator Walter George (D, Georgia), the secretary was asked what would happen if the US ambassador in a given country wanted a project and the ECA administrator considered it a waste of money:

> Senator George: There you come to a practical situation. You must either decide, in that event, that as a matter of sound foreign policy certain projects in country X must be constructive and carried out, or the Administrator's judgment must prevail. Now, what is the situation there?
>
> Secretary Marshall: The matter there, it seems to me, would require the intelligence and judgment of both the Administrator and myself. For purposes of illustration I can exaggerate the affair to the point of saying that there is little the Administrator could do in Europe that would not have some relation to foreign relations. In other words, I would have my hand in almost everything he did. . . . In this respect, following your question, if the exclusive decision were with the Administrator, it would be a very unfortunate thing. On the other hand, if the Secretary of State intruded himself into all manner of decisions regarding the administration that will be more or less commercial, that would be a very unfortunate business. However, you have to trust somewhat to judgment. You always must endeavor to lay down a sound basic organization.[22]

This candid exchange led some senators to worry about the ECA's independence. Marshall was aided by friendly questioning from several Democratic senators. They directed their questions along lines that permitted the secretary to illustrate how the nation had worked through difficult problems in the past. Ultimately the president would decide disputes, Marshall said, and one had to leave room for the president to establish the necessary working relationships. Collaborative efforts were essential among government agencies and just as important between the government and the private sector. Marshall made an impressive witness, and he did not have to call on Gordon or Thorp for assistance.

The testimony of other witnesses elaborated on the cooperative public-private sector endeavor in export promotion, overseas sales of foodstuffs, and the mining industry. Senator Vandenberg had a plan in mind to overcome the difficulty he had raised in his questions—he would commission a study by the prestigious Brookings Institution to recommend solutions to the issue of administrative independence for the ECA.[23] The Brookings report subsequently affirmed the importance of administrative independence and the need for recruitment of high-level technical and managerial talent from the private sector; it also recommended incorporating Section 105 of the Mutual Security Act of 1948 into the legislation. Under this provision disputes between the secretary of state and the administrator of the ECA would be referred to the president for resolution. The provision never had to be invoked during the life of the Marshall Plan. Nonetheless, the Brookings report played its part in the Vandenberg choreography of support for the economic assistance act. Through his efforts Vandenberg ensured adoption of the legislation in his committee, full funding in the Appropriations Committee, and final passage in the full Senate in April 1948. Full Senate passage came after the most memorable speech of Vandenberg's career.

After his testimony Secretary Marshall took off on a grueling speaking campaign across the country.[24] He spoke to thousands of Americans in passionate terms about the necessity of US assistance to Europe and rebutted arguments against the program. He insisted the program must be funded on the scale planned, or the effort would fail. Truman's decision to remain in the background and let Marshall be the public face of the campaign for what was now increasingly referred to as the Marshall Plan was politically wise. Marshall's efforts were the culmination of a long campaign of persuasion built around the analysis and expertise of his many lieutenants, who compiled data, prepared testimony, and backed up his public appearances. Because the plan had worked its way through the executive branch with bruising struggles among agencies and been exhaustively debated in Congress, it now enjoyed solid public backing. Business, labor, citizen groups, and associations had been engaged in the earlier debate, and now many representatives joined in the campaign, with speeches to Rotarians, VFW conventions, chambers of commerce, PTAs, and associations across the country. Because Congress had thoroughly grilled executive officials and the plan had bipartisan backing, civic leaders at the local level were supportive.

Nevertheless, a critical ingredient of the Marshall Plan lay outside the reach of the many Americans in Congress, US executive agencies, and the private sector who labored to enact support for the legislation: the behavior of the Soviet Union. Aggressive Soviet behavior in Czechoslovakia had shocked Americans. The death of Jan Masaryk, a popular Czech leader, under mysterious circumstances had a dramatic impact on American public opinion. Marshall's speeches took on an increasingly anticommunist tone, until anticommunism became the dominant motif of the secretary's final speech of the tour, in Los Angeles. Historians have reached no unanimous verdict on how important this anticommunist motif was or how much the hostile Soviet behavior contributed to the Marshall Plan's passage. Without the provocative Soviet behavior, however, it is possible that the Republican Congress might have enacted the legislation but reduced the administration's funding request and passed a much smaller aid package. Such an outcome would not have been the confidence builder in Europe that the Marshall Plan proved to be. A lesser effort might have suffered the fate of earlier ineffectual postwar assistance programs.

9

The Marshall Plan in Action, 1949–1950

There was only *one* Marshall Plan. There will never be another, because the Marshall Plan sprang from historically determined, special circumstances, which will never be repeated as such. In particular, when I examine the North-South problem—the problem of development of the still underdeveloped countries—it is not a Marshall Plan that is needed: it is something else, a different combination of ideas and actions.
—Robert Marjolin, 1978

People tend to think that the success of the Marshall Plan was due to some special luck or a concatenation of circumstances of the time. I don't think so. I think it was due [in large part] to the special quality of the personnel from top to bottom who manned the Marshall Plan organization when it was in force.
—Milton Katz, 1975

The Marshall Plan enjoyed a unique quantitative record of success. By mid-1951, Western Europe had achieved higher levels of production and consumption, at substantially lower cost, and in much less time, than the goals originally set for late 1952. And the program was almost completely free from corruption. I know of no other sustained cooperative enterprise which matched or surpassed that record. No wonder that voices are regularly raised to call for a "Marshall Plan approach" to other difficult international problems.
—Lincoln Gordon, 2005

In January 1948 Gordon returned to his Harvard teaching duties and was pleasantly surprised to learn that Under Secretary of State Robert Lovett had written on November 20, 1947, to Business School dean Donald David thanking him for Gordon's services. Lovett praised Gordon as "a very competent man," adding, "I hope that his experience down here will prove to be of some value to him in connection with his subsequent duties at the Graduate School. It would give me a little comfort to feel this in view of the loyal and tireless work he put in for us."[1] David thanked Lovett for taking the time to write and said, "We are fortunate to have Gordon on our faculty. . . . I can assure you that his associates here as well as Gordon will be most appreciative of your letter."[2] Gordon taught his course on government-business relations that spring term, but he remained preoccupied with European recovery. He gave three speeches in the Boston area on behalf of the ERP legislation and corresponded regularly with Nitze and other State colleagues. His main writing that spring was an article in defense of the recovery program. He sent a draft to several colleagues in the State Department, asking for reactions. He received a two-page comment from Colonel "Tich" Bonesteel saying that "it might do considerable good" if he "hit hard" at the issue of the broad foreign policy aspects.[3] Bonesteel singled out the journalist Henry Hazlitt as a good target to be attacked. Gordon did his best in the campaign to win public support for the Marshall Plan and to refute opponents like Hazlitt and others.

The spring term sped by. Gordon, preoccupied with selling the Marshall Plan, had reason to believe that if the legislation passed—as looked increasingly likely—he would be offered a role in the agency he had helped to design and sell to Congress and the public. He knew that Richard Bissell would be in line for a senior post in the new agency because of Bissell's close working relationship with both Harriman and Hoffman. In turn, Bissell would recommend a senior position for him. Despite the fact that Gordon liked to portray himself as a man responding to an unsolicited call to duty, he certainly encouraged Bissell's efforts to recruit him for a senior position, and he began to think carefully about the kind of position he wanted.

Should He Return to Government Service?

If Gordon was offered a post, however, it was not a foregone conclusion that he should accept it. It would not be an easy decision, and he had learned enough to be wary of getting stuck in the wrong position. He wanted to be involved, but he was by now an experienced enough bureaucrat to be cautious in what he took on. He also felt some misgivings about asking for yet another leave from Harvard. The Harvard Business School had been good to him. His colleagues liked the breadth of his intellectual interests and his work in government on an important problem. Yet this could not be pushed too far, and it went without saying that taking constant leaves of absence was not the best way to build an academic career. At some point Gordon knew that he must decide whether he was primarily a public servant or an academic. He had discussed this matter with Bissell, whom he found a kindred spirit, and Bissell was struggling with the same problem. The war of course had disrupted both of their lives significantly. For Gordon European recovery was a repeat of the struggle over atomic control: a unique historical circumstance demanding urgent attention. Now the crisis in Europe was playing out against the background of an emerging Cold War. Gordon was older now, had a big family, and thought it was probably time to settle down. But many of his friends were turning toward service with the Marshall Plan, just as earlier his whole generation had gone into wartime service. There was also the question of salary. He was making $7,500 a year as an associate professor in the Business School and next year would be promoted to $9,000. It was likely that government service at the senior level would pay considerably more. (Gordon would make $13,500 plus a housing allowance in Paris in 1949 and $17,500, without housing, when he returned to Washington with Harriman in 1950.) In the end it would probably be a question of the particular job he was offered. There was much in government work that was tedious, and a great deal depended on whom one worked with. Though salary was not the most important factor, it was not the least important either.

Gordon eventually made up his mind that he did not want full-time government service with the new agency in Washington. He had been struck by the amount of time he devoted the previous summer and fall to the preparation for congressional testimony. The burden of the actual testimony was borne by Nitze and Bissell, along with the principals, but he had done much of the background preparation.[4] Much of this labor had been "an exercise in futility" because such items as "net payment balances are small residuals from a host of much larger gross transactions," which are heavily influenced by exchange rates, inflation trends, and other macroeconomic factors.[5] The elaborate "Brown Books" that he and his colleagues had prepared for Congress, showing imports, exports, payment balances, forecasts, and the like for all European countries for the next four years, were voluminous and impressive looking, but they were not very useful for policy-making. Perhaps, however, these were the necessary rituals of American democracy and of deference to "the facts."

Serving abroad, however, seemed more appealing. This would give him some distance from the rough-and-tumble of Congress and domestic politics—and after all, the problem was in Europe. The action was likely to be in Europe since that was where the aid was going. Serving abroad would be less of a grind (or so Gordon thought anyway). There would be fewer political pressures or at least different and more interesting ones. Moreover, the Office of Special Representative would probably be largely independent in practice from ECA headquarters in Washington. Politics of course would be unavoidable, but since the Republicans seemed likely to win the presidency in November, being out of Washington might be advantageous for a New Dealer like himself. Aid to Europe would be a bipartisan program, to be sure, and liberal Republicans like Thomas Dewey, John Foster Dulles, former president Herbert Hoover, Senator Arthur Vandenberg, Paul Hoffman, Harold Stassen, and others who had backed the Marshall Plan were likely to be foreign policy leaders. The Taft wing would remain strong and would probably seek to cut assistance levels if they could. There might well be constant pressures to reduce appropriations for the program. Gordon had registered as an Independent in Massachusetts and was not happy with either party in the state, but he certainly leaned toward the Democrats, and in a policy-level post he could be replaced by a Republican appointee in any change of administration.

Putting aside the political imponderables, Gordon had come up in the spring with a plan for how he would respond if offered an ECA post in Washington. The legislation passed on April 2, 1948, and President Truman nominated Paul Hoffman to be ECA administrator in Washington and Averell Harriman to be the special representative in Paris. The Harriman appointment convinced Gordon that his idea of what to ask for was correct. He wanted to work with Harriman if he possibly could. Within weeks came the call that Bissell had said would come from Paul Hoffman, asking Gordon to come to Washington as director of the program division, a post placing him in charge of one of ECA's major units. The scope and exact duties of the division, said Hoffman, would be worked out between the two of them once Gordon had reported for duty. The job would involve recruiting an analytic staff at headquarters and recruiting the US country mission chiefs. Gordon replied with the counterproposal he had worked out in anticipation of the offer: he would come, but not permanently. He did not want a job (as he said in his draft memoir) "where Congressional presentations would inevitably become the dominant activity." Of course he did not frame his answer in quite these terms to Hoffman. Rather, he proposed that he come to Washington as the *acting* director to set up the division and that he start recruiting right now, while still at Harvard, for both the Washington staff and the country missions abroad. One of his early recruits, he promised Hoffman, would be his successor to take over as permanent director. He had a further condition: he asked to spend August in Paris with the Office of the Special Representative in order to become fully conversant with what was happening on the ground in Europe. Hoffman expressed regret but accepted Gordon's counterproposal.

Gordon began recruiting the heads of the ECA country missions while still in Cambridge. He found the job challenging, but most of those he approached were eager to serve. He arrived in Washington at the beginning of June and recruited as his deputy and successor Arthur Smithies of the Bureau of the Budget, an expert in budgets and fiscal policy. Smithies was a native of Tasmania, with a stammer, a mop of unruly hair, and the slightly distracted air of a Mr. Chips, but these hid an incisive mind. Smithies had published *The Federal Budget and Fiscal Policy* in 1948, which became a widely used text for many years and was a standard work in the ascendant Keynesian tradition. He served for two years and then became chairman of the Economics Department at Harvard from 1950 to 1955 and again from 1959 to 1961. As the very popular master of Kirkland House, Smithies was invariably inveigled by the undergraduates into performing "Waltzing Matilda," which he sang badly off-key, at the annual Christmas party. Another of Gordon's early hires was a promising young Yale graduate named McGeorge Bundy, but the young Bundy moved on to greener pastures within several months. Gordon had better luck in keeping economist Hollis Chenery, who distinguished himself by his subsequent service at the ECA mission in Italy. Doing what he had promised Hoffman—setting up the office and getting it off on a solid footing—Gordon worked hard for two months but was most interested in the foreign offices and looked forward to seeing the Paris side of ECA operations.

Start-Up Phase in Paris: Summer 1948

Gordon arrived in Paris at an opportune time. Negotiations with the Europeans (and among the ECA participating nations themselves) had begun to heat up as the United States pressured them to come up with an agreed-upon formula for distributing the American aid to maximum effect for recovery purposes. Averell Harriman, the newly installed special representative in Europe, in a June speech had issued a pointed challenge to this effect to the ECA's participating nations.[6] When Gordon arrived at Le Havre, he was greeted by his old friend Frank Lindsay from the Baruch team, who was now on Harriman's staff. Lindsay had good news on both the personal and the professional front. He had a guest room in his house, so Gordon could stay with him while in Paris. More important, he conveyed the news that Harriman wanted Gordon to join Lindsay and the ECA's finance officer as part of a three-man US liaison team to work with the OEEC in the negotiations, which were reaching a critical juncture. The negotiations with the Europeans had been going on fitfully and had now reached an impasse, with the OEEC unable to resolve the issue of how the Marshall Plan aid would be allocated among the recipient countries. The OEEC had been originally established in July 1947 to deal with the United States on the aid called for in Secretary Marshall's June Harvard commencement speech and in particular to respond to Marshall's request for a report on European economic needs and a proposal for how the anticipated US aid should be allocated. Harriman had declared upon his arrival that he wanted the OEEC to recommend how the United States should distribute the aid, asserting that it did not want to deal bilaterally with each recipient country.

The European member nations were behaving in a fashion that reminded Gordon of the military services vis-à-vis the WPB: everybody demanded the highest priority for their own needs, with no regard for the overall resource limits. Each country had seemingly unlimited needs, and there was no formula for choosing among the uncoordinated requests for aid. Harriman had tried to change this by challenging the Europeans to come up with a coordinated statement of their needs. The aid was to be given for fifteen months (the maximum permitted by Congress) and was to replace the bilateral country-by-country postwar emergency aid. The OEEC, in response to Harriman, had created a special committee to prepare the coordinated request. To this end each country was to make a presentation to the special committee, and the American liaison team was to assist the committee in evaluating the submissions.

The OEEC operated in tight security and secrecy at first, but European leaders deemed it wise to brief a few Americans from Harriman's staff on their progress. Gordon's inclusion on the liaison team meant that he got to know many prominent Europeans, including Robert Marjolin of France, Eric Rolof of the UK, Dag Hammarskjöld of Sweden, Eric Brofers of Norway, Giovanni Majodi of Italy, and Ernst van der Beugel of the Netherlands. His analytic abilities quickly made him the leader of the American team, and his economic advice was sought out by the European leaders. The allocation process thereupon improved significantly and by the end of the summer proved to be a success, with an agreed-upon formula for allocating US aid and a structured process that was broadly acceptable to the Europeans and to Harriman. The main remaining problem was a dispute with General Lucius D. Clay, US commander of the American zone in Germany, who insisted that the allocation given the Western zones of Germany was inadequate. He threatened to go to Congress to increase the German share. Harriman and Hoffman placated Clay by cutting the aid to other countries and modestly increasing the sum for the American zone in Germany. By the beginning of 1949 the German economic miracle had dramatically changed the German situation. German recovery was proceeding at a faster rate than anything projected by the Marshall planners, and Franco-German rapprochement was making great strides. In September 1949 the Western Allies signed the Termination of the Occupation Agreement and established the Federal Republic of Germany (unifying the three Western occupation zones).

Paris in the summer of 1948 was not all hard work for Gordon. He traveled one long weekend through parts of the war-torn French countryside. Paris had escaped significant war damage, but the larger towns in the countryside were often pockmarked. Gordon spent pleasant evenings at dinner with European delegates to the OEEC. He got to know Colonel Vernon "Dick" Walters, an army officer who was on assignment in Paris.

There was even time for a mild office prank played on Harriman. Harriman was well known for being a difficult and demanding boss with no tolerance for small talk or office bonhomie. On reporting to work one day, Gordon and Frank Lindsay arrived at the OSR headquarters punctually for the regular 9:30 a.m. staff meeting. As other staff members straggled in late, Harriman, not given to chit-chat, fumed and finally started the meeting a quarter of an hour late.

"Gentlemen," Harriman said. "This is not a group of Frenchmen who always begin a meeting 10 minutes late. This is an American group and we should start at the scheduled hour. To encourage this practice, I am going to impose a 100-franc fine [not a large sum] on each latecomer. We will store the fines in a safe place and at the next holiday season have an office party with the proceeds."[7]

The next morning a harried and embarrassed Harriman, caught in traffic, arrived forty-five minutes late. While they waited for Harriman, Gordon penned a note saying, "WAH owes the kitty 100 francs." He placed the note on the table in front of Harriman's seat. When Harriman arrived, he took his seat and glanced at the piece of paper and looked around the room at the faces of his colleagues. After the meeting Harriman scribbled a few words on the bottom of Gordon's note and dropped it in front of him. His scribble read: "Nine-thirty begins when I arrive." Harriman evidently was not troubled by Gordon's assertiveness, for he asked him to stay as Gordon was preparing to leave Paris. The offer put Gordon in an awkward position. He was certainly interested but had family reasons for not being able to accept immediately. Allison was pregnant with their fourth child, and he was expected to return to Cambridge. The job offer was to head the Program Division, one of the three major units of the OSR, and to act as Harriman's economic adviser. This would make Gordon the number-three official at the OSR, behind Harriman and deputy director Milton Katz, a Harvard colleague whom Gordon knew well. The baby was expected in January (daughter Amy would arrive on January 22, 1949), and Gordon proposed that if Harriman were willing to hire an interim director, he could come the next spring. Furthermore, he could stay as long as Harriman wanted. Harriman selected as acting director Shaw Livermore, an old friend of Gordon's from wartime service, and Gordon left with the expectation that he would return to Paris with his family early in spring 1949.

The Marshall Plan in Action: 1949

Gordon's projected return to Europe did not go smoothly. Allison's pregnancy was a difficult one, and she suffered from depression after the baby's birth. Gordon wrote to Paul Nitze in January that he had "decided not to return to Paris in the spring."[8] Matters gradually improved, however, and by May he was able to depart with his family. They flew in an unpressured DC-4 and had long stops for minor repairs at Gander, Newfoundland, and Shannon. In Paris three of their four children came down with polio, which produced anxious moments. Bob, age eight, was temporarily paralyzed, and the Gordons agonized for days until he finally was able to move his legs. Daughter Anne, nine, suffered neurological damage from her bout with polio that stayed with her. Indeed, family illness was a regular part of the Paris assignment, and Gordon's worry over his children detracted from the satisfaction and excitement of his work. Still, the major burden was borne by Allison. Harriman's administrative staff in Paris had arranged for the family to move into a country house in Versailles, which left her struggling with four frequently sick children in a drafty house with inadequate help and no adult companionship for long hours.

Lincoln meanwhile found the political situation in Europe transformed from the previous fall—both for the better and for the worse. In West Germany the threat of famine had vanished, and an astonishing economic recovery had taken place. The Berlin Airlift had not only been sustained over the winter but had performed spectacularly well. The Allied military occupation of the three Western zones was in the process of being replaced by the Federal Republic of Germany, with Konrad Adenauer scheduled to become chancellor in September. In France and Italy, the communist parties were in retreat from their postwar high points. The end of rationing was in sight for most of Western Europe. However, the OEEC division-of-aid allocation process that Gordon had helped to devise was not going well in its second round. The fragile European unity that had been achieved the previous summer was now in danger of fracturing. The OEEC had moved into new headquarters near the Bois de Boulogne, and reporters now hovered around the entrances to pry comments from delegates. The allocation process had become much more open, and thus disputes were openly discussed and rendered more difficult to resolve with quiet diplomacy.

The "dollar gap" remained and was the critical problem for most of the OEEC countries. Issues surrounding the sterling area presented immediately pressing concerns. The financial crisis became full blown in late July, when the British formally asked the OEEC to increase the UK's allocation for 1949–1950, which threw the allocation discussions into turmoil. The crisis facing the pound had some basic elements, one of which was the fact that the Marshall Plan had made provision only for the sterling area's three European countries—the UK, Ireland, and Iceland—and did not include such non-European sterling countries as Pakistan, Iraq, South Africa, Southern Rhodesia, Australia, New Zealand, Burma, Ceylon, and the Faroe Islands. The sterling-area countries not included in the ERP produced a drain on British dollar reserves because the UK supplied dollars to service their debts, cover previous imbalances, and offset the transfers of British capital to the sterling area.[9] Gordon believed that the solution would involve a devaluation of the British pound and proposed to Harriman that he be allowed to pass the word that increasing the British allocation would raise serious questions in Washington. The UK instead should consider devaluation.

Since the OEEC operated under a unanimity rule, the combination of British obduracy and opposition to the British request by other Europeans had produced an ugly impasse. The dispute and the proposed revision to the allocation formula were assigned to a new committee of two, Baron Snoy of Belgium, the OEEC's chairman, and OEEC secretary general Robert Marjolin. The two men succeeded in working out the new Snoy-Marjolin formula, which the British reluctantly accepted, thus defusing the immediate crisis, but the formula did not resolve the underlying problems. The British dollar reserves continued to be drained, and the British preferred to negotiate bilaterally with the United States and Canada about a new solution rather than with the Europeans. The American position, in which Gordon played an important role, was that both sterling devaluation and currency realignment in OEEC countries were necessary to increase intra-European trade.[10] In September the British were forced to accept devaluation of the pound. The amount of the devaluation—from $4.03 to $2.80, a devaluation of 30 percent—took the Europeans by surprise and produced currency adjustments in a number of OEEC countries. Tensions were eased, though the British had demonstrated that they were not willing to surrender even limited sovereignty to European institutions. British dollar reserves recovered in the succeeding months, and, most important, intra-European trade began to increase.

Gordon had come to the conclusion that more far-reaching measures were necessary and communicated his views to Bissell at ECA headquarters. First, he recommended that the Snoy-Marjolin allocation formula should simply be extended for the next two cycles of remaining Marshall Plan aid. This would avoid going through an elaborate deliberation and policy squabble each year. The whole allocation process was becoming counterproductive. The fights over the formula had been so bruising that Gordon feared rehashing the issue with each new cycle. His idea was accepted, with the minor modification that $150 million of US aid be set aside and distributed for special programs determined by American officials to promote cooperative "international investments" by European firms.[11]

Second, Gordon believed that the OEEC should build on the momentum that was developing to limit import restrictions and liberalize trade. What was required was not political integration, but the removal of the barriers to trade that had developed with the Depression and World War II. As Michael J. Hogan notes: "In late September and early October, ECA officials held a series of meetings on the subject of European integration, out of which came important policy papers by Lincoln Gordon of Harriman's staff in Paris and Richard Bissell, Theodore Geiger, and Harold Van B. Cleveland of ECA headquarters."[12] The policy papers had similar diagnoses and prescriptions, reflecting the fact that Gordon communicated daily with Bissell by telephone and teletype. Bissell, recognizing that being on the ground in Europe provided important insights into policy, traveled regularly to Paris, as did many other colleagues at ECA headquarters. The Bissell-Gordon connection, however, had a special significance. Bissell in his memoir described the tensions in the Marshall Plan's administrative structure.[13] Harriman had been deeply offended that he had been passed over for the position of ECA administrator in favor of Hoffman. In the initial days of the Marshall Plan, Harriman, with Katz, his enforcer and hatchet man, was attempting to shut ECA headquarters out of important decisions. Katz made sure that no order was given to any country mission in Europe except through the OSR in Paris. While Katz believed that orders had to come through Harriman, he did not attempt to block communication between ECA headquarters and the field. "But," in Bissell's view, "human factors . . . combined with the dual headquarters structure of the ECA made the potential for conflict high."[14] Bissell saw his relationship with Gordon as the answer to the problem of keeping ECA headquarters informed about what was happening in Paris and the rest of Europe: "I have always felt that Katz [Harriman's deputy in Paris] was most protective of the office's jurisdictional rights, although he could not have been so vocal without Harriman's backing. Nevertheless, neither gentleman's activities influenced my working relationship with others in the office. On my frequent trips I always spent enjoyable and productive time with Lincoln Gordon and his staff in the OSR's Program Division. Washington's working relations with them were very good."[15]

The Gordon and Bissell policy papers came to the same basic conclusion: it was time to abandon the original "salvage function" of the Marshall Plan and to concentrate instead on the goal of breaking down the barriers to economic activity in Europe. The "stifling effects on the process of economic growth" inherent in "the tight compartmentalization" of national economies called for one or more "free trade areas" to promote "mass production and mass consumption."[16] The ultimate goal might be a full-scale European union, but since this could not be achieved in the near future, the objective of US policy should be to help promote the sufficient pooling of power and harmonization of policies to bring about an integrated economy relatively free of currency restrictions and import quotas. The United Kingdom would not participate in any economic union with the continental European nations but should be encouraged to adopt policies that would coordinate with what Europe did.

The next important step came with Paul Hoffman's October 31, 1949, speech to the OEEC ministerial meeting, in which the United States issued a call for European action on "integration." The original draft of Hoffman's speech reflected the thinking of Gordon in Paris and of his fellow economists Bissell, Geiger, and Cleveland in Washington.[17] The draft called for European unification, emphasized supranational institutions, and suggested a timetable for action by the Europeans. The State Department policy-makers (starting with Secretary Acheson) objected to the word *unification*, which they thought could frighten some Europeans, and called for *integration* instead. State Department officials objected to the idea of an American blueprint being imposed on the Europeans and considered that the pace of integration proposed in the draft was much too fast. If the Europeans failed to act according to the specific time-tables that the draft demanded, there could be negative reactions from the Europeans that in turn could trigger cuts in appropriations by Congress. High-level meetings in Washington, involving Acheson, Hoffman, Hoffman's ECA deputy William Foster, Treasury Secretary Snyder, and BOB's Webb, resulted in toning down the draft's demands for timetables, blueprints for action, and calls for supranationality. The speech as delivered to the expectant OEEC audience—this was the first time Hoffman had addressed the organization—was nevertheless a ringing endorsement of the idea of European economic integration. As such, it marked a dramatic shift in US policy away from short-term stabilization, balance of payments adjustments, and recovery goals, toward long-term institutional reforms.

Although pleased that some of his ideas had made their way into the Hoffman speech, Gordon was uncomfortable with the overall thrust of the speech. He was persuaded by the cautions of some of his former colleagues in State, like Ty Wood, who had objected to the draft's emphasis on timetables and US-imposed targets. More seriously, Gordon encountered skepticism from some of his European friends. What did the abstract noun *integration* actually mean? This was a term not included in Marshall's original speech, and the transformation of European institutions was not previously of concern for Marshall Plan supporters or aid administrators. Gordon had to concede that the term was chosen precisely because it had no specific content. For Europeans knowledgeable about American politics, there appeared to be a paradox here. Republicans in Congress had insisted on an independent agency because they were afraid of a New Deal agency bent on central planning at the expense of the free market. They had further insisted on the appointment of a Republican businessman to head the agency, not a Democratic politician who might be inclined to pursue too large a role for government. Now here was the Republican ECA administrator proposing a transformative concept that would make New Deal central planning look like child's play in comparison. Hoffman, in explaining his thinking to Europeans, was fond of the analogy that could be drawn between Europe and the American federal union. The United States had a per capita income of such and such, he would point out, while Europe had lower per capita income levels. Why the difference? Because the United States had a completely open market, and goods moved freely across state borders. Gordon observed: "I found this Hoffman concept too simplistic—too oblivious of deep-seated national differences."[18] Gordon seems to have started out as an advocate of unification along with his ECA economist colleagues and then backed off quickly when he thought more deeply about the problem and when his closest European colleagues objected. He always insisted in later years that the European integration movement was quite separate from the Marshall Plan and that the Marshall Plan's impact on the drive toward European unity was extremely limited. As he frequently pointed out in arguments with colleagues, the Marshall Plan had ceased to exist for several years before the first steps toward the creation of the European community (and then the European Union) took place.

Gordon's retrospective comments may have overstated the position he took at the time, but clearly he developed serious reservations about pushing the pace of integration too far and too fast. The most serious problem, in his view, was that the focus on supranationality was diverting attention from the most urgent need, namely, to restore the normal trading patterns that had existed before the Great Depression and the war. In looking at the European scene, Gordon was struck by the fact that the traditional trading arrangements of the nineteenth and early twentieth centuries had been disrupted by the "beggar-thy-neighbor" policies of the 1930s. Quantitative import quotas had proliferated and were now the norm. Payment mechanisms to facilitate trade were lacking. Exports between European nations in the early postwar days sometimes took the form of barter, as celebrated in the lines from Alfred Friendly's comic Marshall Plan operetta: "Wines for sale; will you swap a little bit of steel for Chateau Neuf du Pape?" In Gordon's analysis, economic relations among nations could be arrayed along a spectrum from total autarky to the completely free movement of goods, people, funds, and investments across national borders. More realistically than either of these extremes, Europe could and should strive for a middle ground, a return to "normal" trade relations, with tariff barriers significantly lowered but not wholly removed, exchange mechanisms with some room for exchange rate adjustments, and the elimination of import restrictions. There should also be strong encouragement of portfolio and direct investment, all of which would promote economic growth and employment.

The European Payments Union (EPU)

The OEEC ministers in November 1949 made a pledge in the wake of Hoffman's October speech to reduce import quotas by 50 percent. This pledge was warmly welcomed in the American delegation in Paris and in Washington, but Gordon worried that pushing too hard toward integration as the major goal could move trade liberalization to the sidelines. Two things were needed now in Gordon's view: a practical program of action the Europeans could agree on and a steady US policy approach that did not overreach and cause trouble. The first of these steps was the plan for a European Payments Union (EPU) that was to be achieved by the target date of the summer of 1950.[19] The EPU was adopted and remained in operation until it was superseded by the European Monetary Agreement of December 1958. Gordon, in a 1997 PBS interview, said that the EPU originated in informal, off-the-record discussions between small groups of Americans and Europeans organized by Robert Marjolin, OEEC's secretary general. Marjolin invited small groups of about eight or nine for dinner at a good French restaurant and then a long evening's discussion of the Marshall Plan. Gordon was the American participant in these meetings. Though a very young man, Marjolin skillfully guided the discussions and drew on the contributions of each of the assembled experts. Gordon recalled: "It was bilingual conversation—we could speak either French or English as we pleased. Everybody knew enough of the other language to understand. There was no time wasted on translations. Very constructive. I think basically always with the common interest in view. And out of that did come ideas, basically, I think the foundation of the European payments union was laid in those, those meetings."[20]

When the Marjolin group discussed the payments union, participants did not limit themselves to technical issues. They discussed what was practicable, what could be sold to national parliaments and to the American Congress, and what was acceptable to the public at home. The EPU's appeal to debtors was obvious enough: not having access to credit was a major worry. If a way could be found to avoid trading against short-term payments imbalances, the debtor nations would be liberated. But there would have to be incentives for countries like Belgium or the Netherlands, whose currencies were already convertible or nearly so. The EPU would function like a bank and would infringe on sovereignty only to the extent that the member states would have to give up import quotas and other restrictive trade practices. Nations were to settle their accounts with the payments union and not bilaterally with individual trading partners. Accounts would have to be settled monthly in gold and dollars, but with provisions made for temporary credits. The EPU concept was hammered into final shape in late 1949 and early 1950. Like the Marshall Plan itself, the EPU concept was not the product of any single man or mind. It came out of a group of dedicated experts who combined very specialized knowledge and a broad grasp of political realities. But the leading figures were Robert Marjolin on the European side and Gordon on the US side.

One of the most vexing issues that had to be solved was the geographical boundaries of the proposed union: Would it be made up of "little Europe" or only the leading economies, whose currencies were almost convertible? Or would the proposed union be inclusive of the whole body of participating Marshall Plan member states? The "little Europe" approach, FINEBEL or FRITALUX, as it was variously known, was first advanced in 1949 to liberalize trade among France, Italy, and the Benelux nations (Belgium, the Netherlands, and Luxembourg). This proposal was not favored by the Americans because it retained some restrictive practices then permitted under OEEC guidelines, and it excluded a large part of Europe. At the opposite end of the spectrum stood the US Treasury and some parts of the State Department, which opposed any regional European payments mechanism or trading bloc. Their reasoning was that regionalism worked against the principles of the Bretton Woods system. Bretton Woods called for a universal system based on current account convertibility as the best means of promoting nondiscriminatory world trade. The position of the Harriman office in Paris, shaped by Gordon, and of ECA headquarters, shaped by Bissell, plus some parts of State, deemed full convertibility for Europe impracticable and pushed hard for the regional concept but favored a more inclusive region than the "little Europe" of France, Italy, and Benelux. Gordon and Marjolin argued that full convertibility would cost Europe 1 to 2 percent in annual gross domestic product and all but wipe out the positive contributions to European growth provided so far by Marshall Plan aid.

Gordon felt confident that events were moving in the right direction with the Europeans in 1950. There were Euro-skeptics and Euro-enthusiasts in each member country, but there were also pragmatists. Marjolin, the architect of the EPU, was a Monnet disciple but more of a pragmatist than a federationist like Monnet.[21] Gordon considered himself to be in the pragmatic camp with Marjolin. The OEEC had tried to formulate a Europe-wide investment code, and the experiment had failed badly. The Europeans were sensible enough to seek pragmatic solutions, and Gordon worked hard to get the United States to support Marjolin. "We are not," Gordon said in a memo to Paul Hoffman, "trying to buy advantage for the United States at the expense of European interest; we cannot bargain as if we were trying to bargain with autocrats for mineral rights. We are engaged in the more difficult task of American leadership in working out with democratic allies a cooperative recovery program."[22] The experience to date with the Marshall Plan had proved that the cooperative approach worked best. The greatest danger was the habitual tendency of Americans to be carried away with their own ideas and to demand short-term results on their own terms.

Gordon saw his main problem in the spring of 1950 as the drift in US policy to demanding more "performance" toward US-imposed integration targets from Europeans as a condition for further aid. The idea was gathering momentum within the US bureaucracy that the Europeans had to be prodded into faster progress on integration. The danger of this approach, for Gordon, was that it would deflect attention and resources away from the real goal of bringing the EPU into operation. In a strongly worded memorandum to Hoffman and Harriman, he argued against a shift to allocating aid on the basis of "performance" measures and timetables on US integration targets. He was, in effect, taking issue with Hoffman's prescription for rallying Congress behind a new theme for the Marshall Plan's next phase. Gordon had prepared the way for his stand with Harriman and Katz and in lengthy long-distance exchanges with Bissell in Washington. They encouraged him to express his views to Hoffman.

"While it is doubtless a caricature of the actual intent," Gordon argued, the attitude conveyed by our policies was that of "lining up the European countries like schoolboys with 'punishments' for the 'bad' and 'prizes' for the 'good.'"[23]

That was at any rate the reaction of many Europeans, who had been turned off by US efforts to use its power to force European cooperation on US terms. Of course, Gordon insisted, some European friends inappropriately viewed US aid as a kind of entitlement. This was wrongheaded on their part, but this entitlement mentality would be fostered if the United States was too heavy-handed in assuming that the Europeans would agree with US interpretations of what was in Europe's interest. Gordon's memo reviewed the whole history of the allocation process and cautioned against re-creating internecine European warfare. This would be the result if the whole aid package was opened up for competition and the Europeans had to fight for shares of the pie based on metrics they did not understand or accept. To throw open the allocation of assistance to a new fight for shares among recipient countries would set back, not encourage, cooperation among the member states. We would be better off, Gordon urged, to limit the discretionary share of Marshall Plan funds to one-third of the total and to focus on the targets already agreed to by the majority of the member states. By far the most critical objective was to implement the EPU. This goal was now within reach, and the United States should make sure that this program was adopted. American influence and lubricating dollars were needed to get the EPU up and running. By facilitating trade, capital flows, technology exchange, and investments, Gordon asserted, export earnings would rise, and the dollar gap would become a thing of the past.

Gordon's arguments were persuasive. They reflected and reinforced the thinking of Harriman, Katz, and other key ECA colleagues and were ultimately acceptable to Hoffman. Gordon's tenacity helped to keep attention focused on the payments union throughout the spring and summer of 1950. The issue of debtor nations joining the payments union in a deficit position was solved by Marshall Plan funds wiping out past debt. The creditor nations should have enjoyed a surplus position on entering the payments union equal to the debts offset by the Marshall Plan funds, but there was no appetite for giving creditor nations further advantages. Counterpart funds had served some of the same functions as the proposed payments union, but counterpart funds did not cover all of the bilateral, triangular, and multilateral trade that would be brought within the proposed EPU. There were not enough counterpart funds in any case. Relations with the British were still delicate by early summer, and the UK's membership in the EPU was a particularly difficult issue. The British economy had recovered significantly with the resolution of the sterling crisis, but the British wanted guarantees of aid under emergency conditions as a precondition for joining the payments union. In May, Milton Katz, now the special representative with Harriman's departure for Washington, reached the Katz-Gaitskill Agreement, which ended the impasse with the British. The United States pledged $300 million to make the payments mechanism work but would not provide the funds until the Europeans, including the British, reached an agreement among themselves on the main features of the plan. The makeshift, year-by-year arrangement on payments was due to expire on June 30, creating an incentive for serious negotiation, because Katz had made it clear that the United States would take no steps on its own to salvage the situation if the EPU negotiations failed.

By the end of June the major issues had been worked out, and final agreement was near. Working closely with Henry Tosca of ECA headquarters in Washington, Gordon had been a critical player in achieving the agreement and making it acceptable to all the OEEC member states. The OEEC's Council of Ministers adopted the European Payments Union in August, and the treaty was officially ratified on September 19, 1950, with the provisions made retroactive to July 1950. A Code of Ethics was adopted in February 1951 to strengthen the obligations of member nations to settle their accounts expeditiously after the end of each month, but with credits available to finance imports.

The liberalization of trade made possible by the EPU became the success story of the second phase of the Marshall Plan. Intra-European trade rose spectacularly, from $10 billion in 1950 to $23 billion by 1959.[24] Even in the first months of the EPU's existence, "intra-European trade ballooned. . . . After only six months of operation of EPU, the index had increased to 140 [from 90]. As intended, the increased trade promoted specialization, investment, competition and innovation and helped, among [other] factors, to lead to 'a period of economic growth which compared favorably with, and may well have exceeded, the rate achieved in any other period in European history.'"[25] In the estimation of Richard Bissell, "the EPU was the greatest achievement of the Marshall Plan since once and for all intra-European trade and payments were freed up from quantitative controls."[26] Averell Harriman thought that "the European Payments Union . . . was a thing which made the Marshall Plan a success and made it possible for Europe to move rapidly after the Marshall Plan was finished."[27] Paul Hoffman, too, believed that "of all the moves that were made, the most important was the organization of the European Payments Union. Once the Payments Union had become available, the upturn in trade was spectacular. It was a major factor in the success of the Marshall Plan."[28]

The Marshall Plan Legacy

For Gordon the summer of 1950 marked both the high point and the end of his Marshall Plan service. Harriman had departed for Washington in late spring to assist President Truman's fight against NSC-68, but the North Korean invasion of South Korea on June 25, 1950, radically underscored the direness of the situation. The Soviet-backed North Korean aggression greatly enhanced the importance of Harriman's role as special assistant to the president for national security but reversed the policy priorities that Truman had assigned him. Truman had wanted Harriman to act as a counterweight to the interagency NSC machinery and its Nitze-inspired budget recommendations for a tripling of defense expenditures. Harriman became the first true national security adviser of the modern era (post–National Security Act of 1947), even though he carried only the title of special assistant to the president. And far from fighting the defense buildup, Harriman became the president's agent in overseeing a great expansion of the nation's military forces and a key adviser on defense issues. Gordon was home in Versailles with a severe cold when he heard the news of North Korea's aggression, and he and his colleagues in Paris immediately began to plan for a shift in Marshall Plan aid toward greater attention to military preparedness. Military assistance had been at least a secondary goal in the thinking of Marshall Plan staff since the North Atlantic Treaty was signed in April 1949. In practice, however, the NATO treaty amounted to little more than a paper guarantee that the United States would not sit on the sidelines in the event of European hostilities, as it had in 1914–1917 and 1939–1941. NATO needed to move from a treaty to an alliance. But before Korea there was little urgency to this effort, and in practice the ECA missions were told not to let military planning interfere with the immediate goal of economic recovery.

Harriman had asked Gordon to join him in Washington as his economics adviser and his key aide on Western European affairs. Gordon's attention was thus to remain focused on Europe, but now in the wake of Korea his attention would shift to military preparedness and military assistance. He had been offered the number-two job in Paris by Katz, who succeeded Harriman as special representative. It was an appealing offer. Katz was Gordon's good friend, his colleague from Harvard, and the two men's views were very close. His family was now finally growing comfortable in Paris, and his wife wanted to stay. But in the end Gordon felt that he owed it to Harriman to come to Washington, and he believed that he had largely done what he could do in Paris, with the EPU about to be fully implemented. Gordon had never worked directly at the White House, and the opportunity was irresistible, all the more so now that the Korean War had broken out and pushed security issues to the front. But most important was the attraction of working for Harriman. Seeing Harriman up close and working with him, though he was a difficult and demanding boss, was to Gordon taking part in history with a great man. Gordon had maneuvered to become a part of Harriman's team and had never wavered in his judgment that Harriman was an exceptional figure.

In subsequent years Gordon had the leisure to reflect often on the Marshall Plan's contributions. The Marshall Plan seemed to him in many ways the perfect government program. Among the various ambitious programs "in the decades following World War II, the Marshall Plan was uniquely successful. It accomplished more than had been hoped, in less time than originally planned, and at substantially less cost. It was the exact opposite of the cost and time 'overruns' which have become our late twentieth century stock in trade."[29] The Marshall Plan validated to him the whole concept of an activist government. Just as the FTC and the New Deal had intervened to rectify the failures of an unregulated marketplace, the Marshall Plan had restored European confidence and set in motion the processes of economic recovery. Yet he was dismayed by what he thought were huge errors and distortions in both public perceptions of and scholarly commentaries about the Marshall Plan.[30]

The first of those errors was the idea that the Marshall Plan paved the way for, or indirectly produced, the drive toward European unity and the European Union. Gordon insisted in his writings over many years that the Marshall Plan and the movement toward European unity were quite distinct. He was willing to concede that the Harriman approach to European self-help helped pave the way for previously nationalistic nations to collaborate on common problems. But this to him was about all that one could claim for the Marshall Plan in regard to European "integration" or "unity." These terms were slogans that helped sell the plan to the American Congress. The OEEC itself did not attempt, beyond the failed experiment in promoting a common investment policy, to promote unification. When the Marshall Plan shut down, the OEEC for practical purposes also shut down. It fell into desuetude after 1952 and then became largely a functionless form until it was reconstituted in 1960 with the addition of Canada and the United States into the Organization of Economic Cooperation and Development (OECD). The OECD has been one of the less significant entities in the pantheon of transnational organizations, existing largely to produce voluminous and well-researched reports for the member governments to ignore. The Schuman Plan, the famous plan for a European Coal and Steel Community, was devised independently by Jean Monnet with no input from any of the Marshall planners.

Gordon was a skeptic about the virtues of European unity at the time of the Marshall Plan, and he remained skeptical throughout his life. In assessing the importance of the Coal and Steel Community, Gordon in his draft memoir in 2005 wavered somewhat from his previous views: "I . . . wrongly assessed it as less important than the European Payments Union which was our preoccupation that spring." But in his published papers and his speeches up to 2000, he invariably stressed the difficulties and drawbacks of a complete monetary union. To have a complete monetary union would require a common currency and fixed exchange rate, and that would need a common fiscal policy. A common fiscal policy among nations with different levels of social, economic, and political development would not be possible. The Marshall Plan succeeded because it was not utopian. Gordon believed that the development of the Euro was a mistake and would eventually come to haunt the Europeans, a position that looks prophetic today, as the Euro has increasingly come to strangle and impede economic growth in Europe.

Another myth that Gordon was intent on puncturing was that the Marshall Plan represented the triumph of *dirigisme*, or a form of global economic planning. There were elements of planning in various countries, such as Monnet's plan to modernize French industry in 1948–1949, but the Marshall Plan as a whole represented mainly the dismantling of the autarkic policies adopted by the European states in the 1930s. The Marshall Plan represented a return to *normal* free market economic relations among the European nations—a return to the patterns that had prevailed in the first wave of globalization in the late nineteenth century. The European Payments Union, exchange rate adjustments, and removal of quantitative trade restrictions epitomized this Marshall Plan thrust toward restoring traditional free market patterns. But the European nations were too weak to be fully integrated into the Bretton Woods system at once, and hence regionalism was an accommodation to reality—perhaps going too far, as with the adoption of the Common Agricultural Policy, which Gordon believed had unfortunate consequences for the world economy.

Gordon did not believe that stabilization policies alone, negotiated individually with each European country, could have returned Europe to prosperity, and certainly not as quickly. He did think that the social, economic, and political fabric of Europe could not have been maintained in the absence of the Marshall Plan assistance. Both communist subversion and counterrevolution from the right were real dangers in early postwar Italy and France. At a retrospective discussion on the thirty-fifth anniversary of the Marshall Plan, the issue of whether the Marshall Plan was really necessary was posed in a provocative paper by Harold Van B. Cleveland.[31] He challenged his colleagues, a group including both academics and many original Marshall Plan participants from Europe and the United States, to reflect on the counterfactual supposition that Americans had approached the European nations individually with an economic stabilization package rather than with the collective Marshall Plan approach.[32] Cleveland drew on historical analogies, a comparison with the Dawes Plan of 1924, and contemporary experience to argue that country-by-country stabilization policies could have produced equally favorable economic results with less provocation to the Soviet Union. Gordon was among those who argued against a key Cleveland premise, namely, that the social and political fabric of postwar Europe would have remained stable without the Marshall Plan. Given the postwar context, one could not assume a stable political framework. France's desire for revenge against collaborators, along with Germany's devastation and the subversive tactics by Italy's Soviet-dominated labor unions, would have likely led to political extremism and ruled out a cooperative recovery effort. This climate, Gordon argued, would have been one of instability and would have undermined the prospects for a rapid economic recovery.

The Marshall Plan, viewed in these broad terms, had helped restore Europe's self-confidence and foster political stability. The Marshall Plan set in motion the normal market forces that had been paralyzed in the Depression, the war, and the war's aftermath. Many unique factors contributed to the Marshall Plan's success, including Europe's strong national traditions, social infrastructure, and exceptional human capital. Such reflections, though, were for the future. In the summer of 1950 Gordon's focus shifted to military security and how the United States could transform NATO into something more than a paper guarantee.

10

NATO: From Treaty to Alliance

The aim of the alliance is to keep the Russians out, the Americans in, and the Germans down.
—Lord Hastings "Pug" Ismay, first NATO secretary general, ca. 1950

The Korean war . . . led to an increasing emphasis on the military phase. In this emphasis, we sought to accelerate rearmament by the Europeans. In doing so, in my judgment, we made a tactical blunder. We overlook[ed] a lesson taught by the Marshall plan. . . . In the degree to which they were in accord with our assessment, they committed themselves to a policy. This signified a commitment of all of their resources, not merely their monetary resources, but their resources of leadership, political resources, political commitments, and bureaucratic resources. . . . The United States followed a very different path in regard to rearmament. . . . We estimated the scale of European rearmament which we deemed appropriate and then offered them large sums of money to help them rearm. Since there was no independent conviction of need arrived at by their own analytical processes, we had recurrent misunderstandings and difficulties.
—Milton Katz, 1975

We are fighting for freedom which means our free way of life. It will serve us little good in fighting for freedom to become regimented. . . . Therefore, we shouldn't go too fast in our rearmament

as to cripple our economy. We are like a boa constrictor swallowing a donkey.
—Dwight D. Eisenhower, supreme Allied commander, 1951

American foreign and defense spending was thus conflicted, if not schizophrenic. On the one hand, there was a perception of high threat. On the other hand, the means adopted to cope with it were slight by later standards and could not meet the felt needs.
—Robert Jervis, "The Impact of the Korean War on the Cold War," 1980

Harriman planned to have a staff in the White House of only six or seven. He was known to prefer lean staffs, whom he would then press relentlessly. In London with Lend-Lease, Harriman's staff started small but grew rapidly until he had some thirty people assisting him, but this job was totally different from what he now faced. A small White House staff meant that Gordon, along with his other colleagues, would have wide responsibilities. Gordon felt some qualms about giving up his Harvard tenure, despite the fact that over the past decade he had spent the bulk of his time in government service rather than in teaching. He was not given to biblical formulations, but Gordon felt that in some deep sense he had put his hand to the plow and could not look back. He was participating in historical events, and this was exhilarating, even if it took a toll. Harriman had spoken to both Katz and Gordon of his intentions to leave Paris after he had discussed his future plans with President Truman in the spring of 1950. Harriman did not want to leave Paris unless Katz agreed to succeed him. Katz had to be persuaded to stay, a decision helped by informal assurances that he would be welcomed back to Harvard Law School when his service in Paris ended.[1] Gordon was able to work out a similar understanding with the business school so that he was not totally burning his academic bridges by staying with Harriman.[2]

The country was now engaged in a shooting war with Korea, which would be of unknown duration. The Soviet Union presented a genuine threat, not merely the threat of subversion and destabilization tactics in a war-ravaged Europe. Gordon, along with other American officials, was aware that some serious steps beyond Korea itself were needed to reassure our allies and to counter the Soviet threat. The fact that the Soviet Union knew and approved in advance of the North Korean invasion seemed to refute the theory that the Soviets presented only the danger of political subversion in Western Europe and posed no threat of direct military action. The North Atlantic Treaty had been signed in April 1949 and had implied new expenditures for troops, but if troops were required, who would provide them? The US strategic nuclear deterrent had to some degree been neutralized by the Soviet atomic bomb, and now American troops were apparently needed for the Asian theater. France was becoming mired in Indochina, which could mean that the United States would have to provide more aid if it expected France to be fully engaged in the defense of Europe as well. Strategy issues in Asia and Europe were becoming intertwined, and the links between economic and military assistance were also becoming more important and more complicated.

It was Harriman's policy always to accept any presidential call to service. He had become fully alive when he cracked FDR's inner circle in 1941 and had made a successful transition to President Truman's service both in the cabinet and with the Marshall Plan. But in those past jobs he had a fairly well-defined portfolio and the full executive authority to carry out his responsibilities. Truman regarded him as a public servant of a high order but did not at this time consider Harriman a politician and did not share his broadest political strategies with Harriman. Now Harriman would be directly attached to the White House, but his exact responsibilities were unclear. He did not have a line department to run, and to begin with, before Korea, the president wanted him to fight against expanding the military budget. The job would be political, but what exactly was his role? Harriman would need to feel his way with the president in his new role and in the new Washington scene. Harriman was functioning vis-à-vis the president the way Gordon was functioning with Harriman.

For the moment Harriman had no operational responsibilities, as in his roles as Lend-Lease coordinator in London, ambassador to the Soviet Union, secretary of commerce, or administrator of the Marshall Plan in Europe. In his new assignment Gordon had a similar problem, but it was in a sense more baffling. He had to wait until Harriman found his niche before he could find his own. Gordon had developed a close working relationship with Harriman and was fully aware that he was a difficult and demanding boss, but Harriman always knew what he was doing. Yet now neither Gordon nor Harriman knew exactly what was in store for them. Gordon was sure that working for Harriman in the White House would be a stimulating experience, but it was going to be different from Paris. It would be more political, require constant self-invention, and call for the ability to find a role in a context of ambiguity and flux. Harriman had an uncanny instinct for intuiting the important emerging issues and positioning himself in the right spot. Gordon felt confident of that. In the meantime a few things were already evident, and one of these was that there would certainly be calls from Congress to reorient Marshall Plan aid toward military objectives. This was bound to be one of Gordon's first assignments.

Economic Recovery versus Military Preparedness

Controlling inflation, promoting intra-European trade, and raising civilian production had been the broadly accepted goals for both ECA planners and European leaders. Some NATO machinery for cooperation with the Europeans had been developed by the spring of 1950, but progress had been slow. In practice, NATO was a treaty commitment but not yet an alliance. The Marshall Plan's focus on the civilian economy was understandable, and undoubtedly economic recovery was a precondition for rearmament. The posture of the Truman administration—and the president was supported by two presidential commissions, various think tanks, the internationally minded business sector, labor, and academic leadership—was that any "defense program of the size now being contemplated" for Western Europe "must be supported by a strong and expanding economic base."[3] This requirement meant contention at home because Americans were not ready for another broad industrial mobilization like that of World War II. The civilian economy could not be taken over as it had been during the world war, but some wartime controls were going to be necessary. Even more seriously, the recovery-versus-preparedness equation was highly controversial and problematic in Europe. The Europeans accepted primary responsibility for their own economic recovery, and they knew that the United States was involved for only a limited period. European and American leaders shared a common definition of the problem and the nature of the solution. The situation was totally different with respect to military preparedness. Many Europeans never accepted the US definition of the threat and did not put the same priority on the need to reorient Marshall Plan aid from an emphasis on economic assistance to an emphasis on military assistance. Moreover, European leaders did not agree among themselves on the threat, and most of those who accepted the need for a strong alliance believed that the United States should bear the main burden.

The outbreak of the Korean War provided the impetus for the US Congress to reorient Marshall Plan assistance. With progress in reviving the European economies ahead of schedule, it seemed to Congress that Europe was now in a position to defend itself and that the United States should assist by reorienting most remaining Marshall Plan funds to defense purposes. So long as a modest amount of American economic aid continued, European countries would continue to grow and to modernize their economies so that they could afford both guns and butter. But certain conditions would be required if these twin goals were to be achieved. First, productivity would have to expand rapidly enough in Europe to provide the resources for both civilian and defense needs. Second, Europe would have to devote increased attention to questions of social equity so that workers would feel they had a stake in society. Union support for productivity gains and the work ethic would be essential. Third, Europe would have to continue on the path toward enough integration to consolidate the economic gains to date, remove the remaining barriers to trade, and create a system for joint military planning. This was the policy thinking of the Marshall planners, but behind the policy debate lay a significant shift in the politics of both Europe and the United States. In the United States the gap had widened between the executive branch and Congress, with an increasingly assertive conservative bloc in Congress demanding more concessions from the administration. In Europe political coalitions had grown less stable in the face of American demands for a greater defense effort.

The productivity targets, Gordon believed, were the key factor. If the ambitious productivity gains were not achieved, growth would not be sufficient to accommodate the conflicting military and civilian demands. Rapid growth had enabled both the United States and Europe to duck some problems that could return with a vengeance if growth slackened. Higher expenditures on defense could easily clash with such other objectives as modernization and social safety net or infrastructure needs. Shortages of critical materials or commodities such as coal would inevitably produce inflationary pressures. Marshall Plan countries were also uncertain about whether and to what extent the Korean War might distract America's attention from Europe. There was one basic issue that the Marshall Plan did not even address: How was Germany to be integrated into Europe economically or militarily?

The French and others retained strong fears of a revived German militarism. Yet if the NATO signatory nations were to defend themselves against potential Soviet aggression, how could they do so without German involvement? An obvious first issue in military planning was the question of the forward defense line—that is, what border would be defended? The West could not construct a defense on the Rhine, because that would leave three current NATO nations or parts of them—Norway, Denmark, and the Netherlands—east of the defensive perimeter. If the Germans were to participate in their own defense, their own territory would have to be defended. Gordon quickly became convinced that the Western allies would have to remove the remaining limitations on Bonn's sovereignty if the Germans were asked to assume defense responsibilities.

Harriman had directed Gordon before the Korean War to begin planning for the NATO force levels, the costs for the various European nations, and how to remove the barriers to the flow of military assistance. He was to outline how Marshall Plan aid could be redirected to defense needs and what other steps would be necessary to make NATO into an effective alliance. Harriman was well aware of the debate within the State Department and the National Security Council (NSC) over the need for a defense buildup. But before Korea it was not evident where the president stood on the issue. Truman before Korea wanted Harriman to assist him in fighting against the pressure for a greatly increased defense budget. Truman was highly suspicious of the implied call in the Nitze-engineered NSC-68 staff report for an astounding tripling of the defense budget. During his World War II Senate investigation of the Pentagon and in his experience as an artilleryman in World War I, Truman had formed the view that the military brass were spendthrifts. He was by instinct a fiscal conservative and a firm believer in balanced budgets.[4] Acheson, on the other hand, had favored the idea of Harriman in the White House for the opposite reason: he thought that his friend Averell, with his connections in the media world, could help create a favorable climate for a defense buildup. Harriman, as was his style, did immediately begin to entertain congressmen and media representatives at his Georgetown home, but without tipping his policy hand.[5]

The Korean War resolved most of the differences over the military buildup and ushered in a new stage in the policy debate. The paradox of high-threat perceptions and relatively modest steps to meet the threat, which was characteristic of American policy before Korea, was now fully exposed and pushed into the center of the policy debate.[6] Although Harriman had been brought back to Washington to help Truman counter the NSC-68 proposal, the president now drew him into the planning for the defense of South Korea. Truman decided to send Harriman to Tokyo to meet with General MacArthur for a strategy review. Harriman departed for the meeting with MacArthur on August 4, accompanied by army general Matthew Ridgway and air force general Lauris Norstad. The aide was to hear and evaluate MacArthur's plans for a bold strategic move to reverse the fortunes of the Korean War.

Early NATO Strategic Planning

Gordon went to London to discuss NATO planning and arrived back in the United States in September. He had learned from Ambassador Charles Spofford in London that the state of the alliance was not good but that some recent progress had been made. The Treaty of Brussels, signed in March 1948, was the first part of Ernest Bevan's two-part strategy for the defense of Western Europe. This alliance would include an inner core—France, Belgium, the Netherlands, Luxembourg, and the United Kingdom—to constitute the nucleus. Britain would act as a "third force" between the rival American and Soviet forces.[7] Britain was in no position, however, to deploy more troops in Europe beyond the small occupation force it then had in Germany. A larger troop commitment would not be possible if the UK wished to maintain its expanded welfare state, recently adopted by the Labor Party.

Neither could the other Brussels signatory nations mobilize significant armies on their own. They wanted American assistance under Article 3 of the NATO treaty and complained that American aid was only a trickle of what had been promised. Only some $45 million out of an appropriation of $1.5 billion in defense funds had actually been spent because the NATO legislation stipulated that aid could not flow until all twelve

NATO nations had ratified the pact. After Korea the Europeans had a new sense of urgency about defense issues and the role of NATO, but this urgency did not last long after the initial shock of the North Korean invasion. Many Europeans still considered economic recovery the main goal and feared that rearmament could derail recovery. Their view was that the remaining Marshall Plan aid should continue to ensure that recovery did not falter because without economic strength there could be no military buildup. The threat was not of a direct Soviet invasion (as George Kennan was arguing within US government circles at this time), but of internal subversion. Even the more hawkish European leaders argued that, if the Americans felt they needed forward bases in Europe to counter the Soviet threat, the Americans should pay for them and not disrupt the still-fragile European economies.

Germany had the resources, but pushing German rearmament too hard and too fast presented a range of difficult problems. Lord Hastings Ismay's quip that NATO's aim was to keep the Americans in, the Russians out, and the Germans down was more than a rhetorical flourish for many Europeans. The initial strategic concept of NATO was that America would provide a nuclear umbrella with a "trip wire" in the form of a small US troop presence. The United States would extend the nuclear umbrella over the Brussels pact countries, plus Canada, Denmark, Portugal, Italy, and Norway. In the famously ambiguous formula of NATO's Article 5, each nation pledged that "an attack against one or more of them in Europe, or North America, shall be construed as an attack against them all; and consequently they agree that . . . each of them . . . will assist the Party or Parties so attacked by taking forthwith . . . such action as it deems necessary, including the use of armed force, to restore and maintain the security of the North Atlantic area."[8] Military action was not automatic; each member state was left to take the actions it deemed "necessary" to aid the victim. The equivocal language was necessary to sell the treaty to the US Congress and to the various European parliaments. But there was considerable uncertainty about the United States' exact role, and—of course—there was another big problem: Germany was not a party to the treaty or a NATO member.

It was going to be necessary, Gordon believed, to resolve the incoherence of Germany's role. He knew that this would not be an easy task. If Germany were removed from the status of an occupied country and then encouraged to rearm, this would have to occur within an integrated framework of European defense, and this meant new machinery had to be invented and new resources devoted to the security cause. Those resources in some part had to be diverted from the civilian economy. German rearmament, for Americans, would also mean that the United States would have to be further "in" than previously supposed. US troops might have to be deployed forward in large numbers to counterbalance large East German and Soviet military forces.

Such ideas ran counter to established views. Secretary of State Acheson had spent most of 1949 after signing the North Atlantic Treaty assuring the French that the United States had no intention of pushing for German rearmament. Harriman had declared when he was still in Paris that while it was desirable to permit full German membership in the OEEC for reasons of economic efficiency, it was quite another thing to think of including the Federal Republic in NATO until "such time as there is concrete evidence that there is a real democratic Germany developing."[9] Acheson had also been assuring Congress that the North Atlantic Treaty meant only that US security was guaranteed; it did not mean a large increase in the defense budget and did not imply the permanent stationing of US troops in Europe. When asked during his Senate testimony if the treaty meant a long-term American troop presence in Europe, Acheson responded, "The answer to that question, Senator, is a clear and absolute 'No.'"[10]

By 1950, however, some NATO machinery had been established, and Pentagon force planners began suggesting sotto voce that a credible defense would have to involve German forces. Chancellor Adenauer, for his part, had developed considerable skill in manipulating American journalists and injecting questions into the US political dialogue to this effect: Could NATO function without German forces? Could the Federal Republic be expected to shoulder the burdens of defense while still having to endure limitations on its sovereignty?

Gordon had to reorient his thinking on strategic issues in Europe, and he also had to grasp equally dramatic shifts on the home front. He knew how the economic assistance budget process worked, but he now had to understand how defense budgeting worked, both on Capitol Hill and within the executive branch. Louis A. Johnson of West Virginia, who had been President Truman's chief fundraiser for his reelection campaign, replaced James Forrestal as secretary of defense with a "hold-the-line" defense budget strategy. The defense budget Congress approved for fiscal year 1949 was $13.8 billion.[11] The Truman administration's request for fiscal year 1950 was $14.4 billion, and the request proposed early in calendar year 1950 for fiscal year 1951 was to be $15 billion. The $15 billion figure was deemed adequate by Dwight Eisenhower and an affordable sum for the national defense. A revolt led by Gordon's old colleague Paul Nitze, now the director of the State Department's Policy Planning Staff, had produced a joint State-Defense comprehensive policy review statement (National Security Council Memorandum 68, NSC-68) in the spring of 1940 calling for a tripling of defense expenditures.[12] The NSC was a mechanism Truman paid little attention to from 1947 to 1949, preferring to get his advice from close personal aides. He did not like to be hemmed in by bureaucratic procedures imposed on him by Congress. The president attended only ten of the seventy meetings of the NSC during the 1947–1949 period, and the NSC rapidly earned a reputation as a paper-shuffling group without real influence. However, the NSC, staffed by Nitze at the State Department, gained in importance, and with Korea President Truman was forced to take it seriously and to come to grips with NSC-68.[13] Harriman's mission began to take on clearer shape. He advised Truman on MacArthur and military operations in Korea, having an input on the vast increase in the defense budget, forging a new strategy for NATO and Europe, reorienting Marshall Plan aid toward more of a defense role and working with ICA headquarters to this end, dealing with the more assertive Congress on a wide range of issues, coordinating a vastly complicated intergovernmental machinery on defense and military assistance, and occasionally taking on troubleshooting assignments for the president. Gordon's role, accordingly, became clarified as well. He advised Harriman on whatever Harriman was working on at the moment, but the majority of Gordon's work involved reconciling military and economic assistance, his liaison with the ECA and State, attending meetings as Harriman's representative, and frequently initiating interdepartmental reviews of policy. He also spent large amounts of time on the industrial mobilization activities and price controls set up during the Korean War and the economic aspects of NATO planning. Gordon had operated at a remove from the pressures of the Washington political scene during his busy but pleasant time in Paris. He knew the

Washington atmosphere would be more highly charged and intense. He had expected and wished for this change in deciding to go with Harriman. He now got his wish.

Time for German Rearmament

Harriman directed Gordon to work on German rearmament and to represent him at all important meetings on the subject that Harriman himself was unable to attend. The two had discussed Germany many times before, while they were in Paris. Now, however, there was an immediate action-forcing mechanism. The NATO defense ministers were meeting in October in Washington to take up officially the question of rearming Germany. Acheson, Marshall, and Harriman would meet with the president during and after this conference to decide US policy on the issue. Gordon was directed to attend the ministerial conference as an observer and Harriman's representative; Acheson would have State Department representatives, and Marshall would be in the chair as secretary of defense of the host country. On the first afternoon Gordon began a friendship with Edwin M. Martin, Acheson's representative from State, which lasted until the two had a falling out over Brazil policy a decade later.

Gordon was struck by the implacable opposition to German rearmament of the French defense minister, Jules Moch. Moch's supporting delegation included his wife. The Mochs had lost a son in World War II who was captured by the Germans in occupied France and shot as a spy. Moch was reported to have observed that he never met a German without asking what that person had done during the war. The Mochs "were bitterly opposed to any form of German participation in NATO. Mrs. Moch was a tall, dark-haired woman wearing black from head to toe. Although allotted a chair near her husband, she preferred to stand most of the time, looking over his shoulder as if to ensure that he conceded not a millimeter. She seemed like the incarnation of Edgar Allen Poe's raven, repeatedly saying 'Nevermore!' [to German militarism]."[14]

The discussion of the second afternoon session turned to defense geography. Should the allied line of defense be on the Rhine or on the boundary between the Western and the Soviet Zone of Germany? The weight of the military advice was overwhelmingly in favor of the forward line. Truman's military advisers had made a clear decision on this issue the previous fall. Acheson, whose public statements at the time of the North Atlantic Treaty's signing in April 1949 had strongly denied any intention of rearming Germany, had changed his position in the face of the unanimous advice of his military planners. He had supported Kennan's arguments for German "disengagement" but had no trouble now reversing his position.[15] By the time of the defense ministerial meeting, he had recognized the impossibility of defending Europe without the inclusion of German forces. The NATO European armies would still be far outnumbered by the Eastern Bloc forces even with substantial numbers of West German troops. By then the German "economic miracle" (*Wirtschaftswunder*) was in full swing, and so was a remarkable political stability under Chancellor Konrad Adenauer. Germany under Adenauer was firmly democratic. Adenauer thought that "rearmament might be the way of gaining full sovereignty. This made it the essential question of our political future."[16] The commitment of large numbers of American troops to Europe still lay in the future, though Gordon had begun to plan for how this could be done. The ministerial discussion went through the afternoon inconclusively until Secretary Marshall, in the hope of forcing a decision, proposed an informal show of hands on the question of German membership in NATO. The vote was ten in favor, with France and Belgium opposed. Marshall then recessed the meeting until the following day.

Gordon and Martin and two other colleagues left the meeting together and paused outside the State Department to discuss the session. A black limousine pulled up, and Acheson got out and, recognizing Martin, walked over to the group.

"You just got out of the NATO defense committee," he said. "How did it go?"[17]

Martin gave a brief summary of the proceedings.

Acheson observed that he, Marshall, and Harriman would meet tomorrow with President Truman to decide on US NATO policy. The key question concerned the inclusion of Germany. Should the United States tell the French that without German participation Western Europe could not be defended? Acheson then sharpened the issue. Without agreement on full German participation, should the United States inform France that the United States would defer action on a NATO command structure and call off General Eisenhower's trip to Europe? This, Gordon thought, would amount to a threat to dissolve NATO before it even got started. He had not dealt with Acheson before and did not know whether Acheson had already answered his own question and this was Acheson's way of testing his staff.

"Ed," said Acheson to Martin. "Do you think this is correct policy? Take as much time as you want before replying."

Martin reflected for what seemed to Gordon "an eon" before he replied in the affirmative.

"Are you absolutely sure of that answer?"

"Yes," Martin said after another pause. "I see no way of defending Europe without full German participation."

Acheson repeated the process with the other two State Department staff members and did the same with Gordon, achieving the same results in each instance.

"Well," said the secretary of state, shaking his head. "That is remarkable. Here we have four intelligent and well-informed experts on European defense who are absolutely sure that West Germany should have full participation in NATO. I think it's likely that tomorrow's meeting will join in that conclusion. But I'm far from certain that it's correct."[18]

Gordon reported to Harriman on the meeting and the after-meeting exchange. As it turned out, the meeting of the defense ministers, as well as the meeting with the president, took an unexpected turn. Acheson's formulation of the day before was rendered moot. The ever-inventive Jean Monnet had come up with an idea that deflected attention away from German participation in NATO. Dubbed the Pleven Plan (after French minister Rene Pleven), the plan called for the creation of a European Defense Community (EDC) outside of NATO. Monnet's scheme offered the prospect of making Germany subordinate to French commanders.[19] Moch had evidently tipped off Paris that the time was ripe to play the French card, and on October 24 he unveiled the Pleven Plan to the NATO defense ministers as the French alternative to German participation in NATO as it was simultaneously announced in Paris. Most American officials doubted whether the concept would be acceptable to French or German public opinion. Opposition from the French right and left was evident at the launching of the Pleven Plan. The right objected that the plan seemed to imply that French officers might be subject to some ill-defined control by other Europeans, and the left remained opposed to German rearmament in any form. The exact terms under which Germans would participate in the European force would have to be negotiated at another forum.

To the Germans the Pleven proposal merely postponed progress toward the restoration of full sovereignty for the Federal Republic. The other four members of the Coal and Steel Community—Italy, Belgium, Luxembourg, and the Netherlands—were invited to join the proposed European Defense Community along with the United Kingdom (the UK rejected the invitation). Americans objected that the Pleven Plan called for lower defense budgets than were envisaged under NATO, a virtual guarantee of an anemic military preparedness effort by the Europeans. The United States considered the French proposal a tactic designed to induce the United States to shoulder a larger share of the defense burden. Nevertheless, the French proposal offered a formula whereby a fracture in the alliance could be avoided, planning for a NATO command structure could proceed, and Eisenhower's morale-boosting trip to Europe could go forward. The NATO defense ministers unanimously agreed in a final communiqué that German forces would be included in the defense of Europe, preferably through implementation of the European Defense Community, but if that effort failed, Germany would then be admitted into full membership in NATO.

Organizational Issues

The November 1950 congressional elections added to Harriman's and Gordon's problems. The Republicans had not taken over Congress, as they had in 1946, but they had gained enough strength to alter the political climate, picking up five Senate seats and twenty-two House seats, which gave them a virtual veto on Senate action and greatly strengthened their position in the House of Representatives. It was not simply a question of numbers. The center of gravity in the political dialogue was shifting. The Republican eastern establishment and the internationally minded Democrats, as well as big business and labor, had been solidly behind the Marshall Plan, the UN, and postwar relief efforts. Now, what had been a noisy but politically ineffectual minority had suddenly become the dominant voices. The Taft wing of the Republican Party—the group Acheson dubbed the political primitive—went on the offensive. One of their targets was the existence of aid programs that had outlived their usefulness. Moderates from both parties supported calls for the Truman administration to straighten out the tangle of foreign aid programs—for economic, military, and technical assistance—with the aim of reorienting aid from economic assistance to military preparedness.

Harriman felt keenly the absence of the authority that he had enjoyed as the "theater commander" for the Marshall Plan in Europe. Under the ECA statute the special representative was subject only to the authority of the ECA administrator in Washington and the president. No one on the ECA Washington staff could issue orders to Harriman's staff in Paris, and Harriman took orders only from Hoffman himself. Any action taken by the Paris staff was based on policies set by Harriman. In the final stages of the EPU negotiations, after he had taken over from Harriman, Milton Katz had used the same authority to stand firm in the negotiations with the UK and Belgium. Now Harriman in the White House faced ambiguity. The NSC machinery was in a shambles. President Truman resented the efforts by Congress to box him in, though in 1950 he had begun to attend more NSC meetings. Truman had added Treasury Secretary John Snyder as an NSC member and frequently solicited his advice on foreign policy as well as more strictly Treasury business. Gordon saw that Harriman was troubled by his ambiguous status but never pushed the president and was invariably cordial and careful in his dealings with Snyder and other Truman favorites. He privately expressed doubts to Gordon about Snyder's capacities. What kind of an organizational game plan should Harriman adopt for his office in these circumstances? Harriman asked Gordon to reflect on this issue and come up with some ideas.

A November 14, 1950, Gordon memo to Harriman addressed the "Functions of Harriman Office." [20] Noting that "as you know a great deal of discussion is going on in the Budget Bureau, the Brookings Institution . . . and elsewhere on the formal functions which it might be desirable for your office to undertake," Gordon declared that he had not yet fully developed his ideas but did want to call attention to the administration's foreign aid programs as an area clearly needing direction by Harriman. Gordon discussed options for both aid to Europe and foreign aid programs for developing nations. He cautiously sketched a strategy for Harriman to make clear his and the president's priorities but to avoid getting too deeply entangled in operational matters. Harriman should wait until "inter-agency disputes are brought to us for resolution" or until he wanted to "take the initiative in organizing interdepartmental machinery," but without "committing the President or yourself until Presidential decisions become appropriate." But Gordon recommended against accepting the chairmanship of interdepartmental committees because it was too big a burden and would work against an honest broker role for the Harriman office. Harriman should be an arbiter, not one of the combatants with an organizational stake in interdepartmental turf battles. This recommendation was in line with Harriman's thinking. The office would mediate interdepartmental disputes through a structured process on behalf of the president.

As Congress imposed more restrictions on Marshall Plan funding, Harriman and Gordon were forced into more and more interdepartmental coordination. In the end they could not avoid congressional limits on the ECA's autonomy. Congress usually preferred the State Department over the ECA because it saw the latter as dragging its feet on converting economic to military assistance. In late 1950 President Truman approved the creation of a new interagency, the International Security Assistance Committee (ISAC), located in the State Department, to oversee the allocation of all economic, military, and technical assistance programs. At Acheson's suggestion, Thomas D. Cabot, president of the Cabot Corporation of Boston, was brought in to chair the new committee. Harriman was represented on the ISAC by Gordon, but State and Defense were the major players in the new system. The dominant policy thrust was to alter Marshall Plan priorities to security objectives. This new "arrangement enhanced the [State] department's authority at the expense of the ECA's autonomy, as did the organizational arrangements developed in Western Europe, where the ECA's mission chiefs and the special representative became subordinate functionaries on a number of rearmament committees directed primarily by officials from the State and Defense departments."[21]

The best that Harriman and Gordon could do to help Harriman's former ECA colleagues was to keep Congress from forcing the ECA to redirect everything to military purposes. Those from the ECA decided they could live with the compromise arrangement because they were still a separate and independent agency with White House backing and had the authority to reprogram up to 10 percent of military assistance funds. The ECA's fortunes, however, grew steadily worse as congressional pressures intensified. In 1951 the administration's strategy of combining military, economic, and technical assistance into one big omnibus bill—on the theory that economic assistance might stay below the radar and be less likely to be singled out for cuts—backfired. Congressional critics were emboldened and saw no reason for any further economic assistance at all in light of the urgent defense needs.

Harriman continued to be frustrated by the seeming uncertainty over his role, and his frustrations spilled over into questioning the performance of his own staff.[22] He pressed Gordon and other staff members to clarify their own roles. A January 24 memo by Gordon and legal adviser Ted Tannenwald spelled out the major areas the office was dealing with—NATO and Germany, foreign aid, strategic materials, export allocations and priorities, loan agencies (World Bank and Export-Import Bank), munitions assignments, and domestic economic stabilization. The memo specified the individuals assigned to each area and their respective roles in areas of joint responsibility. Harriman was a good administrator and asked his staff for reports spelling out what they were doing and how they allocated their time. He gave his people scope to exercise initiative, but he wanted to know what they were doing. He operated with a division of labor in the office. Gordon, for example, followed the Korean War "mainly as a spectator," did not deal with the press, and was not concerned with the Japanese Peace Treaty or other matters outside his own areas of responsibility. But he was drawn into the domestic implications of the war.

While he had a sense of orderliness, Harriman nonetheless did not stand on ceremony when he needed immediate input. From the miscellany of Gordon's reports and memos to his boss, Harriman clearly called on Gordon for his thoughts on numerous subjects and no doubt did the same with other staff members. Harriman was scheduled to have lunch with Paul Hoffman one day and wanted Gordon's opinion of Hoffman's just-published book. Gordon discovered a serious error about troop levels in the book that could be awkward for the US government but then found that one hundred thousand copies had already been printed. It would cost too much to issue an erratum, so he advised Harriman not to mention the problem. Harriman, always wanting to know everything, found out what Hoffman was doing at the Ford Foundation and sniffed out another bit of useful information: Hoffman was working on a plan to recruit Eisenhower to run for the Republican nomination in 1952.

Harriman's curiosity was seemingly limitless, but there was always a purpose to his thinking. The range of queries he addressed to Gordon was instructive of how he might attack a problem. He constantly would ask Gordon questions like: Why was the British Foreign Ministry so passive and seemingly paralyzed and unable to take a position on the Anglo-Iranian oil dispute? What was going on between the World Bank and the US Export-Import Bank, and why were they quarreling? What were the Canadians thinking on the political role of NATO? What was George Kennan's current view on the German question? How many French troops were now in Indochina, and what was the French strategy? The Harriman inquiries reflected the range of the assignments that the president might entrust to him. Harriman had an intuition that seemed to sense how a situation might evolve. This was one reason why Gordon stayed with Harriman: Gordon had received an offer from Foster to replace his friend Bissell as the number-three official in ECA headquarters when Bissell moved up to take Foster's old job as the number-two official. Gordon thought that the job would be more focused on management than on policy, and he was more interested in policy. Gordon brought issues to Harriman's attention, as well as responded to him. Sometimes Gordon urged specific action on Harriman, but more often he merely informed him of a problem, knowing that Harriman would have an instinct for what to do.

Harriman called and visited Gordon so frequently at home that Gordon's children have vivid recollections of him. Three-year-old Amy had a ready excuse for not doing a chore when her mother asked: "I can't; I have to talk to Averell." At a dinner party on one of Harriman's two official visits to Brazil during Gordon's tenure as US ambassador, Allison Gordon was exchanging small talk with guests when she noticed Harriman looking distracted. She turned to him, and he asked her, "How many miles of railroad track are there in Brazil?" She reported to her husband later that Harriman appeared miffed when she could not give the answer.

War Production Board Redux

Allison Gordon and their four children arrived in DC in November 1950, when their newly purchased home was ready for occupancy. On November 26, their first Sunday in the home, Lincoln was awakened by an early morning phone call from Harriman. "The Chinese have come into the

Korean war in force," Harriman said. "We have an entirely new international picture." Harriman told him the president was assembling his foreign policy and military advisers for a midmorning meeting, but Harriman was concerned about developments on the home front. The war could now last a long time and turn into a general war in Asia or even set off a conflict in Europe. There would be the same pressures that the country had faced in World War II: inflation, the need for price controls, allocation of scarce materials, export controls—in short, the kinds of issues Gordon had dealt with at the WPB. Harriman wanted Gordon to attend a crisis meeting on these issues that would take place that morning. The meeting would be chaired by Elmer Staats of the BOB, and Gordon was to call Ted Tannenwald and bring him along because legal issues would certainly come up.

On his way down to the meeting Gordon reflected on his wartime experience and the proposals he and his Harvard Business School colleagues Bertrand Fox and Stanley Teele had made in 1946 to the Munitions Board. He was ready with his recommendations: "We needed to think about painful war scenarios, focused on timely supplies to Korea, without delays in the rearmament of Europe or unintended curtailment of the civilian economy. . . . For several weeks, extending into early 1951, this challenge of partial industrial mobilization occupied most of my time."[23] Between this meeting and the end of February 1951, Gordon had a hand in creating the nineteen new staff and operating units in the federal government that dealt with industrial mobilization.[24]

Gordon continued to address the problems of defense production and industrial mobilization throughout 1951 and into 1952. He was invited to join the Defense Department and take a senior post in the Pentagon's war production programs but made clear his intention to remain with Harriman. The dispute over reconversion that had erupted toward the end of World War II was still vivid to him, and the situation did not look as favorable now in terms of the public support that would be needed to underpin the controls.

The Defense Production Act of 1950 (Public Law 81-774, September 8, 1950) provided the statutory basis for the family of new wartime agencies. The central component of the new system was the Office of Defense Mobilization (ODM), created by Executive Order 10193 of January 3, 1951. Charles E. Wilson of the General Electric Company was recruited to head the office. The ODM served as the umbrella group and a source of policy direction for the various operating units in the executive departments. Wilson shared Harriman's notion that a central staff unit should not be involved in day-to-day operations, but unlike Harriman's office, the ODM had significant powers spelled out in the executive order. Wilson had insisted on seeing the language of the executive order creating the office before agreeing to serve, and President Truman had accepted several changes that Wilson requested. Gordon became Harriman's liaison with the ODM, a task that kept him busy intermittently for the next year and a half.

On the surface the Korean War mobilization bore a close resemblance to that of World War II, and the administrative machinery even looked similar. The critical objectives were similar: to keep prices and wages in check, stabilize rents, allocate strategic raw materials to the most important uses, protect the critical sectors within the civilian economy, and increase production in heavy industry. The chief difference was that during World War II the government had operated within a framework of public support, and the willingness to sacrifice was widespread. The Korean War situation showed what could happen in the absence of broad public and interest group support. Organized labor, far from its World War II "no strike" pledge, fought the wage-stabilization programs from the start.[25] Important business groups, such as the National Association of Manufacturers and the US Chamber of Commerce, opposed direct price controls. The overall fortunes of the industrial mobilization effort waxed and waned with the state of the war. In the period immediately after the Chinese intervention, there was urgency, and the public was more inclined to accept controls and increased taxes. But as the war stabilized, the pressure for strong action diminished, and the burdens of taxes and government controls loomed larger. Mobilization became mixed with the wider ideological differences that divided the political parties and the country. The Republicans in Congress attacked the administration on every front—from its strategic policies to high taxes to specific economic controls.

What was called, somewhat portentously, the Great Debate began on December 20, 1950, when former president Herbert Hoover attacked the Truman administration's declaration of a state of national emergency and its plans for sending more American troops to West Germany. Hoover decried the ingratitude and the rising neutralist sentiment that he saw in

Europe and called for an end to US economic assistance, instead advocating a strong western hemispheric defense as the nation's guiding strategic concept.[26] Republican leaders in Congress did not embrace Hoover's extreme formulation, and Senator Robert A. Taft (R, Ohio) in February 1951 disavowed "those who think we can completely abandon the rest of the world." But Taft still criticized the administration's plan to station four new American army divisions in West Germany and made plain his distrust of entangling alliances abroad and a "garrison state" at home, choked with "unreasonable and arbitrary government regulations."[27] Senator Kenneth S. Wherry (R, Nebraska) had introduced Senate Resolution 8 in January, providing that "no ground forces of the United States should be assigned to duty in the European area for the purposes of the North Atlantic Treaty pending the adoption of a policy thereto by the Congress."[28]

The Truman administration argued that the president had the constitutional authority to deploy troops abroad without congressional authorization and declared that the situation called for urgent action. The administration got the Senate resolution reworded to approve the dispatch of the four divisions in April 1951, which brought to six the number of US divisions in West Germany. Meanwhile the troops in Korea were generally receiving adequate supplies, but the larger Cold War mobilization and rearmament program lagged behind schedule. Despite the urgent pleas of ODM chief Wilson to renew his broad powers, Congress in July 1951 scaled back the ODM's authority. As a result, the year 1951 "was both the apex and denouement of the Korean mobilization. . . . From that point forward, a whole list of economic and political contingencies combined to slow down the ongoing mobilization effort."[29] Charles Wilson continued to battle Congress, strikes, erstwhile business allies, executive branch colleagues, foreign governments, and public hostility to controls for the rest of 1951 and into the new year, until the impending steel workers' strike threatened to paralyze the nation. He resigned when President Truman did not accept his advice to settle with the steel workers. In 1953 President Eisenhower dismantled the whole tottering edifice of the Korean War controls.

The Wise Men and NATO Institutional Reforms

The Korean military situation had stabilized by the summer of 1951. General Ridgway's brilliant generalship had rallied US forces and reversed the retreat begun in the wake of the massive Chinese entry into the war. The firing of MacArthur in April, strongly supported by Harriman, had produced tumultuous protests but in the end yielded widespread support for the president. Removing MacArthur had calmed some European nerves. Nevertheless, the political atmosphere for settling the issue of Europe's commitment to NATO was still not favorable. The noisy dialogue between the administration and congressional critics was amplified when it echoed across the Atlantic and mixed with the equally volatile European political dialogue. Whereas the Marshall Plan had produced a virtuous circle of reinforcing attitudes, the transatlantic dialogue now was different. Public tensions were exacerbated, and this complicated the prospects for agreement among leaders. Inflation had accelerated rapidly in Europe since mid-1950, 20 percent in France and 9–10 percent in Britain, Italy, and Germany. The hoped-for productivity gains in Europe had not materialized despite strong efforts by ECA planners to push programs of technical assistance. Europeans felt that they were being pushed by Americans to use scarce resources for rearmament even as the threat of sudden Soviet military action had diminished.

The problems were manifested in the glacial pace of European rearmament efforts and foot-dragging on financial commitments. General Eisenhower wanted a relatively modest grant from the French government to refurbish NATO's Supreme Headquarters Allied Powers Europe (SHAPE) to house European NATO officials, but the French demurred and told him to use ECA funds. OSR head Katz engaged in arduous negotiations before he could convince French officials that Congress would balk at having to supply $10 million when total US aid to France had already exceeded $1 billion. Troop levels proposed by the European NATO member states came in far below what the Americans considered the necessary minimum. The US decision to deploy more troops to West Germany helped strengthen NATO's capabilities but reinforced the perception that if the Europeans merely stalled, the Americans would do everything on their own.

In launching NATO, in Gordon's view, the United States had forgotten the lessons of the Marshall Plan. The Marshall Plan had been an effort to help the Europeans to help themselves achieve economic recovery within a specified period of time. The Europeans assessed their needs through the mechanism of the OEEC and came up with a plan that they presented to the Americans. The most pressing national problems at the time were the major Europe-wide difficulties of stabilizing currencies and reviving trade. Hence there were strong incentives for acting in concert. The United States agreed to provide such assistance as it could to help Europe deal with its mutually agreed-upon needs. For reasons of administrative convenience as well as program effectiveness, the United States chose to deal with the Europeans collectively, not through bilateral negotiations with each nation. With NATO, the United Sates took the opposite course. It did not wait for an assessment of the threat by the Europeans. The predictable result was that the European governments did not share fully the US assessment.

The NATO defense ministerial meeting that took place in Washington in October 1950, besides adopting the French compromise on German rearmament, had also directed the NATO member states to develop quantitative projections of their defense forces for the next four years. The NATO states were to specify the numbers of infantry and mechanized troop divisions, air combat wings, warships, and submarines, all with weapons, ammunition, and equipment—and indicate which were to be produced domestically and which purchased offshore. They were to present their reports to a NATO meeting in Ottawa scheduled for September 1951. The Ottawa meeting included each country's foreign, defense, and finance ministers. In the case of the United States, Harriman attended as a fourth official delegate in the role of a second secretary of state to assist the overburdened Acheson. Gordon attended as Harriman's deputy. Early in the Ottawa deliberations it became evident, as Gordon put it, that "NATO faced a new kind of existential threat." The sum of the national projections "was far below the minimum needed for Western Europe's effective defense."[30]

To resolve the crisis, the delegates turned to the device of appointing a steering committee of "Wise Men" to come up with a formula for determining European troop commitments. The Wise Men would recommend a plan to a wider "Temporary Control Committee," which would give or withhold approval and submit the plan for a formal vote at the Lisbon ministerial meeting scheduled for February 1952. The Wise Men concept was slightly different from the OEEC formula for distributing Marshall Plan aid. This group of Wise Men included an American in the person of Averell Harriman, with Edwin Plowden of the UK and Jean Monnet of

France as the other two members. Gordon was Harriman's deputy, with Eric Roll as Plowden's deputy and Pierre Uri as Monnet's.

The Wise Men and their deputies assembled in Paris the month after the Ottawa meeting, hoping to finish their work by Christmas. They worked hard, but there were some light moments. The three deputies styled themselves as the "working group" in their early deliberations, only to encounter a rebuff from their bosses. Did these uppity staffers think they were the only ones doing any work? The three deputies privately consoled themselves by adopting the sobriquet of "*les miserables.*" On the occasion of a visit to SHAPE headquarters, the principals and their deputies needed a full-time liaison officer from General Eisenhower's staff. Harriman mentioned that they might be assigned a certain British colonel.

"No, no, no," Monnet said. "He is too wooden and dull. We must ask for that 'Greenpastures.' I like that Greenpastures."[31]

Momentarily puzzled, the Americans soon surmised that Monnet was referring to Lieutenant Colonel Andrew Goodpaster, an enterprising young officer on Eisenhower's staff. The Wise Men and the wise deputies worked together very closely and effectively as a team through nearly three months of "exhausting as well as exhaustive" meetings. The choice of Goodpaster was most fortunate. Goodpaster was an exceptionally able officer and contributed greatly to the success of the endeavor.

The task was, as Gordon described it in his memoir, to "reconcile the requirements of collective security with the political and economic capacities of the member countries." This was like "directing us to square the circle." As it turned out, they could not square the circle. Despite their hard work "it became obvious that we could not close the shortfall between stated requirements for military mobilization and . . . there was no politically feasible way of closing the gap or even coming close." The sense of imminent danger in Europe was receding. Economic recovery, West German political stability, and Soviet political blunders combined to reduce the threat of internal subversion. The gap between European and American perceptions of the threat could not be papered over.

Gordon was struck by the split within Europe on both the German question and the issue of European unity. One episode brought the division home to Gordon as he was preparing the draft report for the Wise Men to present at the Lisbon ministerial meeting. He was working at a conference table with columns of troop figures in front of him. Herve Alphand, France's deputy foreign minister, entered the room looking for Monnet. Monnet was in the habit of conferring daily with Gordon and sometimes worked through the whole day with his American and British counterparts. Gordon told Alphand that Monnet was due shortly. Alphand inquired what Gordon was doing and walked over to his side, his eye running down the column of figures. When he came to the word "Germany," he exploded in a torrent of French and English epithets.

"You, Lincoln Gordon," he shouted. "You've never believed in the EDC! Germany is not a member of NATO and never will be!"

He grabbed Gordon by the shoulders and began shaking him. Gordon pointed out heatedly that the October 1950 ministerial meeting in Washington had provided for standby NATO membership if the EDC failed. Alphand was in a rage, and the two men wrestled and stormed at each other.

Monnet entered the room at this point and exclaimed, "Herve, what's all this shouting about?"

"It's this Lincoln Gordon," said Alphand. "He never believed in the European army and probably never will."[32]

Monnet continued in a stream of rapid French that Gordon only half understood, but he could scarcely believe what he did understand. Monnet calmed and reassured Alphand by telling him that the numbers of French troops or German troops was of no importance. In a few years there would only be European troops. Nationalities would disappear, and in a few years a European consciousness would unite all of Europe.

If the Wise Men could not square the circle, what could they say in their report for the Lisbon meeting? Harriman solved the problem in two ways. First, he directed Gordon "to draft the report as if the military requirements could almost be met but with small type footnotes indicating that any unmet portion in Years I and II would be added to requirements for years III and IV." Goals would be bold but timetables flexible. Second, Gordon was to include a series of institutional recommendations for strengthening NATO that would compensate for the weaknesses in the force levels and defense budgets in the report. The reform ideas emerging from Lieutenant Colonel Goodpaster and SHAPE headquarters and from national working groups were part of the Wise Men recommendations. The participation of national colleagues was crucial to the formal adoption of the ideas by those same colleagues later. The institutional recommendations included moving NATO headquarters from London to Paris, converting the NATO Council into a full-time body with national representatives at the rank of ambassador, and creating a permanent executive with a prominent European designated as NATO secretary general. Harriman and Gordon had a hand in identifying General William Draper as the first American in the US council post and designated Gordon to back him up in the diplomatic aspects of his work as Washington liaison.

The Americans wanted Sir Oliver Franks, British ambassador to the United States, as the first secretary general but were happy to accept the appointment of retired General Hastings "Pug" Ismay, Churchill's wartime chief of staff. The organizational reforms also included the concept of strengthening NATO's "infrastructure" in the form of headquarters facilities, communications, airfields, depots, and roads and transport. The outlays for infrastructure were largely supplied by the United States and justified as bolstering the effectiveness of the American forces stationed in Europe. The Harriman-Plowden-Monnet report finessed the European Defense Community issue again by endorsing the treaty, then approaching a vote in a number of European parliaments, but providing preliminary figures for a German contribution to NATO. The report was published in December and enthusiastically endorsed at Lisbon in February 1952. Secretary of State Acheson, not normally given to overstatement, enthusiastically told the president: "We have something pretty close to a grand slam."[33]

The contribution to NATO's structure was, in Gordon's mind, the main accomplishment of his service with Harriman in the White House: "The [group of Wise Men] had not done all that its terms of reference called for, but it had given NATO sufficient institutional substance to carry it successfully through its dangerous infancy." NATO historian Lawrence S. Kaplan makes a similar point on the significance of Lisbon: "Notwithstanding the hyperbole of the language of Lisbon and the rapid dissipation of most of its promises, the meeting was a watershed for NATO. By 1952 both U.S. aid and the organization it served had expanded in size and scope in a manner not anticipated in 1949. NATO moved from a treaty of alliance to a military organization with a headquarters in Paris. . . . The system seemed to work, whether or not the specific figures of the Lisbon meeting were ever realized."[34]

11

London: A Respite

Our small White House staff received new titles and a few additional high-ranking officials were added, but aid coordination was not a matter of urgency. On that front, unlike Korea and the NATO build-up, significant innovations would have to await a new administration.
—Lincoln Gordon, 2005

Dad once told me that London was his "'least demanding' assignment."
—Robert W. Gordon, 2009

Although the calendar was crammed with intra-Embassy meetings and calls on British Ministers and high officials . . . there were no protracted negotiating crises in the economic area as there had been in the Paris and Washington years with NATO financing or the European Payments Union.
—Lincoln Gordon, 2005

After Lisbon, Gordon set out "to push the military assistance program somewhere near the agreed military goals, even though we knew at the time they were probably too big to be realized. They certainly couldn't be achieved on the time table set out at Lisbon."[1] As it turned out, the goals were never to be achieved. In a shift of strategy the Eisenhower administration adopted the "new look," which introduced tactical nuclear weapons into military planning as a cheaper alternative to increased American troop commitments.[2] Gordon's circumstances changed suddenly in March, when President Truman announced that he would not seek another term. Intense activity connected with the presidential nominating conventions followed. The campaigning, together with the crisis over the steel strike and the president's decision to forego a settlement and instead seize the nation's steel mills, which dominated the news, contributed to an atmosphere of deadlock in Washington and lame-duck status for the administration.

Harriman's presidential ambitions were stirred when Truman decided not to run again. Harriman began spending a large amount of his time on his campaign after calling his staff together to tell them of his plans. The staff had become considerably bigger with the addition of various coordinating responsibilities imposed by Congress with respect to the numerous military assistance programs. Harriman told his assembled staff that he had decided to run for the presidency.

"You're all subject to the Hatch Act," he told them. "I want people to respect it absolutely."

"It was typical of him," Gordon wrote in his draft memoir. "He had absolute integrity in these matters. He said, 'if anybody wants to work on my campaign, he should resign from the government and I'll be glad to hire him at the Harriman for President Committee.'" Only one staff member, Harriman's press officer James I. Lanigan, switched to the campaign staff.[3] Lanigan later went with Harriman to Albany as his press secretary when Harriman was elected governor of New York, defeating Senator Irving Ives, the Republican nominee. If Gordon was at all tempted to join the campaign staff, he did not say so in his draft memoir, and it was not likely, given his distaste for politics. Harriman for his part seems to have compartmentalized his political people and his policy people and viewed Gordon in the latter category. President Truman apparently regarded Harriman at this time in something of the same light.

When Harriman made his decision to run, he did so without seeking Truman's endorsement because he was not sure the president would give it. Truman made it a practice, as did Harriman himself, of keeping his political advisers separate from his policy advisers. When discussing his political strategies, Truman did not want his policy staff present. Harriman knew he had the president's confidence and indeed that he ranked highly—perhaps just below Acheson and Marshall—in Truman's general esteem. He had given generously to Truman's 1948 reelection campaign, ranking behind only Louis Johnson as a donor. But Harriman also knew that Truman had many old friends and cronies from a lifetime in politics and that the president's political instincts had been forged in a background profoundly different from his own. As one of America's richest men, Harriman had no worries over the fundraising to launch his campaign, but his money was also a problem for a Democratic politician. He could be cast as a Wall Streeter and plutocrat.

After he had decided not to run again, Truman sought a successor on the Democratic ticket who would maximize the chances of winning and carrying forward the New Deal/Fair Deal tradition. He entertained some hopes that his old friend Fred Vinson might be talked into the race but quickly abandoned that notion. Truman judged Harriman as "the ablest of them all" but considered that he would be severely hurt by his Wall Street background and by the fact that he had never run for office before.[4] In Truman's memoir he describes his thinking at the time: "There were a number of other good men who were frankly candidates for the Democratic nomination. I understood well enough that historically no candidate could be certain of nomination by the party in power unless he had the support of the President in the White House. I therefore gave careful study and consideration to each of the candidates. . . . The more I weighed the situation, the more apparent it became that Governor Stevenson seemed best qualified on the basis of background, experience, and broad capacity."[5] Yet he gave Harriman a glowing tribute:

> One of the ablest and most deserving contenders for the nomination was Averell Harriman. His record of government service was long and distinguished. Harriman had served in many important posts during the critical war and postwar years. His work in the handling of Lend-Lease from London was outstanding. He served brilliantly as Ambassador to Russia and Great Britain. He was a very able Secretary of Commerce in my Cabinet and did a great job of administering the Marshall Plan in Europe. I held Harriman in the highest regard, and still do, but I felt that with his limited experience in elective politics and no experience in campaigning for an elective office he was somewhat handicapped at this particular time.[6]

Stevenson was a fresh face, had run an outstanding campaign for the Illinois governorship, was an eloquent speaker, and was clearly in the liberal New Deal tradition. But when Truman reached out to Stevenson and tried to get him to jump into the race, the president was frustrated by Stevenson's procrastination. Senator Estes Kefauver of Tennessee, a man whom Truman instinctively disliked and distrusted, as did most party regulars, jumped off to a commanding lead in the primaries and the delegate count. Alarmed, Truman hinted that Senator Alban Barkley would be preferable to the Tennessean but quickly realized that Barkley was not a likely candidate. Truman was surprised, meanwhile, by how vigorously Harriman was championing the New Deal tradition.[7] When someone suggested that Harriman was an inexperienced campaigner and could not sustain his effort, Truman remarked, "You never know what's in you until you have to do it."[8]

On the eve of the Democratic convention, the delegate count stood at Kefauver with 257, or almost halfway to the nomination, Senator Richard Russell of Georgia with 161, Harriman with 112, and Stevenson with a woeful 41.[9] At this point Stevenson finally informed Truman that he wanted to put his name in nomination and asked whether the president would have any objections. Truman replied, "I have been trying since January to get you to say that."[10] The president publicly affirmed his support for Stevenson and swung the Missouri delegation in line behind the Illinois governor.

While his own position was clear, Truman made it plain that he had no objection when party leaders approached him about their backing for Harriman. Truman spoke in similar fashion when Harriman sought a meeting with him shortly before the convention and asked if the president would object to the New York delegation placing Harriman's name in nomination. He told Harriman that of course he had no objection but affirmed that he was committed to Stevenson. He elicited from Harriman a pledge that Harriman would play a constructive role in releasing his delegates and helping to choose the nominee if his own bid fell short.

On the first ballot Kefauver remained in the lead with 340 delegates, Stevenson surged to 273, Russell had 268, and Harriman stood at 123.[11] Stevenson gained on the second ballot, but the outcome was still very much in doubt. Truman decided to send word to the governors of Massachusetts and Arkansas to release their favorite-son delegations to Stevenson on the third ballot and sent word to Harriman to release his delegates. Harriman had already decided to withdraw in favor of Stevenson, a move that was a decisive turning point for Stevenson. Truman was impressed with Harriman's performance throughout the campaign and the convention and was doubly impressed when Harriman swept to victory in the 1954 New York gubernatorial election. Fed up with Stevenson's hesitation, he backed Harriman unsuccessfully for the presidential nomination in 1956, saying that the country needed a president who wanted the job and that Stevenson "lacks the kind of fighting spirit we need to win."[12]

An Opportunity Arises in London

With the Korean armistice talks stalemated, the European situation in a lull awaiting the outcome of ratification votes by six nations on the European Defense Community, and the domestic focus on presidential politics, Gordon found himself in a holding pattern. He "began thinking about another change in working . . . responsibilities." With Eisenhower a likely Republican presidential winner, policy-level positions would mostly go to Republicans. Could he stay below the radar and remain in government? He had no desire to start over as a relatively junior Foreign Service officer or in some other similar capacity. Politics had not been a factor in his work during World War II, at the UN Atomic Energy Commission, or with the Marshall Plan. He had been on the policy side with Harriman, not the political side, but he was certainly a Democrat. As he reflected on the future, he learned that his first boss at the WPB, Bill Batt, currently economics counselor and military assistance officer at the US embassy in London, had decided to retire. Somebody, possibly Batt himself, bruited Gordon's name as a successor.

This was an intriguing prospect. Gordon talked it over with Allison and found her enthusiastic. She had felt that they were just getting accustomed to Paris and Europe when the Korean War broke out. She had enjoyed the brief period the family spent in London in the summer of 1950. Gordon had enjoyed his Rhodes days, and he now felt that he should jump at this opportunity. Besides, it would get him out of Washington and the turmoil and uncertainty of the presidential transition. When Harriman returned from the Chicago convention, Gordon raised the matter.

"Look," Harriman said. "I'm all in favor of this, but I must warn you that there's no tenure to this job. Much as we love Adlai Stevenson, we all know that against Ike he can't be elected president."[13]

Gordon decided to take the chance. He encountered some opposition within the State Department because of his relative youth and lack of management experience, but with Harriman's strong backing he was approved for the post. Batt was delighted and asked that Gordon fly to London for a week so that Batt could show him the ropes and introduce him to important British colleagues. In September Gordon flew to London and spent a week with Batt. He returned in time to help Allison with the final preparations for the move. They sold their Washington home. They decided to travel via ocean liner to have a relaxed period with the children before he took up his new duties. They set sail in late September with Anne, twelve, Bob, eleven, Hugh, seven, and Amy, three.

Gordon's job title included the role of country mission chief for what remained of the Marshall Plan (now as director of mutual security in the Mutual Security Administration, the successor agency to the ECA) and that of economics counselor for the US embassy. The mutual security program included residues of Marshall Plan economic aid but was mainly oriented toward direct NATO support programs. The immediate thrust for Gordon was toward "offshore procurement." By January 1953 Gordon had negotiated an agreement on Centurion tanks, redirected 90 percent of counterpart funds to military assistance, and made progress on several major procurement actions.[14] Under offshore procurement, the United States paid a British contractor for a military item, for example, the Centurion tanks, from military assistance funds and then had the item delivered to the armed forces of a European NATO ally.

Although his embassy calendar was crammed, "there were no protracted negotiating crises in the economic area as there had been in the Paris and Washington years with NATO financing or the European Payments Union." He told his son Bob years later that the London assignment was the "least demanding" one of his professional life. The time in London was pleasant, busy, and filled with an engaging social life. Allison and Lincoln typically went out four to five times a week to social engagements, usually black-tie affairs and occasionally in full formal white tie and tails for the men and gowns for the women. Allison especially warmed to the social and cultural life of London. The conservatives were in power, the sterling and Commonwealth crises had receded, and a comfortable complacency and even a festive atmosphere pervaded the nation as the coronation of Queen Elizabeth II in June 1953 approached.

Yet for Lincoln something was missing. It was the very lack of crises, the absence of being a participant in historical events, that bothered him. With Harriman the job may have been nerve-racking at times, but it was never dull. Gordon liked the US ambassador in London, Winthrop Aldrich: "Winthrop Aldrich as boss—better than reputation—altho naïve on contact with Labor Party."[15] Working for Aldrich, however, was not the same as working for Harriman. Even in his academic work—interviewing for and writing his Oxford dissertation and composing his share of the 836-page book with Fainsod—Gordon had operated under pressure and was evidently comfortable working at a furious pace. As noted earlier, in his 1936 critique of Leslie Howard's portrayal of Hamlet, Gordon had remarked that Howard lacked "intensity" and was therefore merely flaccid. Intensity was important to him, but so was the discipline to control it.

Early in his London tenure Gordon showed himself to be thin-skinned by getting involved in an unnecessary dispute with the chief executive officer of a midwestern US manufacturing company. The US embassy in 1953 was searching for properties that could be purchased at a reasonable price to house embassy personnel. With four children Gordon was high on the list of those who needed more spacious quarters. The apartment where the Gordons lived, which the embassy had rented for Gordon's predecessors, had three bedrooms, was comfortable, and was conveniently located. For the Gordon family, however, it was a tight squeeze. The embassy thus acquired a house with five bedrooms plus a maid's room. The purchase was noted on the inside pages of the London newspapers, including the price and the fact that the first occupants would be embassy official Lincoln Gordon and his family. Soon after, Gordon received a letter from a friend with a clipping enclosed from the newsletter of an American company in the Midwest—an internal publication distributed to stockholders and employees. An article by the company's CEO criticized the purchase of an aristocratic home for "a Harvard professor on leave serving as head of the U.S. aid mission. In addition to squandering billions of our tax proceeds on aid to a socialist government, why does the professor think he has to live like a lord?"[16]

The article carried a photo of the house that had been cropped to disguise the fact that it was a semiattached structure at the end of a row of flats. Gordon should have consulted the embassy's press officer for advice, but "this was my first . . . diplomatic post and I was not yet accustomed to public slander."[17] He sent an angry letter to the editor of the company publication demanding a correction about the cropped photo and a personal apology from the CEO. The editor sent back a "retraction" that compounded the problem from Gordon's point of view. Gordon rejected it as totally unacceptable. He finally learned that the CEO had consulted the company's outside counsel, who had been on the WPB's legal staff during the war, and the lawyer settled the issue.

The Breach with R. H. S. Crossman

Another painful episode involved a public spat with Dick Crossman, Gordon's best British friend from his Oxford days. Gordon was delighted on his arrival in London to renew acquaintance with many British friends and colleagues. His friends from Oxford were largely on the political left, including Dick Crossman, now a Labor Party member of parliament who had moved decidedly to the left wing of the party. Labor was out of power by the time Gordon arrived in London, but Labor MPs were a source of spirited criticism of American policy, and Gordon remembered the trouble that Hugh Gaitskell had caused in nearly scuttling the European Payment Union in 1950. How his dispute with Crosswell got started is not entirely clear. Gordon may have left Crossman off the guest list for an embassy function, which nettled Crossman. In any event, Crossman needled the United States vigorously in parliamentary debate, and the British press picked up on the attack on US policy. Gordon noticed Crossman's sharp criticisms of American policy in the parliamentary debate of July 29, 1953, which included the statement that "it is about time the aircraft industry realized that contracts without appropriations mean nothing in America." Crossman also warned that the UK armaments industry should not believe that Congress would necessarily provide the appropriations.[18] In general Gordon disliked and distrusted the left wing of the Labor Party. At this point the Centurion tank deal was still in process, and Gordon was also negotiating an extensive aircraft purchase. The attack by Crossman angered Gordon, and he fired off a letter to the editor of the *Times* that was published on August 4.[19]

"I wish to call attention," Gordon wrote, "to a serious misstatement of fact concerning the so-called 'Offshore Procurement Programme' for the purchase of supplies in this country by the United States . . . made by Mr.

R. H. S. Crossman." He pointed out that there was in fact already a congressional appropriation for the Centurion tank purchase and declared that negotiations could not begin without a prior appropriation. Crossman shot back the next day: "Mr. Lincoln Gordon's correction of my account of American procurement procedure, which I gratefully acknowledge, does not affect the main point I was making in the defense debate of July 29—namely, that it is not desirable either to accept direct military aid or to rely on offshore purchases in order to maintain an arms production greater than we can afford out of our own resources."[20] Crossman's implication that Gordon was going out of his way to cavil at a minor point stung Gordon, who evidently still had not developed the thick skin required for high-profile public debate. Gordon's voluminous correspondence and the notes he made on his many trips to the UK reveal no contact with Crossman after the 1953 incident.

McCarthyism and Stassen

A more complex problem arose for Gordon and his colleagues in Senator Joseph McCarthy's attacks on communists in the State Department. Ambassador Winthrop Aldrich was so incensed by McCarthy's attacks that he made a special trip back to Washington at his own expense to call on President Eisenhower, a personal friend, to protest the administration's seeming passivity in the face of McCarthy's tactics. He returned shaken by the president's inability or unwillingness to confront McCarthy. Meanwhile Mutual Security Agency (MSA) director Harold Stassen had asked all US embassies in Europe to assess how the McCarthy phenomenon was affecting each embassy's relations with its host government. Aldrich asked Gordon and the deputy chief of mission Julius Holmes to prepare a joint memo responding to the Stassen request. The two men prepared a strong confidential memorandum condemning McCarthy's tactics, which Aldrich strengthened even further before sending it to Washington.

The issue became concrete for Gordon when George Woodbridge, a midlevel economic analyst on his staff, was terminated under a new MSA policy initiated by MSA head Harold Stassen. Stassen, the former governor of Minnesota, was a liberal Republican in the tradition of midwestern progressivism. He had graduated from high school at age fourteen and gone on to the University of Minnesota and then its law school. He had been elected as a crusading district attorney of Dakota County in 1930 at age twenty-three and as governor in 1938. In 1953 Stassen was the only senior Eisenhower official willing to stand up publicly to Senator McCarthy. Although McCarthy had supported Stassen's presidential bid in 1948, as mutual security administrator Stassen had quickly concluded that McCarthy intended to continue the same harassing tactics against the Eisenhower administration that he had employed against the Truman administration. Stassen was particularly incensed by McCarthy's actions in investigating Greek ship owners, because the MSA was then engaged in delicate negotiations with the British and French to ban the use of British and French ports for stopovers, services, or maintenance by any vessels engaged in unauthorized shipment of strategic materials to communist nations. In testimony before McCarthy's subcommittee on foreign aid, Stassen confronted McCarthy and told him that the subcommittee's actions could "undermine" the administration's policy of cutting off trade with the communist bloc. The Stassen-McCarthy clash became the prime topic of an April 2, 1953, presidential press conference.[21] In a classic demonstration of his genius for circumlocution to disarm the press, Eisenhower declared that had he been doing the testifying, he probably would not have used the word "undermine," even though of course it was undeniable that the president and the State Department were the ones duly empowered to negotiate agreements with other governments. Perhaps the word "infringe" would have been appropriate. He was sure that Stassen had probably meant to use the word "infringe" to caution Congress against overstepping its role and exercising executive functions.

The Eisenhower administration meanwhile had embarked on a substantial reorganization of foreign aid operations at Stassen's direction. Under Reorganization Plan 7 of 1953, the new Foreign Operations Administration (FOA) had replaced the old MSA and centralized all foreign aid operations. The reorganization provided a simpler management structure for foreign aid, and Stassen proved to be a strong administrator: "He significantly increased the use of universities and charitable organizations in program implementation and instituted controversial, short-lived screening of personnel long-remembered as the 'Stassenization program,' which moved a number of others out of the agency."[22] The difficulty was that Stassen had to carry through the reorganization at a time of reduced budgets. This meant that he was "in the awkward position of having to carry out the dismantling of the program at the same time that he was warning the Senate Appropriations Committee that the United States would have to continue giving aid to free nations for the 10 years that he expected the Soviet threat to last."[23]

In this context of McCarthyism and reorganization, Gordon clashed with Harold Stassen. The screening of personnel that was part of Stassen's reorganization had blurred the lines between someone released for reasons of downsizing and someone fired on loyalty grounds. Stassen, evidently fearing more attacks by McCarthy, thought he could fend off McCarthy's onslaught by his own house-cleaning. There was trouble in the Paris embassy over the dismissal of seven employees, at least one of whom was apparently dismissed under Stassen's loyalty guidelines. Henry Labouisse, Gordon's counterpart in the US Paris embassy, appealed to Stassen and won reversals in the case of three of his seven dismissed employees. Gordon decided he would make a similar appeal in the case of the dismissed Woodbridge, his economics analyst. Gordon had no close friend at headquarters now to whom he could turn for advice and assistance. Gordon called Stassen's deputy and asked for an appointment with Stassen during a scheduled visit to Washington to discuss the Woodbridge case. Gordon saw Stassen in a number of group meetings but could not get a personal interview to discuss the case. Finally he collared Stassen at the end of a group meeting and asked for an appointment. Stassen said that since they were both scheduled to fly to London on the same flight, they should sit together and discuss the matter then. On the flight Stassen was sympathetic but made no commitment. He did promise to review the file and make a new assessment of the case. After the review, he did not change his mind, and Gordon's analyst was dismissed.

Gordon seethed. He decided to resign and asked Allison how she would feel if he did so. She told him to do what he felt was right. Gordon arranged a meeting with Aldrich and deputy chief of mission Holmes to tell them of his intentions.

"You know our views on this appalling treatment by Stassen," Aldrich said. "He is dismissing dozens of employees without stated cause other than the need for a reduction in force. This brands them all as possibly disloyal citizens. So your impulse to resign is understandable. But consider . . . your resignation will make a one-day article in the *Washington*

Post and the *New York Times.* But as a high-ranking official, your influence might help tilt the balance back toward sanity."[24]

Aldrich and Holmes argued that Gordon would not stop McCarthy or accomplish anything very useful if he resigned. If Gordon stayed on the job, he could accomplish much more in broad policy terms and even help stop McCarthy. Between April and June 1954 McCarthy in effect destroyed himself by launching an ill-advised attack on the Department of the Army. Secretary Dulles, President Eisenhower, most of McCarthy's Senate colleagues, and the public turned against McCarthy. On December 1954, after a lengthy Senate debate, McCarthy was "condemned" by his Senate colleagues by a vote of sixty-seven to twenty-two. The only senator not voting was John F. Kennedy of Massachusetts, who was hospitalized for back surgery. McCarthy continued to haunt the Senate corridors for another two and a half years, largely shunned by his colleagues and drinking heavily until he died of hepatitis in May 1957 at the age of forty-eight.

After deciding to stay on the job, Gordon made an effort to reopen lines of communication with Stassen and to influence policy. He had become interested in Britain's Colombo Plan, a program of technical and economic assistance to British colonies in South and Southwest Asia. Gordon was impressed that, even though Britain's own postwar economic recovery was still incomplete, it was thinking constructively about how to improve the prospects for success in decolonization and how to promote Third World economic development. Accordingly, he proposed a study of potential US cooperation in some fashion with Britain in the Colombo Plan. He was already thinking about something akin to the Marshall Plan for certain developing countries. Stassen was enthusiastic and sought cabinet approval for Gordon's idea but was stymied by strong opposition from Secretary of the Treasury George Humphrey. Humphrey's position was that investment in developing nations was best left in the hands of businessmen, who would invest if market conditions were favorable. With this rebuff, "our mission in London seemed increasingly routinized and distant from the major issues of world policy."[25]

The Pleasant Side of Life in London

If the work in London was not as exciting as earlier assignments, there were compensations from the standpoint of family life. The less frenetic pace gave the Gordons the opportunity for "close and memorable family experiences, especially on holidays away from London." Gordon was in London most of the time, and when he did travel it was mainly on short trips to Paris, Bonn, and other European capitals. Allison enjoyed London and felt more a part of Lincoln's life. The family traveled frequently by car to explore the British and Scottish countryside, enjoyed the festivities of the June 1953 coronation of Queen Elizabeth II, and made a number of excursions to the continent. Their first Christmas in England provided a memorable vacation. The family set off to Devonshire and Cornwall, circling back through the moors of Dunmore, which had many untethered but friendly dogs, and ended up in Chulmleigh, a picturesque and pleasant village, for Christmas. On Christmas morning they hiked to a nearby hill with a model plane designed and built by Bob, where they opened their presents and flew the model plane in unseasonably mild winter weather. They hiked back to the village for a late lunch, in the middle of which they were interrupted by the excited innkeeper. "A long-distance call from America!" It was Bill Batt calling with a Christmas present for his successor. He explained that he had talked with a number of other Republican bigwigs, and he could declare firmly that Gordon would stay on through the change of administration. The family's excursions to the continent included a trip to Bremen, Switzerland, on the eastern end of Lake Lucerne, where Lincoln trekked with his children on several mountain hikes and a strenuous weeklong bicycle trip through the Netherlands and Belgium at Easter time in 1955.

Allison and Lincoln enjoyed the busy social life in London, which sometimes was pleasantly combined with his diplomatic duties. On a rare free Saturday evening they were looking forward to relaxing when both of them noted an item in the papers announcing the appointment of a new minister of international trade, a subcabinet post that would apparently have an impact on trade policy. Lincoln suggested that they should invite the new minister and his wife for an informal embassy dinner for four. The couple turned out to be delightful guests. The new minister's wife had been an enthusiastic chorister at Oxford and was now a member of the Bach Choral Society. Lincoln's passion for choral singing was triggered, and it was agreed that the woman would contact the choral director and arrange for Lincoln to meet with him. The next morning, however, getting cold feet, Gordon tried out his voice at the piano and rapidly came to the conclusion that twenty years of pipe smoking had ruined his voice. He called his new friend and begged off with profuse apologies. She would have none of it. He should surely at least meet with the director and would soon discover he was merely having a case of preperformance jitters. He did not join the choral society, although he did come up with a different musical interest instead. Music was one of his great loves, and he decided to take up an instrument instead of singing. But what instrument? His choice quickly fell on the cello. This instrument was more forgiving if one missed a note in the lower register. With the help of the chorister wife of the trade minister, he was put in touch with a young British cellist in the national symphony who had an excellent record for teaching adult students. So at age forty, Lincoln took up the cello, a decision "which led me into decades of near-addiction as an amateur cellist." He somehow found time to practice three hours on most days when he was not traveling and became an accomplished amateur player.

Moving On

Despite the pleasantness, Gordon determined that he could not postpone his future. He was too old for a junior position in the diplomatic ranks. He was at too high a rank to find any comparable position elsewhere in government service. He did not relish being a foot soldier unless the commander was a Marshall or a Harriman and unless he had some opportunity to make his voice heard in some meaningful fashion. He was an intellectual, but he had been absent from his teaching duties for the better part of the past decade. His children were growing older and would soon be ready to college. How could he afford to educate them? One great crisis after another had led to interesting jobs. More "normal" times meant fewer such jobs and probably more rigid employment settings. To whom could he turn for advice? This was not a matter for Allison, not right now, anyway, before he had a clearer idea of what to do. This was also not something to talk over with an older man like Harriman. Harriman was on a different level. While it was certainly worth consulting Harriman on almost any topic, it would be better to go to him with a concrete plan to discuss. Besides, he could not go to Harriman unless he knew whether he wanted to follow Harriman into politics. He would always be loyal to Harriman and be a part of his circle, but his policy circle was not exactly the same as his political circle. Gordon was not a man who could be helpful to Harriman politically. Gordon felt that he must turn to someone whose career resembled his own. Certain Harvard colleagues could be helpful, but whether he was interested in his old position was one of the things he wanted to decide before approaching Harvard. He had a special rapport with one man and would turn to him.

On December 23, 1953, he wrote to Richard Bissell:

Mr. Richard M. Bissell
3004 32nd Street, N.W.
Washington, D.C.

Dear Dick:

In addition to giving you and Annie the season's greetings, and to inquire about the authenticity of rumors about your going to work for the International Bank, the main purpose of this letter is to ask your friendly advice about my own somewhat obscure future. . . .

I am virtually certain my next move ought to be back to private life in one form or another. This is partly because I see no prospect of one of the very few attractive public positions being open to me, and partly for strictly financial reasons of a kind you are thoroughly familiar with. Moreover, I had a feeling that taking the American scene as it is, it is unwise to advance in one's 40s without a well-established base in private life. . . .

The one specific alternative which is clearly open is to return to the Harvard Business School. . . . [And then there's] the United Nations, the International Bank, and the business or banking world. I know that you have gone through this same set of dilemmas yourself, and I expect that we have enough temperamental affinity so that your reflections would be highly relevant to my own. . . .

If time permitted, there is a great deal I should like to be writing you about several works of common interest, from EDC to sterling convertibility. But I shall refrain and limit myself to repeating Christmas greetings and expressing the hope to see you on one side or another of the ocean before many months elapse.

Love to Annie.

Sincerely,
[signed Linc]
Lincoln Gordon

On January 27, 1954, he received a comprehensive reply from Bissell covering four single-space typed pages of analysis of every aspect of Gordon's (and his own) situation.[26] Bissell noted both the parallels and the differences in their situations and concluded that Gordon was on the right track in seeking to return to private life. He agreed with the virtues of alternate periods of government service and of refreshing oneself outside of government. He had received an enticing job offer from Allen Dulles at the CIA but had turned it down for the moment because Bissell was concerned that he could not educate his children on a government salary. (Like Gordon, Bissell had four children.) Bissell explored the pros and cons of the foundation world and advised against it for Gordon. He told his friend why he himself had not stayed with the Ford Foundation. The real action and major satisfactions lay with the scholars who were the recipients of foundation grants. The scholars performed the actual intellectual work, and the university deans or presidents managed the work. Moving into the business world at their current age was not a good idea either. The most interesting feature of Bissell's letter, however, was that he shifted the focus to the next stages of American foreign policy. Like Gordon, Bissell had worked mostly on the European theater and the political and economic problems of the Atlantic alliance. He now suggested to his friend that US foreign policy should turn away from a preoccupation with Europe to the periphery as the main theater of the Cold War. It was at the periphery where the conditions were ripe for communist subversion.[27] The West had contained communism in Europe, and it was now probable that the Soviet Union would pivot and seek to extend its influence in the Third World.[28]

George Kennan had laid out the classic statement of the containment strategy in a December 1949 address at the National War College.[29] There are five centers of industrial and military power in the world, Kennan argued, and the task of postwar American foreign policy was to check the expansionist tendencies of one (the Soviet Union) by aligning the others (the United States, the United Kingdom, Germany, and Japan) against the Soviet Union. Other nations and regions were of lesser importance since they could not directly threaten US security. Hence the United States did not have to support the forces of the Chinese Nationalists at great cost in blood and treasure to prevent a communist takeover of the mainland, as the Joint Chiefs of Staff were urging at the time. Toward Latin America, Kennan's approach was even more cautious. He articulated a hands-off approach to the region in an internal paper for Acheson in 1950 that had not been published or internally circulated as an official staff paper (and hence was not known to Bissell or Gordon). The term *benign neglect* had not yet been invented, but this was essentially the policy he recommended for the United States vis-à-vis the nations of Latin America.[30] Latin America was a region "where geography and history are alike tragic, but where no one must ever admit."[31] Moscow might seek to exploit the hopelessness of the peoples of the region by seizing power somewhere, but this would probably inoculate the hemisphere against other Soviet efforts at subversion. Washington should take a tolerant attitude toward whatever form of local rule emerged and show restraint in its policies, for Latin America was a region where problems would always be "multitudinous, complex, and unpleasant."[32] Edward G. Miller, assistant secretary of state for inter-American affairs, was enraged by Kennan's report, and as a result all copies were suppressed except for one, which Kennan retained, eventually quoting portions of it in his 1967 memoir.[33] Kennan had, however, used language on other occasions that implied the need for the United States to deter Soviet aggression wherever it might occur, and the Truman Doctrine was widely interpreted to mean that Washington would respond to Soviet aggression anywhere in the world. The North Korean invasion of South Korea in June 1950, with Stalin's almost certain advance knowledge, reinforced the conviction that Soviet probes could be expected anywhere and had to be contained.

The prescription in his friend Bissell's letter clarified Gordon's thinking, which had started with the British Colombo Plan. The Bissell letter not only helped to set Gordon on the path of his next career move but also reinforced a new direction in his thinking. Gordon would return to the Harvard Business School, supplement his income with outside consulting, and shift his intellectual focus. He would begin to redirect his interest to the Third World and the bundle of economic, political, and strategic issues posed by Third World development. This intellectual retooling did not happen instantly—it took several years to ripen, and Lincoln never fully shed his Eurocentric mindset. But the transition did propel Gordon into unfamiliar intellectual and geographical territory. As it turned out, both Bissell's and Gordon's later careers showed that the Marshall Plan and the Cold War were not the best guides for US policy toward Latin America. Kennan's skepticism about US involvement in the region would have been a better guide for US policy than the numerous interventions and initiatives of the Eisenhower, Kennedy, Johnson, and Reagan administrations.

Lincoln in any case thanked his friend for "your extraordinarily interesting letter—I perhaps might better say essay [which] arrived in the morning's mail . . . for which I am more than obliged."[34] In July 1954 Dean Donald David of the Harvard Business School traveled to London and met with Gordon to discuss the offer of a new professorship. Gordon promised to decide his "plans for the future before the end of the year."[35] But he did not wait that long. He wrote to David in October: "I am delighted to accept the offer of the Ziegler professorship. . . . I am particularly happy at the thought of resuming [a] working association with yourself and my many good friends on the school's faculty."[36]

12

Business School Professor, 1955–1960

Alongside the good fit of this job with your background and interests, it will bring you back to the right side of the river.
—Nathan Pusey, Harvard president, to Lincoln Gordon, 1955

Lincoln and Allison and the children enjoyed what was left of the 1955 summer at Lake Sunapee, slept well in the cool evenings, and listened to the wind whistling through the pines and the water lapping on the shore. At summer's end the family returned, refreshed, to their home in Belmont, which they had rented out during the London years. When Gordon first discussed with Donald David the new professorship in international business, the Harvard Graduate School of Business Administration had only one faculty member teaching in that area, an assistant professor who was slated to return to New York. The business school wanted Gordon to develop the field intellectually, to work with other Harvard faculties in creating a new research center, and to recruit new faculty members. The recruitment effort was to focus on finding an additional full professor, an associate professor, and potentially two junior faculty positions in the broadly defined field of international business and economics.[1]

The hiring component gave Gordon pause because he was not familiar with the business school specialties of marketing, finance, management, and the rest or with the leading scholars in those fields. He expressed his misgivings to Dean Stanley Teele, who told him that they wanted him to find another scholar like himself rather than a traditional business school figure. There was at this time, the dean explained, no recognized business school specialty in international business. That was why the new professorship had been created. The typical firm had a vice president for international business, Teele said, but the international side of the firm's activity was usually an afterthought. Now a change was under way. The international dimension had become important in marketing, finance, legal affairs, and production. Gordon's charge was thus to find colleagues broadly interested in the world economy, the changing nature of business enterprises, and trade policy, as well as other government policies that might shape the international business climate.

Recruitment and Institution Building

Gordon's hire for the other full professor slot was a notable success. He brought Raymond Vernon to Harvard, where Vernon spent a long and distinguished career at the business school and the Kennedy School of Government. He became one of the nation's leading scholars in international economic and political affairs.[2] Vernon, a New Yorker like Gordon, had also been born in 1913. He was educated at the City College of New York, with his PhD from Columbia University, and like Gordon was drawn into government service during the war. After the war he became involved with the Marshall Plan, where he first knew Gordon, and then joined the World Bank. Vernon had a brief but highly successful career in marketing with the family-owned Mars Company. Sales of M&M's candies zoomed under Vernon's leadership. Vernon was fond of telling students with a touch of irony, "I will be remembered as the man who put the peanut in the M&M." He was right. Obituary writers found this an irresistible tagline, sometimes with the variant "the man who put the crunch in the M&M's."

Gordon did not do badly with his second hire, either. He worked hard to bring Thomas C. Schelling from Yale to Harvard in 1958. Schelling had worked with him briefly in 1950 dealing with foreign aid and organizational issues during Gordon's White House tour with Harriman, and Gordon was impressed with the young economist's brilliance and articulateness. Although Schelling was located in the Economics Department rather than the business school, he taught courses with colleagues from other faculties. One of those courses was a defense policy seminar cotaught with Henry Kissinger of the Government Department and Barton Leach of the law school, for which Schelling wrote a book on game theory and a study of international conflict, a study that won him the Nobel Prize in Economics in 2005.[3]

Gordon's next foray into administrative matters was more complicated. Late in the fall term of 1955 he received a telephone call asking him to a meeting with Harvard president Nathan Pusey and McGeorge Bundy, dean of arts and sciences. Gordon knew Bundy from having hired him for the ECA's program division in 1948 and was well aware of his meteoric rise as a star in the Government Department and as the "power dean" who ran the academic side of the university. The purpose of the meeting was to inform Gordon that the university had received a large grant from the Ford Foundation to establish a new Center for International Affairs and to invite him to become its first director. The new center was to be a university-wide operation drawing on faculty members from the professional schools, as well as the arts and sciences faculty. The offer was attractive but came at an awkward time for Gordon. He had just moved to the business school and had hardly begun his work there. Several days later Pusey summoned him again. This time Pusey was alone. This was a mistake: Pusey probably should have left the matter in Bundy's hands. Now Pusey displayed the lack of political finesse that was already embroiling him in hot water with the Harvard faculty and student body. Pusey asked if Gordon had come to a decision. He told Gordon that he was anxious to move forward as soon as possible. Gordon said he promised to make a decision within days.

"Good," said Pusey. "Alongside the good fit of this job with your background and interests, it will bring you back to the right side of the river."

The "right side of the river"!? Gordon left the office fuming. He was incensed at Pusey's lack of tact. What did Pusey mean by the wrong side of the river—would this rule the medical school out as well? When he cooled down, Gordon began turning over the possibilities and concluded that he should decline the offer as coming at the wrong time. He could not in good conscience abandon the business school so soon, and the considerable administrative duties did not appeal to him. But he came up with an alternative he thought would appeal to Pusey and Bundy. His proposal was to bring Robert Bowie, a former member of the law school faculty, back to Harvard as the center's director. Gordon would propose himself as an interested faculty associate of the center and advisory board member and pledge to be active in the center's research programs.

Bowie, then serving as the director of policy planning at the State Department, confirmed that he would indeed be interested in the job. Bowie was chafing under the John Foster Dulles regime at State and was anxious to return to Cambridge. President Pusey told Gordon the next week that he had made soundings about Bowie and had found uniformly favorable reactions. Would Gordon undertake to be an intermediary with Bowie? Gordon flew to Washington to talk with Bowie. Bowie did not require much persuasion to accept the offer but raised a problem. As Bowie analyzed how the new center would function, he suggested that while the law and business schools would be important, most of the participating faculty members would come from the arts and sciences (scholars of government, history, and economics and scientists interested in arms control and nuclear issues). This meant that someone from arts and sciences should be involved in running the center.

The Government Department had unused rights to half the time of an associate professor, a line that could be combined with another half-time appointment as assistant or deputy director of the new center to make a full-time appointment. Henry Kissinger had just been turned down for one of two "up or out" tenure lines in Harvard's Government Department, and Bundy conceived the idea of using this vehicle for bringing Kissinger back to Harvard. (In a larger maneuver Bundy also used the occasion to make Stanley Hoffman of the Government Department a tenure offer at the same time.) Kissinger had been offered attractive academic appointments at other universities but had decided to accept a fellowship at the Council on Foreign Relations to be the study director for a study group exploring the topic of nuclear weapons and foreign policy, which eventually led to Kissinger's book *Nuclear Weapons and Foreign Policy*.[4] The striking popularity of this book provided the basis for Kissinger's return to Harvard through Bundy's adroit maneuvering, as the half-time deputy director and as a faculty member in the Government Department. But Bundy had outsmarted himself and failed to consider whether Bowie and Kissinger would be compatible and whether Kissinger could accept a role as subordinate to a colleague (and someone he considered an intellectual inferior). Bundy, in imposing Kissinger on Bowie, ignored or was unaware of the fact that Kissinger had publicly criticized the Dulles doctrine of "massive retaliation," of which Bowie had been a contributing author as director of State's policy planning staff. Kissinger and Bowie did not get on well from the beginning, and their personal animosity was one reason why the Harvard center never quite lived up to its promise.[5] Kissinger continued to freewheel and took no role in the administrative burdens of the center. Bowie fumed as he attempted unsuccessfully to engage Kissinger in the center's activities. The final and irrevocable split between them occurred over an apparently trivial academic issue: whether the words "Harvard Center for International Affairs" should be printed on the title page of the new Kissinger book *The Necessity for Choice*.[6] To Bowie this was a natural and reasonable proposal, but it was resisted adamantly by Kissinger, who considered that the center had had nothing to do with the book. To Bowie this stance typified Kissinger's arrogance and self-aggrandizing practices and constituted the last straw in Kissinger's general failure to pull his weight at the center. To Kissinger, Bowie's request was as an attempt to dictate to a colleague and thus an intolerable affront to his dignity and professional standing. The battle, in Gordon's words in his draft memoir, "was never fully forgiven on either side." Gordon managed to retain his standing with both men after a fashion and continued as a faculty associate and advisory board member with the center. But his personal sympathies were with Bowie, and his friendship with Kissinger cooled after the final blowup. Gordon in the Nixon years blamed Kissinger for scuttling the Alliance for Progress, and as president of Johns Hopkins he publicly criticized Nixon and Kissinger for moving "too slow" in the Vietnam peace negotiations and exacerbating student disturbances on campuses.

Outside Activities

The Gordons enjoyed a busy social life during Lincoln's stay at the business school. They entertained frequently and socialized with the Raymond Vernons, the Frank Lindsays, the Edward Masons, the Arthur Smithies, the Henry Kissingers (until the final split between Bowie and Kissinger), and the Bob Bowies (Bowie and Kissinger were never invited to the same party). The Gordons' next-door neighbors Dick and Ruth Kriebel were extremely close friends and frequent social companions. Lincoln played the cello in a string quartet he organized most weekends at his or Dick Kriebel's house. Kriebel was a fine amateur musician. Lincoln remained close to his mentor Bill Elliott, but because of their age difference the

Gordons did not socialize with the Elliotts. Gordon also became close friends with Don Price, dean of the Graduate School of Public Administration (later the Kennedy School of Government).

Somehow Gordon found the time to do the outside consulting he had discussed in his correspondence with Bissell. As the William Ziegler Professor of International Business, Gordon made about $15,000, and his salary was supplemented by summer school teaching over several years. The supplementary income was needed for his children's tuition bills. Bob went off to Exeter as a boarder in 1955, Anne went first to the Buckingham School and then to the Beaver Country Day School in Chestnut Hills, Hugh went to the Browne and Nichols School and then to Exeter in 1959, and Amy attended the Belmont Country Day School. In 1959 Bob went to Harvard College and Anne to Tufts. College tuition was modest in those days—tuition and fees at Harvard College in 1959 were about $2,000—but Gordon had ample incentive to seek consulting opportunities.

Despite the Ivy League prestige, the business school's working conditions at the time were not plush and did not promote a ready opportunity for faculty members to meet with potential clients. In July 1958, Gordon wrote to Dean Teele saying that he needed an air-conditioner in his business school office.[7] He also asked for "an outside telephone line at our end of the hall, which will be available for incoming calls after hours."[8] Evidently he overcame the obstacles and benefited from the business school's entrepreneurial climate. Over the 1955 to 1961 period, a partial listing of his consulting activities includes the Whirlpool Corporation (1959); the General Electric Company, where he taught a "Value Control Course" and served on an advisory board (1959–1960); Scott, Foresman, and Company (n.d.); A. D. Little & Company (1959–1961); the Stanford Research Institute (n.d.); the Rand Corporation (1956–1957); the Ford Foundation (1958); the US Department of State (n.d.); the Draper Committee (1958–1959); the Committee on Economic Development (n.d.); the Committee on World Economic Policies (1958); and the Senate Committee on Governmental Relations (n.d.).[9]

In addition to his paid consultancies, Gordon participated widely in study groups, task forces, and boards, where he received no compensation other than expenses, including the Longy School of Music Board of Trustees; the President's Committee on National Goals (1960); the

Twentieth Century Fund (now the Century Fund) (1959–1960); the Pan-Am Society of New England, Inc.; the Board of Governors (n.d.); and the Council on Foreign Relations (1956–1961). Increasingly, as his intellectual interests shifted, he began working on projects dealing with economic developments in Latin America.

Interest in the Third World

Gordon had some knowledge of technical assistance programs in his early Marshall Plan days, focused on overall coordination of all aid programs, when he was with Harriman in Paris and the White House from 1950 to 1952. By the end of the Truman administration technical assistance had acquired a rationale somewhat similar to the anticommunist thrust of the Marshall Plan: if Third World countries prospered, they would be less amenable to the threat of communist subversion. Gordon had tried unsuccessfully to interest the Eisenhower administration in joining Britain's Colombo Plan. Eisenhower did not wish to get entangled in British decolonization efforts and in general deemed private-sector investment the best way to promote economic development in the Third World. (Eisenhower's main initiative in Latin America at this point in his administration was the 1954 CIA coup in Guatemala, secretly organized by Richard Bissell.) Gordon's thinking about economic assistance in the Third World took more concrete form as he read in the literature and debated the modernization theories then becoming fashionable in the Harvard-MIT community. The modernization of the nations of Asia, the Middle East, and Latin America was a hot research topic and caught Gordon's attention.[10] But Gordon continued for a time to write articles about the economic aspects of NATO and overall US foreign policy. His gradual shift to Latin America was the result of a number of factors, including new research currents in the academy, the focus of his outside consulting, his new teaching assignments and the preparation of case materials on international business, and as a continuation of his previous intellectual and professional work with foreign aid. The issues of NATO, European security, and East-West relations remained important, but to Gordon these concerns had settled into a pattern. NATO was a reality, the doctrine of containment was accepted in broad outline, and the whole nexus of technical issues surrounding nuclear arms control had moved so far beyond what he had dealt with in 1946 that he would have to devote himself full time to the topic if he wished to make a useful contribution. Further, he was not entirely sure in his own mind whether he belonged to the Nitze and Kissinger hawkish faction or to the more dovish Kennan and Oppenheimer school of thought vis-à-vis the Soviet Union. The evolving disputes involving Harvard's Center for International Affairs and whether there should be a separate European studies program were unpleasant and bound to be frustrating if he kept his focus on European issues. He was tired of focusing on Europe and its messy political issues. Economics and a shift of focus to Latin America seemed to be more satisfying and more in keeping with the concerns of the business school. Had he remained in the Government Department, the situation might have been different, but he had opted for the safer confines of the business school, and he had now to live with that choice. And indeed, there were issues of great intellectual interest and practical importance in a shift to economic development. There was a touch of arrogance in his thinking, too, as he confided to friends that while he found the historical and cultural scholarship about Latin America impressive, the economic, social science, and policy thinking in the field was inferior, and he believed he could make an immediate impact.

He had once largely accepted the universalist premises of the Bretton Woods system as part of his thinking. That was one reason why he had never been an enthusiast for European unification when he was administering the Marshall Plan. The Marshall Plan had revived the economies of the separate European nations by removing the artificial barriers that had arisen during the Great Depression and the world war. Europe should cooperate, but within the framework of the overall international system based on Bretton Woods. The world economy should be guided by a monetary system based on fixed exchange rates and a free trade regime, and both the monetary and the trade regimes should be under UN auspices and supported by all industrialized nations, but with the flexibility for adjustments in certain circumstances. This was the view of the US Treasury that had been a thorn in his side when he was with the Marshall Plan, because Treasury had evidenced almost theological zeal in resisting any compromises or adjustments to the doctrine. Gordon and his ECA and State Department colleagues found it necessary to modify the Bretton Woods system to a degree in creating the European Payments

Union. If the Europeans were now determined to create regional institutions that would integrate their separate national economies further, the United States might not relish the prospects of a protectionist trading bloc but would certainly welcome a more united Europe from the standpoint of US national security interests in the Cold War competition with the Soviet Union.

Europe was one thing, but what about the developing world? Might the Bretton Woods system need further modification in the light of conditions in the Third World? The Soviet Union had in effect excluded itself from the world economy when it excluded itself from the Marshall Plan. This was fortunate because as a centrally planned economy, it was not transparent in its economic dealings, did not allow for private ownership, and did not provide for free trade in goods and services. The Bretton Woods system worked well enough for the industrialized nations, but Gordon began to doubt that Third World nations could develop successfully under the Bretton Woods formula. Significant regional modification was probably in order. Policy changes might include a greatly expanded level of economic assistance going beyond humanitarian aid for poorer nations, specialized technical assistance programs, and perhaps even a coordinated hemisphere-wide Marshall Plan for Latin America. Economists from Latin America were issuing calls for an import substitution approach to stimulate industrialization in key countries, and experimentation was under way in key Latin American countries, notably Brazil.

As he prepared for his new core course in 1956–1957, to be called "International Economic Relations," Gordon first thought of focusing the case materials on India and Pakistan as illustrations of how governments plan for economic growth. The course would begin with the fundamentals of international economics for businessmen, and the empirical, applied part would be "divided roughly half and half between relationships with other advanced countries on the one hand, and relationships with developing countries on the other." As he got into the subject more deeply, he shifted away from the "planned" development of India and Pakistan and other parts of Asia to the "very large amount of development going on in Latin America. It wasn't planned development. . . . It was rather chaotic . . . full of fermentation. There was not only economic development, but also political development—for me an extremely interesting combination of circumstances."[11]

He was aided in his course preparations by a research assistant, Ronald K. Jones, who had been recommended by Dean Teele. Jones was English but had lived for most of his life in Lima, where his father worked for W. R. Grace & Company. Jones was interested in all aspects of development—economic, political, and social—and was especially knowledgeable about investments, public and private, domestic and foreign, in the Latin American economies. The 1950s were marked by a dramatic shift toward manufacturing in the economies of the large Latin American countries—and especially in Brazil.[12] After World War II the more advanced Latin American economies had entered a new phase, importing advanced technologies to improve their manufacturing capacities dramatically. Gordon's intellectual focus both geographically and topically was on what was happening in Brazil. Jones proved to be adept at getting officials of the US Export-Import Bank, the World Bank, and the Inter-American Development Bank to provide case studies for use in Gordon's teaching. Gordon began to teach himself to read Portuguese. He decided that he needed to recruit a team of colleagues from the leading Brazilian universities to assist in the research project.

Gordon organized a major conference at the Harvard Business School in the fall of 1957 that had five country panels: Brazil, Mexico, Venezuela, Argentina, and Colombia. The Brazil panel attracted more participants than any other. The conference took place at the midpoint of the presidency of Juscelino Kubitschek, who served from 1955 to 1961 and who would launch Operation Pan America in 1958. The conference confirmed Gordon's judgment that Brazil was the country he should study. It also convinced him that there were significant gaps in knowledge that needed to be filled. The most erudite observers seemed to Gordon to be historians, especially those who focused on cultural history, whereas contemporary developments were less thoroughly studied and understood. Gordon took a dim view of most of his fellow academics in Latin American studies programs and rather arrogantly concluded that fresh analytical perspectives were urgently needed in the field.

The business school gave Gordon a grant that permitted him to reduce his teaching to half time so that he could focus on his research. He had never enjoyed his teaching duties at the business school, considering the students dull and the routine duties of teaching, such as grading papers, an excruciating bore. He now worked closely with colleagues at

Harvard's new Center for International Affairs to frame a series of studies on economic development, steering clear of the NATO and arms control issues. He took a special interest in Brazil as his part of the overall economic development project. He received support from the center for a trip to Brazil in the summer of 1959 that proved to be an important turning point in his career. In the process he teamed up with a delegation that the Ford Foundation was sending to Chile, Argentina, Uruguay, and Brazil with the mission of outlining a strategy for the foundation to aid development in the hemisphere.

Gordon also spent the spring and summer of 1960 in South America. This time he traveled with Allison to make amends for his lengthy absence of the previous summer. They vacationed for several weeks in Peru and then spent two months in Brazil, where he mixed discussions with Brazilian colleagues with tourism with his wife. They returned to Cambridge in time for him to teach in the fall term of 1960, as the presidential election began to heat up. The Democratic nominee, Senator John F. Kennedy, was well known to and a favorite of many Harvard colleagues. Many Harvard professors worked on his campaign. Gordon scarcely knew Kennedy at the time, but he soon began to catch electoral fever. He took a very limited part in the campaign by preparing a short position paper on economic policy.

A few weeks after the election Gordon received a phone call from Adolf A. Berle of the Columbia University Law School that changed his life. Gordon later liked to tell friends that the call from Berle came totally out of the blue and that he had not the slightest inkling that the Kennedy administration would beckon him back to public service. This was disingenuous on Gordon's part. The particular call from Berle may have been a surprise, but Gordon's insistence that he had not campaigned for a job in the Kennedy administration does not quite fit the facts. Lincoln had devoted considerable effort to preparing the paper "Economic Regionalism Reconsidered," which appeared in *World Politics* in January 1961, in which he argued that the Bretton Woods system should be modified by recognition of the importance of economic regionalism for the Third World. The paper's argument was theoretical, dense, and complicated and reflected his deep knowledge of the economic strategies of Latin American countries and the theoretical writings of Latin American economists. The gist of the argument was that regional arrangements and national strategies such as the "import substitution" policies of a number of Latin American countries, even if not consistent with Bretton Woods principles, could be highly effective for integrating Latin American countries into the world economy. The article did not use the term "Alliance for Progress," since it was largely written before that term emerged late in the presidential campaign, but the policy ideas it discussed lent themselves readily to the new initiatives that were on President-elect Kennedy's and his team's mind. In late November Lincoln sent prepublication copies of the article to Dean Acheson, Dean Rusk, Adlai Stevenson, and possibly other leading Democrats who might be expected to play a role in the Kennedy administration. Stevenson was traveling in Latin America and did not respond, but Gordon received a warm response from Acheson and an invitation to meet with Rusk. At the meeting with Secretary of State–designate Rusk, Gordon was offered the post of assistant secretary of state for economic affairs. Gordon declined this offer in favor of an alternative proposal of his own. It was evident that Gordon had given considerable thought to how he might fit in with the New Frontier, despite the fact that he had played no part in the presidential campaign. Gordon had always liked to portray himself as being "called" to public service, apart from any actions on his own part. This was not quite how he became part of the Kennedy team, for at some point he had become swept up in the excitement of the Kennedy crusade and taken steps that indicated he was interested in and willing to serve in the new administration.

13

The Alliance for Progress and JFK Adviser

We need an economist and that's you.
—Adolf A. Berle to Lincoln Gordon, 1960

The Alliance for Progress, of course, is nothing but terminology.
—Milton Eisenhower, 1980

The tendency to achieve our foreign policy objectives by inducing other governments to sign up to professions of high moral and legal principle appears to have a great and enduring vitality in our diplomatic practice,
—George F. Kennan, *American Diplomacy 1900–1950*

The *Alliance* came to an end with Kennedy's death.
—Arthur Schlesinger Jr., 1986

But the Alliance did not die with any single event. It rather dribbled away.
—Lincoln Gordon, 1980

Lincoln Gordon concludes in his regionalism article that regional blocs, including the Latin American bloc, were going to play increasingly important roles in the world economy. His diagnosis pays special attention to the limited intraregional trade among Latin American countries. The new regionalism, though not spelled out very clearly, would promote intraregional trade and supplement the import substitution strategies of individual countries to limit cheap imports from the industrialized countries.

Gordon's research on Brazil focused on the role of foreign private investment in the Brazilian automotive industry and on policies to promote a more favorable investment climate. But he clearly understood that economic development in Latin America would need much more than merely an improved investment climate. Social reforms would be necessary to improve the lot of the underprivileged. Social reforms, as with the New Deal in the United States, would only come through vigorous government action. He was critical of the passive approach of the Eisenhower administration, as epitomized in the policy positions of Eisenhower's first secretary of the treasury, George Humphrey. The United States, in Humphrey's view, should allow market forces to work, and over a period of time investment in Brazil and other Latin American countries would increase if private property rights were respected. Gordon's criticisms of the Eisenhower administration and his endorsement of far-reaching social reforms appealed to the Kennedy people.

New ideas were in the air, and popular enthusiasm for the newly elected Kennedy was strong and of course especially strong among Gordon's Cambridge friends and faculty colleagues. He was aware that a number of his Harvard friends and colleagues planned to join the Kennedy administration, including Ken Galbraith as ambassador to India, McGeorge Bundy and Carl Kaysen in key national security positions, and Arthur Schlesinger as part of the White House staff. Henry Kissinger was interested too but received only an offer of a part-time consulting role. Gordon took some steps that signaled his interest in the administration and its policy ideas. His *World Politics* paper on economic regionalism was not scheduled for formal publication until January 1961, but he sent an advance copy to Dean Rusk at the Rockefeller Foundation, knowing full well that Rusk was being prominently mentioned for the post of secretary of state. Gordon had no specific contact with his Harvard colleagues who were joining the administration about any particular job, and he had not contacted Harriman yet, but names were floated and rumors circulated as the Kennedy team shifted from campaign to governing mode.

The Berle Task Force

In this climate Gordon took a call from Adolf Berle, a man he knew only slightly at the time but whom he knew to be the Democratic Party's foremost authority on Latin America.

"Have you heard from Sorensen yet?" Berle asked.[1]

"Sorensen?"

"Oh, you know, Ted Sorensen," said Berle. "The president-elect's right-hand man."

Gordon said he had not heard.

"Well, you've been reading in the newspapers that various people are trying to become the head of a task force for Kennedy."

Gordon acknowledged that he was aware of various self-promoting candidates for that role.

"There's only one legitimate task force and I'm the chairman of it. We need an economist and that's you."

"That's all very flattering," said Gordon. "But the fact is I'm not really a Latin American economics expert. I can name you half a dozen people who've devoted their lives to the subject. I've only been at it for a few years, and almost exclusively about Brazil."

Gordon explained that he knew little about the smaller Latin American countries, very little about Central America or the Caribbean, and nothing about the situation in Cuba.

"No, no." Berle cut him off. "We've been through all that. You're the one we want."

Gordon did not know who "we" were but did not inquire. He asked how much time might be involved. Berle indicated that the task force would meet only a few times for half a day and then would probably spend a weekend drafting the report. Some parts could be drafted at home and brought to the windup meetings. That did not seem too daunting an assignment. Gordon agreed to serve.

The task force had its first meeting at the Harvard Club in New York City on December 6. The other task force members present were Arturo Morales from Puerto Rico, Arthur Whitaker from the University of Pennsylvania, and Robert Alexander from Rutgers University, with Richard Goodwin not officially a task force member but representing President-elect Kennedy. After introductions, Berle started the discussion by pounding on the table three times with his hand.

"Now," he said. "We've got to have an under secretary. Got to have a command post! Got to have a command post for Latin America which will have the responsibility for all aspects. Probably better be in the State Department. He's got to have the title of under secretary."

Gordon records the following exchange with Berle in his LBJ Library oral history: "Being on the brash side, I guess, all my life, [I] was the first to speak up. I still didn't call him by his first name—that only came later. I said, 'Look, Professor Berle, you know that's not possible.'"[2]

"Not possible? Why not?"

"You will recall that a week or so ago," Gordon said, "Mr. Kennedy announced the appointment of Soapy Williams [G. Mennen Williams] as assistant secretary of state for African affairs. In making the announcement for that appointment—which he made before he appointed Dean Rusk as Secretary, a peculiar thing—he said that that position would be 'second to none.' Now you're suggesting, in effect, that whoever's in charge of Latin American should outrank Williams."

Gordon observed further that elevating the title of the Latin America assistant secretary would lead to titles being raised all around. Privately, Gordon was nettled by what he took to be Berle's vanity. It was absurd that Berle was not willing to be an assistant secretary given the fact that Averell Harriman was willing to serve as assistant secretary for far eastern affairs. Both Gordon and Goodwin thought Berle was being unrealistic. Goodwin at one point thought he would have to report back to Kennedy that "they had a madman on their hands."[3] Berle did not budge, insisting that without the symbolism of a higher rank for Latin America, nothing important could get done.

The task force at the initial meeting focused on the political issues that were uppermost in Berle's mind.[4] Berle had in mind a kind of political New Deal or a "democratic international" for Latin America. His idea was that the United States should search out and back socially and politically progressive leaders. Berle regarded the Accion Democratica in Venezuela, led by President Romulo Betancourt, as the prototype of the kind of reformist party the United States should support. It should identify a similar leader and party for each Latin American country and help them to become the dominant political force in that country. This was in keeping with President Kennedy's own analysis, Berle said, and with the president's preference for bold symbolic action. As Kennedy had once said, "If the only alternatives for the people of Latin America are the status quo and communism, then they will inevitably choose communism."[5]

While the Berle task force did not dwell on anticommunism as a rationale, the idea of a democratic "third force" was clearly designed to counter the appeal of Castro, the Cuban revolution, and radicalism generally. The threat of external subversion from the Soviet Union and Communist China formed the background for the task force's work. Social and economic inequality created conditions that were ripe for communist exploitation, and the remedy was to support progressive regimes like Betancourt's in Venezuela and progressive ideas like the Kubitschek initiatives in Brazil. This would, in Berle's view, create a firewall against communism. Gordon was somewhat skeptical that the Latin American leaders whom Berle admired were quite as numerous or as uniform in their outlook as Berle imagined. But he did not want to challenge Berle directly or to dispute the priority that Berle placed on the social and political aspects of development. Anticommunism had not been the central thrust of the Marshall Plan, but it was a factor in gaining congressional and popular support for the program in the first place and had all but supplanted the recovery rationale after the Korean invasion. If the Alliance idea were to be sold to Latin American elites, the need to counter radicalism would certainly have to be a part of the appeal.

At the second meeting the task force turned to the economic issues. Trade, investment, balance of payments, commodity prices, and development generally were discussed. Gordon encountered no opposition to the ideas he advanced because they were generally in line with the International Monetary Fund (IMF), the World Bank, and the thinking of Latin American economists. The recipe he called for was consistent with the Puerto Rican development strategy of Muñoz Marín and with the Kubitschek Operation Pan America in Brazil. Gordon called for President-elect Kennedy to include a reference to the Alliance for Progress in his inaugural address and then for an announcement soon thereafter of the details of the new program to a selected audience of Latin American leaders. Further, he called for an immediate message to Congress asking for a $500 million appropriation for the social fund the Inter-American Development Bank (IDB), as promised by the Eisenhower administration at Bogota the previous September.

The third and final meeting of the Berle task force took place over the New Year's holidays in Puerto Rico, where the members attended the third Muñoz Marín gubernatorial inauguration. Here Theodoro Moscoso and other Puerto Rican friends of Berle's joined in the task force's deliberations. The task force embraced both Berle's emphasis on social and political development and Gordon's economic strategy but did not offer any guidelines to resolve potential conflicts between the two broad priorities of social justice and economic development. Berle wrote the first chapters of the report, the transmittal letter to the president, and the organizational recommendations. Gordon wrote the nine-page economic chapter under the title "Approach to Economic and Social Policy," incorporating some minor editorial suggestions from his task force colleagues.

Years later, Gordon expressed his regret that the report was never published. But he understood that it was intended as confidential advice for the president-elect. Berle, always outspoken, had made a derogatory reference about the US ambassador to Nicaragua in the Eisenhower administration, and this, plus other overly candid assessments of developments in specific countries, was apparently enough to keep the document classified for many years.[6] Berle hand delivered the report, dated January 4, 1961, to the president-elect in New York City. He discussed it for an hour with Kennedy and Adlai Stevenson. He reported to his task force colleagues that Kennedy appeared "very pleased."[7]

Point Man for Latin America Policy

When Gordon met with his fellow Rhodes scholar Dean Rusk in December, Rusk told him that he liked both the originality and the realism of Gordon's policy suggestions in the economic regionalism paper. When he asked Gordon to come to Washington as assistant secretary of state for economic affairs, Gordon demurred on the grounds that the present occupant, Edwin Martin, an old friend of Gordon's from the Harriman days, was doing a good job, and there was no reason to change for change's sake. His counterproposal to Rusk was that he devote himself half time—he was sure he could square this with Harvard—to the task of translating the ideas of the Berle task force into an operational program. There were many details to work out and much work to do in getting congressional approval, much as there had been with the Marshall Plan. Rusk accepted the proposal. Soon after the presidential inauguration Gordon got a phone call from George Ball, Rusk's under secretary of state, with an initial assignment.

"Your first job will be to defend the Act of Bogota appropriation [for $500 million] to Passman and his subcommittee," Ball told him.

Gordon began his preparations for what proved to be a three-day session that he later considered one of his most grueling jobs. The hearings were held over March 20, 21, 22, and 23 and covered all aspects of US aid policy for Latin America. Senior administration officials made opening statements, but the brunt of the testimony and preparatory work fell on Gordon. While preparing for the congressional testimony, he assisted Richard Goodwin with the drafting of President Kennedy's speech announcing the Alliance. Goodwin began working on the speech in February and was in touch with Gordon, Berle, State Department officials, and the Mayobre group of Latin American economists. Gordon had a comfortable working relationship with Goodwin and was by this time on familiar terms with Berle. He knew Rusk from the 1930s at Oxford, but he considered it unlikely that Rusk would have time to be a day-to-day participant in the Alliance planning. McGeorge Bundy had no problem with Gordon's part-time role, and the two men had respectful and cordial relations (unlike Bundy's tense relations with Kissinger, whose periodic trips to Washington always seemed to undermine the work of the full-time staff and attempt to outflank Bundy himself). Gordon understood, however, that Bundy was not personally interested in and would not be involved in the details of the Alliance and economic aid policies.

The question of how to interact with the various players in the Latin America policy process in the freewheeling Kennedy White House puzzled Gordon. Kennedy himself had a strong interest in Latin America and from time to time took initiative on his own and sought out advice from various quarters. Gordon as yet had had no direct dealings with President Kennedy and knew him only slightly from Kennedy's visits to the Harvard campus. Gordon did not want to overstep and early on decided to steer clear of security policy, which proved to be fortunate because he was not implicated in the Bay of Pigs debacle. He may have had an inkling that something was afoot with Cuba and for this reason kept his distance. The economic issues were in any case certainly challenging enough to occupy his attention. The planning for the Bay of Pigs was then feverishly under way, under the direction of Gordon's old friend Richard Bissell, now the deputy director of the CIA.[8] Among the While House staffers, Arthur Schlesinger took an interest in Latin American affairs and peppered Kennedy with memos. Gordon had not been particularly close to Schlesinger at Harvard, and it was not clear to Gordon whether Schlesinger had a clearly defined policy role. He could be merely a gadfly and be more involved in domestic politics than in foreign policy. Schlesinger at times circumvented Bundy by bringing his friend Henry Kissinger in to see Kennedy without Bundy's knowledge. Kennedy finally put his foot down and told Schlesinger to clear any Kissinger visit through Bundy.[9] Gordon decided that his best course was to work closely with Richard Goodwin rather than Schlesinger in the White House and to keep closely in touch with a few key players in the State Department. The State colleagues included Ed Martin; John Leddy (who soon moved to Treasury); and Thomas C. Mann, assistant secretary for inter-American affairs. Mann was a career Foreign Service officer but had close ties to important politicians, including his fellow Texan Vice President Lyndon Johnson. Gordon felt that he could count on an appeal to Bundy if the occasion demanded.

Berle remained in the picture after the first task force report had been submitted, but his role was now a confusing one to Gordon. Berle was designated as chairman of a second task force, whose job was to plan the transition to the new administration. The portfolio was to include both broad policy and day-to-day operational matters, including appointments. Gordon became a member of this new task force, along with Leddy and Mann, but the task force quickly bogged down in confusion. The original task force was, in Gordon's view, an excellent example of how the task force device should be used. It was temporary, produced a report with advice for policy-makers, and was then disbanded. The second Berle task force was an incorrect use of the device because it lacked a clear mandate, had no operational role but nevertheless interfered in personnel and other administrative matters, and as a result fostered confusion and inaction. Berle, as chairman, was not a full-time or even a part-time government official and was operating mainly from his Columbia office in New York City. Berle remained in his faculty position with full teaching duties. Kennedy was willing to tolerate the awkwardness for the time being because he hoped that he could still persuade Berle to accept the assistant secretary post in the State Department. Kennedy thus continued to use Berle for special assignments, but he was becoming disillusioned, and Berle for his part was cooling on Kennedy. In February, Kennedy sent Berle to Brazil to meet with the newly installed president Janio Quadros, who had succeeded the term-limited Kubitschek. Berle's mission was twofold: to size

up Quadros and to persuade him to join with the United States in diplomatic efforts to isolate Cuba. Kennedy had not informed Berle about
the Bay of Pigs operation, both to maintain secrecy and because he was
not sure Berle would support the planned invasion. JFK was right in this
intuition. Berle was appalled and totally disillusioned with the Kennedy
administration when the invasion took place. Berle's mission to Brazil at
any rate was a total failure. Quadros flatly refused to back any US effort
to isolate Cuba, and he even refused to appear for a joint press conference
with Berle after their meeting.

Kennedy drew from this trip the lesson that Berle could no longer
work magic in the hemisphere. The Kennedy administration thus gave
up on Berle and turned increasingly to Gordon as its key Latin America
adviser. Gordon became the chief adviser in the planning for the Charter of Punta del Este and in the informal talks with the Latin American
experts of the Inter-American Economic and Social Council (ECOSOC).
He acted as the go-between with the Harvard-MIT development experts
and the Latin American economists. Gordon was given the choice by
Rusk of becoming assistant secretary of state for inter-American affairs
when Tom Mann departed for Mexico or US ambassador to Brazil. Gordon chose the latter post. He suspected that he did not have the political
instincts to function as assistant secretary in the hothouse atmosphere of
Washington. He knew little or nothing about Central America and the
Caribbean and did not speak Spanish at the time. He had begun to read
Portuguese with some fluency and even to speak it, eventually acquiring
the second-highest State Department category in Portuguese-language
skills.[10]

Meanwhile, Gordon had begun to surmise that his suspicions were
correct about imminent action with Cuba. There had been a briefing in
February in Tom Mann's office at which a CIA officer had alluded to
pending actions in Cuba. Goodwin had attended the same briefing and
expressed similar uneasiness to Gordon after the meeting. Evidently security became tighter, and there was no further hint of the pending action
in Cuba in the meetings Gordon attended. The Bay of Pigs action took
place in April, and in June Kennedy dispatched US UN ambassador Adlai
Stevenson and Gordon on a seventeen-nation visit to confer with Latin
American leaders. This was a fence-mending gesture in two senses: to
reach out to the hemisphere's leaders and to reach out to Stevenson, who

had been humiliated when he was kept in the dark about the Cuban invasion and had unwittingly lied to the UN. Stevenson and Gordon were not tarred with the Bay of Pigs debacle. Stevenson privately was so angered that he had considered resigning, and Kennedy had devised the mission to placate his irate UN ambassador, as well as to mend fences with Latin American leaders.

Gordon chose the Brazilian assignment over the assistant secretary job on several grounds. One was based on Galbraith's choice to go to India rather than take a job at home. Galbraith wanted an important country, but not one of the most sought after. That way he could be the undisputed leader in policy for the country. As India was to Galbraith, so Brazil was to Gordon. Galbraith had been much more active in the campaign and was therefore in a better position than Gordon to ask for what he wanted. So Gordon considered himself lucky to have the choice. Brazil was a large country and probably the most important one in the hemisphere. Too, Gordon had fallen in love with Brazil on his first visit there. In contrast, being in the spotlight in Washington and responding to daily crises would be less pleasant. He was more naturally a technocrat-statesman than a politician. In June, while Gordon was on the visit to Latin American capitals with Adlai Stevenson, JFK telephoned him to make a direct appeal that he change his mind and take the assistant secretary job. Gordon persuaded the president that he was better suited for the ambassadorial post. Rusk and JFK then wanted him to set off immediately for Brazil. Gordon convinced them that he could be more useful if he continued with the preparations for the Punta del Este conference. This conference would be critical to the success of the Alliance for Progress. Every ambassador in the hemisphere would in some sense stand or fall on the success or lack of success of the Alliance, Gordon argued, and he promised to leave for Brazil right after the Punta del Este conference and as soon as he could be confirmed. In the meantime he would meet with President Quadros on the June visit and begin dealing with his future problems as ambassador.

The Punta del Este Conference

The Kennedy administration's Latin American policy before the Bay of Pigs (April 14–17) was operating on two separate tracks: the security track, with plans for the Cuban invasion, and the economic and political track, emphasizing the reforms of the Alliance for Progress. The Bay of Pigs forced the two tracks to converge into one. US policy was now pursuing social and economic development as a "third way" to counter communist penetration in the hemisphere. Overcoming the economic backwardness that perpetuated social inequality would presumably put an end to the domination of Latin American countries by privileged elites. As the threat of communist subversion in Europe had helped generate support for the Marshall Plan, Kennedy administration strategists hoped that the communist threat in the region would generate congressional support for the Alliance for Progress at home and persuade elites in the hemisphere to surrender some of their privileges. The problem was that the United States would have to depend on the very governments that it was decrying as plutocratic and dominated by privileged elites to carry out the sweeping reforms called for in the Alliance for Progress.

President Kennedy's March 13 speech outlining the Alliance had called for a ministerial conference in the summer to plan for its implementation. A preparatory conference would be convened in May in Washington, under the auspices of the Organization of American States (OAS), to plan the agenda for the Punta del Este conference later in the summer. The Washington sessions drew heavily on a contingent of economists from ECOSOC in order to avoid the appearance of the United States imposing its agenda on Latin Americans. The Washington meeting's aim was to prepare the preliminary working papers for Punta del Este. Two sets of documents were to be prepared: a set of technical papers spelling out the Alliance program elements and a "Declaration of the Peoples of Americas" committing the member states of the OAS to implement the program.[11]

The preparatory work followed closely the ten points broadly outlined in President Kennedy's March 13 speech. In Gordon's view the presidential speech had simply restated the Berle task force recommendations: "While the speech of March 13 was written by Dick Goodwin, the substantive content of it is practically all my own handiwork. The speech is simply an expansion of the task force recommendations."[12] Actually, elements of the speech—specifically, JFK's call for commodity price stabilization and the speech's relative neglect of private investment—reflected a clear difference of emphasis from Gordon's task force chapter. Gordon's reaction to the Kennedy speech at the time was cautious. Kennedy for his part apparently was not entirely satisfied with the Berle report: he deemed it advisable to seek more explicit Latin American input on the speech, possibly to cushion the likely shock of and critical reaction to his pending action in Cuba. The president had telephoned Jose Antonio Mayobre, Venezuela's ambassador to the United States, in February and told him that he was planning a major address and wanted the ambassador to help him get ideas and suggestions from Latin American colleagues. Mayobre then invited nine eminent Latin American economists to provide President Kennedy their suggestions.[13] The group included Felipe Herrera, president of the IDB; Jorge Sol Castellanos, executive secretary of ECO-SOC; Felipe Pazos, a Cuban who had been president of the Cuban Central Bank before he defected; and Raul Prebisch, executive secretary of the UN Economic Commission on Latin America.

The Mayobre group recommended a long-term program of external capital assistance, commodity price stabilization, changes in the agrarian land tenure system, technical assistance to help Latin entrepreneurs, and recognition by the United States that "it would not always be easy to overcome the resistance by the privileged groups without agitation and disturbances."[14] The speech should, said the group, fire the imagination of the masses of the Latin American peoples in order to generate the pressure necessary to move politicians. Not every member of the Mayobre group was pleased with Kennedy's speech. There was concern that its ringing tone and ambitious goals raised expectations beyond what could be delivered. Political leaders from the large Latin American countries had their own reservations. President Arturo Frondizi of Argentina wrote Kennedy that his emphasis on social reform was misplaced and that the real problem lay in the need for rapid industrial development. The Alliance's emphasis should be on the more advanced sectors of the leading South American economies and on expanded trade with both North America and Europe.[15] Roberto Campos, Brazil's ambassador to the United States, was already on record as favoring a top-down strategy of economic development for his country. President Janio Quadros, Kubitschek's successor, did not like the big-development bureaucracies that seemed to be envisaged under the Alliance. He worried that the Alliance might give too big a role to OAS and UN bureaucrats at the expense of his own room to maneuver. But since everyone was hoping for a slice of what was seen as a large pie, and since Kennedy's youth and idealism had wide popular appeal in most of their countries, the Latin American politicians muted their public criticism of Kennedy's proposals.

In his role as the link between Latin American experts and development economists from Harvard and MIT, Gordon drew mixed reviews from his Latin American colleagues. Felipe Pazos complained that the North Americans were "totally unprepared" to formulate plans for Latin America. They had little empirical data of their own and were not sufficiently familiar with the basic concepts and recent work of leading Latin American economists. The US team had "no philosophy, no thinking behind [its] position."[16] Gordon bristled at the criticism and maintained that he and his American colleagues were fully aware of the work of Prebisch and others and contended that the US team was reticent only because it had wanted to leave the initiative to the Latin Americans.

As a means of gaining visibility for the upcoming conference, Kennedy considered going to Punta del Este himself. The picturesque Uruguayan resort town where the conference would be held would be all but vacant in the southern winter, so security would be manageable for high-level attendees. JFK's presence would induce other heads of state to attend, which would potentially offset some of the negative aftereffects from the Bay of Pigs fiasco. Kennedy was not sure, however, whether the political atmosphere had calmed down enough for him to undertake the trip. The preparatory meeting in Washington had not given him enough guidance for deciding whether or not he should go to Punta del Este. It had been a meeting of experts who could not respond as representing their governments or in particular say where their political leaders stood on Castro. The Stevenson-Gordon visit, however, during which the two would confer with the presidents of seventeen Latin American countries, would gain intelligence on whether Kennedy should attend the conference. Stevenson was probably the most prestigious American leader besides Kennedy himself in Latin American eyes, and he was not implicated in the Bay of Pigs.[17] In accompanying Stevenson, Gordon would answer questions about the Alliance and generally provide technical backup. By this time word that Gordon would be the US ambassador to Brazil had also become public.

A third individual was added to the delegation to reassure State Department realists and to bring additional experience to bear in Latin America. Ellis Briggs, who joined the team, was a senior career diplomat who had served as US ambassador in Uruguay, Peru, and Brazil. Briggs was a puzzling choice in some respects, for he was completely unsympathetic to the Alliance for Progress concept. He later denounced the Alliance as a "blueprint for upheaval throughout Latin America" and offered his sympathy for those "hard pressed" Latin American heads of state to whom Kennedy's exhortations "sounded suspiciously like the Communist Manifesto in reverse. . . . If there is a more pernicious doctrine than one which impels the sponsor of an economic and social program to throw gasoline into his neighbor's woodshed, it has yet to come to the attention of history."[18]

The Stevenson team visited the South American capitals over the period June 3–22. At each stop Stevenson asked the president if he would be willing to attend the Punta del Este conference, and the answer was usually equivocal. The implication was that the timing of the meeting— coming so soon after the Bay of Pigs—would cause domestic political problems for Kennedy. Stevenson continued to gain a general sense of where the various South American presidents stood on the Alliance's future and on relations with Cuba. Most Latin American leaders believed that Cuba was a problem for the United States, but not for them.[19] The Stevenson team saw that it was not going to be easy to gain acceptance of the idea of isolating Cuba and that the price tag for them to go along with the US plan was going to be high. Matters came to a head at the final stop of the trip, in Bogota, Colombia. The team's meetings over two days with Colombian president Alberto Lleras Camago produced a formula for dealing with Castro that Stevenson could bring back to Kennedy. Like Venezuela's Betancourt, Camago, who combined a deep understanding of Latin American politics with an unusual grasp of the US domestic scene, believed that Cuba under Castro should be isolated. His plan proposed a two-stage process: First, Cuba would be given the opportunity to expel "external hostile forces" threatening the hemisphere. If it failed to do so, then Cuba would be suspended from the inter-American system and placed in a sort of political quarantine.[20] But the problem, in Camago's analysis, was that the large Latin American countries like Mexico, Brazil, Argentina, and Chile would be willing to go along with such a plan only if the United States made a major financial commitment at the Punta del Este meeting. Further, he said, it was not easy for politicians from the big countries to view a bearded revolutionary from a small Caribbean island as a serious threat. As one Mexican diplomat put it, "If we publicly declare that Cuba is a threat to our security, forty million Mexicans will die laughing."[21]

Stevenson submitted his report to President Kennedy on June 27, 1961. In the end Stevenson recommended that the president not go to Punta del Este. The Brazilians had asked for a delay in the conference date, and this presented an opportunity for Kennedy to decline. Instead he sent Secretary of the Treasury C. Douglas Dillon as the head of the US delegation. The policy that would be pursued would be along the lines outlined by Camago. Gordon, showing more emotion than was customary for him, told Stevenson in a warm letter that the trip "was an enormously rewarding experience for me" and that "everyone has his private pantheon, and in mine there are some empty niches reserved for prominent, public figures who keep their eye on the critical issues, and who retain a capacity to look at—and laugh at—themselves objectively."[22] He evidently meant to include the cerebral and witty Stevenson in his pantheon.

The Punta del Este conference—officially a meeting of the country representatives of ECOSOC—took place over August 5–17, 1961. In the southern winter the delegates had the beach resort town on the eastern tip of Uruguay all to themselves. The conference conducted its sessions in the halls of the town's municipal casino, wired for simultaneous translation in English, Spanish, Portuguese, and French. The casino had no central heating, and the delegates conducted their business in sweaters and overcoats. The dramatic tension from the start centered on the sharp contrast between Ernesto "Che" Guevara as head of the Cuban delegation and Treasury Secretary Dillon on the US side. Che was dressed in green military fatigues and an open-necked shirt, always with a long cigar in his mouth and accompanied by four usually heavily armed bodyguards (who could be persuaded to park their weapons at the door only after delicate negotiations). Dillon, tall, blue eyed, and formally dressed in a blue pin-striped suit, looked very much the wealthy, patrician Republican Wall Street investment banker whom Kennedy had appointed to give a bipartisan flavor to his cabinet.

Dillon's first appearance was limited to reading a welcoming message from President Kennedy in which he reiterated Kennedy's pledge of $1 billion for the Alliance's first year's operation. The delegates were expecting something more dramatic from Dillon. The US delegation had run into a problem in deciding whether to announce a specific figure for the ten-year US aid pledge. Assistant Secretary of State Ed Martin insisted that the delegation lacked the authority to pledge a specific amount. Dillon, backed by Goodwin and Gordon, maintained that he had this authority by virtue of implicit guidance from the president. Without a concrete commitment the United States would look foolish and might jeopardize the effort to isolate Cuba. Dillon came up with the figure of $20 billion for the ten-year period and carried the day. The Alliance's ten-year projected life cycle was Gordon's invention, based on the notion that the Marshall Plan's original life span was four years and that, since the Alliance was at least twice as difficult, a longer time frame would be prudent.

Dillon's announcement of the $20 billion target made headlines across South America. The pledge drew a scornful two-and-a-quarter-hour rebuttal from Guevara, who reminded the delegates that "many times the promises made here have not been ratified up there."[23] Che mockingly told the delegates that the idea of the Alliance was based on US fear of communism and that any assistance they received should "bear the stamp of Cuba."[24] In the plenary sessions Che peppered Dillon with questions. Che was courteous and on his good behavior in the working sessions, however, sometimes offering helpful technical suggestions to the delegates drafting the charter.

There were numerous lines of fracture among the delegations. The small countries, led by Uruguay, Paraguay, and Ecuador, wanted emergency assistance immediately. Uruguay's president Eduardo Victor Haedo threatened to denounce the proceedings "if we don't see some money fast."[25] The weight to be accorded experts from the inter-American machinery as opposed to national planners was a bone of contention, with several delegations complaining of a threat to national sovereignty. The pace of social reform, the changes in agrarian land tenure, the mechanisms for commodity price stabilization, and economic integration and trade sparked controversies that were often resolved by equivocal language that left each country free to interpret the meaning as it chose. Title I, item 6, dealing with agrarian reform, declared that the American republics would work together "to encourage, in accordance with the characteristics of each country, programs of comprehensive agrarian reform leading to the effective transformation, where required, of unjust structures and systems of land tenure and use." The delegates were amused when both Guevara and Dillon raised their hands in favor of this artful compromise.

Since the charter and the accompanying declaration were not treaties, but rather joint agreements among the signatory nations, the documents carried no legally binding commitments. The show between Cuba and the United States did not prevent the delegates from laboring long hours to produce the charter, a complicated document with four titles, seven chapters with subitems, and an appendix, plus the "Declaration of the Peoples of the Americas," which affirmed the spiritual and political unity of the Americas and set forth the goals of democratic development underlying the charter. At the conference's last session all the delegations except Cuba voted to approve the charter, and Guevara loosed a bitter assault on the Alliance, denouncing it as an instrument of economic imperialism.[26] Dillon rose and asked for the chance to reply. He stated that the United States would never "recognize the permanence of the present regime in Cuba," thus sealing the enmity between the United States and Cuba for the rest of the century and beyond. Despite the dramatic US-Cuba showdown, the Punta del Este delegates departed with a sense of high accomplishment and optimism.[27]

The Alliance for Progress: Retrospect and Prospect

Gordon returned again and again for the rest of his life to his experiences in Brazil and to the question of what went wrong with the Alliance for Progress. He wrote his daughter Amy, a day after his eighty-fifth birthday, "I have had two big disappointments in my life," one of which was the failure to make the Alliance for Progress a success in Brazil.[28] At other times he thought he was being too harsh and hasty in judging the Alliance a failure; it was certainly not a complete failure in his mind. He was not usually given to introspective self-analysis. He had his mother's self-assurance and believed that most problems lent themselves to reasoned solutions. But he could not shake the conclusion that with the Alliance something had gone very wrong. What was it? He was not sure whether the failure was big or small, whether the effort was utopian and misconceived from the start, or whether the failure—if indeed it was a failure—lay in flawed implementation. Was the past record of US commercial dealings with South American countries the problem, or was the problem instead the Alliance's lack of concern with private investment? Or was the Alliance simply doomed by unforeseen events like the Kennedy assassination or Johnson's decision to pull out of the 1968 race?

He came to various provisional conclusions at different times but was never fully satisfied with them. Early in his tenure as US ambassador to Brazil, he concluded that not enough emphasis was being placed on the "self-help" dimension of the Alliance.[29] The lack of region-wide coordination and priority setting, such as had happened through the OEEC machinery with Marshall Plan aid, was another problem he singled out.[30] Gordon told an interviewer in 1980, when he was asked if JFK's assassination had doomed the Alliance, that "the Alliance did not die with any single event. It rather dribbled away."[31] This judgment seemed too harsh in 1988, when he reflected on the Alliance's successes and failures for a twenty-fifth-anniversary volume.[32] The infusion of capital, the training of Latin American administrators, scientists, and other technical experts, and the upgrading of Brazilian universities that occurred via the Alliance in the 1960s had paved the way for later economic progress:

> I . . . believe that the balance sheet of the Alliance for Progress remains on the positive side. Between 1960 and 1980, Latin America did make significant advances in the continuing transformation from Third World dependency to independent action on the world stage—a transformation that will somehow surmount today's international debt crisis. During the 1960s, the Alliance helped lay the foundations for the surge in production of he 1970s, and for notable improvements in literacy, health, and life expectancy. Above all, its investments in human resources— in technical and administrative skills to complement the region's humanistic tradition—have made possible an ongoing modernization, looking ultimately to full incorporation into the First World.[33]

Cultures change more slowly than economic policies or political alignments, and thus it is hardly surprising that it took time for modernization to occur. One factor that seemed of major importance to Gordon in retrospect was that the Punta del Este conference, and the Alliance as a whole, represented mainly the work of experts and did not include enough participation by politicians. Had the heads of state been represented, as JFK had wanted, there would have been more political "buy in" for the Alliance. He tried to rectify the lack of political support by organizing a 1967 meeting for heads of state, but LBJ's withdrawal from the 1968 presidential race cut short this possibility for improvement. "Then," Gordon noted, "the Alliance was repudiated by Nixon and Kissinger in favor of a new era of neglect. For that mistake, all the Americas—North, Central, and South—continue to pay a heavy price."[34] All in all, "the diagnosis in 1961 and the array of proposed policies, reforms, and outside assistance were correct in their essentials. But there were two critical errors." On the US side, "we erred in not promoting from the very beginning arrangements appropriate to a more genuine partnership."[35] On the Brazilian side, "two successive presidents—Janio Quadros and Joao Goulart—were not [interested] in economic and social progress but rather the pursuit of personal and illegitimate power."[36] Gordon does not spell out what he means by the US failure to develop a "genuine partnership," but presumably he means that the Alliance was imposed on Brazil and other Latin American countries rather than, as in the Marshall Plan, developed by the recipient governments. Gordon goes on to contradict himself on the partnership point, however, by saying that he worked closely with some state governments in Brazil and ignored or worked around the national government, a stance that would not usually be conducive to forging a partnership with the host country. Gordon, the ultimate technocrat, blamed politics and his political enemies, not flaws in the Alliance's conception, for its failures.

None of the participants in framing the Alliance from North or South America—and certainly not Gordon himself—simplistically believed that the Marshall Plan concept could be applied without adaptation in the Latin American context. Alliance for Progress planners understood that the Latin American problem demanded much more than the Marshall Plan's effort to rebuild traditional economic relationships that had been disrupted by war. In this case, the framers knew, the social order had to change in order to achieve the reform goals, and change fundamentally. But they still had the Marshall Plan analogy in mind, and the goals sought by the framers of the Alliance thus could not be achieved without the cooperation of the participating governments. The fundamental Marshall Plan analogy, however, was misconceived. Harriman had invited the Europeans to define their own needs and to do so collectively. The United States had not tried to change the European social order or the internal political structures of the various countries. The Europeans had technical and human capital that was not present in equal measure in Latin America. The communist threat in South America was markedly different from the postwar European context. And of course the history of US relations with its neighbors in the hemisphere was entirely different from US-European relations, culturally, politically, and economically. Latin American governments simply could not tolerate the massive social upheavals implied by the redistributive politics of the Alliance for Progress. Yet if they did not embrace social change, what chance was there to achieve the Alliance's ambitious goals?

Gordon had believed, when he first saw conditions in Sao Paolo in the 1950s, that Brazil was like the New York City of his boyhood. In the 1920s New York had an elite class—the four hundred families that dominated the city's social and economic life—but it also had a large class of immigrant families, like his own, striving to realize the American Dream. As in 1920s New York, there was tremendous social mobility in Sao Paolo, with its booming economy and its emerging middle class of professionals and service workers. Democratic movements had emerged in a number of South American countries, as Adolph Berle had predicted. But as the US's Brazilian ambassador, he gained deeper knowledge of the country and recognized that these were utopian dreams. Instead of bringing about a New Deal for Brazil, as he had hoped, he was drawn into seemingly endless and messy disputes over expropriations of US utility companies in Brazil and related measures that blocked private investment in the country. He tried to reverse course and make the Alliance goals more modest and practical, but he still encountered opposition in Brazil and disappointment in Washington.

These doubts, second guessing, and reappraisals all lay in the future. At the end of the Punta del Este conference, Gordon was filled with hopes for his new assignment. An unusual development occurred as he prepared to leave for his new post, however, that took him by surprise and presented him with an immediate crisis. President Quadros of Brazil suddenly resigned, and a succession crisis confronted the country.

14

Ambassador to Brazil

What kind of a parliamentary regime is this; is it like Britain, France, Germany, or something else?
—Lincoln Gordon's first question on arrival in Brazil, 1961

But we continue hoping for the best and doing what we can to influence developments favorably.
—Lincoln Gordon, letter to a friend, August 22, 1963

My considered conclusion is that Goulart is now definitely engaged in a campaign to seize dictatorial power.
—Lincoln Gordon, March 26, 1964, cable to the State Department

As one of his last official acts before he resigned on August 25, 1961, President Janio Quadros presented "Che" Guevara with the nation's highest honor for foreigners, the Cruzeiro do Sul. This capped off to his critics the eleven months of unpredictable and bizarre actions that had marked his maverick presidency. Gordon and the State Department took the Guevara visit and related moves as more than a twist of Uncle Sam's nose, but the full implications were unclear. Gordon had met Quadros in June on the Stevenson visit, and Quadros had given the Americans three hours instead of the scheduled one hour. He had learned of Gordon's appointment as ambassador and expressed his desire to work closely with the new US envoy to make the Alliance for Progress a success in Brazil. But Quadros's actual performance in office grew increasingly erratic. He did little to advance any kind of program, let the economic stabilization effort slide, and showed his disdain for the Brazilian congress and the usual routines

of politics. A balance of payments crisis and accompanying runaway inflation were developing, and no effective program was in sight to deal with
them.

Now the new US envoy would have to deal with Joao Goulart—or
"Jango," as he had been known since boyhood—who had gained the presidency after the constitutional crisis that followed in the wake of Quadros's resignation. Goulart, as vice president, was the legal successor, but
he encountered fierce resistance from the military. Jango was a large land-
owner and one-time neighbor and protégé of the late president Getulio
Vargas. Jango's father had been a Vargas business partner and neighbor
in the state of Rio Grande do Sul. Goulart was a poor student, held back
and then dismissed from school after the fifth grade. He persevered, however, displaying the remarkable recuperative powers that he was to demonstrate throughout his political career. His passion was soccer, at which
he excelled to the point that he made the national youth team as a teen-
ager. This led him into a life of dissipation, as a result of which he con-
tracted a venereal disease and became gravely ill. He recovered at home
under the care of his beloved older sister, but the disease left him with a
permanent stiffness in his left leg and ended his soccer career. He fell into
a depression but bounced back, and with the help of a gift of land from
his father, he became a prosperous rancher. Goulart helped to organize
Vargas's presidential bid in 1950, and Vargas tried to persuade Jango to
enter politics. Jango initially refused but soon changed his mind and won
election to the state assembly along with his brother-in-law Leonel Brizola
(who had married his favorite sister).

Vargas persuaded Jango to take a leave of absence from his provincial
legislative duties and join him at the national level. Jango took the lead
in the campaign to raise the minimum wage and subsequently served as
labor minister for Vargas from 1953 to 1954, earning the undying enmity
of Brazil's business interests and the political right. Jango was a populist in the Vargas mold and an implacable foe of the rich and powerful.
Jango became well known to the Brazilian public when it became known
that President Vargas, prior to his 1954 suicide in the presidential palace in Rio, had entrusted his suicide letter to Jango. In 1955 he was chosen to run as the vice presidential candidate of the Brazilian Labor Party
(PTB), which had forged an electoral coalition with the party of presidential candidate Governor Juscelino Kubitschek. Many groups tried to

block the nomination of Goulart, but he fought back adroitly and kept his place on the ticket. Goulart served harmoniously with the term-limited Kubitschek and was narrowly reelected vice president when Quadros succeeded Kubitschek as president in 1960. Jango did not enjoy good relations with Quadros and set off on an independent course that included courting Communist China as part of his own personal foreign policy.

Goulart's succession to the presidency under the extraordinary circumstances of Quadros's sudden resignation was not a foregone conclusion. Opposition from the military ministers in Quadros's government and from business on the political right produced a parliamentary deadlock. Indeed, Quadros had counted on precisely this reaction in the hope of being returned to power with enhanced powers by the military leaders who opposed Jango. But Goulart and his brother-in-law, now Governor Brizola of Rio Grande do Sul, outmaneuvered the generals by first taking over command of the armed forces in their state so that the generals opposing Jango knew they would have to fight their brother officers. Then Brizola forged a compromise in the parliament under which his brother-in-law would become president, but the presidential regime would be replaced by a parliamentary system with a prime minister and cabinet ministers appointed by the prime minister, thus limiting the powers of the presidency. Goulart appointed Tancredo Neves, a veteran centrist politician, as prime minister and pledged to pursue an economic stabilization program under the internationally respected economist and planning minister Celso Furtado. Goulart and Brizola extracted a concession providing for a plebiscite in January 1963 to determine whether the parliamentary system should be continued or replaced by a return to the presidential system.

Lincoln and Jango, Phase One: October 1961 to June 1962

Gordon was confirmed by the Senate on September 8 and arrived in Brazil in mid-October. He asked Niles Bond, the minister-counselor who had been in charge of the embassy prior to Gordon's arrival, "What kind of parliamentary regime is this; is it like Britain, France, Germany, or something else?" Bond's answer was that it was too soon to tell. The centrist cabinet appointed by Prime Minister Neves included the center-left San Tiago Dantas as foreign minister and the center-right Walter Moreira

Salles at Treasury. Goulart appeared to be working cooperatively with the cabinet. Gordon presented his credentials to Goulart in Brasilia on October 19 and had private meetings with him and with the leading cabinet ministers. His fluency in Portuguese (despite his self-described "flat-as-a-tortilla" accent) was a great asset in establishing friendly relations. President Goulart was cordial and said that he hoped to work closely with the new envoy. Goulart expressed his admiration for President Kennedy and voiced his desire to meet with the American president soon.

The first few months, in Gordon's view, amounted to a good start. The embassy negotiated agreements for Peace Corps activities in Brazil and for a regional accord to collaborate in Recife with the Brazilian regional development agency (the Superintendancy for the Development of the Northeast, or SUDENE). This region was one of the poorest in the country and of special interest to the Americans as a central challenge to Brazil's development goals. Gordon began his extensive travels and meetings with federal and state officials and leaders of public opinion, many of whom looked to potential US technical and economic assistance. On November 29–30 Gordon returned to Washington to argue for allocating one-third of total American aid under the Alliance for Progress to Brazil. If the Alliance was going to transform Latin America, success in Brazil, the largest and most important country in the hemisphere, would lead the way. Success here would breed success in the rest of the hemisphere.

Gordon's approach, which was successful for Brazil in this instance, was based on the premise that he would leverage his contacts with President Kennedy and the White House staff on policy initiatives, short-circuiting the State Department. He knew that JFK, like FDR before him, did not like or trust the State Department bureaucracy. JFK had drawn the lesson from the Bay of Pigs episode that career bureaucrats, the generals and the CIA, had boxed him in and misled him. So Gordon sought to deal directly with the White House without too obviously side-stepping his State Department colleagues. He believed that this was what Harriman had done with both Presidents Roosevelt and Truman. From observing Harriman in action, Gordon judged that not getting bogged down in formal channels and going directly to the top were key to success. Such an approach required unusual political skills, however, and these Gordon did not have. The informal policy-making style had some significant drawbacks: decisions could emerge that were not fully staffed out or thought out. Moreover the analogy between the Alliance and the Marshall Plan was already missing some key components: in this case the United States, not the Brazilians or other Latin Americans, was deciding where US economic assistance would go. There was no OEEC-like mechanism for establishing priorities from Latin America as a whole and even within Brazil itself. Gordon "was troubled . . . by the failure of the Brazilian government to establish effective mechanisms for coordination of Alliance programs and projects as a whole."[1]

The new ambassador grew concerned as he traveled around the country by the antiforeign, anticapitalist, and anti–North American sentiments he encountered. "I had become generally aware of the popularity of Marxist theory among Brazilian professors of social science," he wrote in his 2003 *Supplement* to *Brazil's Second Chance,* but "I was not prepared . . . for the depth and intensity of this sentiment."[2] In the time before the Cuban missile crisis there was a popular idea that the United States had lost the space race and was now technologically inferior to the Soviet Union. The fear of communism that had been a rallying cry for the Marshall Plan in Europe did not seem to exist or to exist to the same degree in Brazil. It surprised Gordon that important sectors of public opinion were so hostile to the United States and so skeptical of US military power. To counter this view, Gordon insisted in April 1962 that the projected Goulart visit to the United States should include a visit to Strategic Air Command (SAC) headquarters in Nebraska to demonstrate US military and technological strength. Gordon became convinced that US efforts in cultural and educational diplomacy lagged behind the decades of skillful Soviet propaganda activities in Brazil and other Latin American countries. Although Gordon was an economist, primarily interested in the economic success of the Alliance, he certainly shared the Cold War views of the Kennedy administration and most of his national security colleagues at the time. The dangers of Castroism and the need to combat the drift toward pro-Soviet sympathies were exaggerated in Gordon's thinking and in the thinking of most of his contemporaries at the time but were part of the US motivation behind the Alliance. Kennedy administration policy-level officials were probably slightly more hardline than State Department career officers, who were more inclined to view the hemisphere's leftism as nationalist in origin.

As a result of his early contacts, Gordon decided to intensify his outreach activities to Brazilian audiences. He stepped up his travels around the country, both on official business and on family vacations. For their Christmas vacation in December the family drove to Ouro Preto from Rio via Petropolis and Belo Horizonte, staying in the hotel at Ouro Preto designed by Oscar Niemeyer, visiting the church with the Aleijadinho soapstone sculptures of the prophets, and exploring the countryside, before ending up at a beach resort north of Rio for Christmas. In 1962 there were twenty-three trips, including three returns to Washington for consultations. On each of his return trips to Washington, Gordon met with President Kennedy, and he always maintained direct lines of communication with the White House.

Meanwhile, Gordon's independent access to the White House was a delicate point of protocol. Kennedy had an unusual interest in Brazil, and there were contacts with his ambassador that would be scarcely imaginable in a current presidency. Gordon had a favorite story he liked to tell friends illustrating his White House ties. He came into his office one morning and told his secretary Mary Stevenson to get the president on the line for him, meaning President Goulart. As he rehearsed his opening line in Portuguese for Goulart, a different accent—the Boston-inflected English of JFK—came over the line: "Linc, is there a problem down there?" Not usually at a loss for words, the flustered ambassador confessed the mistake and apologized. Kennedy laughed and asked for a report on recent developments.

Despite his efforts to pay attention to cultural diplomacy, pressing political problems still occupied the bulk of Gordon's time and attention early in his tenure. The new parliamentary system appeared to have stabilized by the end of 1961, but with the president exercising full powers and the prime minister apparently having little or no power, the compromise worked out at the transfer to Goulart did not have the intended consequence. Gordon's initial dealings with President Goulart had two main objectives: to get Goulart to move more rapidly toward full implementation of the Alliance for Progress and to persuade the president to support the US position on expelling the Castro regime from the OAS system. While meeting with Gordon in mid-February, the president told the American that he was dissatisfied with the "hybrid system" that had paved the way for his succession. The system was neither truly presidential nor quite parliamentary. The result of this flawed system, Jango told the envoy, was that members of congress and the cabinet acted on the basis of short-term electoral considerations and blocked measures in the broad national interest. He therefore proposed to fortify his position through the device of "disincompatibilization"—that is, he wanted a constitutional requirement making holders of executive office who wanted to run for elective offices resign their executive positions four to six months in advance of the election.[3] With congressional elections coming in the fall of 1962, he would thus force his cabinet members to resign and replace them with a cabinet of technicians. The new ministers would be men of "great integrity, reputation, and capacity drawn from all regions and groups in the community"—all of them without political ambitions and devoted to democratic progress.[4]

Gordon decided that it was time to play the JFK card and proposed a presidential visit by Goulart to Washington. This visit would consolidate US relations with Goulart and possibly enhance the prospects for influencing the Brazilian president at a critical juncture. The visit took place in April and included stops in Washington, New York (where Jango was given a ticker-tape parade), Chicago, and Omaha, Nebraska, SAC headquarters. The trip was a great success. Goulart made an address to a joint session of Congress, a rare honor for a foreign head of state, and met with a number of cabinet members, including the secretaries of state and the treasury. Most important were the private meetings with President Kennedy. The two men developed a genuine rapport, and Goulart invited Kennedy for an early return visit to Brazil, an invitation Kennedy quickly accepted. Brazilian finance minister Moreira Sales at the same time negotiated an economic stabilization plan and aid package with US treasury secretary Dillon. President Goulart pledged to negotiate a broad agreement whereby Brazil would, in purchasing foreign-owned utilities, provide generous compensation; in addition he promised to resolve a dispute that had arisen when his brother-in-law in Rio Grande do Sul in February 1962 nationalized International Telephone and Telegraph (IT&T) facilities in his state. Brizola's action in this instance had led directly to the adoption of the Hickenlooper Amendment by the US Senate, calling for a cutoff of US aid to countries nationalizing US companies without compensation.[5] Governor Brizola two years earlier had expropriated a subsidiary of another US-owned utility, still a simmering dispute between the United States and Brazil.

Gordon and his embassy colleagues were hopeful that the Goulart visit had laid the basis for early progress on the Alliance, for more effective macroeconomic stabilization policies, and for a general improvement in US-Brazilian relations. But "this hopeful prospect came to an abrupt end in June and July."[6]

Troubles Mount: July to December 1962

As the congressional elections of fall 1962 approached, the Goulart government relaxed its fiscal discipline, and inflation accelerated. Labor strikes increased, and shortages of basic foods and other essential commodities were frequent, which led to shop break-ins and other public disorders. Inquiries from the US embassy to follow up on the agreements reached in the Goulart visit to Washington were politely pushed aside or deferred. The hopeful outlook established by the presidential visit rapidly dissipated as Governor Brizola stepped up his vehement attacks on the United States, which Goulart disavowed in private but failed to repudiate publicly.

With the honeymoon between himself and Goulart over, Gordon reflected on his situation. He and Goulart were as different as one could possibly imagine. Gordon was rational, direct, secular, and unpretentious—an intellectual with a slightly moralistic streak. He was something of a Victorian gentleman with an ethic of hard work. Jango, on the other hand, was a politician not interested in or comfortable with long technical arguments, a man steeped in Catholicism of the reformist variety, with an almost mystical sense of his own destiny as an embodiment of the Vargas tradition. Goulart was courteous, affable, and seemingly quick to agree with the American envoy when pressed on a point, but he would quickly forget or find it inconvenient to follow up on any agreements. It was a recipe for a troubled relationship, and the troubles soon came.

Protracted negotiation over profit remittances by foreign-owned businesses was a case in point. Legislation had been introduced in the Brazilian congress to limit such remittances, and the business community became alarmed over potential interruptions in the flow of badly needed foreign investment capital. President Goulart was pressed to water down or veto the objectionable provisions and appeared to agree that this legislation could dry up private investment. But in the end he heeded the arguments of his leftist brother-in-law and allowed the bill to become law without any amendments. Meanwhile, Goulart was having difficulty in gaining congressional approval for his new cabinet selections after forcing the resignation of the old cabinet. Goulart's first choice for prime minister, San Tiago Dantas, was turned down by the congress. Auro Maura Andrade, Jango's second choice, was confirmed easily but then abruptly resigned the post. The United States got an unpleasant Fourth of July surprise when President Goulart finally named Francisco Brochado da Rocha, an ally of his brother-in-law Brizola and the state official in charge of Brizola's expropriations, as prime minister. In retaliation Gordon recommended the postponement of JFK's visit to Brazil. JFK was initially reluctant to accept Gordon's recommendation for a postponement but finally agreed after setting two conditions. The first was that the visit be postponed to a certain date, and the trip was rescheduled for November. The second was that Gordon return to Washington to give him a full briefing on the Brazilian situation. Gordon departed for Washington in late July and met with Kennedy on July 30.

The July 30 meeting was notable for several reasons. It was the first time that Kennedy used his new secret taping system.[7] The publication of the tape in 2001 became a minor sensation in the watchdog community, which viewed the tape as evidence of US backing for a military coup against Goulart. A careful reading of the transcript, though, does not support this interpretation. That the Brazilian military should have been discussed was hardly surprising in the wake of the Argentine coup of March 29–30, which was fresh in everyone's mind. This coup was a blow to the Alliance for Progress because President Arturo Frondizi had been regarded as a strong supporter of the Punta del Este vision. Gordon's pertinent remarks on the subject of a military coup in Brazil were as follows:

I don't think we want to encourage a coup. What we want to do with Goulart, I think, is two things: we want to make use of the fact that he does have a tremendous regard for you [President Kennedy] and he is very proud that this relation with the U.S. [president] has been established. And there are certain [positive] things. . . . I think we'll get this IT&T case settled and soon and finally . . . I hope we can avoid other expropriations this time. I think we can make some headway on the utility thing. It's mostly negative, but I think we've got to use [your prestige with him] as much as we can.

The main thing is, at the same time, to organize forces which are both political and military, either to reduce his power . . . [or] in an extreme case to push him out, if it comes to that. And this would depend on some overt actions on his part.[8]

A few minutes later in the meeting, White House staffer Richard Goodwin remarked: "We may very well want them [the Brazilian military] to take over at the end of the year if they can."[9] To this Gordon replied: "We have that military front. And as I see it their function is first to keep Goulart on the rails [i.e., within constitutional limits]."[10] Neither Gordon nor Kennedy, in short, agreed with Goodwin. That they discussed the possibility of military intervention in Brazil was understandable in view of the recent coups in Argentina and Peru, and of course the men were well aware of the military's failed effort to block Goulart from becoming president in 1961 and of the military's past role in Brazilian politics.

The more relevant criticism of the July 30 meeting is that it showed the shortcomings of the informal Kennedy style of decision-making. President Kennedy approved Gordon's request to spend $5 million on a campaign to support candidates friendly to the United States in the Brazilian congressional and gubernatorial elections that fall. Gordon's proposal followed the advice of the CIA staff at the embassy and called for the United States to provide assistance to democratic forces, along an analogy with the Marshall Plan's support for the Einaudi government against the communists in Italy. According to Gordon's intelligence sources, Soviet and Cuban agents had infiltrated the trade union movement and were maneuvering to elect radicals in the fall 1962 elections. Gordon had not vetted the proposal through the regular State Department machinery. Had he done so, it is likely that the proposal would at least have been scaled back in size and perhaps dropped altogether. Assistant Secretary of State Ed Martin worried that his old friend Gordon was becoming unduly alarmist and had exaggerated the threat of communist influence in the Goulart administration.[11] Nor had the proposal been reviewed through the regular interagency national security decision-making machinery, where State's opposition would have been raised. Gordon and Martin's friendship softened their policy disagreements, but the gap between them was widening in the course of the year. JFK at the July meeting initially questioned the amount of the proposed expenditure to influence the elections but finally agreed. This effort backfired and strengthened the position of leftist candidates, including Miguel Arraes, who was elected governor of the northern state of Pernambuco, whose capital city was Recife. Brazil's major development agency was located in Recife, and the governor's support was badly needed if the Alliance was to succeed in the northeast. Gordon came much later to regret the US intervention, but he continued to defend the action for many years.[12]

When Gordon returned to Brazil after his meeting with Kennedy, he found the political situation in an even more unsettled state. Goulart's treasury minister informed Gordon that he was resigning because of the lack of strong government backing for his economic stabilization policies. Governor Brizola was attacking the Peace Corps with such vehemence that the physical safety of the volunteers was threatened. Goulart promised to provide police protection but as usual made no public criticism of his brother-in-law. Progress had not been made on the IT&T compensation issue or on the promise to purchase foreign-owned utilities at a fair price. Gordon finally negotiated an agreement to compensate IT&T for $10 to $12 million and averted the application of the Hickenlooper Amendment, which could have cost Brazil hundreds of millions in US aid cuts. Dealing with nationalization of American utilities took up an enormous amount of Gordon's time and was one of the most frustrating aspects of his tenure in Brazil.

One bright spot in Brazilian-US relations, which proved to be only temporary, came with the Cuban Missile Crisis of late October, when Brazil for a time abandoned its pro-Soviet, pro-Castro stance and sided with the United States. President Goulart seemed to support unequivocally the strong US stance, surprising Gordon and military attaché Colonel Vernon Walters when they came to brief him on the situation. Brazil supported the United States on an OAS resolution calling for the removal of the missiles.[13] Most important, starting on October 27, just four days after Kennedy's speech announcing the naval blockage of Cuba, Brazil played a potentially important role in highly secret negotiations as a mediator between Castro and the United States in an effort to secure the removal of the Soviet missiles via diplomacy. The Brazilian effort at negotiations soon disillusioned Gordon, however, who communicated his

The Gordon family on vacation in New Hampshire, ca. 1918. Top row: Bernard Gordon, Dorothy Gordon, unidentified woman family friend. Bottom row: Frank, about age seven, and Lincoln, age five. Frank resembles his father, Lincoln his mother.

Photos are from the Gordon family personal collection unless otherwise credited.

Dorothy Gordon in gypsy costume early in her career as a folksinger and performer, ca. 1920. She wanted to be an opera singer, but her voice was too weak in those preamplification days. According to family lore, she took up her stage career at her son Lincoln's suggestion (his first bit of policy advice to an elder). She rapidly professionalized her performances, toured the US Northeast, performed in London and Europe, and then moved to the radio, remaining highly successful until her death in 1970.

Dorothy Gordon at the piano, singing and surrounded by children, ca. 1921. Lincoln is sitting beside her, dressed in a suit and turning the pages of the sheet music. Lincoln did this on stage with his mother during her early career as a performer.

Bernard Gordon at Chetwood, ca. 1930.

Portrait of Allison as a girl, ca. 1928.

Lincoln and Frank with Lake Sunapee in the background, ca. 1920.

Lincoln as a youth at the family's summer compound at Lake Sunapee, near the town of Gorgas Mills, New Hampshire, ca. 1928.

Lincoln in his twenties as an assistant professor of government at Harvard, before he left for government service in Washington, DC, during World War II, ca. 1938.

Darkwater, before the hurricane, 1938.

Allison and Lincoln Gordon on their wedding day, June 25, 1937, in the garden of her parents' home in Brookline, Massachusetts.

Bernard Baruch being quizzed by a Senate Committee, Washington, DC, February 28, 1938. Senator James F. Byrnes (left), chair of the Senate Unemployment and Relief Committee, is questioning Baruch. (Library of Congress.)

W. Averell Harriman, ca. 1942, at his desk in London as Lend-Lease administrator. (Library of Congress.)

Crimean conference, Livadia Palace, Crimea, Russia, February 1945. Left to right: Secretary of State Edward Stettinius, Major General L. S. Kuter, Admiral E. J. King, General George C. Marshall, Ambassador Averell Harriman, Admiral William Leahy, and President F. D. Roosevelt. (Library of Congress.)

George C. Marshall takes the oath of office to become secretary of state, January 21, 1947. Chief Justice Fred Vinson appears in the foreground. In the background is President Harry S. Truman. (Library of Congress.)

Milton Katz, ca. 1939. (Library of Congress.)

A bound report on the operation of the Marshall Plan on its second anniversary is presented to General George C. Marshall (right), the father of the plan, by Secretary of State Dean Acheson (left) and ECA administrator Paul Hoffman in Washington, April 3, 1950. (Library of Congress.)

Brazilian president Joao Goulart at a ticker-tape parade in New York City, April 1952. (Library of Congress.)

Lincoln with Queen Elizabeth II at the opening of a US exhibition in London in 1953.

The Gordons' Gloucester Road house in London, ca. 1953.

Lincoln at Harvard Business School, ca. 1960.

Lincoln conferring with President Kennedy in the Oval Office, February 1962. (John F. Kennedy Presidential Library.)

Mrs. Maria Teresa Goulart, wife of Brazilian president Joao Goulart, October 27, 1961. Brazilians considered Matia the world's most beautiful First Lady. (Library of Congress.)

Lincoln looks on as President Kennedy greets President Goulart at Andrews Air Force Base, April 3, 1962. (Library of Congress.)

A remark by President Kennedy prompts a smile from his guest, President Joao Goulart of Brazil, as they pose with advisors in his White House office after lunching together in the executive mansion, April 3, 1962. (Library of Congress.)

Ambassador Gordon descending from a US Air Force plane on a visit to a Brazilian regional capital city several days after the March 30–April 1 military coup. Brazil requested that Gordon make the previously scheduled visit to illustrate that calm prevailed in the country. (Library of Congress.)

Left to right: Brazilian president Humberto Castelo Branco, Lincoln Gordon, an unidentified American, and Ambassador Roberto Campos enjoying a laugh at a meeting in late 1964.

Lincoln as assistant secretary of state for inter-American affairs and Latin American representatives, ca. 1966–1968.

Lincoln taking the oath of office as ambassador to Brazil, February 1961. In the center in the background is Secretary of State Rusk, with Lincoln and Allison Gordon beside him. The man on the left is unidentified. (Library of Congress.)

Ambassador Gordon shaking hands with Prime Minister Tancredo Neves after arriving in Brazil, March 1961. (Library of Congress.)

Lincoln as assistant secretary of state, listening as President Johnson makes a point in an Oval Office meeting, January 1967. (LBJ Library.)

Lincoln, seated second from left with Allison beside him (wearing glasses), en route to the LBJ ranch in preparation for the meeting of the OAS presidents, 1967.

Lincoln playing the cello, 1962. He played regularly from 1954 into the early 1980s. With long hours of practice he became a proficient amateur player, but his practices and sessions with a string quartet kept him away from his family for many hours. Allison joked that his passion for music (an avocation she did not share) was at least preferable to his having an affair.

Allison in Rio de Janeiro, ca. 1962.

Lincoln in his presidential office at Johns Hopkins, [196?]. Official photo by Bachrach Photographers.

Lincoln, Kenneth Flamm, John Steinbruner, Cherryl Eschbach, Brookings Institution, 1987.

Lincoln on the Amalfi Coast, ca. 1992, on one of his many travels in his later years.

Family photo taken at Darkwater, on the occasion of Lincoln's ninetieth birthday, 2003.

Lincoln in the woods, ca. 1990.

Lincoln with his granddaughter Kate Gordon when he was in his eighties. She was with him on his last day.

disenchantment to Washington. The initiative—the brainchild of Secretary Rusk and Assistant Secretary Martin—was doomed from the beginning by Castro's obstinacy and bellicosity. Castro not only rejected the Brazilian suggestion that he ask his Russian allies to remove the missiles already in place in return for Cuba rejoining the OAS system. He also wrote to Khrushchev urging a Soviet attack on the United States. Notwithstanding the difficulty of dealing with Castro, the Kennedy administration considered that the Goulart government had grossly mishandled the assignment. The upshot was a souring rather than an improvement in US-Brazil relations. The problems, as meticulously detailed by James Hershberg, included the Brazilians getting off on the wrong foot by sending the wrong man as courier, General Albino Silva instead of the US-preferred Bastian Pinto. Albino Silva did not follow the script laid out for him by the Americans. The Brazilians subsequently failed to observe the strict confidence and secrecy that they had promised to follow. Goulart himself, in the middle of the delicate negotiations, appeared to qualify his country's support for the US-backed OAS resolution, even hinting to his leftist constituency at home that his mediation efforts were designed to restrain the United States and aid Fidel Castro.[14] Goulart's ambivalent conduct during the crisis "caused an even further decline of his reputation among U.S. officials, who remained convinced that Brazil yearned to 'help Cuba re-enter the inter-American community and build up Castro as a true Latin American revolutionary.'"[15]

The ill-fated missile crisis episode in US-Brazilian relations began when Ambassador Gordon and military attaché Colonel Vernon Walters brought President Goulart the text of President Kennedy's October 22 speech, which Walters read in a fluent Portuguese translation. Goulart told the two Americans that Brazil would support the United States in the UN and the OAS and that he was delighted his friend Kennedy was standing up to the Soviets and defending the whole continent from external aggression. He even appeared slightly disappointed, in Gordon's recollection of the meeting, that the United States had not immediately bombed the missile sites. Goulart asked that his ambassador in Washington be allowed to see the intelligence pictures and asked for a daily report from Gordon on the naval dispositions. The mediation efforts, which were designed to secure the removal of the Soviet missiles already in place, appealed to Goulart's sense of himself as a man of destiny. But his duplicity and lack of discretion contributed to the failure of the mission. The Americans were divided in their estimates of whether Goulart had simply botched a sensitive assignment or was seeking to aid Castro and present himself as a hemispheric third force opposing both US and Soviet imperialism.

When the Soviet vessels turned around and headed back home in the face of the US blockade, Goulart invited Gordon to the presidential residence and poured out a generous tumbler of scotch (his favorite drink) for each of them to toast the victory. Gordon could not help seeing the Brazilian president in a favorable light on this occasion. Jango seemed to Gordon then the pure *gaucho,* a warmly human and appealing figure without his usual political guile. Despite the Russian reluctance to challenge the naval blockade, there was still the problem of removing the missiles already in place in Cuba, and it was for this purpose that Brazil's help was sought. There then ensued the missteps described above. Gordon's and the Kennedy administration's hopes that Brazil could negotiate the removal of the missiles were rapidly disappointed. The failure to move Castro, whether or not the result of Goulart's deceptions and missteps, caused Kennedy to turn toward diplomacy brokered by his brother, whereby the Soviets ignored Castro and agreed to remove their missiles from Cuba in return for an implicit US commitment to remove intermediate-range missiles from Turkey at a later date (which occurred six months later).

There remained the question of Kennedy's previously scheduled visit to Brazil. The November date had already been postponed once again to December 17, before the missile crisis. It was now obvious that the postcrisis diplomatic maneuvering around Berlin would preoccupy Kennedy, and in any case his desire to accommodate Goulart was gone. He could easily dispense with the visit and do so with a plausible excuse. Despite Kennedy's disillusionment with Goulart's erratic behavior during the missile crisis, he recognized that Brazil, with the Cuban question now off the agenda as a leading US foreign policy concern, would be the most important focus of US policy in the hemisphere. JFK did not want to exacerbate further US relations with Brazil. The question of the visit was thrown to Gordon and the embassy for a recommendation. Someone on Gordon's staff, possibly Walters, floated the idea of substituting Attorney General Robert Kennedy to replace his brother for the December visit. The attorney general was known to be the president's closest adviser, and the Brazilians would be happy to have him if they could not have the president. The idea was vetted through the White House NSC machinery and approved at an NSC meeting in December with President Kennedy in the chair.

RFK arrived in Brazil in mid-December, so the meeting took place on the date set for the presidential visit and in time for the attorney general to return to Washington for the Christmas holidays. A three-hour meeting took place between Bobby Kennedy and President Goulart on December 17, with only Gordon and Jose de Seabra, the State Department's leading Portuguese-to-English interpreter, sitting in on the session. Gordon worried that the absence of any of Goulart's ministers would lead to distortions or misunderstandings of what was said at the meeting. Both Gordon and de Seabra took notes to have a record of any agreements.[16] The United States had prepared an ambitious agenda of items for the attorney general to raise with President Goulart, including technical issues of the balance of payments problem, the treatment of American businesses, communist influences in the Goulart government, and questions of how Goulart would use his soon-to-be-reclaimed full presidential powers.[17] Issues of foreign policy and the postponed visit of President Kennedy were also discussed. Attorney General Kennedy raised a series of US criticisms of Brazil's policies but did so in a manner that Gordon considered arrogant and undiplomatic. Among Kennedy's criticisms was Brazil's failure to curb population growth and its refusal to confront the Catholic Church over birth control. The irony of Kennedy, a Catholic and the father of nine children, lecturing Goulart on birth control was not lost on Gordon. Goulart's responses to this and to other criticisms amply illustrated, for Gordon, the limitations of summit diplomacy. Jango gave a rambling rejoinder to Kennedy's opening remarks, lasting more than an hour. It was difficult to reach any clear understandings because the president was not fully conversant with the details of the policy issues. While Goulart was eager to please and reiterated his admiration for President Kennedy, his stated desire for closer relations with the United States was mixed with discursive commentary and complaints about US policy that left RFK and Gordon confused. Privately Gordon was shocked by Kennedy's behavior toward the Brazilian president and laid much of the blame for the frustrating session at RFK's feet.

A lunch with Planning Minister Celso Furtado helped salvage something from the Kennedy visit. Furtado gave a cogent analysis of a new three-year plan for economic stabilization that impressed Kennedy and Gordon and revived their hopes for improved US-Brazilian cooperation in economic policy. Gordon's overall verdict on the RFK-Goulart meeting was that it was "possibly useful but certainly inconclusive."[18]

Renewed Hopes: January to May 1963

The new year brought a measure of stability to the domestic political scene in Brazil and an improvement in US-Brazilian relations. Goulart's victory in regaining his full presidential powers in the January 6 plebiscite meant that the form of government was no longer a point of contention and constant friction. The Christmas holiday season and the southern summer contributed to the lull in political battles. The presidential cabinet appointed by Goulart included ministers less hostile to the United States and was welcomed in the embassy and Washington. Gordon was hopeful that an improved climate for badly needed foreign investment might follow from the government's new stabilization strategy. But his hopes were tempered by the stubborn economic problems that continued to worsen—inflation, fiscal deficits, balance of payments problems, and production slowdowns. It became increasingly clear that substantial US assistance in the form of "program aid" (general support to assist in the budget and balance of payments) was going to be necessary along with "project aid" (of the Agency for International Development [AID] and the Alliance for Progress). In February a team from the US Treasury Department arrived in Brazil to negotiate the terms of the US aid package. The team's work led to an agreement in mid-March between Finance Minister Dantas on the Brazilian side and AID administrator David Bell on the US side that promised that continued US "support [would] be given to a technically satisfactory Brazilian program for economic stabilization . . . but on a 'short-leash' basis permitting periodic review and making possible the withdrawal of support on either economic or political grounds."[19]

In negotiating the agreement, Dantas was received in Washington more like a head of state than a minister of finance. He met with President Kennedy, Treasury Secretary Douglas Dillon, Attorney General Bobby Kennedy, the secretaries of labor and agriculture, the managing director of the IMF, and several senators and representatives, in addition to attending negotiating sessions with David Bell. Despite the attention, Dantas balked initially at the terms of the agreement. He complained to Gordon about the small initial aid installment and said that he was inclined to abandon the whole effort. Gordon assured him that the proposed $400 million was a generous sum from Congress and that Congress would insist on benchmarks and periodic reviews before it would appropriate funds. The Dantas-Bell agreement laid the foundation for continued US support both for "program loans" and for certain "project loans"—mostly infrastructure loans for highways, power plants, health centers, and public works. Brazil for its part pledged to adopt anti-inflationary fiscal policies and a variety of social reforms.

Anticipating that he would be greeted with appreciation if not fanfare upon his return home, Dantas instead encountered a storm of protests, criticism, and venomous attacks led by Brizola and his leftist allies. Goulart equivocated and did not repudiate his brother-in-law publicly or give full support to his finance minister. Gordon continued to press Goulart to repudiate Brizola when he should have recognized that Jango would never do this, for both personal and political reasons. Goulart assumed, correctly from a hard-headed political assessment, that he could have both the benefits of US assistance (the Americans would not walk away from the agreement they had just negotiated) and the continued support of his own political base. He had merely to straddle the issue. While Gordon and his diplomatic colleagues might occasionally despair at President Goulart's failure to master the details of policy, none doubted the president's dexterity as a political high-wire artist.

Goulart meanwhile was pushing the Brazilian congress to adopt a constitutional amendment to permit payment for land expropriations through long-term bonds rather than with cash. This effort burnished Goulart's image as a reformer. Gordon surmised, based on a conversation with Goulart, that the proposal had not been a serious one, but a tactical move to keep his political opponents off-balance. During a friendly conversation with the US ambassador on various topics, President Goulart had asked Gordon's opinion "as an economist" on the merits of achieving land reform by expropriating strips of land along federal highways and public works. Gordon replied that such a step would have to take into account the effect on the value of neighboring land and how to distinguish land that was highly productive from land that was not already in use. Jango responded: "I can see that that makes sense to you as an economist, but my plan squeezes those PSD *coloneis* [colonels] where it hurts!"[20]

Rapid Deterioration: June to December 1963

Despite signs that the Dantas-Bell targets were slipping and Brizola was gaining strength, Gordon felt confident enough to request a month's stateside vacation from Assistant Secretary Ed Martin. Martin sensibly worried that this might be too long a period for Gordon to be away. Gordon pressed the request, and Martin eventually granted it. Gordon spent the period from June 2 to June 30 in New Hampshire with his family. He returned to find the political landscape changed for the worse. In June Goulart had shaken up the cabinet again and dismissed San Tiego Dantas, Celso Furtado, Army Minister General Amaury Kruel, and several others who had been publicly attacked by Brizola. The shakeup set off a flood of press speculation and rumors that a coup was imminent. Analysts in the US State Department Brazil desk and at the embassy took the view that changes in the key ministries of war and finance did "give cause for concern but not for despair."[21] A good sign was that Brizola, despite campaigning hard for the job, had been passed over once again by his brother-in-law for finance minister in favor of the centrist Carvalho Pinto.

President Goulart had met briefly with President Kennedy at the papal installation ceremony in Rome in March, and there had been something of a renewal of the Goulart-Kennedy friendship. Now Jango invited Lincoln to the presidential palace to tell him about his private meeting with Kennedy. The Brazilian president was in an ebullient mood and wanted to reassure the American ambassador that his cabinet reshuffle of June was not an anti-US move or a radical step. The changes, Jango explained, were merely camouflage for the replacement of General Kruel from the war ministry. The departure of Dantas was only necessary, said Goulart, because of the minister's failing health. Goulart gave a detailed analysis of the tensions within the military and a lucid account of the feud between Brizola and Governor Carlos Lacerda that Gordon believed pointed toward an intensifying political instability. Nonetheless, Gordon's reporting telegram to Washington was cautious but not alarmist: "My general impression [of] this talk was that Goulart is considerably surer of himself than in either February or April talks. He appeared especially relieved by [the] solution of [the] military crisis. [He] continues to be difficult or impossible to pin down on policy questions, partly because [he] resists being pinned down but equally because he continues uneducated and ill-informed on all policy substance. . . . In personal attitude toward me, he could not have been more cordial. He appeared very happy with [the] way in which President Kennedy had talked with him in Rome."[22]

However, economic conditions worsened and produced turmoil in July and August. An unusual problem developed at this time that complicated Gordon's official life and may have deepened his antipathy for Goulart. Before this date the two men were not on the same wavelength intellectually but personally were not hostile. After this episode any vestiges of trust seemingly disappeared. On August 8 three major Rio newspapers published front-page stories about an alleged dinner party hosted by Ambassador Gordon for seventeen visiting American businessmen. The dinner party, for which no date was given, was allegedly intended to organize support for Governor Lacerda in opposition to Kubitschek for the Brazilian presidential elections scheduled for 1965.[23] The story was a total fabrication, and the embassy press office issued an immediate and unequivocal denial. However, Gordon, always thin-skinned when anyone attacked his integrity, deeply resented the attack and immediately understood that his relationship with Goulart was irrevocably damaged. He was worried about the impact of the story on his relations not only with Goulart but also with Kubitschek and other politicians. Gordon sought out Kubitschek urgently at his home to deny the story. Kubitschek took from his pocket a copy of a paper that had been distributed in Brasilia containing a list of the guests at the alleged dinner. The paper also included a summary of Gordon's supposed "opening remarks." The paper had been distributed to reporters at a briefing at the presidential palace several days before. Kubitschek apparently believed the American's vehement denials.

President Goulart agreed to see Gordon for a private conversation, at which the first topic was the mythical dinner party. Gordon denied that the event had ever taken place and told the president that the story had obviously been invented to damage US-Brazilian relations. Goulart said that he had first read the story in the newspapers and that the details had subsequently been confirmed by his intelligence service. Gordon said he would like to know the supposed date so that he could definitively refute the story. Goulart waved this aside and assured Gordon that he took the

American at his word and accepted the denials. The conversation then turned to other subjects, but in diplomacy, the stronger the denial, the more the original falsehood is likely to be believed. At a later point in the conversation Goulart suddenly returned to the dinner: "Do you mean to say that there was no meeting at all?"[24] Gordon repeated his denials but reported in his telegram to Washington that President Goulart's advisers were still telling him that the story was true and that Goulart probably believed them.[25]

With reports flowing in from many quarters of work stoppages, social unrest, extralegal and political maneuvers, and rumors of potential coups in the newspapers, Gordon decided it was time to step back and send an overall appraisal of the situation to Washington.[26] He had now become convinced "that Goulart's aim [was] to perpetuate himself in power through repetition of Vargas's 1937 coup looking toward Peronist type regime of extreme anti-American nationalism" and that Goulart was being "pushed aside, like General Naguib in Egypt, to make way for some communist Nasser."[27] The general situation seemed very unstable to Gordon, who urged: "In these circumstances, our aim should be to help frustrate his [Goulart's] authoritarian proclivities and maintain prospects for genuine election in 1965." To achieve US goals would "require great improvements in some of our current operating methods, for example, in rapid action on aid projects. . . . But our great card in this game is presidential visit."[28]

Gordon's analysis set off a vigorous debate in the embassy and Washington over the merits of rescheduling the long-delayed trip by President Kennedy to Brazil, now back on the agenda because of the warm meeting between Kennedy and Goulart in Rome. In the net Gordon considered that the advantages outweighed the disadvantages and recommended that President Kennedy make the trip to coincide with the annual meeting of inter-American ministers of finance to discuss the Alliance for Progress. The presidential visit might attract other heads of state to the ministerial meeting, and a possible presidential tour of several Brazilian regions might considerably improve US-Brazil relations. President Kennedy accepted the recommendation, and his visit was tentatively rescheduled for November. With the Kennedy visit in the offing, a potential upswing in US-Brazil relations seemed possible, when suddenly the "rebellion of the sergeants" in September threw matters into turmoil. The episode began when noncommissioned officers (*sargentos*), apparently incited by Brizola, angrily protested against a Supreme Court decision denying their eligibility under the constitution to hold elective office. The threat to military discipline temporarily grounded all military air transport and caused ominous rumblings in the officer ranks. The deteriorating situation caused another postponement of the Kennedy visit.

In October, while Gordon was in Washington with Carvalho Pinto to renegotiate Brazil's external debt, came the stunning news that Goulart had requested from the congress a "state of siege" (i.e., a declaration of martial law). In this atmosphere of deep crisis, Carvalho Pinto hurriedly returned to Brazil, as did Gordon. The congressional center and right united to reject Goulart's request for martial law. This move brought an end to Goulart's maneuver for emergency executive powers but did not end the crisis. Goulart for a time then sounded conciliatory and chastened, but his demeanor did not fool his critics from both left and right, who continued to distrust the president. By this time television was available in Rio de Janeiro and Sao Paulo, and Gordon watched demonstrations at which US nemesis Leonel Brizola, flanked by uniformed marines sent by the left-wing Admiral Aragao, denounced the congress and called for its abolition.[29] Brizola offered money and tactical guidance to guerilla "Groups of Eleven" that would be dedicated to revolutionary change. Gordon learned of reports that were difficult to assess, to the effect that Goulart had wanted the congress to reject his state of siege so as to lay the groundwork for the abolition of congress and a military takeover by forces friendly to him.[30]

The Goulart personnel move that most riled his political opponents was his removal of General Kruel and replacement of him with General Assis Brasil. On October 14 Gordon reported to Washington the reaction of San Tiago Dantas: "To Dantas, [the] most significant immediate development was the prospective formal appointment and investiture of General Assis Brasil as head of military household. . . . Dantas said this would be first time that [a] strong military figure from [the] 'extreme negative left' would occupy this position. . . . He believed Assis Brasil to be involved with [the] group which had been stimulating subversion among sergeants. . . . He saw dangerous possibilities of Spanish-type civil war."[31]

By this time Gordon had "[become] convinced that a breakdown of the constitutional order might lead to civil war in Brazil."[32] Tensions had increased between the Goulart government and the state government of Sao Paulo, and a state official told Gordon that Goulart would use state police forces to resist any federal attempt to take over the state and appoint a new governor. On October 16 Gordon sent another somber assessment to Washington citing the "urgency [of] various types [of] contingency planning."[33] He did not specify what types of contingency planning he had in mind, but he evidently had discussed the topic with Assistant Secretary of State Ed Martin and White House staffer Ralph Dungan on his last visit to Washington. Martin's and Dungan's reactions were the exact opposite. Martin was skeptical of Gordon's dire warnings and considered it much more likely that Goulart was simply trying to survive until the election in 1965. He consequently convened a review of the Brazilian situation by State's Bureau of Intelligence and Research (which subsequently upheld his view). Dungan was receptive to Gordon's warnings but made no recommendation to Kennedy pending the review by the Bureau of Intelligence and Research.

JFK's assassination in November shocked Washington and Rio in almost equal measure. For the moment it quieted Brazil's domestic political disputes. Tensions eased during the extended grieving period that was observed throughout Brazil. The youthful American president had been universally admired in Brazil. Gordon, like other US ambassadors, was ordered to stay at his post and represent the nation at the various commemorative events in the host country. The period of mourning in Brazil was followed by the Christmas holidays. Over the Christmas holidays Gordon apparently felt no sense of imminent danger, since he took Allison, Hugh, and visiting family friend Ruth Kriebel on a vacation trip through Bahia via his personal car and without escort of any kind. They encountered friendly crowds, and the local mayors in the small towns along their way insisted on celebrating their arrival. The embassy press office had released their itinerary, unknown to the ambassador, who had assumed they might be able to enjoy going incognito. Gordon remembered this vacation as one of his most pleasant times in Brazil. The three small-town mayors he encountered each insisted that he and his party tour the town, stay for a special luncheon, and mix with local citizens. The mayors, though by coincidence representing the nation's three major political parties, had a similar message: "Keep Jango and those crazy feds out of our hair; we're fine here at the local level!"

The Failure of the Alliance for Progress

The close economic cooperation envisaged under the Furtado three-year plan and the Dantas-Bell plan was no longer possible as political conditions deteriorated. US program aid was accordingly suspended in October of 1963, but project assistance continued on a modest scale at both the federal and the state levels. US project assistance was not limited to the state governments that were hostile to the Goulart regime, as leftists contended, but was limited to what Gordon dubbed "islands of sanity." By this he meant jurisdictions that had the administrative capacity and fiscal control to identify sensible projects and fund them via debt financing. The aid included projects in Minas Gerais, Bahia, and other states where the governors were neutral or pro-Goulart and also aid for federal highway and power projects where standard lending arrangements were acceptable to both donor and recipient.[34] Gordon was not willing to close down the Alliance for Progress program altogether, even though it had fallen far short of its original ambitions and was the target of opposition from numerous nationalist politicians. That nationalists opposed the Alliance stiffened Gordon's determination to preserve it, even if in attenuated form. Some appropriated funds from the US Congress remained unspent for lack of satisfactory projects.

Gordon gave a detailed assessment of what he thought was wrong with the Alliance program in Brazil in a long letter of December 28, 1962, to Theodoro Moscoso, US coordinator of the Alliance for Progress in the Agency for International Development.[35] On the relation between social progress and economic development, he told Moscoso, "I still find in Brazil . . . a mistaken tendency to regard social investment as 'assistencia' or 'palliative' in character. . . . I remain unrepentedly convinced that education and health investment in people is as productive as or more productive than most physical investments." Even housing investments, if properly organized, could yield high social returns. On broad reforms such as tax and land reform, he said, "I feel very strongly that we have popularized a much too simple stereotype of Latin American conditions, and given the impression generally that tax reform and land reform are simple things, being held back only by a reactionary oligarchy." Phony reform proposals that were advanced only to be rejected by the political center and right thus reinforced the rationale for dictatorial powers exercised by a Peron- or Vargas-style populist executive.[36] Gordon stopped short of saying that the United States should abandon all efforts toward basic social reform but cautioned that reform should not be viewed as a prerequisite for—but merely one element of—an economic development strategy. His views of December 1962 represented an almost total retreat from his call for "a New Deal for Latin America" and from the original reformist impulse behind the Alliance.

But Gordon did not mention in his memo to Moscoso a more immediate cause of the Alliance's failures in the northeast of Brazil: the administrative chaos in the US AID mission in Recife. This was a problem for which he bore a large measure of the responsibility. When Gordon had arrived in Brazil, the US AID mission in Recife and the embassy in Rio were feuding over how best to administer the Alliance in the northeast of the country and how to interact with the Brazilian technicians in SUDENE, the government agency in charge of the region's development. Bruno B. Luzzano was named head of the US AID mission in Recife in April 1961. He favored a small, low-profile mission staffed by Americans with a good grasp of the Portuguese language and a feel for the Brazilian way of doing things.[37] The embassy in Rio favored a larger office and a more assertive US role vis-à-vis SUDENE. The US embassy should not act merely as a bank to fund projects developed by the Brazilians, the approach favored by Luzzano in Recife. Luzzano was highly competent but had an abrasive personality and did not have good relations with the local press in Recife. He and Gordon disliked each other from the start. Luzzano was not a Kennedy-style New Frontiersman with a go-getter personality. Gordon was arrogant and a poor administrator in Luzzano's estimation, and Gordon considered Luzzano obstinate and unimaginative. Their relations were all but doomed when Gordon sided with the embassy on the need for a large mission in Recife.

When Gordon met with Kennedy in July 1962, they discussed the situation in Brazil's northeast, which had been an important part of the JFK-Goulart discussions in April. In response to a question from the president, Gordon indicated his dissatisfaction with the AID mission's leadership in Recife, the capital of the state of Pernambuco. They discussed the possible replacement of the mission head, and JFK proposed a man he thought would be ideal, a person then working for Sargeant Shriver at the Peace Corps. The president directed Richard Goodwin to secure the man's release from Shriver. Thus encouraged by presidential backing, Gordon on his return to Brazil fired Luzzano and sent him back to Washington. Unfortunately, the replacement from the Peace Corps did not come through, and Gordon was obliged to appoint John C. Dieffenderfer from the embassy staff as acting director of the Recife mission. Several months later he made the appointment permanent. Dieffenderfer worked hard but suffered from two major flaws: he lacked political skills in the complex diplomatic relations with the Brazilians, and his knowledge of Portuguese was limited. The Recife mission never functioned effectively, and relations with the Brazilian state government were poor. Pernambuco governor Arrais cold-shouldered Dieffenderfer, partly as a result of US efforts in support of his opponent in the 1962 gubernatorial elections. Gordon was quite ready to blame Goulart for the failure of economic stabilization in the country but was less forthcoming in acknowledging his own failures in Recife.

For most of his term as ambassador, Gordon laid great stress on the need to improve the climate for foreign direct and portfolio investment as probably the major contributor to Brazilian growth. This was a theme that dated from his research in the 1950s. Efforts to enhance human capital were another key dimension for him—on par at least with capital improvements. Loans for large-scale capital improvements were certainly desirable if it could be demonstrated that increased economic activity would be able to service the loan. He had one other large policy idea that he repeatedly pushed whenever he had the opportunity. This was the notion of a common market for Latin America. He got the idea onto the agenda for the 1963 annual meeting of finance ministers in Rio. The proposal was for new collaborative machinery to promote more intraregional trade and investment among Latin American countries. This idea was modeled on the OEEC machinery of the Marshall Plan in Western Europe, but with some adaptations for Latin America.

The majority of finance ministers approved the creation of the CIAP (Inter-American Committee for the Alliance for Progress), but the Brazilian delegation opposed it. President Goulart's opening speech at the conference totally ignored the proposal and instead focused on preparations for the 1964 UN Conference on Trade and Development (UNCTAD), at which developing countries would demand "concessions" from industrialized nations. President Goulart threw a festive state dinner for the US representative to the meeting, Governor Averell Harriman, and his wife, Marie. But at the postdinner meeting of the principals (Goulart and Harriman, with Gordon acting as interpreter), no meeting of the minds took place. Goulart stuck to his complaint that the prices of commodities fluctuated wildly and in recent years had fallen. Harriman replied that prices moved in response to market conditions. Goulart rejoined: "That is why I don't like markets."[38]

The Run-Up to the Military Coup

In early January 1964, on Gordon's return to Rio from the vacation in Bahia, Samuel Wainer called on him at the US embassy to report on his private dinner the previous evening with President Goulart.[39] This was an unusual visit for the American ambassador. Wainer was a protégé of the late President Vargas, who had subsidized him in founding the populist *Ultima Hora* newspaper and was a friend and supporter of the Goulart regime (for which he was exiled after the military coup). Nevertheless, Wainer had formed a cordial relationship with Gordon and felt enough confidence in him to give him a completely uninhibited account of President Goulart's state of mind. Wainer's account appeared to confirm that Goulart was agitated, "pacing up and down like a caged tiger and banging his fist on a table." The president had described his situation to Wainer as having to choose one of three courses of action: (1) He "could just do the routine presidential things for another two years, cutting ribbons to inaugurate projects and making speeches on ceremonial holidays." This apparently was an unappealing alternative. (2) He "could follow Janio's [Quadros's] example and resign." This also was not an attractive option. (3) He "could GO FOR IT!"[40] What Goulart meant by this was not entirely clear to either Wainer or Gordon. But Gordon recalled from earlier casual conversations with the president that his favorite politicians were Getulio Vargas and Juan Peron. This recollection seemed to confirm Gordon's growing conviction that Goulart might attempt an "auto coup"—that is, a preemptive strike against his political opponents if he felt completely blocked from action within the established order.

In the meantime, the rumors of coups and countercoups from the left and right swirled around the capital and kept US embassy officials busy trying to check their veracity. The reports became commonplace and originated from journalists, diplomats, businessmen, foreign intelligence sources, students, government contacts, and supposedly well-informed individuals. The reports were often couched so as to discern US intentions or to elicit potential US reactions to attempted coups. Most reports lacked credibility and were merely boastful puffery. US diplomats were instructed to say that US policy was to support Brazilian democracy and that the United States expected elections to take place in 1965, at the expiration of the original Quadros term as president. Gordon remained in Brazil until January 20, 1964, when he departed for a three-week trip to the United States.

Gordon was scheduled to meet with Thomas C. Mann, the new assistant secretary of state for inter-American affairs and special assistant to LBJ in the White House, and to consult with Treasury officials. The interesting development was Mann's new role as both State Department official and immediate adviser to LBJ in the White House, something like the arrangement Berle had sought unsuccessfully under Kennedy. Mann was a Texan and an old friend of LBJ's, and the president had now called him back from Mexico and put him in charge of policy for Latin America. Mann thus had even more authority than Berle had sought from Kennedy. The shift to the hardline Mann with broadened powers could nudge US policy toward Latin America in a more hawkish direction. At a minimum, thought Gordon, the Mann appointment might mean a clearer policy line on Brazil. The intelligence review on Brazil initiated by Ed Martin had come down in Martin's favor and against Gordon's assessment of Goulart's intentions. White House staffers were not persuaded by the State Department's analysis, however, and Gordon's proposal for contingency planning was adopted. The contingency plan for Brazil prepared in the State Department, with input from Gordon and the embassy, was intended to clarify US reactions to various circumstances. But like many documents of its kind, the plan was so filled with qualifications, equivocal language, and cautious formulations that no clear policy conclusions emerged. The plan seemed to be a compromise between Martin's views and Gordon's: on the one hand the United States was in favor of encouraging Brazil to stay on its democratic course to new presidential elections in 1965, and on the other hand the United States would not publicly support Goulart under specified circumstances if his actions precipitated a military revolt against him.

Gordon first attempted through Mann to arrange a meeting with President Johnson. Meeting with the president had been a privilege Gordon enjoyed in his close association and personal relationship with Kennedy. Gordon did not know where he stood with LBJ and wondered if Johnson distrusted him as a Kennedy protégé. Mann refused the request for Gordon to see the president. The president was too busy. Furthermore, Johnson had decided to make a practice of not meeting with ambassadors on their visits to the United States. Did the president at least have time for a photo op, Gordon queried, since this would help him in Brazil? Even this request was denied. Gordon would have to content himself with a meeting with Mann, and Mann's own schedule was consumed with crisis management.

Gordon did, however, meet with Mann three times, briefly on Wednesday, January 22, and then for three hours on Saturday, January 25, and briefly once more before Gordon's departure for Brazil on February 9. Gordon was eager to talk with Mann not only for policy reasons but also out of personal considerations. Gordon had received a letter from President Robert F. Goheen of Princeton in June asking him if he were interested in a position as dean of Princeton's new Woodrow Wilson School.[41] This inquiry had ripened into a firm offer in the fall of 1963. Years later Gordon told his son Bob that he turned down the Princeton job because Allison considered the Princeton atmosphere too "clubby" and hostile to women. This does not quite jibe with what he told an LBJ oral history interviewer on July 10, 1969: "I'd been asked a month before the assassination by President Goheen whether I would be interested in going there as dean of the Woodrow Wilson School of Public and International Affairs. They'd just gotten 35 million dollars. As he said, it was the one important job in academic administration that didn't involve fundraising. I was thinking about it fairly seriously."[42] Gordon was serious enough to raise the Princeton matter with Tom Mann, whom he knew well and could count on for a frank and discreet opinion. Mann was adamantly opposed to the idea of Gordon leaving his post, insisting that the crisis situation in Brazil made it impossible to get anyone up to speed quickly, and called for Gordon to stay on the job. Gordon agreed to stay on through 1965.[43]

Since the meeting with Mann lasted three hours, it is likely the two men covered a range of topics. One item suggested in Gordon's correspondence of this period was the matter of Goulart's health. Goulart was known to have a serious heart condition, and he was reported to have had several emergency visits to his doctor recently. Another matter on Gordon's mind was his standing in the new administration. Since Gordon knew Mann well, he would naturally have raised this issue with him. Gordon was uncertain where he stood in the pecking order with President Johnson. Was the president's refusal to meet with him a snub? It is uncertain how much Gordon knew then about the new administration, but he was certainly aware of the reported tensions involving the Bobby Kennedy loyalists and LBJ. Mann assured Gordon that the president fully shared Mann's own confidence in him and wanted him to stay in his post. Although Mann was much less enamored of the Alliance for Progress than was Gordon, he told Gordon that LBJ wanted continuity in the Alliance and was anxious that the program be seen as having survived the death of Kennedy.

On broad policy toward Brazil, the new administration broke no new ground. US policy remained in the somewhat ambivalent posture of seeking to get through to the 1965 elections if at all possible but at the same time to begin planning for what to do if a coup or a civil war situation occurred. It went without saying that the United States should assist elements favorable to US interests and oppose a pro-Soviet, pro-Cuban government in Brazil. The "Mann Doctrine" was not yet formalized as US policy but was in the process of discussion in the State Department. Under this doctrine the United States would give a higher priority to the nondiscriminatory treatment of US trade and investment in Latin American policy than to formal features of governance. In practice this meant that military regimes could be tolerated if they followed the accepted rules of free commerce as spelled out in the inter-American system. Mann announced this policy to the US ambassadors to Latin American countries, assembled for a three-day Washington conference held from March 14 to 16, 1964. Mann was quoted as saying (in leaked press accounts of the conference) that "the United States will not in the future take an *a priori* position against governments coming to power through military coup."[44]

During Gordon's January visit to Washington, the news came from Colonel Walters in Rio that army general Humberto Castelo Branco had issued a warning to Goulart's war minister "that a pro-government coup would be met with resistance by elements of the armed forces and that he, Castelo Branco, would join such elements."[45] Reports followed shortly detailing a quixotic attempt by San Tiago Dantas to form a "popular front" collation. This initiative predictably gained no support and quickly vanished. In what he expected to be an atmosphere of deepening crisis, Gordon returned to Brazil on February 9. To his surprise he instead found an eerie lull. The political combatants had seemingly exhausted their energies for the moment, and the result was a kind of calm before the storm. For the next month the business of diplomacy as usual dominated Gordon's attention.

US embassy officials pinched themselves and wondered if this extraordinary country had regained its footing and if their dire assessments of imminent civil disorder were exaggerated. The embassy expended much effort in preparing for a visit by John J. McCloy, former assistant secretary of war, high commissioner to Germany, and head of the World Bank, who was representing the US-owned Hannah mining interests in Brazil. The company was worried about potential expropriation under a Goulart decree and wanted to reaffirm its interest in long-term investment in Brazil. Gordon loved such visits. Spending time with the great figures of the war and postwar eras reminded Gordon of happy days. The Brazilians received McCloy warmly and organized a state dinner in his honor, capped off with a three-hour personal meeting with President Goulart. Goulart was at his affable best with McCloy and appeared not to have a care in the world.

Gordon was scheduled to fly to Washington on the evening of March 13 for three days of meetings with President Johnson and Mann. All US ambassadors in Latin America were to attend what was billed as a review of US policy for the hemisphere. At the end of the three days Gordon was asked to stay on to meet with Mann and others for a review of the Brazil situation. The political lull had been suddenly shattered on the day Gordon left Brazil for Washington by the Comício da Central (a rally at the Central Railway Station in Rio), which launched the country back into a constitutional crisis. Gordon had watched the rally on television before departing for the airport. The crowd was a colorful throng of some ten thousand people, thousands of them bussed in from various parts of the country and many waving hammer-and-sickle flags. Gordon watched in fascination as Brizola gave a fiery denunciation of the congress. When it came Goulart's turn to speak, Gordon was struck by the change in the president's demeanor from the calm manner in which he had received McCloy. He was now a highly excited, almost agitated, and perspiring figure as he stood at the podium and addressed the throng. Anti-Goulart forces, funded by the CIA, organized an even larger counterdemonstration known as "the Family March with God for Freedom," with the aim of keeping Goulart from taking the unilateral steps against the congress that his highly emotional and somewhat incoherent speech had suggested.

Thus, during Gordon's visit to Washington, a cabinet-level review of Brazil policy took place. Gordon in his remarks to the cabinet stressed the fluidity of the situation, indicating that there could be a pro-Goulart coup, an anti-Goulart coup, or a split within the military that could precipitate prolonged armed conflict. He recommended an acceleration of the planning for what became the "Brother Sam" naval task force, intended as a show of US strength. CIA director John McCone added that oil tankers should be dispatched to Sao Paulo to counter any interruption of fuel supplies for friendly forces and for the city's power needs. These plans were agreed to in principle, but no specific dates were assigned for the departure of the naval task force or of the tankers. Gordon was instructed to return to Brazil, conduct an urgent review of the situation, and report back to Washington as soon as possible. In a private meeting with Secretary of State Rusk just before his departure for Brazil on March 21, Gordon was instructed to conduct the review and formulate policy recommendations within one week.

Gordon conducted the review with his senior staff over the period March 23–25. Colonel Walters brought to the review a copy of a message from General Castelo Branco to senior army officers, alerting them to the dangers of a general strike by the leftist labor organization the CGT (Commando Geral dos Traballadores). Walters also told his colleagues that Castelo Branco was heading a group of senior army officers to develop contingency plans to stop Goulart if he attempted any clearly unconstitutional action.[46] Gordon drew together the threads of the review into the lengthy "top secret" cable he sent to Washington on March 26.[47] Gordon noted that "my considered conclusion is that Goulart is now definitely engaged in [a] campaign to seize dictatorial power. . . . The immediate tactics of the Goulart palace guard are concentrated on pressures to secure from the Congress constitutional reforms unattainable by normal means, using a combination of urban street demonstrations, threatened or actual strikes, sporadic rural violence, and abuse of the enormous discretionary financial power of the federal government . . . coupled with a series of populist executive decrees of dubious legality." The March 26 cable's recommendations included the call for the Brother Sam naval task force to be sent to Brazilian waters as a show of force and the prepositioning of "small arms of non-U.S. origin" to be distributed to the anti-Goulart forces, the arms to be prepositioned "as soon as requirements [are] known."[48]

On March 25, as Gordon was putting final touches on the cable, the "sailors' revolt" began in Rio de Janeiro, giving added urgency to the policy review. President Goulart was on a fishing vacation and rushed back to take charge of the government's response to the sailors' revolt. The sailors' revolt stretched out over the course of a week and blended into the events of the actual coup. Led by Jose Anselmo dos Santos under the sobriquet of "Corporal Anselmo" (and later exposed as a probable agent provocateur), some two thousand sailors demanded better living conditions for themselves, as well as the right to vote, and pledged their support for President Goulart's broad social and constitutional reforms. After intense and confused negotiations, a settlement of sorts was reached that granted some of the sailors' demands. As the leaders of the revolt departed the premises in triumph, however, they were promptly arrested for mutiny by troops under the command of officers who did not recognize the "settlement." Goulart thereupon issued pardons to the mutineers, thus creating an open breach with the military leadership, intent on reestablishing discipline in the ranks.

On March 30 Goulart stuck his thumb in the military's eye with a speech to a gathering of noncommissioned officers in which he paid lip service to military discipline but called for military support of his broad reform agenda.[49] Goulart's speech was filled with references to religion, patriotism, and tradition that evidently were meant to soften the radical edges of his rhetoric. But several passages alarmed his enemies, including a reference to the constitution as a "living" document meant to be flexible and capable of amendment through presidential actions like the January 1963 plebiscite restoring full presidential powers. If Goulart were to organize a plebiscite on his reforms, his enemies assumed that he could set the terms of who would vote and thus could empower illiterates to vote for the first time (and of course the illiterates would vote as Goulart requested).

Colonel Walters was now telling his embassy colleagues that he had solid information that a military coup against Goulart was at last at hand—and would possibly be triggered by a meeting of nine anti-Goulart state governors scheduled for Wednesday of that week. He could not, however, be certain of the exact date.[50] Washington was so informed. Gordon spoke at length on the telephone on the evening of March 30 with Secretary Rusk. After Rusk and Gordon spoke, Rusk telephoned President Johnson at his Texas ranch to inform him of developments and get his approval for instructions to Gordon.[51] Gordon received the telegram from Rusk the next morning, calling for clarification of the small-arms requirements that might be needed but instructing Gordon to refrain from any direct contacts with Brazilian authorities.[52] The secretary's cable was quickly overtaken by the cascading chain of events.

The Coup: March 31 to April 2, 1964

Gordon and his military advisers in the embassy became aware on the morning of March 31 that some kind of military activity was taking place in Minas Gerais, the state just north of Rio de Janeiro, but were unsure whether the actions signaled the beginning of a coup. Gordon and Walters looked anxiously for reports of action in Sao Paulo from the Second Army, but no military activity of any kind was reported in Sao Paulo. Gordon passed on what the embassy knew in an early teletype conversation with Rusk, George Ball, and Tom Mann.

Ball and Mann telephoned LBJ at his ranch in the afternoon to brief him on the situation. (LBJ was planning to return to Washington that evening.) Ball did most of the talking, telling the president that the naval task force had finally been dispatched earlier that day after a meeting with Secretary of Defense McNamara but could not arrive before April 10. He told the president that the situation might clarify itself in the meantime so that the administration would have time to assess what the task force's mission might be. The tankers with aviation and automotive fuel could not arrive until about April 13, Ball reported. Ball noted that Ambassador Gordon agreed that probably the next critical juncture would come with a meeting of nine state governors opposed to Goulart, which was scheduled for the next day, Wednesday, April 1. LBJ exhorted them to stay on top of the situation and to tap the best thinking from Defense, the CIA, and State.[53]

Machine-gun fire was heard in Rio during the day on March 31, but Gordon and his key aides in the embassy still had no firm reports of military activity in Sao Paulo or of organized troop movements anywhere outside the state of Minas Gerais. Considerable political maneuvering was taking place in Brasilia at the congress, apparently with the result that Goulart's position was slipping but with no definitive assessment yet possible. That evening Gordon decided to assemble a small circle of his key aides the following morning but instructed the remainder of the large embassy staff to stay home. Gordon and his team had no knowledge as they broke up for the evening of the fateful conversations then taking place between General Kruel and President Goulart.

The first telephone conversation between General Kruel and President Goulart took place at about 10:00 p.m. on March 31. The military situation was not yet settled. General Castelo Branco, ostensibly the head of the coup plotters, had attempted but failed to halt General Olímpio Mourão Filho's premature moves in Minas Gerais. Castelo Branco then ordered troops to occupy and barricade the Ministry of War building and the military school in Rio de Janeiro. Other minor actions took place around the country, but the decisive forces under General Kruel in Sao Paulo had not been committed. Goulart's military aide, General Argemiro de Assis Brasil, was confident he could defeat the rebels and apparently convinced the president that he had matters in hand. General Kruel was the godfather of Goulart's two children. They had had their differences, but Goulart believed he could talk Kruel out of support for the conspirators. Thus, it was a confident Goulart who took Kruel's first call. Kruel asked Goulart to break with his leftist supporters by firing his justice minister and his chief of staff and by outlawing the CGT. In return for this assurance, Kruel said, he would not join any military action against the president and would disavow General Mourão in Minas Gerais. Goulart replied that such a step would amount to a humiliation and would render him merely a "decorative President." Goulart told Kruel, "General, I don't abandon my friends. . . . I would rather stick with my grassroots. You should stick to your convictions. Put your troops out on the street and betray me, publicly."[54]

Kruel called twice more, repeating a variant of his demands, and received the same answer. After the final rebuff he decided that he would oblige the president and ordered his troops into action the following morning, on April 1.

Goulart's bold stance with Kruel was based on a total misreading of the military situation. The Assis Brasil (and Goulart) strategy proved to be disastrous. Two of Goulart's three military chiefs of staff were out of action for various reasons. Goulart's main military support was located in his native southern Brazil, and the plan devised by Assis Brazil called for shifting a general from the southern Third Army to the southeast to take over command of forces previously commanded by Castelo Branco. The order was botched, and the general never arrived to take command. Four of Goulart's other generals, in the states of Parana and Rio Grande do Sul, were on vacation and were not in contact with Assis Brasil. Two other pro-Goulart generals who sought to return to their posts in Curitiba ran into bad weather and were forced to land in Porto Alegre and were thus separated from their commands. An air force general loyal to the president made it back to his base in the north but, lacking ground forces, was quickly surrounded and forced to surrender.

Gordon and his team of key aides spent the morning of April 1 sweltering on an upper floor of the embassy in Rio while they tried to piece together what was happening. Receiving reports that a mob of student radicals was heading toward the embassy, Gordon had ordered the air conditioning turned off out of fear that they might be asphyxiated if students started a fire on the ground floor and smoke billowed through the cooling system. Gordon ordered the air conditioning turned back on when he learned that troops under Castelo Branco's command had headed off the students, occupied the student union headquarters, and arrested a number of students. The team remained caught up in the swirl of rumors but at least was now confused in air-conditioned comfort.

Realizing that his situation was now desperate, Goulart left Rio in the afternoon of April 1 for Brasilia and arrived around 4:00 p.m. for a last-ditch attempt to rally political support. He rapidly determined that his situation was hopeless and stayed for only a short time, gathering his wife and two children and departing for Porto Alegre aboard an air force aircraft. It was not clear at this point whether he would organize resistance to the plotters and issue a ringing statement in the nature of Vargas's suicide letter. Some sort of word had to be sent to the congress, which had briefly interrupted its session in anticipation of hearing from him. His aide Darcy Ribeiro urged the president to strike a fighting stance. Tancredo Neves then composed a ringing statement for Goulart in the tradition of the Vargas suicide letter and the Quadros resignation statement, calling on Brazilians to resist the forces of imperialism and fascism. Goulart tape-recorded it for release to the media before he departed for Porto Alegre, but the quality of the recording was not good, and it was heard only once, on a radio station with limited range. Jango and his family took refuge in Third Army headquarters, where troops under the command of General Floriano Machado were now the only forces still loyal to him. Goulart's brother-in-law Leonel Brizola, also at Third Army headquarters, characteristically urged him to pursue armed resistance. General Machado, on the morning of April 2, advised Goulart that a strong force under General Kruel was heading toward Porto Alegre and that he could not hold out for long. He recommended that the president leave the country for Uruguayan exile if he wished to avoid capture. Goulart and his family left Porto Alegre on an air force C-47 cargo plane but did not go immediately into Uruguayan exile. He stayed at his ranch near Uruguay before crossing the border on April 4 and then began an exile that lasted until his death in 1976 of a heart attack at a villa near Buenos Aires.

Only seven civilians were killed in the coup. Casualties included two students shot during a demonstration at the governor's palace in Recife, three in Rio, and two in Minas Gerais.[55] No troops died in any of the coup's military actions. While the coup did not follow the plan laid out by the conspirators, it was certainly decisive. Goulart was gone from the scene into exile in Uruguay (and later Argentina), his turbulent term in office a closed chapter. The military sent Brizola into exile in Uruguay and moved to arrest suspected radicals across the country, purged the labor movement of "subversives," and began a process of selecting nonpolitical technocrats for key economic and other government posts. Brazil's leftists, as Joseph A. Page states in summing up the coup's outcome, "consoled themselves by blaming the United States for the coup. Although Washington applauded the military intervention and even had naval forces on alert not far from the coast of Brazil, the fact is that the overthrow of Goulart required no outside aid. Those who place responsibility on the Yankees are merely reflecting Brazil's inferiority complex, the conviction that Brazilians can accomplish nothing of real significance on their own."[56] Page's summary errs in only one minor respect: the US naval task force never got anywhere near Brazil, having gotten under way the day of the coup and having been recalled the second day. The large issue remained of what the coup leaders would do next: Would they choose to rule the country directly or keep themselves in the background with civilians chosen by them nominally in charge? What parts of the formal constitutional structure and governmental machinery would they preserve? How far would they go to punish suspected subversives? And not least important, what would be the US relationship with the new regime?

15

Assistant Secretary

There's one more thing. You know how I feel about leaks.
—Lyndon B. Johnson, offering Lincoln Gordon the job
of assistant secretary, 1966

On April 2, Gordon and his team felt confident enough to report to Washington that the coup was over. Civil order had been restored in most of the country, with the situations in Recife and Porto Alegre still uncertain.[1] They indicated that Brizola had been arrested (incorrect) and that Goulart had fled the country (premature). Meanwhile, at about 2:30 a.m., the speaker of the lower house, Ranieri Mazzilli, had been sworn in as acting president. This news was passed on by twenty-four-year-old Robert Bentley, an American diplomat who was stationed in Brasilia to observe and report on the activities of the congress. The young US diplomat was in the room next to the swearing-in and telephoned the news immediately to the embassy in Rio. Gordon relayed it to George Ball, listening on an open telephone line to the Rio embassy. Ball was acting secretary of state in Rusk's absence and asked if Gordon thought the swearing-in was legal. Gordon asked Bentley for his opinion. Bentley replied that it looked like it was legal and proper to him.

Ball thereupon on his own initiative sent a congratulatory telegram to Mazzilli that in effect would confer US recognition, but for some reason the telegram never arrived. This was all to the good, because LBJ was infuriated at not having been awakened and given the news of the swearing-in immediately. The National Security Council met at noon and discussed whether recognition was necessary. Later the next day President Johnson sent a congratulatory telegram at Gordon's recommendation that was drafted by Gordon. The congratulatory telegram was a move that

Gordon later regretted as too hasty and as giving the false impression that the United States had orchestrated the coup. The LBJ telegram declared that "the American people have watched with anxiety the political and economic difficulties through which your great nation has been passing, and have admired the resolute will of the Brazilian community to resolve these difficulties within a framework of constitutional democracy and without civil strife."[2]

Gordon awoke on the morning of April 3 enormously relieved that the United States would not have to confront disorder or civil war. He recommended to Washington that the Brother Sam naval task force be recalled immediately but that the petroleum tankers be allowed to continue southward for a few days until conditions in the inflation-ridden economy could be further assessed. The immediate Brazilian need seemed to be for food, which the embassy provided through AID. The tankers were also subsequently turned back, with no leaks of these classified operations appearing in the Washington or Brazilian media. But the impression of US involvement was reinforced by an April 4 newspaper article in which Governor Carlos Lacerda, a center-right nationalist and Goulart foe, alleged that Ambassador Gordon had expressed "satisfaction and relief that the Brazilian armed forces had in such a brief time and without bloodshed succeeded in obviating the necessity of military intervention by the U.S. to prevent Brazil from falling into the Soviet orbit."[3] Lacerda went on to say that it was fortunate Brazil had been spared "a type of Latin American Viet Nam."[4] Gordon did not deny having paid a call on Lacerda but vehemently denied having made any such statements. The Brother Sam naval task force remained unknown and played no part in Brazilian or US domestic politics until its existence came to light in 1977.

The Carlos Fico Critique of US Involvement

A great deal of ink has been spilled over alleged US involvement in the 1964 coup, including Lincoln Gordon's purported role. The most scholarly critique was a 2009 book by the Brazilian historian Carlos Fico of the Federal University of Rio de Janeiro, *O grande irmão: Da Operação Brother Sam aos anos de chumbo: O governo dos Estados Unidos e a ditadura militar brasileira* (Big brother: From Operation Brother Sam to the years of lead: The United States government and the Brazilian dictatorship).[5] I cannot deal with every point made by Fico, but I will address his main arguments. The book jacket announces portentously that "this is not a spy novel, but a complete historical narrative of the diplomatic relations between the United States and Brazil." The back cover contains these headings:

SECRET PROJECTS DEVISED BY FOREIGN DIPLOMATS
CLANDESTINE DELIVERIES OF ARMS
MILLIONS OF DOLLARS SPENT TO SUBORN POLITICIANS
SECRET MILITARY BASES
PLANS FOR THE ASSASINATION OF A GOVERNOR
CLANDESTINE EQUIPMENT FOR THE DETECTION OF
NUCLEAR EXPLOSIVES

Fico writes from the perspective of a Brazilian nationalist and as a man of the political left, but the book is a scholarly treatise without sensationalism. Through his careful discussion of the events and issues, he takes some of the sting out of the harshest criticisms of Gordon. Fico's main arguments may be summarized as follows: (1) Beginning as early as 1962 the US government engaged in a campaign to destabilize the Joao Goulart government. (2) A contingency plan of December 1963, written by Gordon and others, pretending to be an objective analysis of Brazilian conditions, was in fact rigged to produce a rationale for a US show of force and assistance to military conspirators against Goulart. (3) Knowledge of US intentions was probably leaked by sources in the US embassy to Brazilian military officials and thus helped to shape the course of events (creating, in effect, a self-fulfilling prophecy). And (4) in the whole process Gordon was uniquely influential in the US government's Cold War stance and policy blunders. The Americans, according to Fico, "overreached [*excederiam-se*] themselves in the business of 'Operation *Brother Sam*.' Gordon most of all had gone too far, as the one with principal responsibility for the campaign of destabilizing Goulart and the bizarre naval task force. The activities of Ambassador Lincoln Gordon and the military attaché Vernon Walters initiated a phase never before seen of the interference by the United States in Brazil's internal politics."[6]

The policy misjudgments in which Gordon played a major role included the following: the decision to spend some $5 million to influence the 1962 Brazilian congressional elections; the ill-considered naval task force and shipment of arms and petroleum under the code name of Brother Sam; the hasty decision to recognize the speaker of the lower house, Ranieri Mazzilli, as president via a congratulatory telegram from President Lyndon Johnson before it was determined that President Goulart had actually left the country; and the failure of the US government to oppose or at least distance itself from the military government of Castelo Branco. Fico's broader claim, that the United States engaged in a campaign to destabilize the Goulart government from the beginning, rests on the doubtful proposition that cultural diplomacy was actually subversion. Fico considers even benign cultural exchange programs as "seduction" and insists that any exchanges involving parliamentarians were attempts to suborn politicians. But cultural exchange programs funded by contributions from Brazilian business groups and private individuals brought youths from a variety of regions and backgrounds to the United States with no political motives other than to enhance understanding between the two countries. Gordon arranged for one such group of young leaders to visit President Kennedy. This was a popular program, and Gordon's interest and support helped make him a popular ambassador. Scientific exchanges were a special interest for Gordon, and he took pride in encouraging them.

Fico acknowledges that Brazilian scientists were highly enthusiastic about programs of scientific exchange between their own and US universities and considered that US technical assistance contributed to the progress of Brazilian science. But overall, according to Fico, Brazilian politicians and military leaders became overly dependent on the United States and lost their bearing. General Castelo Branco, for example, is blamed for being indiscreet and talking too much to his friend Vernon Walters, the US Army attaché. Walters, of course, Fico acknowledges, was simply doing his job when he reported everything Castelo Branco told him to Ambassador Gordon and to Washington. Similarly, Fico's castigation of Gordon for interference in Brazil's internal affairs is softened somewhat by his criticism of Brazilian politicians for being weak and seeking out the American for advice on numerous matters.

Further, Fico wavers in describing when the destabilization campaign began and when it reached its greatest intensity. He correctly discerns no sharp discontinuities between the Kennedy and Johnson policies toward Brazil but seems to suggest that the campaign to destabilize Goulart assumed more serious proportions after Kennedy's death. Of course, since Goulart shifted sharply to the left, the US attitude toward him was changing at this time. Even as relations with the Goulart government deteriorated, the US embassy was still attempting to play the card of the Kennedy presidential visit to improve relations prior to Kennedy's assassination. Gordon's August 1963 telegram to Rusk warning of the dangers of a two-stage coup did not signify a US policy to destabilize the Goulart government because Ed Martin and others did not accept Gordon's analysis. Rusk seems to have had his doubts, too, for he accepted Martin's call for the State Department's Bureau of Intelligence and Research (INR) to arbitrate the dispute between Martin and Gordon. The report of the Bureau of Intelligence and Research came down squarely on Martin's side: "It is definitely not apparent . . . that Goulart is embarked on a course of establishing an authoritarian regime in Brazil . . . but instead that the bulk of available evidence points to a decision on his part simply to finish out his term . . . turning over office to a duly elected successor in January 1966."[7] The INR assessment was concluded, however, before Goulart called for a state of siege and dramatically escalated the battle with his political opponents in the congress.

Gordon's support in the White House meant that US policy remained divided between the Gordon and the Martin perspectives in the period leading up to the Kennedy assassination. As Ralph A. Dungan of the White House staff wrote to President Kennedy: "As you will see from the attached, there is some difference of opinion as to the nature of the problem and consequently, how we address ourselves to it. While I think Linc tends to be a little bit emotional and is very easily offended by apparent attacks on his own integrity, I am more inclined to his view of Goulart and his administration than I am to the INR analysis which ascribes most of Goulart's aberrations to rampant nationalism."[8] But since these policy debates and the contingency plan were highly secret matters within the US government, it is difficult to see how Brazilians, who knew nothing of the contingency plan, could have been affected or their domestic politics influenced.

Given the fast-moving events of the coup, what could the United States have actually done to support Goulart even if it had wanted to? Fico acknowledges that US influence in Brazil's domestic politics was always limited, but at the same time he insists that the United States exercised great influence by encouraging the anti-Goulart conspirators. Fico concedes that Goulart was incompetent in his handling of his own commanders and in his interactions with the key commanders opposing him. In the last chapter of his book Fico comes to the conclusion that the 1964 *golpe* was in the final analysis a Brazilian affair but that the United States stood in the background ready to prevent the emergence of a Castro-type regime in Latin America's largest country. As to what the United States could have actually done, Fico does not answer that question. His overall judgment of the Brother Sam task force never settles on a consistent theme: he portrays it as a farcical action belonging in a comic opera or as a menacing display of gunboat diplomacy.

Fico argues that Gordon was forced to support Castelo Branco and the military government in whatever steps it undertook because he was unwilling to admit his original mistake. Gordon doubled down and excused every military misstep because he had mistakenly aided Goulart's overthrow in the first place. Gordon certainly believed that the initial order brought by the military was preferable to the chaos of the last stages of Goulart's presidency, but Fico exaggerates the differences between Gordon and other US policy-makers, especially Gordon's differences with Rusk. Gordon is contrasted in Fico's account with a more reasonable and cautious Rusk, but as Fico's analysis unfolds the reader sees that Gordon reacted more strongly against the military's Second Institutional Act of October 1965 than did Rusk. The First Institutional Act—or "the Act," which at the time was not seen as requiring amendment and further measures—stripped specified individuals of their political rights but did not totally revamp the constitutional order. The Second Institutional Act reshaped politics and the constitutional system dramatically by abolishing all existing political parties and establishing a new government party and an "opposition" party in their place. The Second Institutional Act also outlawed the direct election of the president, all state governors, and local executives. By making executives appointive rather than popularly elected officials, the military could more readily control the country. Gordon regarded the Second Institutional Act as an inflection point in the path toward authoritarian rule. He also opposed a standing army for the OAS, was against a combat role for Brazil in Vietnam, and faulted Castelo Branco for not building a base of popular support from which he could resist the demands of his more hardline fellow officers. While certainly a patriot and a dedicated public servant, Castelo Branco was in Gordon's view too deferential to the United States for his own good. The general thus left himself open to criticism from some of his fellow officers that he was insufficiently nationalist and was a toady of the United States.

Fico asserts that it is a "myth" that Castelo Branco was a moderate who wanted to restore constitutional government, but he subsequently demonstrates that Castelo Branco was strongly opposed to, and opposed by, more extreme military factions. Critics of Gordon, including Fico, seem willing to acknowledge that the United States was faced with complex and agonizing moral and political choices in the aftermath of the coup. In diplomacy as in life, to be human is to err—and Gordon's critics might have granted him some margin for error, except for one thing: he rarely acknowledged error and never adopted the stance of a penitent.

In a 2005 interview at age ninety-two, with Brown University's James N. Green, one of his sharpest critics, Gordon came as close to conceding error on Brazil as he ever did: "With the advantage of hindsight, I can justly be accused of naïveté in believing that constitutional democracy would be restored after a short period of emergency [rule]. . . . In previous changes of regime, the Brazilian armed forces had always returned authority promptly to civilian hands."[9] But he shortly added: "I don't believe I would have done anything differently."[10] Another critic, his own daughter Anne, in 2009 said of her father: "In spite of being a progressive democrat who supported FDR's New Deal and other programs . . . his antagonism to left-leaning reform movements in Latin American was, in my opinion, short-sighted and ultimately harmful to the people of that region. I wish that his mind had not disintegrated as it did, because I will never be able to tell him that in my own work, I have tried to make up for the harm that he caused to others in spite of all his best intentions."[11]

The Aftermath of the Coup

In the coup's immediate aftermath US policy and Gordon's own actions mixed support and caution toward the military regime. Far from immediately blessing the military takeover, Gordon contacted civilian politicians to express his hope that Brazil would preserve as much of the constitutional structure as possible and that any direct military rule would be short-lived. He urged a return to civilian rule as early as practicable, in keeping with past military interventions. His meeting with Governor Carlos Lacerda was for that purpose. He sought out Kubitschek to urge the former president to use his influence to help preserve Brazil's basic constitutional structure. Gordon deemed Kubitschek (known as JK to Brazilians) the political figure most likely to become president again in the next election. But what would the military leaders do? LBJ's telegram to Mazzilli had not conferred recognition of a military regime as such; it had congratulated the Brazilians on maintaining continuity, as prescribed in the constitution.

The coup leaders had arrested thousands of left-wing activists and labor supporters in the course of establishing order, but many of these were released once the coup had clearly succeeded and stability was restored. The stated goals of the coup—reestablishing discipline in the armed forces and preventing a communist takeover of the government— did not require the military to rule directly. But it quickly became evident that the generals could not agree on a civilian politician to take over the government. Costa e Silva initially wanted Mazzilli to serve out the remaining part of Goulart's term, paving the way for his own succession. Other military leaders did not support this idea. The difficult questions were how the military was to exercise its authority and how much of the existing constitutional structure and political order was to be preserved. The issue of how extensive the cleaning out of radicals should be was even more pressing to some military leaders. The "moderates" under General Castelo Branco initially prevailed but did not entirely win over the military "hardliners," who demanded that subversives be removed from the congress, the diplomatic corps, and executive agencies. As a result, mildly repressive measures were adopted to ensure that there would be no backsliding into the chaos of the late Goulart period.

On April 9, the first of what later became a series of five "Institutional Acts" (Actos Institucionais) was drafted by the military and passed by the congress to give it the force of law. The First Institutional Act (later known as "AI-1") stripped some 150 politicians, including such figures as former President Kubitschek and the internationally renowned economist Celso Furtado, of their political rights for a period of ten years. Most but not all of those stripped of their right to engage in political activity were vocal supporters of former president Goulart or of his brother-in-law Brizola.

The measure certainly showed the military's distrust of radical politicians and local commanders and broadly defined what was meant by a "radical." In jailings across the country, hot spots such as Recife witnessed the most sweeping police actions. Within fifty days of the promulgation of the First Institutional Act, many of those imprisoned were released, and the repressive measures were eased. But how far the correctives should go and how long the purge should last became a subject of bitter dispute in the country and within the military itself.

The military government of President Castelo Branco did not construe AI-1 as giving it authority to outlaw any political party, curtail press freedoms, or interfere with preparations for state and local elections. It did not interfere with the workings of the congress or intervene in the normal functions of the judiciary. An atmosphere of relative calm prevailed in most of the country from June 1964 through the rest of the year and into 1965. The atmosphere of relative calm was the image the military strove to present to the world. It largely succeeded in getting favorable press treatment in North America and Western Europe. The coup was hailed for being bloodless, and the relative calm in the country was portrayed as proof of the military's restraint. Nevertheless, the calm was deceptive. In certain parts of the country—notably in Recife—there were jailings, beatings, and pursuit of dissidents in the ranks of the clergy and the universities. Ambassadors serving abroad who had been appointed by Goulart were scrutinized, and some were recalled.[12]

On April 15, the congress, following a constitutional provision requiring it to name a new president within thirty days of a vacancy in the presidency, "elected" General Castelo Branco as Brazil's new president. Gordon had briefly considered resigning as a symbolic protest against the First Institutional Act but decided that this gesture would accomplish little. Castelo Branco pledged on taking office to serve out only the unexpired portion of the Quadros-Goulart term and to leave behind "a united nation." He projected a reassuring presence. Gordon held his first private meeting with the new president in Brasilia on April 20, 1964. He congratulated the general and told him that Washington "looked on [the] April Revolution as [a] possible turning point . . . provided proper use [is] made of [the] opportunity."[13] At the same time he issued a warning against "revolutionary excesses" and indicated that the withdrawal of political rights from renowned figures such as Celso Furtado had been "especially badly received" in Washington.[14] The remainder of the meeting focused on the Alliance for Progress, the renewal of US economic assistance, and broad international political issues. Gordon left the meeting generally encouraged.

Only a few weeks before, the country had been on the verge of chaos, and now it seemed to be on the path to renewed economic growth and a return to democracy. The military, Gordon hoped, would make the difficult decisions needed to fight inflation and stabilize the economy. US officials were favorably impressed with the military's initial appointments to key positions. No one at this point, not even the military officers themselves, imagined that the return to civilian rule would not come for another twenty-one years. Gordon did not hesitate to recommend that the United States should work with the Castelo Branco government. If Castelo Branco failed, more extreme military factions would assume power. The policy direction Gordon recommended was that the United States should restore economic assistance for balance of payments purposes, spend the project aid that had been appropriated but left unspent, seek additional funding for economic assistance, and cooperate in training and assistance to the Brazilian military and police forces. He sought to follow this course and did not waver in his support for Castelo Branco—up to the Second Institutional Act (AI-2) in October 1965.

Gordon tried to persuade Castelo Branco not to adopt the Second Institutional Act and criticized it strongly once it was enacted. He wanted to go further in distancing the United States from the regime than Washington was willing to accept. At this time Rusk was more inclined than Gordon to believe that the United States had no choice but to continue to work with the military regime. Gordon later considered, in an exchange with one of his critics on torture, that "my greatest failure as ambassador [was] my inability in 1965 and 1966 to persuade President Castelo Branco to undertake the building of a new kind of political infrastructure, for which he had an unrivalled opportunity" and that could have prevented "the recent depressing cycle of growing urban terrorism and arbitrary repression."[15]

Gordon's attitude toward Castelo Branco was complex. He criticized the Brazilian military ruler in a 1970 reply to human rights advocate Ralph Della Cava for failing to build a democratic coalition during his first year in power, but he took pains on other occasions to express his admiration for the general.[16] Gordon took umbrage, for example, at a *New York Times* obituary at the time of Castelo Branco's death and wrote a letter to the editor calling the article a "caricature." He attributed patriotism and leadership qualities to the general. Castelo Branco in some ways, said Gordon, reminded him of General Marshall. The *Times* did not print the letter, which was probably all to the good, since Gordon's critics would have cited it as further evidence of his endorsement of repressive rule.

Gordon's direct involvement with Brazil for practical purposes ended with the Second Institutional Act on October 25. In a state of resignation he seems to have psychologically disengaged from his ambassadorial duties, or perhaps he was simply worn down by the pressures and the constant series of crises. In early November Dean Rusk made a trip to Brazil for a ministerial meeting and persuaded Gordon to stay on for another year. Late in November Gordon departed for Washington and afterward went to New Hampshire for a scheduled rest with his family at Darkwater. He spent the whole month of December in New Hampshire, with Allison and three of their four children. During this time there was a sudden change of signals: Gordon was not to go back to Brazil for another year after all. In January 1966 he was already serving in his new assignment on an acting basis, awaiting his February Senate confirmation as assistant secretary. He returned briefly to Brazil to say his goodbyes and left the country on February 6, 1966. The Brazilian military government awarded him the Cruzeiro do Sul, the same honor that President Quadros had bestowed on Che Guevara on the eve of Gordon's arrival as ambassador.

Return to Washington

In the postcoup period Gordon was both a favorite of his Washington bosses and an occasional thorn in their sides. He had gained favor from Mann and LBJ for his steady performance during the coup but soon after let it be known that it was unhelpful for Washington to appear to gloat. The sort of thing he had in mind was the tone of a telephone conversation between Mann and President Johnson in which Mann commented: "I hope you're as happy about Brazil as I am." The president replied: "I am." Mann observed further: "I think this is the most important thing that's happened in the hemisphere in three years." The president said: "I hope they give us some credit, instead of hell."[17] Gordon contributed to the problem himself by a talk he gave at the Brazilian war college a month after the coup. He asserted that the "Brazilian Revolution" was on a par with "the Marshall Plan, the end of the Berlin blockade, the defeat of communist aggression in Korea, and the solution of the missile crisis in Cuba as one of the critical moments in world history at the mid century."[18]

Gordon later felt that this was an overblown assessment, but one observer was intrigued by the analysis. In his first private conversation with President Johnson, which took place in June, Gordon found himself being grilled about the war college speech. The president wanted to know the reasoning behind Gordon's assessment. Whether LBJ was entirely persuaded by Gordon is not clear, but the president did support Gordon's request for greatly increased aid for Brazil. The flap over the postcoup gloating was resolved in characteristic fashion by the State Department. The department decided that it concurred with Ambassador Gordon about the problem of bad publicity resulting from loose talk by US officials but concluded that the blame lay with the embassy itself. Thus the department decided to send an admonition to Ambassador Gordon to the effect that the embassy limit its public comments about the recent changes in Brazil's government. Under Secretary Ball warned that it was "especially important that views on communism, subversion, etc., emanate from Brazilian sources . . . so . . . that such news will not be attributable to the U.S."[19]

When US Marines were sent to the Dominican Republic on April 29, 1965, the opportunity emerged for Brazil and hence Gordon to play important roles in US policy. The Dominican Republic had been in a state of political ferment since the assassination of the dictator Raphael Trujillo in 1961. A government of the left, led by President Juan Bosch, was overthrown by a military coup in September 1963, but the military regime lost public support and splintered into rival factions. In the spring of 1965 civil war erupted. President Johnson, acting on the advice of the US ambassador W. Tapley Bennett, decided to send US troops to evacuate American and other foreign nationals and to prevent the emergence of another Castro stronghold at the US doorstep. LBJ initially dispatched five hundred marines, but these forces were augmented by an additional twenty thousand army troops. The Johnson administration in consultation with the OAS quickly decided that the solution to the Dominican crisis would require converting the US forces occupying the country into an inter-American peace force while plans for a new presidential election were worked out. Preliminary canvassing showed that Brazil was the only large country showing any interest in sending troops to the Dominican Republic.

LBJ sent Averell Harriman to Brazil to meet with President Castelo Branco. Harriman arrived on May 3, and he and Gordon flew to Brasilia the next day for a luncheon with Castelo Branco and Foreign Minister Vasco Leitao du Cunha. The Brazilians said that Brazil would be willing to supply troops if the OAS approved the plan for a multilateral force. The Brazilian foreign minister proved to be very helpful in gaining a favorable OAS vote for the plan. A Brazilian general became the commander of the multilateral force, and Castelo Branco took a close personal interest in the operation. The Brazilians provided two thousand troops, and the small Caribbean countries Honduras, Nicaragua, El Salvador, and Costa Rica added a slight additional number. The US troops were largely withdrawn by September 1965, and the Brazilians ran the country while preparations were made for a new presidential election in 1966. Gordon's skillful handling of the negotiations with Brazil won him credit with President Johnson.

The administration conceived another policy initiative that did not prove to be a happy collaboration with Gordon. The administration sounded him out in the summer of 1965 along with other US ambassadors about a plan to recruit Latin American troops for the Vietnam War.[20] LBJ was sending Secretary Rusk around the world to explain and gain support for a US peace initiative in Vietnam and was not directly involved with this initiative. Gordon could not tell whether the idea had LBJ's personal blessing, but he regarded the notion of soliciting Latin American forces for Vietnam as one of the worst proposals he had ever encountered. He managed to undercut the scheme by citing strong Brazilian opposition, to the immense relief of other US ambassadors.

After his December vacation in New Hampshire, Gordon stopped in Cambridge for a luncheon seminar on Brazil at Harvard's Center for International Affairs. He was scheduled to leave for Washington later in the afternoon to spend a few days in consultations before returning to Rio. As the seminar was winding up, the director's secretary came into the room and said that Ambassador Gordon's office in Washington was urgently trying to reach him. Gordon reached Jack Kubish on the Brazil desk, who told him that George Ball wanted to talk to him and transferred the call to Ball's office.

"I've been trying to track you down," Ball said. "Where are you right now?"[21]

Gordon said he was at Harvard but would be leaving shortly for Washington.

"Don't move. Stay there for a few minutes and give me the number," Ball said. "The President wants to talk with you. You will get a call in a minute or two."

The phone rang again in a minute, and LBJ was on the line. The president addressed him as "Linc" for the first time. In their previous meetings the president had been formal. The president explained that he had decided that Sergeant Shriver could not continue to run both the Peace Corps and the domestic poverty program. Therefore he was moving Shriver to the poverty program and putting Jack Vaughn in the Peace Corps job. This left open the job of assistant secretary for Latin America, which the president wanted him to take. Johnson went into an eloquent description of Gordon's virtues, his steadiness under fire, great analytical skills, pragmatism, idealism, good character judgment, and so on. Gordon knew that this job had a reputation as a "meat grinder" and was aware that there had been five or six assistant secretaries for Latin America in as many years. It was one of the worst jobs in Washington and in addition carried the responsibility of coordinator of AID programs. His instinct was that this position was not his cup of tea. On the other hand he remembered something that Kennedy had once told him: the geographical assistant secretaries in the State Department were the key policymakers for their countries and were as important as members of the cabinet. He also remembered that his mentor Harriman had never turned down a presidential request.

"Mr. President," he said, "I'm very flattered and gratified by your confidence, but I'd like to point out that I had a recent conversation with Dean Rusk and we had tentatively agreed that I'd stay on for another year in Brazil."

"That's all right," the president said. "I've talked to Dean—he's out in the Pacific—and he's fully on board with the idea. And so are George Bill and Tom Mann."

Gordon told the president that he was honored and would be receptive to serving but asked if he could at least have some time to reflect and talk it over with his wife. Gordon had read somewhere that LBJ frequently relied on Lady Bird's advice. He promised he would have an answer by the next morning and would be in Washington later that day to meet with George Ball. Johnson said that he had reporters coming in to see him at 4:00 p.m., and he wanted to announce the Shriver and Vaughan moves and would ideally announce Gordon's appointment at the same time but agreed that it was wise for Gordon to talk with his wife.

"There's one more thing," said the president. "You know how I feel about leaks. You're not planning to discuss this with anyone else, are you?"

After learning that only Rusk, Ball, and Mann had been consulted, Gordon assured the president that except for his wife, he had no intention of talking with anyone else. Gordon was picked up at National Airport by Jack Kubish, who drove him to the State Department for his appointment with George Ball. Kubish, a good friend, had spent two years with the AID mission in Rio. He appeared to have something on his mind and finally told Gordon that rumors were flying around the department that he would succeed Vaughn as assistant secretary. The White House operator had called around that morning to locate him, and later someone from the White House had asked the public affairs office for a biographical sketch. Were the rumors true? Gordon attempted to deflect the question by saying that this was perhaps why George Ball wanted to talk to him.

Gordon was discussing the pros and cons of taking the job with Ball when Ball's executive assistant stuck his head in: "That goddammed Dan Kurzmann of the *Washington Post* has been running up and down the sixth floor saying he knows Lincoln Gordon is going to be named assistant secretary and he doesn't believe Jack Vaughn's denials and says he's going to print the story."

"Oh my God, call Bill Moyers [LBJ's press secretary] and warn him. Tell him it wasn't us. This is the sort of the thing that could make the President change his mind," Ball said.

Gordon excused himself to put in a call to his wife, then returned to tell Ball that he had a green light.

"That's good," said Ball. "Now I can tell you that the president said that if you accepted he wants to see both of us for breakfast tomorrow morning at 8:30. He has a press conference and a swearing-in ceremony for Robert Weaver at 10:00."

When Ball picked Gordon up the next morning, he had bags under his eyes and looked anxious.

"What's the matter?"

"The president called me last night at 12:30. Woke me up out of a sound sleep. Mad as hell. He'd read the story in the early edition of the *Post*. Demanded to know who leaked it. He wanted somebody's head in the State Department. He had half a mind to send you packing back to Brazil. I don't know what mood we'll find him in."

When they arrived at the White House, they were ushered upstairs to the residence, where the president had already started on his breakfast. There were two places set for the guests. LBJ greeted the men cordially and directed a question to Gordon about Brazil. Gordon gave a brief answer, and LBJ asked for Gordon's view of the Alliance for Progress. Gordon replied that unfortunately it was now seen as a bilateral US aid program, and not as a joint or a multilateral effort, and that we had not gotten straight the relation between the social reforms and the program's economic goals. LBJ remarked that he had looked into the program shortly after he became president and noticed that less money was actually spent than had been appropriated for Brazil, and he believed that overall the program as not as efficiently run as it could be. Did Gordon agree? LBJ and Gordon talked for nearly an hour, while Ball sat and occasionally murmured in agreement. The president had said nothing about either the assistant secretary position or the news story. LBJ finally glanced at his watch and mentioned that he had to prepare for the swearing-in ceremony. Ball and Gordon rose awkwardly to take their leave. Vice President Hubert Humphrey was waiting to consult with the president. LBJ greeted him and motioned to Ball and Gordon.

"Hubert, you know George Ball of course. Do you know Linc Gordon, our new assistant secretary for Latin America?"

LBJ gave a smile and wink to Gordon, and the new assistant secretary did his best to grin back. The president decided that they would add the announcement of Gordon's appointment to the morning ceremony. Gordon could see that the president had enjoyed the morning's cat-and-mouse game, and he surmised that the president was not quite through with this process. LBJ looked at Gordon.

"Now who do you suppose leaked that story to the *Post*?"

"Mr. President," said Gordon, "I think I can tell you what happened. When I was picked up at the airport yesterday I was told that rumors were flying all over the State Department. The White House operator had called a number of offices looking for my number and then someone on your staff called and asked for a biographical sketch. Shriver and Vaughn had been announced. There was a vacancy and these people are in the business of drawing inferences. Probably 50 people in the building by the afternoon had some inkling and you can't keep that secret. What you should have done was to have George Ball call me privately and then if necessary arrange a meeting with you."

The president's eyes narrowed momentarily, and then his face broke into a crinkly grin.

"Well, I suppose you're right," he said.

The Job of Assistant Secretary

Gordon took up his new duties on an acting basis immediately. His confirmation hearings could not be scheduled until February, and he would have to return in the meantime for an orderly exit as ambassador. LBJ wanted Gordon's assistance on the final stages of the Dominican negotiations, so he directed that his new appointee move immediately into Jack Vaughn's vacated office in the State Department. The first order of business for Gordon was to closet himself with Ellsworth Bunker to discuss the status of the Dominican negotiations. Bunker had been commuting between Santo Domingo and Washington and working with an OAS team to set the conditions for the new presidential election. Two sticking points confronted Gordon and Bunker: the status of the ex-president Juan Bosch and the status of W. Tapley Bennett, the US ambassador, who had become the target of unrelenting congressional attacks. The solution was already evident in outline. Bosch should be in—allowed to be a candidate in the presidential election—and Bennett should be out—moved to his next post as US ambassador to Portugal.

But LBJ was leery about any agreement that included Bosch. He feared that Bosch's election might mean greater Castro influence or even a communist government in the Dominican Republic. With respect to Bennett the president considered him a distinguished diplomat who was being pilloried by Senator Fulbright and the press. He resisted Bennett's transfer because it might appear that he was giving in to Fulbright's demands for Bennett's removal or being swayed by clamor in the press. At several points LBJ had been on the verge of transferring Bennett to Portugal, only to be infuriated by press leaks announcing the transfer. He pulled back and confounded the media. Gordon's contribution was to persuade LBJ that the United States must accept the principle that the presidential election should be fair and that this meant the United States should be prepared to live with Bosch if he won. Gordon had known the deposed Dominican president and recommended renewed US contacts with Bosch. Bosch had been exiled to Puerto Rico during the military regime. At a critical White House meeting Gordon told LBJ that the burden of dealing with Bosch day-to-day would fall on him as assistant secretary. While he knew Bosch would be difficult to deal with, he was prepared to do so, he said, adding that an open election "is the only stance for us to take."[22] The outcome was fortunate: Joachim Balaguer, a centrist, won handily in the May 1966 election. Gordon attended Balaguer's presidential inauguration in July as part of a US delegation that included Vice President Humphrey, Senator Bourke Hickenlooper, and Congressman Hale Boggs.

And finally Gordon, Bunker, and the soon-to-depart national security adviser McGeorge Bundy nudged President Johnson to complete the transfer of Ambassador Bennett to Portugal. Bennett was the last American diplomat who had been in the embassy at the time of the US military intervention to be reassigned. His move to Portugal represented a symbolic wiping of the slate and solved the practical problems of his lame-duck status and the status of his successor, who was already on hand as chargé d'affaires. Fulbright continued to attack the Johnson administration's foreign policy but now shifted to a new target: Vietnam and the escalating US military commitment there.

The assistant secretary job, as Gordon had anticipated, proved to be grueling. But he and Allison settled into a comfortable house at 1915 Twenty-Third Street NW and enjoyed the urban amenities and Washington's social life. The Twenty-Third Street home was, by Allison's reckoning, the sixteenth house they had owned and the forty-seventh move of their nomadic diplomatic existence. Gordon's typical day started at 8:00 a.m. with either a working breakfast or an early morning staff meeting, followed by meetings throughout the morning with foreign dignitaries, officials from other US executive departments, or a congressional presentation. A luncheon, often with a speaking engagement, would typically follow. There were frequent ceremonial visits to the White House, with foreign diplomats presenting their credentials to the president. More staff meetings and briefings in the State Department, award ceremonies, visits with US ambassadors returning home for consultations, and sessions with business groups from Latin America or American businesses wanting to invest in Latin America were routine features of the afternoon. The day would be capped off by a diplomatic reception from approximately 5:00 to 7:00 p.m., usually with Allison, for whom such events were torture. The day would usually end around 10:00 p.m., after a dinner party or other formal diplomatic event. With the numerous Latin American countries having national days and special commemorations, there was a seemingly endless series of events where protocol demanded Gordon's appearance.

Crises would mean urgent phone calls with his State colleagues, other departments, the White House staff, and sometimes the president. His dealings with the rest of the US government were sometimes routine but at times amounted to crises or minicrises in their own right. His most frequent regular contacts were with the departments of Agriculture, Treasury, and Commerce, often in his capacity as coordinator of the AID program for Latin America. As Kennedy had advised him, he was often the senior State Department official dealing with a problem affecting one of the countries within his jurisdiction. He had an easy relationship with his old friend Dean Rusk, who gave him considerable leeway in framing Latin American policy and resolving disputes with other agencies. Rusk was increasingly preoccupied with Vietnam and did not have much time for Latin America. Gordon usually dealt directly with the cabinet officer whose support he needed or whose department was causing him problems. Gordon had cordial professional and close personal relations with Agriculture Secretary Orville Freeman and mostly adversarial relations with Henry "Joe" Fowler, the secretary of the treasury, despite the fact that he and Fowler had been acquainted since their War Production Board days. The disputes principally involved balance of payments questions and "conditionality" issues tied to loans to Latin American countries. When he could not resolve a dispute with his old WPB colleague, he and Rusk would turn to the president for resolution, and LBJ would usually side with them over Treasury.

Another aspect of the job that brought Gordon into frequent contact with President Johnson was an unending series of personnel issues. Gordon was responsible for, or at least had to sign off on, the appointment of every ambassador to a Latin American, Central American, or Caribbean country and frequently even the deputy chief of mission position. He was surprised at the close attention LBJ paid to many of the appointments. Both LBJ and Gordon, for example, wanted to name his successor in Brazil quickly. LBJ asked for a recommendation, and Gordon proposed William D. Rogers, a Washington lawyer who was a close personal friend and an experienced Latin American hand (not to be confused with William P. Rogers, the New York lawyer who was Nixon's first secretary of state). Rogers had been a personal lawyer for Gordon, and Lincoln endorsed him in the strongest terms. But Gordon had gotten no reaction from the president by the time he departed for his brief farewell to Brazil trip. Nor did he hear anything on the matter for weeks after his return from Brazil. This was unusual, for once LBJ had gotten his teeth into a matter, Gordon knew that he did not let go. There had to be something else at issue here. As it turned out, Gordon had not done his "political due diligence"—he somewhat innocently had assumed that the president meant it when he directed Gordon to find the best man as his replacement. So Gordon called John Macy, the White House personnel chief, who had invariably leveled with him when he asked about any personnel issue, to inquire about the holdup. Macy indicated the nature of the problem: Rogers was known to be a friend of Bobby Kennedy's. Macy did not need to elaborate on why this recommendation had not gone forward.[23] LBJ's dislike for Robert Kennedy was well known in the upper reaches of the government. RFK's thoughtless snubs of Johnson aboard Air Force One after his brother's assassination had removed any chance of the two men ever reconciling their already deeply antagonistic relationship.

There was another reason for LBJ's opposition to Rogers that Gordon had unaccountably forgotten when he proposed Rogers's name. Rogers had resigned in protest as deputy coordinator of the Alliance for Progress in 1965 over the Dominican invasion. LBJ was hardly going to appoint Rogers to any future position in his administration. LBJ eventually accepted Gordon's second choice as his successor: John W. Tuthill, a Foreign Service officer who served as US ambassador to Brazil from July 1966 to January 1969. Tuthill was fortunate to escape the fate of his successor, Charles Burke Elbrick, who was kidnapped in September 1969 by urban guerillas as he drove to work.[24] The Tuthill term as ambassador was notable mainly for his launching of what he dubbed Operation Topsy, an effort to scale back drastically the numbers of US officials at the embassy. The embassy bureaucracy had grown like Topsy, especially in the period after the coup, when the United States, at Gordon's instigation, increased its economic and military assistance to the Castelo Branco government. By the time he departed Brazil, Tuthill had succeeded in reducing the number of US officials from all departments by nearly one-third, from just under 1,000 to 719.[25] His actions received cabinet-level support in the Johnson administration and led to efforts to reduce the staffs at US embassies around the world. Gordon had departed the government by the time Tuthill's moves were in full force and never recorded his reactions to Operation Topsy.

The Meeting of the Presidents

As assistant secretary Gordon traveled frequently to Latin America. On a trip in March 1966 he picked up an idea that became the signature effort of his term in office. At a meeting in Buenos Aires, President Arturo Ilia of Argentina surprised the delegates by proposing a hemisphere-wide meeting of the heads of state to discuss economic integration in Latin America. Gordon and delegates from most Latin American countries were hearing the proposal for the first time, and, having no instructions, they did not know how to react. Gordon, along with several Latin American colleagues, arranged a temporizing response: the proposal was praised as a good idea in principle and forwarded to the secretary general of the OAS for detailed review. President Ilia had a particular interest in the proposal, which he embraced as a means to keep himself in power. Rumors were swirling, and reports appeared in Argentine newspapers to the effect that military leaders were plotting a coup to remove Ilia.

As Gordon reflected on Ilia's proposal, he recognized that it bore a resemblance to the original Kennedy idea, dropped for various reasons, of launching the Alliance for Progress at a conference of the hemisphere's presidents. It could be a vehicle for mobilizing political support for and reinvigorating the Alliance. LBJ was won over to the idea and asked Gordon to organize the US government's response. Gordon set up a task force to organize the effort. Progress was slow, however. The OAS was a logical partner to help organize and to act as host for the conference, but the organization's machinery was slow-moving in the extreme. Gordon complained of pettifogging lawyers who did not understand the economic issues and felt stymied by a maze of procedural requirements that delayed timely decisions. The OAS's internal problems reflected the foot-dragging of some member states.

As an alternative to the presidential meeting, security adviser Walt Rostow suggested to Gordon that the president was a naturally restless man who liked to travel and proposed that they recommend to LBJ that he make a trip of his own to various Latin American capitals. The president was enthusiastic. Planning for the trip went forward but reached an impasse when a military coup in Argentina in late June 1966 changed the political landscape. In the aftermath of the Argentinean coup, Gordon told the president, it was impossible to go to Argentina. Yet if he visited other countries and did not visit Argentina, it would be an affront. The proposed trip was placed in limbo. The United States and the OAS, meanwhile, struggled to find a formula to deal with the military government in Argentina. The military elements behind the "Argentine Revolution" had decided that the military in the past had made a mistake in preserving the trappings of civilian rule. This time the military leaders were determined not to leave even a fig leaf of civilian authority. LBJ saw on television scenes of police clubbing students in Buenos Aires and told Gordon to call off the whole idea of a presidential trip.

Attention shifted back to the potential heads-of-state meeting. In August, Johnson delivered a speech drafted by Gordon on the anniversary of the 1961 Punta del Este conference, in which he endorsed the hemispherewide presidential meeting. Since no one was then mad at the Uruguayans, the idea of Punta del Este as the site for such a gathering gained favor. In September the region's foreign ministers were all present in New York for the opening of the UN General Assembly. Informal sessions were held to discuss the presidential meeting, and Argentina participated in the discussions. The foreign ministers, while issuing no formal declaration, reached a general understanding on three points: (1) the idea of the heads-of-state meeting was important for the region and should be pursued; (2) the process was moving too slowly and needed to be accelerated and the agenda spelled out; and (3) the meeting could not take place before April

1967, and the exact date and place should be set at the January meeting of foreign ministers in Buenos Aires.

Gordon and his team worked hard throughout the fall in preparation for the foreign ministers. An important addition to the effort came with the appointment of Sol M. Linowitz as US ambassador to the OAS and American delegate to the Inter-American Committee of the Alliance for Progress (CIAP). Linowitz was a highly successful businessman who had helped transform a small upstate New York company into the world-famous Xerox Company, one of America's twelve largest firms in 1966, of which he was chairman of the board. He was a Bill Gates of the time, enormously wealthy but looking for a new challenge in life, which he now found in government service.[26] Gordon and Linowitz had not known each other before, but they immediately formed a close working relationship. The two men were almost the same age and had both grown up in secular Jewish families in the Northeast. Linowitz was an accomplished violin-ist and a patron of music and found a kindred spirit in Gordon. Linowitz brought new energy, prestige, and considerable salesmanship skills to the post as US ambassador to the OAS.

He and Gordon established a committee of internationally respected Latin American figures to advise the OAS. The committee was made up of Prebisch of UNCTAD (the United Nations Conference on Trade and Development); Herrera of the Inter-American Bank; Carlos Sanz de Santa Maria, chairman of the CIAP; and Jose Antonio Mora, secretary general of the OAS. It seemed like a replay of Punta del Este to Gordon, who had worked with three of the four men at the earlier conference. The evocation of the original Punta del Este, however, had a problematical side. The committee produced a long technical report that was a document written for experts, and Gordon feared a repetition of the original conference's shortcomings. A preoccupation with technical issues would defeat the purpose of the presidential meeting. Gordon's skill as a draftsman came in handy now. He revamped the lengthy report into an annotated table of contents and a more manageable agenda, with decision items singled out. A very brief description of the issue to be addressed replaced the lengthy technical analysis. They now had a five-page succinct document, instead of an overly detailed seventy-page document, which Sol Linowitz took to the OAS council. He returned late that evening and said, "It worked like magic. These fellows have been floundering about now for so many months that they were in favor of anything, anything that really looks like a way out."[27] This was the breakthrough they presented to President Johnson. Linowitz by this time had conceived of a trip on LBJ's behalf to the presidents of the principal countries to review the agenda for the presidential meeting. The presidents would, if all went well, give their final blessing to the effort and instruct their foreign ministers for the January meeting. LBJ quickly embraced the idea and decided that he would send Gordon and Linowitz to the region for the purpose Linowitz suggested.

"You and Sol," he instructed Gordon, "are going on these two trips. . . . Sol . . . up the West Coast of South America meeting with presidents, you . . . up the East Coast. . . . I want the two of you toward the end, as the last stop in your trip, to meet in Mexico City with President Diaz Ordaz. Tell him everything you've learned, get his advice, and report back to me."[28]

Treasury attempted to block the Linowitz-Gordon trip in the interagency negotiations prior to their departure. Gordon and Linowitz took the issues in dispute to the president, who ruled in their favor, subject to gaining congressional approval for any future budgets incorporating proposals from the meeting of the presidents. The travel arrangements were complex. Linowitz went first to Central America, while Gordon traveled to Europe to fulfill a previous longstanding commitment. The next leg of the trip involved a rendezvous in Buenos Aires, where the two men would map their strategy. It was an exhausting trip, especially for Gordon, who had to cross the Atlantic twice as well as make the long trek to the southern cone. Linowitz visited Chile, Peru, and Colombia and then proceeded to Panama City in mid-December to meet up with Gordon, who in the meantime had focused on Argentina, Brazil, and Venezuela. The two amigos paused in Panama City only long enough to brief each other and then headed for Mexico City. In Mexico they had long meetings with key members of the Mexican cabinet at Diaz Ordaz's request before they saw him. Several of the ministers expressed reservations about the high-level meeting. The Americans expressed their view that one of the agenda items would be favorable treatment in US trade policy in favor of exports from developing countries. Mexico, which had no interest in foreign aid, was deeply interested in trade, and the evident skepticism of the Mexican commerce minister turned to support. After a cordial meeting with Diaz Ordaz, the diplomats departed for the LBJ ranch in Texas.

Their plan was to check into the St. Anthony Hotel in San Antonio and then telephone the Texas White House for further instructions. Gordon had never been to the ranch and was looking forward to the visit. Linowitz had been there once before, but he, too, anticipated Texas hospitality. However, their call to Jake Jacobsen, the liaison official at the ranch, revealed a problem. Jacobsen explained that the president would not be able to see them tonight but would send a helicopter for them in the morning. They sought advice from the maitre d'hôtel on local restaurants and had a leisurely dinner, took a stroll, and on returning to the hotel found an urgent message: "Call the Ranch immediately!" This time Jacobsen declared that there had been a misunderstanding and that the president and Mrs. Johnson had wanted to invite the men for dinner. Jacobsen asked if he could send the helicopter at once so that the two could bring their bags and stay the night.

They had been told to look for a chauffer with a red hat when they disembarked from the helicopter. There was a sedan waiting for them, but their chauffer was not wearing a red hat. Instead it was the president himself, in his usual ten-gallon hat. When they arrived at the ranch, the president took them for a brief tour in the darkness and could not disguise the pride and satisfaction he took in his surroundings. The men then sat down for a full briefing with the president, who was animated and exuberant over the prospects for the meeting of the presidents. This would be a historic meeting, he was convinced, a milestone in the hemisphere. The report ended around 12:30 a.m., but the president was only warming up. Linowitz and Gordon would hold a press conference tomorrow morning, he said, and spread the good news. He dictated what they should say: stress the strong interest throughout the hemisphere, the enthusiasm of the presidents, the final choice of the date and site by the foreign ministers, the historic opportunities. "Let's take a walk," he said. He picked up two of his personal secretaries to join them, and the group strolled around the compound. The president was expansive, energetic, and eloquent as he skipped from topic to topic. The secretaries drifted away, but LBJ wanted to talk more to his guests. A naval petty officer arrived to give him a message, but the president talked on. He became indignant when he touched on the subject of excerpts he had read from a forthcoming book by William Manchester on the JFK assassination. All wrong, the president insisted; it misstated everything and missed the point. The president appeared ready to go on all night, but at around 2:30 a.m. he noticed that his guests were beginning to droop. He declared that they needed sleep and ordered them to bed.

The next morning everyone rose early, and LBJ took the men off for a full tour of the grounds. LBJ, who drove, slowed often to point out a landmark or explain a point of animal husbandry. The press conference went smoothly, and by noon Gordon and Linowitz were headed back to Washington, trying to digest the three weeks of nonstop action. The Christmas holidays would provide some badly needed rest.

16

Johns Hopkins President

The Committee should return with one of these names as a candidate for President, [and] the Executive Committee would find any of them acceptable.
—Executive Committee, Board of Trustees, Johns Hopkins University, November 1966

Fundamentally looking back on it, even at that time looking back on it, I think it was probably a mistake for me to have accepted the job.
—Lincoln Gordon, oral history interview, 2006

Who was that woman?
—Faculty member to Ross Jones, at presidential inauguration, February 1968

Lincoln Gordon was more than tired—he was, in fact, worn out. The recent trip was a blur, like some old speeded-up newsreel. He had been going all out since 1961 and was under pressure for much of the time. And for all of his efforts, what did he have to show for it? He could not delude himself that his recent activities had been great successes for America or for him personally. He had tried to recover some of the greatness of the Marshall Plan in the form of the Alliance for Progress, and the project had failed. Brazil had ended up as a dictatorship that was growing more repressive by the day. The Latin American field, which he had once dismissed as a second-rate academic field and a low priority in US foreign policy, was being subordinated to Vietnam. He had not thought much about Vietnam and did not want to think about it. His two older children were nagging him about where he stood on LBJ's Vietnam policy. The kind of unity and consensus that had always marked the band of brothers that made up the foreign policy establishment was showing cracks. America's future—and his own—seemed clouded. This was especially troubling to him because his religion, as it were, was America and America's mission in the world. He had a deep faith in America as a force for good in the world, and he felt that one's life could derive meaning by being a part of each new chapter in the American story. Now the consensus that sustained American efforts abroad was cracking, and the sure-handedness that marked US efforts in Europe seemed to be lacking in the less familiar worlds of Latin America and Asia. In the State Department there was an old joke that if you were uncertain of your objective, the answer was to redouble your efforts. He had redoubled his efforts, but the objective was still not clear, and the fatigue he felt was not like the good fatigue of the war and the Marshall Plan.

Yet in addition to the fatigue he felt a certain sense of expectancy. It had always been the case that when one chapter closed there was something else, another challenge that turned up. That was the American story that had been true for him. You just had to work hard, show up as they said, and your efforts would eventually pay off. He had something of that feeling of expectancy now. The conceptual work for the heads-of-state meeting had now been largely accomplished. The thing was set in motion, and some other challenge would emerge. He had helped to usher in the Alliance for Progress; he could depart now after setting it back on a corrective course. The meeting would go forward, and the period of implementation would follow. That should be the task of somebody else. He could not keep up the pace of the assistant secretary job, and he had a feeling that he had more or less reached the end of the string with President Johnson. The president had treated him well; he could not complain. But he had an uneasy feeling that he was sitting on top of a volcano that might explode at any minute. Vietnam was bound to affect everything. Latin America would be pushed further into the background. It was time to go, but where could he go? He could not go back to Harvard. They had sold their home in Belmont, and he had lost contact with the Harvard community. One did not go backward in one's career or in life. The Princeton opportunity was gone. He needed some big new opportunity. He wished he had his mother's flair; she could always reinvent herself by blazing some new path.

On getting back to Washington he stopped briefly at his office, and when he arrived home Allison had dinner waiting for him. As he sat down to dinner the phone rang.

"It's him again," said Allison.

"Who?"

"The man from Baltimore."

Lincoln took the phone and was conscious that both fatigue and a trace of irritability showed in his voice. The caller identified himself as Charles Garland, chairman of the Board of Trustees of Johns Hopkins University. He and his colleagues were engaged in a search and had identified Ambassador Gordon as at the top of a short list of candidates to succeed Milton Eisenhower as president of the university. Would he be willing to speak with Garland and several of his colleagues, probably right after Christmas? They would also want him to visit the Homewood campus and speak with Milton Eisenhower. Garland suggested January 1 as a possible date since it was a holiday. Milton had indicated his availability to spend an entire afternoon with Gordon at the board's request.

"Well, what did he want?" asked Allison.

"It was the chairman of the board of Johns Hopkins University. They want to talk to me about being president of the university."[1]

Lincoln had been dimly aware that there was an upcoming vacancy at Johns Hopkins. He had sought to enlist Milton Eisenhower's help on an inter-American project, but Milton had begged off on the grounds that he was devoting his full energies to raising funds for a favorite Hopkins project prior to his retirement. Gordon became aware of the subsequent rumors that members of the Johnson administration could be under consideration for the Hopkins job. Such persons would include Secretary John Gardner, Health, Education, and Welfare (HEW). Gardner was the first choice of every college Board of Trustees searching for a president. Dean Rusk and Harlan Cleveland could also be logical candidates, and there were others. Lincoln was on friendly terms with Francis O. Wilcox, dean of the Johns Hopkins School of Advanced International Studies. He had given occasional lectures there for Wilcox, but he had no idea whether Wilcox might have suggested his name. But he had made no overt effort to solicit a nomination or support from Wilcox or anyone else. According to the mores of the day, one did not seek out such a position but must await a "call." Now such a call had come, and the Hopkins presidency was an enormously attractive prospect—it would give him an honorable exit from his current position. Here was a chance to return to his first love—teaching, research, and learning. Too, Hopkins was located scarcely an hour outside of Washington. He could keep his hand in and offer advice to his former government colleagues. It was not a faculty position, of course, but he could use the position as a kind of bully pulpit. He could speak out on issues, renew his acquaintance with a number of research fields, and interact with the renowned scholars on the faculty. There were models of earlier Hopkins presidents being intellectual leaders and shapers of public opinion—Daniel Coit Gilman, Frank Goodnow, Isaiah Bowman during the war, and of course Milton Eisenhower.

Gordon did not do what he usually did when contemplating a new assignment. He did not map out his priorities, manage expectations, or negotiate the terms on which he would be evaluated. He admitted as much later, when he acknowledged that he had started off "naively ignorant of the complexity of university finance."[2] He did not think hard about what it meant to move from the highly structured environment of government service, where he was taking policy direction from a political leader, to being the leader himself and setting the overall policy direction. He did not think about whom he might recruit, as Harriman had recruited him, to serve as his deputy or adviser. He did seek out advice before accepting the position but found "the advice given in good faith but in hindsight extraordinarily misleading . . . by such well-informed sources as Kingman Brewster, John Gardner, McGeorge Bundy, and Milton Eisenhower."[3] The problem was that he had been "selected by the old-fashioned system" and took "office precisely at the moment of transition from the golden age of presidential authority and expanding resources to the era of external and internal disillusionment."[4] The Hopkins trustees had asked him to meet with Milton Eisenhower, and he spent four hours closeted with the current president, getting an upbeat account of all aspects of Hopkins. "I have no doubt that I painted things in pretty glowing terms," Milton Eisenhower later said.[5]

The Trustees Find Their Man

Lincoln had always resisted any role in academic administration. He had never been even a department chairman. Furthermore, his entire academic experience had been at Harvard, with the exception of three years at Oxford. There was no headhunter firm to vet him and conduct preliminary interviews. The Hopkins trustees handled the recruitment themselves, through a screening committee of trustees headed by federal district judge Harrison Winter and with Chairman Garland as a member ex officio. The search, like most faculty appointments then, operated through an "old boys' network." The committee, however, was not casual or careless in its work: it took its responsibilities seriously and worked very hard over a long period. When Gordon was finally contacted, it was to inform him that he headed a very short list, so that in effect he had already been chosen.

There were, however, serious flaws and misunderstandings from the start that cast a shadow over the Gordon presidency. One was the apparent lack of communication between Milton Eisenhower and his successor over the report of a committee that Milton had convened in 1964 to plan for the university's future. Milton had appointed William McElroy, chairman of the Biology Department, as the head of the Hopkins Committee on Long-Range Planning, but he had kept one of his own aides on the committee to keep the recommendations within bounds. The committee, in the heady post-*Sputnik* atmosphere, got out of Milton's control and became a vehicle for the "growth" proponents on the faculty. Milton and his dean of arts and sciences, Wilson Shaffer, disapproved of the way McElroy directed the committee and were horrified by its recommendations. McElroy and his cohorts, in effect, had gone to the individual departments and asked, "How many more people do you need?" The answer was usually "about twice as many as we have now."[6]

The committee report, when it came out in 1966, recommended a significant expansion in both faculty and staff positions without any increase in undergraduate enrollment or other steps to generate revenue. Eisenhower and Shaffer believed that McElroy had misunderstood the nature of the university. Hopkins was a small, elite research university with an excellent reputation that had been built around a small, high-quality faculty, staff, and student body. The McElroy Report disparaged what it termed an archaic management structure, which it said was no longer adequate to handle the growing complexity of Hopkins's affairs. The inference was clear that Eisenhower's approach was inadequate for the future. Milton, though privately seething, made no official comment and took no action on the recommendations, leaving the matter to his successor. He apparently believed that he had subtly indicated to Gordon his discomfort with the report. If he had, Gordon missed the signal: he attempted to implement the committee's proposals for expansion just as the economy went into recession and federal research funds nosedived.

A second and related misunderstanding was that Gordon got the impression that fundraising was well in hand and that what was expected of him was intellectual leadership. The rosy picture of the university's finances that Milton painted during the courtship of Lincoln reinforced the impression left by the trustees.[7] This was a mistake, for as Steven Muller later told Milton Eisenhower's biographers, "fund-raising at a private university is never done" but is always an urgent requirement for the president.[8]

The university had made great strides under Milton's stewardship. Eisenhower doubled the school's endowment, raised $75 million for buildings and $30 million for scientific equipment, increased faculty salaries by 70 percent, and added new departments in the history and philosophy of science and in mathematical statistics. Milton strengthened the medical school and the Hopkins School of Advanced International Studies (SAIS) both in Washington and at SAIS's Bologna branch. Although university finances were apparently on a sound footing, a more aggressive development office was considered necessary by everybody and was part of the planning for the university's centennial celebration in 1976. A new and aggressive fundraising campaign was thus in the offing, but how to organize and conduct the campaign was left to Eisenhower's successor. The university would have to spend money to raise money, but the climate for raising money was changing, and no one wanted to end up spending much to raise little. Hopkins had a strong tradition in graduate education, but if the undergraduate programs at Hopkins could be strengthened and the size of the undergraduate student body increased—there were 1,704 undergraduates and 2,038 graduate students in 1967—the resources for growth would be more nearly at hand.[9]

If Gordon was surprised at how quickly the appointment was made, it certainly did not seem that way to the trustees. By the time they settled on Gordon, the trustees had been through a protracted search process stretching over seven months. The trustees had initially made a number of soft inquiries and several concrete offers and been rebuffed. The disappointments lent a note of growing urgency to the process. In September 1966 they set forth an ambitious list of the criteria for the next Hopkins president. A sounding was made to John W. Gardner, but he declined to be considered. The screening committee sent letters to fellow trustees, Johns Hopkins deans, members of the faculty, alumni associations, visiting committees, and foundation officials asking for names and began sifting through the responses. Judge Winter reported to the executive committee on November 7, 1966, on the search committee's work.[10] It had assembled a list of approximately 130 candidates; after several meetings with a joint search committee of faculty and deans, the list was whittled down. Judge Winter and several committee members then made a trip to New York to meet with officials from the Carnegie, Ford, and Rockefeller Foundations to get reactions to the names remaining on their list. The list by this time was down to 30 or 35 persons. The committee then met with Milton Eisenhower, and this further reduced the list to 21 names. The deans and faculty committee was again consulted and asked to give comments in writing on each candidate and to rank the candidates. Judge Winter and Ross Jones, secretary of the Board of Trustees, met in Washington with Dr. Logan Wilson, president of the American Council of Education (ACE), to review the list. This meeting and the written evaluations from the deans and faculty committee resulted in a list of 12 candidates. The trustees at their November 7 executive committee meeting produced a final list of 10 individuals, who were discussed at length.

The finalists were: Harlan Cleveland, the US ambassador to NATO and former assistant secretary of state for international affairs and publisher of the *Reporter;* George Alexander Heard, chancellor of Vanderbilt University; James M. Hester, president of New York University; Douglas Maitland Knight, president of Duke University; Herbert E. Longennecker, president of Tulane University; Clark Kerr, Roger W. Heyns, and Franklin D. Murphy, all three administrators in the University of California system; David B. Truman, provost of Columbia University and former dean of Columbia College; and Lincoln Gordon.

The screening committee's report to the executive committee included summary written comments on each candidate. The comments on Cleveland raised "a question of whether he would stick to being President" and noted that "he has been removed from the academic community for some time."[11] About Gordon the screening committee reported: "He is an expert in foreign affairs and the word the Committee receives is that he is probably not interested in academic administration."[12] The most significant decision made by the executive committee that evening, however, as reported in the secretary's summary, was that "there was a consensus that the trustees approved the list and that the committee should proceed with the plan as outlined by Judge Winter. If the committee should return with one of these names as a candidate for president, the Executive Committee would find any of them acceptable."[13]

While no one at the November 7 meeting praised Gordon, no one had anything negative to say about him. In Cleveland's case, the written report calling attention to whether he would "stick to being President" seemed to imply a lack of commitment and staying power. One trustee recalled "an earlier association with Mr. Cleveland and asked Mr. Garland [the board chairman] to review comments from the faculty and foundations about Cleveland."[14] While this subsequent review turned up nothing damaging, the comment left the impression that there may have been a skeleton in Cleveland's closet.

The trustees usually met as a whole three times a year, and in between the executive committee met at least once a month. The screening committee, working closely with Charles Garland, decided on four names from the list of ten to be sounded out as to availability and interest in the Hopkins post. The four finalists were Hester, Knight, Heard, and Truman.[15] Judge Winter had contacted each of the four candidates, Garland told his colleagues at the executive committee meeting in December, and NYU's Hester had taken himself out of consideration at once, Knight had expressed some initial interest but then had withdrawn, and Heard and Truman had expressed strong interest. Judge Winter had a preliminary meeting with Heard in Washington and met with Truman in New York City. On the basis of these meetings the screening committee decided that Heard was their first choice. Heard, a political scientist with a national reputation who had been chancellor of Vanderbilt University since 1963, looked to be an excellent candidate from every point of view. The committee invited him and his wife, Joan, to campus for what they hoped would be a successful conclusion to their search. Before the visit could be arranged, however, Heard called to say that upon careful reflection, his loyalty to his own university prevented him from contemplating a move.

The trustees were disappointed but quickly moved on to David Truman. Truman was an ideal candidate, too, just a whisker below Heard in their estimation. He had many of the same qualities as Heard, and he had the advantage of being a rising and not an already risen star. The trustees reasoned that since Truman was not yet a university president, his interest in the Hopkins post would be strong, and his own institution would be less likely to stand in the way of his professional advancement. A visit to the Hopkins campus for Truman and his wife, Eleanor, was tentatively scheduled for the first week of January, since a visit during the semester break would allow Truman discreetly to leave his own campus.[16] In Truman, the trustees thought they finally had a candidate who truly wanted the job. They had found the search a grueling process, but nothing had gone drastically wrong so far, and they were anxious to wind matters up. Truman had been a highly successful dean of Columbia College before becoming the university's provost. He was admired by his colleagues, was liked by students, and was all in all an admirable choice. The trustees went all out to land their man. Truman was impressed by Hopkins, but like the Heards, Dave and Ellie Truman had deep ties in their own university and community. They had many close friends at Columbia and in New York. They loved the city and their spacious apartment on Riverside Drive just a block from the Columbia campus. Dave, as one Columbia colleague remarked to me then, "is blue [Columbia's school color] down to his underwear."

Moreover Truman had reason to believe that Grayson Kirk, Columbia's president and successor to General Eisenhower, was contemplating retirement within a year or two. Truman, as provost, was widely considered the likely successor to Kirk. The future of course was uncertain. The Hopkins offer was a bird in the hand. Was a bird in the hand worth a bigger bird in the bush? Truman consulted his closest friends on the faculty, and they told him to get a sounding on what the trustees were thinking. He was reassured that he had strong backing on the board if he could just wait a year or two. Truman decided to take his chances at Columbia.[17]

The Hopkins trustees took the news on Truman hard. They had pulled out all the stops and had fallen short. The trustees decided that they had too hastily dismissed the California candidates. Garland had asked for provisional authority from the December 5 executive committee meeting to contact Berkeley's Roger Heyns as a potential backup to the four finalists. With Truman out, there was no cause for panic, but the trustees considered the situation serious. They had gone through half of their short list of ten and had reservations about three of the remaining names. Many other universities were seeking to fill their top post, and the demands on chancellors, presidents, and provosts were multiplying, making recruitment a challenge. The thought of reopening the whole search was daunting. Could they persuade Milton to stay on for a year or two? Garland squashed any idea of trying to persuade his best friend to stay on. It was not fair to Milton. He had done enough. Fortunately several strong candidates remained on the short list. It was time to give serious consideration to availability—to look at someone not attached to another university or research laboratory now who really wanted the job. The two remaining candidates were both senior government officials: Lincoln Gordon and Harlan Cleveland.

It did not take the screening committee long to make its choice. Gordon was the older of the two by five years, had more government experience, had been associated with a more prestigious institution (Harvard vs. Syracuse), and had more scholarly publications. Gordon had his PhD, and Cleveland did not, an important consideration for Judge Winter. Moreover Cleveland was overseas, and Gordon was right here in Washington. The only knock on Gordon was that he might not be interested in academic administration. That was easy enough to determine: ask him. The next board meeting was scheduled for January 19. It would be nice to wrap matters up officially at that meeting, but in the meantime the executive committee could act with the full authority of the board.

When Garland and his colleagues met with Gordon after Christmas, it was a case of love at first sight. They were dazzled by his learning, articulateness, and affable personality, and he even *looked* like a university president. His mop of white hair, his pipe, and his scholarly demeanor embodied what a university president should be. Garland hastened to tell Milton Eisenhower the good news and arranged for the meeting with Gordon on Monday, January 2. Lincoln, Allison, and Amy (about to enter Bard College in the fall) visited the Homewood campus, Allison and Amy touring the campus while Lincoln met with Milton. The meeting with Eisenhower went well and evidently accomplished its purpose. Gordon was sold on the university, and the trustees were sold on him. Garland polled his colleagues, and a formal offer was made and accepted before the full board met on January 19 to ratify the decision.

The most delicate negotiations involving the appointment occurred among Rusk, Gordon, and President Johnson. Gordon met with Rusk on January 3 and told him what had happened over Christmas and New Year's. When Gordon explained the situation, Rusk smiled. "Well," he said. "That explains one thing."

Gordon asked what he meant.

"I've been getting calls from this reporter asking me to confirm or deny that I was leaving to become president of Johns Hopkins," said Rusk.

The two talked about the job of a university president and about Hopkins, which Rusk knew well from his days at the Rockefeller Foundation. Rusk then volunteered to run interference with and soften up the president at a luncheon meeting for which he was about to depart.

"He might be unwilling to let you go," Rusk said.

This thought had occurred to Gordon, too, and he had taken pains to explain to Rusk that he would stay through the presidential meeting in April and would not report to Hopkins until July 1. He wanted to leave in early June so that he might have a vacation at Lake Sunapee. Gordon stopped by Rusk's office later in the day and got a report. The president was gracious and less upset than Rusk had feared.

"He wants to meet with you, though, to talk about it," Rusk said.

Gordon called Marvin "Pa" Watson, LBJ's appointments secretary, and arranged to see the president.

Johnson greeted him cordially and said, "You know, if I had any qualifications—which I don't—that's exactly the job I'd love to have if I weren't doing this. I would like to think that, if I asked you to stay, you would, but I've thought about it and I don't think I have a right to ask that. You've served for how long now?"[18]

Gordon said that he had been in Brazil since 1961, so he was nearly six years on the job.

"I only send soldiers to Vietnam for one year. You've been in Brazil a lot longer than most of your predecessors. You will stay through the presidents' meeting, of course?"

Gordon promised that he would.

President Johnson went on to say that he wanted a recommendation for Gordon's successor. They discussed the Punta del Este meeting and some other issues. LBJ wanted to throw a party for Gordon. The president "could not have been nicer, was most gracious."[19] The sailing was quite as smooth as it had appeared to Gordon in his interview. Rusk told him sometime later that he had gotten a call from the president the same evening after he had talked to him about Gordon's departure. Johnson talked for some time, going over the same ground, and in a less than conciliatory frame of mind. Finally LBJ talked himself back to his original position. "Well, if I'm going to agree to this in the end I might as well be gracious about it," he told the secretary of state.

At four o'clock in the afternoon of January 17, 1967, the White House press office released an exchange of letters between the president and the Honorable Lincoln Gordon. President Johnson said in part: "I congratulate both you and The Johns Hopkins University. You have brought to Latin American affairs in the last six years a rare combination of experience and scholarship, idealism and practical judgment. . . . After you have assumed your new post, I shall be counting on you from time to time to serve your country in an advisory capacity."[20]

Ambassador Gordon replied:

It has been a special privilege and pleasure to work directly with you. . . . My willingness to leave the Department of State at this time is due only to the opportunities for continued service to the national interest afforded by the Presidency of The Johns Hopkins University which for ninety years has distinguished itself for pioneering innovations in higher education and for major contributions to the advancement of knowledge and to the shaping of constructive national and international policies. A valued part of The Johns Hopkins tradition is the advisory services of its Officers and Faculties in many fields of national policy-making, a tradition which I shall certainly expect to maintain.[21]

The Hopkins Presidency: The Honeymoon Phase

Gordon enjoyed something of a honeymoon in his early days as president of Hopkins. He was enormously relieved to be out of government and out of (so he thought) the line of fire. He wanted to stay active professionally in policy and public affairs. He gave speeches, wrote papers, and attended conferences in his first six months on the job. He spoke for an old friend at Southern Methodist University on the problems of Latin

America and Brazil; spoke for the president of the University of Maryland system on power, freedom, and accountability in higher education; and prepared papers on foreign economic policy, the linkages among Europe, the United States, and Latin America, and the future of foreign aid. He later believed that it was probably a mistake to be away from campus so much while trying to learn the ropes at Hopkins.[22] Hopkins had a tradition of inaugurating its presidents formally on February 22 to correspond with the date in 1876 when Daniel Coit Gilman was installed as its first president. This may have contributed to Gordon's idea that he could ease into the job and safely devote time and energies to outside activities. The time between July 1967 and the inauguration on February 22, 1968, would in any case give Gordon the opportunity to prepare his vision statement and outline his plans for the presidency. He hoped to draw on the planning process under the direction of Provost William Bevan for ideas, and he would use the bicentennial date of 1976 as a kind of focal point for his plans. The bicentennial was a convenient target for planning purposes, fund drives, and the setting of goals for the university.

In his first six months as president he received "six or seven honorary degrees" from other colleges and universities, a customary honor for the presidents of major universities. One came before he even took office: he received an honorary Doctor of Letters from Rutgers University in May 1967. He cherished it in particular because of the other recipients, who included the composer Aaron Copeland, the novelist Catherine Drinker Bowen, and James Fisk, president of the Bell Laboratories.[23]

His administrative duties included many talks before Hopkins alumni groups and Rotary functions to bolster fundraising. Since he did not trust himself to speak in public without a text, Gordon usually prepared his remarks in advance and would then either read from or glance at his notes while speaking. It seemed to him that he was spending an enormous amount of time crisscrossing the country in unavoidable but largely pointless activity just as he was trying to learn the personalities and ins-and-outs of the university. He was also dogged by the controversies that had followed him from Brazil. He had never developed the thick hide of a politician and even smarted at jibes from student journalists that he should have ignored.

A pleasant aspect of his new life was that he could learn new things— it was like becoming a student again. He was particularly intrigued by the problems of international health and the activities of the School of Hygiene and Public Health and formed a close personal relationship with John Hume, the school's dean. He received a letter from Brazilian colleagues pointing out that Brazil's whole public health system owed much to Hopkins, including the fact that virtually all of the leaders of Brazil's public health system had studied at Hopkins. The School of Hygiene and Public Health had trained health leaders from all over Latin America, South Asia, and the Far East and was conducting many research programs overseas. The school had an arrangement with Lebanon to run a teaching hospital and treated patients from all of the oil states. Gordon learned that Hopkins had weathered the financial storm in the 1930s by pioneering the practice of treating Middle Eastern royalty at the Hopkins Baltimore hospital. Wealthy Middle Eastern families paid cash for their treatments and often became important donors for clinical programs. Although the School of Nursing was slated to be phased out, Gordon was drawn into many of the problems of that transition. In general he felt very comfortable in dealing with professional women.

Gordon recruited David Rogers as dean of the School of Medicine, and Rogers proved to be a bold administrator. Rogers brought African Americans into his clinical faculty, developed many new programs, and occasionally trod on the toes of senior professors, who were accustomed to ruling their departments with an iron fist. He was so confident an administrator that he rarely called on Gordon for assistance. Gordon would get complaints from some medical school professors about Rogers's high-handed tactics, but he felt confident that Rogers was usually right and backed him even though he knew the dean could be abrasive at times. Gordon also took special interest in the activities of SAIS and his old friend Fran Wilcox, the SAIS dean, who made the new president a member of the faculty.

Despite the exchange of flowery letters with President Johnson when he left government, Gordon was only rarely summoned back to the White House. One occasion when he was called on was in March 1968, shortly before LBJ's historic speech to the nation announcing his decision not to seek renomination in 1968. The event was a luncheon at the White House to honor German chancellor Ludwig Erhard. The president would seek an opportunity to speak with Gordon, but the subject was not specified. He gladly accepted the invitation because he had a topic he wanted to discuss with the president. While Vietnam was not yet the dominating campus issue it was shortly to become, Gordon saw how strongly students and faculty felt about the draft issue and considered that the abolition of the draft and the creation of a volunteer army would ease campus tensions. He had held some discussions with his presidential peers from other schools, had exchanged letters with HEW Secretary Gardner on the draft status of graduate students, and had written several articles for the *Baltimore Sun* on the topic. He did not have a specific proposal but wanted to broach the notion of a presidential commission to study the draft issue.

At the lunch Gordon was seated at Erhard's right, with the president on Erhard's left; interpreters were seated nearby. The conversation was proceeding awkwardly. Gordon's spoken German, never fluent, had deserted him entirely. He was making small talk with the aid of an interpreter. Gordon noticed that Johnson seemed preoccupied and was clearly not paying attention to what was said. The president had already spent part of the morning with Erhard. Suddenly Johnson leaned across Erhard and said to Gordon, "Linc, what is your opinion of Vietnam?"

An interpreter attempted to translate for Erhard, but the president waved him aside.

"Mr. President," said Gordon. "You know Vietnam is not my area. I was your Latin American man. I have no knowledge of Vietnam."

LBJ was not to be put off.

"Come now, that's nonsense. You're an American. You're a citizen. Of course you have views on Vietnam. Everybody does. What are yours?"

Gordon protested weakly that he could not give an off-the-cuff answer but promised to write up his views in a memo and send it promptly. Erhard looked on in surprise, understanding some of what was said but not quite believing what he heard.

Under the circumstances there was no chance to talk with the president about the draft. He hurried back to Baltimore and worked on his memo, which he sent to the president via Walt Rostow on March 25. In later years he viewed this memo as taking the Clark Clifford position and recommending that it was time to cut our losses in Vietnam and pull out. The message was in reality more qualified, though, beginning with the statement that he "was neither a hawk nor dove."[24] But the thrust was against any deeper involvement in Vietnam and pessimistic about US leverage in negotiations with the North Vietnamese. The memo could not have been reassuring to the president if he had expected support from his strongly anticommunist former assistant secretary. Gordon presented options for the president based on varying assumptions about the prospects of maintaining a strong US position in Asia even if South Vietnam fell. All US support had to be premised on a stable local government and the determination of our local allies to defend themselves, an assumption that was lacking with South Vietnam. He did not directly criticize the administration's policy, possibly taking a cue from Harriman, who had refused to criticize the president publicly at a time when Acheson, Clifford, Kennan, and others were breaking with LBJ over Vietnam. But Gordon's memo could not have been read as anything other than a strong, if nuanced, critique of the administration's Vietnam policy. He never knew whether LBJ actually saw it. The president was not looking for analysis—he was looking for support. That he did not get it from what he thought might be a reliable source was just one more straw moving the president toward his decision not to run again.

Administrative Challenges

Gordon's professional activities at times blended with his presidential duties. He testified before the Maryland state legislature urging general state support for private higher education as one of his early initiatives. The state already gave capitation grants for medical students, but Gordon won a significant broadening of state support for private higher education. His office took the initiative in creating an association to lobby the state legislature and to represent the interests of private higher education in dealings with the Maryland Education Department. He became an enthusiastic participant in the work of the Association of American Universities (AAU), the interest group of the presidents of the major research universities and their graduate school deans. He worked, among other issues, on tax policy and charitable deductions—matters of obvious interest to Hopkins and other research universities.[25]

Despite the fact that Gordon was always "more interested in substance than in administering things," he found certain management issues unavoidable, and they increasingly absorbed his time and energies.[26] Even the comparatively minor issue of the presidential residence on the Homewood campus proved troublesome. Nichols House had been purchased and renovated as a home for Milton Eisenhower so that he could entertain and be near his office. Allison found "this place . . . a monster without service" and inadequate to handle the representation functions of the presidency.[27] She persuaded her husband that they should bring several trusted Brazilian ex-servants from the Rio embassy to Baltimore to help them run the presidential residence. This move raised eyebrows on campus, and some old-time faculty, accustomed to Milton Eisenhower's frugal ways, saw the move as lavish and pretentious, representing a kind of "imperial presidency." This was galling at a time when the university's financial pressures were mounting. Nevertheless, Gordon found the immediate staff resources available to him, beyond the household problem, quite inadequate. Allison's comments in a letter to her friend Ruth Kriebel reflect her husband's frustrations: "L. has [sic] without the help who were supposed to do the job he has had to do for a year. And those leftovers from the old regime were terrible—and those brought in to help the first year were awful."[28]

Gordon was careful never to criticize his predecessor publicly, but he quickly concluded that Milton had relied too much on "amateurs" from within Hopkins on some highly technical matters. He believed that such technical matters could have benefited from outside expertise.[29] For example, university vice president Bruce Partridge persuaded Gordon to hire outside consultants for construction on the Homewood campus. Gordon credited Milton with often finding talented insiders, but to Gordon there was a world of difference between talented amateurs and real professionals. Gordon considered Partridge "very competent" and believed he had found someone who could handle the administrative problems that Gordon found irksome. But Partridge soon departed to become president of the University of British Columbia in Vancouver, leaving a gap at a key position.[30]

Far from shoring up central administration in line with the McElroy recommendations, Gordon found himself having to operate with an even leaner team than had served Eisenhower. Gordon recruited Benjamin Willis, a retired air force general who had had a successful career in government, to run the sponsored-research office, but Willis found the Hopkins terrain difficult to navigate. He could not help Gordon on the central problems of financial management. After a long search Gordon recruited Robert Kerley from the University of Kentucky as vice president for administration but soon had a falling out with him. Their personal relationship deteriorated to the point where they were scarcely on speaking terms before Kerley departed. The only one on Gordon's staff who was thoroughly comfortable with the university's finances was a young accountant from Peat, Marwick & Co., Robert C. Bowie (no relation to Gordon's Harvard friend Bob Bowie). Bowie was only twenty-nine at the time he arrived at Hopkins in 1966 as the accounting firm's on-campus auditor. Kerley had hired Bowie away from Peat, Marwick & Co. to be the university's comptroller. Kerley then shortly left Hopkins for a position in California. A senior person Gordon thought he had recruited withdrew ten days before he was scheduled to arrive on campus and took a post in industry. As described by Allison, "a V.P. for finance threw up his contract 10 days before coming."[31] Gordon would have done better to promote Bowie, but he had few interactions with the auditor and failed to recognize his talents.

The trustees wholeheartedly agreed that the university needed to recruit new high-level administrative talent, but it proved easier to state this as a goal than to achieve it. A new fundraising campaign was under discussion that would require recruitment for the office of development. Gordon upgraded the university's previously informal arrangement for legal advice when he brought in Ellen Fishbaum as the university's first in-house general counsel. He was particularly pleased to recruit a professional woman for the legal post. He believed that Hopkins should have more women on both the administrative staff and the faculty. Personnel matters of all kinds, from appointments to fringe benefits to the wages of the university's maintenance crews, demanded his attention.[32] He did not have, and sorely missed, a deputy chief of mission like he had in Brazil or a planner who could do for him what he did for Harriman.

Hopkins's unique internal governance system gave broad powers to a twelve-person academic council elected from the tenured faculty. The president convened the meetings of the council but had no vote. The council's jurisdiction was in theory narrowly focused on academic issues, but no one ever accused the council of having a narrow definition of its powers. When the council felt a broader expression of faculty views was appropriate, a larger general assembly meeting was called to which the entire Homewood faculty, tenured and nontenured, was invited. Both the council and the assembly had only advisory powers, but the recommendations of the council were typically routinely accepted by the university's president and trustees. This structure meant that the university's president would have to exercise political dexterity of a high order if he wanted his priorities to be adopted. To the Hopkins senior faculty, Milton Eisenhower had seemed the ideal president. He flattered them, raised money for them, and did not invade their turf (or when he did, he did so with a light touch). Now here was Lincoln Gordon: a horse of apparently a quite different color. This was an intellectual who styled himself as a reformer by temperament. Gordon had, for example, created a new center for urban affairs to reach out to the local community and help solve the urban crisis. The faculty did not mind anyone trying to reform society. Coeducation was all right, too, but reform in how the university was run? Reforming society was one thing, but reform of the university was quite a different matter.

Gordon recognized that following the popular Milton Eisenhower was going to be a challenge, and he tried in various ways to reach out to the faculty. But he earned a reputation for talking too much and not listening to the faculty. Early in his administration he invited a small group of influential faculty members to lunch to get their views on the university's problems. According to Alfred Chandler, one of the faculty participants, Gordon "talked away. When it was all over we looked at each other and asked, what was that? He didn't ask us how we were doing, how funds were, anything like that."[33] On another occasion Gordon invited Wilton Shaffer, Eisenhower's longtime dean of arts and sciences, to stop by for a talk. "I came over," Shaffer recalled. "And I was there for an hour and I don't think I said three sentences."[34]

To students of the "me generation," Gordon seemed like an archaic figure. Patriotism and discipline were not ringing slogans even with the hardworking and straight-laced Hopkins student body. The incredulous students saw that the man actually *believed* that America was a force for good in the world. Gordon had once observed that General Marshall's Victorian manner and absolute integrity made him seem like someone from a different century. To many Hopkins students, President Gordon also seemed like a man from a different century. Yet for all his difficulties, there was excitement as Gordon's inauguration approached on February 22, 1968. For Gordon personally there was a "heavy weight of LA [Latin American] concerns and connections in 2nd half of 1967—overlapping with JHU demands."[35] But he could not have been happier to be out of the pressures of government service. His later assessment was brief but pungent: "Note shift in atmosphere from 1967 to 1968!"[36]

The Presidential Inauguration of February 22, 1968

The inauguration of Lincoln Gordon as the ninth president of Johns Hopkins was a gala occasion. The festivities lasted several days and included a lavish alumni banquet with President Nathan Pusey of Harvard the speaker. Forty college and university presidents attended the inauguration ceremony, led by Harvard's Pusey, Yale's Kingman Brewster, Courtney Smith of Swarthmore College, Detlev Bronk of Rockefeller University, and Gordon's predecessor Milton Eisenhower. City and state notables included Baltimore mayor Thomas D'Alessandro and Maryland's secretary of state C. Stanley Blair. Governor Spiro T. Agnew was away traveling. Trustees, community leaders, foundation officials, representatives from business and from the arts, educators, and other assorted luminaries joined family members for an elaborate banquet in advance of the ceremonies. Twelve hundred spectators crowded into the auditorium of Shriver Hall for the ceremony, which lasted more than two hours. The whole assemblage of academic luminaries just before the campus explosions of that spring made the affair resemble a grand ball on the eve of the battle of Waterloo. The world they knew was about to change, and this celebration was the swan song for the comfortable old order, which would suddenly disappear with the tumultuous campus upheavals only a few weeks later. Seen in retrospect—in the light of the events that shattered the cloistered calm of America's elite campuses—the glittering spectacle was an astounding symbol of the end of an era.

The day was cold and clear. The academic procession began the formal ceremony, with the forty university presidents solemnly marching in full academic garb. Led by Chief Marshall Charles S. Singleton bearing the silver mace, the presidents slowly filed onto the stage and took their seats behind Dr. Gordon. His Eminence Lawrence Cardinal Sheehan performed the invocation. Chairman of the Board Garland welcomed the assembled guests and paid tribute to past Hopkins presidents in the audience. He read from a letter sent to him by President Lyndon Johnson congratulating Hopkins and Dr. Gordon; thanking Milton Eisenhower for his service to the nation; and asserting, "I welcome and shall continue to encourage the interchange because I firmly believe that it strengthens both the government and the universities."[37] Garland told the audience that the "primary function of the Board of Trustees is to select the President of the University. . . . Lincoln Gordon was the obvious and enthusiastic choice to become our ninth President."[38] The Maryland secretary of state lauded the contributions of Johns Hopkins to the state. Mayor D'Alessandro spoke of the special pride the city took in its great university. Chief Marshall Singleton read a message from Dr. Felix Battiglia, rector of the University of Bologna, extolling the role of the university in Western culture. Courtney C. Smith, president of Swarthmore College, spoke on behalf of Oxford University and as American secretary of the Rhodes scholarship trust, delivering a witty and erudite tribute that "stole the show" in Gordon's estimate. Smith would be dead within months, succumbing to a heart attack in his Swarthmore office at age fifty-two, in the middle of a student strike and occupation of the admissions office.[39] Nathan Pusey, then in his fifteenth year as Harvard's president, gave a greeting on behalf of American universities. The chief marshal got into the act again and wound up the preliminaries with a slightly over-the-top introduction of the new president: "Sir, May you continue to court our Lady of Wisdom . . . may you keep a perpetual date with her in the arduous years ahead as you have so clearly done during the past months. . . . There is, we know, a very old expression in the languages of men which, translated to English, says simply: 'Thank you for existing.' Dr. Gordon, I hold that the faculties of the University could find no more fitting words of address, of sincere and cordial salutation to you. . . . Sir: 'Thank you for existing.'"[40]

In handwritten notes penned in his nineties, Gordon gave this appraisal of his inaugural address: "My Feb 22, 1968—Inaugural Address @ JHU—much too long + too *ambitious!*"[41] He was correct in this appraisal. His speech was an erudite and wide-ranging analysis that "charts the immediate future of Johns Hopkins and comments on many of the major issues facing American higher education today" and that, "owing to its particular pertinence . . . is being published and distributed to all alumni and to other friends of the University."[42] As an analysis it was penetrating and an example of graceful prose, but as a guide to his priorities for the university, it was less successful. So many reforms were suggested that his listeners were confused. It was not certain whether Hopkins would end up on its present course or whether some wholesale overhaul was in the offing. The address predicted major changes in how elite universities would relate to society, sketched the implications of universal higher education, and proposed radical new methods for financing the nation's research universities. But the tone was confident if not complacent: elite universities, it almost went without saying, would remain cherished institutions in our society. Universities like Hopkins would remain vital to the nation in an increasingly technological age.

A few themes could be picked out as auguries of his later battles with his Homewood faculty. He called attention to the more than seven thousand students in the Evening College to illustrate the broadening Hopkins educational mission. The issue of an expanded Evening College would become highly controversial two years later. Gordon called for careful planning and declared that "much of this thinking must be done in groups which cross traditional departmental and divisional lines."[43] Interdisciplinary programs, the merging of faculties, and the consolidation of departments were red flags for traditionalists on the Homewood campus. Gordon expressed his need to fight against "a kind of national withdrawal from the world" based on the idea that "engagement is inherently imperialistic."[44] One day, he said, "Vietnam will again be at peace, but the problems of world order . . . will persist."[45] This appeared to be pooh-poohing the Vietnam issue and drawing a line in the sand to some war critics on the faculty. Most notably, however, the inaugural address emphasized budgetary pressures and how financial issues could affect the university. Gordon detected an accelerating growth in expenditures relative to revenues and questioned the traditional model of how research universities were financed. That Gordon placed such focus on financial issues ensured that his Hopkins stewardship would be judged on how well he dealt with finances.

Gordon read from his written text in a monotone. When he was finished, a polite ripple of applause rose from the weary audience after what was by now nearly three hours of speeches. A diminutive woman jumped to her feet and began cheering enthusiastically and waving her arms. She continued well after the applause had died away. After the benediction, as the crowd of over one thousand slowly filed out of the Shriver auditorium, a faculty member approached Ross Jones, secretary of the Board of Trust-ees, and asked: "Who was that woman?"

"That was Dorothy Gordon, the president's mother."[46]

Signs of Trouble, 1968–1969

The warm feelings from the inaugural festivities did not last long. Anti-war disturbances erupted on campuses scarcely one month after Gor-don's installation. In March serious protests at Columbia began when six students, dubbed "the IDA Six," disrupted a university baccalaureate ceremony. The university's alleged ties to the Institute of Defense Analy-ses (IDA), which triggered the protest, consisted of two professors hav-ing served briefly as consultants to that organization.[47] Demonstrations against Columbia's plans to build a gymnasium in Morningside Park fol-lowed. Senator Eugene McCarthy's strong showing in the New Hamp-shire primary and LBJ's March 31 announcement that he would not run again launched a tumultuous campaign season and set off mushrooming campus protests across the country.[48] In April the protests against the Columbia gym escalated into a major crisis when members of the Students for a Democratic Society (SDS) occupied several university buildings and forced the university to shut down. These dramatic events captured the attention of the nation's media, and campus unrest rapidly spread.

The Hopkins demonstrations were mild in comparison, but the mood on the Homewood campus was tense. For Gordon and other university presidents the protests at Columbia and other campuses became a topic of absorbing interest and concern. AAU presidents held meetings to dis-cuss how to deal with the protests. President Gordon dispatched the law-yer who serviced the university's legal issues to New York to meet with Columbia officials on how to deal with the occupations of university buildings. After meeting with his lawyer, Gordon became convinced that the use of injunctions was an effective tactic against planned demonstra-tions. "We had injunctions up our sleeves and in every drawer against every contingency," said Ross Jones, Hopkins vice president and secretary of the board.[49] Preparing for the legal battles led Gordon to create the in-house office of legal counsel. He also decided to speak pointedly against what he termed student anarchists, which seemed an overreaction to some faculty members.

One venue for Gordon's public criticism of student radicals was particularly ill chosen and gained him the reputation for being unnecessarily confrontational. He chose Parents Weekend for a seemingly unprovoked attack on student radicals, when there had not yet been protests at Homewood. The student newspaper the *News-Letter* reported, "Before 200 students and parents attending 'Parent's Weekend' . . . Dr. Lincoln Gordon delivered a major policy address in which he defended President Grayson Kirk's handling of the Columbia student demonstrations."[50] The paper described the talk as lasting "one hour and 45 minutes" and quoted Gordon as saying that "the [Columbia] students attempted to grab power for the sake of power." Gordon "felt it betrayed ignorance on the student's [*sic*] part to demand representation on the board of trustees."[51] The role of the trustees, according to the paper's version of what President Gordon said, "was merely a fund-raising one," and if the students thought they could raise more money than the trustees, they were welcome to a seat on the board.

The student paper did not enjoy a high reputation for accuracy in its reporting. There was no journalism school at Hopkins and no faculty advisers to the student journalists. Gordon nonetheless displayed his thin skin and unwisely rose to the bait. Three weeks later, in a talk intended to reassure the student body, Gordon complained that his remarks at Parents Weekend were not a "major policy address."[52] He had spoken informally from notes, which the *News-Letter* reporter had failed to mention. Gordon implied malice or incompetence on the student journalists' part. He alluded to radical behavior by students in Latin America and at Columbia University. The president's relations with the student paper thus went from bad to worse and never recovered. He later developed a rocky relationship with the *Baltimore Sun,* complaining regularly that the paper had gotten a story wrong.[53] This was unfortunate because his initial treatment by the *Sun* had been favorable.

In September Gordon picked up the cudgels again as he welcomed the new freshman class. He stated that "the University will not tolerate anarchists" as part of his welcome to the freshmen.[54] But it would be misleading to suggest that Gordon was always picking fights or that the campus was about to explode. The Hopkins scene was still relatively calm compared to what was happening at Columbia, Swarthmore, Brown, Cornell, Berkeley, and many other campuses. Gordon himself was not sure why

Hopkins had so far been spared and was inclined to attribute the relative calm to good luck. While he would not gain high marks for courting the press, Gordon was an active presence on campus and engaged students at numerous campus events. He met informally with students who sought him out or asked for advice. His general approach to any problem, whether student or faculty grievance, was to say, "Let's discuss it." One Hopkins colleague remembered witnessing a scene on a beautiful fall afternoon when President Gordon was speaking animatedly to a cluster of students sitting on the grass. Gordon was describing a visit to Germany during the 1930s, when the Nazis were taking over German universities. He was earnestly warning against the dangers of politicizing the university such as happened with Germany in the 1930s and more recently with Venezuela's universities. The students seemed mesmerized as Gordon held forth; they turned their faces to the sun as they drowsily listened to the hum of the president's voice. The colleague remembered thinking that he was witnessing a kind of tranquility through verbal anesthesiology.

Yet the budgetary situation in the fall of 1968 still appeared under reasonable control. Administrative weakness, however, made it hard to get a firm grip on the university's finances. Growth as envisaged in the McElroy Report was still on the agenda. What did it matter to the faculty that there was coming and going among the deans and assistant deans, signs of administrative untidiness, or quarrels with the student newspaper? So long as the university's finances were sound, the faculty members would simply go about their business. The faculty had a tradition of surviving the foibles of any administrators. During World War II President Isaiah Bowman shared the uneasiness of Baltimore's old families at the large numbers of Jewish émigré scholars on campus. Gordon's transgressions were picayune so far, compared to what the faculty had endured under Bowman. Nor was there anything for the trustees to view with alarm. They had gone through an arduous search and had no taste for another such effort. Gordon had formed strong bonds with several of the trustees, including the new chairman Robert D. H. Harvey, Judge Harrison Winter, D. Luke Hopkins, and Ernest Stebbins. Gordon had shown a willingness to work with the trustees to modernize the university's management structure and to plan the ambitious new $100 million fundraising campaign. There was every reason to believe Hopkins would make a successful transition from an "amateur style of administration to a modern university with a world-class standing." Knowledgeable observers knew that there were cleavages among the trustees. There were thinly disguised battle lines between the medical complex in East Baltimore and the Homewood campus and deep divisions between the medical school and the hospital. Internal power relations on the board had not yet settled after the retirement of its long-time chairman Charles Garland (who had stayed on during Gordon's first year at Milton's request to help ease the transition). The Hopkins trustees and their faculty friends formed a closely knit but quarrelsome family. The new medical school dean David Rogers proved a formidable administrator who stood up to the hospital barons, but he was not ready for a showdown in his early days as dean. The hospital had its own Board of Trustees and was tied to the university and medical school only through joint trustees—that is, those who served on both the hospital's and the university's boards.

The Hopkins faculty was watchful, however, because their new president had signaled in his inaugural address that he might seek major changes. Dr. Gordon had described himself as a reformer by temperament and had outlined a laundry list of potential reforms. Beyond this, the 1968 presidential election had swept Richard Nixon into office on a wave of national protest against the student unrest. Disruptive student behavior was a prime example of what the electorate disliked, and voters had first shown their dislike by electing Ronald Reagan, who ran against the Berkeley radicals in the 1966 governor's race in California. Nixon had picked up on Reagan's theme when he denounced the "bums" who were ruining the nation's universities. Moreover the US Congress had shown a strong inclination to force universities to take stronger steps against disruptive student behavior, adopting Section 411 of the Health, Education, and Welfare Appropriation Act of 1969, which stipulated that federal student aid or research funds would be cut off if an applicant for aid or a grant "has been convicted by any court of general jurisdiction" of using force or trespassing on university grounds.[55] Such federal actions complicated Gordon's job of running the university. Gordon feared that such gestures could make matters worse by leading to more student and faculty protests. The state of Maryland was also threatening actions that could affect the state's colleges and universities. Hence the mood on the Hopkins campus was uneasy. How Lincoln Gordon would react to the new environment was uncertain. To faculty members on the left he sounded like Nixon, but his eagerness for dialogue with student radicals alarmed conservatives. He had called demands that classified research be halted at the university's Applied Physics Laboratory (APL) "absurd," but his defense of the laboratory was not always reassuring to hardliners on the faculty and on the board. There was a willingness to cut him some slack in these difficult times, but there was also an underlying anxiety. Many people would be quick to blame Gordon for any missteps.

The Death of Dorothy Gordon

Lincoln and Allison Gordon were expansive hosts at Nichols House, the president's campus home, organizing events and dinner parties. Lincoln was fond of including his mother in such gatherings on her frequent visits to campus. Richard Macksey, professor emeritus of the humanities, recalled an invitation from the president's office to attend a dinner party to honor Archibald MacLeish, the poet and former librarian of congress. When Macksey and his wife arrived, they found Dorothy Gordon acting as hostess in her daughter-in-law's absence. Macksey knew her, since he had appeared as a guest on one of her *Youth Forum* shows. Macksey remembered Dorothy as "a prodigious talker" who totally monopolized the evening with her insider's knowledge of the problems facing the *New York Times* and the Sulzberger publishing family. Only her son could begin to keep pace with her conversationally. The guest of honor sat listening as Dorothy and Lincoln ping-ponged their observations across the table. Afterward the Mackseys and MacLeish departed together, and MacLeish remarked with a smile, "When Linc and his mother get together, it is something. I can't get a word in edgewise."[56]

Dorothy was a frequent visitor on the Homewood campus in the first years of her son's presidency. She had missed him during his long service in Brazil. His official trips to Washington were busy affairs, and he could not usually get to New York to visit her. He missed the conversations with his mother, in which the two of them would go on for hours on any topic. Dorothy was always in or near performance mode. On her eightieth birthday, Lincoln and Frank gave her a diamond pin in the shape of a bee, and of course Lincoln composed two sonnets for the occasion, one entitled "To a Queen Bee":

The connotations of the bee are many:
Honey; the hive; the busy buzz; the sting.
In fourscore years this Queenliest of any
Has learned to buzz as well as how to sing.
Her hives swarm with brash and eager youth
Debating, probing, searching at each forum.
Her honey (and her sting) tame these uncouth,
Who manifest incredible decorum.
Her drones comprise a string of VIP's.
No wonder that her busy buzz's scope
Ranges from urban topics to Chinese;
From drugs to better ways to choose a Pope.
And so, we generations in your thrall
Salute O Queen, the liveliest of us all.[57]

Dorothy's health began to fail in 1969. While she continued work-ing, she had to restrict her travel. Lincoln made frequent trips to New York on fundraising and alumni business and for monthly meetings of the board of the Equitable Life Assurance Company, of which he was then a member, invariably visiting his mother on these trips. Her death of stomach cancer in May 1970 was a heavy blow and coincided with the ris-ing burdens of the Hopkins presidency. Though it had been obvious that she was suffering from a terminal illness, her death when it finally came was a shock for him. His father had died in 1944, and Gordon had only dim memories of him, but Dorothy had been such a presence and so vital a force in his whole life that he found it hard to imagine her gone. He reacted as he usually did when depression returned, by working harder.

Rising Student and Administrative Problems

A string of problems began in the spring of 1969 and continued into the fall term, including student protests and a threatened student strike over the ROTC presence on campus, the desegregation of admissions, the tangled academic calendar, the unionization of blue-collar university employees, student rights in university governance, the status of the Evening College, and reactions to mounting federal and state regulations regarding student disturbances. Taken together, the problems created enough dissatisfaction with Gordon that the coalition that eventually deposed him began to take shape. In March student protesters briefly occupied Homewood House, the administration building, to protest the low wages of the university's hourly workers. The university considered employing an injunction, but the protesters seemed surprised by their own boldness and left the building before Gordon had to do anything to evict them. This protest did not draw major attention or press coverage. In April, however, relations with undergraduates took a turn for the worse when Gordon had to react to a Baltimore police arrest of three students on drug charges. When the students protested their arrests, the police used tear gas and mace to disperse them. Gordon told the students that the university would consult with the police, raise bail money for the three arrested, look into the circumstances under which the police came on campus, and investigate the allegations of police brutality. The student newspaper charged that Gordon knew of the police raid in advance and had condoned it. When he denied this, he was criticized by hardline faculty for vacillating and pandering to the students.

In early May the SDS staged a sit-in at Homewood House to demand an end to the ROTC on campus. Gordon used the injunction powers for the first time to good effect. The students avoided university disciplinary action and possible criminal penalties by obeying the injunction and leaving the building. But they elicited from Gordon a pledge to discuss university decision-making with students. In the subsequent discussions with students, he rejected their demand for a voice on the academic council.[58] Gordon characterized the tactics used by the SDS in occupying Homewood House as "inappropriate . . . unnecessary, undesirable and likely to be counter-productive."[59] Dissatisfied, a group of students attempted to interrupt an academic council meeting to state their grievances. Their actions resulted in disciplinary action by the university. Gordon's new dean of arts and sciences, George Benton, insisted on suspensions for some of the students and opposed what he saw as Gordon's efforts to appease student radicals. Benton saw Gordon's efforts to reduce the sentences against the students as a sign of weakness, while more liberal faculty members considered the president's handling of the incident too harsh. Relations between Gordon and Benton had been strained before this incident but now hardened into hostility and deep mutual antagonism.

In the fall 1969 term antiwar sentiment on campus was on the upswing. The student council and the student newspaper called for a moratorium on October 15 to protest the war and demanded that President Gordon suspend all classes on that day.[60] Some fifty faculty members announced that they did not intend to hold classes on the moratorium day. Gordon reminded them that they were obligated to hold makeup classes for any they postponed. While Gordon insisted that the university could not officially sanction the moratorium, he reminded students that class attendance was strictly voluntary and that students could simply skip classes if they chose to do so. This stand pleased no one. It appeared to be a backhanded way of endorsing the moratorium while pretending to oppose it. Nonetheless, the moratorium day went off without major trouble. Some three thousand students gathered on the Homewood campus but did not disrupt classes or occupy university buildings. This was probably because Gordon had arranged a standby injunction to prevent anyone from occupying university buildings. The assembled students marched downtown to City Hall, where they staged a peaceful protest.

Convinced that dialogue was the best way for the university to respond to the war, Gordon organized a convocation in November to discuss Vietnam policy. His own thinking had evolved beyond that of being "neither a hawk nor a dove"—he was now opposed to any escalation of the war but equally opposed to a precipitous withdrawal from Vietnam. He said in an interview with the *Sun* that the Nixon administration was not moving quickly enough to end the war.[61] Gordon may have become a dove, but he was not enough of a dove for the student protesters or the antiwar faculty. He let his hair down in an address at Bowdoin College on October 21, when he declared that New Left prescriptions for reforming universities "would return to the medieval tradition of theology as the unifying touchstone. In their system, all the answers are known in advance, the only function of the university being to rationalize the answers in theological terms—in this case, neo-Marxist theology."[62]

The Bowdoin speech ruffled feathers on the Homewood campus for another reason as well. The Hopkins faculty members who followed the president's pronouncements noted Gordon's views on the future role of liberal education. He told the Bowdoin students that future political leaders would see that "much of higher education will be frankly and almost exclusively vocational." Contrary to critics' view, Gordon declared, the trend toward vocational education was not to be deplored: "The right kind of professional education can be as liberal and liberalizing as education supposedly designed to produce well-rounded persons."[63] Traditionalists on his Homewood faculty saw such remarks as signs of Gordon's enthusiasm for the Evening College and his desire to alter the predominant role of graduate education at Hopkins. This was in line with Gordon's well-known admiration for the medical school's clinical-education model, which combined practice with theory. The speech was actually an eloquent and nuanced defense of the importance of liberal learning for the twenty-first century, the kind of liberal education that could best be provided by an institution like Hopkins, with its strong links to graduate and professional education.

In November the trustees voted to accept President Gordon's proposal that the undergraduate student body become coeducational starting in the fall term of the 1970–1971 academic year. The coed action came at some cost to his standing with the board. Several trustees were incensed that the president had issued a press release before the trustees had officially acted on the proposal. While Gordon did not apologize for his actions, he privately conceded that he should have brought the trustees in on the decision earlier. He had similar problems with the thorny problem of the conflicting Hopkins academic calendars. Hopkins had one calendar for the Homewood campus, based on a two-semester system; another for the medical school, featuring an additional short session in between its semesters; and a third calendar for the public health school, based on a three-quarter system. The administrative problems of the calendar became mixed with broader issues of governance. A proposal surfaced to create a tripartite university senate composed of faculty, student, and administrative representatives.[64] Gordon was "skeptical and uncertain" about the proposal but was open to persuasion. He observed that university governance consisted of a number of discrete subject areas—academic appointments, student relations, long-range planning, curriculum, finance—and each area had evolved distinct administrative arrangements. Combining the areas into one senate with overall jurisdiction would produce an unwieldy system. There would be poor attendance except when one's particular area was on the agenda. He would like to have a better understanding, he told the *News-Letter,* of what problem his colleagues thought needed fixing with the current decentralized system.[65] Something was afoot that Gordon did not quite understand, an unfocused discontent of some kind. Nonetheless, he managed to bring about the calendar reform and dispose of the senate proposal.

Unionization of hourly workers emerged as a critical issue in December. Gordon favored a significant increase in pay for hourly employees, but very rapidly it became evident that much more was at stake than a one-time wage adjustment. College and university employees—including maintenance crews, library staff, kitchen and cafeteria workers, and seasonal workers—typically were not unionized in those days. Yet colleges and universities were usually among the largest employers in a city or region. Hopkins was not the first university to unionize large parts of its nonacademic staff, but the rapid shift in December 1969 gave key impetus to the unionization movement in higher education generally. Gordon did not seek the approval of the Board of Trustees before allowing unions to organize Hopkins workers. An angry board member prior to the January board meeting queried Gordon about the chances of reversing the decision on unionization. Adopting the confiding tone this trustee apparently used with Milton Eisenhower, whose center-right politics coincided with the trustee's own, the trustee inquired if the "liberals" were becoming a troublesome force on campus. Gordon replied that the issue was quite settled; the decision was one of those pressing day-to-day operational issues that required a quick decision by the president. Gordon argued that unionization of the workers would be good for the university in the long run. But he succeeded only in convincing the trustee that he was one of the liberals taking over the university.

On another important issue—the admission of racial minorities to the undergraduate student body—Gordon decided to follow Milton Eisenhower's practice and *not* consult the trustees. Milton had decided on his own initiative in 1956 to increase gradually the very small number of minority students. This was two years after the *Brown* school desegregation decision and a year before Milton's brother signed into law the Civil Rights Act of 1957. Milton's aim was to gain a minority presence on campus without precipitating a divisive debate among trustees. Gordon now discovered that the number of minority students had leveled off in the last several years, and therefore he determined to double the number of minority students admitted for the next year. Thereafter he would make further gradual increases for "three or four years."[66] After this had been accomplished, he rather naïvely believed the problem would be more or less solved, and admissions officers could operate on a color-blind meritocratic basis.[67] Whether he could have continued with this policy was mooted by his premature departure.

Gordon had never aspired to being a university administrator. In retrospect, he believed that he should not have taken the job. He told a Hopkins interviewer in 2006: "Fundamentally looking back on it, even at that time looking back on it, I think it was probably a mistake for me to have accepted the job."[68] He shared the faculty's typical disdain for administration. When he actually became a university president, it came as a surprise and a providential escape when he badly needed an exit from the Johnson administration. Now his old doubts returned. But he had made the commitment to serve, and he could not walk away from it. The issues that had been accumulating to date, however, were nothing compared to what was in store the following year. In the fall of 1969 he could still point to a budget in balance. In January 1970 he was obliged to announce that the university had slipped into a budget deficit of $530,294.[69] Since there was a continuing effort to improve cost accounting, he said, it was entirely possible that this reported deficit would be less. It was also possible that the newly discovered deficit was only the tip of a larger iceberg.

Year of Crisis, 1970

Of Gordon's many problems the financial crisis was the most serious, for it was inextricably linked to the university's other problems, from student unrest to labor relations to governance. If student disturbances continued, donor giving and even student-tuition income could decline. Tight budgets could force cuts in academic staffing, which would upset the faculty. It would be doubly galling if the president increased the administrative staff for fundraising purposes and monitoring the budget and at the same time cut faculty positions. Federal research funds were more important than ever but could be jeopardized by issues like the ROTC on campus, military recruiting, and arguments with the navy over classified research on campus and at the Applied Physics Lab. Milton Eisenhower had taken steps to limit classified research in the medical school and in engineering but had assumed that other federal research funding would be available to replace those losses.

The $100 million fundraising campaign also proved to be a major headache for Gordon instead of a solution to his problems. Early in Gordon's tenure the trustees had launched the ambitious new project and set the target at $100 million, a figure far greater than anything the university had ever undertaken. The development office would have to be upgraded and expanded to achieve the campaign's ambitious goal. An outside professional firm would have to be hired. Planning for the campaign started slowly. In 1969 Gordon finally found the person he believed could be an effective vice president for development: Ellery B. "Woody" Woodworth, cofounder of Maryland public television and a member of the Maryland Council of Higher Education. Gordon persuaded Woodworth to take the job after a dazzling four-hour exposition on his goals for the university. Woodworth reported for work in July and rapidly began hiring new staff for the campaign. Problems with the hospital, however, developed early. The hospital displayed a massive disinterest in any university-wide campaign, refusing to provide its donor list and ducking important meetings. Even more irritatingly, the barons of East Baltimore kept revisiting issues that Woodworth thought had been resolved. The underlying problem was that the trustees themselves were deeply split on the wisdom of the fundraising campaign. Crossman Cooper, a powerful joint trustee, made no bones of his skepticism about merging the hospital with broader university fundraising. The trustees lacked a strong chairman, with the retirement of Garland, to give President Gordon clear direction or strong backing for his initiatives. Early in 1970 President Gordon selected an outside firm from New York, Jones & Co., to spell out the campaign's details, even as the hospital continued to throw roadblocks along the path, sometimes allied with the medical school and sometimes antagonistic to both the medical school and the Homewood campus. Gordon decided to force the issue at a trustee meeting, since critical decisions were not getting made.

At this meeting Gordon and Woodworth at last presented their plan for the campaign, which had been prepared with the assistance of the professional fundraising firm from New York, and scheduled the unveiling and full-dress presentation for the Board of Trustees. Copies of the report and plan were distributed to the board members at the meeting, and Gordon opened the presentation with an overview of the plan. Woodworth made a brief statement and asked the representative from Jones & Co. to outline the plan's details. Before the presentation was completed, however, an angry, red-faced Crossman Cooper, one of the powerful joint trustees, threw his copy of the plan down on the table and exploded:

"This is outrageous! Anyone who expects the trustees to come up with these sums is out of his mind."

He rapped his knuckles on the column of figures indicated as the trustees' share of the campaign and went on to denounce the whole plan as incompetent. This time, unlike the issue of coeducation or the unionization of university workers, other trustees joined in the criticism. The $100 million campaign was dead on arrival. The president had suffered a heavy blow. He had no alternative other than to direct Woodworth to dismantle his office. Woodworth now had to devote his time to firing most of the people he had just hired.[70]

Meanwhile, Hopkins provost Bill Bevan decided to leave Hopkins to become the executive secretary of the American Association for the Advancement of Science (AAAS). He had come to Hopkins in 1966 hoping to be in the running to succeed Milton Eisenhower but had been passed over by the trustees when they hired Gordon. When George Benton came on as dean of arts and sciences, he pushed Bevan to the side and left him powerless. Bevan's departure meant that Gordon had to search for a provost while also trying to recruit a new vice president for administration and attempting to keep on board a demoralized development officer who was being forced to fire most of his staff. Dean Benton wanted the provost job, but under no circumstances would Gordon elevate him to the position. Gordon would have liked to fire Benton, but he could not risk a faculty backlash and vacancies in all of the top administrative ranks.

The problems came in all sizes and variants for President Gordon. A medical school faculty member went berserk and threatened to shoot a colleague. This was one problem where the medical school dean was happy to call for the president's assistance. Gordon enlisted the university's chaplain, Chester Wickwine, to form a three-man hostage negotiating team to deal with the situation. The mentally unbalanced professor was talked into surrendering and seeking therapy. Shortly thereafter Gordon discovered that his house in Washington, which he and Allison were trying to sell, had been occupied by squatters and turned into a commune. He had to prod the DC police repeatedly before they finally evicted the squatters. In the meantime Congress was threatening further punitive action against universities that tolerated student militancy. Gordon asked the trustees to reverse their previous decision to suspend temporarily military recruiting on campus and instead to hold a university-wide referendum on the issue. He favored on-campus recruiting by the military and had every reason to expect he would win the vote with strong support from the health campuses. But the Nixon administration's Cambodian invasion occurred on the eve of the referendum, and Gordon narrowly lost the vote and drew fire from Dean George Benton over his handling of the whole recruitment issue. He had opposed Gordon's initial decision to ask the trustees for a temporary suspension of recruiting as appeasement of campus radicals. For his part Gordon considered that confusion in the administration over the voting by Benton's office was partly responsible for the defeat. The underlying deterioration in the relationship between the president and his dean was underscored. By now the two men were scarcely on speaking terms.

The fiscal crisis was still the major issue for Gordon and for the university. Because of the lack of cooperation from Benton, the beleaguered president had to confront the fiscal crisis largely on his own and even contend with what he considered virtual insubordination on Benton's part. After failing to recruit his intended replacement for departed university vice president Kerley, Gordon had elevated Benjamin Willis to the post but soon found that Willis was out of his depth in this role. He did not significantly aid Gordon's understanding of the university's complex financial issues and was hampered by Benton's failure to cooperate on the arts and sciences finances. Benton surmised that Gordon would not risk firing him and saw no reason to cooperate with a president apparently bent on cutting the arts and sciences budget. Benton had been the virtually unanimous choice of the faculty to succeed Allyn Kinball as dean and believed that he, and not the inexperienced president brought in from the outside with no knowledge of Hopkins, was uniquely equipped to save the university. He was strong-minded, willful, and tenacious and had supreme confidence in his own ability. Benton was a down-to-earth Chicagoan, a scientist with conservative political views, and harbored a suspicion of Gordon as a weak-minded, loquacious, and arrogant eastern snob. Benton's lack of support for the president's policies became so obvious that it appeared to Gordon that Benton was almost trying to provoke a confrontation. Gordon was enough of a politician to sense Benton's design and to stay above the catfight Benton apparently wanted. But he was not enough of a politician to sense Benton's wider design to recruit faculty allies to force the president's eventual ouster.

Gordon labored hard over the summer on a plan to deal with the fiscal crisis and other problems. In September he communicated his findings and recommendations to the Hopkins community in the form of a lengthy letter to fifty thousand alumni, faculty, and the parents of all current students. In reporting on the academic year just concluded, he attempted to reassure the alumni and parents concerning the "tensions" of April and May, emphasizing that "in comparison with the serious incidents on so many other campuses, our problems were minor."[71] The president pointed to the absence of any destruction of property, personal injury, or interruptions of normal university functions but gave an account of various student protests. He explained the suspensions of ten students and their failure to graduate on time (they were readmitted in the fall semester).[72] Then Gordon moved on to a detailed analysis of the institution's gloomy financial situation.[73] He reported that the deficit for the 1969–1970 academic year just completed was $2.9 million and that the projected deficit for the 1970–1971 academic year that started on July 1 had risen to $4.3 million, although he hoped that some savings could be made to reduce that figure. A number of steps to cut costs had been taken already, the president reported, and more steps would be taken. Tuition would be raised from $2,500 to $2,700. Academic salaries were to be frozen starting the next academic year. The development office had already been cut by $300,000, and further cuts were anticipated. The president indicated that while the medical school was currently in deficit, its prospects were bright inasmuch as the school was the recipient of a $2,000 per capita payment from the state of Maryland for each medical student. Prospects for continued federal research support and donor giving were favorable. The major source of the deficit lay in the Homewood campus with the arts and sciences department, which had grown too quickly. Savings would have to be made in all Homewood academic departments, and for that purpose all faculty appointments would have to be subject to careful review. The administration planned to cut the operating deficit in half for the 1972–1973 academic year and then cut it down to $1 million the following year.

The financial news stunned the Homewood faculty. The pay freeze, though it was not scheduled to take effect until the next year, struck like a thunderclap. Nothing like this had happened for a decade or more. Gordon tried to explain that it was entirely possible that the preliminary estimates were exaggerated and that he intended to expand the comptroller's office so that he could more accurately grasp the magnitude of the problem. His reasoning fit the narrative of a bloated central administration whose only solution to a problem was to hire more bureaucrats. It was surprising to Gordon how the deficit had increased so suddenly and so sharply. In fact, as it turned out, the projected deficit of $4.3 million for 1972–1973 turned out to be an exaggeration.[74] Gordon did not know this at the time, however, and neither did the faculty. Gordon was thus unable to offer much reassurance to the Homewood faculty. There were rumors of a 10 percent cut in the size of the arts and sciences faculty, a proposal never advanced by the president. Gordon believed that Benton was fanning the flames of faculty discontent by spreading false rumors and again considered firing him. Once again he decided that this move might backfire and give Benton an ideal weapon to use against him.

Gordon did not know Benton when he appointed him. Benton was a distinguished meteorologist who had been away from the university on an extended leave at the National Oceanic and Atmospheric Administration (NOAA). Benton had received such strong recommendations from all faculty quarters that Gordon did not seriously consider anyone else as successor to the retiring dean, Allyn Kimball. Among Benton's accomplishments was his work in World War II on the atmospheric conditions hampering the effectiveness of the B-29. This work of Benton and his colleagues had led to the discovery of the jet stream. Gordon felt that Benton's having been away from the university during the student disturbances would be an advantage. Even the initial meeting between the two, however, suggested sharply differing views on student protests and the respective jurisdictions of president and dean. The signs of trouble were unmistakable when Benton requested a meeting to brief Gordon on the benefits of the arts and sciences and to outline his plans for the president—at a time before Benton had officially assumed office. It was a tour de force performance and showed Benton to be intimately familiar with the work of every department and nearly every faculty member. But to Gordon there was something disconcerting about the presentation: Benton appeared to resent any questions. The dean-designate, moreover, had a very broad definition of his sphere of authority. Gordon was not a man quick to take offense, but he could not help finding this performance patronizing. As soon as Benton officially became dean in the spring of 1970, he began to drag his feet in passing on information to the president. The referendum vote on military recruiting hardened the animosity between the two men when Benton took over the referendum's administration and issued press releases on his own. Both men favored recruitment on campus, but they were not on the same page when it came to the wording of the referendum. Other incidents over the summer reinforced Gordon's distrust. Gordon sent requests for information from Benton's office, but cooperation was grudging, and Gordon found out that Benton had instructed his staff not to work with the president's office. Homewood tuition, for example, was to Benton an arts and sciences matter, not a presidential one. (Gordon ignored this and raised tuition.) Benton also closed a small department without, in Gordon's view, giving the chairman of the department a fair hearing. Gordon could not live with this dean, but he could not get rid of him either.

The Faculty Steps In

In the fall Gordon took two important steps in addition to his budget actions. He decided to reverse the suspension and once again permit military recruiting on campus because of the threat of losing Defense research funds, and he completed the search for a provost to replace the departed Bevan. Working closely with the trustees, he hired Dr. Steven Muller, a political scientist and Cornell's vice president. Gordon invited any trustee from the Baltimore area to hear the presentations of the two finalists, Muller and a candidate from a midwestern public university. The midwesterner seemed the more academically distinguished of the two to Gordon, but the trustees unanimously preferred Muller on the strength of his presentation of a financial strategy for Hopkins. The appointment of Muller as the new provost was to take effect in January 1971, but Muller had been given until July 1 to report to Hopkins on a full-time basis. In the meantime Muller was to work part time and make occasional trips to Hopkins.

Allison Gordon was afraid that her husband was getting worn down by the stresses of the job. She never felt quite at home at Hopkins; she did not view the Hopkins community as welcoming, though they did have some friends in the larger Baltimore area. Allison was no longer young; she was four years older than her husband but looked older. She had smoked cigarettes all her adult life, and at sixty she had begun to show signs of the ill health that dogged her later years. Faculty wives were not quite like diplomatic wives in supporting the good causes of the ambassador's wife. The wives of the younger faculty members were increasingly independent and wanted careers of their own. Allison was not happy, and she was especially unhappy at how Lincoln was being overworked and underappreciated. Her anger boiled over one morning when a small crowd of colleagues came to Nichols House to pick up Lincoln for a breakfast meeting. He was still dressing when she burst into the room.

"You're killing him! You're killing him!" she cried. She demanded that they respect his age and his need for sleep and ease the punishing schedule and then hurried out of the room.

Gordon complicated his situation with the Homewood faculty by announcing his intention to create up to fifteen new positions for the Evening College. This was the last straw for faculty traditionalists. To expand the inferior and marginal Evening College while hollowing out the "real" university was to them intolerable. Benton consolidated his position as champion of traditional faculty interests. He and his faculty allies developed the idea of a faculty committee to investigate the finances and the apparent overstaffing of central administration, and they decided to present this proposal at the next meeting of the faculty's general assembly. The issue of university finances was scheduled to be the sole topic of the December 11 session of the general assembly, at which the president and his top aides would present a full briefing on their plans to stabilize the budget.

The central administration distributed a substantial financial report to each faculty member in advance as background for the meeting. President Gordon called the meeting to order at 4:05 p.m., with 85 faculty members present (that number soon grew to 120), and presented a detailed explanation of the university's finances over the past five years, expanding on the analysis of his September letter to the alumni, parents, and faculty.[75] Savings were to be sought wherever possible, salaries frozen for the next year, tuition increased for the current year, and administrative positions cut immediately. He announced a new plan to revise the accounting procedures for estimating indirect costs that would increase cost recovery from the federal government. He called for the admission of more undergraduates to generate more tuition revenue. He reported on the recommendations of the 1966 McElroy report, and their implementation to date, and defended the ratio of administrative staff expenditures to the total operating budget as being below Harvard's 9 percent, Yale's 8 percent, and similar figures for other Ivy League institutions. The figure for Hopkins was on par with the 6 percent ratio of the University of Pennsylvania.

Benjamin C. Willis, the acting vice president for administration, gave a history of his office since 1964. John P. Young, associate provost for planning and advanced policy studies, pointed out that the "substantial increases" in the budget of the provost's office since the fiscal year 1967 had been in accord with the long-range goals of the McElroy report and amounted to "about 273% more than the budget of Provost Macaulay's time [before 1966]."[76] The increase had been "occasioned by necessary liaison with the federal government, the establishment of an 'overall University Long Range Planning' officer, coordination of interdivisional program development, the establishment of a University Director of Information Processing and other responsibilities generated by the increased size and complexity of the university."[77] Ross Jones, vice president for university affairs, explained that his office, formed in 1968, had been created to administer a number of functions that had previously been part of the provost's office. Ellery Woodworth, vice president for development, painfully aware of the troubles surrounding his office, observed that private gifts over the last two years had averaged $11 million and that the overhead cost of 5 percent was within the national average for fundraising activities.

The meeting was then thrown open to questions. The faculty, having grown accustomed to Milton Eisenhower's style of running the university quietly and seemingly on a shoestring, was unmoved and slightly dazed by the recitation of roles, offices, functions, and institutional expansion. The frequent references to the McElroy report were not persuasive to many present, even though they had once been its ardent champions. There was now no faculty constituency behind the McElroy report, since McElroy had left the university soon after the report was issued. The skeptical questioning began slowly but quickly gathered momentum. What was the expected increase in university income per student if more undergraduates were admitted? President Gordon replied that as much as 75 percent of the gross tuition would accrue to income since few additional costs were anticipated. Coeducation might result in increased costs for dormitories down the line, however, because parents might want their daughters living on campus.

Professor Niehans turned the discussion in a more difficult direction by commenting that the administration's presentation was merely a defense of past expenditures and offered no solutions. He offered a motion with three parts: (1) The general assembly should endorse the formation of a committee on administrative costs. (2) The assembly should require that the committee be a faculty committee and not an administration committee. And (3) the assembly's steering committee should be empowered to advise the dean on whom to appoint to the committee. That the motion proposed the dean and not the president as the official to receive and act on the committee's advice was not accidental. Benton's hand was behind this recommendation. The proposal was clearly a faculty effort to wrest budgetary powers from central administration and place them in the more friendly hands of their own dean.

President Gordon opposed the motion, warning that such a committee would take up an enormous amount of faculty and administrative time and largely redo work that had already been done. Moreover, there was not enough time for the formation of such a committee because the budgetary review process was well under way. Dean Benton had remained aloof from the discussion so far. He had not participated in the administration's initial presentation, as if to signal that he was not a part of central administration. He now intervened on behalf of the motion and against the president. He declared that such a committee should be "encouraged."[78] In an effort to appear conciliatory, however, the dean recommended that departmental chairmen should be logical members of the committee since they already had a detailed knowledge of and had been part of the ongoing budget process. Their involvement in the preliminary budgetary planning made them the appropriate liaison between the faculty and central administration. Benton finessed the issue of whether he as dean or Gordon as president would act on the committee's recommendations. He portrayed the committee as an open-minded set of advisers who would be of great assistance to the budget professionals. But most of those who backed the committee did not have a high view of the administrative staffers who had prepared the budget. The faculty members believed that they understood the problem more clearly than did the central administration: the administration *was* the problem.

The administration had overspent, padded the rolls with unnecessary bureaucrats, and in particular enlarged the development office to a ridiculous extent and then failed to raise the funds it had promised. Worst of all—and what greater sin could there be?—the administration had had the temerity to propose faculty cuts to compensate for its own extravagance. By being unresponsive, dragging its feet, and offering excuses, the administration had demonstrated its incapacity to deal with the problem. But the proposed committee on administrative costs was less a research team convened to offer advice than a grand jury. George Benton was playing the role of district attorney, and the man in the dock was Lincoln Gordon.

17

What Now?

The battle itself would have injured the University and . . . from my own viewpoint the battleground was not worth winning.
—Lincoln Gordon, letter to D. Luke Hopkins, 1971

But as I realized that there was no one else that I knew who could do it, because it had to be done quickly and therefore you had to know the place intimately, both personnel and finance and organization, I said, "All right. The institution is more important than any individual, I'll go back." But I assure you I thought it was the end of Milton Eisenhower's reputation.
—Milton S. Eisenhower, 1980

Your career has epitomized the almost Jeffersonian ideal of the engaged intellect.
—Milton Russell, letter to Lincoln Gordon, 1980

There is the occasional glimmer of hope that one is contributing something to the education of our new political masters concerning the world's complexities in a time of great troubles. If that latter aspect can be contributed during my second year . . . I shall be more than content.
—Lincoln Gordon, letter to Don McGranahan, 1981

With the faculty committee investigating him, Gordon made a serious tactical mistake. He chose to be absent from Homewood for most of January 1971 instead of staying home and focusing on the immediate crisis. He departed after announcing the appointment of Dr. Muller of

Cornell as the university's next provost. The announcement, Gordon hoped, would give him some breathing room. The proposed trip for Gordon was an around-the-world journey with his health dean, John Hume. The itinerary was to travel from east to west rather the more usual west to east, based on the theory that the jet-lag problem was thus more manageable. Gordon and Hume would start with several days of intensive meetings in Japan and then travel to India for two weeks. They would spend the time at a clinic that was engaged in health services for the poor as part of a Hopkins research project. Finally, Gordon would go home on his own via Europe for a stopover at a Ditchley Park conference in England.

The trip hurt Gordon in several ways: he was not there during a critical period when he should have been trying to co-opt the faculty committee, and Dean Hume, one of Gordon's strongest allies, was not there to support him. Benton, in the president's absence, used the time well. He consolidated his grip on the committee and worked closely with the committee's chairman, Professor George E. Owen of the Physics Department, to build toward a bold objective. The actions of Benton and Owen were pivotal in Gordon's downfall. Benton and Owen formed a skillful Mr. Outside and Mr. Inside combination. Benton as dean had access to staff resources and could supply the committee with information. The work of persuading faculty colleagues to support his committee's recommendations fell to Owen. The physics chairman was one of the most respected and formidable figures on campus. The duo was an odd couple in many ways: Owen was a political liberal, Benton a political conservative; Owen was tall, handsome, and outgoing, Benton heavy featured and stolid in appearance and demeanor. An intellectual polymath, gifted musician, and talented artist and draftsman, Owen commanded the respect of humanists, social scientists, and hard scientists alike. He was a bold, forceful, inspired teacher and an ingratiating personality, whereas Benton was a bulldog-like individual with tenacity rather than charm. Benton remained in the background and let the committee do its work under Owen's leadership.

Owen made the rounds of his colleagues and kept them informed on the committee's work. The committee, as it looked into the costs of the library, development office, and provost's office, quickly concluded that at least $1.2 million of the arts and sciences deficit was attributable to administrative bloat and overstaffing. The registrar, the library staff, and in particular the development office were identified as the chief culprits. The remedy was obvious: cut administrative staff, and spare the faculty. Gordon had, the committee concluded, not focused enough on cuts in his own staff; it ignored the fact that Gordon had expanded the Homewood faculty by 70 percent, in line with the McElroy recommendations and other expressions of faculty intent up to 1969. One proposition the Owen committee could clearly agree on was the demand for an immediate 10 percent across-the-board cut in central administration, a figure that was considered moderate by many committee members, who wanted a 20 percent cut. Yet as they dug into the budgetary complexities, their original simplistic ideas did not always hold up. Nonetheless Owen, in an impressive display, managed to get 248 Hopkins colleagues to endorse the 10 percent cut and the report as a whole. The report was completed and presented to the Hopkins community on January 25, 1971, while Gordon was still away.

The assumption was that Gordon would accept the committee's recommendations and agree to "work with" the faculty. And if he did not follow the faculty's suggestions? Calling for the president's resignation was not yet the plan, though Owen, Benton, Philosophy Department chair Maurice Mandelbaum, and some other faculty leaders might have privately discussed this step. Stephen Ambrose and Richard Immerman suggest in their biography of Milton Eisenhower that "shortly after the beginning of the 1971 spring semester," board chairman Robert Harvey received a letter from a faculty committee demanding Gordon's resignation.[1] This account does not quite square with the timing of the critical faculty meetings of February 11 and February 19, and thus the call to Harvey was probably near the denouement of the succession drama. Ambrose and Immerman probably refer to the letter addressed to President Gordon requesting his resignation that was hand-delivered to Gordon in March. The tumultuous events of spring 1971 went through several overlapping and difficult-to-sort-out stages before culminating in their sudden and dramatic ending.

There were two broad categories of objections that Owen encountered when he was asking colleagues to sign on to his committee's recommendations (and laying the groundwork for wider steps if necessary). Some colleagues found the clandestine scheming unbecoming to the dignity of the university. The chairman of the History Department, Orest Ranum, a Minnesotan of Norwegian descent and a man of character, told Owen that he found his tactics repugnant. The campaign against Gordon reminded Ranum of the dishonorable conduct of many of his Columbia colleagues in undermining President Grayson Kirk in April 1968. Ranum had moved to Hopkins from Columbia for a fresh start after student radicals destroyed the only copy of a manuscript he had been working on for years when they occupied and trashed Hamilton Hall. Ranum lunched with Gordon frequently.

"He was the most cultivated man I knew," Ranum told me. "He talked and I listened. I was a good listener, maybe too good a listener. I should have warned him about the problems."

Ranum urged Owen to bring his grievances directly to Gordon and not connive behind the president's back. The conspirators took his warning to heart, but only partly. They did indeed confront the president directly in his office, but only after organizing a secret meeting of the academic council to take an informal vote on a motion of no confidence in Gordon. There may have been informal contact with one or more trustees before March. If there was an earlier faculty letter to Chairman Harvey before the letter was delivered directly to Gordon, Eisenhower may have suggested to Harvey that he reject any letter from the faculty and tell the disgruntled faculty members to go through the president.

The second objection that Owen encountered from colleagues was the caution against a hiatus in the university's leadership. Should the conspirators succeed in forcing Gordon out, they must reflect on the damage to the university that could result from a prolonged period of disarray. It would be irresponsible to destroy a president and leave a vacuum. This was a serious objection. Even Benton could see that while he might harbor the desire to be president, to thrust himself forward as Brutus over his fallen leader's body would not be tolerated by the trustees. Gordon had some opponents on the board, but he could probably still count on majority support, especially against any action that was the work of a small circle of conspirators. One of George Owen's selling points in winning support was the need for unanimity in the faculty, including the junior faculty, in opposition to the president. To achieve a high degree of unity, however, Owen recognized that he could not beat something with nothing. He would have to answer the question of what came next if Gordon was forced to resign. Fortunately he had the answer right at hand at 12 Bishops Road, just off the Homewood campus.

Milton Eisenhower and the Faculty Coup

Milton Eisenhower had continued to entertain students regularly at dinners prepared by his cook, Margy, since his retirement. He talked regularly with friends on the faculty. He was known to be in despair over recent developments and particularly over the budget deficits, which he loathed above almost anything. Milton had encountered deficits when he first arrived at Hopkins and considered the financial stability he left behind as his greatest legacy. But it would require the most delicate diplomacy to persuade Milton to come out of retirement. Milton was seventy-one, with an insurance age of seventy-two (his closest birthday). He had advised Ike in 1956 that a second term as president might bring crises that could tarnish his reputation and suggested that the safest course would be not to run again. But the Eisenhower brothers had a commitment to duty, and he knew that Ike would in the end follow the path of duty. Milton, as the youngest of the six Eisenhower brothers, had one of the largest egos in the family. His carefully cultivated and relaxed man-of-the-people manner masked a tremendous ego, an enormous capacity for hard work, and supreme self-confidence. There was also a bit of vanity. He was quietly proud of his designation as one of America's ten best-dressed men and never appeared in public without one of his elegant, conservative suits, which always looked like they had just been pressed. He loved his gray fedora hats, which he thought gave him a jaunty air. A group of Maryland Republicans once paid a call on Milton and asked him to run for the US Senate, pledging him solid financial support. Milton replied that he would be willing to run, but only if they could spare him from having to compete in a Republican primary. The anti-Gordon Hopkins conspirators knew they would have to make the most earnest entreaties to move Milton by a call to duty well beyond what they had any right to ask. They would have to rally the man out of retirement, and they would have to ask him to step into the middle of a crisis.

Milton told Neil Grauer, a recent Hopkins graduate who had become one of his many friends, "Godammit, if I had moved to Palm Springs, this wouldn't be happening!"[2]

When asked in 1980 whether he felt frustration that Hopkins could not get along without him or pride at being considered the indispensable man, he replied:

> Neither one. I was selfish. I was almost 72 years old. I wasn't as agile as I once was, didn't have the stamina and energy. I knew that I had left one of the best records that Hopkins had ever had. Many mean things had to be done, fine people let go, drastic cuts made. My overpowering feeling was, if I go back I'll ruin everything I've ever done as far as my own personal standing at the institution is concerned. It never occurred to me otherwise.
>
> And I thought that was asking a good deal. But as I realized that there was no one else that I knew of who could do it, because it had to be done quickly and therefore you had to know the place intimately, both personnel and finance and organization, I said "All right. The institution is more important than any one individual, I'll go back." But I assure you that when I went back I thought that was going to be the end of Milton Eisenhower's reputation.[3]

Milton had the time to determine how he would react if was asked to return. He appeared angry, but his anger was feigned, carefully calculated to protect his reputation and give him some protective cover if things turned out badly. Why did Lincoln Gordon and Milton Eisenhower not enjoy more cordial relations? Except for the holdover of Garland as board chairman the first year, and Turner as medical school dean for one year, Gordon had an entirely new slate of deans and other officers around him, most of whom had to learn their jobs just as Gordon had to learn his. Gordon had inherited from Eisenhower an able young man, Wayne Anderson, who became his personal assistant and with whom Gordon formed a close personal bond. Since Anderson was close to both men, he might have played a role as a middleman between them, but Anderson was a promising administrator and soon received an attractive offer of advancement elsewhere. Anderson's departure meant that Gordon lost the young man's knowledge of Hopkins, as well his contacts with Eisenhower. Gordon recognized that Milton could be a valuable resource and approached him for advice not long after assuming office. Lincoln was impressed with

Milton's deep knowledge of the personalities and of any Hopkins situation they discussed, but there was no rapport between them. Milton, despite his self-confidence, had always felt some unease in the presence of many of his prestigious Homewood faculty members. Milton did not have a PhD and did not consider himself a scholar. This feeling could be overcome, but it took time with the faculty members who became his friends, and he evidently felt some diffidence in his initial meetings with Gordon. Gordon was a modest man despite his assertive intellectual style and for his part felt some awe in the presence of this president's brother, a man world famous in his own right. Lincoln was at ease with many different people, but he wished he had a little more of his mother's natural social grace. He knew that he had a tendency to ramble, but this was sometimes nervous talk while he was trying to circle around to the point. He felt that it might seem artificial if his questions to Milton lacked focus or were not of sufficient gravity to be put to his distinguished predecessor.

Gordon tried to break the ice by arranging an informal dinner at Nichols House, where he and Milton, dining alone, discussed "three or four topics of university business." The discussion was rather strained. Gordon worried that he might be embarrassing himself or his guest by trying too hard. Neither man had a taste for small talk. There was the awkwardness, too, of Gordon making changes in the Hopkins administration, as recommended by the McElroy report. Gordon had only belatedly come to understand that Milton was skeptical of the McElroy concepts and deeply resented the inference that his administration was an amateur operation. The experiment of an intimate dinner with Milton Eisenhower was not repeated, and Eisenhower was never invited back to Nichols House as a guest or even to ceremonial events. The contact between the two men dwindled and then ceased altogether. As Gordon's own situation grew more serious in 1970, he did not seek and Eisenhower did not volunteer any advice.

There is no question that others did seek out Milton's counsel in the course of the crisis and did pass on to him bulletins on campus developments. A turning point apparently came when Eisenhower told close associates on the faculty in the early spring of 1971 that he was uncomfortable discussing his successor's handling of the situation. He told friends that he wanted no record and no trace of his having participated in any discussions of his successor's fate. Of course it was understood that he would never make any public criticism of Gordon. He wanted no comment of his on the topic to appear in any document or written record of any kind. It would be unprofessional for him to be involved in any way with any plan, or even to have knowledge of any plan, to diminish the authority or the reputation, let alone the job tenure, of the president of Johns Hopkins University. Yet a Rubicon of some kind had been crossed. The situation at his beloved university had deteriorated to the point that serious persons were considering asking for the president's resignation. As difficult and distasteful as it was for him, Milton Eisenhower was drawn into the discussion.

Milton Eisenhower was not immune from grievances against this man, who should not have gotten into such trouble and plunged the university into such turmoil. Gordon evidently did not have the right instincts for navigating the crisis. Milton had harbored suspicions of the Kennedy team that invented the glitzy term "Alliance for Progress" and arrogantly implied that this idea signaled a new and bold concept in American foreign policy. He considered that they had slighted his brother's role and his own by implying that this grandiose-sounding approach was different from Ike's policy, when in fact it *was* the Eisenhower policy, slightly dressed up. The Alliance for Progress was a public relations term for what in fact was continuity with President Eisenhower's policy.[4] There was arrogance about Kennedy and his team; the whole campaign to "get the country moving again" was nothing but political rhetoric, as if the country had done nothing under Dwight Eisenhower. Moreover Kennedy had authorized and then mishandled the Bay of Pigs and had had the gall to hint that the whole thing was Ike's and the generals' fault rather than the result of his own loss of nerve and failure to authorize the second air strike that would have destroyed Castro's remaining two planes. If Ike had gone ahead with this scheme, he certainly would not have botched it as Kennedy did. And then that cockamamie Tractors for Freedom scheme to pay a ransom of five hundred bulldozers to Castro get the Bay of Pigs prisoners back! Milton had agreed to serve as cochairman of that damned scheme, along with Eleanor Roosevelt and Walter Reuther, to raise $28 million for the ransom. He then was the first one of the three cochairmen to resign when Kennedy bungled the negotiations and allowed Castro to make a fool of him.

Gordon certainly shared the naïve assumptions of the Kennedy people then, and Gordon's approach to the Hopkins presidency smacked of the same arrogance. How could he buy into the Bill McElroy tomfoolery when Milton had tried to warn him off? Was the man tone deaf? Gordon had said he wanted to keep the university out of politics—he was certainly right there, but he seemed to have a bee in his bonnet about Latin American radical students. He had started out picking fights with the students. Gordon looked great on paper but lacked political sense and pretended to be above politics. He kept pretty quiet about Vietnam when Johnson was president and then let loose with a barrage of criticism when Nixon and the Republicans came back in. The personal snub had hurt—and down deep for Milton it was an intolerable snub when Gordon never even invited him to ceremonial functions or called on him for advice. When Milton had said he that did not want to interfere but wanted to be helpful, Gordon never followed up with so much as a phone call. The plain meaning was that Milton's advice was not wanted or valued.

What the conspirators got from Milton Eisenhower cannot be known—was it merely a general sense that he took in the gravity of the situation? No one can say for sure. The recollections of those with any direct knowledge of events vary widely. Dr. Déjà Owen, the widow of George Owen and an active octogenarian psychiatrist still seeing patients, thought the whole thing "was Milton's idea." Ross Jones, who worked closely with Milton for most of his first Hopkins presidency and his return, and remained in close touch with him until Milton's death in 1985, denies that Milton had any direct knowledge of the conspirators' plans. Mrs. Charlotte Benton, the widow of George Benton, refused to be interviewed. She did not want "to put words into my husband's mouth" but said enough over the phone to indicate that in her view "Lincoln did himself in."

What seems likely is that Milton knew enough about the situation to surmise that the trustees would be turning to him—and that he, with the greatest reluctance and kicking and screaming, would in the end return for a temporary period. When the delegation from the trustees did finally arrive at his home, Milton had a ready quip for them: "Do you want me to return in a wheelchair?"[5]

Lincoln Gordon Resigns: March 1971

When the Owen committee report was published in January, calling for an immediate 10 percent cut in administrative costs, it was accompanied by a petition signed by 248 Homewood campus faculty members.[6]

This was an impressive display of unified faculty opinion, since at the time the total Homewood faculty numbered only 292.[7] Gordon knew that he would have to respond much more forcefully than he had in his December 11 presentation to the assembly. If he incorporated many of the report's suggestions into his revised budget, he hoped, the faculty would be reassured. The showdown would come at the next meeting of the general assembly, now rescheduled for February 12 after a week's initial delay.

This time Lincoln Gordon was not flanked by aides but instead sat alone on the dais in Shriver Hall, facing the faculty. This was a fitting symbol of Gordon's isolated position. Gordon was the only administrator to speak at the meeting, other than a brief report by Dean Benton on the academic council's recent personnel actions. President Gordon called on Professor Owen to report on the work of the Owen committee, and Owen summarized the highlights, noting in particular that personnel in central administration had increased from 30 in 1966 to 81 in 1970—a two-and-half-fold increase—while faculty positions had grown much more modestly—from 246 to 292. He concluded his report by stating that 248 members of the faculty had signed the petition supporting the recommended cuts in administrative expenses.[8] President Gordon praised the committee for "its diligence in handling the complex material with which it dealt." He noted the close cooperation between the committee and his own staff and acknowledged that the committee had identified areas where potential savings could be achieved. He expressed his hopes for further close collaboration and then outlined his own plans to reduce the deficit for the next fiscal year by 43 percent. He announced that he had already made cuts in central administration by the 10 percent requested by the committee. The president pointed out that accurate figures on many of the questions were difficult to achieve, and he called attention to the continuing efforts by the comptroller to improve the data on expenditures. Gordon struggled to explain the formulas for imputing a "tax" on the various university divisions to support central administration, and his explanations seemed to raise suspicions from the faculty. A chorus of faculty voices demanded clarification from the president as soon as he finished speaking.

A high—or low—point came in the discussion of the complex accounting issues when a professor questioned whether Gordon had made the 10 percent cut requested by the committee by not counting certain library costs that were simply shifted to another budget. The professor contended on the basis of a quick calculation that Gordon had only cut his own costs by 6 percent. The student newspaper quoted the professor as saying, "I cannot regard these reductions as fair dealing."[9] So to the president's problems was now added the charge that he was being evasive. Benton and Owen made no effort to rebut the charge. For the next two hours the president was battered by hostile questions. The central issue, as Professor Bela Belassi of the Economics Department summed it up, "was one of expanding administration versus expanding instruction."[10]

Gordon emerged from the February 12 meeting considerably weakened. The narrative of an out-of-control central administration was more firmly entrenched than ever. There were rumors that the president was planning to present more fudged figures. Benton never defended the president and by his silence appeared to confirm the worst suspicions. Indeed, he fanned the flames by suggesting that the president had exaggerated the need for faculty cuts. The cuts could be more gradual and stretched out over a period of years through attrition. Benton hinted that he had opposed the unpopular faculty cuts and the pay freeze that Gordon had unilaterally imposed and suggested, "We do not necessarily have to adopt the 10-percent figure that rapidly."[11]

Since the February 12 assembly meeting had come to no clear resolution, another meeting was called for February 19. Gordon had to be out of town that day and delegated his duties to the acting provost John Young and the vice president for administration Benjamin Willis. Attendance was down to 110 faculty members, but the atmosphere was tense and expectant. Several routine matters were to be discussed first, and Young asked Dean Benton to handle this discussion. Benton took the opportunity to take charge of the entire meeting. He had by the time of the second assembly meeting emerged as the champion of traditional faculty rights and the core Hopkins belief that the senior faculty ran the university. Dean Benton expounded on the arts and sciences budget, seeking to draw a contrast between central administration's bloat and dissembling and his own frugality. In a display of chutzpah that comes through even in the dry prose of the minutes, Benton declared that he "did not think that illusory figures which made non-existent reductions seem real were truly responsive to the situation in which the university found itself."[12] This act of insubordination, in challenging the "illusory figures" of the Gordon administration, suggests that the conspirators by now were convinced that they could force Gordon from office. Dean Benton wound up his statement with an emotional appeal for the faculty to affirm his view of the university's academic traditions and the integrity of his approach and priorities, rather than "illusory figures which made non-existent reductions seem real" and "were not responsive to the situation in which the university found itself," so that the minutes of the February 19 assembly meeting conclude: "Confidence in Dean Benton and in the work of the Faculty Committee on Administrative Finance was expressed."[13]

Benton had in effect declared himself in charge of the Homewood campus and received the blessing of an official faculty body. With this power grab, Benton apparently believed that Gordon would see the handwriting on the wall and resign, paving the way for Benton himself to be named the interim president. He was surprised when the president did not in fact resign. When briefed by aides about the February 19 meeting, Gordon believed that several courses of action lay open to him. First, he could acquiesce to an enlarged conception of the dean's powers. Second, he could reassert his own authority and make it clear that the dean of arts and sciences was his subordinate and ask for Benton's resignation. Third, he could ignore Benton and the faculty and appeal to the trustees for support. If it occurred to Gordon that he was ironically weighing his options somewhat in the fashion that Goulart had weighed his in the face of overthrow, he did not mention this to anyone or record it in his notes. Unfortunately for his chances of survival, Gordon equivocated and embraced a contradictory approach that neither placated the faculty nor clearly asserted his own powers.

In the week following the second general assembly meeting, President Gordon announced that he had found an additional $162,000 in savings in the central administration budget.[14] This did nothing to assuage faculty critics, who saw the action as another instance of the president being dragged into confessing that his figures were wrong. In the first week of March Gordon shifted to a hard line and reaffirmed his decision to create fifteen new full-time teaching positions and a new satellite campus in Columbia, Maryland, for the Evening College. His decision was taken without consulting the academic council because the Evening College was under the jurisdiction of a separate dean, not under Dean Benton and the academic council. The decision enraged Gordon's enemies in the arts and sciences faculty, who considered the step an act of arrogance. His critics conceded that he had courage but deplored the inept timing of the decision. To the worldlier faculty critics nothing could have been worse in a university president than Gordon's combination of high integrity and political insensitivity.

Gordon also attempted to assert himself by taking an action that amounted to spitting in the faculty's eye: he approved a student council proposal for heavier faculty teaching loads, the creation of a new social relations major, and more undergraduate seminars instead of lecture courses. Again he acted without consultation with the academic council, this time on the rationale that the council would block anything he proposed. But this move left him vulnerable on procedural grounds because teaching loads and the curriculum were clearly academic matters within the faculty's purview.

The conspirators decided that if Lincoln Gordon would not resign on his own, he would have to be forced to resign. It was widely suspected that Allison Gordon was not happy, and it could not escape notice that Lincoln himself was not enjoying life in the hot seat. On the morning of Wednesday, March 10, a letter asking for President Gordon's resignation was ready to be delivered to his office by three of the faculty conspirators. The letter asking for the president's resignation, by careful design, gave no reasons or specific grievances. The conspirators reasoned that spelling out the grievances would be painful to Gordon, and they may have also feared that he might challenge or outargue them over any stated grievance. Listing no specific cause would be preferable to enumerating his faults. The coup was a calculated risk since technically, under the university's statutes, the president was supposed to convene all council meetings. If the conspirators, who included George Benton, George Owen, and Maurice Mandelbaum, had gained any kind of council endorsement, this could only have been deemed unconstitutional under university rules. Similarly, under informal practice, no faculty proposal could be officially acted upon by trustees unless it came through the university president.

The three-man delegation must have had some trepidation as they approached the president's office. Other accounts have referred to a "committee of five" (Ambrose and Immerman) or to a "gang of six" (the *News-Letter*) as the leaders of the faculty revolt. But it was a three-man delegation—probably including Owen and Mandelbaum, but not Benton—

that marched to Homewood House to present the letter and ask President Gordon to resign. Dean Benton was not included out of obvious concern that Gordon would resist any proposal coming from Benton. The group evidently had decided to take a more-in-sorrow-than-in-anger approach, according to Ross Jones, who witnessed their arrival and noticed their countenances. One of the participants was a man Gordon regarded as a close friend, probably Mandelbaum, because there was a letter of apology from Mandelbaum in Gordon's papers.[15] The three arrived at Homewood House at midmorning and brushed past Ross Jones, who sat at his desk in the outer office. Although the president's door was open, Jones cautioned the men that the president was busy.

"He'll see us," one said, grim faced.

Jones remembers all three as having somber demeanors. The three entered Gordon's office and closed the door. They delivered the letter and asked him to read it. Gordon asked for an explanation of why they or the academic council had taken the action. By prior agreement the men gave no reasons, saying the letter requesting the president's resignation did not intend to specify any cause, and they were simply messengers and had no authority to discuss grievances. The president pointed out that if they were acting on behalf of the academic council, such action did not technically conform to university statutes, which authorized him to convene council meetings. A recent meeting of the council had taken place with Gordon in the chair, but there had been no talk of his resignation. To what council action were they referring? What was the time and date of the meeting? Were the men simply bluffing, or had they informally consulted with several fellow council members, or were they intuiting the "general will" of the faculty? Official records show that the council had met on November 25, 1970, and January 26, February 9 and 24, and March 10, 1971, and that at none of these meetings was there any discussion of the president's performance or his potential resignation. Gordon said in 2006 that one of the men later told him, "We didn't handle the situation well," to which Gordon readily assented.[16] Nothing more is known of what transpired that morning in the president's office. After approximately twenty minutes the three men emerged from the office looking grim. One said to Jones softly, "Leave him alone for a while. Don't bother him with anything. He has things to think about."

The president did not linger long. He took the short walk back to his

Nichols House residence, where he found Allison sipping coffee and reading the newspaper. He told her that "the academic committee has voted to request my resignation, reasons unstated."

"Thank God," said Allison. "I have not had a happy life in this Baltimore community. They've never really accepted us as part of their preferred way of life and I don't know that I want to continue sharing that preferred way of life. My advice is to accept it."

So far as Lincoln was concerned, "this [Allison's reaction] was the end of the decision. I wasn't going to fight it." His wife cast the deciding vote. This had been an unpleasant experience for him, but he had fared better than some of his friends. Courtney Smith had died of a heart attack in his Swarthmore office in the middle of a student occupation of the building. Merle Fainsod had died of a heart attack after struggling to establish peace among warring factions at Harvard. Charlie Hitch was taking a pounding but hanging on as president of the University of California system. A feeling of relief but also failure came over Gordon. The state of mind of both Lincoln and Allison is suggested in a letter Allison drafted but never sent to her friend Ruth Kriebel:

Dear Ruth,

L. has resigned from Johns Hopkins. It was the result of a faculty-administrative conflict—and of all things L. lost this round. We were quite relieved—at least I am. . . . He will take a long rest this summer, I hope. The rascals want him out tomorrow—which the trustees I suspect will not permit.

There has been a most disloyal Dean—and showing up to be utterly dishonest. The affair has been so nasty—that it will be nice to be in clear air. What happened was unbelievable.

The faculty have not taken the student troubles to heart—the students who wish to be taught—and they have been talking of the good old days—with larger research grants—lots of graduate students—plenty of assistants—and are miffed that those days are gone because they will have to teach. No one has had an increase in salary these days—for the 1st time in 10 years—and they think without L. they can pluck the money out better.

We are without an Administrative Dean . . .—a V.P. for finance threw up his contract ten days before coming—so L.

has [*sic*] without the help who were supposed to do the job he has had to do for a year. And those leftovers from the old regime were terrible—and those brought in to help the first year were awful. There is no style—or was none. Actually—it will be easier for us to move now than it would be six years hence. Where to we do not know—nor care much at this point.

But I really wonder what will happen to this poor place—especially if the Dean who commandeered this [illegible] takes over as he wishes. . . .

We have sold our Washington house praise be—so that headache is over—and we have not lost money on it. Squatters turned it into a commune and a [illegible] for a week—and the police [illegible—finally?] turned them out. I think Washington might be a place to live. . . . New York is so dirty—crowded and expensive and I will *not* live in a suburb.

How I hate to sort out things—and get everything hanged up again. 16th house—48th move—better while I can still crawl around—than a few years hence. . . . How are you?
Love,
A–[17]

A striking aspect was Gordon's stoicism and total lack of self-pity despite the deep resentment he felt. He kept his dignity and aplomb in the face of bitter disappointment. Ross Jones saw him at noon that same day in the faculty club, having lunch with an editor from the *Johns Hopkins Magazine.* He was chatting animatedly and looking unfazed. Later in the afternoon Lincoln made a trip downtown to see board chairman Robert Harvey. He received assurances of Harvey's backing if he chose to fight it out with his faculty critics. In Harvey's estimate there would be enough support from the board for Gordon to prevail. Gordon also sought out his friend Judge Winter, one of his strongest defenders, and received similar assurances of support. Whether the assurances were quite as firm as Gordon believed cannot be known. Gordon's assessment of his position, as he told his friend D. Luke Hopkins of the board in a letter later in the summer, was this: "I never doubted that a successful battle could have been fought at Hopkins, not only with trustee backing but with the ultimate support of the faculty as well. Nevertheless, it seemed clear to me in

March (and I have not revised that opinion) that the battle itself would have injured the University and that from my own viewpoint the battleground was not worth winning."[18]

A press conference was arranged for the morning of Friday, March 12. Through his long life Gordon never revised the opinion expressed in the letter to his friend Hopkins. He never reflected otherwise in writing on his presidential experience, and he rarely mentioned it in conversations with friends or family. After he resigned he received a letter from Brad Jacobs of the *Sun* suggesting that "what occurred at the Hopkins is inevitably of national significance." In light of potential lessons for the whole of higher education, the Hopkins case "seems too important to be left to speculation by outsiders, especially to outsiders only partially informed and not altogether objective."[19] He offered Gordon two thousand words to present his side of the story and "keep the record straight."[20] Gordon chose not to take advantage of Jacob's offer. He might at some future time offer his own reflections, but "this . . . is not the best time for that purpose."[21] He did not see any point in prolonging the controversies or attempting to justify himself. There never was a best time for him to tell his side of the Hopkins story. He remained on friendly terms with Steven Muller, the man whom he had chosen as provost and who succeeded Milton Eisenhower less than a year later as Hopkins president.[22] Gordon was not invited to the Hopkins centennial celebration in 1976, but he was invited back in 1998, as one of four living ex-presidents to appear at an inaugural ceremony, and gave a gracious two-minute speech to the assembled guests. He wrote of this appearance to his children and included a copy of his remarks.

Gordon's 1971 letter to D. Luke Hopkins contains his only explicit analysis of the causes of his Hopkins undoing. Unsurprisingly he identified Benton as the villain. "The bitter aspect of it," he wrote Hopkins, "is that the faculty group concerned would not have been misguided on its own, but was systematically misguided by a Dean of my own unwise choosing and more unwise retaining."[23] In his letter of resignation and at the press conference on March 12, Gordon stated, "I have concluded that the best interests of the University will be served by younger and more vigorous leadership in the difficult years which lie ahead." This was the quote carried by newspapers across the country on Saturday, March 13, 1971.

Aftermath at Hopkins

The story of Gordon's time at Hopkins was not quite finished. The March 12 resignation that the trustees accepted raised a problem. The resignation was to take effect upon the trustees' selection of a successor, a process that was to be concluded "not later than June 1972." The "1972" was a typo; the date was meant to be June 1971. The mistake created momentary confusion, since June 1972 was more than a year in the future. Further, the negotiations with Milton Eisenhower had informally begun but encountered several unforeseen bumps. Milton was willing to return for a temporary period but had made up his mind to use his leverage and impose conditions beforehand. It was obvious that the board was in no position to reject any reasonable conditions that Milton might ask. Milton at seventy-two would be the oldest president of any major US university and very likely the oldest college president in US history. But he understood that the leverage he enjoyed was now greater than it had been when he came to Hopkins in 1956. At that time he had lost his wife to cancer and had already decided to leave Penn State. Ike was having health problems and needed him more than ever. Milton knew that he could now get concessions from the trustees that he could not get once he was back in office. So Milton pressed his advantage by first insisting that the board immediately elect a woman trustee. The trustees accommodated him by naming the gifted Marjorie G. Levinson, who was to serve from 1971 to 1989. Milton then asked for and received a commitment that the trustees would name four younger trustees, including at least one Hopkins faculty member and one recent graduate. He also wanted a current student as a trustee. The distinguished scholar Alfred D. Chandler was named to one of the positions, and he served from 1971 to 1981. Recent Hopkins graduates Russell S. Passarella, who had been a student body president, and Stephan P. Mahinka joined the board, the former serving from 1971 to 1974 and the latter from 1971 to 1976. Milton further wanted a pledge of $1.5 million from the trustees to use at his discretion—and this was the initial funding for the new undergraduate student union that bears his name.

The final condition was more difficult because it did not lie within the trustees' power to grant. Milton wanted the new provost in place before he took up his responsibilities. The ideal solution was to have Steven Muller come early to take up the provost duties at the same time that Milton resumed the presidency, but Muller was not scheduled to arrive until July 1, and Gordon's sudden departure changed the picture. An early meeting was in both men's interests, and by good fortune Muller was in Baltimore house-hunting when he learned of Gordon's resignation. Muller knew enough about the Hopkins situation to know that he should seek out Milton, and Milton knew enough of Steven's compelling story to seek him out. Muller was forty-three, athletic, and extremely good-looking, with large expressive eyes. He was noted for his sense of humor. One Hopkins colleague who worked closely with Muller described him as a "combination of stand-up comedian, master politician, and competent political scientist all rolled up into one."[24] Muller and Eisenhower met for three hours. Milton opened the discussion by saying that he would like Steve to report for duty immediately.[25] Could he come earlier than July 1? Muller said he was not sure; he was committed to Jim Perkins, Cornell's president, until July 1.

"I'll take care of that," said Milton. Milton called Perkins—he knew every major university president—and explained the situation.

There was no problem. Perkins was quite willing to release Muller early if this would be helpful. Did Muller have any other problems?

Well, there was the awkward fact that he would be taking a chance. Suppose he moved his family to Baltimore and bought a house, and then Hopkins a year from now named a new president. Where would that leave Muller?[26] A new president might well want his own provost.

"If you are as good as you think you are, I'll see to it that you become president," said Milton Eisenhower. "If you are not, it's better to find it out sooner than later."

Milton was as good as his word. After the March 25 Board of Trustees meeting, where Milton and Lincoln exchanged respectful letters and Milton was officially named the interim president, Milton announced that the transition would take place on April 5 and that Dr. Steven Muller would be available to take up his duties as provost at the same time. The board established a search committee for a permanent president, but it quickly became apparent that this was merely a pro forma gesture. It was understood from the start that Muller was serving in a kind of probationary status. Eisenhower was quickly convinced that Muller was as good as he thought he was, and Milton proceeded to make him the tenth president of Hopkins.

Steven Muller was installed as Johns Hopkins president in February 1972 with less fanfare than was the case with the gala celebration at Lincoln Gordon's inauguration. The pomp of the Gordon inauguration belonged to a different age. Muller became the longest-serving president in the history of Johns Hopkins, with the exception of the university's founder, Daniel Coit Gilman. Muller's impact on the university was second only to that of Gilman. He served for eighteen years, until 1990, when his term abruptly ended under circumstances strangely reminiscent of what had happened to Lincoln Gordon. Muller was accused of overspending, administrative laxity, and creating a large deficit. He was abruptly removed by the trustees, but without the turmoil that marked Gordon's exit.

Milton Eisenhower moved swiftly after taking over as interim president. His first decision was to cancel the new furniture order for Garner Hall, the new administrative building nearing completion. He directed those moving into the building simply to move in their old furniture. This action saved as much as $500,000, according to an estimate by Robert C. Bowie, and was highly popular with the faculty.[27] Milton cut his own salary drastically, down to one-third of Gordon's last salary. Milton's stated goals were simple: cut costs, increase giving, improve the quality of undergraduate life, and increase the number of undergraduates to raise more tuition income. Institutional lore has it that Milton, in inspecting the administrative offices upon his return as president, commented to an aide, "Who are all these people—where did they come from?" Milton understood that symbolic gestures were needed to restore confidence.

He decided that he would speak to the entire Hopkins community on April 15. Milton was an unusually gifted public speaker, having a great voice, a commanding air, and an ease at marshaling facts persuasively without notes. Dwight Eisenhower's aides in the 1952 campaign wanted Milton to go on the stump and speak for his brother all over the country, but Milton refused. He believed it was his role to give private advice to his brother and to stay in the background. Milton gave the best speech at the 1964 Republican convention in San Francisco, when he placed Governor William Scranton's name in nomination for president and gave a rousing defense of Eisenhower Republicanism. Milton had been given a plastic replica of a wheelchair with the inscription "We'll all help push!" when he returned to the presidency. As he strode onto the stage at Shriver Hall precisely at 4:00 p.m. on April 15 to speak to a jam-packed and expectant crowd, impeccably dressed as usual and having committed most of what he wanted to say to memory, Milton carried the wheelchair replica to use as a prop. Smiling broadly with the famous Eisenhower grin, he raised the wheelchair replica and read the inscription. Milton proceeded to use this as the theme of his speech, calling for sacrifice and assistance from all members of the Hopkins community but radiating confidence as he meticulously described the problems facing the university and the steps he would take to deal with them. In substance his solutions to the university's problems amounted to what Gordon had tried to do, but the Hopkins community was now ready for the message. When he finished, there was total silence in the auditorium, and Milton was afraid for a moment that the speech had fallen flat. For fifteen seconds the audience sat silently. Milton began to walk slowly off the stage. Then the audience rose as one in a burst of thunderous applause, and Milton gave another broad grin and waved the wheelchair replica.

Eisenhower was able to restore confidence almost overnight. Students who had never known him observed that Dr. Milton was back. Milton maintained his open-door policy as before; anyone in the Hopkins family could make an appointment to see him on any matter. It was a remarkable display of leadership. The plan, so similar to what Gordon had proposed at the February 12 general assembly meeting, which Benton had denounced, was quickly approved and put into effect. Working with Robert Bowie to understand the university's finances, Milton now concluded they were worse in some ways but better in others. He added $800,000 to the current deficit but noted the gains already made by Gordon's cost-cutting steps. The endowment had not been touched. Milton called for an increase of six hundred in the undergraduate student body, a step Gordon had urged. He continued to make cuts in the development office and shelved plans for the $100 million campaign, postponed the additional faculty Gordon proposed for the Evening College, and cut the faculty ranks by attrition. As was his practice, Milton picked from the ranks an individual whose judgment he trusted to manage the university's finances, choosing Robert C. Bowie, the thirty-three-year-old comptroller. Eisenhower's reliance on Bowie did not escape the notice of Provost Muller, who, after he became president, elevated Bowie to the position of vice president for administration in 1973 and in 1980 promoted him to a senior vice president post. Among his contributions, Bowie developed a new system for indirect cost recovery on federal research grants that he had begun at President Gordon's direction. Bowie's system resulted in the recovery of an additional $2 million in indirect costs from the federal government. Bowie remained at Hopkins for another decade and a half, until he departed in 1987 over what he regarded as unwise practices resulting in unfavorable trends in the university's finances.[28]

Meanwhile the student protests disappeared as rapidly as they had arrived at Homewood. The student protests at Hopkins had never quite reached the intensity they had at some other campuses, but they were nonetheless surprising because of the Hopkins tradition as a preprofessional, career-minded, and politically apathetic campus. The rapid end to the campus disturbances was due in large part to the winding down of the Vietnam War and President Nixon's decision to end the draft. The end to the draft was a cause that Gordon had championed along with other AAU university presidents. The altered mood on campus was underscored when Hopkins undergraduates, who may have lagged behind in antiwar demonstrations, took a national lead in launching the "streaking" movement in 1974, originally intended as an attention-grabbing activity to assist in charitable fundraising. Hopkins students first "streaked" across the campus clad only in sneakers to raise funds for the hospital. The hospital rather stuffily refused the money as tainted because it had been raised via a breach of the peace, but the medical school cheerfully took the donation. Streakers appeared all around the country in short order. The streak across the football field at halftime became the favorite venue. A faculty group at Hopkins joined in the fun by declaring that it would have no objections if a group of coeds should care to streak through the faculty club.

A New Start in Life

President Gordon said in "A Statement to the Johns Hopkins Community," issued March 17, that "the opportunity to begin another new chapter in life in late middle age has strong personal attractions for me." But this was mostly whistling in the dark. Despite the tensions on the job, the sudden end to his presidency left him in a state of shock. His resiliency returned slowly, and his strong disinclination to replay the past helped to restore his equilibrium, but the initial notes he made in the wake of the resignation show the uncertainty that he faced and his painful groping for a new foothold. In handwritten notes penned in New York City and dated March 17, 1971, he lists the following under the heading "Fields of Interest Internationally": "Ec. [economic] system, Pol/mil. [political/military], L.A. [Latin America] Area, Eur. Area." He also lists domestic interests: "Health Care Delivery, Technology Assessment, and Education [broken down into subcategories]," analyzing each area and supplying question marks where he thinks that he has no chance for a new position. He ruminates on places to live. Here he is clearer; he limits himself to *"East Only."* The choices are: "1.) Wash. (very strongly preferred), 2.) ?Boston?, and 3.) NYC—(considerable antipathy—Allison)."[29] He has a section on "Finances" where he lists sources of income. His marginalia indicate that he is worried. His arrangement with Equitable Life Assurance Society is "not likely" to continue. SAIS is termed "a good base," but doubts are expressed on how long he could use SAIS as a base or what a teaching salary would be. The Council on Foreign Relations is mentioned as a possible fellowship source, but with a question mark. The Center for International Affairs at Harvard is listed with this notation—"deputy?"

In notes dated Sunday, March 21, 1971, Lincoln cites the United Nations Development Program as a possibility; the United Nations Association (UNA) is also mentioned, but with doubts about how much leeway the board might give UNA executives. He lists the names of people he should consult in New York and Washington. Matters have taken a clearer shape for him by March 31, when a memorandum labeled *"PRIVATE & CONFIDENTIAL,"* sent by Benjamin G. Willis, outlines for Dr. Gordon and Dr. Eisenhower the terms agreed upon as "terminal financial arrangements with Dr. Lincoln Gordon."[30] These terms were neither generous nor grudging; they were approximately the norm for the era before chief executives and university presidents began to receive excessive salaries and golden parachute severance packages. Gordon was to receive his presidential salary through June 30; an additional four months of salary, from July 1 to October 30, based on the annual salary equivalent of a full professor at SAIS of $27,000; temporary office space at SAIS in Washington for that period (with no teaching or other duties); moving expenses for the shipment of furniture and personal items from the presidential residence; and a one-time payment of $5,000 to cover rental and relocation costs. Unfortunately, Willis did not have the letter hand-delivered to Gordon and Eisenhower, and when he placed it in the regular campus mail, he neglected to mark the envelope "private." The result, in what must have seemed a final indignity to Gordon, was that the letter was opened by secretaries, stamped as received on April 2, and treated as routine mail, with the result that the severance terms were viewed by many eyes and became common knowledge.

But the nightmare was over at last, and Gordon was free to search for his new start. The severance package relieved his immediate financial worries and helped steer him toward Washington as his permanent location. Allison liked Washington, strongly disliked the prospect of New York City, and was adamantly against living in the suburbs anywhere. Employment opportunities for Lincoln seemed more promising in Washington than in Boston, and it had been a decade since they had lived in Boston. So for their seventeenth house—the forty-ninth move in their marriage—the Gordons purchased a house on a pleasant, tree-lined street in the section of Washington they wanted at 3069 University Terrace, NW.

In settling into his new home, Lincoln undertook an elaborate woodworking project to build bookshelves for his substantial personal library. His private papers include elaborate architectural drawings and three pages of detailed requirements for lumber, fasteners, fixtures, and the like. In July he had an offer of a visiting professorship that amused his wife and children. They tried to picture their New Deal husband and father in the role of Richard Nixon Professor at Whittier College. The president and the dean of Whittier College, President Nixon's alma mater, had invited Gordon to come to California for the spring term 1972 as Visiting Richard Nixon Professor. He had ruled out any location other than the East and had a ready excuse for declining the offer.

Gordon zeroed in on a role at the World Bank as his best opportunity. He had had a preliminary meeting with Robert McNamara, president of the World Bank, shortly after leaving Hopkins and apparently had received some encouragement. During the summer and fall Gordon talked informally with eleven World Bank officials, some of whom he knew well. In October he wrote a memorandum to McNamara on "Proposed Assignment as Consultant to the World Bank Group," identifying the following as major areas of concern: (1) problems of private investment in relation to development and bank policy; (2) population-control strategy in relation to work in nutrition and health; (3) enlarged employment opportunities and improved income distribution for project formulation; and (4) evaluation studies of various organizational relationships with the UN, regional banks, and bilateral aid agencies.[31] He had evidently misjudged his prospects, for nothing materialized with the bank.

After this misfire there was no more laying out of his options or meditations for the future. He simply began doing what he would do with the rest of his life. He fell into the activity that was second nature—and was both vocation and avocation. He wrote. Fish swim, birds fly, and writers write. Lincoln resumed writing about issues that interested him. Fortunately his children were adults now, and the pressures of raising a family were somewhat diminished, but he owed them and Allison more of his time and attention. Yet he had to do something professional and did not have enough money to retire. He clearly understood that it was not going to be easy at his age to find a desirable job. Failure breeds contempt, and he saw already that erstwhile friends were not rushing to help him. He owed it to his family and to himself to pick himself up and not to dwell on what had gone wrong at Hopkins. He returned to the topics of foreign aid, development strategy, and the limits of congressional oversight—his most recent intellectual pursuits before Hopkins. As in earlier periods in his life he was comfortable in the role of adviser, policy analyst, and strategist, not as someone in charge of running a big organization. He would use SAIS as his base, but only temporarily. Staying on the Hopkins faculty would be too uncomfortable for him and awkward all around, given the circumstances of his departure as president.

His first foray was in defense of foreign aid in a paper entitled "New Myths for Old: Senator Church and Foreign Aid."[32] Defending the Kennedy administration against Church's charge that it had exaggerated the prospects for a "benign take-off into self-sustaining growth," Gordon conceded that "we overrated the possible speed of development and reform of the then apparently democratic regimes of Argentina, Brazil, and Peru. But the record has been better than he acknowledges, not only in overall growth but in the enlargement of the middle classes, the increase in social mobility, and the participation of wider segments of the population in the modern economies."[33] This was his first of many retrospective reflections on his Brazilian experience that occupied him off and on for the rest of his life. He also began to speak regularly on foreign aid issues. In a New York City talk early in 1972 he endorsed Jacob Viner's critique of the linear-stages model of economic development. Foreign aid will not simply enable an economy to "take off" like a jet plane speeding down a runway; rather, economies can whirl in place like a helicopter and even crash back to earth. Yet on moral and pragmatic grounds Gordon defended a patient approach to foreign aid and argued against revolutionary shortcuts like those taken by Sukarno in Indonesia, Nkrumah in Ghana, and Castro in Cuba. He was back in the pragmatic idealist posture that LBJ had applauded.

Gordon did not seek a permanent teaching position at SAIS for reasons of his history at the university. But he doubted that teaching in general was his ideal venue. He had liked the idea of being a professor more than he had liked being a professor, and the Vietnam troubles had left a hangover that made academic positions much less attractive for someone like himself. Antiwar faculty sentiments had changed the atmosphere for ex-government officials on many campuses The gap between basic research and the policy research he preferred had grown. His instincts told him that he would have more freedom and scope for his kind of research in one of the Washington "think tanks" that had grown in importance in recent years. These entities were sprouting as the principal intellectual resource for policy-makers, displacing the Ivy League universities and New York law and investment firms that had earlier been the source of the "in and outers" supplying an important source of talent for government. The outsiders had become insiders. Former officials and ex-congressmen remained in Washington; worked in the think tanks, law firms, associations, consultant firms, and research centers in the area; and participated in the ongoing "inside the beltway" policy debates that often replicated the political battle lines within the government. This provided a more limited source of talent and fresh views than had been the case during World War II and the Marshall Plan days, but the older fluidity and easy access to the policy process were no longer possible in the more complicated Washington scene. The new system had its virtues, too. As Washington had become a city where layer after layer of high-level appointive and elected officials stayed on after leaving office, a pool of talent and experience developed that acted as a magnet for attracting further talent to the city.

The Washington think tanks of course came in a great variety and presented many kinds of research opportunities for Gordon as he pondered his career moves. Beginning in the 1970s, a new breed of more ideological and advocacy-oriented think tank had emerged, but Gordon preferred the more traditional professional atmosphere. The Woodrow Wilson International Center for Scholars of the Smithsonian Institution was one of the newer additions to the Washington think tanks, but it promised a nonpartisan and serious atmosphere for research as Gordon began to look for a new base of operation. Created by an Act of Congress in 1968, the Wilson Center's mission was to serve as a bridge between the "world of learning and the world of policy." As a newcomer the center had not developed a specific mission and style of operation. It had no ideological ax to grind, which appealed to Gordon. Like its sister institutions the center did not confer academic tenure. This was a factor contributing to the more flexible style of operations that was a chief virtue of the Washington think tanks. A given institute could rapidly staff up or shift its intellectual focus in response to government needs. At his age Lincoln did not worry about tenure. Benjamin Read, the Wilson Center's first director, invited Gordon in 1972 to join the staff of the fledgling organization. Read told Gordon that he had in mind a core group of six to ten researchers who would explore the problems of "sustainable growth." Gordon happily accepted the offer and joined the center in July 1972.

Last Jobs: The Wilson Center, Resources for the Future, and the CIA, 1972–1984

The center provided a pleasant environment for Gordon to resume his career as a policy intellectual. But progress was slow in the recruiting and fundraising for the economics research group that Gordon was to direct. Wilson Center director Ben Read left to become the president of the German Marshall Fund, and James H. Billington succeeded him. Billington had a different vision of what the center should be. His aim was to focus on selecting historians and political scientists from the academic world to come to the Smithsonian for a year to finish a book manuscript nearing completion. Billington did not, however, wholly abandon the original notions that had led to Gordon's hiring. He asked Gordon to serve as "coordinator" of the growth group while also finishing his own book.

Gordon had no "desire for administrative responsibilities" but "would not find them wholly allergic if they were in moderate dosages."[34] Gordon worked on a potential joint project with the OECD in Paris and with a research group in Japan and in January 1975 wrote a memorandum outlining his ideas. If the center were to go in the direction proposed, Gordon pointed out that some of the appointments for visiting humanities scholars would have to be redirected to the economics effort. Billington was not willing to move in this direction. Gordon concluded that he should focus on his own work. He sought a two-year renewal of his contract in 1974 but was granted only one year for the present. He had formulated an ambitious project that was eventually became one of his major works, *Growth Strategies and the International Order* (1979).[35] He was less certain that the Wilson Center could provide the atmosphere for the kind of work he wanted to pursue and did not want to narrow the focus of his proposed book so that it could be completed in one year.

Resources for the Future, 1975–1980

Fortuitously, Gordon noticed a Ford Foundation announcement that it had just awarded a $10 million grant to the Washington think tank Resources for the Future (RFF) and that Charles J. Hitch, president of the University of California system, would be leaving his post to become the president of RFF in July 1975. Gordon sent a letter of congratulations to his old friend, with whom he had maintained an intermittent correspondence since their Oxford days and World War II. He offered Hitch and his wife, Nancy, his guest room when they came to Washington to hunt for a house. Hitch accepted the offer and invited Lincoln in turn to work with him on a World Future Society conference. The renewal of contact with Hitch resulted in an invitation to join the RFF staff—the "best decision I ever made at RFF," Hitch later said. In mid-1975 Lincoln joined the RFF staff as a senior fellow working on the interrelated problems of energy, environment, and economic growth, with special attention to developing nations.

The next five years were happy and productive ones for Lincoln. His high energy, ebullient spirit, work habits, and wide-ranging intellect made him popular and admired at RFF. His colleagues were occasionally bemused by his learned conversations on almost any topic. His loquacity became legendary, and he took much good-natured ribbing. Liberated from heavy administrative responsibilities, his playful streak showed itself. For example, he sent around from time to time missives to his colleagues like the following:

1652—A BANNER YEAR!

1. Founding of Cape Town
2. Cromwell's recall of the Governor of Maryland
3. Start of the first Anglo-Dutch War (mostly at sea)
4. Start of the Shogunate in Japan
[How could anyone possibly forget it???] [36]

He formed close personal friendships with a number of colleagues, including the economist Joy Dunkerly, who coauthored reports with him. He had worked with Hans Landsberg before and now formed a close collegial relationship with him. Charlie Hitch remained one of his oldest and best friends and was a frequent social companion, often visiting Darkwater in the summer. Charlie and Lincoln frequently debated esoteric points of economic theory that went beyond what the RFF was doing or what other staff members could understand. It was as if they were back at Oxford, experiencing the birth of Keynesianism. A particular pleasure for Lincoln was that the RFF was colocated with the Brookings Institution in the Brookings annex. RFF shared a cafeteria with Brookings, and there were many contacts and collaborations between the two. RFF's areas of expertise in energy, agriculture, and the environment complemented the foreign policy, national security, macroeconomics, budget, public administration, and governance issues that were the focus of Brookings scholars. When Lincoln went to the cafeteria for lunch, he had the choice of the economics, foreign policy, or government studies table and joined in the discussions that were standard over lunch. Gordon thrived in this atmosphere, rebounding from the depression and fatigue following Hopkins. SAIS was right across the street from Brookings, so he could keep up with some of his colleagues there. The Carnegie Endowment was nearby, and so were other think tanks. The whole array of research centers near DuPont Circle formed an "invisible university" that suited him perfectly.

He made many friends at Brookings and had the pleasure of renewing his contacts with one of his oldest friends, Walter Salant, who was associ-ated with the Brookings Economic Studies Department. Walter had been a year ahead of Lincoln at Fieldston, the valedictorian and intellectual leader of the senior class when Lincoln was a junior. Gordon and Salant were not close friends until England, where both spent time in graduate study. When Walter died in 1997, Lincoln said at the memorial service that Walter "was a man with many friends and no enemies," a man who did not trumpet his own achievements, who was always respectful and supportive of others.[37] Lincoln rarely allowed himself to show his deepest feelings, but he did so on this occasion. He wished that the same thing could be said of him—that he was a man with only friends and no ene-mies—but he knew that this was not true in his case. At Hopkins most of his critics did not dislike him personally; they merely considered him mismatched for the job. But some—George Benton and a few others—did hate him, and he had quarreled with a number of his other adminis-trators. His Brazil experience left him with implacable foes on the left in that country and with the enduring hostility of a circle of leftist intellectu-als and watchdog critics in the United States. The human rights advocates in foreign policy reviled Gordon and regarded him as the poster boy for everything wrong with US foreign policy.

Gordon for the most part brushed off the slings and arrows that came his way, even though they hurt. He was busier than ever in his RFF years. The 1930 Fieldston yearbook description of him as tireless and always busy was also apt for his years at RFF. He was a busy man, churning out reports, books, and articles at an amazing rate; commenting on drafts by colleagues; and participating in projects on the work of the Overseas Development Council (ODC), the Atlantic Council, the Council on For-eign Relations, and other organizations on whose boards he served. He served on the science advisory committee for the Bureau of Oceans, Inter-national Environmental, and Scientific Affairs (OES) of the State Depart-ment, the Population Crisis Committee, the National Defense University, the Marshall Scholarship Fund, the Committee for Economic Develop-ment (CED), the advisory panel of the US delegation to the UN confer-ence on new and renewable energy, and other nonprofit and government entities. He served as cochairman with Robert Marjolin of the thirtieth-anniversary celebration of the Marshall Plan in Paris and coedited the conference papers. Participation in the reviews and celebrations of the

Marshall Plan came like clockwork every five years and was a constant in his life.

Despite this busy schedule he was spending more time with his family and becoming more the pater familias, enjoying his children on family vacations and doting on his grandchildren. Winter vacations were a special favorite of his, and he specialized in organizing cross-country skiing expeditions. As he wrote to his friends Don and Nancy McGranahan in January 1978:

> Dear Chaps,
>   This is a gloomy, mild, rainy, foggy, London-like Sunday, less than a week back from . . . a lovely cross-country skiing holiday at Darkwater. We felt like revolving inn-keepers most of the week, with all four of our own progeny together with us for a few days for the first time in eight years, and at least twenty of their friends in clumps of assorted sizes for one or two night stands. But we discovered several new trails, including some that look very interesting as possible summer or autumn hikes. . . . The snow was deep but old, with too much ice crust, so that trails already broken were much better than virgin ones (beware of pushing that analogy too far). One pair of skis—on my own feet at the time—were both broken off 40 cm. from the tips by running into an ice bank piled up by a highway plow; the wearer was undamaged and the local sporting goods dealer most sympathetic about discounts on a replacement.[38]

He regretted not having spent more time with his own children when they were young, and he now took particular interest in his grandchildren. On his numerous trips to Europe he usually enjoyed a stopover to visit his close friends Don and Nancy McGranahan in Geneva. In the wintertime they took long cross-country skiing hikes in the Swiss Alps, and in summer they hiked and climbed mountains. The only dark side to his enjoyment of these hiking and skiing excursions was that Allison could not accompany him, due to her failing health. Allison turned seventy in 1979 and, a heavy cigarette smoker throughout her life, was now beginning to show the symptoms of emphysema and congestive heart disease.

Gordon's pleasant days at RFF would end when the funding from the Ford Foundation's large initial grant ran out. Hitch told him: "As you know, I have not been able to include you in the limited number of researchers that I have constituted as a core group."[39] But Gordon's work "would be funded for at least a year," and after that he could retire on favorable financial terms, or if funding could be secured he could continue as senior fellow. Gordon turned sixty-five in September 1978 but had no desire to retire.

Although Gordon was fully occupied with his research and service on numerous boards, he did not wholly abandon direct engagement in policy. In late summer 1977 the two Panama Canal treaties proposed by the Carter administration were running into public opposition that threatened their Senate ratification. Lincoln threw himself into the cause of bolstering the support for Senate ratification of the agreement President Carter had negotiated with Panama. The issue seemed to Gordon so obviously important for the country that it reminded him of the campaign to sell the Marshall Plan to a reluctant public. He decided to concentrate his efforts on the revived Committee on the Present Danger (CPD), which had been formed in 1950 by Paul Nitze and Dean Acheson to promote the massive rearmaments envisaged under NSC-68 and to "prevent a Korea in Europe."[40] By the mid-1960s the committee had become dormant, but two days after President Carter took office, it was revived. Carter's flat refusal to hire Nitze in any capacity in foreign or defense policy had helped to convince Nitze that Carter was soft on the Soviet threat. The committee would later provide the core of President Ronald Reagan's national security team after 1980, but now it was revived with the mission of combating the communist threat and the dangers posed by Carter's weak foreign policy. The committee included such figures as William D. Casey (later CIA director), Richard V. Allen (later Reagan's first national security adviser), George Shultz (secretary of the treasury and secretary of state), and Eugene V. D. Rostow (dean of the Yale Law School and Walt Rostow's brother); in 1979 the committee included Reagan himself. Preventing the ratification of SALT II was the committee's key objective, and it appeared to Gordon that the committee might be mobilized to fight the two Panama treaties. If this happened, Gordon believed, the odds were against Senate ratification. A two-thirds vote of course was required for Senate ratification, and more than twenty senators were already committed to vote against ratification on the grounds that the treaties violated US sovereignty.

Gordon telephoned Eugene Rostow, chairman of the CPD executive committee, and urged him to support the administration and to prevent any hasty CPD action to oppose the treaties. Gordon also warned against premature commitments by CPD members in their individual capacities before they had studied the issues. Rostow had some reservations about the treaties but was impressed with Gordon's arguments, which relied heavily on the details of the LBJ administration's negotiations he had conducted with Panama while he was assistant secretary of state. He had been a key participant in these negotiations, which were on the way to success but unfortunately failed when a military coup deposed the civilian government and derailed the talks. The United States had received strong assurances then on a host of key issues, and Gordon pointed out that the protections of critical US interests were even stronger in the current agreement. The Carter proposal was the best deal the United States could get, and ratification was vital for the future of US relations with the hemisphere. Rostow urged Gordon to present a detailed analysis of his position, bringing in the historical perspective and focusing on key technical issues of neutrality, passage through the canal, and the security arrangements for US naval forces. He should explain the provisions for the twenty-year transition period and what safeguards remained once sovereignty over the canal passed to the Panamanians in 1998. Rostow would present Lincoln's paper to the CPD executive committee, which would study the arguments and make recommendations to the members on what official CPD actions, if any, might be warranted. Gordon wrote a three-page letter to Rostow "to follow up on our telephone conversation of mid-August, in which I suggested it would be appropriate and desirable for the Committee on the Present Danger to take a public position in support of the ratification of the recently negotiated treaties relating to the Panama Canal."[41]

Rostow thanked him for the letter, which "I am transmitting at once to the Executive Committee for study."[42] Rostow noted that "a number of our members will publicly support ratification" but that "a number of others are opposed or doubtful. The Executive Committee has agreed to study the problem carefully, and to decide—after the study—whether attempting to reach a collective position is feasible and desirable."[43] In the end the CPD did not reach a collective position and did not raise its voice against the treaties. Gordon's effort to keep the committee out of the camp of opponents played a part in the treaties' very narrow victory in the Senate. The Senate ratified the treaties in March 1978 by one vote more than the required two-thirds.

When Gordon finally left RFF on September 1980, he was sixty-seven years old, but he left to take a new job. He received a warm and affectionate farewell from his RFF colleagues. They threw a big party marked by friendly toasts and good humor, a pleasant contrast from his departure from Hopkins and his somewhat cool parting from the Wilson Center. His RFF colleagues even gave him a dose of his own medicine when Hans Landsberg composed a sonnet called "On Lincoln Gordon's Departure from RFF," which included these jibes:

> You broadened our scope, extended our vision;
> And in due course one learned not to ask you the time of day
> Unless one wanted to know clock making, astrology, and
> Relativity along the way. . . .
> In landing you, Linc, they've got quite a find;
> But one wonders if they fully grasped the consequences
> Of letting Linc Gordon graze without any fences.[44]

In February 1981 Emery Castle wrote Gordon a warm letter in which he informed Gordon that the RFF board had voted to award him the title of senior fellow emeritus. This carried with it no salary, but the privilege of office space and secretarial services whenever he might need a base. The board extended this recognition because of "our regard for your contributions to RFF and as well as that we believe a continuing association will bring credit to RFF."[45] His colleague Milton Russell wrote him a moving tribute, saying in part: "Your career has epitomized the almost Jeffersonian ideal of the engaged intellect; as its personification, your example has been important to us all."[46] All this was a pleasant note on which to depart for his final government post.

Central Intelligence Agency, 1980–1983

The reference to "they" in the Landsberg poem referred to the Central Intelligence Agency. To Gordon's surprise, he had been offered a new job in government. Bob Bowie, his good friend from Harvard, had told him of a position opening up on the four-member senior review panel of the CIA's national foreign assessment center, the committee known under the rubric of the "wise men." He had had no desire to return to government when Jimmy Carter was elected president in 1976. He did not view the Georgian as on a par with the nation's great wartime and postwar leaders. He noted that his friend Nitze, who had campaigned hard for a role in the administration, was rebuffed, and he was certain that the human rights faction of Carter's foreign policy team would be adamantly opposed to him. But the job now appealed to him. It would beef up his government pension with today's higher salaries. It also seemed ideal for Gordon in other ways. Bowie argued that the panel was important because it helped produce the national intelligence estimates that reviewed the quality of the intelligence work of Defense and State, as well as the CIA. The intelligence estimates were public documents and could influence the wider policy debate. Further, the panel worked with the top CIA policy-makers. The senior review panel had nothing to do with the clandestine side of the CIA.

The other members of the panel were Bill Leonhart, a distinguished retired diplomat whom Gordon knew; General Bruce Palmer, also known to Gordon; and Herbert Rothenberg, a retired CIA scientist whom Gordon did not know but who had a good reputation. The panel members were supposed to be individuals with broad experience in government and in the private sector—and to be nearing the end of their careers so that they were beyond the suspicion of trying to advance themselves bureaucratically. Gordon was interested. He wrote to the McGranahans the day before he reported for duty:

Dear Chaps,

I was planning to take that occasion to communicate the rather surprising news that I am about to start a new job—to be precise, with tomorrow the first day. Much to my surprise, I was approached at the end of July at the instance of Bob Bowie to replace Klaus Knorr of Princeton as a member of four-man body. . . . I concluded that the job would not only be interesting but also had a fair chance of exerting useful influence on matters of importance. The appointment is completely non-political and I was assured would be most unlikely to be directly affected by the November 4 election outcome (although it could obviously be much affected indirectly). So I took a deep breath and accepted. Now with the start imminent, I am naturally looking forward with some eagerness to learning whether it was a wise or foolish decision. I tried to discount the flattery involved in being asked to do something new at this age, but was probably not entirely successful.[47]

Gordon still worried that if he took the job, his appointment might be rescinded if Reagan won the 1980 election. The CIA director, Admiral Stansfield Turner, had assured him that "there is an increasingly important role for the Review Panel, and your contribution to it will be most important."[48] Gordon felt sufficiently concerned to discuss the problem with Emery Castle in mid-October, but Castle assured him that RFF would be a safe harbor in the event that something went awry. A presidential transition looked more and more likely as Reagan surged in the campaign's late stage. This safe harbor at RFF proved to be unnecessary. The CIA post was protected as a high-level career appointment, and Gordon thought he could in any case count on the fact that he knew Bill Casey, Frank Carlucci, and other Reagan appointees. The Reagan CIA team made no immediate organizational changes that affected the review panel's status.

The first major assignment for Gordon and the review panel arose when the panel was asked to mediate an acrimonious interagency dispute over Soviet intentions in Central and Latin America. Secretary of State Alexander Haig made a speech in April 1981 accusing the Soviet Union of fostering worldwide terrorism, citing Soviet activities in Central and Latin America as an example of the threat. Gordon's role was a familiar one: to fashion a middle ground in the dispute. He argued against the most extreme positions taken by other analysts. Gordon told his son Hugh later that his greatest contribution at the CIA was to tone down the extreme assessments of both the Soviet Union's intentions and its capabilities. This role was not in keeping with the view of him as a relentless cold warrior. Since he was one of the original NATO framers, he rather relished his new position.

The battle over the Reagan administration's first national intelligence estimate came to a moderately successful conclusion. A staff report of the subcommittee of the House Select Committee on Intelligence stated: "The NIE [National Intelligence Estimate] stands as a fine example of intelligence professionalism under difficult circumstances."[49] The first year on the job was generally satisfying and stimulating for Gordon. He was learning much both substantively and about the process of intelligence production. He was intrigued by intelligence's relation to policy-making. He wrote to his first CIA boss, Bruce Clarke, in October 1981: "I am in a good position to observe the evolution of international affairs; it has been and continues to be a new learning experience on the . . . delicate art of intelligence production; and it has led to a whole new range of personal acquaintanceships with people I value. Beyond that, there are occasional glimmers of hope that one is contributing something to the education of our new political masters on the world's complexities in a time of great troubles. If that latter aspect can be enhanced during my second year . . . I shall be more than content."[50]

He did not continue to be upbeat. At one point he found himself acting as the national intelligence officer-at-large representing the CIA in interagency skirmishes. He felt the need to get guidance and backing from CIA director Casey, and this task gave him some pause, since by then it had become clear to Gordon that he and Casey did not see eye-to-eye on a number of issues. Casey sometimes acted unilaterally and took little notice of the panel's and other staff inputs. Gordon went through several drafts for a letter to his director. Most memos Gordon wrote came straight from his typewriter, with few or no corrections, but not this one. He wrote:

> Dear Bill: The purpose of this letter is to request your guidance concerning the final stages in handling the current Draft NIE on Soviet Support for International Terrorism. . . . My request is either for reassurance that you approve that course of action or for alternative instructions if you feel otherwise. I understand my role . . . to be *representing you* in your capacity as head of the Intelligence Community. Having accepted the responsibility, I would find it very embarrassing to have the rug pulled out from under me. . . . I am prepared to be a good soldier and to take my chances in No Man's Land, but I should not like to be shot in the back by my Commanding Officer![51]

This was apparently too much for his commanding officer. Their hitherto frosty relationship grew even chillier. From what can be gleaned from the records, it appears that a series of reorganizations took place that left the review panel in a state of limbo. Lincoln maintained a role in certain policy areas, such as nuclear issues and Latin American matters, by virtue of his background and hence was consulted with some regularity by colleagues. But the review panel did not regain the power it had enjoyed in its first year. The CIA experience contributed to a shift in intellectual focus for Gordon to new policy topics and areas of interest or perhaps to older areas of interest dating back to the Marshall Plan and NATO periods of his life. The implications of potential Soviet weakness rather than the threat of overwhelming Soviet power slowly ripened in his mind and became a new focus of his thinking. He saw indications of this weakness in the intelligence estimates of Soviet vulnerabilities in its relations with Eastern Europe. Gordon increasingly sided with those in the intelligence community who found the portrait of a growing Soviet threat dubious. The CIA was under pressure to provide evidence that justified the US military buildup, but Gordon saw growing evidence of Soviet weakness. This was a new direction in his thinking and a departure from conventional wisdom on the Soviet Union. His interests also shifted back toward Europe. He became more concerned with broad political questions than with the problems of economic growth. He had, for the moment at least, said what he had to say on those topics, and he wanted to move on to the "political" side of political economy, more in line with his interests as an undergraduate.

The CIA assignment was an anticlimactic end to his career in public service. He had learned much and had toned down some excessive estimates of Soviet power. The discovery of potential cracks in the Soviet empire seemed to him a matter of significance. He was now seventy, not likely to be hired by anyone at this age, but he was not ready to retire or stop working when he had a new idea. He had been giving some thought to what to do now. He was not wealthy, but he had enough to live on from his government and university pensions. There was no reason to give up writing and research, provided that he could find the right venue.

18

Elder Statesman

Although somewhat cramped financially by the slump in endowment returns, and facing dozens of new competitors (some of them highly partisan or single interest promoters), Brookings remains the policy "think tank" par excellence.
—Lincoln Gordon, Christmas letter, December 2003

The Brookings Institution remains a most cordial host institution, providing well-based assessments of events and conditions in the public domain, both domestic and foreign.
—Lincoln Gordon to Josh Billings, August 7, 2006

An obvious choice would be to return to RFF if the offer for an office and secretarial support still stood. There was, however, a problem: the RFF was no longer in the Brookings annex. As RFF had grown, it needed more space. RFF's president, Emory Cassell, approached Brookings president Bruce K. MacLaury with a proposition. Would Brookings sell to RFF the property it owned on P Street immediately behind the Brookings buildings? RFF could then build its own office, and RFF and Brookings would maintain their close intellectual partnership. MacLaury discussed the overture with his own board and returned with a bold counteroffer. The Brookings trustees were unwilling to part with the property but proposed that Brookings and RFF merge. This was a bridge too far for the RFF trustees, since Brookings was roughly twice RFF's size and had much greater financial resources, making it likely that Brookings would be the senior partner and set the terms for the merger. RFF decided to vacate the Brookings annex and relocate to new facilities nearby. In practical terms this meant, as Gordon saw it, that the easy contact with Brookings scholars, the cafeteria discussions, the tradition of the Friday lunch, and use of the Brookings library would be foregone. Moreover, the topic he was most interested in—the potential implosion of the Soviet empire—was much closer to the work of Brookings than it was to that of RFF. Therefore he approached the Brookings director of foreign policy studies, John Steinbrunner, to inquire if Brookings might welcome him as a visiting scholar without pay. He would generate his own support for the direct costs of any research projects and would offer any book-length manuscript to the Brookings Institution Press. Steinbrunner and Brookings president MacLaury welcomed the idea. In 1984 Gordon took up residence at Brookings, attached to Foreign Policy Studies, where he would remain for the next quarter of a century, functioning in both the role of an active researcher and that of an elder statesman.

The Soviet Empire and Eastern Europe

Although he enjoyed attending numerous Brookings seminars showcasing the work of colleagues, Gordon was not tempted to play the role of simply being an avuncular presence. He continued to work on two tracks: a short-term agenda (writing reviews and articles and giving talks) and a larger agenda (a major research project). He had one peculiarity in mapping out any major research effort. Like Dickens, he could not begin without a title. By mid-1984 he had found his title, and the research project jelled in his mind. The title of the book would be *Eroding Empire* to indicate the growing Soviet weaknesses. The subtitle flowed from the title: *Western Relations with Eastern Europe.*[1] The focus would be on how the Western nations, in anticipation of the Soviet empire beginning to crumble at its extremities, should respond in the face of an erosion of Soviet control over its satellite nations. He outlined how he would approach the topic, the list of European contributors who would be part of the research team, and his own role as editor and chapter contributor. He had secured a preliminary commitment from German sources to finance the direct research costs, provided that he secure start-up funds from an American source. To this end Gordon turned to his mentor Averell Harriman. Harriman's health by this time was failing, and he was almost totally deaf, so that communication was difficult. (Harriman died two years later at the age of ninety-five from bone cancer.) Through Harriman's longtime secretary Gordon learned that Harriman's own foundation had already fully committed its funds for that year, but a luncheon was arranged to discuss his new project. The lunch resulted in a gift of $10,000 that Harriman arranged for the project. This initial funding enabled Gordon to proceed with a Paris meeting of his contributors and paved the way for the German grant. He was later to obtain additional funding from the Hudson Institute, which became a cosponsor of the project.

Gordon wrote the introduction, a chapter on Washington's evolving attitudes toward Eastern Europe, and the concluding chapter. Other chapters featured an analysis of Germany's *Ost Politik,* British policies, French perceptions, the Eastern European setting, and internal political trends. Lincoln reported to his friends Don and Nancy McGranahan in July 1986 that he was in the midst of the Brookings review of the manuscript, which would "go out tomorrow to qualified outside readers . . . [who] are to report back one of three verdicts: (a.) excellent, should be published as is; (b.) good, but should be improved by modifications along such and such lines; or (c.) hopeless; Brookings should not publish it at all."[2] He judged the third as not likely and noted that the "probabilities of (b.) are greater than (a.)" By the fall a favorable verdict from the anonymous readers was in, and final revisions were made. The book appeared in 1987, with the title *Eroding Empire* in bold letters at the top. The volume consisted of nine chapters, three written by Gordon, and was 328 pages long, with an appendix of 14 pages of statistical tables. It was well received at Brookings and in the wider scholarly community. It had the good fortune of appearing at a time when *glasnost* and *perestroika* were in the air, and US-USSR strategic arms negotiations pointed toward a thaw in the Cold War.

Allison's Death

Lincoln was comfortable in his surroundings and happy in his work. He made several trips to Europe to consult with his collaborators, which usually afforded him the opportunity to meet up with old friends and acquaintances. A less happy part of this time of his life was Allison's failing health. Her condition had deteriorated sharply. She was older than

Lincoln by four years, but she seemed older and frailer than her years. She suffered from emphysema and related pulmonary and cardiac disorders that sapped her strength. She had a premonition that she might not last until their fiftieth wedding anniversary, so the couple decided to hold a big celebration in 1982 for their forty-fifth anniversary. They invited a group of fifty friends—all that could fit into their small backyard—for the party, and Lincoln presented her with a sapphire and the sonnet reprinted at the head of chapter 5.

In February 1987, Lincoln told the McGranahans the "sad news [that] on January 20, after nine days in the Georgetown University Hospital, Allison's heart finally gave out and she died at three o'clock that morning."[3] He reported that "her condition had been getting poorer since August, but there was a kind of reprieve in the fall which made for a good Thanksgiving party in Baltimore." Daughter Amy, together with her husband and young son Nicholas, joined them, along with son Hugh and his wife, Bridget. There was also "a quite good Christmas party at home, with Anne and Hugh." Allison had still been cooking dinners for the family two weeks before her death. "It was," Lincoln told Don and Nancy, "not a painful death, and Allison was spared a prolonged invalidism—a possibility which had been worrying and frightening her."[4]

The family held a secular memorial service at which Lincoln spoke for ten or fifteen minutes, "followed by each of the children in order of seniority." He had his and the children's remarks printed up in a handsome booklet that he sent to the McGranahans and to other friends who were not able to attend the memorial service. He reported that he was "bearing up reasonably well." What Allison's loss meant to him can be best seen in his remarks at the memorial service, in his sonnet to her composed five years earlier, and in the occasional references to her in his correspondence. He wrote Ruth Kriebel when she lost her husband that he could understand how deeply Dick's death affected her because he knew what Allison's death meant for him. He wrote Josh Billings: "On a personal note, I repeat my condolences on the loss of your wife. Having had that experience 18 years ago, I know that life goes on but is never quite the same."[5] In notes written in 2002 for his proposed memoir, three items were outlined for the concluding chapter: "Vast component of luck," "Loss of Allison too soon," and "Compensation from children and grandchildren. Salute to them."

Brazil Again

Lincoln was regularly asked to give a talk, to write a paper, or otherwise to reflect on aspects of his career. Seminars on Latin American problems and Third World economic development were frequent. He kept in touch in the 1970s and 1980s with Elio Gaspari, a Brazilian journalist then stationed in New York who was for many years the semiofficial historian of the 1964 coup and the twenty-one years of Brazilian military rule. Gordon followed Brazilian developments but did not undertake serious research on Brazil until the late 1980s. In 1986 a major effort was organized to mark the Alliance for Progress on the occasion of the twenty-fifth anniversary of its birth. Gordon was invited to the conference along with other living participants, and each wrote a paper. In preparing his paper, Lincoln was forced to revisit his role and to reflect on the successes and failures of the Alliance in Brazil. The Eastern Europe project was then in its final stages. His attention was shifting with that book finished, and he began to think about his next research effort. Brazil naturally came to mind. Why had the Alliance failed in Brazil, and why was economic and political development in Latin America so different from the experience of Western Europe and North America? Many of the peoples that inhabited Brazil were transplanted Europeans, so why were there such sharp differences? Or were conditions that different? Perhaps it was only a matter of time before the normal laws of economics as understood in the United States and Europe applied in Brazil as well.

It was more than an intellectual puzzle to him. It was a personal affront, a deep disappointment, and a mark of failure for him personally and for the US role in the world. Brazil was a challenge to the American liberal consensus. Brazil had declared a general amnesty in 1979, and the military began to prepare for the return of civilian rule, which was finally restored in 1985. Normal macroeconomic policies and party politics seemed in the offing when Tancredo Neves, a centrist politician from the premilitary regime, won the presidency, but Neves became ill and died before he could take office. His vice president took over, but the electoral system was still partially controlled by the military, so that the first popularly elected president since Jango's overthrow had to wait until the election of 1989. An assembly to draft a new constitution was created in 1988. Inflation, the old problem, had resumed and soared to an annual rate of more than 25 percent.

Gordon had not been back to Brazil since the return of civilian government in 1985. (He and his wife had gone there on holiday briefly in the 1970s without fanfare or press notice.) He regarded the challenges of establishing sound economic policies and stable democratic authority as still the critical issues facing the country. With the European book completed, he now turned his attention fully to Brazil. How would he approach the task? He decided that the research would have to be on a broad scale, encompassing the historical trends for the past half century at least, and would have to cover political and social trends as well as economic developments. He would of course draw on the considerable recent scholarship on Brazil, both American and Brazilian, but his own experience would come into play as well. There would be no point in a team effort here; the project would be his, and it would be his intellectual swan song, for he was now approaching his seventy-fifth birthday.

In a casual conversation in late 1987 or early 1988, he said that he had a title for his next book: *Brazil's Second Chance.* Not long afterward, by coincidence, an investment-broker friend of mine asked me if Brookings would organize a seminar in Argentina and Brazil for a small group of portfolio investors. I asked Lincoln if he would help me organize the seminar and accompany me on the trip. He readily consented, and we agreed on a convenient time. The trip would give him the opportunity to get his Brazil research under way. "On balance it was a rewarding trip," he wrote his children after we had returned, "even though the travel schedule was strenuous."[6] It was strenuous because we had two long overnight flights (going and returning), and three very early morning departures (Buenos Aires to Sao Paulo, Sao Paulo to Rio, and Rio to Brasilia) and because he "was pursued unmercifully by eager journalists."

The trip gave a jumpstart to Lincoln's work on *Brazil's Second Chance.* He enthusiastically took up the research and arranged to spend three more weeks in Brazil in June to conduct more interviews. He made further trips to Brazil in 1991 and 1992. While the start was promising, however, progress slowed, and then the work bogged down altogether. There were many reasons why the work progressed slowly. He was busy with multiple projects, committees, papers, entertainment, and social commitments. He was active on a project involving Russia and Ukraine. He was also called on, as the only surviving program vice chairman of the War Production Board, to serve as an expert witness in Superfund litigation.

He was happy to have these opportunities because he was paid $1,000 a day as an expert witness (a part of court costs usually borne by the losing side in the lawsuit). His testimony attempted to rebut the company's contention that the federal government in World War II had condoned pollution in the emergency.[7]

He had not been able to travel in the last stages of his wife's illness, but after her death he felt free to take vacations that involved travel. He took a month-long trekking visit to Nepal and northern India in October–November 1990, sending his children a sixteen-page, single-spaced report summarizing the daily journal entries he made on his trip.[8] In the course of 1992 he traveled to Brazil, Spain, Greece, Turkey, China, India, France, Italy, the Grand Tetons, and elsewhere in the United States.

His attention also strayed from his research for another reason: he fell in love. On December 14, 1990, he wrote his children that there is "news from papa this Christmas season" that "has to do with falling in love—enthusiastically and irrationally—with Edith Bennet Page whose (inadequate) picture is enclosed."[9] Edith was an attractive divorcee, age fifty-three to his seventy-seven, whom he had met in October at a dinner party. Edith "is intelligent, attractive, and energetic, enjoys life, has an excellent sense of humor, and shares my attitudes and tastes in an astounding variety of matters."[10] He would have liked the letter to his children to be an announcement of an impending marriage. However, Edith had been nursing her elderly father and was worried about the prospect of having to care for two frail old men and discouraged his hopes of a permanent liaison. He had to be content with a "temporary" relationship that lasted seven years. With me he was more direct: "I'm in love with her and want to marry her, but she won't have me."

Lincoln was not a man to give up easily, though, whether he was on the tennis court, figuring out an economics problem, or wooing Ms. Page. He continued to argue his case, but on a trip to Spain in 1991, Edith was so definitive that he had to abandon his hopes of marrying her. He reported to his children: "In one major respect, however, it was a deep disappointment. . . . Edith has made it clear that she is obsessively preoccupied with the age gap between us and that my lingering hopes of a long-term association should be abandoned. . . . Edith says with candor and regret that she only wishes that I were 20 years younger but cannot put the fact out of her mind. . . . While indeed disappointed I am not devastated."[11] He therefore decided to bow to the inevitable and make the best of the situation. She left him in 1997 to marry a recently widowed family friend closer to her own age.

Progress on the book was slow, however, for a reason not directly related to his travels, love life, or consulting. The chief reason for the slow progress was that the book became a trope for the fate of Brazil itself. He could not make progress on the book unless Brazil made progress as a country. Finishing the book depended on Brazil becoming a more finished country—taking advantage of its second chance. The presidential election of 1989 had been marred by a last-minute staged kidnapping perpetrated by the winning candidate, Fernando Collor de Mello, the governor of the small northeastern state of Alagoas. Collor was adroit at using television to influence public opinion and alleged that the kidnapping was the work of groups associated with the political left. The sensational charge on television on the eve of the second round of the election was enough to defeat the candidate from the left, Lutz Inancio Lula da Silva ("Lula"). Lula had made his way into the runoff election by narrowly edging out Gordon's old nemesis Leonel Brizola for second place in the first-round balloting. Brizola had rebuilt his political fortunes in Rio after returning from exile in Portugal in 1979. Brizola supported Lula in the runoff, uttering one of his more colorful remarks to a reporter who asked him why he was supporting Lula now after bashing him in the first round: "Politics is the art of swallowing toads [*engolir sapo*] and wouldn't it be nice to see the rich having to swallow the Bearded Toad [Lula]!" The nefarious winner, Fernando Collor, was forced to resign in 1992, as he was about to be impeached by the Brazilian Senate for corruption in government contracting. The only good that Gordon saw in this donnybrook was that Brizola was implicated in the scandal and was thus dragged down with the president. Thus began Brizola's slide into political oblivion.

Gordon nevertheless was hopeful in his assessment of the Brazilian situation. He soon saw reasons for hope when a significant currency reform was enacted in 1994 that broke the back of the inflationary spiral that had plagued the country for so long. Brazil also elected Fernando Enrique Cardoso as president in 1994, and he became one of the nation's great political leaders of the modern era. Cardoso was succeeded by Lula, the first leftist president since Jango. Lula surprised and reassured the political center by his mainstream macroeconomic policies and like Cardoso served two terms.

Progress by Brazil meant progress by Lincoln in his research. In January 1995 Lincoln wrote his friend Josephine Saner, "I have made some headway on Brazil, where politics and economics have finally taken a major turn for the better."[12] In December 1996 he reported in his annual Christmas letter to friends, "I am now just past the halfway mark on Brazil, with analysis of economic structures completed, social structures half done, and political structures on the next drawing board." As a visiting scholar Lincoln was lower on the pecking order than other senior researchers, but his steady output of papers and his collegiality helped to protect him from bureaucratic slings and arrows. He was forced to move his office from the foreign policy floor to a cubicle in the library stacks but grew quite pleased with his new surroundings. He loved to talk to the younger scholars and learn what they were working on. Many colleagues liked him and found him a source of knowledge and wisdom. But there were detractors, too, who found him verbose and tiresome. Some regarded him as a relic. One younger researcher remarked to me: "When I saw him coming down the hall, I'd duck back into my office and close the door."

Since at Brookings one lives and dies by the book, the Brazil book's birth pangs presented some danger that Lincoln might be downsized off the staff even if he was not paid and indeed contributed generously to the institution. None of the regular foreign policy staff wanted to be located in the library, so Lincoln was effectively insulated from the institution's fierce competition for offices. He quite liked his location surrounded by books and quickly formed friendships with a number of the librarians. He benefited from tutorials provided by library colleagues on how to use the computer; send and forward emails; access and navigate the Internet; and cope with passwords, the new phone system, and other paraphernalia of the information age. Through emails and the Internet he found it easier to keep in touch with Brazilian colleagues and keep up with recent developments in the country. He found the information age a mixed blessing: it helped him immensely in his research but confounded him repeatedly with its complexities.

Brazil's Second Chance, Last Hurrah, and Unfinished Memoirs

In March 1997 Gordon wrote to Brookings president Michael Armacost and its head of foreign policy Richard Haass that "the draft of Chapter V of my Brazil study, entitled 'The Social Dimension,'" had just been sent to the Twentieth Century Fund (now the Century Foundation). He presented a timetable for the completed manuscript to Haass in April 1997, specifying completion dates for the remaining chapters. He told Haass that he had recently had a Brazilian visitor "well wired into the political and business establishments there [who] claimed to have been carrying an informal message from President Cardoso expressing great interest in my book and hoping for an early visit on my part."[13] He told the visitor that he did not want to make another trip to Brazil until he had finished the book. He did not quite make his deadline, completing the manuscript in mid-2000 and sending it off to the Brookings Institution Press. Negotiations for a Portuguese translation were consummated shortly after the publication by Brookings in 2001, and an accompanying *Supplement* dealing with the United States and his own role in the 1964 coup was planned. The *Supplement* became a small book and required him to do considerable archival research.

The Brookings Institution Press published *Brazil's Second Chance* in May 2001 and the *Supplement* in 2003. A Sao Paulo publisher brought out Portuguese translations, which attracted widespread interest in Brazil, and Lincoln made a three-week promotional tour for the book in Sao Paulo and Rio that became his "last hurrah" in the country. The tour attracted a surprising amount of publicity in the Brazilian press and on television. He still spoke Portuguese, but somewhat haltingly now. To some he remained the villain and stirred memories of the hated period of repression. To others who had not been even alive when he was US ambassador, he appeared as an eccentric old man in strange old-fashioned suits and wide ties. Lincoln had probably not bought a new suit since the 1970s.

Lincoln told friends after the Brazil books were published and as he approached his ninetieth birthday that he had no desire to stop working, but at the same time he did not feel up to tackling another big project. Sometime in 2002, though, he changed his mind and decided that he would after all undertake another major effort, namely, writing his memoirs. He credited "two strong recommendations from outside the family," one from Steve Bundy, McGeorge Bundy's son, and the other from Pedro Malan of Brasilia, with persuading him to embark on the memoir.[14] Evidently he did not need much persuading. He cited as a reason for writing the memoir his desire to contribute "what I have learned over seven decades of varied activities in an era of profound change."[15] He gave a different reason to Brookings colleague Michael Callingaert at a Friday lunch. When asked what he was working on these days, now that the Brazil book was finished, he said: "I'm working on a book of memoirs because I don't want to be kicked out of Brookings for doing nothing." The force of habit was not to be discounted as motivation. What was the one thing he had done all his life and done well? Write. So he wrote. He had written his way to a Harvard summa, to a Rhodes scholarship, to the Harvard faculty, to his progression up the bureaucratic ranks, so why not continue? In notes dated December 2002 he sketched out eighteen chapters of the projected memoir and later scaled back the number to nine. Contrary to his usual practice, he did not have a title in mind before starting to write. The notes at the top of the page had this heading: "[Possible title: *Participant in a Transforming World*]." This indefinite formula perhaps explains why he did not have any idea of what large theme the book would have and what criteria would guide his choice of material.

He was not given normally to introspection, second-guessing, or replaying past actions, and he considered the "tell-all" book an anathema. Lincoln was a man of the old school. One did one's duty and expected nothing in return. One did not engage in self-justification or condemn others. But what was a memoir if it did not refight old battles, if it were shorn of the stuff of controversy and the clash of personalities? He had no patience for such questions; the answers would emerge from the actual writing. One should plunge ahead with the task and let the story tell itself. He would start with his childhood in New York and then move to his Harvard and Oxford years and then return to Harvard and all the rest. Strangely, the older events seemed clearer than the more recent. He would start with the old days and work his way forward. Chapter 1 would talk about his childhood and Harvard and Oxford, a draft completed by the summer of 2003. He finished chapter 2, which dealt with the War Production Board and World War II, in 2004. By this time he had begun to make visits to the John F. Kennedy Presidential Library in Boston, where he had deposited his papers in 1973.

Chapter 3 of the draft memoir dealt with the work of the United Nations Atomic Energy Commission in 1946. He consulted his papers in the JFK Library extensively for this chapter. The most interesting part of this chapter is his memory of a meeting between Baruch and Wallace in which Baruch attributed a paper prepared by Gordon to somebody else. This angered Gordon, and he wrote a note for the historical record and had it put into the files at the JFK Library. He did not like Henry Wallace, and he had a hard time disguising the fact in this chapter; he did not want to step over the self-imposed mental barrier to his present task. Ironically, Lincoln's own policy views were probably closer to Wallace's than to Baruch's, but to explore this would have taken him into criticisms of his old boss Baruch, and he did not think it was proper to do that. He acknowledges that Wallace was willing to make concessions in order to gain Soviet agreement to atomic controls and hints that Baruch was more inflexible. But Lincoln only hints at his policy disagreements with Baruch.

Chapter 4 addressed the Marshall Plan, which occupied him for most of the remainder of 2004. It was with relish that he returned to the Marshall Plan era, for it relieved him from thinking about the contemporary scene. He took a dim view of the foreign policy of the George W. Bush administration and put a rosy glow on the Marshall Plan era as a time of consensus and unselfconscious patriotism. It was comforting to return to this time when consensus apparently reigned in American foreign policy. This chapter took up much of 2005, and chapter 5 took up the rest of the year, dealing with Harriman as Truman's national security adviser and himself as Harriman's adviser on NATO. This was the last year he was able to write before health problems began to slow him down.

Lincoln was not entirely confident that he knew what he was doing with this project, partly because his powers were failing but also because the memoir genre was new to him. He decided in 2005 to show drafts of the early chapters to a small group of friends for their reactions. One was Joy Dunkerly. She told him: "Where is the emotion? There is no emotion here. The reader doesn't know what you feel about anything." She was not sure of his reactions to her comments. To his son Bob the memoir had interesting historical vignettes but "did not reveal much of himself." Gordon began to think more seriously about who might publish the memoir. He had had previous discussions with Margery Thompson of the Association of Diplomatic Studies and Training, and so he wrote her in April 2005 and sent her chapter 4, on the Marshall Plan, along with a table of contents. He asked for her comments but noted that "since a complete MS is still many months away, this question may not yet be ripe."

An encounter with Brazilian journalist Elio Gaspari in June 2005 brought home to Lincoln the challenges of his projected memoir chapter on Brazil. Gaspari and Gordon were featured at a seminar at Harvard's new Latin American Center, which drew some fifty to sixty students. Then the two men spent several hours discussing Brazilian politics, during which Gaspari "startled me by saying that I could and should have prevented the intra-military coup of 1965 led by General Arturo Costa e Silva against President Humberto Castelo Branco [that] thwarted the president's plan for a prompt return to constitutional and civilian democracy. Elio had never before suggested that I had the power to prevent the Costa e Silva coup."[16] Lincoln dismissed the charge: "I can only conclude that his (understandable) antipathy to the military regime had made him forget the *de facto* weakness of U.S. influence on Brazilian politics in 1965."[17] Despite this dismissal the charge disturbed him. He had been deeply disappointed by the Second Institutional Act and by his own failure to head it off. He had been stung by the exchange in 1970 when human rights activist Ralph Della Cava blamed him for condoning torture in Recife in 1964. Yet he had emerged largely unscathed in Elio Gaspari's volume dealing with the 1964 coup. Lincoln confided to his son Hugh that this charge coming from a man he regarded as a friend had hurt: "I don't know what I could have done. I don't know what he expected me to do."

The issue would have to be addressed somehow in the memoir. He knew that more US documents had been declassified in 2004 and that these documents had been used by Brazilian scholars to cast new and damaging light on the United States and his own position. It was as if Gaspari were now opening a new front in the war of words over Brazil's military dictatorship. This would complicate his task in writing the memoir, for he could apparently not rest on the answers he had given in the Brazil book and the *Supplement.* He would have to revisit the whole damned subject of Brazil and also debate the Alliance once again. He would have to study the new Brazilian scholarship. He wrote to his friend Josh Billings that the next chapter was "still in its infancy." This was an overstatement: chapter 6 was stillborn. No progress at all was made. He had hit a wall.[18]

Unlike many scholars, whose greatest works remain unwritten or are forgotten in a corner of the brain, Gordon prided himself on his tenacity and on finishing what he started. This was part of his persona. He abided by the gospel of hard work and finishing any project undertaken, whether it was clearing a path in the woods to the site where his mother and father were buried, installing shelves in the house, a trek in Nepal, or completing a book. But the memoir was a tougher nut than he had anticipated, and now he had gotten to a point where he could not see his way forward. How could he deal with Brazil in simply a descriptive fashion and explain Hopkins without identifying the villains? He was in a good relationship with Hopkins now, and writing his version of events would only open up old wounds. Between the falls, the numb feet, the fatigue, and the memory lapses, the memoir, and indeed any kind of writing, became difficult if not impossible. He wrote no more Christmas letters or "Chers enfants" reports to the children. He continued to enjoy Brookings, as it "remains a most cordial host institution, providing well-based assessments of events and conditions in the public domain, both foreign and domestic."[19] In moments when his mind was clear, he continued to reflect on the problems facing him on the memoir. He would have to deal with the two "big disappointments" of his life: first, the failure to make the Alliance for Progress a success. Was it merely that "the accidents of Brazilian politics made it impossible to achieve that goal at that time"?[20] Given his view of history as the product of human agency, he knew that he could not pass over the Alliance's failure as simply due to "accidents of Brazilian politics."

And what of the second big disappointment, the Hopkins presidency? He had made his peace with Hopkins and been welcomed back into the fold as a distinguished ex-president. In a memoir he could not simply say that he had failed to achieve important educational advances because "we were caught up in the youthful reaction against the war in Vietnam and then in a phase of declining federal budget support."[21] He could not tell the story of his presidency without telling of the disloyal dean and naming names. But this would compromise the statesmanlike posture that he admired. He owed loyalty to the university that he had led. This public airing of dirty laundry would not fit his own sense of self or his ideal of public service.

The Year 2003: "For the Gordon Family It Has Been a Banner Year"

"However 2003 goes down in global history," Gordon wrote in his Christmas letter for that year, "for the Gordon family it has been a banner year."

The year saw a gathering of three generations of his family at Darkwater to celebrate his ninetieth birthday. The next day the Lincoln Gordon family "received an adequate cash offer for Darkwater, our family summer house since 1937," and the sale allowed for much-needed home renovations and improved the fortunes of the extended Gordon family. The children and grandchildren were "all in good health and in frequent communication with one another."[22] Amy had published a new novel, *The Gorillas of Gill Park,* which had a five-star rating from Amazon.com. The "grandchild generation looks more promising than ever," and there was the prospect of a fourth generation. Had Lincoln been inclined to biblical allusions, he might have said that his cup runneth over. That was his sentiment as he reached the age of ninety in relatively good health, in the bosom of his large family, and financially secure with the sale of Darkwater.

When Lincoln returned to Washington, there were more birthday celebrations at Brookings, the Atlantic Council, and the homes of friends. The Atlantic Council party was a luncheon at Washington's Metropolitan Club hosted by General Andy Goodpaster and attended by a group of his old friends who had served with him over the years. Brookings feted him as an elder statesman, and as he observed in the Christmas letter for the year: "Although somewhat cramped by the slump in endowment returns, and facing dozens of new competitors (many highly partisan or single-interest promoters, but some of high quality in narrowly specialized fields), Brookings remains the policy 'think tank' par excellence." There were enjoyable family visits to his home in Washington. His daughter Amy, Amy's husband, Tim, and her son Hugh "Hickory" Lawson and a classmate friend spent a week with him, and they visited Mount Vernon, attended a concert at the Kennedy Center, toured the Washington monuments by moonlight, and saw other Washington sights. They paid a visit to Peter Savage and his wife, Ina, in Baltimore. Peter had been a Fulbright Scholar during Lincoln's service as ambassador and was later a CIA officer in Brazil. He had married Ina, who had been very close to Allison as her embassy secretary. She was like a big sister to Amy. Peter warned them that Ina had been diagnosed with early-onset Alzheimer's disease and was having trouble with her memory. Ina did not recognize either Lincoln or Amy. Ina died just a few weeks before Lincoln wrote in his 2003 Christmas letter: "I hope never again to witness Alzheimer's at first hand."

19

Going Gently

How much longer?
—Lincoln Gordon, December 2009

Gordon remarked once that his idea of a proper death was to have a heart attack while playing tennis at a friend's home. He then considered for a moment and said that on second thought he would prefer it not to be a friend's court. That would be putting the friend to the trouble of notifying the coroner, and so on, so better that it be a stranger's court. He liked this quip, for he used it on other occasions and refined it further. In a 1993 letter he remarked, "My own preferred exit is via a fatal heart attack on a tennis court belonging to someone I dislike."[1] As usual he had a theory to support his thinking. Based on an article he had read in *Scientific American* on the "old" old, he believed that "once you get to 90, you are likely to be in good health until some rapidly acting terminal illness or event."[2] He might have had the example of his brother in mind. While he was dining out, Frank, at the age of eighty-eight, as his widow Dot told me in 2011, "just keeled over right in the middle of the lasagna."

Lincoln was not to get his wish for a quick exit, and his theory on aging did not prove to be quite accurate either. His decline over the final years was gradual, marked by memory loss, falls, numb feet, anxiety, confusion, and a general decline of mental and physical vitality. Despite the year 2003 being one of his happiest, it was also when his health problems became serious. He had a laminectomy (disc surgery), with complications in the form of numbness and tingling in the leg. The recovery from this surgery was slow, despite exercises that sometimes took up to half a day. He would jocosely invoke his ailments to account for his deteriorating tennis game, but this was galling to him because tennis to him was still a serious and highly competitive sport.

In early 2007 a combination of factors—falls, reports from his friends to family members of growing numbers of dementia episodes, and the opening of an attractive new assisted-living facility in his neighborhood—brought matters to a head. Lincoln was finally persuaded to sell his house and move to the new facility. The new assisted-living facility was in the same neighborhood, and this was an important factor in the family's thinking. Lincoln would be near his friends and have easy access to the nearby Sibley Hospital, to Brookings, and to Washington's cultural amenities. There were preliminary indications that space was available. In the spring of 2007 I had my last conversation with Lincoln. As I approached Brookings one day, I ran into him coming out of the building. I hadn't seen him in some time. He greeted me warmly, and we paused for a chat. He was in an ebullient mood, having just received a firm offer for his house. I had no knowledge of his health problems at the time. He looked to me as he had looked nearly twenty years before, when we were chased around Brazil by the paparazzi. He asked me to guess what he had paid for the house originally in 1971.

I said I didn't know.

He told me that he had paid in the high thirties and had gotten almost a million. I congratulated him and asked where he was going to live now. He explained that an assisted-living facility had opened in his neighborhood and emphasized its convenience and comfortable apartments. I told him that it sounded like a very sensible arrangement. I did not see him again for some months. Evidently not long after my encounter with him another Brookings colleague, Henry Aaron, ran into him under less happy circumstances. Henry said that he had been walking through the Brookings cafeteria when he noticed Lincoln sitting alone at a corner table. Henry remembered the crestfallen expression on his face. He had never seen him look like this. Gordon explained—and it was painful to hear—that he had just been turned down by the assisted-living home because he had failed a short-term memory test.

The buyers of the home accommodated the Gordon family by extending the date of occupancy. Gordon's son Hugh came up with an alternative that suited his father's needs well: the Collington Episcopal retirement community in Mitchelville, Maryland, about an hour's drive east of Washington, where many retired Foreign Service officers lived. Collington provided residents with a range of living arrangements and medical services. Lincoln moved into the Collington facility in the summer of 2007 and had an apartment of his own. He had a room for his files that would serve as an office. For some eighteen months he lived almost independently, taking his meals in the dining hall but not requiring skilled nursing care. He tried to resume work on his memoirs but could not sustain the effort. He made friends with Marge Crisler, an intelligent, forceful woman who was wheelchair bound and a lively and engaging companion. Lincoln liked to push her wheelchair not only because it made him feel useful but because he could lean on the chair and not have to use a walker. She for her part adopted a protective and motherly air toward him and remained his friend even after he could no longer carry on a conversation. His dementia gradually worsened, and he was moved to the intensive care wing.

Lincoln had his good days and his bad days. On a good day he told his daughter Amy that he had called an assembly to calm down the campus after a murder had occurred at the small college of which he was president. He reassured his colleagues by promising to get to the bottom of the matter (evidently a recall of the real episode during his Hopkins presidency when he talked a deranged colleague who was threatening to shoot another Hopkins faculty member into surrendering). On a bad day he hallucinated that he had gone to the boathouse at Lake Sunapee and discovered his father's body hanging from a rafter. His condition worsened over the course of 2009. In November the family was notified that he was nonresponsive, but this proved to be a false alarm. His condition remained grave, but he continued to eat, sit upright, and interact with the nurses and see family members. He was now three months past his ninety-sixth birthday.

On December 18, 2009, Kate Gordon drove to Collington from Washington to visit her grandfather. It was a bright, crisp winter day. Snow was in the forecast for later in the afternoon. She brought with her CDs of some of his favorite Mozart music, including one of the cello pieces he used to play. She had her laptop with the soundtrack from Walt Disney's *Fantasia* and the kaleidoscopic dancing shapes from the movie, which he liked to watch. He opened his eyes when Kate entered the room but did not speak. They listened to Mozart, and she read him an article on climate change from the *New Yorker* and gave him the latest family news. She reached her father, Bob, and his siblings on the cell phone and had each give him greetings. When the nurse brought his lunch, she went downstairs to get a bite in the cafeteria. In the shop she was pleased to find a CD of Mozart's *The Magic Flute.* He would like that. It was one of his favorites. She would be sure to give it the German name and pronounce it correctly. She smiled to herself, for Collington was really an excellent facility. The staff was extremely attentive. The care of her granddad was outstanding. She went back upstairs. He had scarcely touched his lunch. She told him that she had found a CD of *The Magic Flute.*

"Good," he said.

They listened to the Mozart, and she thought at one moment his fingers moved on the coverlet as if he were fingering his cello. He watched the *Fantasia* figures on the laptop and was absorbed by the dancing shapes. Then he dozed off to sleep. She pulled up his covers and sat down again. She had a feeling of exquisite well-being. The room was very comfortable for her grandpa. It was clean and warm and spacious, and she felt glad that he was in this nice place. She felt drowsy herself. The light had shifted in the room, and there was a beautiful yellow glow. She was aware of a cat's-paw patter of snow on the windowpanes. The light sprinkle of snow, the warmth of the room, and the sleeping figure of her grandfather added to her own drowsiness. She settled back in the chair, thinking that she perhaps would take a short nap herself. The snow had picked up slightly; now it was many cats brushing the windowpane, and there was the sound of an occasional gust and the moan of wind. She may have fallen asleep for a moment. Suddenly she was startled awake. Her grandfather was speaking, or was he? She glanced around to see if anyone else had entered the room. Had he actually spoken the words?

"How much longer?"

His eyes were open, and he was looking directly at her. She could not quite register his meaning. How much longer for what—the recording? Or did he mean to ask how much longer she was staying? She looked at the frail old man, scarcely recognizable as her grandfather. He seemed to be pleading for something. She thought she finally understood. She drew her chair close to the bed and took his hand. He could still return a slight pressure. She spoke in a low voice, but with a confidence that surprised her. She told him that it was all right for him to let go now. He had done his duty. He had cared for the family his whole life, and they were fine now. They were going to be all right, thanks to him. He did not have to hold on any longer. He could rest. It was time for him to think of himself and just rest. His eyes closed. He was sleeping.

She sat and listened to his breathing. The snow was pattering insistently on the window, and gusts rattled the windowpanes. The light had changed again. It was still beautiful but dimmer. It was the afternoon. She looked out the window. Snow had dusted the cars in the parking lot, and the bushes were frosted with a white topping. She had better get home, she thought, before the roads got bad. It was Friday, and there would be traffic. She lingered over her grandfather. He was breathing evenly but shallowly. She noticed again the comfortable warmth of the room as she heard the wind outside. She heard the snow against the window, and the wind whined. She knew she must leave but lingered at the bedside. As she left the room, Kate had the feeling she would not see her grandfather again. Lincoln Gordon died later that night.

Epilogue

There is no doubt that Lincoln Gordon enjoyed brilliant successes in his early career. The successful wartime mobilization depended on the recruitment of talented professionals from outside the government, and Gordon was one of those most in demand. He served throughout the war in increasingly important posts and at the war's end was one of the WPB's key decision-makers. In the postwar period he and his colleagues from the eastern universities and business establishment, along with a small circle of counterpart European professionals, made the Marshall Plan a reality, and they did so working largely out of the limelight while the political leaders got most of the publicity and the credit. Working in relative obscurity for the most part, this cadre of brilliant and mostly young officials—led by Gordon on the US side and Robert Marjolin on the European side—planned, organized, and implemented the policies that produced the spectacular postwar European economic recovery. The enormously important contributions of this supporting cast to the better-known "Wise Men" deserve to be recognized and remembered.

The young professionals were able to accomplish so much in part because of their personal qualities—their intellectual capacities, broad experience, and indefatigable work habits. These factors, however, were not sufficient and were assisted by favorable circumstances. The exceptional leaders whom this supporting cast served, Americans like Averell Harriman and Europeans like Jean Monnet, recognized and developed the talents of their deputies and gave them the scope and backing they needed. Harriman aided Gordon's personal development and fostered the success of the policies that Gordon and the others devised. Moreover, the success of the Marshall Plan depended on the fact that the goals sought were modest and attainable: the United States did not try to remake but merely to help rebuild Europe as it had existed before the war. It did not try to impose its own political and economic system on Europe nor to revolutionize the European social order. It sought rather to assist the participating nations in the Atlantic partnership to rebuild their economies and social systems as they saw fit. Gordon and Marjolin knew each other and each other's political leaders and institutions so well that they shared a common strategic vision, political outlook, and set of cultural values. The threat from the Soviet Union furthermore lent urgency to the policy deliberations and provided strong political backing to the recovery efforts and to the development of a Western security framework.

The circumstances, in short, were well suited for key staff men like Gordon, for the nation's political and military leaders, and for the shared vision of the circle of internationally minded American and European statesmen. The Atlantic community was made up of like-minded nations whose political elites recognized the need for joint action but respected their individual national identities and aspirations. America's political leaders had entered the "good war" united behind a burst of patriotism and were committed to winning the war even if many had only recently been converted to intervention. The coalition of Democrats and a group of liberal Republicans mostly from the Northeast, under the leadership of FDR, had taken the nation step by step "into the war and into the world" over the 1939 to 1941 period.[1] The immediate postwar period required statesmanship of the same order to keep America from slipping back into the kind of retrenchment that had followed World War I. The prewar coalition built by President Roosevelt had to be rebuilt by President Truman after the war to sustain the national unity needed for great purposes. The postwar challenges were daunting, and Truman drew on some of the same figures and some new statesmen first of all to rebuild and then to defend Western Europe. Gordon, though a Democrat and an ardent New Dealer, was primarily a technocrat in his wartime service and had worked easily with the Republican businessmen who largely staffed the WPB. After the war he worked with internationalist Republicans like Arthur Vandenberg and Paul Hoffman, who were key figures in the Marshall Plan and the NATO alliance. Foreign policy was bipartisan not only by tradition but by necessity because of divided government. The bipartisanship, though, was always fragile and was often honored in the breach.

In Gordon's later career the broad factors that had worked in his favor earlier were either missing or quite different in character. Gordon's brilliant early successes were in consequence followed by a number of set-backs and failures—partly attributable to his own miscalculations but also reflecting the larger failings of the nation and of American foreign policy. Clues to the later setbacks could be found in the earlier accomplishments, which were not as unequivocal or as unqualified as they appeared at the time. While a broad national consensus prevailed during World War II, intense political and bureaucratic conflicts bubbled beneath the surface and reemerged as the war drew to a close and the country prepared for peace. These conflicts became difficult to manage within the WPB as it shifted its focus to demobilization and as Congress debated how much military preparedness would be needed after the war. Gordon did not consider himself temperamentally suited for politics, and his doubts were reinforced as political conflict returned with a vengeance at the war's end. As an economist he had a marked distaste for logrolling and usually sought the technically correct solution to a problem. He was a kind of throwback to the "civic republicanism" of the Founding Fathers—that is, he believed that public affairs should largely be entrusted to a small circle of patriots who operated above party, faction, and narrow group interests. These disinterested statesmen would make decisions solely based on the national interest. When the nation's leaders (i.e., his political supervisors) set overall policy directions and the country was united behind those broad goals, Gordon and technicians like him could shine, and their analytical abilities could be fully exercised as they carried out orders. But as Gordon rose higher in the ranks, he faced more complex choices, and the political crosscurrents that swirled around him meant that he had to grapple with tougher issues. He was no longer merely an economic analyst but one of the political bosses himself. The issues he decided became less amenable to purely technical solutions. Toward the end of the war, with victory in sight, the political divisions within the WPB erupted into public conflict. Gordon, along with many others, was less sure-footed in the demobilization phase than he had been during mobilization. He favored small business over big business, distrusted the military brass's positions on a number of issues relating to demobilization, and generally sought a planned and more deliberative pace of loosening wartime controls than was popular with many politicians and business leaders. Therefore in late 1944 and in 1945 Gordon found himself on the losing side in many bureaucratic battles. He did not like to lose, and unlike experienced politician, he did not have a charitable attitude toward his opponents, whom he deemed to be pursuing parochial interests.

His distaste for political infighting and opportunistic compromise kept him from seeking higher office or pursuing an overt political role. As he told John Lord O'Brian in 1943, he did not think he was cut out for politics. After the war he was offered the position of assistant secretary in the Department of the Interior, and he could have stayed on in other high-level capacities, but he did not relish the political atmosphere in which he would have had to work. As a confirmed New Dealer who believed that government had a positive role to play in a free market economy, he was frustrated by the postwar reaction against government and against the expanded welfare state sought by FDR's New Deal and Truman's Fair Deal. When the resurgent Republicans campaigned on the slogan of "Had enough?" (referring to wartime controls and big government) and appeared likely to win big in the 1946 congressional elections, Gordon opted to return to Harvard.

The attraction of teaching, however, proved to be short-lived. He returned to government due to the crisis in Europe and the Truman administration's determination not to repeat the mistake made after World War I of abandoning international responsibilities. The challenge of rebuilding the devastated economies of Western Europe and fighting communism brought him back into public service. Once again a national emergency provided the right circumstances for his talents. His role in designing the Marshall Plan repeated and surpassed his wartime achievements. In putting the organizational design into the Marshall Plan, he was largely sheltered from having to deal directly with Congress. After another brief return to teaching, he reentered public service to help implement the Marshall Plan as a key aide to Averell Harriman in Paris and then followed Harriman back to the White House to work on NATO and the Korean War mobilization. His postwar service as wise man to America's "Wise Men" in the creation of the new world order built around American leadership was followed by more routine duties as economics counselor in the US embassy in London. This phase of his public career was less rewarding because he did not have a great figure like Harriman or Marshall to work for and because he was removed from the center of policy-making. The more routine duties of the London office and his role as manager of a large staff were not his cup of tea, and this time (in 1955) he was happy to leave government and return to Harvard and teaching duties.

But he could not resist the excitement of the New Frontier and returned to public service after drafting the economic strategy of the Alliance for Progress, serving as President Kennedy's chief adviser on Latin America and then as US ambassador to Brazil. This marked a new stage in his public service. The going became more difficult because he was thrust into the role of leader himself, rather than key adviser to a powerful political figure, and because he had to operate outside the more familiar Atlantic context that had been the focus of his entire professional life. It proved difficult for Gordon to repeat his early successes for reasons relating to his own misjudgments, the grandiose ambitions of the Kennedy administration, and the changed circumstances of US foreign policy. Gordon was now functioning as a close policy adviser to President Kennedy while serving as a country ambassador, an unusual role made possible by Kennedy's freewheeling style, his distrust of bureaucratic channels, and his confidence in Gordon. The brilliant staffer to Harriman was thus now playing a new role, a role resembling that of Harriman vis-à-vis President Truman. There was a critical difference. Whereas Truman and his close advisers had fairly clear ideas of what they wanted to accomplish in Europe and in their relations with the Soviet Union, Kennedy and his close advisers, including Gordon, did not have clear ideas of what they wanted to accomplish in Latin America. The ideas they did have were contradictory, confused, and unsuited for Latin America. The Kennedy team wanted to replay the Marshall Plan in an unfamiliar context. Meanwhile the US government had grown larger, more complex, and more bureaucratized—and less amenable to the kind of personalized decision-making that had marked FDR's leadership during World War II. Truman's refusal to be pinned down by the NSC machinery imposed on him by the Republicans in Congress after the war further inclined Kennedy, like most modern Democratic presidents, to favor looser White House operations built around the president himself rather than a powerful chief of staff. Truman had, however, gradually adopted more formality in how he ran his White House and later in his presidency had attended NSC meetings more regularly. Eisenhower had run a more orderly, military style of White House and delegated authority to his cabinet officials. Kennedy reacted against Ike's hierarchical, military style in favor of a decentralized team of aides and loyalists with close personal ties to him. The rise of television and the mass media had opened up politics and made America's political system more permeable to outside pressures and more subject to volatile swings in public opinion, even as large bureaucracies with powerful constituencies were proving to be increasingly difficult to manage and control. The Kennedy style was based on personal charisma and the cultivation of popular appeal and celebrity, and JFK, with journalistic experience himself, became the first modern president to cultivate reporters and press contacts as a routine feature of his governance style.

The Alliance for Progress, in whose creation Gordon played a key role, was in part a public relations initiative, an effort to dramatize JFK's commitment to bold action, which was intended to distinguish his approach to Latin American policy from that of his Republican predecessor. But the Alliance conception was flawed from the start because it rested on a misleading analogy with the Marshall Plan and with the Cold War strategy of containing communism. Europe's very different economic, political, and social circumstances, and the Marshall Plan's carefully circumscribed policy objectives, contrasted with the sweeping social and economic transformation sought by the Alliance for Progress. JFK's New Frontiersmen wanted to forge bold new approaches in policy that would mark a departure from what they saw as Eisenhower's caution and stick-in-the-mud conservatism.

As US ambassador to Brazil, Gordon quickly recognized the flawed conception of the Alliance but lacked the political clout and the administrative skills to bring about a midcourse correction in US policy toward Latin America. He struggled but failed to make the Alliance for Progress successful in practice. He had more success in persuading the Kennedy and then the Johnson administration to take a hardline stance against the demagogic government of Brazilian president Joao Goulart. But this influence came at the expense of the more cautious policies advocated by the State Department and career Foreign Service officers.

Gordon had chosen the ambassadorial post in part to escape the political pressures of the Washington scene. He thought that being in the field in a major Latin American country would give him broad influence in shaping US policy. His direct relationship with President Kennedy and with the White House staff meant that he at times skirted the State Department and escaped departmental supervision. If he managed to escape some of the usual Washington bureaucratic and political pressures, however, Gordon discovered that he had jumped from the frying pan into the fire, having to deal with the boisterous politicians, populist politics, and rising nationalism of Brazil. In the end he could not escape political pressures at home and could not alter the Brazilian political climate, which constrained what the United States could accomplish in the country. He tried to counter Brazilian radicals with tactics borrowed from the Marshall Plan playbook for dealing with communist subversion in Italy and France. The Cold War tactics misfired in Brazil and strengthened the radicals. In the end the US influence on domestic Brazilian political developments was limited. Nonetheless, the US government and Gordon personally were criticized for interfering in domestic affairs and blamed for Brazilian military rule. After the 1964 military coup, the United States was widely castigated both at home and in Brazil for the demise of that country's civilian rule and the military's excesses. Brazil became a lightning rod for the rise of the "human rights" movement as a force in US foreign policy. The human rights movement contributed to the growing split in the foreign policy establishment initially triggered by the US engagement in Vietnam. Gordon persuaded President Johnson to go all out in support of the "moderates" in the Brazilian military but resisted getting Brazil into Vietnam as a US ally. But the moderate military rulers and their technocratic ministers did not build any coalition with Brazil's civilian politicians or seek a base of public support in the country and were consequently soon overthrown by more hardline military factions. The military rule thereupon became increasingly repressive. To Gordon's astonishment and to that of most civilian politicians in the country—who had accepted the military's initial assurances that civilian rule would be restored soon—the military rule lasted twenty-one years. The worst excesses of military rule came after Gordon had left the country, but he continued to be dogged by critics who blamed him for everything that had gone wrong.

LBJ recalled Gordon from Brazil in 1966 to be assistant secretary of state for Latin American affairs. He labored with limited success to breathe new life into the Alliance for Progress and was frustrated by the administration's growing preoccupation with Vietnam. He tried to transfer control of the Canal Zone to Panama but could not bring the effort to fruition during his time as assistant secretary (and a military coup in Panama not long after he left office shelved the project for a decade). Gordon did assist in restoring civilian rule in the Dominican Republic and eliminating the vestiges of the US military intervention there. His old depression returned as Vietnam pushed Latin American concerns to the back of the administration's policy agenda. Gordon sought but could not find a ready exit from the Johnson administration. The offer of the presidency of Johns Hopkins University unexpectedly brought him the opportunity to leave government on favorable terms.

But the setbacks with Brazil and the Alliance for Progress were followed by an even more painful period as president of Johns Hopkins. The changes that were undermining the foreign policy establishment were also producing wrenching changes in American higher education. His own leadership shortcomings and lack of experience in academic administration were fully exposed in the tumultuous changes sweeping through the nation's colleges and universities. He discovered how difficult it was to operate without a strong supporting staff and in crisis circumstances where there was no time for on-the-job learning. He was ousted in a coup engineered by disgruntled faculty members and a disloyal dean. The arc of Gordon's life seemed almost to follow the script of the typical Hollywood biography: brilliant early success followed by humiliating failure and a period in the wilderness. There was, however, to be no miraculous comeback and return to public favor with a new hit performance. The remainder of his life was spent largely outside the public spotlight. At the same time he could never quite escape his critics and continued to be dogged by charges that he was guilty of condoning human rights abuses and promoting military rule in Brazil.

Yet Gordon achieved a quiet redemption in the nearly four decades remaining in his life through an outpouring of scholarly books and articles, service on the boards of numerous nonprofit and government organizations, and behind-the-scenes support for policy causes that mattered to him. He returned to the roles that were second nature and at which he had excelled earlier: as an adviser to others, as a thinker and writer, as a valued colleague. He was an indefatigable member of numerous boards and excelled in the role of someone who could see both the forest and the trees and synthesize partial perspectives into a coherent whole. He combined, as Lyndon Johnson said of him, pragmatism with idealism. These qualities were much in demand in the burgeoning new world of Washington think tanks and policy analysts. Liberated from the day-to-day responsibilities of the line manager, he was busy and productive again. Like the precocious young boy who had turned the pages of the sheet music for his mother, Lincoln as an elder statesman was back in the comfortable role of adviser to others, harmonizing different kinds of specialized expertise into coherent policy ideas for those who performed on the political stage.

Perhaps more important, he took an increasingly active role in the lives of his children and grandchildren and enjoyed the quiet satisfactions of family life. He regretted not having spent more time with his children when they were young and became a devoted and doting grandfather. Some of his best scholarship was produced as he continued to be an active researcher in his seventies and eighties. He remained as busy as ever—as he struck his classmates at the Fieldston School. He even displayed some late-blooming political skills when he helped to rescue the Carter administration's Panama Canal treaties by persuading friends on the Committee on the Present Danger not to oppose Senate ratification.

His last hurrah in public service came at the end of the Carter administration, when Carter's CIA director named him to a "committee of wise men" at the agency. His tenure carried into the Reagan administration, and he enjoyed some initial success in shaping a national intelligence estimate on Russia. But his outspokenness incurred the ire of Reagan's CIA director Bill Casey, who froze Gordon out of important policy decisions. A planning or advisory group can only be successful if the decision-maker wants to be advised. The US government of the 1980s had become more deadlocked, and policy-makers sought out the advice they wanted to hear.

The problem, it seemed to Gordon, had deep roots. When he had started teaching Harvard students in the 1930s, his job was to fill the minds of a rather passive and ill-informed student body with knowledge in the place of ignorance. Students then, like Americans generally, were inclined to listen respectfully to those in authority and to accept the views of political leaders if the leaders made a sincere and reasoned appeal for support. There were, to be sure, many Republicans in the Harvard student body and faculty then who disliked FDR and the New Deal intensely. Yet leaders could still generally bridge differences and cooperate on a course of action. They could deliberate among themselves, listen to knowledgeable experts, and persuade the public, especially on the grave foreign policy and security problems facing the nation. Something had happened, though, with Vietnam, the student disturbances, and the rise of ideological politics. America had become a more polarized nation. Both the public and political leaders were deeply divided. Old friends and colleagues like Eugene Rostow and Paul Nitze, both Democrats, had publicly condemned Carter's defense policies and teamed up with Republicans. The CIA had Team A and Team B to discern Soviet intentions, suggesting a difference in worldviews even among the experts. Ideology divided everybody into rival camps, not like it had during World War II, with the Marshall Plan, and with NATO. Some of this was nostalgia, he knew, but there was no doubting the reality of his current impressions. Gordon had known Bill Casey slightly from his previous government service and had had respectful dealings with him, but there was no such contact between them now. Casey regarded him as belonging to a different and implacably hostile ideological camp. Gordon did not seek a second term as a CIA wise man because he knew that Casey would not reappoint him, and he had no desire to serve further.

The unselfconscious patriotism that had united a relatively small group of elite policy-makers and their advisers at one time and earned them a reputation for being free of narrow partisan or group interests seemed like a distant memory to Gordon now, a thing of the past. The Vietnam War had splintered the foreign policy establishment. The New Deal consensus that favored an activist government and that had been largely accepted by the Republican administrations of Eisenhower, Nixon, and Ford had come under serious challenge from an invigorated conservative movement. The tone of politics and the context of public service were altered for the worse. Gordon once described his ideal public servant, General George Marshall, as a man who "belonged to a different century." Now Gordon himself felt like a man from a previous century, and indeed his long life stretched into the twenty-first century.

His final active years, spent at the Brookings Institution, which seemed to him a bastion of civility and the old bipartisan tradition, retraced the trajectory of his earlier career. He first focused on Europe. His 1987 book *Eroding Empire* dealt with the problems of Europe, but this time from the perspective of Soviet weakness and an unraveling Soviet empire. The end of the communist threat, in Gordon's view, vindicated US Cold War foreign policy, though he was ambivalent about the respective importance of US military strength in this regard as against the West's diplomatic restraint and latent Soviet weakness. He migrated in his thinking from his old colleague Paul Nitze's stress on military strength and the "equilibrium of forces" toward George Kennan's belief in political containment and the eventual implosion of the Soviet system.

The difficulty of deciding which Cold War policy camp he belonged to—combined with the conviction that the main direction of European policy had been settled—had led him in the late 1950s to take up the challenge of the Third World's economic and political development. The collapse of communism, whether inspired by the West or by internal forces, had become the final chapter in the story of US policy toward Europe. So Gordon again shifted his intellectual focus to Brazil and to the puzzle of Third World development. He had to understand why Brazil had followed a pattern of development different from that of Europe and North America and why his vision of the Alliance for Progress had failed.

For more than a decade he labored to produce his final work of scholarship, *Brazil's Second Chance*, in 2001. This was a masterly survey of the social, political, and economic history of contemporary Brazil that showed how that nation had finally joined the ranks of the industrialized economies. He accompanied this study two years later with a short volume explaining and defending the US (and his own) role in the Brazilian military coup in 1964. At age eighty-nine he made a promotional book tour to Brazil that drew wide publicity in the press and on TV. The trip stirred old controversies because a secret and previously unknown tape of a 1962 conversation between Ambassador Gordon and President Kennedy dealing with Brazil had been coincidentally published in the United States shortly before Gordon's arrival in Brazil. The secret tape, whose publication revealed for the first time the existence of President Kennedy's taping system, showed Kennedy aide Richard Goodwin favoring a military coup in Brazil, Ambassador Gordon recommending a clandestine CIA program to influence Brazilian state elections, and President Kennedy objecting only to the cost of the proposed effort to influence the elections. Those who believed that the United States was responsible for the 1964 military coup found vindication in the tape's revelation, and Gordon, who had not been aware of the taping system, found himself on the defensive with the Brazilian media.

In his nineties, Gordon set out to write his memoirs, as Dean Acheson, George Kennan, Bernard Baruch, Vernon Walters, Richard Bissell, and others among his friends and acquaintances had done, but he undertook the task too late. His mental powers were slipping, and he did not relish the usual purposes of a memoir. By his own lights he should not indulge in self-promotion or -justification. He did not admire the tell-all memoir or aspire to write one. His memoir, which was never finished, contained warm recollections of his childhood years, his special bond with his mother, and his college hijinks and vignettes of his public service in World War II, the Marshall Plan, and NATO. He did not go deeply into his own motives and the complexities of events. He stopped before he reached the difficult years of Brazil, the State Department, and Johns Hopkins. He evidently had no taste for and could not relive these painful experiences. In any case, he had said most of what he wanted to say in his books, speeches, and articles since he stepped back from public service.

In his final years his thoughts turned away from the depressing contemporary scene to the America he loved and knew best: the New York City of his youth, Lake Sunapee in New Hampshire, the intellectual and cultural vitality of Harvard, the New Deal era, the patriotism of World War II, and the selfless effort to rebuild Europe and fashion a new world order based on US leadership. In his mind's eye America was always the land of opportunity, the unique country that had enabled an immigrant family like his own to realize the American Dream. It seemed to him that his life had not been a failure even though, as for most public men, his failings were remembered more than his achievements. He believed that despite its disappointments, his life had had integrity. He had been steadfast in his belief in reason applied to public affairs and in America's special mission in the world. He had provided for his family and served his country faithfully. He had not flinched or wavered in the face of adversity. He was a totally secular man and never invoked scripture, but something in his life—his dutifulness, his steadfastness, and his work ethic—called to mind Luke 9:62: "And Jesus said unto him, 'No man, having put his hand to the plough, and looking back, is fit for the kingdom of God.'"

Acknowledgments

I was fortunate to have a subject who was unusually fastidious in keeping notes, reports, diplomatic cables, copies of correspondence, a diary, copies of his published and unpublished writings, past employment records, and a host of other materials. Because I knew him as a Brookings colleague (and we had many mutual friends), I had some advantages as a biographer. Sometimes of course the written record is surprising, and you learn things through a lengthy immersion with the documents that you did not anticipate. What you think you know about someone can be wrong, and at the very least studying the paper trail of a life and reflecting on its critical turning points can confirm, deepen, and enrich what you knew or suspected at the beginning. Besides his private papers, Lincoln Gordon also left an array of published books and articles, many growing out of aspects of his career and commenting on historical events that he had seen up close. Like the pragmatist and activist he was, he did not write philosophical treatises but responses to particular circumstances and events. Yet they do reflect a consistent worldview: he was a rationalist, an optimist, a believer in progress and science, a quintessential American. But all of this, however, was tempered by the realism that comes from the bumps and bruises of a high-profile public career.

While this is not an "official" biography, I could not have done it without the encouragement, support, and generous assistance of Lincoln Gordon's family. The family gave me access to Gordon's voluminous private papers and copies of his correspondence, memorabilia, photos, and scholarly writings and helped me in so many ways that I can hardly enumerate them all. I am especially grateful to Hugh Gordon and Amy Gordon for running interference for me with the JFK Presidential Library, reading drafts of the chapters dealing with the family's history, translating documents from Portuguese, and exchanging dozens of emails on various aspects of their father's career. At the library in particular Hugh Gordon and Amy Gordon helped me gain access to the seventy-three boxes of their father's papers. The JFK Library had decided that none of Gordon's extensive papers, most of them deposited in 1972, could be accessed directly by scholars until the papers as a whole had been "processed." But the library's curators dutifully made available to the Gordon family copies of any documents I requested, with the knowledge that the materials would be transmitted to me. In addition to Hugh and Amy, I had the pleasure of meeting and talking with all of Lincoln's children and a number of other family members, notably Bob Gordon and Ann Gordon. Lincoln's grandchildren also participated, and I can see why he liked them so much. Kate Gordon, Emily Gordon, and Laura Dickinson shared their remembrances of their grandfather with me, and Kate Gordon shared her memories of his last day and a contemporary email she sent to family members, which I relied on in chapter 19. George Gordon discovered his grandfather's diary on a visit with his father and aunt to the JFK Presidential Library. Gino Segre provided valuable technical assistance with the photographs that the family kindly allowed me to use in the book. The Frank Gordon family—Frank's widow, Dot, and her three daughters and their husbands—were gracious hosts during a Gordon family reunion at Lake Sunapee in August 2011 and shared many memories with me. Other members of the extended Gordon family shared stories as well. It was a great pleasure to get to know all of the Gordons, and my pleasant association with the family helped lighten the labor of the project. I hope that the family will feel that I have done him justice in these pages. I hope also that the uncommon but little-known colleagues who served with him and their families will feel that their voices have been heard along with his. I think he would have wanted it that way.

The staff of the JFK Library was most cordial to Lincoln Gordon when he was working on his memoirs there. He very much enjoyed his visits to the library, which were a source of satisfaction in the final period of his life. The draft chapters of his unpublished memoir were of great value to me in explaining his early life and his career up to the age of forty (roughly until his initial participation in the Alliance for Progress). The direct quotes and dialogue that I sprinkle throughout the book come from his draft memoir, as well as from four oral history interviews and other interviews he granted scholars and journalists. In a few instances I slightly edited the dialogue for clarity.

On nearly every facet of Gordon's public service there is a vast body of scholarly literature that provides the context and setting for the story I tell in this book. A small army of highly competent and dedicated scholars continues to produce important new contributions on America's entry into World War II, Lend-Lease, wartime mobilization and administration, the early UN's atomic energy policy disputes, the Marshall Plan, European economic integration, the European Payments Union, NATO, the Alliance for Progress, and many other important topics of the Cold War era. Many of Gordon's colleagues told their own stories in memoirs, and there are excellent biographies of most of the prominent postwar figures. I relied heavily on this body of work and have tried to indicate my specific indebtedness in the footnotes.

Gordon's service in Brazil required reference to Portuguese sources. Hugh Gordon kindly translated a number of sources for me and provided an excellent translation of Caros Fico's 2008 book on Brother Sam and the Brazilian military governments during his father's tenure as ambassador (except for the final chapter, which Rui Neiva translated). Rui Neiva, then a PhD candidate at the School of Public Policy at George Mason University, translated the final chapter of Fico's book, acted as research assistant, and assisted me with other Portuguese sources, including the memoirs of Brazilian politicians, the speeches of Goulart and others, and official government documents (now available in growing numbers on the Internet).

No one who undertakes a biography or other research today can fail to make extensive use of—and be amazed by—what is available on the Web. At one's fingertips is a vast trove of materials that makes the job of writing about the past both easier and harder. I have tried to indicate in the footnotes the online sources that I found useful and to point the reader toward convenient sources. Email likewise gives one access to scholars across the country and abroad who are helpful in numerous ways, from pointing out sources to offering their own interpretations of events. While the Web makes the historian's and the biographer's job easier, it also complicates the task. One is overwhelmed by the mass of what is available and with the tempting opportunities to chase down side stories. It is easy to be diverted from one's main focus. I found myself at times spending whole mornings or afternoons looking at the intriguing personalities who drifted in and out of Gordon's life and public service. On the theory that a biography is like a statue, the author has to chip away at a large block of material to get down to the essence of the story.

Since I had never written a biography before this effort, I sought advice from friends. Jean Edward Smith, who has written distinguished biographies of Ike, FDR, Grant, and others, offered this excellent advice: "Proceed chronologically." Sanford Lakoff wisely counseled me to pay attention to the housekeeping, logistics, note-keeping, and scholarly apparatus of the project. Allan Silver supplied the metaphor of the statue and urged me to focus on the public life of my subject and the larger themes in my narrative, as well as supplying important references and incisive questions throughout.

Brandon Ledford and Kunal Kumar, students from George Mason University, provided valuable research assistance at various stages, along with Rui Neiva. Robert Lapeyruse, a kind volunteer from the Columbia Lighthouse for the Blind and a friend, read for me and helped me navigate through the papers at the Harriman Collection in the Library of Congress and the National Archives. His generous spirit and keen mind were greatly appreciated. Marjorie Crow, who has worked with me for more than thirty years, copyedited the manuscript with her usual care and skill. Ronald Goldfarb of Ronald Goldfarb Associates represented me ably and provided useful comments on several chapters. His associate Gerrie Sturman helped me to professionalize the presentation of the manuscript. Brett Geranan, my computer tutor, was at hand to assist with the endless computer problems.

Margery Thompson of the Association of Diplomatic Studies and Training (ADST) encouraged me when my spirits flagged and secured detailed and useful reviews of the manuscript from two anonymous reviewers. I thank her and ADST for including the book in their diplomatic studies series and her reviewers for their useful comments on the draft manuscript.

Ambassador Luigi Einaudi read an early draft of the chapter on the Alliance for Progress and offered shrewd advice on the book, as well as sharing his profound knowledge of Latin America with me. Fred Jasperson of the Institute of International Finance tutored me on the financial and economic issues of Brazil and of Latin America. Joseph A. Page of the Georgetown University Law School shared his experiences with Brazil's military government and his deep knowledge of Brazil. Peter Savage provided useful insights from his long experience with Brazil and many details about Lincoln Gordon's ambassadorship.

For the Johns Hopkins events, I am indebted to Ross Jones, Richard Macksey, Orest Ranum, Ellery Woodworth, Robert C. Bowie, Déjà Owen, Mrs. Steven Muller, Mame Warren, Hopkins archivist James Simpert, and Richard Immerman of Temple University, coauthor of the Milton Eisenhower biography.

Sanford A. Lakoff, professor emeritus at the University of California at La Jolla, went beyond the call of duty and friendship in providing guidance on this project. He read the entire manuscript twice, offered an invaluable critique in both large and small matters, and advised me on dealing with publishers. Lawrence S. Kaplan of Georgetown University, a distinguished NATO historian, read the manuscript closely and provided many valuable comments. Allan Silver, professor emeritus of sociology at Columbia University, read various parts of the manuscript and the research plan and advised me at critical stages in the writing. I am grateful for his advice and his friendship.

My colleagues at Brookings and the Cosmos Club shared many stories and remembrances of Lincoln with me, as did many other friends and associates who knew him and worked with him at one stage of another of his career.

Stephen Wrinn, director of the University Press of Kentucky, was unfailingly supportive, and it was a pleasure to deal with him and his colleagues Allison Webster, Iris Law, and Mack McCormick. The press's anonymous reviewers contributed valuable comments. Carol Sickman-Garner skillfully copyedited the penultimate version of the book and improved the clarity of my presentation.

My wife, Elise, put up with my compulsiveness and eccentricities, encouraged me, corrected many errors, deciphered texts, offered large observations, and assisted in myriad other ways even as she was busy with her own heavy workload. I cannot thank her enough. I am grateful to everyone mentioned here and the many others who helped to clarify my thinking and save me from mistakes but must of course absolve them of responsibility for any remaining errors and shortcomings. I am reasonably sure that no one will dispute the assertion that I bear full responsibility for any infelicities of style, errors of fact, or failures of imagination.

Appendix A

Lincoln Gordon's Family Tree

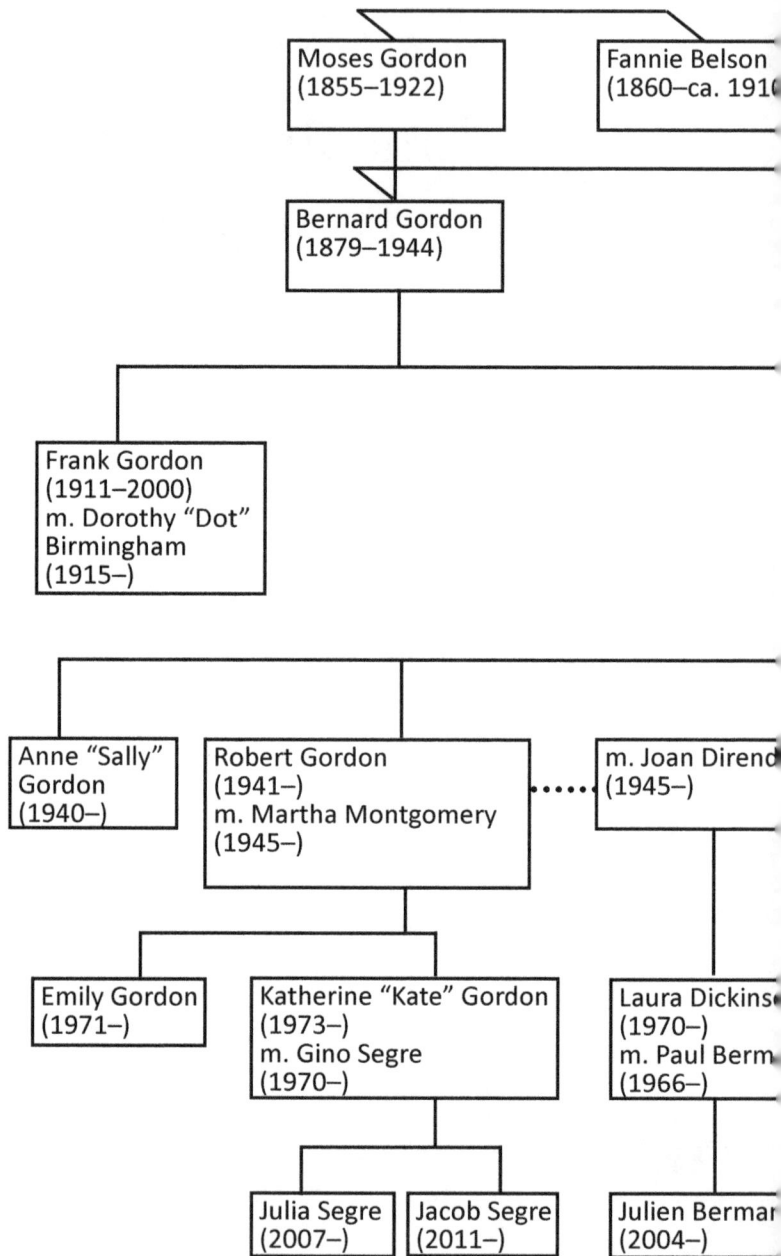

Moses Gordon
(1855–1922)

Fannie Belson
(1860–ca. 191[0]

Bernard Gordon
(1879–1944)

Frank Gordon
(1911–2000)
m. Dorothy "Dot"
Birmingham
(1915–)

Anne "Sally"
Gordon
(1940–)

Robert Gordon
(1941–)
m. Martha Montgomery
(1945–)

m. Joan Dirend[
(1945–)

Emily Gordon
(1971–)

Katherine "Kate" Gordon
(1973–)
m. Gino Segre
(1970–)

Laura Dickins[
(1970–)
m. Paul Berm[
(1966–)

Julia Segre
(2007–)

Jacob Segre
(2011–)

Julien Berma[
(2004–)

Jacob Schwartzmann — Tilley Spiewack

o Lerner
859–1926)

Rose Schwartzmann
(1860–1907)

rothy "Ooma" Lerner
889–1970)

braham Lincoln "Linc" Gordon
913–2009)
. Elizabeth Allison Wright
909–1987)

ugh Gordon
945–)
. Shiela "Brid-
t" Murnaghan
951–)

Amy Gordon
(1949–)
m. Richard Lawson
(1942–)

· · · · · · ·

m. Tim
Young
(1946–)

eorge
ordon
991–)

Jane
Gordon
(1993–)

Nick Lawson
(1983–)

Hugh "Hickory" Lawson
(1987–)

Source: The information here was gathered from "Lincoln Gordon, 1913–2009: Collected Memories," a pamphlet prepared for Lincoln Gordon's Cosmos Club Memorial Service, Washington, DC, March 2010, by Hugh B. Gordon, with the assistance of Robert W. Gordon, Amy Gordon, and Anne Gordon (mimeograph).

Appendix B

Exchange of Letters with President Johnson on Departure as Assistant Secretary of State

January 19, 1967

Dear Mr. President:

The purpose of this letter is to submit to you my resignation as Assistant Secretary of State for Inter-American affairs and United States Coordinator for the Alliance for Progress, effective June 30, 1967. As you know, the reason for this action is to permit me to accept the position of President of The Johns Hopkins University.

With this move, I shall have completed some six years of full-time service in the field of inter-American affairs under the direction of President Kennedy and yourself, first in the formulation of the Alliance for Progress, then as United States Ambassador to Brazil, and now in my present post. During these years, cooperation among the governments and peoples of this Hemisphere has taken on a major new dimension. Without weakening the long-standing tradition of common action in matters of international policy and mutual security, our nations have moved together to accelerate economic and social progress under free institutions. Under your leadership, the United States has made clear its firm dedication to this cause and is giving vigor and continuity to these cooperative efforts.

Today the Alliance for Progress is a vital and growing enterprise, whose principles are at the core of governmental action programs throughout Latin America. The CIAP and the Inter-American Development Bank are well-established institutions, growing steadily in effectiveness. With the amendment to its basic Charter worked out last year, the Organization of American States will become a more powerful instrument of inter-governmental cooperation. I am confident that the forthcoming Inter-American Meeting of Presidents will consolidate substantial progress of recent years and give new impetus to the needed major advancements in the pace of economic growth, in the broadening of social justice, and in closer integration among the nations of the Hemisphere. As this movement goes forward, we can see the growing confidence of Latin America in its capacity to create prosperity in freedom, and to play that full and positive part in world leadership for which its talented peoples and great resources are so well suited.

It has been a great privilege for me to participate at the center of these events. It has been a special privilege and pleasure to work directly with you on them, to enjoy your unflagging support, and to have the certain knowledge of your deep personal interest in the freedom and welfare of Latin America and in the strengthening of inter-American relations on the basis of true mutual respect and partnership. Only those who have worked closely with you on these matters can know the time and energy you have devoted to pressing forward the active collaboration of the United States in support of Latin America's economic and social progress. These purposes have been fully shared by my old and good friend Secretary Dean Rusk.

My willingness to leave the Department of State at this time is due only to the opportunities for continued service to the national interest afforded by the Presidency of The Johns Hopkins University which for ninety years has distinguished itself for pioneering innovations in higher education and for major contributions to the advancement of knowledge and to the shaping of constructive national and international policies. A valued part of The Johns Hopkins tradition is the advisory services of its Officers and Faculties in many fields of national policy-making, a tradition which I shall certainly expect to maintain.

With gratitude, affection, and esteem, I am
Sincerely yours,
/s/ Lincoln Gordon

The President
The White House
Washington

FOR RELEASE NOT BEFORE 4:00 P.M.
Thursday, January 19, 1967
Office of the White House Press Secretary

THE WHITE HOUSE
EXCHANGE OF LETTERS BETWEEN THE PRESIDENT
AND THE HONORABLE LINCOLN GORDON, ASSISTANT
SECRETARY OF STATE

Dear Linc:
I accept with real regret your letter of resignation of January 19, 1967.
Given the distinguished position you will occupy from July 1, as I told
you when we talked, I have no choice. Our great educational institutions
are fundamental to the progress of our society and play a major role of
lifting the level of education on the world scene. They require the kind
of leadership you will, I am sure, provide.
    I congratulate both you and The Johns Hopkins University.
    You have brought to Latin American affairs in the last six years a
rare combination of experience and scholarship, idealism and practical
judgment. Your career in public service illustrates the change through
which we have passed in recent years: from a primary focus on Europe
to a balanced global policy. You made a major contribution after the war
to European reconstruction, but then turned to the great adventure of
Latin American economic and social development.
    You helped formulate and bring to life the Alliance for Progress; at
a critical time you served with great distinction as our Ambassador to
Brazil; in the past year you have helped lead the Alliance for Progress to
a point where it is no longer a concept or a hope, but a working reality.

In the weeks and months ahead we shall be working together to increase the momentum of the Alliance and, especially, to make the Inter-American Meeting of Presidents the greatest possible success.

After you have assumed your new post, I shall be counting on you from time to time to serve your country in an advisory capacity. You will leave your post in Washington with the thanks and gratitude of all of us.

Mrs. Johnson joins me in very best wishes to Allison as well as to yourself.

Sincerely,
/s/ Lyndon B. Johnson

Honorable Lincoln Gordon
Assistant Secretary of State
Department of State
Washington, D.C.

Appendix C

Confidential Report to the President on Vietnam Policy

March 24, 1968

NOTE ON POLICY IN VIETNAM

The writer of this note has no pretensions to expertness on Southeast Asia. He has never publicly expressed an opinion on our policy in Vietnam. He has no political or personal axes to grind. He has no access to secret sources of information. He is neither hawk nor dove.

<u>Premises:</u>

1. If responsible authorities in the United States had been able to foresee the present situation, different decisions would have been made in 1954, 1962, and 1965. The scale of the present commitment in men and money and the current level of casualties are disproportionately high in relation to the importance of South Vietnam as such. With different U.S. policies, South Vietnam and Laos would have come under Ho Chi Minh's control. This would have been unfortunate, but not catastrophic for free Asia, assuming that reinforcing measures were taken in Thailand, Burma, Malaya, Singapore, Pakistan, and India. Dominoes may fall or not, depending on their internal specific gravity and their external support.
2. The effect of the large U.S. commitment, especially since 1965, has

been to increase the danger of falling dominoes. An overt or disguised U.S. defeat would now entail much greater risk of all Communist control of all Southeast and South Asia than would the quiet loss of South Vietnam in 1955.

3. Most current "dove" proposals for deescalation and negotiation, including the "enclave concept," amount to more or less disguised surrender (whatever their proponents may think). This would not be the case of a shift from "search and destroy" emphasis to "clear and hold," or to a limitation of bombing or to a limited area north of the DMZ.

4. Under present battlefield and internal U.S. political conditions, it would be absurd to expect North Vietnam to enter serious negotiations for anything but rapid absorption of the South on their terms.

Critical Problem:

1. The critical problem today, as at all times since 1954, is whether there exists or can be developed sufficient internal national cohesion in South Vietnam to make its defense meaningful. Diem gave it that appearance for a while, but this proved illusory. The new constitutional arrangements provide some protective coloration, but there is no convincing evidence of a solid political or social structure underneath. Without it, even an outright military surrender by North Vietnam would not promise a viable free South.

2. The only reliable test of this capacity is greater responsibility for South Vietnam for providing military and administrative self-help. The time for that test is sooner rather than later.

Conclusions for Policy:

1. We should increase our bargaining power with the South Vietnam regime by making it credible that our solidarity with them depends on their performance. Elements in that performance include a larger military manpower effort, a larger *national* (not American) pacification effort, greater control of corruption, and a broader political base of government. They must be made to feel

that we have options other than unconditional support.

2. We should provide unlimited arms and military training for South Vietnam, but not expand the American manpower commitment there unless it is indispensable to the safety of our own troops.

3. We should adopt a more objective and critical posture in public appraisal of Vietnamese developments.

4. We should reenforce economic and social development, assist internal security efforts, and promote political cooperation in the peripheral countries of South and Southeast Asia where there does exist internal national cohesion. We should make clear that our commitment to such support is related to their self-help and will be maintained regardless of the outcome in Vietnam.

5. If South Vietnam demonstrates the capacity and will to assume greater responsibility, we should be prepared to back them with unlimited arms assistance and substantial economic assistance for a very long haul. As ARVN numbers are greatly expanded, there should be a token reduction in the size of the American military manpower commitment. If no such capacity or will are demonstrated within a few months, we should consider negotiations to save as much face as possible, assure the safety of our own forces, and rescue as many conspicuous anti-communist South Vietnamese as possible. At the same time, the commitment to support the nations demonstrating internal cohesion should be reemphasized. In short, if there is to be a failure in Vietnam, the onus should be unmistakably where it belongs—not on American will or resolution or interest in freedom and order in the Pacific, but on the irremediable weaknesses of the Vietnamese society and polity.

6. While neutralization of the area under international guarantee is fanciful under present conditions, this concept should be kept alive for use when the time has come for negotiation, especially as a means of engaging the Soviet Union in any settlement.

Appendix D

Exchange of Letters with Eugene Rostow on Panama Canal Treaty

Panama Canal, 1977

Resources for the Future
1755 Massachusetts Avenue, N.W.
Washington, D.C. 20036

September 29, 1977

Eugene V. Rostow, Esq.
208 South Ronan Street
New Haven, Connecticut 06511

Dear Gene:

I am writing to you in your capacity as Chairman of the Executive Committee of the Committee on the Present Danger. The purpose is to follow up our telephone conversation of mid-August, in which I suggested that it would be appropriate and desirable for the Committee on the Present Danger to take a public position in support of ratification of the recently negotiated treaties relating to the Panama Canal.

My special interest in the Panama Canal issue, in addition to general concern for national security and welfare, arises from my experience as Assistant Secretary of State for Inter-American Affairs in 1966 and 1967, when the last serious negotiation on this subject was taking place between Panama and the United States. Although the direct negotiating responsibility at that time was in the hands of Robert B. Anderson and John Irwin, I was regularly consulted and kept fully informed and also joined them in consultations with the Joint Chiefs of Staff, President Johnson, and several senators. During that period, we gave extensive consideration to the security issues involved as well as the political and economic aspects. As you know, the text of draft treaties was agreed by the negotiators in 1967, but they were repudiated in Panama after a coup d'état, before they could be formally signed or presented to our Senate.

Against that background, I have reviewed the texts of the treaties recently signed by President Carter and now under consideration by the Senate Committee on Foreign Relations. I am satisfied that the new treaties provide even stronger protection for American security interests than the 1967 drafts, both during the transitional period until the end of 1999 and under the provisions in the second treaty for permanent neutrality thereafter, including my sea-level canal to be built in Panama as well as the existing canal. In other respects, the new treaties appear to provide somewhat greater direct economic benefits to Panama, but those differences are not important compared to the vital question of our national interest in assurance of a canal which is continuously open and usable, without restriction of our commercial or military traffic. On that central point, ratification and implementation of the new treaties would not only be an improvement over the 1967 drafts, but also a clear improvement over the alternative of seeking to maintain the 1903 Convention by unilateral force. As a supplementary but not inconsiderable point, failure of ratification would poison our relations with the Latin American region as a whole, impeding other transactions of affirmative importance to our national security and welfare.

The relevance of the Panama Canal issue to the objectives of the Committee on the Present Danger is, of course, a matter for you and your colleagues to determine. As a strong supporter of your basic objective of pursuing secure peace with freedom, I would urge a positive response, bearing in mind the connection between the Panama question and the wider strategic struggle between the Soviet Union and the Atlantic Alliance. Failure of ratification of the Panama treaties would strengthen the Soviet-supported anti-American attitudes and organizations all over Latin America. In some circumstances which are not implausible, defense of the canal might necessitate a substantial diversion of our security forces away from their priority objectives of strategic deterrence.

As you know, the reported statements of the chief Panamanian negotiator have raised some question as to whether the permanent neutrality treaty does in fact permit the United States to intervene unilaterally if necessary to protect that neutrality effectively. Article IV states that: "The United States of America and the Republic of Panama agree to maintain the regime of neutrality established in this Treaty, which shall be maintained in order that the Canal shall remain permanently neutral, notwithstanding the termination of any other treaties entered into by the two Contracting Parties." I would expect any impartial authority to interpret that language as unequivocally conferring upon the United States the right of unilateral intervention to ensure the permanent neutrality of the canal and to maintain the specific conditions and provisions which constitute the "regime of neutrality" established in the treaty. Since a question has been raised, however, it would seem to me appropriate that the Committee on the Present Danger make its support contingent upon clarification of this question through legislative history or other appropriate means.

In considering this matter, you will naturally be aware that a public expression of support by the Committee on the Present Danger may help to determine the outcome of what appears to be a very closely balanced issue of high public policy. The membership and record of your Committee are testimonials to a profound concern with national security, completely free of taint or suspicion of motivation by narrow partisanship or special interest. Your collective views should therefore carry weight in sectors of public opinion which may be decisive.

I should be happy to discuss this matter at first hand with you or any of your colleagues, or to assist in any other way in its further consideration. Meanwhile, with warm personal regards.

Sincerely,
Lincoln Gordon
Senior Fellow

YALE UNIVERSITY
LAW SCHOOL
NEW HAVEN, CONNECTICUT 06520

EUGENE V. ROSTOW (203) 436–2234

October 3, 1977

Honorable Lincoln Gordon
Resources for the Future
1755 Massachusetts Avenue, N.W.
Washington, D.C. 20036

Dear Linc,

Thank you for your cogent letter of September 29, which I am transmitting at once to our Executive Committee for study.

It is clear at the moment that a number of our members will publicly support ratification of the Panama Treaty, and that a number of others are opposed or doubtful. The Executive Committee has agreed to study the problem carefully, and to decide—after that study—whether attempting to reach a collective position is feasible and desirable.

My own position is sympathetic to the goals sought through the Treaty, as I told you when we spoke on the telephone last month. My present concern is not only with the problem of neutrality, which you discuss, but with the relationship of the notion of neutrality to the Rio system.

Yours cordially,
EVR/SM
Cc: Mr. Tyroler

Appendix E

Correspondence with Richard Bissell on ERP's Early Troubles

"Darkwater,"
Georges Mills, N.H.

September 13, 1948

Mr. Richard M. Bissell, Jr.
Assistant Deputy Administrator
Economic Cooperation Administration
Washington 25, D.C.

Dear Dick,

The main purpose of this letter is to cover a few matters not very adequately touched on in our rather rambling quarrel last week concerning the best disposition of ECA forces—and especially yourself—over the next few months. You will appreciate that only a feeling of considerable depth and intensity leads me to sit down indoors to do this on a magnificent New Hampshire morning! In all seriousness, it does seem to me that the way in which this matter is handled may well make a crucial difference in the success of the ERP's first year and therefore in its survival.

The problem is obviously one of that genre dear to the hearts of economists—making the best of scarce personnel and organizational resources over a limited period of time, with appropriate regard to both current production and to capital formation. You would argue, as I understand it, that genuine progress has been made in building up in ECA-Washington an effective organization capable of rational program analysis and objective evaluation of ERP progress and requirements. You are concerned that your removal from Washington for a period of four to six weeks on end might jeopardize those gains. And you fear that such analysis and objectivity may be sacrificed to a basically unsatisfactory process of brilliant improvisation and semi-political negotiation (which may be fun for the improvisors but is otherwise not very defensible) if undue weight is now rested on ECA-Paris. Beyond which I have no doubt that you view without relish the idea of stepping into a thoroughly unsatisfactory administrative situation—especially within so short a time of getting the one in Washington reasonably straight.

This view (which I have perhaps overstated) seems to me to overlook a number of circumstances peculiar to the position of the Harriman mission as it ideally should be—and perhaps even more the woeful gap between the ideal and the reality. There is nothing simple about the four way relationship among participants and the OEEC, country missions, ECA-Paris, and ECA-Washington. At present both Paris and Washington are given to bitter complaints on the inadequacy of information and reciprocal consultation—and there is justice on both sides. There must indeed be far more adequate reporting from Paris, but there ought also be more transfer to Paris of the fruits of the Washington process of capital formation. Paris cannot act as a mere transmission belt in the manner of the Soviet missions. The State Department is legitimately criticized for so treating its missions. Given the existence of OEEC and the responsibilities we want it to assume to the European program proper (as distinguished from the American supply program) and [text unreadable] the peculiar position of the U.S. as a non-member participant-adviser to OEEC, we must find some means of providing full understanding of our aims and our analyses at the point of impact. We cannot afford a dichotomy between reasoned analysis in Washington and off-the-cuff improvisation and negotiation in Paris.

It does not follow that we should attempt to duplicate the Washington organization in Paris or to move the entire Washington personnel for periodic OEEC crises. It does follow that Paris must be equipped with a cadre of permanent personnel with full understanding of the fundamentals of the program; that the flow of information both ways must be complete; that there must be frequent and intimate personal contact among all senior officers on both sides; and that there must be some real flexibility at the point of direct contact with OEEC.

I believe that it would be disastrous to permit the present disorganized condition of the Paris mission to persist in the hope that its evil effects can be made good through review and control from Washington. This line would make impossible the creation of a proper working relationship with OEEC, which seems to me of crucial importance. A proper relationship would, for example, have avoided the absurd procedures adopted by OEEC in the allocation first of dollar aid and then of intra-European aid—procedures largely responsible for the recent crisis on the first annual program, for the general rush to maximum debtor positions on intra-European account, and for a serious threat to the working out of any effective means of working out the intra-European trade and payments problem.

When it comes to developing the shape of the long-term program, there will be far more numerous instances in which even a recognition of the relevant issues will require the best available talent in Paris this autumn. The mere framing of the questions on which Washington's advice should be sought will require a calibre of understanding which is now lacking and which I gather Henry Arthur cannot provide. Yet these are the issues and this is the process which may well determine the entire success or failure of the program and the longer-run prospects of Western European economic and perhaps political cooperation. This is the point at which, if at all, the over-complicated process of dividing American aid will give way to the facing of such issues as the needed patterns of trade between Europe and other major trading areas; the place of Germany in the European economy; the realism with which internal financial disorder and distorted exchange rates are faced; the possibilities of effective joint planning of capital development; avoiding the dissipation of assistance in mere increased consumption or in wasteful capital development; and any number of others.

I cannot state too strongly the concern that the long-term program work may be undertaken without the kind of drive and vitality essential to its success. The OEEC Secretariat cannot provide it; the British probably will not; the Paris Mission is not now equipped to do it; and I believe that your presence can. I would not for a moment relax the necessary efforts to transform the Paris mission into a permanently effective agency or to create the proper relations between the Paris and Washington offices, and I should certainly move ahead at once with the transfer of Ty Wood for a period of months. But on the substance of the long-term program I see no adequate substitute for your own participation—preferably from October 1st onwards but at a minimum from October 15 to November 15.

I find a few points left over from my Paris notes which were not passed on last week.

1. Guarantees: I hope that this problem can be settled by the establishment of a notional $50m "kitty" to start with outside the $487m, with good projects approved over and beyond the regular allocations. I very much doubt the likelihood of more than this being committed before April 2. . . .
2. As part of the needed reforms in Paris, a far more adequate job is required on country mission indoctrination and coordination. There is no consistent understanding at present of responsibilities in connection with the country programs or even of the broader purposes of the entire operation.
3. Steps must be set in motion in connection with the OEEC procedures on the 2d annual program to avoid a repetition of the recent fiasco—particularly in the watertight compartment treatment of extra-European and intra-European assistance.
4. Frank Lindsay has suggested the desirability of initiating a survey of long-term prospects for European exports in extra-European markets—presumably a job for Commerce. This seems to me a potentially fruitful notion.
5. (This is a purely personal one)—My brother used to employ as a secretary one Dorothy Coyner, who is now in one of the ECA missions overseas. He hopes to hire her back next year and would like to get in touch with her. Can you have one of the girls find out from the personnel office where she is?

We return to Cambridge next Monday. If you want to discuss any of these matters by phone, I can be reached at Sunapee (N.H.) 93 ring 3 for the rest of this week.

With best regards,
Sincerely,
Lincoln Gordon

Notes

1. Dorothy and Dad

1. The daughters as well as the parents all had Hebrew names originally. I adopt Anglicized usage and refer to them by the names they used in their new country.

2. This story made its way into one of Dorothy's biographical entries. See *Jewish Women in America: An Historical Encyclopedia* (New York: Routledge, 1997).

3. Contemporaries of Abraham Lincoln Gordon's, Walt Whitman Rostow and his brother Eugene Victor Debs Rostow, have similar historical names from this period.

4. Lincoln Gordon (LG hereafter), draft of unpublished memoir, chapter 1, Feb. 11, 2004, LG's personal papers.

5. "Dorothy Gordon's Recital," *New York Times,* Dec. 29, 1929. The accompanist was Adele Holstein.

6. LG, unpublished memoir.

2. Secular Humanism at Fieldston

1. Mimeo sheets from the "Fieldglass," a school yearbook for Lincoln Gordon's class, preserved in the Gordon family records.

2. This figure is cited in Jean Edward Smith, *FDR* (New York: Random House, 2007), 585. The GI Bill, passed by Congress in 1943, helped move the nation toward the dramatic expansion of college attendance occurring after the war.

3. The reference is to Percy Bysshe Shelley, "Ozymandias of Egypt," in *English Poetry: From Collins to Fitzgerald,* 2 vols. (Danbury, CT: Grollier Enterprises, 1980), 2:515, http://www.bartleby.com/41/515/html (full citation for the online edition at http://www.bartleby.com/br/04101.html) (accessed Oct. 20, 2014).

4. "Fieldglass" (mimeo), n.d., "Last Will and Testament" (Class of 1929).

5. LG, "Pre-College Years," four-page draft with handwritten edits (not part of LG's unpublished memoir), LG's personal papers.

6. LG, diary entry, Mar. 1, 1937. LG's diary was discovered in the JFK Presidential Library by George Gordon, Hugh Gordon's son, on an expedition to the library in Boston on my behalf. A copy was made for me.

7. LG, diary entry, Mar. 1, 1937.

8. Aline Bernstein Saarinen died on July 13, 1972, in Paris, where she was head of NBC's Paris News Bureau, the first woman to have held the post of head of an overseas news bureau. See the following biographical sketches of Aline: "Aline Bernstein Saarinen (1914–1972)," http://www.jewishvirtuallibrary.org/jsource/biography/Saarinen.html (accessed Oct. 20, 2014); Cathleen McGillighan, "The Purpose-Driven Wife," *Daily Beast*, www.thedailybeast.com/reporting/2009/11/05/the-purpose (originally published in *Newsweek*) (accessed Sept. 2012).

9. LG, "Pre-College Years."

10. See Smith, *FDR*.

11. LG, "Pre-College Years."

12. LG, "Pre-College Years."

13. "Fieldglass" (mimeo), n.d.

14. "Lincoln Gordon, 1913–2009: Collected Memories" (mimeo), pamphlet prepared for Cosmos Club Memorial Service, Washington, DC, Mar. 2010, by Hugh B. Gordon, with the assistance of Robert W. Gordon, Amy Gordon, and Anne Gordon. The family's remembrances were reprinted in this handsome pamphlet for circulation to family members and close family friends.

15. LG to Dorothy Gordon (DG hereafter), May 1, 1930, LG's personal papers (original lent to the author by the Gordon family). Unless otherwise noted, all letters are from LG's personal papers.

16. Henry Adams, "The Dynamo and the Virgin (1900)," chapter 25 of *The Education of Henry Adams* (New York: Houghton Mifflin, 1918).

17. This monument was dedicated in May 1902. Its marble and granite pillars and its platform stand above and overlook Riverside Park at Eighty-Ninth Street. From this spot one has grand views of the Hudson River and Riverside Park, stretching both north and south.

3. Harvard in Three Years

1. LG, unpublished memoir, chapter 1, completed July 2, 2004.

2. Hugh B. Gordon to the author, email, Feb. 2011.

3. Frank Gordon to his Princeton classmates, Class of '33, copy in LG's personal papers. Judge Medina later drew criticism from Supreme Court Justice William O. Douglas and others for bias in his handling of the case. For a discussion of the case, see Noah Feldman, *Scorpions: The Battles and the Triumphs of FDR's Great Supreme Court Justices* (New York: Twelve Publishing, 2010), 340–44.

4. William Yandell Elliott, *The Pragmatic Revolt in Politics* (New York: Macmillan, 1928). LG could recite passages from this study many years later and considered the themes of the book very timely for the upheavals and tensions of the post-communist era.

5. Walter Isaacson, in his biography *Kissinger* (1992; New York: Simon &

Schuster, 2005), 62–64, gives a colorful, if somewhat unflattering, portrayal of Elliott and appears to side with Carl J. Friedrich, Elliott's rival, in the legendary battles between those two giants of the Harvard Government Department.

6. LG to Bernard Gordon (BG hereafter), Mar. 6, 1931.

7. LG, unpublished memoir, chapter 1, July 2004.

8. This dialogue comes from LG's unpublished memoir, chapter 1.

9. LG to BG, Sept. 20, 1930.

10. LG, unpublished memoir, chapter 1, 2004.

11. Charles H. McIlwain, *Constitutionalism—Ancient and Modern* (Ithaca, NY: Cornell University Press, 1947).

12. Elliott, *Pragmatic Revolt in Politics,* passage quoted in LG's unpublished memoir, chapter 1.

13. LG, "The Federal Trade Commission and the Courts" (honors thesis, Harvard College, Apr. 1933), preface (copy lent to the author by the Gordon family).

14. LG, "Federal Trade Commission and the Courts," 99.

15. LG, "Federal Trade Commission and the Courts," 99.

16. LG, "Federal Trade Commission and the Courts," 113.

4. An American at Oxford

1. LG to DG, Oct. 5, 1933.

2. I borrow the dialogue from LG's unpublished memoir, chapter 1, July 2004.

3. LG to BG and DG, July 12, 1934, Marburg.

4. LG to DG and BG, July 12, 1934, Berlin.

5. LG, *The Public Corporation in Great Britain* (Oxford: Oxford University Press, 1938).

6. As Gordon states in the acknowledgments, "In any realistic study of contemporary institutions, investigation of documentary sources must necessarily be supplemented with a large degree of personal information."

7. LG, *Public Corporation in Great Britain,* 314.

8. LG, *Public Corporation in Great Britain,* 314.

9. LG to DG and BG, July 19, 1935.

5. Allison

1. LG to BG, Jan. 12, 1937.

2. The course lectures eventually became the basis for Merle Fainsod and Lincoln Gordon's book *Government and the American Economy* (New York: W. W. Norton, 1941). The book was reissued with the addition of two chapters in 1948, and a third edition came out in 1959.

3. Please see chapter 2, note 6, for an explanation of how Lincoln Gordon's diary was found.

4. LG, diary entry, Feb. 8, 1937.

5. LG, diary entry, Mar. 6, 1937.

6. LG, diary entry, Mar. 15, 1937.

7. Conversation with Dorothy "Dot" Gordon, Aug. 2011, at a Gordon family celebration I attended at Lake Sunapee, New Hampshire.

8. Allison Gordon (AG hereafter) to her children Anne, Bob, and Hugh, Oct. 22, 1961. Amy, twelve, the youngest daughter, was with the Gordons in Rio from 1961 to 1963.

9. Hugh B. Gordon, in "Memorial Service for Allison Gordon," pamphlet privately printed for the family and close friends, 22.

10. Robert W. Gordon, in "Memorial Service for Allison Gordon," 14–18.

11. Lynne Olson, *Those Angry Days: Roosevelt, Lindbergh, and America's Fight over World War II, 1939–1941* (New York: Random House, 2013).

12. Michael Fullilove, *Rendezvous with Destiny: How Franklin D. Roosevelt and Five Extraordinary Men Took America into the War and into the World* (New York: Penguin, 2013).

13. Fullilove, *Rendezvous with Destiny*, 5.

14. LG, unpublished memoir, chapter 1, July 8, 2004.

15. One of his papers was published in 1942 as a chapter entitled "Fuel and Power," in National Resources Planning Board, *Industrial Location and National Policy* (Washington, DC: Government Printing Office, 1942).

16. Fullilove describes in gripping detail how FDR sent Harry Hopkins to the UK to describe the Lend-Lease plan to Churchill and how he got Congress to pass the legislation. See Fullilove, *Rendezvous with Destiny*, 104–52ff.

17. Fainsod and Gordon, *Government and the American Economy*, 821.

6. Mobilizing for War

The epigraphs are drawn from the following sources. LG prepared his "mobilization paper," from which the first quote is taken, for inclusion in a book to be published by the Industrial College of the Armed Forces in 1995. Plans for the volume's publication were dropped due to the illness of the editor. LG attached the paper as an appendix to chapter 2 of his unpublished memoir, dated Oct. 15, 2004. Felix Frankfurter is quoted in Smith, *FDR*, 570. Also see the original letter, cited in note 16 below.

1. LG, mobilization paper, in unpublished memoir, chapter 2. For historical reviews of the wartime mobilization, see Alan Brinkley, *The End of Reform: New Deal Liberalism in Recession and War* (New York: Knopf, 1995); and James T. Sparrow, *Warfare State: World War II Americans and the Age of Big Government* (Oxford: Oxford University Press, 2011).

2. Alexander J. Field, *A Great Leap Forward: 1930s Depression and U.S. Economic Growth* (New Haven, CT: Yale University Press, 2011), 26.

3. LG, mobilization paper.

4. Field, *Great Leap Forward*, 81–88.

5. Donald M. Nelson, *Arsenal of Democracy: The Story of American War Production* (New York: Harcourt, Brace, 1946), 30. This memoir by Nelson, who served as WPB chairman from 1942 to 1944, presents an insider's view of the World War II mobilization but needs to be supplemented by Brinkley's more analytical treatment in *The End of Reform*; especially relevant for our purposes are Brinkley's analysis of the 1942 Nelson-Eberstadt fracas (193–99) and his account of the simmering Nelson-Wilson dispute that led to Nelson's departure from the WPB in August 1944 (239–46).

6. *Time*, Feb. 24, 1941, cover story on Donald M. Nelson, then director of the Division of Purchases for the Office of Production Management (OPM).

7. Olson, *Those Angry Days.*

8. Fullilove, *Rendezvous with Destiny,* 153–97. More generally with respect to the US domestic political scene, see Brinkley, *End of Reform;* Olson, *Those Angry Days;* Susan Dunn, *1940: FDR, Willkie, Lindbergh, Hitler—The Election amid the Storm* (New Haven, CT: Yale University Press, 2013).

9. W. D. Evans, quoted in Field, *Great Leap Forward,* 24.

10. Field, *Great Leap Forward,* 76–77.

11. LG, unpublished memoir, chapter 2, Oct. 15, 2004.

12. This dialogue comes from LG's recollection in chapter 2 of his unpublished memoir.

13. As a boy in St. Paul, Minnesota, I dutifully aided my older brother in flattening our tin cans every week, tying them up in a neat package, and placing the package in the alley for pickup. We also observed Mr. Batt's injunction to eat meat (Spam) only once a week.

14. Charles Higham, *Trading with the Enemy: An Expose of the Nazi-American Money Plot* (New York: Delatorre, 1983), chapter 7.

15. Smith, *FDR,* 570.

16. Frankfurter to FDR, in Max Freedman, ed., *Roosevelt and Frankfurter: Their Correspondence, 1928–1945* (Boston: Little, Brown, 1967), 329, also quoted in Smith, *FDR,* 570.

17. Robert C. Perez and Edward F. Willett, *The Will to Win: A Biography of Ferdinand Eberstadt* (New York: Greenwood Press, 1989).

18. James F. Byrnes, *All in One Lifetime* (New York: Harper & Brothers, 1958).

19. Nelson, *Arsenal of Democracy,* chapter 20, "Reconversion: War within a War."

20. The following dialogue is Gordon's recollection as recorded in LG, unpublished memoir, chapter 2, Oct. 15, 2004.

21. LG, unpublished memoir, chapter 2. The quote is Gordon's recollection of O'Brian's words.

22. Charles E. Wilson of General Electric had the sobriquet of "Electric Charley" to distinguish him from Charles E. ("Engine Charley") Wilson of General Motors Co. "Electric Charley" Wilson before his WPB service had served in the New Deal's National Recovery Administration and was later to serve as director of

the Office of War Mobilization (OWM) during the Korean War. He resigned from the OWM post in a huff in April 1953, when the president did not take his advice on accepting a settlement of the steel seizure dispute.

23. Wilson had a ferocious temper. Scuttlebutt had it that he had lunged at an army general in a fury, lifted him up by the lapels, and shaken him as he delivered a tongue-lashing. The incident is cited in Paul G. Pierpaoli, *Truman and Korea: The Political Culture of the Early Cold War* (Columbia: University of Missouri Press, 1999), 51.

24. James Agee, "Atomic Bomb," *Time,* Aug. 20, 1945.

7. Controlling the Atom

Epigraph: Bernard Baruch is quoted in Richard G. Hewlett and Oscar E. Anderson Jr., *The New World, 1939/1946: A History of the United States Atomic Energy Commission,* vol. 1 (University Park: Pennsylvania State University Press, 1962), 619.

1. See Sparrow, *Warfare State.*

2. LG's personal papers, sections dealing with Harvard Business School, for March through April 1958, in this case copies of Harvard Business School General File; Friedrich to Professor Heros (Xerox).

3. Isaacson, *Kissinger,* 63–64.

4. LG, unpublished memoir, chapter 3, "The United Nations Atomic Energy Commission," Jan. 10, 2005.

5. Seymour E. Harris wrote to LG on October 5, 1944, expressing sympathy over the death of Bernard Gordon. He was engaged in research on mobilization and sought input from Gordon on a variety of issues during the war.

6. See LG to Ralph Epstein, Apr. 27, 1947: "I just turned down appointment as associate dean of Public Administration under Ed Mason."

7. Richard Rhodes, *The Making of the Atomic Bomb* (New York: Simon & Schuster, 1985); Hewlett and Anderson, *New World,* 619.

8. Smith, *FDR,* 579.

9. A facsimile of the note is in Rhodes, *Making of the Atomic Bomb,* 388.

10. Henry L. Stimson, with McGeorge Bundy, *On Active Service in Peace and War* (New Haven, CT: Yale University Press, 1948), 636.

11. Walter Isaacson and Evan Thomas, *The Wise Men: The Friends and the World They Made* (New York: Simon & Schuster, 1986).

12. Hewlett and Anderson, *New World,* 551ff.

13. I first learned of Marks's association with Acheson from his son, Jonathan Marks, an undergraduate in Leverett House at Harvard when I was a tutor there in 1962. Herbert Marks died in 1960 at the young age of fifty-three. Though his life was short, he was one of the unsung generation that made a great contribution to the nation. He served with Acheson in the State Department from 1945 to 1946 as the point person on atomic issues before joining the newly established Atomic Energy Commission (AEC) as general counsel in December 1946.

14. Hewlett and Anderson, *New World,* 532–33.

15. Lilienthal acted as chairman of the group of consultants. Lilienthal was recommended to Acheson by Herbert Marks, who as assistant general counsel at the TVA had worked with Lilienthal before the war. The Acheson-Lilienthal Report is available at www.learnworld.com/ZNW/LWText.Acheson-Lilienthal.html (accessed Sept. 2012).

16. John Lewis Gaddis, *George F. Kennan: An American Life* (New York: Penguin, 2011), 201–22.

17. Isaacson and Thomas, *Wise Men,* 361.

18. David McCullough, *Truman* (New York: Simon & Schuster, 1992), 494.

19. Bernard M. Baruch, *Baruch: My Own Story* (New York: Henry Holt, 1957).

20. The scene and dialogue come from LG, unpublished memoir, chapter 3.

21. The Smyth Report was aimed at explaining nuclear energy to the public. See Henry DeWolf Smyth, *Atomic Energy for Military Purposes* (Princeton, NJ: Princeton University Press, 1945). The quote is from LG's unpublished memoir, chapter 3.

22. LG, unpublished memoir, chapter 3, Jan. 2005

23. Hewlett and Anderson, *New World,* 582–84.

24. Oppenheimer told Gordon in a 1947 letter that "our association was one of the bright spots in an otherwise dismal situation" (letter in LG's personal papers).

25. Hewlett and Anderson, *New World,* 590.

26. Lincoln Gordon, oral history, 1974, Harry S. Truman Presidential Library, www.trumanlibrary.org/oralhist/gordonl.htm.

27. Quoted in Alex Ross, "Uncommon Man: The Strange Life of Henry Wallace, the New Deal Visionary," *New Yorker,* Oct. 14, 2013, 104–9.

28. Ross, "Uncommon Man," 107.

29. LG, unpublished memoir, chapter 3.

30. LG, unpublished memoir, chapter 3.

31. Wallace's thinking is spelled out in his 1948 book *Steps to Peace* (New York: National Wallace for President Committee, 1948), written as part of his campaign for the presidency in 1948.

32. McCullough, *Truman,* 517.

33. Hewlett and Anderson, *New World,* 603. See the *New York Times,* Oct. 4, 1946, for a front-page article that adds the words "as to the facts" after "not being fully posted."

34. Hewlett and Anderson, *New World,* 597–607.

35. "Statement by Baruch on Controversy with Wallace and Texts of Exchanges between Them," *New York Times,* Oct. 3, 1946.

36. Thomas Devince, *Henry Wallace's 1948 Presidential Campaign and the Future of Postwar Liberalism* (Raleigh: University of North Carolina Press, 2013).

37. Ross, "Uncommon Man," 108.

38. Ross, "Uncommon Man," 108.

39. Graham Farmelo, *Churchill's Bomb: How the United Sates Overtook Britain in the First Nuclear Arms Race* (New York: Basic Books, 2013), 321–22.

40. LG, unpublished memoir, chapter 3, "The United Nations Atomic Energy Commission," Jan. 10, 2005 (quoting from his memorandum in the JFK Presidential Library).

41. James Chace, "A Sharing of the Atomic Bomb," *Foreign Affairs* (Jan.–Feb. 1996).

8. Birth of the Marshall Plan, 1947–1948

The epigraphs are taken from the following sources. For an account of the origins of George C. Marshall's speech, see Charles P. Kindleberger, in US Department of State, *Foreign Relations of the United States,* 1947 (Washington, DC: US Government Printing Office, 1947), 3:241–47, reprinted as "Origins of the Marshall Plan: Memorandum by Mr. Charles P. Kindleberger," in Stanley Hoffman and Charles Maier, eds., *The Marshall Plan: A Retrospective* (Boulder, CO: Westview Press, 1984), 115–21. The Milton Katz quotation is from Katz's oral history, 1975, Truman Presidential Library, 93, http://www.trumanlibrary/oralhist/katzm.htm. For Gordon's quote, see LG, "Lessons from the Marshall Plan: Successes and Limits," in Hoffman and Maier, *Marshall Plan,* 55.

1. See Thomas G. Patterson, ed., *Cold War Critics: Alternatives to American Foreign Policy in the Truman Years* (Chicago: Quadrangle Books, 1971), 18–33, 76–114, 114–39.

2. Charles P. Kindleberger, "The American Origins of the Marshall Plan: A View from the State Department," in Hoffman and Maier, *Marshall Plan,* 7–12.

3. Marshall's speech was based on a conceptual paper written by George Kennan, director of the Policy Planning Staff, and the speech itself was largely drafted by Charles Bohlen. See Gaddis, *George F. Kennan,* 264–70.

4. Gaddis, *George F. Kennan,* 264–70.

5. The speech evidently had some of Marshall's own editing. The Bohlen draft drew on the May 27 Will Clayton memo; the work by George Kennan's Policy Planning Staff; and the ideas of Charles Kindleberger, Walt Rostow, Miriam Camp, Tom Blaisdell, and other economists.

6. LG, unpublished memoir, chapter 4, June 2005; LG, oral history, 1974, Truman Presidential Library.

7. See Greg Behrman, *The Most Noble Adventure: The Marshall Plan and How America Helped Rebuild Europe* (New York: Free Press, 2008), 45–48.

8. This group of young officials included Charles Kindleberger, Walt Rostow, Miriam Camp, Thomas Blaisdell, Harold Van Buren Cleveland, and others. See Kindleberger, "American Origins of the Marshall Plan," 7–12. This essay is to be distinguished from Kindleberger's memo of 1948 cited in note 1 above.

9. LG, diary entry, Oct. 19, 1936.

10. James Reston, "Vandenberg Pays Tribute to Framers of Plan / Seven Are Named to State Under-Secretary in Drafting Measure," *New York Times,* Jan. 10, 1948.

11. Reston, "Vandenberg Pays Tribute."

12. LG, "Recollections of a Marshall Planner," *Journal of International Affairs* 41, no. 2 (1988), 233–45.

13. LG, oral history, 1974, Truman Presidential Library.

14. The Harriman Committee reported on November 7, 1947, and generally rebutted critics on the left (notably Henry Wallace) and the right (Henry Hazlitt) who had attacked the proposed recovery program. See Michael J. Hogan, *The Marshall Plan: America, Britain, and the Reconstruction of Western Europe, 1947–1952* (Cambridge: Cambridge University Press, 1987), 96–97. The Harriman Committee report was largely drafted by Bissell and reflected Bissell's Keynesian views of how US aid would revive the European economies.

15. LG, unpublished memoir, chapter 4, "The Marshall Plan and European Economic Recovery," June 2005.

16. Hogan, *Marshall Plan,* 102–4.

17. LG, unpublished memoir, chapter 4, June 2005.

18. Hogan, *Marshall Plan,* 103, note 40, citing LG to C. H. Bonesteel, memorandum, Sept. 23, 1947, and Minutes of the Committee on European Recovery, Oct. 7, 1847.

19. Hogan, *Marshall Plan,* 103–4.

20. Donald Stone to James E. Webb, memorandum, Dec. 3, 1947, cited in Hogan, *Marshall Plan,* 104, note 45.

21. Testimony of Secretary Marshall and others, US Senate Committee on Foreign Relations, *ERP Hearings, 1948,* Part 1 (Washington, DC: US Government Printing Office, 1948), Jan. 8, 9, 10, 12, 13, 14, 18, 1948.

22. US Senate Committee on Foreign Relations, *ERP Hearings, 1948,* Part 1, 24.

23. US Senate Committee on Foreign Relations, *ERP Hearings, 1948,* Part 1, 74. The conclusions and recommendations of the Brookings Report are reprinted in US Senate Committee on Foreign Relations, *ERP Hearings, 1948,* Part 2 (Washington, DC: Government Printing Office, 1948), 855–60.

24. Behrman, *Most Noble Adventure,* 152–62.

9. The Marshall Plan in Action, 1949–1950

The epigraphs are taken from the following sources. For the Marjolin quotation, see the Organization for Economic Cooperation and Development, *From Marshall Plan to Global Interdependence* (Paris: OECD, 1978), 214–15. The Katz quotation, from his 1975 oral history for the Truman Presidential Library, is quoted in Behrman, *Most Noble Adventure,* 329. For Gordon's quote, see LG, unpublished memoir, chapter 4, June 2005.

1. Robert Lovett to Dean David, Nov. 20, 1947.

2. Dean David to Robert Lovett, Nov. 24, 1947.

3. "Tich" Bonesteel to LG, Feb. 27, 1948.

4. Richard Bissell, in *Reflections of a Cold Warrior: From Yalta to the Bay of Pigs* (New Haven, CT: Yale University Press, 1996), 44, observed, "Testifying before the House Appropriations Committee . . . with perhaps six hours of continuous presentation . . . was the hardest work I have ever done."

5. LG, "Lessons from the Marshall Plan," 54.

6. Nicklaus Mills, *Winning the Peace: The Marshall Plan and America's Coming of Age as a Superpower* (New York: John Wiley, 2008), 171–86.

7. LG, unpublished memoir, chapter 4, June 2005 (the dialogue reported by Gordon was slightly edited by me for clarity).

8. LG to Paul Nitze, Jan. 31, 1949.

9. Hoffman and Maier, *Marshall Plan,* 127.

10. Hogan, *Marshall Plan,* 258–68.

11. The definition of cooperative international investments proved to be elusive, and this portion of Marshall Plan aid remained unspent.

12. Hogan, *Marshall Plan,* 271.

13. Bissell, *Reflections of a Cold Warrior,* 30–73.

14. Bissell, *Reflections of a Cold Warrior,* 51.

15. Bissell, *Reflections of a Cold Warrior,* 51.

16. Hogan, *Marshall Plan,* 272, citing LG to Averell Harriman and Milton Katz, memorandum, Oct. 11, 1949.

17. Hogan, *Marshall Plan,* 270–75.

18. Hogan, *Marshall Plan,* 270–75.

19. The Council of Ministers of the OEEC adopted the EPU in August 1950 and officially ratified it in September 1950, but the date it came into being was made retroactive to July 1, 1950.

20. These are excerpts from Lincoln Gordon, interview with Eric and Linda Christenson, producer Ira Klugerman, for a 1997 PBS documentary on the Marshall Plan, to coincide with a Marshall Plan reunion held in 1997 (LG's personal papers).

21. Robert Marjolin, *Le travail d'une vie* (Paris, 1983).

22. LG to Paul G. Hoffman and Averell Harriman, memorandum, "ECA Strategy–Performance and Incentives," Feb. 12, 1950.

23. LG to Hoffman and Harriman, "ECA Strategy–Performance and Incentives."

24. Barry Eichengreen and Jorge Briga de Macedo, "The European Payments Union: History and Implications for the Evolution of the International Financial Architecture," OECD, Mar. 2001; Behrman, *Most Noble Adventure,* 280–81.

25. Behrman, *Most Noble Adventure,* 281.

26. Behrman, *Most Noble Adventure,* 281.

27. Behrman, *Most Noble Adventure,* 281.

28. Nicklaus Mills (*Winning the Peace,* 180–81) concurs with the view that the EPU was "the most important institutional achievement of the Marshall Plan in its early years" but views the decisive impetus for the EPU as coming from Hoffman's October 31 speech to the OEEC council.

29. LG, "Lessons from the Marshall Plan," 53.

30. LG, "Myth and Reality in European Integration," *Yale Review* 45, no. 4 (Sept. 1955): 634–36; LG, "Economic Regionalism Reconsidered," *World Politics* 13 (Jan. 1961): 231–33; LG, "The Marshall Plan Legacy," *NATO Review* 55, no. 3 (June 1987): 14–19; LG, "Does the Euro Portend a Federated Europe?" luncheon talk for the National War College Alumni Association, Oct. 22, 1998.

31. Harold Van B. Cleveland, "If There Had Been No Marshall Plan . . . ," in Hoffman and Maier, *Marshall Plan,* 59–64, 65–70 (commentary).

32. Participants at this conference from the Marshall Plan included Harriman, Milton Katz, Lincoln Gordon, Charles Kindleberger, Cleveland, Eric Roll, and Miriam Camps (now with an "s" on her name since her marriage).

10. NATO

The epigraphs are taken from the following sources. Ismay is quoted in "NATO," *Wikipedia,* http://en.wikipedia.org/wiki/NATO (accessed Aug., 22, 2011). Katz's statement comes from his oral history, 1975, Truman Presidential Library. General Eisenhower's remark is drawn from an interview with Eric Johnston, Economic Security Agency (ESA) administrator, Oct. 2, 1951, quoted in Paul G. Pierpaoli, *Truman and Korea: The Political Culture of the Early Cold War* (Columbia: University of Missouri Press, 1999), 119. The final quotation comes from Robert Jervis, "The Impact of the Korean War on the Cold War," *Journal of Conflict Resolution* 24, no. 4 (Dec. 1980) 567.

1. W. Averell Harriman Papers, US Library of Congress, box 1012, Milton Katz folder.

2. Memorandum on Contacts with Averell Harriman, 1947–1968, Mark Chadwin, interviewer, Feb. 1968, President's Office, Johns Hopkins University, Baltimore, MD, Harriman Papers, box 868, Lincoln Gordon folder.

3. President Truman's 1950 remarks, quoted in Hogan, *Marshall Plan,* 389; and see the sources cited at 389, note 14.

4. Pierpaoli, *Truman and Korea,* 18–21; also see the sources cited at 18, note 3.

5. Whether it was for Acheson's reason, Harriman upon returning to Washington organized a series of dinner parties at his Georgetown home to become acquainted or to renew acquaintances with congressmen and to mix them with figures from the news media. James Lanigan, Harriman's staff member in charge of public and media relations, handled the arrangements for these affairs. See Benjamin O. Fordham, *Building the Cold War Consensus. The Political Economy of U.S. National Security Policy, 1949–51* (Ann Arbor: University of Michigan Press, 1998), which presents an analysis based on extensive archival research showing that budget cutters such as Louis Johnson tried to influence the media, but they were outgunned by Acheson and Harriman, who had more extensive media contacts.

6. Jervis, "Impact of the Korean War on the Cold War." See also Robert Jervis, *Perception and Misperception in International Politics* (Princeton, NJ: Princeton University Press, 1976), 86–89.

7. Hogan, *Marshall Plan,* 380–426; Robert H. Terrell, "The Formation of the Alliance, 1948–1949," in Lawrence S. Kaplan, ed., *American Historians and the Atlantic Alliance* (Kent, OH: Kent State University Press, 1991), 11–32.

8. Appendix C, p. 228, reprinted in Lawrence S. Kaplan, *The United States and NATO: The Formative Years* (Lexington: University Press of Kentucky, 1984). Kaplan reminded me in a private conversation that the Article 5 formula was borrowed from the Rio Treaty of 1947, where it was first used.

9. Quoted in Kaplan, *United States and NATO,* 136.

10. Quoted in Ernest R. May, "The American Commitment to Germany, 1949–1955," in Kaplan, *American Historians and the Atlantic Alliance,* 52.

11. Warner R. Schilling, "The Politics of National Defense: Fiscal 11950," in Warner R. Schilling, Paul Y. Hammond, and Glen H. Snyder, eds., *Strategy, Politics, and Defense Budgets* (New York: Columbia University Press, 1962), 46.

12. Paul Y. Hammond, "NSC-68: Prologue to Rearmament," in Schilling, Hammond, and Snyder, *Strategy, Politics, and Defense Budgets,* 267–378; "History of the National Security Council, 1947–1997," Office of the Historian, US Department of State, http://www.fas.org/irp/offdocs/NSChistory.htm (accessed Sept. 2011).

13. NSC-68 remained classified as "top secret" until 1975. Some knowledge of its proposals was available before that date. Clark Clifford observed in a public comment in the 1950s, without alluding to the exact nature of NSC-68's proposals, that expenditures of at least $40 billion would be involved if the report's ideas were fully implemented. The full text of NSC-68 is published in Thomas H. Etzold and John Lewis Gaddis, eds., *Containment: Documents on American Policy and Strategy, 1945–1950* (New York: Columbia University Press, 1978), 385–442.

14. LG, unpublished memoir, chapter 5, Sept. 30, 2005.

15. Gaddis, *George F. Kennan,* 371–403. Acheson liked to argue and was quite open to controversial positions, but as a Washington lawyer and not a diplomat, he was extremely pragmatic and had no trouble reversing himself in a flash with no second thoughts.

16. Quoted in Walter Lefeber, "NATO and the Korean War: A Context," in Kaplan, *American Historians and the Atlantic Alliance,* 38.

17. LG, unpublished memoir, chapter 5, Sept. 30, 2005.

18. LG, unpublished memoir, chapter 5, Sept. 30, 2005.

19. For the details of the Pleven Plan, see Kaplan, *United States and NATO,* 158–68.

20. Harriman Papers, box 310, Lincoln Gordon folder.

21. Hogan, *Marshall Plan,* 390.

22. Memorandum on Contacts with Averell Harriman, 1947–1969.

23. LG, unpublished memoir, chapter 5, Sept. 30, 2005.

24. Pierpaoli, *Truman and Korea,* 49–81.

25. As Paul Pierpaoli notes, "The labor walkout, which began on February 15,

was the most serious and destabilizing crisis of the period. The labor representatives to the tripartite wage board walked out of in protest of the new wage catch-up formula which was designed to address the inequities of the January freeze and to mollify workers whose wages had not kept pace with prices. Three weeks later, on February 28, organized labor withdrew completely from all mobilization posts, including the Economic Stabilization Agency" (*Truman and Korea,* 86).

26. Richard Stebbins, *The United States in World Affairs 1951* (New York: Harper & Brothers, 1952), 48–56; Hogan, *Marshall Plan,* 383–85; Pierpaoli, *Truman and Korea,* 56–58.

27. Quoted in Hogan, *Marshall Plan,* 386.

28. Stebbins, *United States and World Affairs 1951,* 50.

29. Pierpaoli, *Truman and Korea,* 86.

30. LG, unpublished memoir, chapter 5, Sept. 30, 2005.

31. LG, unpublished memoir, chapter 5, Sept. 30, 2005.

32. LG, unpublished memoir, chapter 5, Sept. 30, 2005.

33. Dean Acheson, *Present at the Creation: My Years in the State Department* (New York: W. W. Norton, 1969), 626.

34. Lawrence S. Kaplan, *A Community of Interest: NATO and the Military Assistance Program, 1949–1951* (Washington, DC: Office of the Secretary of Defense, Historical Office, 1990), 168–69.

11. London

The first two epigraphs are taken from the following sources: LG, unpublished memoir, chapter 5, Sept. 30, 2005; and Robert Gordon, remarks delivered at memorial service for Lincoln Gordon, Cosmos Club, Washington, DC, Mar. 27, 2010. The Gordon family printed a booklet with the speeches that were delivered at the memorial service, plus numerous family photographs ("Lincoln Gordon, 1913–2009: Collected Memories"). The third epigraph is taken from LG, unpublished memoir, chapter 5, Sept. 30, 2005.

1. LG, unpublished memoir, chapter 5, Sept. 30, 2005.

2. Glen H. Snyder, "The 'New Look' of 1953," in Schilling, Hammond, and Snyder, *Strategy, Politics, and Defense Budgets,* 379–524.

3. LG in his unpublished memoir incorrectly remembers the name as "Lanahan." It was Lanigan.

4. McCullough, *Truman,* 889.

5. Harry S. Truman, *Memoirs,* vol. 2, *Years of Trial and Hope* (New York: Doubleday, 1956), 493.

6. Truman, *Memoirs,* 2:493.

7. McCullough, *Truman,* 903. Harriman was "proving a spirited champion of the New Deal–Fair Deal program in a way that made Truman glow."

8. McCullough, *Truman,* 903.

9. McCullough, *Truman,* 904.

10. McCullough, *Truman,* 904.

11. McCullough, *Truman,* 904.

12. McCullough, *Truman,* 959.

13. LG, unpublished memoir, chapter 5, Sept. 30, 2005.

14. LG to William L. Batt, Jan. 3, 1953. He tells Batt that he will have difficulty in "living up to the expectations which you . . . have apparently created."

15. Handwritten note, ca. 1953, LG's personal papers.

16. LG, unpublished memoir, chapter 5, Sept. 30, 2005.

17. LG, unpublished memoir, chapter 5, Sept. 30, 2005.

18. *Hansard,* July 29, 1853, columns 1393–94.

19. LG, "U.S. Purchases in Britain/Funds for Offshore Procurement," letter to the editor, *Times,* Aug. 4, 1953, 7.

20. R. H. S. Crossman, "U.S. Purchases in Britain/Need to Prepare for Future Cuts," letter to the editor, *Times,* Aug. 5, 1953, 7.

21. "Ike Soothes McCarthy and Stassen," *New York Times,* Apr. 3, 1953.

22. Samuel Hale Butterfield, *US Development Aid: Failures and Achievements in the Twentieth Century* (Westport, CT: Praeger, 2004), 38.

23. Vernon W. Ruttan, *United States Development Assistance Policy: The Domestic Politics of Foreign Economic Aid* (Baltimore, MD: Johns Hopkins University Press, 1996), 71.

24. LG, unpublished memoir, chapter 5, Sept. 30, 2005.

25. LG, unpublished memoir, chapter 5, Sept. 30, 2005.

26. Bissell's letter foreshadows many arguments of his memoir *Reflections of a Cold Warrior.*

27. In his memoir Bissell uses almost the same language as in his letter to Gordon and calls attention to NSC Paper 141, which he coauthored at the end of the Truman administration. He calls NSC-141 the "last will and testament" of the Truman administration. See the extended discussion of the periphery point in *Reflections of a Cold Warrior,* 74–84.

28. Bissell's coauthors on NSC-141 were Paul Nitze of State and Frank Nash of Defense. As noted above, NSC-141 was the final statement of Truman foreign and national security policy, which reflected Truman's thinking as he left office.

29. Gaddis, *George F. Kennan,* 331–34.

30. Gaddis, *George F. Kennan,* 395–89. See also Nicholas Thompson, *The Hawk and the Dove: Paul Nitze, George Kennan, and the History of the Cold War* (New York: Henry Holt, 2009), 267–70.

31. Quoted in Gaddis, *George F. Kennan,* 385.

32. Gaddis, *George F. Kennan,* 385.

33. The full document was not published until 1976. See Gaddis, *George F. Kennan,* 386.

34. LG to Richard Bissell, Feb. 1, 1954.

35. LG to Dean Donald David, Oct. 19, 1954.

36. LG to David, Oct. 19, 1954.

12. Business School Professor, 1955–1960

The epigraph is taken from LG, unpublished memoir, recollection of a conversation with Pusey, in chapter 6, "A New Focus: Economic and Political Development," Aug. 2007. This is the last fragment, only six pages long and filled with cross-outs. He was ninety-four years old and could not sustain his intellectual effort.

1. "Lincoln Gordon and the Alliance for Progress: An Annotated Oral History," Craig VanGrasstek, interviewer and editor, Sept. 8, 1980, 1–3.

2. Vernon first supervised (in 1956) a Harvard-run, large-scale project on the New York metropolitan region. He started full-time teaching at the Business School and the Graduate School of Public Administration (later the Kennedy School) in 1959. His best-known works include *Sovereignty at Bay* (1973) and *Big Business and the State: Changing Relations in Western Europe* (1974).

3. Thomas C. Schelling, *The Strategy of Conflict* (Cambridge, MA: Harvard University Press, 1960). Schelling is currently a professor emeritus at the School of Public Affairs, University of Maryland, College Park.

4. Henry A. Kissinger, *Nuclear Weapons and Foreign Policy* (New York: Harper and Row, published for the Council on Foreign Relations, 1957). The other appointments were at the University of Chicago and the University of Pennsylvania; Kissinger had also been negotiating with Columbia University through Philip E. Mosely, on leave from Columbia while serving as overall director of studies for the Council on Foreign Relations.

5. See Issacson, *Kissinger,* 107ff.

6. Henry A. Kissinger, *The Necessity for Choice: Prospects of American Policy* (New York: Harper and Row, 1961).

7. LG to Dean Teele, July 25, 1955, LG's personal papers, box 2, "HBS Undated Correspondence" folder.

8. LG to Dean Teele, July 25, 1955.

9. LG's personal papers, box 23.

10. On the concept of "modernization" in the social sciences generally, see Bruce L. R. Smith, A. Lee Fritschler, and Jeremy D. Mayer, *Closed Minds? Politics and Ideology in American Universities* (New York: Brookings Institution Press, 2008), 51–61.

11. LG, unpublished memoir, chapter 6, Aug. 2007.

12. This became the subject of Gordon's research and a major book at the Harvard Business School. See Lincoln Gordon and Engelbert L. Grommers, *United States Manufacturing Investment in Brazil: The Impact of Brazilian Government Policies 1956–1960* (Boston, MA: Division of Research, Graduate School of Business Administration, Harvard University, 1962).

13. The Alliance for Progress and JFK Adviser

The first epigraph is taken from "Lincoln Gordon and the Alliance for Progress," 7. LG also cites this conversation with Berle in almost identical terms in his 1974

Truman Presidential Library oral history interview and his LBJ Presidential Library oral history interview, July 10, 1969, Paige E. Mulhollan, interviewer (http://www.lbjlib.utexas.edu/Johnson/archives.hom/oralhistory.hom/Gordon-L/Gordon.pdf). I have amalgamated and slightly edited the versions into the dialogue here. LG also included references to the events of this chapter in the partially completed chapter 6 of his draft memoir, which closely tracks the above-cited sources.

The remaining epigraphs are drawn from the following sources: Milton Eisenhower, interview with Craig VanGrasstek, Sept. 5, 1980, quoted in "Lincoln Gordon and the Alliance for Progress," note 33; George F. Kennan, *American Diplomacy 1900–1950,* quoted in Enrique Lerdau, "The Alliance for Progress: The Learning Experience," in L. Ronald Scheman, ed., *The Alliance for Progress: A Retrospective* (New York: Praeger, 1988), 165; Arthur Schlesinger Jr., "Myth and Reality," in Scheman, *Alliance for Progress,* 71; LG, quoted in "Lincoln Gordon and the Alliance for Progress," 33.

1. See the note about the first epigraph, above.

2. See the note about the first epigraph, above. The three versions of the exchange with Berle are almost identical, and I have combined them with slight editing on my part.

3. Jerome Levinson and Juan de Onis, *The Alliance That Lost Its Way* (Chicago: Quadrangle Books, 1970), 55.

4. Beatrice Berle and Travis Jacobs, eds., *Navigating the Rapids, 1918–1971: The Papers of Adolph A. Berle* (New York: Harcourt, Brace, and Jovanovich, 1973); Levinson and de Onis, *Alliance That Lost Its Way,* 52–58.

5. Levinson and de Onis, *Alliance That Lost Its Way,* 56.

6. The Berle task force report has still not been officially published but is now available to researchers and the public at the JFK Presidential Library in Boston (Pre-Presidential Papers, box 1074), unedited and declassified. Berle referred to US ambassador Whalen as "widely believed to have been in the pocket of the late dictator, Antonio Somoza, and of his son who succeeded him" (15). A summary of the report is available online at US Department of State, *Foreign Relations of the United States, 1961–1963,* vol. 12, *Inter-American Republics,* https://history.state.gov/historicaldocuments/frus1961-63v12 (accessed Oct. 20, 2014); "Document 2: Report from the Task Force on Immediate Latin-American Problems to President-elect Kennedy," Jan. 4, 1961 (copy in LG's personal papers); and in "Document 5: Draft Memorandum from the Consultant to the Task Force on Latin America (Gordon) to the President's Special Counsel (Goodwin)," Mar. 6, 1961 (copy in LG's personal papers). The full report is thirty-four double-spaced pages, and Gordon's chapter is nine pages (24–33).

7. "Lincoln Gordon and the Alliance for Progress," 26; and Berle and Jacobs, *Navigating the Rapids,* 725–26.

8. JFK, according to Arthur Schlesinger Jr., first learned of the Bay of Pigs planning on Nov. 17, 1960. See Arthur Schlesinger Jr., *A Thousand Days: John F. Kennedy in the White House* (Boston: Houghton Mifflin, 1965).

9. The president told Schlesinger that while he occasionally found Kissinger's ideas interesting, it would lead to chaos if Bundy did not clear all such visits and handle national security issues. Bundy knew that the president found Kissinger's ponderous style tiresome, and he had been cool to the proposal to bring Kissinger on as a full-time staff member. The cool Bundy and the tightly wound Kissinger had been wary of each other since Kissinger feuded with Bowie and disrupted Bundy's plans for the Harvard Center on International Affairs. See Isaacson, *Kissinger*, 112–15, on Kissinger's stint as a White House consultant during the first year of the Kennedy administration.

10. A State Department language test rated him as "excellent" in each of five measures of language competence (reading, oral comprehension, speaking, etc.), earning a "2" (with the highest rating being "1" and signifying native speaking competence). He was "good" in French, "fair" in Spanish, and "poor" in most measures of German-language competence. Gordon told me that he taught himself Portuguese by carefully studying an economics textbook in Portuguese and understanding every single sentence, verb tense, and idiomatic expression.

11. The documents are reprinted in full as appendixes in Levinson and de Onis, *Alliance That Lost Its Way*, 349–71, and in LG, *A New Deal for Latin America: The Alliance for Progress* (Cambridge, MA: Harvard University Press, 1963), 113–42.

12. "Lincoln Gordon and the Alliance for Progress," 27.

13. Levinson and de Onis, *Alliance That Lost Its Way*, 56–58.

14. Levinson and de Onis, *Alliance That Lost Its Way*, 75.

15. Levinson and de Onis, *Alliance That Lost Its Way*, 69–70.

16. Quoted in Levinson and de Onis, *Alliance That Lost Its Way*, 63.

17. See *Foreign Relations of the United States, 1961–1963*, vol. 12, *Inter-American Republics*. President Kennedy, Adlai Stevenson, and Assistant Secretary of State Harlan Cleveland planned the trip.

18. Quoted in Schlesinger, "Myth and Reality," 69.

19. Ellis Briggs, memo, n.d., LG's personal papers.

20. Levinson and de Onis, *Alliance That Lost Its Way*, 62.

21. Levinson and de Onis, *Alliance That Lost Its Way*, 62.

22. LG to Adlai Stevenson, July 7, 1961.

23. Levinson and de Onis, *Alliance That Lost Its Way*, 66.

24. Levinson and de Onis, *Alliance That Lost Its Way*, 66.

25. Levinson and de Onis, *Alliance That Lost Its Way*, 70.

26. Castro himself took a more benign view of the Alliance for Progress. Castro told Jean Daniel in 1963, "In a way it was a good idea; it marked progress of a sort. Even if it can be said that it was overdue, timid, conceived on the spur of the moment . . . despite all that I am willing to agree that the idea in itself constituted an effort to adapt to the extraordinarily rapid course of events in Latin America." Quoted in Schlesinger, "Myth and Reality," 70.

27. C. Douglas Dillon, "Prelude," in Scheman, *Alliance for Progress*, 61–66.

28. LG to Amy Gordon, Sept. 14, 1998.

29. LG, *New Deal for Latin America,* chapter 7, "Productive Tensions in the Development of the Western Hemisphere," 90–112; LG, speech, Aug. 8, 1962, Salvadore, Bahia.

30. LG, "Punta del Este Re-Visited," *Foreign Affairs* (July 1967): 634–38.

31. "Lincoln Gordon and the Alliance for Progress."

32. LG, "The Alliance at Birth: Hope and Fears," in Scheman, *Alliance for Progress,* 73–79.

33. LG, "Alliance at Birth," 78–79.

34. LG, "Alliance at Birth," 78–79.

35. LG, "Alliance at Birth," 78–79.

36. LG, "Alliance at Birth," 78–79.

14. Ambassador to Brazil

1. LG, *Supplement, Brazil, 1961–1964: The United States and the Goulart Regime* (Washington, DC: Brookings Institution Press, 2003), to LG, *Brazil's Second Chance* (Washington, DC: Brookings Institution Press, 2001), 4.

2. LG, *Supplement,* 4.

3. LG, *Supplement,* 6.

4. LG, *Supplement,* 6.

5. The Hickenlooper Amendment provided for a cutoff in US aid for any country expropriating US-owned companies without adequate compensation. Ironically, the Hickenlooper Amendment was formally invoked only once in the ensuing decade, applied against Ceylon in 1963. It was never used against Brazil, Peru, Argentina, or any other Latin American government. For a discussion from the Brazilian perspective of how the US government used the amendment to "blackmail" the Brazilian government into generous indemnity terms for expropriated US companies, see Alexandre M. Saes and Filipe P. Loureiro, "From Foreign to State Investment in the Brazilian Electric Power Sector: The Expropriation of the American Foreign and Power in Brazil," 2012, http://www.fea.usp.br/feaecon/RePEc/documentos/AlexandreSaes08WP.pdf.

6. LG, *Supplement,* 7.

7. A transcript of this meeting was later published as chapter 1 of Timothy Naftali, ed., *The Presidential Recordings, John F. Kennedy: The Great Crises,* vol. 1 (New York: W. W. Norton, 2001), 9–25.

8. Naftali, *Presidential Recordings,* 17, reprinted in LG, *Supplement,* 10.

9. Naftali, *Presidential Recordings,* 19.

10. Naftali, *Presidential Recordings,* 19, reprinted in LG, *Supplement,* 10. See also the discussion in LG, *Brazil's Second Chance,* 65ff.

11. Edwin M. Martin, *Kennedy and Latin America* (Lanham, MD: University Press of America, 1994), 77–78, 295–97.

12. Gordon, in the 2003 *Supplement* to *Brazil's Second Chance,* acknowledges that his actions were mistaken and issues a public apology (11). As late as June 2001

he was still defending the US intervention in the 1962 elections, linking this action to the related US efforts to defeat a "remittance" bill preventing repatriation of profits from foreign private investment that were supported by many prominent Brazilians. He argued this case in a June 1, 2001, letter, friendly in tone, to Professor Thomas E. Skidmore, a Brown University historian and strong critic of Gordon's ambassadorial tenure, after Skidmore attacked Gordon's campaign financing and other policies at a forum at the Lotus Club in New York City. Gordon rarely made any concessions to his critics. In a 2003 interview with James N. Green, Skidmore's colleague and successor as professor of Brazilian history at Brown and also a strong critic of Gordon's tenure as ambassador, Gordon stated that he "would not have done anything differently in Brazil." Thank you to Professor Green for sharing this interview with me.

13. The triangular US-Cuba-Brazil relationship during the missile crisis is meticulously analyzed by James G. Hershberg in a two-part article in the *Journal of Cold War Studies*: "The United States, Brazil, and the Cuban Missile Crisis, 1962," part 1, *Journal of Cold War Studies* 6, no. 2 (Spring 2004): 3–20, and part 2, *Journal of Cold War Studies* 6, no. 3 (Summer 2004): 5–67.

14. Hershberg, "United States, Brazil," part 2, 37–58.

15. Hershberg, "United States, Brazil," part 2, 59; and see the cables cited in note 166 on that page.

16. The Robert Kennedy–Joao Goulart Meeting, Dec. 17, 1962, Embassy Airgram A-710, reprinted as appendix A, LG, *Supplement,* 41–56.

17. Goulart had arranged for a plebiscite on January 6 that would vote for or against restoration of the presidential system. The vote was five to one in favor of restoring full presidential powers.

18. LG, *Supplement,* 15–17.

19. Quoted in LG, *Supplement,* 19. The full text of the memorandum is available in *Foreign Relations of the United States, 1961–1963,* vol. 12, *Inter-American Republics,* 493–98.

20. LG, *Brazil's Second Chance,* 125–30; LG, *Supplement,* 21, note 31.

21. "Analysis of New Brazilian Cabinet," June 26, 1963, memorandum for Mr. McGeorge Bundy (White House), by Brazil desk, Department of State (then CONFIDENTIAL), quoted in LG, *Supplement,* 22.

22. Embassy Telegram 106, July 17, 1963 (SECRET), quoted in LG, *Supplement,* 23.

23. LG, *Supplement,* 23.

24. Embassy Telegram 345, Aug. 17, 1963 (then SECRET), quoted in LG, *Supplement,* 24.

25. Embassy Telegram 345, Aug. 17, 1963.

26. Rio telegram EMBTEL 373 to State Department, Aug. 21, 1963. See the discussion in LG, *Brazil's Second Chance,* 60–66.

27. Quoted in LG, *Brazil's Second Chance,* 63.

28. LG, *Brazil's Second Chance,* 63.

29. LG, *Supplement,* 28–29.

30. The informant was Samuel Wainer, an intimate friend of President Goulart's, who, like Jorge Serpa, was on good terms and in regular contact with the American ambassador. Wainer also reported that the president was "physically increasingly exhausted and psychologically desperate." See Embassy Telegram 982, Nov. 2, 1963 (then SECRET), quoted in LG, *Supplement,* 29. Part of the telegram that Gordon does not quote is instructive because it lays out Goulart's thinking and strategy for the immediate period ahead. Wainer reported that Goulart "knows he cannot administer . . . [and] that time is too short for him to make any real constructive record as President, but he will not simply resign, being unwilling to go down in history as a total failure. . . . [The president believes] he should 'give up my mandate for basic reforms.' . . . The frustrated attempt for the state of siege in October, however, was premature. The intention was to have it refused by Congress and then to close Congress, whereupon Goulart would decree two big reforms immediately—(a) agrarian reform and (b) electoral reform which would give the vote to illiterates, sergeants, and enlisted men—the decree to be affirmed by plebiscite in 60 days followed by new popular election for presidency in which everyone would be eligible except Goulart himself. The problem . . . was that too many people mistrusted Goulart's real willingness to abandon office, and it was this mistrust on the left, as well as natural opposition on the right, which frustrated plan."

31. Embassy Telegram 811, Oct. 14, 1963 (then SECRET), quoted in LG, *Supplement,* 28–29.

32. LG, *Supplement,* 28.

33. Embassy Telegram 841, Oct. 16, 1963 (then SECRET), LG's personal papers. The first paragraph reads as follows: "On return here I find situation in some ways worse than I had expected, highly unstable, more likely than not to undergo substantial further deterioration, although not without some hopeful possibilities. None of this leads me to question agreed recommendations in last week's policy paper, but it adds urgency to various types [of] contingency planning discussed at White House and with [Assistant Secretary of State Edwin] Martin and [White House staffer Ralph] Dungan."

34. LG, *Brazil's Second Chance,* 64. Cf. the argument of Jeffrey Taffet, in *Foreign Aid as Foreign Policy: The Alliance for Progress in Latin America* (New York: Routledge, 2007). Taffet appears convinced that aid under the Alliance for Progress in Brazil was doled out only to completely friendly state governments.

35. LG to Moscoso, Dec. 28, 1963.

36. This is the basis for his criticism of Goulart, which Gordon elaborated in lengthy letters to Ed Martin, assistant secretary for inter-American affairs. Martin never accepted Gordon's argument and usually took a softer position on Goulart's motives. Martin did not, however, argue against support for the military leaders when the coup actually came.

37. Joseph A. Page, *The Revolution That Never Was: Northeast Brazil 1955–1964* (New York: Grossman Publishers, 1972), 124.

38. LG, *Supplement,* 30, note 43.

39. LG, *Supplement,* 32–33. See also LG, *Brazil's Second Chance,* 66–68; Phyllis Parker, "U.S. Policy Prior to the Coup of 1964" (PhD diss., University of Texas), first published in 1977 in Portuguese under the title *1964: O papel dos Estados Unidos no golpe de estado de 31 marco* [1964: The Role of the United States in the coup d'état of March 31] (Rio de Janeiro: Editora Civilizacao Brasileira, 1977) and then in English under the title *Brazil and the Quiet Intervention, 1964* (Austin: University of Texas Press, 1979).

40. LG, *Supplement,* 32.

41. Robert F. Goheen to LG, June 7, 1963. Goheen was writing "at the suggestion of several of your friends and admirers on the Princeton campus, Pendleton Herring, Lester Chandler, and Chandler Patterson." LG's penciled marginalia indicate he answered the letter on July 2, 1963.

42. LG, oral history, July 10, 1969, LBJ Presidential Library (pp. 1–12 of the written text version). LG's allusion to fundraising may have been a case of the wish being father to the thought. A dean's job always involves fundraising even with a generous endowment. This same misconception occurred in 1967, when LG was misled into believing that the Johns Hopkins presidency would not involve much fundraising.

43. LG, oral history, July 10, 1969, LBJ Presidential Library (pp. 1–13 of the written text). LG also wrote a letter from his Cosmos Club room on the evening of January 25 describing the meeting with Mann and telling his wife that he had agreed to stay on through 1965 (LG's personal papers).

44. James N. Green, *We Cannot Remain Silent: Opposition to the Brazilian Military Dictatorship in the United States* (Durham, NC: Duke University Press, 2010), 36.

45. Embassy Airgram A-871, Jan. 20, 1964 (then SECRET).

46. LG, *Supplement,* 34–35.

47. Embassy Telegram 3824, Mar. 26, 1964 (then TOP SECRET), sent through CIA communications, reproduced in full as appendix B in LG, *Supplement,* 57–62, available at "National Security Archives," http://www2.gwu.edu/~nsarchiv/ (accessed Oct. 20, 2014). This Web site was developed at George Washington University by critics of US foreign policy on the political left to promote critical discussion of national security issues and to declassify national security documents.

48. Embassy Telegram 3824, Mar. 26, 1964. The "National Security Archives" Web site erroneously suggests under the heading "Brazil 1964" that the United States was aware of and had already backed the coup as of March 26 and had prepositioned the arms for the coup backers. The audio of a critically important March 31 conference call in which President Johnson discusses the Brazilian crisis with State Department officials George Ball and Tom Mann is available at http://millercenter.org/scripps/archive/presidentialrecordings/Johnson/1964/03_1964 (accessed Oct. 20, 2014). This conversation makes clear that the United States did not have prior knowledge of or authorize the military coup. The president can be heard asking his staff to "do everything that we need to do." This conversation, however, took place

after the United States had learned that the coup was under way and does not indicate that the United States knew of, backed, or organized the coup in advance.

49. See the sources cited in "1964 Brazilian Coup d'Etat," *Wikipedia,* http://en.wikipedia.org/wiki/1964_Brazilian_coup_d'%C3%A9at (accessed Oct. 20, 2014). The *Wikipedia* entry quotes heavily from the first volume of Elio Gaspari's multivolume account of Brazil's military rule. I am grateful to Hugh Gordon and Rui Neiva for translations of Goulart's speeches, Gaspari's analysis, and Carlos Fico's *O grande irmão: da Operaçao Brother Sam aos anos de chumbo: O governo dos Estados Unidos e a ditadura militar brasileira* (Rio de Janiero: Editora Civilizacao Brasileira, 2008). I discuss Fico's analysis in detail in the next chapter.

50. Army Intelligence Report C-24, Mar. 30, 1964 (then SECRET, declassified in 1994), in LG, *Supplement,* 34–35, note 48. Vernon Walters later, in his memoir *Secret Missions* (New York: Doubleday, 1978), makes the claim that he pinpointed the date of the coup as March 31, but that is not what he said in his contemporary report. LG, *Supplement,* 34–35, note 48, quotes language from Walters's report. Cf. Green, *We Cannot Remain Silent,* 33–48.

51. Michael R. Beschloss, ed., *Taking Charge: The Johnson White House Tapes, 1963–1964* (New York: Simon & Schuster, 1997), created confusion by editorializing that "the CIA has warned Johnson that a coup it is supporting against the government of Goulart is imminent" in order to explain an LBJ allusion in a call of March 30 to his press secretary George Reedy. There was no such CIA report. See LG, *Brazil's Second Chance,* 67.

52. LG, *Supplement,* 35, note 50, 70–73 (State Department telegram 1296 to American Embassy in Rio de Janeiro, Mar. 30, 1964, 9:52 p.m., Washington time). Gordon was instructed to "prepare recommendations on types of arms most likely to be needed," but "without consulting Brazilian authorities just yet." See also LG, *Brazil's Second Chance,* 66–68.

53. An audio of the March 31, 1964, conversation may be found at http://millercenter.org/scripps/archive/presidentialrecordings/Johnson/1964/03_1964 (accessed Oct. 20, 2014).

54. Elio Gaspari, *A ditadura envergonhada* (Sao Paulo: Cia das Letras, 2002), 90, quoted in "1964 Brazilian Coup d'État" (*Wikipedia*).

55. Gaspari, *A ditadura envergonhada,* 90, quoted in "1964 Brazilian Coup d'État" (*Wikipedia*). For an account of the coup in Recife, see Page, *Revolution That Never Was,* 195–202.

56. Joseph A. Page, *The Brazilians* (Reading, MA: Perseus Books, 1995), 213.

15. Assistant Secretary

1. Gordon summarizes these events in his *Supplement,* 37–40. See also Page, *Revolution That Never Was,* 195–202, which gives an interesting account of the situation in Recife.

2. Quoted in Green, *We Cannot Remain Silent,* 22.

3. LG, *Supplement,* 39.

4. LG, *Supplement,* 39. Lacerda repeats the story in his memoir, but without the Vietnam reference. See Carlos Lacerda, *Depoiemento,* 3rd ed. (Rio de Janeiro: Editora Frontiera, 1977), 310.

5. I am grateful to Hugh Gordon for an excellent translation of all but the last chapter of the Fico book and to Rui Neiva for translating the last chapter. Professor Fico published a reader in 2004 with selections about the 1964 coup, *Além do golpe: Versões e controvérsias sobre 1964 e a ditadura militar* (Rio de Janeiro: Editora Record, 2004). Neither of these volumes is available in English. According to Worldcat.org, the 2004 reader is also out of print in Brazil. Professor Fico blogs on his Web site about post-1984 Brazilian history. See *Brasil Recente,* http://www2.uol.com.br/historiaviva/reportagens/carlos_fico_parte_da_sociedade_queria_solucao_autoritaria.html (accessed Oct. 20, 2014).

6. Fico, *O grande irmão,* chapter 3, 7 (trans. Hugh Gordon).

7. James N. Green and Abigail Jones, "Lincoln Gordon's Evolving Doctrine: Changing Times Necessitate New Arguments," unpublished paper, n.d., 5.

8. Green and Jones, "Lincoln Gordon's Evolving Doctrine," 5.

9. LG, interview with James N. Green, Aug. 5, 2005, quoted in Green and Jones, "Lincoln Gordon's Evolving Doctrine."

10. LG, interview with James N. Green, Aug. 5, 2005, quoted in Green and Jones, "Lincoln Gordon's Evolving Doctrine."

11. Anne Gordon, in "Lincoln Gordon, 1913–2009: Collected Memories." Anne concluded her remarks by saying, "I wish his altruism had not hurt so many people. But now that he is gone, he has left me with enough money to keep my Center open for a few more years. I will strive to help those who have been hurt by poverty, gang violence, abuse, and discrimination [to] help find a voice, and in my way, continue to carry out the best part of my father's legacy."

12. Page, *Revolution That Never Was,* "Notes from a Recife Jail," 257–66, recounts his arrest and detention in Recife in November 1964 when the local police mistakenly believed he was escorting Ralph Nader (as he had done the year before). Page was released after several days of imprisonment, but while in jail he heard prisoners in neighboring cells being beaten and tortured.

13. Department of State, incoming telegram, Rio de Janeiro to Washington, Apr. 20, 1964, quoted in Green, *We Cannot Remain Silent,* 23.

14. Department of State, incoming telegram, Rio de Janeiro to Washington, Apr. 20, 1964, quoted in Green, *We Cannot Remain Silent,* 23.

15. LG, letter to the editor, *Commonweal,* Aug. 7, 1970, in an exchange with Ralph Della Cava on torture in Brazil (398–99).

16. LG, letter to the editor, *Commonweal,* Aug. 7, 1970, 178–79, 198, in response to Ralph Della Cava, "Torture in Brazil," *Commonweal,* Apr. 24, 1970. Della Cava blamed Gordon for condoning torture after the military coup and bearing major responsibility for the repression, which reached its most extreme stages after Gordon had left the country. Gordon's response denied the charge and blamed

Costelo Branco for failing to fight hard enough for a democratic regime in his first year in office when he had he chance.

17. Beschloss, *Taking Charge,* 306.

18. Quoted in Green, *We Cannot Remain Silent,* 37.

19. State Department to Rio de Janeiro, telegram, Apr. 17, 1964, NSF, Brazil, volume 4, group 2, LBJ Presidential Library, quoted in Green, *We Cannot Remain Silent,* 40.

20. In his oral history held at the LBJ Presidential Library (July 10, 1969), LG said, "There were a couple of things in connection with Vietnam. And there, I never could tell whether the President was personally involved or not. Along with all other ambassadors, I was asked to explore the possibility of Brazilian forces or other contributions to Vietnam. I resisted this. I think I had good foresight in that particular case, and with hindsight, I feel even happier that I did. I think it would have just created a shambles in Inter-American relations if any Latin American country had contributed forces. That is certainly the case in Brazil. It would have been a disaster" (19).

21. These and the following quotes come from LG's oral history, July 10, 1969, LBJ Presidential Library.

22. LG, oral history, July 10, 1969, LBJ Presidential Library, 27.

23. Robert A. Caro, *Passage to Power* (New York: Alfred A. Knopf, 2012), refers to the LBJ-RFK relationship as a "great blood feud" of American politics; see chapter 23.

24. This act by the Revolutionary Movement 8th October (MR-8) was followed by other diplomatic kidnappings and murders and helped propel Brazilian military rulers toward the most repressive phase of the long military rule. The kidnappers released Elbrick after seventy-eight hours in exchange for nineteen imprisoned leftist students.

25. John W. Tuthill and Frank Carlucci, "Operation Topsy," *Foreign Policy,* no. 8 (Autumn 1972): 62–85, figures on 85.

26. Sol M. Linowitz, *The Making of a Public Man: A Memoir* (New York: Little, Brown, 1985).

27. LG, oral history, July 10, 1969, LBJ Presidential Library, 38.

28. LG, oral history, July 10, 1969, LBJ Presidential Library, 38.

16. Johns Hopkins President

The first two epigraphs are drawn from the following sources: Minutes, Executive Session, Executive Committee, Board of Trustees, Johns Hopkins University, Nov. 7, 1966, box 2, "Minutes of Board of Trustees up to 1970," Johns Hopkins University Archives, Milton Eisenhower Library, Homewood campus, Baltimore, MD (p. 5955 in Hopkins numbering); LG, oral history, part 2, Aug. 14, 2006, 48, Johns Hopkins University Archives.

At the inauguration ceremony of Lincoln Gordon as president of Johns Hopkins University, on February 22, 1968, the question in the third epigraph was posed to Ross Jones, secretary of the Johns Hopkins Board of Trustees, after Dorothy Gordon jumped to her feet and cheered wildly for her son while the audience in Shriver Hall gave a polite ripple of applause.

1. LG, oral history, part 1, Aug. 11, 2006, Mame Warren, interviewer, Johns Hopkins University Archives.

2. LG to David Riesman, July 17, 1962, commenting on a paper Riesman had written entitled "The College Presidency," which he sent to LG for comment.

3. LG to David Riesman, July 17, 1962.

4. LG to David Riesman, July 17, 1962.

5. Stephen E. Ambrose and Richard H. Immerman, *Milton S. Eisenhower, Educational Statesman* (Baltimore, MD: Johns Hopkins University Press, 1983), 229.

6. Ambrose and Immerman, *Milton Eisenhower,* 230.

7. In his oral history, part 2, Aug. 14, 2006 (Mame Warren, interviewer, Johns Hopkins University Archives), Lincoln Gordon said that Milton Eisenhower apologized to him several years later for giving him a misleading impression about the ease of raising funds to cover potential budgetary shortfalls.

8. Muller pointed this out in commenting on the Lincoln Gordon presidency in an interview he gave to Stephen Ambrose and Richard Immerman for their biography *Milton Eisenhower* (236–39). This taped interview was said to be available to the public at the Johns Hopkins University Archives but could not be found.

9. "Education: Academic Democracy," *Time,* Jan. 27, 1967, http://content .time.com/time/magazine/article/0,9171,843397,00.html (accessed Oct. 20, 2014).

10. Minutes, Executive Session, Executive Committee, Board of Trustees, Nov. 7, 1966, Johns Hopkins University Archives.

11. Minutes, Executive Session, Executive Committee, Board of Trustees, Nov. 7, 1966, 5953.

12. Minutes, Executive Session, Executive Committee, Board of Trustees, Nov. 7, 1966, 5954.

13. Minutes, Executive Session, Executive Committee, Board of Trustees, Nov. 7, 1966, 5954.

14. Minutes, Executive Session, Executive Committee, Board of Trustees, Nov. 7, 1966, 5955.

15. Report delivered by Mr. Garland of the Screening Committee in Judge Winter's absence, Minutes, Executive Session, Executive Committee, Board of Trustees, Dec. 5, 1966, Johns Hopkins University Archives.

16. The visit may have occurred during the last week of December. It is possible that Truman called off the visit and reached his decision before the date on which he and his wife were scheduled to be on campus. The Hopkins board minutes do not say. I know that Truman met with Judge Winter in New York and that Truman received an offer, but I am not sure whether Truman and his wife made the scheduled visit to the Hopkins campus.

17. David Truman did not become president of the university. His candidacy was fatally damaged by the tumultuous events that shook the university in the spring of 1968. The Columbia trustees in the wake of the crisis appointed Andrew Cordier, dean of the School of International Affairs and an official with longtime diplomatic experience at the United Nations, as interim president of the university and later named Michael Sovern, dean of the law school, as Columbia's president. Truman left Columbia and spent the rest of his career as president of Mount Holyoke College in South Hadley, Massachusetts.

18. LG, oral history, July 10, 1969, LBJ Presidential Library, 45–47.

19. LG, oral history, July 10, 1969, LBJ Presidential Library, 45–47.

20. LBJ to LG, Jan. 19, 1967.

21. LG to LBJ, Jan. 19, 1967.

22. LG, oral history, part 1, Aug. 11, 2006, LG vertical file, Johns Hopkins University Archives.

23. LG, oral history, part 1, Aug. 11, 2006, Johns Hopkins University Archives. Milton Eisenhower was awarded thirty-one honorary degrees during his eleven-year tenure as Hopkins president.

24. See the Memorandum to President Lyndon Johnson, Mar. 24, 1968, included here as appendix C. The reader can judge for him- or herself whether my characterization is apt.

25. In 1969 he testified before Congress on behalf of the AAU universities.

26. LG, oral history, part 1, Aug. 11, 2006, Johns Hopkins University Archives.

27. AG to Ruth Kriebel (draft), Mar. 10, 1971. This letter was never sent. In it Allison describes their arrival at Hopkins and tells her friend of her husband's resignation from the Hopkins presidency, describes the faculty-administration battles that led to her husband's resignation, and identifies a "power struggle" between her husband and a "disloyal Dean" (George S. Benton).

28. AG to Ruth Kriebel (draft), Mar. 10, 1971.

29. LG, oral history, part 1, Aug. 11, 2006, Johns Hopkins University Archives.

30. Partridge had the misfortune of being fired after only a year on the job, when it was discovered that he had misrepresented his academic credentials on his curriculum vita. He had claimed to have a PhD when he in fact had not completed his program of doctoral studies.

31. LG, oral history, part 1, Aug. 11, 2006, Johns Hopkins University Archives.

32. In handwritten notes, dated June 27, 2005, when he was doing research for a chapter of his memoir that would deal with his Hopkins presidency, he wrote, "Sept. '67 . . . [Many *personnel* actions—Grad School Admissions, employment issues, etc.]." The ten pages of notes were intended to be the basis for a chapter of his memoir, but he never got far and stopped writing altogether in August 2007.

33. Ambrose and Immerman, *Milton S. Eisenhower,* 233.

34. Ambrose and Immerman, *Milton S. Eisenhower,* 232.

35. Handwritten notes, June 27, 2005, LG's personal papers. Thanks to Hugh Gordon and Amy Gordon for sending me the original handwritten notes.

36. Handwritten notes, June 27, 2005, LG's personal papers.

37. Pamphlet prepared for the president's inauguration at Johns Hopkins University (Baltimore: n.p., n.d.), 4.

38. Ibid., 3–4.

39. The strike and occupation of the admissions office by twenty black students began on January 8, 1969. The students demanded that the college admit more black and "high-risk" students.

40. Pamphlet prepared for the president's inauguration, 10.

41. Handwritten notes, June 27, 2005, LG's personal papers.

42. Pamphlet prepared for the president's inauguration, frontispiece.

43. LG, inaugural address, in pamphlet prepared for the president's inauguration, 14.

44. Ibid., 17.

45. Ibid., 17.

46. Ross Jones, interview with the author, Dec. 20, 2011, Homewood campus.

47. I was one, and Professor I. I. Rabi of the Physics Department was the other.

48. A good popular history is Michael T. Kaufman, *1968* (New York: Roaring Brook Press, 2009); see also Joe W. Haldeman, *1968* (New York: Morrow, 1995).

49. Jones, interview with the author, Dec. 20, 2011. In LG's handwritten notes of June 27, 2006, one entry reads, "Berkeley, Col, Harvard—our siblings draft *injunctions*—first use in April '69 (??)."

50. "Gordon Scores Students for Recent Columbia Coup," *News-Letter,* May 10, 1968 (Xeroxed by Kennedy Library due to deterioration of the original).

51. "Gordon Scores Students for Recent Columbia Coup."

52. Lincoln Gordon, "Student Relations at Johns Hopkins," draft of informal presentation by President Lincoln Gordon for open meeting for students, Shriver Hall, May 20, 1968 (mimeo), LG's personal papers.

53. "A Letter to the Editor, Dr. Gordon's Position," *Baltimore Sun,* May 11, 1969. The letters and commentaries to editors of newspapers and journals in the United States and Brazil about Gordon's alleged role in the 1964 events are so numerous that I gave up attempting to list them all. The substance of LG's arguments is well presented in *Brazil's Second Chance* and the *Supplement.*

54. "Gordon's Chronology," in "GORDON RESIGNS," special issue of the Hopkins *News-Letter,* vol. 25, Mar. 13, 1971.

55. "Gordon Criticizes HEW Laws on Federal Aid," *News-Letter,* Apr. 18, 1969. Gordon wrote to HEW Secretary Robert Finch urging him to let Section 411 lapse and arguing that such federal provisions were unnecessary and counterproductive. He declared that universities would expel disruptive students, who would automatically lose their federal financial aid.

56. Richard Macksey, interview with the author, Dec. 2011, Homewood campus.

57. LG, sonnet in honor of Dorothy Gordon's eightieth birthday, Apr. 4, 1969, LG's personal papers.

58. "Hopkins Head Bars Student Voice in Policy; SDS Posts Five Demands on

UM Building: Gordon Is Opposed to Allowing Youths to Vote on Academic Council," *Baltimore Sun,* May 9, 1969.

59. "Hopkins Head Bars Student Voice in Policy."

60. "Gordon Does It Again," editorial, *News-Letter,* Oct. 3, 1969.

61. "Hopkins President Terms Nixon Viet Policy 'Too Slow,'" *Baltimore Sun,* Oct. 9, 1969.

62. "Gordon Faults Leftist 'Theology,'" Brunswick, ME, Oct. 21, 1969 (Xerox clipping from LG vertical file, Johns Hopkins University Archive; the name of the newspaper is illegible, but it could be the *Baltimore Sun*).

63. "Gordon Faults Leftist 'Theology.'"

64. "Gordon Unclear on Governance Controversy," *News-Letter,* Dec. 5, 1969.

65. "Gordon Unclear on Governance Controversy."

66. LG, oral history, part 2, Aug. 14, 2006, Johns Hopkins University Archives.

67. LG, oral history, part 2, Aug. 14, 2006, Johns Hopkins University Archives.

68. LG, oral history, part 2, Aug. 14, 2006, Johns Hopkins University Archives, 48.

69. "Gordon's Chronology," Mar. 13, 1971.

70. The description of the meeting is based on Ellery Woodworth's recollection in an interview with the author, Dec. 2011, Homewood campus.

71. "Gordon Details Hopkins Unrest," *Baltimore Sun,* Sept. 18, 1970.

72. This episode occasioned a sharp dispute between Lincoln Gordon and George Benton. Benton, representing a "hardline" faction, insisted that the students had shown disrespect for authority and must be punished. Gordon attempted to soften the penalty, arguing that the students were reportedly peaceful (he had left the meeting early and did not witness the incident) and did not violently disrupt the meeting. Benton prevailed.

73. "The Plight of the Hopkins: A Grim Story in Statistics," President Lincoln Gordon to the Alumni of Johns Hopkins University, n.d. (probably Sept. 1970), excerpt, LG vertical file, Johns Hopkins University Archives.

74. The exaggeration in the size of the deficit was discovered by Robert C. Bowie, who worked closely with Milton Eisenhower from April 1971 on and then with Provost Steven Muller. President Muller in 1973 made Bowie vice president of administration and then senior vice president in 1980. Bowie left Hopkins to become treasurer of Rollins College in Florida in 1987 and then went to the Florida Institute of Technology in a similar post from 1991 to 1995 before retiring.

75. Minutes, meeting of the General Assembly of the Faculty of Arts and Sciences, Dec. 11, 1970, Johns Hopkins University Archives.

76. Minutes, meeting of the General Assembly of the Faculty of Arts and Sciences, Dec. 11, 1970, 3.

77. Minutes, meeting of the General Assembly of the Faculty of Arts and Sciences, Dec. 11, 1970, 3.

78. Minutes, meeting of the General Assembly of the Faculty of Arts and Sciences, Dec. 11, 1970, 4.

17. What Now?

1. Ambrose and Immerman, *Milton Eisenhower,* 234.

2. Ambrose and Immerman, *Milton Eisenhower,* 228.

3. Milton Eisenhower, Jan. 1980, quoted in Ambrose and Immerman, *Milton S. Eisenhower,* 235.

4. Milton S. Eisenhower, *The Wine Is Bitter: The United States and Latin America* (Garden City, NY: Doubleday, 1963), 8, 12.

5. Ambrose and Immerman, *Milton S. Eisenhower,* 1–7.

6. Minutes, meeting of the General Assembly of the Faculty of Arts and Sciences, Feb. 11, 1971, Johns Hopkins University Archives; "GORDON RESIGNS," Mar. 13, 1971.

7. Cited by Professor Bela Belassi, from Minutes, meeting of the General Assembly of the Faculty of Arts and Sciences, Feb. 19, 1971, Johns Hopkins University Archives, 5.

8. Minutes, meeting of the General Assembly of the Faculty of Arts and Sciences, Feb. 12, 1971, Johns Hopkins University Archives, 2.

9. Art Levine, "Gordon's Downfall Foreseen," in "GORDON RESIGNS," Mar. 13, 1971.

10. Minutes, meeting of the General Assembly of the Faculty of Arts and Sciences, Feb. 19, 1971, 5.

11. Levine, "Gordon's Downfall Foreseen."

12. Minutes, meeting of the General Assembly of the Faculty of Arts and Sciences, Feb. 19, 1971, 4.

13. Minutes, meeting of the General Assembly of the Faculty of Arts and Sciences, Feb. 19, 1971, 5.

14. Levine, "Gordon's Downfall Foreseen."

15. LG, oral history, part 2, Aug. 14, 2006, Johns Hopkins University Archives.

16. LG, oral history, part 2, Aug. 14, 2006, Johns Hopkins University Archives. The next several quotes are from also from the Johns Hopkins oral history.

17. AG, handwritten letter, LG's personal papers. The letter is dated March 10, 1971, but this may have been a mistake, or else she was anticipating LG's resignation, because he did not actually resign on March 10.

18. LG to D. Luke Hopkins, June 29, 1971.

19. Brad Jacobs to LG, Mar. 18, 1971.

20. Brad Jacobs to LG, Mar. 18, 1971.

21. LG to Brad Jacobs, Mar. 19, 1971.

22. Gordon sponsored Muller for membership in Washington's Cosmos Club, writing a strong and warm nominating letter to the Admissions Committee.

23. LG to D. Luke Hopkins, June 29, 1971.

24. Ellery B. Woodworth, who worked for Muller during his entire presidential term, gave me this description. I met Steve Muller on several occasions and found him extremely likable and impressive.

25. My account of the meeting comes from Mrs. Steven Muller, based on what he told her. Steve Muller was still alive at the time I wrote this chapter, but he suffered from dementia and could not be interviewed. He died early in 2013.

26. Muller, when he became president in 1972, chose not to live in Nichols House because he did not want his teenage daughters exposed to the fishbowl atmosphere of living on campus.

27. The figure of potentially as much as $500,000 was cited to me by Robert C. Bowie, who became Milton's "go-to" accountant in getting the budget under control.

28. Bowie left to join Rollins College in Florida as vice president and treasurer (see chapter 16, note 74). Bowie left Johns Hopkins when he began to feel that his influence on President Muller was diminishing and that the university's finances were beginning to get out of control again.

29. LG's personal papers.

30. The letter is from LG's personal papers and has "envelope *not* marked private" written in his handwriting at the top.

31. Copy of memorandum, Oct. 11, 1971, LG's personal papers.

32. The essay, directed against Senator Frank Church (D, Idaho), dated November 10, 1971, was submitted to the *Washington Post* for publication as an op-ed piece. The *Post* apparently did not publish it. Gordon identifies himself during this period as professor of international economics, Johns Hopkins School of Advanced International Studies.

33. Copy of memorandum, Oct. 11, 1971, LG's personal papers.

34. LG to Charles J. Hitch, Feb. 1, 1971.

35. Other works grew from his initial work at the Wilson Center and came to fruition at RFF.

36. N.d., LG's personal papers.

37. Text of remarks at memorial service for Walter Salant, LG's personal papers.

38. LG to Don and Nancy McGranahan, Sunday, Jan. 8, 1978.

39. Charles J. Hitch to LG, Sept. 28, 1978.

40. Martin Walker, *The Cold War: A History* (New York: Macmillan, 1995), 245.

41. LG to Eugene V. Rostow, Sept. 29, 1977.

42. Rostow to LG, Oct. 3, 1977.

43. Rostow to LG, Oct. 3, 1977.

44. Hans S. Landsberg, Oct. 2, 1980, spoof letter addressed to the RFF staff for use at the party celebrating LG's service.

45. Emery N. Castle to LG, Feb. 6, 1981.

46. Milton Russell, director, Center for Energy Policy Research, RFF, to LG, Sept. 29, 1980.

47. LG to Don and Nancy McGranahan, Oct. 19, 1980.

48. Stansfield Turner to LG, Aug. 20, 1980.

49. "US Intelligence Performance on Central America: Achievements and Selected Instances of Concern," Staff Report on Oversight and Evaluation of a Sub-

committee of the Permanent Select Committee on Intelligence, Sept. 22, 1982 (Washington, DC: Government Printing Office, 1982), 9.

50. LG to Bruce Clarke, Oct. 2, 1981.

51. LG to Bill Casey, Apr. 4, 1981.

18. Elder Statesman

1. Lincoln Gordon, with J. F. Brown, Pierre Hassner, Josef Joffe, and Edwin A. Moreton, *Eroding Empire: Western Relations with Eastern Europe* (New York: Brookings Institution Press, 1987). This study was sponsored by the Brookings Institution and the Hudson Institute.

2. LG to Don and Nancy McGranahan, July 17, 1986.

3. LG to Don and Nancy McGranahan, Feb. 17, 1987.

4. LG to Don and Nancy McGranahan, Feb. 17, 1987.

5. LG to F. Tremaine Billings, Sept. 7, 2006.

6. LG to his children, Apr. 27, 1988 (one of the "Chers enfants" letters he wrote regularly to Anne, Bob, Hugh, and Amy, following the tradition established by Allison of writing to the children with news from Brazil).

7. He participated in eighteen such suits, mostly in the 1990s. A number of the suits concerned the copper mining industry. The issue usually was whether the federal government had authorized or condoned effluent discharges in the interests of speeding up wartime production. Gordon testified that the federal government had done no such thing.

8. Lincoln Gordon, "Notes on a Trekking Visit to Nepal," Nov. 1990, LG's personal papers.

9. LG to his children ("Chers enfants" letter), Dec. 14, 1990.

10. LG to his children, Dec. 14, 1990.

11. LG to his children, Dec. 14, 1990.

12. LG to Josephine B. "Jo" Saner of Springfield, IL, Jan. 11, 1995.

13. LG to Richard Haass, Apr. 8, 1997.

14. LG, Christmas letter to friends, Dec. 2002.

15. LG, Christmas letter to friends, Dec. 2002.

16. LG, Christmas letter to friends, Dec. 2005.

17. LG, Christmas letter to friends, Dec. 2005.

18. He attempted to work on chapter 6 from time to time but got nowhere. The last fragment of his draft memoir is a rambling six pages that starts to explain his shift in intellectual interests toward Latin America and Brazil while he was at the Harvard Business School in the late 1950s. The text is full of cross-outs, interlineations, and editorial comments to himself. It is dated August 2007.

19. LG to Josh Billings, Aug. 7, 2006.

20. LG to Amy Gordon, Sept. 13, 1998.

21. LG to Amy Gordon, Sept. 13, 1998.

22. LG to Amy Gordon, Sept. 13, 1998.

19. Going Gently

1. LG to Josephine Saner, Jan. 11, 1995.
2. LG to Josephine Saner, Jan. 11, 1995.

Epilogue

1. Fullilove, *Rendezvous with Destiny*.

Selected Bibliography of Lincoln Gordon's Scholarly Writings

Books and Monographs

Lincoln Gordon. "The Federal Trade Commission and the Courts." AB, honors thesis, Harvard University, 1933.

Lincoln Gordon. *The Public Corporation in Great Britain*. Oxford University Press, 1938.

Merle Fainsod and Lincoln Gordon. *Government and the American Economy*. W. W. Norton & Company, 1941.

Lincoln Gordon. "Economic Aid and Trade Policy as an Instrument of National Strategy." Graduate School of Business Administration, Harvard University, 1956.

Lincoln Gordon and Philip Caryl Jessup. "International Stability and Progress: United States Interests and Instruments." Graduate School of Business, Columbia University, 1958.

Lincoln Gordon and Engelbert L. Grommers. *United States Manufacturing Investment in Brazil: The Impact of Brazilian Government Policies, 1946–1960*. Harvard University Press, 1962.

Lincoln Gordon. *A New Deal for Latin America: The Alliance for Progress*. Harvard University Press, 1963.

Lincoln Gordon. "Conditions for Investment in Countries at Different Levels of Development." International Chamber of Commerce, 1976.

Lincoln Gordon. *From Marshall Plan to Global Interdependence: New Challenges for Industrialized Nations*. Organisation for Economic Co-operation and Development, 1978.

Lincoln Gordon. "International Stability and North-South Relations." Stanley Foundation, 1978.

Lincoln Gordon. *Growth Policies and the International Order*. McGraw-Hill, 1979.

Joy Dunkerley, William Ramsay, Lincoln Gordon, and Elizabeth Cecelski. *Energy Strategies for Developing Nations*. Johns Hopkins University Press, 1981.

Lincoln Gordon. *Changing Growth Patterns and World Order*. Resources for the Future, 1982.

Lincoln Gordon. "The Future of Western Policies toward Eastern Europe: Report of a Review Conference Sponsored by the Defense Intelligence College, September 1985." Hudson Institute, 1986.

Lincoln Gordon, ed. *Eroding Empire: Western Relations with Eastern Europe*. Brookings Institution Press, 1987.

Lincoln Gordon and Timothy W. Stanley. "Integrating Economic and Security Factors in East-West Relations." Atlantic Council of the United States, 1988.

Karen Dawisha, Lincoln Gordon, and John W. Kiser III. "Change in Eastern Europe: Soviet Interests and Western Opportunities." Atlantic Council of the United States, 1989.

Lincoln Gordon. "Searching for a New Economic Model." Atlantic Council of the United States, 1990.

Lincoln Gordon. *Brazil's Second Chance: En Route toward the First World*. Brookings Institution Press, 2001.

Lincoln Gordon. *Brazil 1961–64: The United States and the Goulart Regime*. Brookings Institution Press, 2003.

Articles and Book Chapters

Lincoln Gordon. "The Port of London Authority." In *Public Enterprise*, ed. W. A. Robson. George Allen & Unwin, 1937.

Lincoln Gordon. "The Public Corporation in Great Britain." *Public Administration* 16, no. 4 (1938): 466–91.

Lincoln Gordon. "Government Controls in War and Peace." *Bulletin of the Business Historical Society* 20, no. 2 (1946): 42–51.

Lincoln Gordon. "An Official Appraisal of the War Economy and Its Administration." *Review of Economics and Statistics* 29, no. 3 (1947): 183–88.

Lincoln Gordon. "ERP in Operation." *Harvard Business Review* 27, no. 2 (1949): 129–50.

Lincoln Gordon. "L'intégration économique européenne." *Politique étrangère* 14, no. 6 (1949): 523–38.

Lincoln Gordon. "Libertarianism at Bay." *American Economic Review* 39, no. 5 (1949): 976–78.

Lincoln Gordon. "An Expansionist Policy for Production." *Institution of Production Engineers Journal* 32, no. 5 (1953).

Lincoln Gordon. "Myth and Reality in European Integration." *Yale Review* 45, no. 1 (1955).

Lincoln Gordon. "Economic Aspects of Coalition Diplomacy—The NATO Experience." *International Organization* 10, no. 4 (1956): 529–43.

Lincoln Gordon. "The Organization for European Economic Cooperation." *International Organization* 10, no. 1 (1956): 1–11.

Lincoln Gordon. "NATO and European Integration." *World Politics* 10, no. 2 (1958): 219–31.

Lincoln Gordon. "N.A.T.O. in the Nuclear Age." *Survival: Global Politics and Strategy* 1, no. 2 (1959).

Lincoln Gordon. "Private Enterprise and International Development." *Harvard Business Review* 38, no. 4 (1960): 132–38.

Lincoln Gordon. "Economic Regionalism Reconsidered." *World Politics* 13 (1961): 231–53.

Lincoln Gordon. "Punta Del Este Revisited." *Foreign Affairs* 45, no. 4 (1967): 624–38.

Lincoln Gordon. "A Healthy University in a Sick Society?" *Journal of Medical Education* 45, no. 11 (1970): 847–53.

Lincoln Gordon and Samuel A. Stern. "The Judicial and Administrative Procedures Involved in the Chilean Copper Expropriations." *American Journal of International Law* 66, no, 4 (1972): 205–13.

Francisco Orrego-Vicuña and Lincoln Gordon. "Economic Development, Political Democracy, and Equality: The Chilean Case." *American Journal of International Law* 67, no. 5 (1973): 213–21.

Lincoln Gordon. "Environment, Resources and Directions of Growth." *World Development* 3, nos. 2–3 (1975): 113–21.

Lincoln Gordon, Allen Lesser, and Richard H. Ullman. "Correspondence." *Foreign Affairs* 53, no. 3 (1975): 575–80.

Lincoln Gordon, C. A. Pryor, Robert W. Schoning, David Pimentel, John Krummel, and William Dritschilo. "Food, Energy, and Population." *Science,* new series 193, no. 4258 (1976): 1070+, 1073–76.

Lincoln Gordon. "Introduction." In *Brazil: Awakening Giant,* ed. Phillip Raine. Public Affairs Press, 1978.

Lincoln Gordon. "Foreign Policy Challenges for a President: Between Cold War and Détente." *Atlantic Community Quarterly* 22, no. 2 (1984): 172–82.

Lincoln Gordon. "The Alliance at Birth: Hopes and Fears." In *The Alliance for Progress: A Retrospective,* ed. L. Ronald Scheman. Praeger, 1988.

Lincoln Gordon. "Recollections of a Marshall Planner." *Journal of International Affairs* 41, no. 2 (1988): 233–45.

Lincoln Gordon. "Assessing Brazil's Political Modernization." *Current History* 97, no. 616 (1998): 76–81.

Lincoln Gordon. "Varieties of Nationalism: A Half Century of Brazilian-American Relations." *Brookings Institution Papers* (2003).

Book Reviews

Lincoln Gordon. Review of *Government Corporations and Federal Funds,* by John McDiarmid. *Yale Law Journal* 48, no. 5 (1939): 922–25.

Lincoln Gordon. Review of *Government Corporations and State Law,* by Ruth G. Weintraub. *Columbia Law Review* 39, no. 7 (1939): 1278–80.

Lincoln Gordon. Review of *Power in Transition,* by Ernest R. Abram. *Journal of Land & Public Utility Economics* 17, no. 2 (1941): 255–56.

Lincoln Gordon. Review of *Public Policy and the General Welfare,* by Charles A. Beard. *Annals of the American Academy of Political and Social Science* 218 (1941): 195–96.

Lincoln Gordon. Review of *The Managerial Revolution: What Is Happening in the World,* by James Burnham. *American Economic Review* 32, no. 3, part 1 (1942): 626–31.

Lincoln Gordon. Review of *Public Administration in Perspective: Reflections on Public Administration,* by John M. Gaus. *Public Administration Review* 7, no. 4 (1947): 263–67.

Lincoln Gordon. Review of *Knudsen--A Biography,* by Norman Beasley. *Military Affairs* 12, no. 2 (1948): 120–21.

Lincoln Gordon. Review of *The Economic Reconstruction of Europe,* by Geoffrey Crowther. *American Economic Review* 39, no. 2 (1949): 553–55.

Lincoln Gordon. Review of *The West at Bay,* by Barbara Ward. *American Economic Review* 39, no. 2 (1949): 548–50.

Lincoln Gordon. Review of *The Political Economy of American Foreign Policy: Its Concepts, Strategy, and Limits,* by W. Y. Elliott, Frank Altschul, R. M. Bissell, C. C. Brown, H. van B. Cleveland, Theodore Geiger, H. D. Gideonse, E. S. Mason, and D. K. Price. *Review of Economics and Statistics* 38, no. 1 (1956): 108–10.

Lincoln Gordon. Review of *National Monetary Policies and International Monetary Cooperation,* by Donald R. Hodgman. *Journal of Finance* 30, no. 3 (1975): 935–37.

Lincoln Gordon. Review of *US-Brazilian Reprise, Requiem for Revolution: The United States and Brazil, 1961–1969,* by Ruth Leacock. *Journal of Interamerican Studies and World Affairs* 32, no. 2 (1990): 165–78.

Index

Aaron, Henry, 397

Accion Democratica, 221

Acheson, Dean: Acheson-Lilienthal report on US proposals to the UNAEC, 91–93; Committee on the Present Danger and, 375; European integration issue and, 149, 150; German rearmament issue and, 170, 172, 173–74; launching of NATO and, 184, 187; opposition to Henry Wallace, 112; response to Gordon's "Economic Regionalism Reconsidered" article, 217; return to private law practice in 1947, 123; support for Harriman as adviser to Truman, 167; US postwar atomic policy and, 89, 90–91

Acheson, George, 31–32

Acheson-Lilienthal Report, 91–93, 94, 95

Adenauer, Konrad, 170, 173

Agee, James, 83

AI-1. *See* First Institutional Act

AI-2. *See* Second Institutional Act

Aldrich, Winthrop, 194, 196, 198–99

Alexander, Robert, 220

Allen, Richard V., 374

Alliance for Progress: Argentine coup and, 246; Brazil and, 234–36, 237, 241, 242, 259–62, 406; Castro's views of, 457n26; countering of communist penetration in Latin America, 228; Milton Eisenhower's views of, 350; Gordon's "Economic

Regionalism Reconsidered" article, 216–17; Gordon's retrospective analysis on the failure of, 385–87, 388–90; Kennedy and, 222, 224, 228–30; Marshall Plan analogy, 236–37, 242, 406; overview and assessment of Gordon's contribution to, 2, 3, 234–36, 237, 406; planned meeting of Latin American presidents and, 294, 301; Punta del Este conference, 226, 227–34, 235–36; twenty-fifth anniversary, 385

Alphand, Herve, 186

Ambrose, Stephen, 345

American Communist Party, 110

Americanism, 7, 14–15, 301

Anaconda copper company, 69

Anderson, Oscar E., Jr., 109

Anderson, Wayne, 348

Anselmo dos Santos, Jose, 268

anticommunism: Alliance for Progress and, 228; Berle task force on Latin America policy and, 221–22; George Marshall and, 137

antiwar students: at Columbia University, 322; at Johns Hopkins, 322–24, 325, 328–29, 364

Appleby, Paul, 110–11

Argentina, 246, 294, 295

Armacost, Michael, 389

Assis Brasil, Argemiro de, 257, 270, 271

assistant secretary for inter-American affairs: Dominican negotiations, 290–91; Gordon's decision to

assistant secretary for inter-American
affairs *(cont.)*
    move to Johns Hopkins, 300–303,
    310–11; interactions with Johnson
    on personnel issues, 293–94; at
    Johnson's Texas ranch, 298–99;
    LBJ offers the position to Gordon,
    286–90; overview and assessment
    of Gordon's service, 3, 407–8;
    planning for the meeting of Latin
    American presidents, 294–99,
    301; typical working day, 291–
    92; working relationships in the
    Johnson administration, 292
Association of American Universities
    (AAU), 315
atomic bombs: development of, 88–89;
    end of World War II, 82–83;
    Gordon's analysis of US nuclear
    diplomacy, 112–17; US bomb tests
    in the Pacific, 98–99; US postwar
    atomic diplomacy, 89–91. *See also*
    UN Atomic Energy Commission
Atomic Development Authority (ADA),
    100, 114
auto industry: World War II
    demobilization issues and, 82

Balaguer, Joachim, 291
Ball, George, 223, 269, 274, 285, 287,
    288–89
Balliol College, 39, 40–41
Baltimore Sun, 323
Barnard, Chester I., 91
Barnett, Vince, 111
Barrie, J. M., 29
Baruch, Bernard: in Gordon's
    unfinished memoirs, 391–92; US
    representative to the UNAEC,
    92, 93–110; Henry Wallace
    and, 99–100, 106–10, 111; War
    Production Board controversy and,
    74

Batt, William L., 70–71, 73, 192, 193,
    200
Battiglia, Felix, 320
Bay of Pigs invasion, 224, 226–27, 228,
    350
Beach, Northrop ("Nors"), 30–32
Belassi, Bela, 353
Bell, David, 252
Bennett, W. Tapley, 285, 290–91
Bentley, Robert, 274
Benton, Charlotte, 351
Benton, George: dispute with
    Gordon over student protesters,
    328, 468n72; Gordon's forced
    resignation and, 345, 346, 351,
    353–54, 355, 356, 359; provost
    position at Johns Hopkins and,
    334; undermines Gordon during
    the 1970–1971 fiscal crisis, 335–36,
    337–38, 339, 341, 342, 344
Berchtesgaden, 45
Berle, Adolf A., 216, 219–23, 224,
    225–26, 237, 263
Berle Task Forces, 219–23, 225, 456n6
Bernstein, Aline, 20–21
Betancourt, Romulo, 221
Beugel, Ernst van der, 144
Bevan, Ernest, 123, 168
Bevan, William, 312, 334
Bidault, George, 123
*Big Brother: From Operation Brother
    Sam to the Years of Lead* (Fico),
    275–80
Billings, Josh, 384
Billington, James H., 369–70
Birdsell, Thomas E., 126
Birmingham, Dorothy ("Dot"), 53, 396
Bissell, Richard: 1954 CIA coup in
    Guatemala and, 212; Bay of Pigs
    invasion and, 224; European
    integration issue and, 148, 149;
    European Payments Union and,
    153, 154, 156; Gordon's 1954

decision to return to the Harvard
Business School and, 202–3, 204–5;
Gordon's wartime association with,
77; Harriman Committee and, 127;
Marshall Plan and, 139, 140

Blair, C. Stanley, 319

Boas, Ralph P., 19

BOB. *See* Bureau of the Budget

Bonesteel, Charles H., 126, 127, 139

Boorstin, Daniel, 58

Bosch, Juan, 285, 290, 291

Bowdoin College, 329

Bowie, Robert (Harvard law professor),
208–10, 376–77

Bowie, Robert C. (comptroller at Johns
Hopkins University), 317, 362,
363–64, 470n28

Brazil: 1963 US aid package, 252–53;
1964 coup, reaction, and aftermath,
269–73, 274–75, 280–84, 407, 411;
Alliance for Progress and, 234–
36, 237, 241, 242, 259–62, 406;
Adolf Berle's mission to, 225–26;
Comício da Central rally, 266–67;
Cuban Missile Crisis and, 248–50;
development of Gordon's interest in,
212–17; Dominican Republic crisis
and, 285–86; events prior to the
1964 military coup, 262–69; Carlos
Fico's critique of US involvement in
the 1964 coup, 275–80; Gordon as
US ambassador (*see* US ambassador
to Brazil); Gordon's impressions
of Sao Paolo, 237; Gordon's last
research and books on, 385–87,
388–90, 411; Gordon's travels in,
243; Goulart and land reform,
253–54; Goulart's political career
and rise to presidency, 239–40,
243–45; Goulart's political troubles
in 1962, 245–46; Hopkins School
of Hygiene and Public Health
and, 314; human rights movement
and, 2, 407; Institutional Acts,
279, 281–82, 283, 284; Kennedy's
planned visit to, 246, 250, 256;
Robert Kennedy's visit to, 250–52;
Marxism in, 242; nationalization
disputes, 244, 248; parliamentary
system and, 240, 243–44; political
deterioration in 1963, 254–58;
political events in the 1980s
and 1990s, 385, 388; Quadros's
presidency and resignation, 237,
238–39, 240; reaction to Kennedy's
assassination, 258; "sailors' revolt,"
268; US 1964 contingency plan,
263; US AID mission in Recife,
260–61; US Cold War perspectives
and, 242; US intervention in the
1962 elections, 247–48, 458–59n12

Brazilian Labor Party, 239

Brazil's Second Chance (Gordon), 385–
87, 388–90, 411

Bretton Woods system: European
Payments Union and, 153, 160;
Gordon's argument for modifying
in the case of Third World
countries, 214, 216–17; Gordon's
views of European unification and,
213–14

Brewster, Kingman, 319

Briggs, Ellis, 230–31

British Broadcasting Corporation
(BBC), 46, 47

Brizola, Leonel: 1964 coup and, 272,
274; 1989 Brazilian presidential
election and, 388; attacks on San
Tiago Dantas, 252; attacks on the
Peace Corps, 248; attacks on the
US, 245; at the Comício da Central
rally, 266; Joao Goulart's rise to
the Brazilian presidency and, 240;
nationalization of US enterprises,
244; political deterioration in 1963
and, 254, 257

Brochado da Rocha, Francisco, 246
Brofers, Eric, 144
Bronk, Detlev, 319
Brookings Institution: Gordon joins in 1984, 381–83; Gordon's contact with through Resources for the Future, 371–72; Gordon's last research and books on Brazil, 385–87, 388–90; Gordon's ninetieth birthday celebration, 395; Gordon's work on his memoirs, 390–94, 412; overview of Gordon's time with, 410–12; report on the Economic Cooperation Administration, 136
Brookings Institution Press, 390
Brooks, E. Penn, 72
Brother Sam naval task force, 267, 268, 272, 275, 279
Bundy, McGeorge: Gordon hires for the Economic Cooperation Administration, 142; Harvard Center for International Affairs and, 208, 209–10; in the Johnson administration, 291; in the Kennedy administration, 219, 224; Kissinger and, 224, 225, 457n9
Bundy, Steve, 390
Bunker, Ellsworth, 290
Bureau of Intelligence and Research, 278
Bureau of Research and Statistics, 60
Bureau of the Budget (BOB), 128, 132–34
Bush, George W., 392
Bush, Vannevar, 88–89, 96
Byrnes, James F., 74, 75; influential in Bernard Baruch's appointment as US representative to the UNAEC and, 93–94, 95; opposition to Navy atom bomb tests in the Pacific, 98; US postwar atomic policy and, 89–91; Henry Wallace and, 107, 112

Cabot, Thomas D., 177
Callingaert, Michael, 391
Camago, Alberto Lleras, 231–32
Camp, Miriam, 128–29
Campos, Roberto, 229
Cardoso, Fernando Enrique, 388
Carter, Jimmy, 374, 375, 377
Casey, William D., 374, 379–80, 409, 410
Cassell, Emory, 381
Castellanos, Jorge Sol, 229
Castelo Branco, Humberto: 1964 coup in Brazil and, 265–66, 267, 271, 277, 279, 280, 281; 1965 meeting with Harriman, 286; Gordon's postcoup meeting with and views of, 283–84; as president of Brazil, 282–83
Castle, Emery, 376, 378
Castro, Fidel, 248–49, 457n26
cello playing, 201, 210
Center for International Affairs (Harvard University), 208–10, 213, 216
Central Electricity Board, 46, 47
Central Intelligence Agency (CIA), 376–80, 409, 410
Chace, James, 116
Chandler, Alfred D., 318, 360
Chenery, Hollis, 142
Chetwood house, 9–11, 52
Churchill, Winston, 93
CIA. See Central Intelligence Agency
civic republicanism, 403
Civilian Production Administration, 85
Clarke, Bruce, 379
class system: British, 39–40
Clay, Lucius D., 71, 144
Clayton, William, 107, 121–23
Cleveland, Harlan, 306, 307
Cleveland, Harold Van B., 148, 149, 160
Cold War: containment doctrine,

100, 119, 203–4; emergence of, 93; Gordon's analysis of in *Eroding Empire,* 410–11; impact of Wise Men and their aides, 1–2; origin of term, 90; US perspectives toward Brazil and, 242
Cole, G. D. H., 46
Collington Episcopal retirement community, 397–400
Collor de Mello, Fernando, 388
Colombo Plan, 199, 212
Columbia University, 308, 322, 466n17
Comício da Central rally, 266–67
Committee for European Economic Cooperation, 129
Committee on the Present Danger, 374–76
Common Agriculture Policy, 160
Compton, Arthur, 96
Conant, James B., 89, 96
Congress of Industrial Organizations, 109
Connolly, Tom, 95
Constitutionalism (McIlwain), 33
containment doctrine, 100, 119, 203–4
Controlled Materials Plan, 73
Cooper, Crossman, 333, 334
Copeland, Aaron, 104
copper and the copper industry, 69, 73, 471n7
Costa e Silva, Arturo, 281, 393
Council on Foreign Relations, 209
Crisler, Marge, 398
Crossman, Dick, 44, 45, 48, 195–96
Cruzeiro do Sul, 238, 284
Cuba: Bay of Pigs invasion, 224, 226–27, 228, 350; Kennedy's Latin America policy and, 228, 229, 230–31, 232
Cuban Missile Crisis, 248–50
Czechoslovakia, 123, 137

D'Alessandro, Thomas, 319, 320

Dantas, San Tiago, 240, 252–53
Darkwater house, 10, 22, 53, 58, 395
David, Donald, 87–88, 98, 139, 205, 206
D-Day, 77
"Declaration of the Peoples of the Americas," 228, 234
Defense Production Act of 1950, 180–81
depression: Allison and, 146; Lincoln and, 75–77
de Seabra, Jose, 251
Deutschbein, Max, 44
Diaz Ordaz, Gustavo, 297
Dieffenderfer, John C., 261
Dillon, C. Douglas, 232–33, 244
Dominican Republic, 285–86, 290–91, 408
Draper, William, 187
Dulles, John Foster, 71
Dungan, Ralph A., 258, 278
Dunkerly, Joy, 371, 392
Dunster House, 30, 32, 49, 51

Eberstadt, Ferdinand: with Bernard Baruch at the UNAEC, 90, 95–96, 97, 99, 102, 108, 109; with the War Production Board and Gordon's boss, 73–74
Economic Cooperation Administration (ECA): chain of command, 130; congressional approval of, 136, 137, 141; European integration issue and Gordon's analysis, 148–51; Gordon as acting director of the program division, 141–43; Gordon's organizational plan for, 128–29; Paul Hoffman as head of, 130, 141; International Security Assistance Committee and, 177; negotiations within the Truman administration to establish as an independent agency, 130–34; Senate hearings on, 134–36. *See also* Marshall Plan

"Economic Regionalism Reconsidered" (Gordon), 216–17, 218–19
Ecuador, 233
EDC. *See* European Defense Community
Eisenhower, Dwight D.: 1951 defense spending and, 171; dismantling of Korean War controls, 182; introduces tactical nuclear weapons into NATO planning, 188; McCarthyism and, 196, 197, 199; NATO and, 183; presidential management style, 405. *See also* Eisenhower administration
Eisenhower, Milton: first Johns Hopkins presidency, 304–5, 318, 332; Gordon's selection for the Johns Hopkins presidency and, 302, 303, 306, 309; as interim president of Johns Hopkins, 360–64; Johns Hopkins' faculty coup and, 347–51; Johnson's praise of, 319–20; Nichols House and, 315–16; personality of, 347; relationship with and views of Gordon, 348–49, 350; Tractors for Freedom scheme and, 350
Eisenhower administration: McCarthyism and, 196–99; perspective on social reform, 219; perspective on the Third World, 212; reorganization of foreign aid operations, 197–98
Elbrick, Charles Burke, 294, 464n24
Elliott, William Yandell: feud with Carl Friedrich, 86; as Gordon's mentor, 29, 32, 33, 34, 88; Gordon's relationship with, 210–11; recommends Gordon for Balliol College, 41; with the War Production Board, 64
EPU. *See* European Payments Union
Equitable Life Assurance Company, 327

Erhard, Ludwig, 313, 314
Eroding Empire (Gordon), 382–83, 410–11
Ethical Culture Fieldston School, 19–26, 372
ethical culture movement, 19
European Coal and Steel Community, 159, 175
European Defense Community (EDC), 174–75, 187
European integration, 148–51
European Monetary Agreement, 152
European Payments Union (EPU), 152–57, 160, 213–14, 450n19
"European Recovery and American Aid" (Harriman Committee report), 127
European Recovery Program steering committee, 125–27

Faber & Co. publishers, 48
Fainsod, Merle, 50, 60–62, 63, 86, 357
Federal Budget and Fiscal Policy, The (Smithies), 142
Federal Republic of Germany, 144, 146. *See also* West Germany
"Federal Trade Commission and the Courts, The" (Gordon's Harvard thesis), 34–36
Fico, Carlos, 275–80
Fieldston School. *See* Ethical Culture Fieldston School
FINEBEL, 153
First Institutional Act (AI-1), 279, 281–82
Fishbaum, Ellen, 317
Ford Foundation, 203, 208, 216
Foreign Operations Administration, 197
Foster, William, 150
foundation grants, 203
Fox, Bert, 71, 111
France: German rearmament issue

and, 172, 174–75; involvement in Indochina, 163; Pleven Plan, 174–75; SHAPE refurbishing controversy, 183

Frankfurter, Felix, 72–73

Franks, Oliver, 187

Freeman, Orville, 292

Freudenberg, Albert, 10

Friedrich, Carl J., 86, 87

Friendly, Alfred, 151

Fritanix. *See* FINEBEL

Frondizi, Arturo, 229, 246

Fulbright, J. William, 291

Furtado, Celso, 240, 251–52, 254, 281

Galbraith, John Kenneth, 63, 87, 219, 227

Gardner, George K., 28

Gardner, John W., 302, 306

Garland, Charles, 302, 307, 308, 309, 319, 320, 325

Gaspari, Elio, 385

Geiger, Theodore, 148, 149

George, Edwin B., 68–69

George, Walter, 135

Gilman, Daniel Coit, 362

Goheen, Robert F., 264

Goodpaster, Andrew, 185, 186

Goodwin, Richard: 1962 meeting with Kennedy and Gordon on Brazil, 247, 411; Berle Task Force and, 220, 221; Gordon's working relationship with, 224, 225; Kennedy's speech outlining the Alliance for Progress and, 224, 228; at the Punta del Este conference, 233

Gordon, Abraham Lincoln: 1960 vacation in South America, 216; Americanism and, 7, 14–15, 301; birth of his children, 86, 145, 146; children's education, 211; criticism of Nixon and Kissinger, 210; death of Allison, 383–84; death of mother Dorothy, 326–27; depression during

the war, 75–77; honorary degrees, 313; language competencies, 457n10; life story in the context of twentieth century American history, 4–6; marriage to Allison, 21, 51–57; George Marshall and, 131–32; music and cello playing, 200–201; personal characteristics, 124–25, 194–95; poetry and sonnets, 20, 78–79, 326–27; relationship with brother Frank, 27; tennis and, 22, 397; view of history, 5

—academic career: at the Harvard Business School (*see* Harvard Graduate School of Business Administration); instructor in government at Harvard, 48, 49–50, 57–59, 60; at Johns Hopkins University (*see* Johns Hopkins University presidency); Woodrow Wilson School offer, 264

—books and articles: *Brazil's Second Chance,* 385–87, 388–90, 411; "Economic Regionalism Reconsidered," 216–17, 218–19; *Eroding Empire,* 382–83, 410–11; following the Johns Hopkins presidency, 367–68; *Government and the American Economy,* 50, 60–62; *Growth Strategies and the International Order,* 370; "International Control of Atomic Energy," 112–16; "New Myths for Old: Senator Church and Foreign Aid," 367; *The Public Corporation in Great Britain,* 46–48, 50

—childhood and youth: birth of, 8; Ethical Culture Fieldston School and developing sense of self, 19–26; family history, 7–11; influence of mother Dorothy on, 11–14, 15, 16, 29–30; values and beliefs learned in the family environment, 7, 15–17

Gordon, Abraham Lincoln *(cont.)*
—college education: Harvard
    University, 27–27; Oxford
    University, 34, 37, 39–43, 46–48;
    Rhodes scholarship, 34, 37; travels
    in Europe, 37–38, 43–45
—later years: with the Brookings
    Institution *(see* Brookings
    Institution); with the Central
    Intelligence Agency, 376–80, 409,
    410; family life, 373; ninetieth
    birthday year, 394–95; overview
    and assessment of, 3, 408–12;
    physical decline and death of,
    396–400; relationship with Edith
    Page, 387–88; research and books
    on Brazil, 385–87, 388–90;
    Resources for the Future, 370–76,
    381–82; Superfund litigation and,
    386–87; travels and vacations,
    386, 387; unfinished memoirs, 17,
    390–94, 412; Woodrow Wilson
    International Center for Scholars,
    369–70
—public service career: aide to
    Harriman as adviser to Truman,
    3, 157–58, 163, 164–65, 171–72,
    175–79; analysis of US nuclear
    diplomacy, 112–16; assistant
    secretary for inter-American affairs
    (see assistant secretary for inter-
    American affairs); on the Berle task
    force for Latin America policy,
    219–23 *(see also* Latin America
    policy); development of interest
    in Brazil and the Third World,
    212–17; distaste for and lack of
    political skills, 403–4; "Economic
    Regionalism Reconsidered"
    article, 216–17, 218–19; European
    Recovery Program steering
    committee, 125–27; on the
    International Security Assistance

Committee, 177; Johnson solicits
    views on the Vietnam War, 313–14;
    joins the Kennedy administration
    in 1961, 216–17; Marshall Plan
    and *(see* Marshall Plan); NATO
    and *(see* North Atlantic Treaty
    Organization); overview and
    assessment, 17–18; overview
    and assessment of, 2–4, 401–12;
    Panama Canal issues, 374–76,
    407–8; relationship with Harriman,
    145, 178–79, 201–2; Walter Salant
    and, 36; UN Atomic Energy
    Commission service, 96–106, 108–
    10, 111; with the US embassy in
    London, 192–96, 198–201; views of
    Henry Wallace, 110–11, 392; work
    on industrial mobilization during
    the Korean War, 180
—World War II: impact on the
    career of, 17, 58–62; postwar
    career options, 85–88; service
    with the Civilian Production
    Administration, 85; War
    Production Board service, 63–64,
    68–70, 73–74, 75–55, 77–79, 80,
    84, 85
Gordon, Allison (née Wright): 1960
    vacation in South America, 216;
    birth of children, 60, 145, 146;
    childhood and family history,
    51–52; death of, 383–84; depression
    and, 146; on the emotional and
    physical impact of Marshall Plan
    service on Lincoln, 124; first
    meets Lincoln, 21, 51; on Bernard
    Gordon, 8; Harriman and, 179;
    Harvard social life, 210–11; health
    problems, 339, 373; homes in
    Washington, 179, 291, 366; life
    at Johns Hopkins, 316, 338–39;
    life during World War II, 69; life
    in Brazil, 54–55, 56, 258; life in

London, 192, 199–200; life in
Paris, 146; married life, 52–57;
personal characteristics, 51; reaction
to Lincoln's resignation from Johns
Hopkins, 357–58; unfinished novel
of, 56–57; visit to Johns Hopkins
University, 309
Gordon, Amy: birth of, 145, 146;
college education, 211; death of
mother Allison, 384; Harriman
and, 179; novel writing, 395; visit to
Johns Hopkins University, 309
Gordon, Anne: birth of, 60; college
education, 211; critique of Lincoln's
impact on Latin America, 280;
death of mother Allison, 384; polio
and, 146
Gordon, Bernard: abstinence, 12; birth
of sons, 8; death of, 10–11; division
of the Lake Sunapee property, 52;
education of Lincoln and Frank,
19, 20; Lake Sunapee home, 9–10;
marriage to Dorothy Lerner, 8,
9; George Medalie and, 15–16;
parents of, 8–9; values and beliefs
transmitted to Frank and Lincoln,
15–17
Gordon, Dorothy (née Lerner): birth
of sons, 8; broadcasting career,
7, 13, 15; death of, 13–14, 327;
death of Bernard Gordon, 10–11;
education of Lincoln and Frank,
19, 20; eightieth birthday, 326–27;
influence on Lincoln, 11–14, 15, 16,
29–30; at Lincoln's Johns Hopkins
inauguration, 321–22; marriage to
Bernard Gordon, 8, 9; relationship
with Allison, 52; travel to England
and Europe with Lincoln, 37; visits
to Nichols House, 326
Gordon, Frank H.: birth of, 8;
childhood personality, 11; college
education, 24, 27; death of, 396;

education of, 20, 24; marriage to
Dorothy Birmingham, 53; mother
Dorothy's eightieth birthday and,
326; with the Office of US Attorney
for the Southern District of New
York, 27; relationship with brother
Lincoln, 27; values and beliefs
learned in the family environment,
15–17
Gordon, Hugh B.: birth of, 86; college
education, 211; death of mother
Allison, 384; Lincoln's last years
and, 397; travels in Brazil in 1963,
258
Gordon, Kate, 398–400
Gordon, Moses and Fannie Belson, 8–9
Gordon, Robert W.: birth of, 60;
childhood in London, 200; college
education, 211; on Lincoln's
unfinished memoirs, 392; polio
and, 146; remembrance of mother
Allison, 56
Gorillas of Gill Park, The (Lawson), 395
Gorsky, Anatoly, 105
Goulart, Joao: 1962 visit to the US,
244–45; 1964 coup against,
269–72, 274; 1964 meeting with
John McCloy, 266; compared to
Gordon, 245; Cuban Missile Crisis
and, 248–50; events prior to the
1964 military coup, 262, 265–69,
460n30; exile and death of, 272;
Carlos Fico's critique of the 1964
coup against, 275–80; Gordon's
assessment of political ambition
in, 236; Gordon's initial dealings
with, 241, 243–45; Inter-American
Committee for the Alliance for
Progress conference, 261–62; JFK's
and Gordon's 1962 meeting about,
246–47, 411; Robert Kennedy's
1962 meeting with, 251–52; land
reform and, 253–54; political

Goulart, Joao (cont.)
deterioration in 1963, 254–58;
political troubles in 1962, 245–46;
relations with JFK, 244, 254; rise to
the presidency of Brazil, 239–40
Goulart, Marie, 54–55
Government and the American Economy
(Fainsod & Gordon), 50, 60–62
Grauer, Neil, 347
Great Britain: Colombo Plan, 199;
Marshall Plan allocation crisis
in 1949 and, 147–48; nuclear
power and, 113; Treaty of Brussels
defensive alliance and, 168. See also
United Kingdom; US embassy in
London
Great Debate, 181–82
Green, James N., 280
Gromyko, Andrei, 98, 101–2
Gross, Ernest, 127
Groves, Leslie, 96, 110, 113
Growth Strategies and the International
Order (Gordon), 370
Guatemala, 212
Guevara, Ernesto "Che", 232, 233,
234, 238

Haass, Richard, 389, 390
Haedo, Eduardo Victor, 233
Haig, Alexander, 378
Hamlet (Shakespeare), 125
Hammarskjöld, Dag, 144
Hancock, John: with Bernard Baruch
at the UNAEC, 95–96, 99, 102,
104, 105, 106–7, 108; Gordon's
1947 memorandum on the US
stance toward nuclear power,
112–16
Harriman, Averell: adviser to Truman
with Gordon as aide, 3, 157–58,
163, 164–65, 167–68, 171–72,
175–79; William Blatt and,
70; chairman of the President's

Committee on Foreign Aid, 127;
curiosity of, 179; death of, 383;
European Payments Union and,
153, 154, 155, 156; funding for
Gordon's Eroding Empire project
and, 382–83; German rearmament
issue and, 170, 172, 174; Dorothy
Gordon and, 13–14; Gordon's
assignment to the US embassy
in London and, 192, 193; Joao
Goulart and, 262; Korean war
and, 179–80, 183; Marshall Plan
allocation crisis in 1949 and, 147;
Marshall Plan special representative
in Paris, 141, 143–44, 145, 176;
meeting with Castelo Branco in
1965, 285; presidential aspirations,
189–92; relationship with Gordon,
145, 178–79, 201–2; strategy
review on Korea in Tokyo in
1950, 168; tensions in Marshall
Plan administration and, 148–49;
Washington dinner parties, 167–
68, 451n5; Wise Men and NATO
institutional reforms, 184–85, 186,
187
Harriman Committee, 127, 449n14
Harriman-Plowden-Monnet report,
187
Harris, Seymour E., 88
Harvard Graduate School of Business
Administration: 1957 conference
on economic development in Latin
America, 215; Gordon joins, 87–88;
Gordon's developing interest in the
Third World, 212–17; Gordon's
development of an international
business program, 206–8; Gordon's
"International Economic Relations"
course, 214–15; Gordon's outside
activities, 210–12; Gordon's
temporary leaves from, 97–98, 124,
140; Gordon's view of teaching,

215; Gordon teaches at, 111, 118–19, 120, 139, 201–5; William Ziegler Professor of International Business, 205, 206–7, 211

Harvard University: Center for International Affairs, 208–10, 213, 216; Gordon in the Government Department, 48, 49–50, 57–59, 60, 86–87; Kissinger and, 207–8, 209–10; Arthur Smithies and, 142

—Gordon's undergraduate years: classes and activities, 28–30; determination to graduate in three years, 27, 28; intellectual development, 32–34; social life, 30–32; thesis, 34–36. *See also* Harvard Graduate School of Business Administration

Harvey, Robert D. H., 324, 345, 358

Hauser, Philip M., 108, 112

Hazlitt, Henry, 139

Health, Education, and Welfare Appropriation Act of 1969, 325

Heard, George Alexander, 306, 307

Herrera, Felipe, 229, 296

Herring, Pendleton, 32, 53, 99

Hershberg, James, 249

Herter, Christian, 128

Hester, James M., 306, 307

Hewlett, Richard G., 109

Heyns, Roger W., 306, 308

Hickenlooper Amendment, 244, 248, 458n5

Hiroshima, 82, 83

history: Gordon's view of, 5

Hitch, Charles, J., 370, 371, 374

Hitler, Adolf, 45, 82

Hoffman, Paul: appointed head of the Economic Cooperation Administration, 130, 141; European integration issue and, 149–51; European Payments Union and, 154, 155, 156–57; Gordon's position

in the Marshall Plan and, 142; Harriman and, 178

Hoffman, Stanley, 209

Hogan, Michael J., 148

Holcombe, Arthur, 59

Holmes, Julius, 196, 198

honorary degrees, 313

Hoover, Herbert, 66, 181–82

Hopkins, D. Luke, 324, 358, 359

Hopkins Committee on Long-Range Planning, 304–5

Hopkins School of Advanced International Studies (SAIS), 305, 313, 365, 368, 3676

Hopkins School of Hygiene and Public Health, 314

Hopkins School of Medicine, 314

housing: World War II demobilization issues and, 81–82

human rights movement, 2, 407

Hume, John, 314, 344

Humphrey, George, 199, 219

"IDA Six," 322

Ignatieff, George, 99

Ilia, Arturo, 294

Immerman, Richard, 345

India, 227

Indochina, 163

Institute of Defense Analyses, 322

Inter-American Committee for the Alliance for Progress, 261–62

Inter-American Development Bank, 222

Inter-American Economic and Social Council, 226, 228, 232

"International Control of Atomic Energy" (Gordon), 112–16

"International Economic Relations" (Harvard Business School course), 214–15

International Security Assistance Committee, 177

International Telephone and Telegraph, 244, 248
"iron curtain" speech, 93
Isaacson, Walter, 86–87
Ismay, Hastings ("Pug"), 169, 187

Jacobs, Brad, 359
Jacobsen, Jake, 298
Japan, 82–83
John F. Kennedy Presidential Library, 391
Johns Hopkins University: 1969 convocation to discuss Vietnam, 329; academic council issue, 328; Applied Physics Laboratory, 326; becomes coed, 330; Robert Bowie and, 317, 362, 363–64, 470n28; Committee on Long-Range Planning, 304–5; endowment and fundraising, 305; Evening College, 321, 339, 354–55; internal governance system, 317–18; minority students issue, 331–32; Nichols House, 315–16, 326; School of Advanced International Studies, 305, 313, 365, 367, 368; School of Hygiene and Public Health, 314; School of Medicine, 314; "streaking" movement, 364; student antiwar protests, 328–29, 364; students' views of Gordon, 318; unionization of hourly workers, 331. See also Johns Hopkins University presidency
Johns Hopkins University presidency: Milton Eisenhower, 304–5, 318, 332, 360–64; Steven Muller, 361–62
—Lincoln Gordon: 1969 Bowdoin College speech on the future of liberal education, 329–30; 1970–1971 fiscal crisis, 332–34, 335, 336–37, 339–42, 343–47; 1971 around-the-world journey, 343–44; administrative challenges, 315–19; assessment of, 332, 408; December 1970 general assembly, 339–42; dispute with George Benton over student protesters, 468n72; Milton Eisenhower and the faculty coup, 347–51; Milton Eisenhower's relationship with and views of Gordon, 348–49, 350; Evening College expansion, 321, 354–55; faculty pay freeze, 336–37; faculty relations, 318, 324, 325–26, 330, 339–42, 343–47; forced resignation and personal aftermath, 345, 351–59, 360, 364–69; fundraising and, 305; Dorothy Gordon's death and, 327; in Gordon's unfinished memoirs, 394; Dorothy Gordon's visits to Nichols House, 326; honeymoon phase, 311–13; inauguration ceremony and inaugural speech, 319–22; initial flaws and misunderstandings, 304–5; on-campus military recruiting issue, 335, 338; personal assistant, 348; relationship with George Benton, 334, 335–36, 337–38, 341, 342; relationship with the Board of Trustees, 324–25, 330, 331, 333–34; relations with the student paper and *Baltimore Sun,* 323; replacement of provost Bill Bevan, 334, 338; selection and recruitment, 302–4, 305–9; severance package, 365–66; student and administrative problems in 1969, 327–32; student antiwar protests and, 322–24, 325, 328–29; students' views of Gordon, 318
Johnson, Louis A., 170–71
Johnson, Lyndon B.: Dominican Republic crisis, 285–86, 290–91;

entertains Gordon at the Texas ranch, 298–99; interactions with Gordon on personnel issues as assistant secretary to Latin America, 293–94; Robert Kennedy and, 293; letter for Gordon's inauguration at Johns Hopkins, 319–20; Thomas Mann and Latin America policy, 263, 264–65, 266, 267; meetings with Gordon, 285; offers Gordon the position as assistant secretary to Latin America, 286–90; planning for the meeting of Latin American presidents and, 294, 295, 297–99; plan to recruit Latin American troops for Vietnam, 286; reaction to Gordon's departure for Johns Hopkins University, 310–11; response to the 1964 crisis in Brazil, 269, 274–75, 281, 284–85, 407; solicits Gordon's views on the Vietnam War, 313–14

Johnson, Samuel Houston, 59

Jones, Ronald K., 215

Jones, Ross, 306, 322, 340, 351, 356, 358

Judd, Walter, 119

Kaplan, Lawrence S., 187

Katz, Milton: deputy to Harriman in Paris, 145, 149; European Payments Union and, 154, 155, 156; France and the SHAPE refurbishing controversy, 183; Gordon's wartime association with, 77; Katz-Gaitskill Agreement, 156; Marshall Plan special representative in Paris, 158, 163, 176

Katz-Gaitskill Agreement, 156

Kaysen, Carl, 219

Kefauver, Estes, 191

Kellogg-Briand Peace Treaty, 101

Kennan, George: containment doctrine and, 203–4; European Recovery Program steering committee and, 127; Marshall's 1947 speech outlining the Marshall Plan and, 120; skepticism about US involvement in Latin America, 204, 205; US–Soviet policy and, 93, 169

Kennecott copper company, 69

Kennedy, John F.: 1960 presidential election, 216; Alliance for Progress and, 222, 228–30; assassination, 258; Bay of Pigs invasion, 224, 226–27; Berle transition task force, 225; Ralph Dungan's communication concerning Gordon in Brazil, 278; Milton Eisenhower's views of, 350; Gordon's informal access to as ambassador to Brazil, 241–42, 243, 247; Joao Goulart and, 244, 254; Kissinger and, 457n9; Latin America policy and, 225, 226, 405; meetings with Gordon on Brazil, 246–48, 260; planned visit to Brazil, 246, 250, 256; presidential management style, 405–6; Punta del Este conference and, 230–32; taping system in the White House, 246, 411. See also Kennedy administration

Kennedy, Robert, 250–52, 293

Kennedy administration: Gordon's colleagues in, 219; Gordon's entry into, 216–17, 219, 223; Kissinger and, 219, 224, 225, 457n9; Latin America policy (see Latin America policy)

Kerley, Robert, 316–17

Kerr, Clark, 306

Keynes, John Maynard, 42

Kindleberger, Charles, 127

King, Harry, 69

Kirk, Grayson, 308

Kissinger, Henry: Robert Bowie and, 209–10; McGeorge Bundy and, 224, 225, 457n9; Gordon's criticism of, 210; at Harvard, 29, 86–87, 207–8, 209–10; Kennedy administration and, 219, 224, 225, 457n9; repudiation of the Alliance for Progress, 236
Knapp, J. Burke, 126
Knight, Douglas Maitland, 306, 307
Knowlson, James, 70, 73
Knox, Frank, 62, 66
Korean War: American mobilization, 179–82; Gordon's work on industrial mobilization, 179; impact on Harriman's role with Truman, 157, 171; impact on NATO, 169; impact on the Marshall Plan, 157, 166–68; labor opposition to wage stabilization during, 181, 452–53n25; military stabilization in 1951, 182–83; US 1950 strategy review in Tokyo, 168; US perceptions of the Soviet Union and, 163–64
Kramers, Hendrik, 103
Kriebel, Dick, 210, 384
Kriebel, Ruth, 210, 258, 384
Kruel, Amaury, 254, 257, 270–71
Krug, Julius A. ("Cap"), 77, 80–81, 87
Kubish, Jack, 287, 288
Kubitschek, Juscelino, 215, 222, 239, 240, 255, 281

labor: opposition to wage stabilization during the Korean War, 181, 452–53n25; shortages during World War II, 68
Labouisse, Henry, 198
Lacerda, Carlos, 254, 275, 281
LaGuardia, Fiorello, 120
Lake Sunapee (NH), 9–11, 16, 52–53, 206

Landsberg, Hans, 371, 376
Lanigan, James I., 189
Latin America: 1957 Harvard conference on economic development in, 215; Bretton Woods system and, 215; development of Gordon's interest in, 212–17; economic development in the 1950s, 215; Gordon's common market idea, 261; Anne Gordon's critique of Lincoln's impact on, 280; Gordon's views of economic regionalism, 218–19; Hopkins School of Hygiene and Public Health and, 314; Kennan's skepticism about US involvement in, 204, 205; LBJ's plan to recruit troops for Vietnam, 286; planning for the meeting of Latin American presidents, 294–99, 301; Punta del Este conference, 226, 227–34, 235–36; social reforms and, 219. See also Brazil
Latin America policy: Bay of Pigs invasion, 224, 226–27, 228; Adolf Berle's mission to Brazil, 225–26; Berle task force, 219–23; Dominican Republic crisis, 285–86, 290–91, 408; Gordon as point man for the Kennedy administration, 223–27; Gordon's and Stevenson's southern trip following the Bay of Pigs, 226–27, 230, 231–32; Gordon's assignment as US ambassador to Brazil, 226, 227 (See also US ambassador to Brazil); Kennedy administration's lack of clear goals for, 405; Latin American criticism of Gordon, 230; Thomas Mann and, 263, 264–65; Panama Canal issues, 374–76, 407–8; prior to the Bay of Pigs, 227–28; Punta del Este conference, 226,

227–34, 235–36; US concerns with
Cuba and, 228, 229, 230–31, 232.
See also Alliance for Progress
Lawson, Amy, 395. *See also* Gordon,
Amy
Leach, Barton, 207–8
Leddy, John, 225
Leitao du Cunha, Vasco, 286
Lend-Lease, 61
Leonhart, Bill, 377
Lerner, Dorothy. *See* Gordon, Dorothy
Lerner, Leo, 7–8, 14
Levinson, Marjorie G., 360
Lilienthal, David E., 91–92, 94, 447n15
Lincoln, George ("Abe"), 126–27
Lindsay, A. D., 41
Lindsay, Frank, 99, 145
Linowitz, Sol M., 296–99
Lippmann, Walter, 90
Littauer School, 88
Livermore, Shaw, 145
London. *See* US embassy in London
London Port Authority, 46, 47
Longennecker, Herbert E., 306
Lovett, Robert, 124, 128, 133, 134, 139
Lula da Silva, Lutz Inancio ("Lula"),
388

MacArthur, Douglas, 168, 182
Machado, Floriano, 272
Macksey, Richard, 327
MacLaury, Bruce K., 381, 382
MacLeish, Archibald, 327
Macy, John, 293
Mahinka, Stephan P., 360
Majodi, Giovanni, 144
Malan, Pedro, 390
Manchester, William, 298
Mandelbaum, Maurice, 345, 355–56
Mann, Thomas C.: 1964 crisis in
Brasil and, 269, 284–85; in the
Johnson administration, 263; in
the Kennedy administration, 225;

meetings with Gordon on Brazil,
264–65, 266
Mann Doctrine, 265
Marjolin, Robert, 144, 147, 152–54,
372, 401, 402
Marks, Herbert S., 91, 99, 112, 446n13
Mars Company, 207
Marshak, Jacob, 42
Marshall, George C.: 1947 speech and
the origin of the Marshall Plan,
120–21; 1948 Senate hearings on
the ECA, 134–36; anticommunism
and, 137; creation of the ECA
and, 131–32, 133–34; fiftieth
anniversary of the Marshall Plan,
12–13; German rearmament issue
and, 172, 173; as Gordon's ideal
public servant, 410; Gordon's
impressions of, 131–32; selling the
Marshall Plan to the American
people, 136–37
Marshall Plan: 1948 Senate Foreign
Relations Committee hearings
on, 134–36; Alliance for
Progress and, 236–37, 242, 406;
anniversaries of, 12–13, 372–73;
congressional approval of, 136,
137, 141; emotional and physical
toll on Gordon, 124–25; Gordon's
public support for the passage
of, 139; Gordon's reflections on,
158–61, 392; Gordon's role in
the negotiations establishing the
ECA, 130–34; Gordon's views
of the Bretton Woods system
and European unification,
213–14; Gordon's work on the
organizational structure of, 121–30;
International Security Assistance
Committee and, 177; Marshall's
1947 speech and the origin of, 120–
21; negotiations within the Truman
administration to establish

Marshall Plan *(cont.)*
    the ECA as an independent agency,
    130–34; overview and assessment
    of Gordon's contribution to, 2, 3,
    401–2, 404; reasons for the success
    of, 401–2; selling to the Congress
    and the country, 134–37; Soviet
    response to, 137
—administrative history: allocation
    crisis in 1949, 146–48; economic
    recovery versus military
    preparedness, 157, 165–68, 169;
    European integration concept,
    148–51; Gordon and the European
    Payments Union, 152–57; Gordon
    and the start-up phase in Paris,
    1948, 143–45; Gordon as acting
    director of the program division,
    141–43; Gordon as country mission
    chief in London, 193; Gordon on
    productivity targets and military
    preparedness, 166; Gordon's
    associates from the War Production
    Board, 77; Gordon's decision to
    accept a position in, 139–42;
    Gordon's salary, 140; Harriman
    asks Gordon to head the Program
    Division in Paris, 145; Harriman as
    special representative in Paris, 141,
    143–44, 145, 176; impact of the
    1950 US congressional elections on,
    175–76, 177–78; impact of trade
    liberalization, 156; Milton Katz as
    special representative in Paris, 158,
    163, 176; the problem of Germany,
    167; reasons for the success of,
    401–2; tensions in administrative
    structure, 148–49; US concern with
    "performance" measures, 154
Martin, Edwin A.: 1964 crisis
    in Brazil and, 278; German
    rearmament issue and, 172, 173,
    174; Gordon's ambassadorship

to Brazil and, 247–48, 258;
    intelligence review on Brazil, 263;
    in the Kennedy administration,
    223, 225, 233; relationship with
    Gordon, 172; views of Joao
    Goulart, 460n36
Marxism, 33, 242
Masaryk, Jan, 137
Mason, Edward, 32, 60
May, Stacy, 60
Mayobre, Jose Antonio, 229
Mazzilli, Ranieri, 274–75, 281
McCarthy, Joe, 196, 199
McCarthyism, 196–99
McCloy, John J., 89, 93, 266
McCone, John, 267
McElroy, William, 304, 340
McGranahan, Don and Nancy, 373,
    384
McIlwain, Charles, 32, 33
McMahon Act, 113, 119
McNamara, Robert, 366–67
Medalie, George Z., 15–16, 28
Medina, Harold J., 27
meritocracy, 15, 40
Mexico, 296
Miller, Edward G., 204
Milne, A. A., 29
M&M's, 207
Moch, Jules, 172
Monnet, Jean, 159, 174, 184–85, 186
Mora, Jose Antonio, 296
Morales, Arturo, 220
Morgenthau, Henry, 66, 70, 72
Morrissey Collection hoax, 56
Moscoso, Theodoro, 222, 259
Maura Andrade, Auro, 246
Mourão Filho, Olímpio, 270
MSA. *See* Mutual Security Agency
Mueden, Emma, 19
Muller, Steven, 305, 338, 359, 360–62,
    363–64
Muñoz Marin, Luis, 222

Murphy, Franklin D., 306
music, 200–201, 210
Mutual Security Act of 1948, 136
Mutual Security Agency (MSA), 193,
    196, 197

National Defense Advisory Committee,
    60
national intelligence estimates, 378–79
nationalization, 244, 248
National Resources Planning Board,
    59–60
National Security Council (NSC), 171,
    176, 274, 405
National Security Council
    Memorandum–68 (NSC-68), 157,
    167, 168, 171, 452n13
National Security Council
    Memorandum–141 (NSC-141),
    454nn27*28
NATO Council, 187
Nazi Germany: Gordon's travels to,
    43–45; World War II and, 58, 59,
    61
Necessity for Choice, The (Kissinger), 210
Nelson, Donald M.: reconversion issue
    and, 79–80; Roosevelt replaces at
    the WPB, 80–81; Henry Wallace
    and, 119; War Production Board
    service, 64, 68, 72–74, 75, 76, 77
Neves, Tancredo, 240, 271–72, 385
New Deal: Gordon's early interest in,
    42–43; Supreme Court cases, 48
"New Myths for Old: Senator Church
    and Foreign Aid" (Gordon), 367
New Republic, 110
New Zealand, 58
Nichols House, 315–16, 326
Nitze, Paul: 1950 defense spending
    issue and NSC-68, 171; Jimmy
    Carter and, 377, 410; Committee
    on the Present Danger and, 375;
    European Recovery Program

steering committee, 126, 127;
    Marshall Plan and, 123
Nixon, Richard: Gordon's criticism of,
    210; repudiation of the Alliance for
    Progress, 236; student response to
    the 1968 election, 325
Norris, George, 42
Norstad, Lauris, 168
North Atlantic Treaty, 157, 170
North Atlantic Treaty Organization
    (NATO): 1951 Ottawa meeting,
    184; Eisenhower and tactical
    nuclear weapons, 188; German
    rearmament issue, 167, 169–70,
    172–75; Gordon and early strategic
    planning, 168–70; Gordon's
    contribution to NATO structure
    as Harriman's deputy, 185–86,
    187, 188; Gordon's criticism of
    US policies in the launching of,
    183–84; Gordon's shift of interest
    to the Third World, 212–14;
    Lisbon meeting, 186, 187, 184185;
    movement from treaty to alliance
    in 1950, 157, 165, 167; SHAPE
    refurbishing controversy, 183; Wise
    Men and institutional reforms,
    182–87
Northrop, F. B., 126
Norton, William, 60
NSC. See National Security Council
nuclear diplomacy: Gordon's analysis
    of, 112–17; postwar, 89–91. See also
    atomic bombs; UN Atomic Energy
    Commission
Nuclear Weapons and Foreign Policy
    (Kissinger), 209

OAS. See Organization of American
    States
O'Brian, John Lord, 64, 76
ODM. See Office of Defense
    Mobilization

OEEC. *See* Organization for European Economic Cooperation
Office of Defense Mobilization (ODM), 180–81, 182
Office of Price Administration (OPA), 63, 67, 84–85
Office of Special Representative (OSR): in the ECA chain of command, 130; Gordon requests service with, 142; Harriman in Paris, 141, 143–44, 145, 176; Milton Katz in Paris, 158, 163, 176; in the Marshall Plan organization, 129
Office of US Attorney for the Southern District of New York, 27
Office of War Mobilization, 75, 82
offshore procurement, 193, 195–96
O Grande Irmao (Fico), 275–80
"On Lincoln Gordon's Departure from RFF," 376
OPA. *See* Office of Price Administration
Operation Barbarossa, 61
Operation Overlord, 77
Operation Pan America, 222
Operation Topsy, 294
Opie, Redvers, 42
Oppenheimer, J. Robert, 91, 94, 96, 99
Organization for European Economic Cooperation (OEEC): allocation crisis in 1949, 146–48; European Payments Union and, 143–44, 152, 154, 156, 450n19; German membership, 170; reconstituted as the Organization of Economic Cooperation and Development in 1952, 159
Organization of American States (OAS): Dominican Republic crisis and, 285–86, 290; launching of the Alliance for Progress and, 228; planning for the meeting of Latin American presidents and, 295–97

Organization of Economic Cooperation and Development, 159
OSR. *See* Office of Special Representative
Owen, Déjà, 351
Owen, George E., 344–47, 351, 352, 353, 355–56
Oxford University, 34, 37, 39–43, 46–48
Oxford University Press, 50
"Ozymandias" (Shelley), 20

Page, Edith Bennet, 387–88
Page, Joseph A., 272, 463n12
Palmer, Bruce, 377
Panama Canal, 374–76, 407–8
Paraguay, 233
Partridge, Bruce, 316, 466n30
Passarella, Russell S., 360
Pazos, Felipe, 229, 230
Peace Corps, 241, 248
Peel, Margaret, 43, 45
penny, 69
Pepper, Claude, 105, 119
Perkins, Jim, 361
Phelps Dodge copper company, 69
Pinto, Carvalho, 254, 257
Pleven Plan, 174–75
Plowden, Edwin, 184–85
poetry, 20. *See also* sonnets
Poland, 123
polio, 146
Pound, Dean Roscoe, 35
Pragmatic Revolt in Politics, The (Elliott), 29, 33
Prebisch, Raul, 229, 296
presidential elections (US): of 1952, 188–92; of 1960, 216
President's Committee on Foreign Aid (Harriman Committee), 127, 449n14
Price, Don K., 211
"Price of Free World Victory, The"

(Wallace "common man" speech),
104–5
Princeton University, 24, 27, 264
Public Corporation in Great Britain, The
(Gordon), 46–48, 50
Punta del Este conference, 226, 227–
34, 235–36
Pusey, Nathan, 208, 209, 319, 320

Quadros, Janio: Alliance for Progress
and, 229, 236; Adolf Berle's mission
to, 225–26; Gordon's meeting with,
227; presidency and resignation,
237, 238–39, 240

Rabbit Is Rich (Updike), 56
radio: Dorothy Gordon and, 7, 13
Ranum, Orest, 346
Read, Benjamin, 369
Reagan, Ronald, 374, 378
Reconstruction Finance Corporation, 69
Reith, Arthur, 47
Reorganization Plan of 1953, 197
Resources for the Future (RFF), 370–
76, 381–82
Reston, James, 104
Reuther, Walter, 350
RFF. *See* Resources for the Future
Rhodes scholarship, 33, 37
Ribeiro, Darcy, 271
Richard Nixon professor, 366
Ridgway, Matthew, 168, 182–82
Rogers, David, 314, 325
Rogers, William D., 293
Roll, Eric, 185
Rolof, Eric, 144
Roosevelt, Eleanor, 350
Roosevelt, Franklin Delano: atomic
energy development and, 88–89;
liberal internationalist Republican
supporters, 61–62; management
of the home front and, 74–75;
Donald Nelson and, 72–73, 74, 80;

recreation of the National Defense
Advisory Committee, 60; responses
to the approaching war, 66–67;
Henry Wallace and, 75, 104–5;
wartime political coalition, 402
Roosevelt, Theodore, 9
Ross, Charles, 106
Rostow, Eugene V. D., 374, 375, 410
Rostow, Walt, 295
Rothenberg, Herbert, 377
Rusk, Dean: 1964 crisis in Brazil
and, 267, 269, 278, 279; Gordon's
assignment as US ambassador
to Brazil and, 226, 227, 284;
Gordon's departure for Johns
Hopkins University and, 310–11;
Gordon's entry into the Kennedy
administration and, 217, 219,
223; relationship with Gordon as
assistant secretary to Latin America,
292
Russell, Milton, 376
Russell, Richard, 191
Rutgers University, 313

Saarinen, Aline Bernstein, 442n8
Saarinen, Eero, 21
"sailors' revolt," 268
SAIS. *See* Hopkins School of Advanced
International Studies
Salant, Walter, 36, 372
Sales, Walter Moreira, 240–41, 244
SALT II, 374
Sanger, Margaret, 16
San Tiago Dantas, Francisco de, 246,
254, 257, 266
Sanz de Santa Maria, Carlos, 296
Sao Paolo, 237
Savage, Peter and Ina, 395
Schelling, Thomas C., 207–8
Schlesinger, Arthur, 219, 224–25
Schuman Plan, 159
Searle, John, 95–96

Second Institutional Act (AI-2), 279, 283, 284
Selective Service Act, 61
Senate Foreign Relations Committee: 1948 hearing on the Marshall Plan, 134–36
Shaffer, Wilson, 304, 318
SHAPE. *See* Supreme Headquarters Allied Powers Europe
Shriver, Sargent, 260, 287
Shultz, George, 374
Silva, Albino, 249
Singleton, Charles S., 319, 320
SKF ball-bearing company, 70–71
Slee, Noah, 16–17
Smith, Courtney, 319, 320
Smith, Herbert, 19, 21
Smith, Jean Edward, 72
Smithies, Arthur, 142
Snoy et d'Oppuers, Jean Charles (baron), 147
Snoy-Marjolin formula, 147, 148
Snyder, John, 176
social reforms, 219
Soldiers' and Sailors' Monument, 26
sonnets, 20, 78–79, 326–27, 376
Southard, Frank A., Jr., 126
Soviet Union: CIA review panel and, 378; emergence of the Cold War, 93, 100; Gordon's analyses of US nuclear diplomacy and the Soviet Union, 114, 115, 116–17; Gordon's analysis of in *Eroding Empire*, 382–83, 410–11; Gordon's views of, 119–20, 380; relief and emergency aid received in 1946, 123; response to the Marshall Plan, 123, 137; US containment doctrine, 100, 119, 203–4; US perceptions of during the Korean War, 163–64; US postwar atomic policy and, 89–90, 100; US–Soviet interactions in the UNAEC, 100–103

Spirit of the Common Law, The (Pound), 35
Spofford, Charles, 168
Staats, Elmer, 180
State Department: 1964 contingency plan for Brazil, 263; admonition to Gordon about comments on Brazil, 285; creation of the Marshall Plan and, 127; European integration issue and, 149–50; European Payments Union and, 153; International Security Assistance Committee, 177; Mann Doctrine, 265; negotiations establishing the ECA as an independent agency, 131–34; relations with Gordon as ambassador to Brazil, 247–48. *See also* assistant secretary for inter-American affairs
Stebbins, Ernest, 324
Steinbrunner, John, 382
Stevenson, Adlai, 190–92, 217, 223, 226–27
Stimson, Henry, 62, 66, 89
Stone, Donald C., 128, 132–33, 134
Strategic Bombing Survey, 87
"streaking" movement, 364
Students for a Democratic Society, 322, 328
Superfund litigation, 386–87
Supreme Court: Gordon's Harvard thesis on, 34–36; New Deal cases, 48
Supreme Headquarters Allied Powers Europe (SHAPE), 183
Sweden: William Batt and the SKF ball-bearing company, 70–71
Swope, Herbert Bayard: with Barnard Baruch at the UNAEC, 90, 94, 95–96, 99, 102, 103, 108, 109

Taft, Robert A., 182
Tannenwald, Ted, 178, 180

Taylor, Glen, 119
Teele, Stanley, 98, 111, 124, 206–7
television: Dorothy Gordon and, 7, 13
Tennessee Valley Authority, 42, 46
tennis, 22, 397
Termination of the Occupation
    Agreement, 144
"think tanks," 368–69
Third World: development of Gordon's
    interest in, 212–17; Gordon's views
    of the Bretton Woods system and,
    214, 216–17. See also Latin America
Thomas, Charles A., 91
Thompson, Margery, 392
Thorp, Willard, 123, 127–28, 134
Tilson, Kay, 53
"To a Queen Bee" (Gordon), 326–27
Tolman, Richard, 96, 99
Tosca, Henry, 156
Tractors for Freedom, 350
Treaty of Brussels, 168
Trotskyism, 33
Truman, David B., 306, 307–8,
    466n17
Truman, Harry S.: 1950 US
    congressional elections and, 175–
    76; 1952 presidential election and,
    188–92; appointment of Bernard
    Baruch US representative to the
    UNAEC, 92, 94–95; atom bomb
    tests in the Pacific and, 98; defense
    spending issue and, 157, 164, 167,
    168, 171; end of World War II,
    83; FDR and, 75, 105; Harriman
    as adviser to, 3, 157–58, 163,
    164–65, 167–68, 171–72, 175–79;
    International Security Assistance
    Committee, 177; Korean War and,
    157, 168, 171, 181–82; Marshall
    Plan organization and, 129–30;
    posture toward European recovery-
    versus-military preparedness, 165;
    postwar political coalition, 402;

presidential management style, 405;
    President's Committee on Foreign
    Aid, 127; response to Churchill's
    "iron curtain" speech, 93; US
    postwar atomic policy and, 89–90;
    Henry Wallace and, 98, 106–11,
    112
Truman Doctrine, 204
Turner, Stansfield, 378
Tuthill, John W., 293–94
Twentieth Century Fund, 390

UN Atomic Energy Commission
    (UNAEC): Acheson-Lilienthal
    Report on US proposals to, 91–93;
    atomic energy developments
    and diplomacy leading to the
    creation of, 88–91; Bernard
    Baruch as US representative to,
    92, 93–110; creation and mission
    of, 91; Gordon's later analyses of
    US nuclear diplomacy, 112–17;
    Gordon's service with, 96–106,
    108–10, 111; Great Britain and,
    113; the Kramers report, 103–4;
    US atom bomb tests in the Pacific
    and, 98–99; US–Soviet interactions
    in, 100–103; the Wallace affair,
    106–11
United Kingdom: European Defense
    Community and, 175; European
    economic union and, 149;
    European Payments Union and,
    155–56; relief and emergency aid
    received in 1946, 123. See also Great
    Britain; US embassy in London
United Nations Rehabilitation and
    Relief Administration (UNRRA),
    120, 123
University of Marburg, 44
UNRRA. See United Nations
    Rehabilitation and Relief
    Administration

Updike, John, 56
Uri, Pierre, 185
Uruguay, 232, 233, 272
US Agency for International
    Development (US AID): mission in
    Recife, Brazil, 260–61
US ambassador to Brazil: 1964 coup,
    American response, and aftermath,
    269–73, 274–75, 280–84, 407;
    Allison and family life in, 54–55,
    56, 258; comparison of Gordon's
    and Goulart's personalities, 245;
    Cruzeiro do Sul awarded to
    Gordon, 284; Cuban Missile Crisis,
    248–50; Dominican Republic crisis,
    285–86; events prior to the 1964
    military coup, 262–69, 411; failure
    of the Alliance for Progress, 234–
    36, 237, 259–62, 406; Carlos Fico's
    critique of Gordon's purported
    involvement in the 1964 coup,
    275–80; Gordon's assignment to,
    226, 227; Gordon's confirmation
    and arrival in Brazil, 240; Gordon's
    informal access to Kennedy, 241–
    42, 243, 247; Gordon's key policy
    ideas, 261; Gordon's replacement,
    293–94; Gordon's travels in Brazil,
    243, 258; Joao Goulart's 1962 US
    visit, 244–45; from January to
    May 1963, 252–54; from June to
    December 1863, 254–58; Robert
    Kennedy's visit to Brazil, 250–
    52; LBJ's plan to recruit Latin
    American troops for Vietnam and,
    286; meetings with and views of
    Castelo Branco, 282–84; meetings
    with Goulart, 241, 254, 255–56;
    meetings with Kennedy, 246–48,
    260; meetings with LBJ, 285;
    meetings with Thomas Mann, 263,
    264–65, 266, 267; meeting with
    Janio Quadros in 1961, 238; from

October 1961 to June 1962, 240–
    45, 411; overview and assessment
    of Gordon's service, 3, 405, 406–
    7; postcoup period and return to
    Washington, 284–90; response
    to Kennedy's assassination, 258;
    retrospective reflections on, 367–
    68; US intervention in the 1962
    elections, 247–48, 458–59n12
US Congress: Marshall Plan and, 124,
    128, 134–36, 137
US embassy in London: family life,
    199–201; Gordon's assignment
    to, 192–95; Gordon's breach
    with R. H. Crossman, 195–96;
    Gordon's decision to return to the
    Harvard Business School, 201–
    5; McCarthyism and Gordon's
    conflict with Harold Stassen, 196,
    198–99; overview and assessment of
    Gordon's service, 404–5
US Navy: atom bomb tests in the
    Pacific, 98–99; Brother Sam task
    force, 267, 268, 272, 275, 279

Vandenberg, Arthur, 89, 107–8, 126,
    134, 136
Vargas, Getulio, 239
Vaughn, Jack, 287
Venezuela: Accion Democratica, 221
Vernon, Raymond, 207, 455n2
Vietnam War: antiwar protests (see
    antiwar students); Gordon's
    criticism of Nixon and Kissinger,
    210; Johnson solicits Gordon's views
    on, 313–14; LBJ's plan to recruit
    troops from Latin America, 286
Viner, Jacob, 368
Vinson, Fred, 190

W. W. Norton & Sons publishers, 60
Wainer, Samuel, 262, 460n30
Wallace, Henry: FDR and, 75, 104–5;

in Gordon's unfinished memoirs, 391–92; Gordon's views of, 110–11, 392; later career of, 110, 119; response to Churchill's "iron curtain" speech, 93; "The Price of Free World Victory" speech, 104–5; Truman's firing of, 108; views and criticism of US postwar atomic policy, 89, 90, 98, 99–100, 104–5, 106–10, 112; "Where I Was Wrong," 111

Walters, Vernon, 144, 248, 249, 267, 269, 277

Warburg, James P., 119

war mobilization: challenges facing the US, 64–68. *See also* War Production Board

War Production Board (WPB): Controlled Materials Plan, 73; Gordon's depression and attempt to join the army, 75–77; Gordon's relevant work experiences prior to, 59–60; Gordon's service with, 63–64, 68–70, 73–74, 75–55, 77–79, 80, 81–82, 84, 85; inter- and intra-agency disputes and controversies, 67; Julius Krug as chairman, 77, 80–81; leadership and administrative problems, 70–74; Donald Nelson as chairman, 72–74, 75, 76, 77, 79–80; overview and assessment of Gordon's service with, 403–4; planning for Operation Overlord, 77; reconversion issue, 79–80, 81–82, 84–85; replaced by the Civilian Production Administration, 85; Superfund litigation, 386–87

Washington "think tanks," 368–69

Webb, James E., 128, 134, 150

Western Europe: William Clayton's 1947 assessment of, 122–23; European integration, 148–51; issue of economic recovery versus military preparedness, 157, 165–68; relief and emergency aid in 1946, 120; Treaty of Brussels defensive alliance, 168

West Germany: economic recovery, 146; European Defense Community and, 174–75; formation of, 144; Marshall Plan and, 144; rearmament issue, 167, 169–70, 172–75; US debate on sending troops to during the Korean War, 181–82

"Where I Was Wrong" (Wallace), 111

Wherry, Kenneth S., 182

Whitaker, Arthur, 220

Whittier College, 366

Wickwine, Chester, 334

Wilcox, Francis O., 302, 313

Williams, G. Mennen, 221

William Ziegler Professor of International Business, 205, 206–7, 211

Willis, Benjamin, 316, 335, 340, 353, 365, 366

Willkie, Wendell, 66–67

Wilson, Carroll S., 91

Wilson, Charles E., 74, 80, 180–81, 182, 445–46n22, 446n23

Wilson, Logan, 306

Wilson Center, 369–70

Winne, Harry A., 91

Winter, Harrison, 304, 306, 307, 309, 324, 358

Wise Men: the Cold War era and, 1–2; Gordon's postwar service to, 404; the Marshall Plan and, 401; NATO institutional reforms and, 184–87

Wood, C. Tyler, 121–22, 150

Wood, Robert E., 72

Woodbridge, George, 196, 198

Woodrow Wilson International Center for Scholars, 369–70

Woodrow Wilson School of Public and International Affairs, 264
Woodworth, Ellery B., 333–34, 340
World Bank, 366–67
World Politics, 216–17
World War I, 65, 66
World War II: atomic bombs and the end of, 82–83; beginning of and impact on Gordon's career, 58–62; FDR and management of the home front, 74–75; Gordon's service with the War Production Board, 63–64 (*see also* War Production Board); US mobilization challenge, 64–68
WPB. *See* War Production Board
Wright, Allison. *See* Gordon, Allison
Wright, George, 52
Wright, Goddard, 52

Young, John P., 340, 353
Youth Forum (radio program), 13, 326

Ziegler professorship. *See* William Ziegler Professor of International Business

STUDIES IN CONFLICT, DIPLOMACY, AND PEACE

SERIES EDITORS: George C. Herring, Andrew L. Johns, and Kathryn C. Statler

This series focuses on key moments of conflict, diplomacy, and peace from the eighteenth century to the present to explore their wider significance in the development of U.S. foreign relations. The series editors welcome new research in the form of original monographs, interpretive studies, biographies, and anthologies from historians, political scientists, journalists, and policymakers. A primary goal of the series is to examine the United States' engagement with the world, its evolving role in the international arena, and the ways in which the state, nonstate actors, individuals, and ideas have shaped and continue to influence history, both at home and abroad.

ADVISORY BOARD MEMBERS

David Anderson, California State University, Monterey Bay
Laura Belmonte, Oklahoma State University
Robert Brigham, Vassar College
Paul Chamberlin, University of Kentucky
Jessica Chapman, Williams College
Frank Costigliola, University of Connecticut
Michael C. Desch, University of Notre Dame
Kurk Dorsey, University of New Hampshire
John Ernst, Morehead State University
Joseph A. Fry, University of Nevada, Las Vegas
Ann Heiss, Kent State University
Sheyda Jahanbani, University of Kansas
Mark Lawrence, University of Texas
Mitchell Lerner, Ohio State University
Kyle Longley, Arizona State University
Robert McMahon, Ohio State University
Michaela Hoenicke Moore, University of Iowa
Lien-Hang T. Nguyen, University of Kentucky
Jason Parker, Texas A&M University
Andrew Preston, Cambridge University
Thomas Schwartz, Vanderbilt University
Salim Yaqub, University of California, Santa Barbara

Books in the Series

The Gulf: The Bush Presidencies and the Middle East
Michael F. Cairo

Diplomatic Games: Sport, Statecraft, and International Relations since 1945
Edited by Heather L. Dichter and Andrew L. Johns

Nothing Less Than War: A New History of America's Entry into World War I
Justus D. Doenecke

Grounded: The Case for Abolishing the United States Air Force
Robert M. Farley

The American South and the Vietnam War: Belligerence, Protest, and Agony in Dixie
Joseph A. Fry

Obama at War: Congress and the Imperial Presidency
Ryan C. Hendrickson

The Conversion of Senator Arthur H. Vandenberg: From Isolation to International Engagement
Lawrence S. Kaplan

The Currents of War: A New History of American-Japanese Relations, 1899–1941
Sidney Pash

So Much to Lose: John F. Kennedy and American Policy in Laos
William J. Rust

Lincoln Gordon: Architect of Cold War Foreign Policy
Bruce L. R. Smith